VITAL
INTERESTS

VITAL
INTERESTS

The
Soviet Issue
in
U.S. Central American
Policy

edited by

Bruce D. Larkin

Lynne Rienner Publishers ◆ Boulder/London

Published in the United States of America in 1988 by
Lynne Rienner Publishers, Inc.
948 North Street, Boulder, Colorado 80302

and in the United Kingdom by
Lynne Rienner Publishers, Inc.
3 Henrietta Street, Covent Garden, London WC2E 8LU

Library of Congress Cataloging-in-Publication Data

Vital interests : the Soviet issue in U.S. Central American policy/
  edited by Bruce D. Larkin.

    Bibliography: p.
    Includes index.
    ISBN 1-55587-111-9 (lib. bdg.) :   ISBN 1-55587-112-7
(pbk.) :
    1. Central America—Foreign relations—United States.   2. United
States—Foreign relations—Central America.   3. Geopolitics—Central
America.   4. Central America—Foreign relations—Soviet Union.
5. Soviet Union—Foreign relations—Central America.   6. United
States—National security.   7. Central America—National security.
I. Larkin, Bruce D., 1936-
F1436.8.U6V58 1988
327'.09728—dc19   87-37458
                                                                 CIP

British Library Cataloguing in Publication Data
A Cataloguing in Publication record for this book
is available from the British Library.

Printed and bound in the United States of America

Contents

Contributors

Russell H. Bartley is Associate Professor of History at the University of Wisconsin-Milwaukee. He has authored numerous books and articles on the history of Russo-Latin American relations and is a correspondent for the Mexico City daily *unomásuno*.

Rubén Berríos is affiliated with the Department of Economics of the University of Pittsburgh.

E. Bradford Burns is Professor of History at the University of California at Los Angeles and author of works on the Central American conflict.

The **Committee of Santa Fe**: On the reissuance of the Santa Fe document in 1981 the Committee's members were described as follows:

L. Francis Bouchey is Executive Vice President of the Council for Inter-American Security. He is the co-author of the recent monograph *Guatemala: A Promise in Peril* and of the book *International Terrorism— The Communist Connection*.

Roger Fontaine serves as the National Security Council's Latin America specialist. He has been Director of the Latin American Division at the Georgetown University Center for Strategic and International Studies and Resident Fellow at the American Enterprise Institute.

David C. Jordan is Professor of Government and Foreign Affairs at the University of Virginia. He is a member of the Board of Directors of the U.S. Strategic Institute and is a member of the Institute for Foreign Policy Analysis. Professor Jordan is co-author of *Nationalism in Contemporary Latin America*.

Lt. General Gordon Sumner, Jr. (USA-Ret.) was Chairman from 1975-1977 of the Inter-American Defense Board. He was assistant to General Douglas MacArthur during the Korean War and is on leave as Chairman of the Council for Inter-American Security. General Sumner is currently Special Advisor to the Assistant Secretary of State for Latin American Affairs.

Lewis Tambs is Professor of History at Arizona State University. He is the author of more than 30 books and articles. Professor Tambs spent 14 years abroad as a scholar and researcher, as an independent contractor in Venezuela, and as an engineer for a major petroleum firm. More recently, Professor Tambs has served as US Ambassador to Costa Rica.

Edward Cuddy is Professor at Daemen College.

W. Raymond Duncan is a Distinguished Teaching Professor of Political Science and Director of Global Studies at the State University of New York (SUNY) College at Brockport. His most recent books are *Soviet Policy in Developing Countries* (ed.), (New York: Robert E. Krieger, 1981) and *Soviet Policy in the Third World* (ed.), (New York: Pergamon, 1980). He has written numerous articles and essays on Soviet and Cuban policy in Latin America and he traveled to Cuba in January 1983.

Marc Edelman. Marc Edelman is Assistant Professor of Anthropology at Yale University. He was Research Director of the North American Congress on Latin America, an independent research organization in New York founded in 1966. He holds a doctorate in anthropology from Columbia University, where he has also studied international relations. Edelman has done research in Nicaragua, Costa Rica, Mexico, the United States, and the Soviet Union. He is an editor of a forthcoming anthology on Costa Rican politics and the author of numerous articles on Central American history and development.

Barbara Epstein is Professor of History at the University of California at Santa Cruz.

Carl G. Jacobsen was formerly head of the graduate program in Soviet and East European Studies at the University of Miami and is now a senior research associate at the Stockholm International Peace Research Institute.

Jeane Kirkpatrick, former US ambassador to the United Nations, is Professor of Political Science at Georgetown University.

Bruce D. Larkin is Professor of Politics at the University of California at Santa Cruz. He is the author of *China and Africa, 1949-1970: The Foreign Policy of the People's Republic of China*.

William Ratliff is a Research Fellow at the Hoover Institution on War, Revolution and Peace in Stanford, California.

David Ronfeldt is a staff member of the RAND Corporation.

Peter W. Schulze, a specialist in Soviet affairs, is affiliated with the Friedrich Ebert Foundation in Bonn, West Germany. In 1985-1987 he was a visitor at the Institute of International Studies, University of California, Berkeley.

David G. Sweet is Associate Professor of History at the University of California at Santa Cruz and Chair of its Committee on Latin American Studies.

Mary Vanderlaan is Associate Professor of Political Science at Hartwick College and author of *Revolution and Foreign Policy in Nicaragua* (1986).

Laurence Whitehead is an Official Fellow of Nuffield College, Oxford.

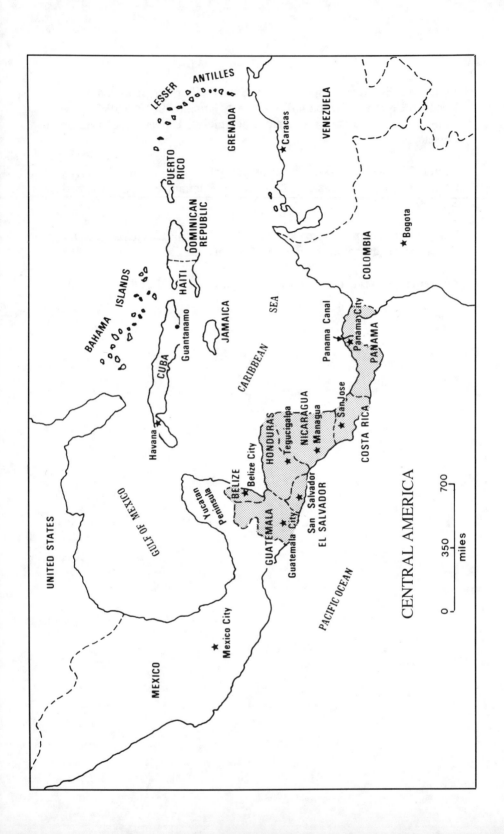

CENTRAL AMERICA

Introduction

Bruce D. Larkin

The Reagan administration's case for intervention in Nicaragua has relied on two claims: that the Sandinistas have denied internal democracy, and that Sandinist Nicaragua, allied with the Soviet Union and Cuba, threatens security interests. As the United States has not undertaken to overthrow other foreign governments that fail to meet the standards of internal democratic practice, even governments in Central America, the weight accorded Nicaragua's willingness to associate with the Soviet Union and Cuba may be a major source of the administration's Nicaragua policy. Even if that were not true, the argument that security interests are in the balance has been made repeatedly by the administration, and by the president himself, and therefore has come to form part of the fabric of public understanding of the administration's policy.

The object of this volume is to bring together representative statements that Managua's policies and dispositions threaten security, assessments and critiques of that claim, and evidence of Soviet and Cuban activity and capabilities from which the reader may better judge the charges and countercharges.

In late 1987 the White House declared an intention to seek from Congress perhaps $230 million to support the *contras* for the remainder of the Reagan presidency; by the day of the crucial congressional vote on 3 February 1988 it faced tough going asking just $36 million, but persisted doggedly. More than a year after the attorney general stunned America by announcing that profits from the sale of weapons to Iran had been directed to the *contras*, and in the midst of congressional testimony from Lt. Col. Oliver North, Admiral John Poindexter, and others who stood at the center of a questioned National Security Council operation, the White House has elected to insist that *contra* support is a matter of principle and necessity.

•

Two concerns led me to call a conference on this subject at the University of California at Santa Cruz in October 1985. I perceived policy toward Central America as unsound, directed to neither desirable nor attainable ends, and corrosive of statecraft in a world demanding Washington's attention. I also

1

believed, on the basis of some of the many reports identified in the articles that follow, that the administration was deceiving the public and practicing a dangerous disregard of constitutional requirements. My concerns did not turn on the facts developed since November 1986, but on other grounds: that *contra* support meant pointless death and disruption; that *contra* support was waging war, albeit through proxies, against treaty prohibitions and in defiance of constitutional requirements; that forces were being used to intimidate the Sandinistas, despite denials; that the United States was undermining the drive for pacific settlement of disputes by its contempt for the World Court; and, more generally but most importantly, that administration policy relied upon a portrayal of an endangered America that contradicted common sense.

Those who gathered in Santa Cruz did not address all of the questions raised by policy in Central America. We did not take up the Constitution, or international law, the internal Nicaraguan polity, or the War Powers Act. Instead, we focused on the security claims: on the claims that the Soviet Union threatened the United States, or its interests, through Central America, and especially through Nicaragua.

To papers based on those given at Santa Cruz we have added some direct but distinct versions of arguments that security is at risk and some scholarly assessments published in journals or elsewhere but not widely circulated among the general public.

Scholars, like other people, choose to do what they do because they believe the result may matter. In the essays that follow the reader will discern some careful efforts to set out facts and to contradict error, attesting to the motive, whether in scholarship or public policy, to get things right. The reader will also find essays whose authors believe that getting things right requires bold, fundamental recasting of how those who make policy think about the issues here, and what acts they choose; and their essays stretch our thinking about how the administration's claims may be understood. It is lively and informed argument, rather than a bloodless claim to detachment, for which this volume strives. This is, then, not a dispassionate volume. Whatever my own final conclusions may be, the reader has here a diversity of views and evidence on which to base an independent judgment.

THE CLAIM

This work is divided into four parts. The first consists of several quite distinct versions of the claim that security interests are at risk because the Sandinistas govern in Managua. The second contains critiques of that view, the third assessments of the Soviet and Cuban roles, and the fourth proposed reconceptions of desirable policy.

The report of the Committee of Santa Fe was written before the November 1980 presidential election, which brought Ronald Reagan to the White House. It is a blueprint—a proposal. It has no official standing, and even advocates of a strong military presence in the Caribbean have spoken of the report as "discredited," a "right-wing" manifesto. Still, of its five authors one was subsequently the National Security Council's Latin American specialist, and a second was named by President Reagan as ambassador to Costa Rica.

The Santa Fe document retains a following precisely among those who have been most active in their support of the *contras*, and contains some remarkable suggestions: the most startling, perhaps, is that the United States should offer Cuba material inducements to give up its ties to the Soviet Union, failing which "a war of national liberation against Castro must be launched."[1] This could be read in conjunction with reports that the White House rejected early proposals by Secretary of State Alexander Haig to use force against Cuba and Nicaragua.[2]

Jeane Kirkpatrick's article *U.S. Security & Latin America* was published just as the Reagan Administration took office, and she was about to assume the post of ambassador to the United Nations. A critique of Carter administration policy, it calls for a policy "that will protect security interests and make the actual lives of actual people in Latin America somewhat better and somewhat freer." Carter policy in Central America, according to Kirkpatrick,

> interacted with the presence there of weak regimes and Cuban-supported insurgents to transform the region into a battleground in an ideological war that the administration did not understand and could not acknowledge.

Carter "underestimated the fragility of order in these societies and overestimated the ease with which authority, once undermined" could be restored. It failed, Kirkpatrick insists, to understand *politics*.

Dr. David Ronfeldt, an analyst at the RAND Corporation, authored a widely-read study of the Caribbean Basin, of which one chapter—on the "future conflict environment"—is reproduced here. He calls attention not only to dimensions of the Soviet and Cuban roles, but also to growing efforts by West European states to be political actors in the region. The "decisive requirement" for strategy, he says, is "to 'de-Sovietize' Cuba, or at least to contain and diminish its close military collaboration with the USSR." The United States needs a "primarily nonmilitary" strategy in the Caribbean Basin, but must ensure that the Soviet Union gains no military position outside Cuba. Ronfeldt describes himself as a "mainstream" analyst.

As Kirkpatrick insists on the need to consider the independent political life of each country, so Dr. William Ratliff argues the need for close attention to the particular facts of each case. Ratliff, a Research Fellow and Scholar/Curator of the Latin American Collection at the Hoover Institution, takes to task critics of the administration certain of whose views he character-

---

[1] Part V, Proposal 4.
[2] See Whitehead, critique.

izes as myths: myths that the United States is an enemy of freedom, that Nicaragua "is no threat to the United States," that the United States brought the East-West conflict to Central America and forced Managua to align with Moscow (that the Sandinista government is nonaligned), that support to the *contras* sparked a Nicaraguan arms race, and that the *contras* are "all marauding Somocistas." The facts, he argues, are different, and the East-West conflict has become a factor in Central America.

The final three items in this section are speeches by President Reagan and Secretary of State Shultz. They address the subject of this volume unambiguously. "How," says President Reagan, speaking of Nicaragua, "can such a small country pose such a great threat?" "Central America is vital to our own national security. . . ." And "Nicaragua is becoming a Soviet base every day that we debate and debate and debate—and do nothing."

CRITIQUES

The critics represented here take five rather different tacks. Marc Edelman directly addresses work by those who identify with the administration's claims:

> Administration spokespeople have bombarded the Congress and public with a barrage of half-truths and outright distortions which . . . has successfully narrowed the spectrum of acceptable discourse about Central America. A coterie of analysts writing in prestigious foreign policy journals has contributed significantly to the Reagan Administration's efforts to shape a consensus around its Central America policies by lending what otherwise would be transparently tendentious arguments an appearance of scholarly legitimacy.

Edelman takes as his role holding these texts to the fire of empirical evidence.

Mary Vanderlaan and Barbara Epstein develop the contradiction inherent in calling, at the same time, for negotiation and coercion. The "dual strategy" that Vanderlaan discusses is the administration's call for both military aid to Nicaragua's neighbors and the *contras* and declared support for reform, human rights, and democracy. She places this squarely in the context of President Reagan's claim that "the national security of all the Americas is at stake in Central America."[3] And she argues there is a difference between the administration's words and its actions.

The Vanderlaan account says something of maneuvering within the administration in the 1981-1983 period. Barbara Epstein spoke with a number of the key figures concerned with Central American policy in a series of interviews conducted in 1985 and 1986. She tells graphically of the contest between advocates of negotiation and of invasion, come to rest in 1986 in reliance on a policy of neither negotiation nor invasion by troops, but "low-

---

[3]   Citing a 27 April 1983 speech.

intensity warfare" sustained into an indefinite future by funding of the *contras*.

The principal approach of the next essay, by Laurence Whitehead, is the force of domestic politics on framing the issues. Whitehead's stated task is "exploring the ways that American internal politics have helped to shape Washington's stance toward the crisis in Central America." While demurring from having accomplished a "full" assessment of administration claims that America's vital interests are threatened by Cuba and the Soviet Union in Central America (on which he acknowledges there remains an "unresolved debate"), he argues that the initiative in Washington lies with an "ideological right," which has failed, paradoxically, to convince the Pentagon, Congress, the media, or much of the public. And perceptions of Central America in Washington, Whitehead insists, "have a surprisingly loose relationship to local realities."

We then come to two articles that remind that there are very different perceptions in Europe, than in Reagan's Washington, of what is being done in Central America. George Philip, writing in the Royal Institute of International Affairs' *The World Today*, portrays the protagonists seeking "to win the sympathies of the outside world." He sees the Soviet objectives as essentially propagandistic, but finds fault in the conventional Reagan interpretation of Nicaragua. And he reminds that Latin American assessments of Nicaragua are rooted in their own concerns. Peter Schulze, a German student of Soviet affairs, explains how we might understand a "European policy" on Central America, and how Europe's own place vis-à-vis the Soviet Union leaves many European analysts altogether skeptical of the key proposition of Reagan policy in Nicaragua. It is also curious to read Schulze's piece alongside David Ronfeldt's expressed concern for European interest in Central America as an unacceptable intrusion on Washington's home ground.

SOVIET AND CUBAN ACTIVITIES

The articles in this section provide a broad evidential basis for judging the Soviet role in Central America. The first five are similar in that each presents a version of Soviet interests in Central America, typically by characterizing Soviet policy prior to 1979 and then interpreting Soviet-Nicaraguan relations since 1979. Each is distinctive, motivated by somewhat different questions, and they illustrate well both the varying readings to which the evidence is open, and some understandings widely shared among analysts. The sixth study is a detailed discussion of trade and aid.

Russell Bartley describes the history of traditional Russian interest in Latin America, calls attention to the role of prevalent notions and popular culture in sustaining in the United States images of Soviet intentions and policy slogans, and explores the proposition that the Soviet Union seeks conventional economic and political scope in its relations with Latin America.

The Jacobsen Report sets out in much careful detail the record of Soviet and Cuban activities in the period 1980-1984: it is widely distributed here for the first time. Originally prepared as a report to the Department of State, funded by its program of external research, the Jacobsen Report received scant distribution from the Department. In particular, it took umbrage at Dr. Jacobsen's conceiving it useful to compare Soviet, Cuban, and East European contributions to Nicaragua with those of other countries, or to show (again by comparisons) how small a part of their global interest was directed at Nicaragua.

Jiri Valenta's article is distinctive not only for its review of Soviet policy to 1981, but because it is believed to have circulated widely among policymakers after it was first published. Valenta perceives the Soviet Union and Cuba as implementing an "anti-imperialist" policy in Central America, ready to exploit revolutionary opportunities, but judges "deep socioeconomic cleavages" to be the prime cause of the Central American crisis.

The second of Marc Edelman's pieces published here focuses on Soviet-Nicaraguan relations and their interplay with the developing policy of war against Nicaragua through the *contra* proxy. Through careful tracing of the chronology, and an alertness to claims that are contradicted by evidence, Edelman argues in effect for a reading of the evidence fundamentally at odds with that of the administration.

W. Raymond Duncan dwells especially on the constraints that limit Soviet and Cuban action in the Caribbean and Central America. Rubén Berríos and Marc Edelman document the relative trade and aid dependence of Nicaragua on different sources in the period up to 1984.

RECONCEPTIONS

Finally, we have a set of three interpretive studies, each offering a quite different and personal view of Central America, and each in effect challenging the relevance of the Reagan administration's policy. Edward Cuddy argues that America's Cuban policy, and by extension its Central American policy, is that of an obsessive compulsion for control; only by abandoning the "Cuban obsession" will America be able to see with clear eyes. E. Bradford Burns, a distinguished American historian of Latin America, insists that we should be attentive to the main issue, that of the need for social and economic change in Central America, and that the Soviet question is a distraction from reality. David Sweet identifies pathological anticommunism as the main source of distortion; he calls for a policy based on our best values, abandoning hegemony, appreciating the reasons that impel men and women to revolt against tyranny, and seeking reconciliation through self-criticism and repentance.

•

One result, surprising to many, of the Iran-*contra* scandal is a determined effort by the Republican party and loyal White House defenders to contend that the *contra* cause was and remains proper. Certainly the claim that we address in this book remains at center stage. In that vein Representative William S. Broomfield, ranking Republican member of the House Foreign Affairs Committee, in his introductory remarks immediately prior to Secretary of State Shultz's testimony on the Iran-*contra* case, advised in the following language, televised live across the nation:

> I think the greatest disappointment with this whole matter stems from the transfer to the Nicaraguan resistance of funds generated by arms sales to Iran in a matter [sic: manner?] the committee has yet to ascertain. Many of us in Congress, Mr. Secretary—both Republicans and Democrats— have worked very hard within the halls of Congress to secure Congressional approval of support for the *contras*. The strategic interests of the United States in continuing to stand with the Nicaraguan freedom fighters has not changed.[4]

Visions of a threat to the United States and its interests continued to be circulated and play some role in forming understandings of policy requirements. In spring 1987 William Safire, columnist for *The New York Times* and onetime Nixon White House speechwriter, no consistent supporter of the Reagan administration but a widely-read conservative, surveyed the likely consequences of a "negotiated settlement" with the Sandinistas.[5] Assume a settlement, he argued, and then consider the consequences of a Gary Hart or Jack Kemp presidency in January 1989. In the "Hart" scenario:

> In go a few medium-range missiles, capable of taking out Miami and Houston. . . . Does anybody seriously foresee President Hart dispatching U.S. ships to blockade Nicaragua and bombers to destroy the installations and kill the Soviet advisers?

And in the "Kemp" scenario, Kemp denounces subversion of Honduras and El Salvador by Nicaraguan-sponsored guerrillas and asks Congress for a formal declaration of war:

> Democrats in Congress, joined by Cohen-Kassebaum-Rudman swingers, would instantly choke up: War? Send in the Marines to an endless quagmire to protect a few corrupt dictators? What are you, some kind of jingo nut?

And in Safire's own view:

---

4   *New York Times*, 9 December 1986.

5   *New York Times*, 9 April 1987.

> A swing group in Congress knows why the Communists have not suc-
> ceeded in subverting El Salvador: it is only because Soviet-backed
> Cubans and Sandinistas have their hands full with the *contras* in
> Nicaragua. If Congress collapsed the *contra* movement . . . Com-
> munism would surely resume its expansion on our continent.
>
> A small but real war is now being waged in Central America. . . .
> The Communist side is not in this war to settle, though it will readily
> sign a list of promises while the bone is in its throat; as always,
> Communists will carry their revolution as far as opposition weakness
> permits. If our side does not win this war with the *contras*, we are going
> to have to stop Communist expansion with another force. That would
> mean the North Americanization of the war.[6]

Safire's point isn't to advocate sending in the Marines but to argue that failure
to support the *contras* today would lead to a policy impasse in the future in
which troops were required but could not be sent.

•

Financial support for the conference and the preparation of this volume
was provided by the Comparative and International Studies Organized Research
Activity of the University of California at Santa Cruz. Several of my
colleagues at UC Santa Cruz have made special contributions to this venture.
James Mulherin proposed the conference and has provided guidance throughout. Without the counsel and encouragement of David Sweet, and in particular
his suggestion of articles for inclusion and preparation of the Bibliography,
this volume would not have reached completion. Others who have taken a role
at one or another stage of the process include Sonia Alvarez, David Mayers,
Michael Brown, and my late colleague Ralph Guzmán. Marie Francois has
played an essential role in making these papers ready.

Bruce D. Larkin

[6] *New York Times*, 9 April 1987.

PART 1

THE CLAIM

1

A New Inter-American Policy for the Eighties

The Committee of Santa Fe (Lewis Tambs, editor)

FOREWORD

During the last several years, United States policy toward the other nations within the Western Hemisphere has been one of hoping for the best. Too often it has been a policy described by The Committee of Santa Fe as "anxious accommodation," as if we would prevent the political coloration of Latin America to red crimson by an American-prescribed tint of pale pink.

Whatever the pedigree of American policy toward our immediate neighbors, it is not working. The hemispheric region south of our border has become America's Balkans, alluding to the tinder box area of southern Europe that exploded into the First World War.

The young Caribbean republics situated in our strategic back yard face not only the natural growing pains of young nationhood, but the dedicated, irrepressible activity of a Soviet-backed Cuba to win ultimately total hegemony over this region. And this region, as Professor Tambs has described it on occasion, is the "soft underbelly of the United States." It is not analogous to Vietnam, nor even to Angola or Afghanistan, important as they may be as global factors in America's equation of continental security.

It is the principal assumption of this study that our country must adopt and embark upon a new policy for inter-American defense and development. In the course of implementing such a policy, we believe that the U.S. Department of State and all of our country's auxiliary foreign policy agencies should

† Editor's Note: The members of the Committee of Santa Fe are L. Francis Bouchey, Roger Fontaine, David C. Jordan, Lt. General Gordon Sumner, Jr. (USA-Ret.), and Lewis Tambs. Lewis Tambs was editor of the report. Ronald F. Docksai, President of the Council for Inter-American Security, which published the report, wrote the foreword. An editorial note to the second printing [1981] states that the authors "are now in a position to make their proposals become policy. Dr. Roger Fontaine, for example, serves as the National Security Council's Latin America specialist. Lt. General Gordon Sumner, Jr., is Special Advisor to the Assistant Secretary of State for Inter-American Affairs."

predicate policy options on the principle that ours is the responsibility of supporting rather than undermining pro-Western governments within our hemisphere. That this is not in itself a self-evident axiom of American policy formulation successfully illustrates the severity of the problem with which this study deals.

During the Carter Presidency, U.S. policy in the Americas has resembled a pathfinder without an azimuth. The pathfinder reads his compass, yet with no idea of True North, he is lost. Able as he may be, however short the journey or simple the directions, he is lost. Like our proverbial pathfinder, Carter foreign policymaking has been a sincere but desperate meandering search through the woods of the world, looking for familiar landmarks to set a bearing. Illustrations are everywhere:

- After seven months of indecision, the White House finally agreed to the shipment of U.S. processed nuclear fuel to India for the peaceful development of India's domestic reactor capability. This decision came in the wake of the Carter Administration's refusal to do so for the Government of Brazil. Despite Brazil's appeal to the American State Department in light of the Indian decision, American foreign policy spokesmen have reiterated the U.S. determination not to ship nuclear fuel abroad. Presently, Brazil is seeking its requisite high technology fuels from the Soviet Bloc.

- The United States, late last year, consummated an agreement with the Government of Canada for America's purchase of natural gas with an explicit provision declining a similar arrangement with Mexico. Ironically, the decision came at a time when the United States has attempted to bring our nation and Mexico closer together, even to the extent of President Carter's appointment of an additional Office of U.S.-Mexican Affairs.

- Over one third of America's off-season crops are grown in Mexico, though irregularities in pricing and shipping contribute to an ambiguous inter-American economic arrangement and the conflagration of border problems. Critical as is the need to standardize such a bilateral arrangement, months of negotiations have produced a deadlock while it is determined whether the U.S. Embassy in Mexico or President Carter's recently appointed additional Mexican affairs office has original jurisdiction in the negotiations process.

- Nicaragua is the size of Illinois, having 1.8 million people, which in 1990 is projected to be 3.5 million. El Salvador's 3.4 million people are crowded into a country of 8200 square miles, slightly smaller than

Connecticut. By 1990, this number will grow to 5.9 million Salvadoreans. These and the remaining ever-populating countries of Central America face the same economic and social upheaval beleaguering every developing country in the world in which over half the respective population of each is migrating to the cities.

Leaving behind their farms or plantations fields, these people seek new employable skills and the jobs that go with them. It has been American overseas investment, multinational and otherwise, which has supplied the missing link. Concurrently, the Carter Administration has tried to encourage such foreign U.S. business activity on the one hand through the Administration's advocacy of tax law changes while, on the other, discouraging and at times seeking to forbid such U.S.-Latin American economic relations in the name of human rights.

For too long, ignorance concerning Latin America in the United States has been matched only by a lack of interest. This is measured not merely as a focus of popular discussion, but by its presence within the policymaking realm of the U.S. State Department, where much more attention is paid to Europe, and even to Asia and the Middle East.

And yet the 7000 miles of land mass stretching from the Rio Grande to Cape Horn is not only physically larger and strategically critical, but potentially richer than our own country. It is an area of continental vastness which in latitude stretches across a fourth of the globe, an area comprising 16 per cent of the world's geography and 10 per cent of the world's people.

The interest of the Soviet Union in a strategic presence within our own hemisphere was clearly demonstrated in 1962 during the Cuban Missile Crisis, and in 1970 when, it has been learned, the Soviets constructed a submarine base at Cienfuegos. To the extent that they would deploy nuclear facilities within our hemisphere, the Soviets would only do so with the support of the host government involved. The degree to which the United States ignores the nations to our south presents an opportunity if not an implicit invitation to the Soviet Union to cajole these nations through the offer of trade credits, technology and markets for South American produce. To the extent that Latin Americans believe that the United States does not care about their future, and that we are insensitive to any concept of a common hemispheric destiny, we are by omission encouraging our southern neighbors to embrace the Soviet bear.

Not through economic power alone can we regain lost ground in the protracted struggle to offset Soviet influence where it counts most. In his recently published biography of Theodore Roosevelt, Edmund Morris describes President Roosevelt's habit "of reminding people that his famous aphorism 'Speak softly and carry a big stick' proceeds according to civilized priorities. Persuasion comes before force. In any case, it is the availability of raw power, not the use of it, that makes for effective diplomacy."

The United States appears weak and indecisive, unknowledgeable and insensitive to the problems of our hemispheric neighbors. The United States has been more than just a wallflower during the Carter years of U.S.-Hemispheric policymaking: our national image has been one of breaking the spirit if not the letter of the Inter-American Treaty of Reciprocal Assistance we originally signed in 1948.

America must once again assume the role of the unquestionably cohesive force in building a Western Hemispheric community. The analysis and recommendations of The Committee of Santa Fe are based on this assumption, pointing in the direction our foreign policymakers can embark. To the extent that *A New Inter-American Policy for the Eighties* can hold the attention of such policymakers, suggesting to them a new azimuth, it will fulfill our desire to contribute to the making of a sound policy for inter-American security, peace and liberty.

> *Ronald F. Docksai*
> *President*
> *Council for Inter-American Security*

•

INTRODUCTION

Foundations for a Fresh, Forward-Looking Foreign Policy

Nations exist only in relation to each other. Foreign policy is the instrument by which peoples seek to assure their survival in a hostile world. War, not peace, is the norm in international affairs.

For the United States of America, isolationism is impossible. Containment of the Soviet Union is not enough. Detente is dead. Survival demands a new U.S. foreign policy. America must seize the initiative or perish. For World War III is almost over. The Soviet Union, operating under the cover of increasing nuclear superiority, is strangling the Western industrialized nations by interdicting their oil and ore supplies and is encircling the People's Republic of China.

Latin America and Southern Asia are the scenes of strife of the third phase of World War III. The first two phases—containment and detente—have been succeeded by the Soviet strategy of double envelopment—interdiction of the West's oil and ore and the geographical encirclement of the PRC. America's basic freedoms and economic self interest require that the United States be and act as a first rate power.

The crisis is metaphysical. America's inability or unwillingness either to protect or project its basic values and beliefs has led to the present nadir of indecision and impotence and has placed the very existence of the Republic in peril. For though foreign policy and national strategy are based on the triad of climate, geography and the character of the people, it is the latter—the spirit of the nation—that ultimately overcomes. And America has forgotten that basically it is the political will behind the policy that counts; that it is the purpose behind the instrument of foreign policy that prevails.

America is everywhere in retreat. The impending loss of the petroleum of the Middle East and potential interdiction of the sea routes spanning the Indian Ocean, along with the Soviet satellization of the mineral zone of Southern Africa, foreshadow the Finlandization of Western Europe and the alienation of Japan.

Even the Caribbean, America's maritime crossroad and petroleum refining center, is becoming a Marxist-Leninist lake. Never before has the Republic been in such jeopardy from its exposed southern flank. Never before has American foreign policy abused, abandoned and betrayed its allies to the south in Latin America.

It is time to seize the initiative. An integrated global foreign policy is essential. It is time to sound a clarion call for freedom, dignity and national self interest which will echo the spirit of the American people. Either a *Pax Sovietica* or a worldwide counter-projection of American power is in the offing. The hour of decision can no longer be postponed.

•

Inter-American Relations—Shield of New World Security and Sword of U.S. Global Power Projection

The Americas are under attack. Latin America, the traditional alliance partner of the United States, is being penetrated by Soviet power. The Caribbean rim and basin are spotted with Soviet surrogates and ringed with socialist states.

No great power is sufficiently strong to conduct hemispheric foreign policies as if the different regions of the world were isolated and did not impact on each other. Historically the Latin American policy of the United States has never been separated from the global distribution of power, and there is no reason to assume that what happens in the 1980s between great states in one area of the world will not affect power relationships on other continents. The Monroe Doctrine, the historic cornerstone of United States-Latin American policy, recognized the intimate relationship between the struggle for power in the Old World and the New.

The three great principles of that doctrine were:

1. "no further European colonization in the New World";
2. "abstention" by the United States from European political affairs; and
3. opposition by the United States to European intervention in the governments of the Western Hemisphere.

The Monroe Doctrine, along with the No Transfer Principle, thus formed the first and fundamental basis of United States-Latin American policy and focused on the impact of the European power rivalries on the Western Hemisphere. The U.S. security objective was to prevent any expanding European power from making strategic gains in the New World as a result of the wars, shifting alliances, or revolutions in the Old World.

The Monroe Doctrine served as a sensitive political device for determining a threat to the security of the Republic. The Doctrine proclaimed that certain activities in the Western Hemisphere could not be interpreted "in any other light, than as the manifestation of an unfriendly disposition towards the United States." The Doctrine prohibited non-American powers from acquiring territory, introducing alien systems, or intervening in the Western Hemisphere. The Doctrine was multinationalized and made compatible with the Organization of American States by the Caracas Declaration of 1954, which stated that:

> The domination or control of the political institutions of any American state by the international Communist movement, extending to this Hemisphere the political system of an extracontinental power, would constitute a threat to the sovereignty and political independence of the American states, endangering the peace of America, and would call for a meeting of consultation to consider the adoption of appropriate action in accordance with existing treaties.

U.S. global power projection rests upon a cooperative Caribbean and a supportive South America. The exclusion of Old World maritime powers from Cuba, the Caribbean and Latin America has helped the United States generate sufficient surplus power for balancing activities on European, Asian and African continents.

Latin America, like Western Europe and Japan, is part of America's power base. Any United States power base, be it in Latin America, Western Europe or the Western Pacific, cannot be allowed to crumble if the United States is to retain adequate extra energy to be able to play a balancing role elsewhere in the world. For a balancing state like the United States, there is no possibility of flexible global action if its power is immobilized or checked in any one area. Indeed, in areas vital to any nation's power potential, preservation of the status quo is not enough. The United States must seek to improve its relative position in all its spheres of influence. If there is a loss of will with respect to the importance of improving a nation's relative power position, it will be only a matter of time until the inactive state is replaced by a competitor.

The United States is being shoved aside in the Caribbean and Central America by a sophisticated, but brutal, extracontinental super power manipulating client states. Soviet influence has expanded mightily since 1959. The Soviet Union is now ensconced in force in the Western Hemisphere and the United States must remedy the situation.

Prior to stating the Committee of Santa Fe's specific recommendations for a responsible U.S.-Latin American policy for the 1980s, the premises and consequences of recent U.S.-Latin American policy must be comprehended and the necessary principles and assumptions for the dangerous 1980s must be presented.

The roots of the present security dilemma of the United States are in the early 1960s—the Bay of Pigs fiasco in 1961, followed by the Kennedy-Khrushchev Agreement ending the Cuban missile crisis of 1962, where the escalation of a threat beyond what had been previously considered tolerable brought acceptance of what had been previously unacceptable. The apparent adoption in Washington of the position during the Vietnam War that Latin America was not strategically, politically, economically nor ideologically important further eroded the U.S. position. And the post Vietnam detente premises of Presidents Richard Nixon and Gerald Ford (that even an intransigent and disruptive Soviet Union lacked the capacity to disrupt an international system now more plural in its power distribution as it involves China as a *de facto* U.S. ally in the containment of the Soviet Union) became the basis for U.S. policy.

President Jimmy Carter's Ibero-American policies, undergirded intellectually by the reports of the Commission of United States-Latin American Relations and the Institute for Policy Studies (IPS), are the culmination of this accommodation process whereby Latin America is excluded from U.S. strategic concerns and independent Latin American regimes are abandoned to extracontinental attacks by the international Communist movement.

Latin American governments were well aware that the Carter Administration, upon taking office, sought to normalize relations with Cuba. The Commission and IPS reports called for basic changes in the U.S. approach to Latin America in general and the Caribbean in particular. Arguing that military security need not be the overriding goal and ordering principle for U.S. policy in Latin America; that the United States should not continue the policy of the isolation of Cuba; that "Cuba's material support of subversive movements in other Latin American countries has diminished in recent years"; that the United States should end the Cuban trade embargo; and that "an equitable new agreement with Panama regarding the Canal would serve U.S. interests not only in Panama but throughout Latin America," the Commission and IPS engineered the end of the American presence in the Caribbean. The Institute for

Policy Studies report was optimistic regarding the socialist governments of Jamaica and Guyana and used the phrase "ideological pluralism" to encourage a receptive U.S. attitude toward pro-Soviet socialist models of political and economic development.

President Carter reflected this attitude at his Notre Dame speech in 1977 when he declared that the United States had overcome an "inordinate fear of Communism." The pardon of convicted Puerto Rican terrorists, the casual attitude toward Fidel Castro's efforts to push the nonaligned movement substantially closer to the Soviet world view, and the cordial reception at the White House in 1979 of three Sandinista members of the Nicaraguan revolutionary junta, which included a member trained in Cuba, became characteristic of U.S.-Latin American policy.

The United States is reaping the consequences of two decades of neglect, short-sightedness and self-deception. Now, the Carter Administration faces a Soviet Union entrenched in force in the Caribbean and a possible Marxist and pro-Cuban oriented Central America. In contrast to simplistic U.S. policies, the Soviet Union has employed sophisticated tactics for enhancing international Communist connections in Latin America and for reducing the U.S. presence. Havana accepts Moscow's doctrine that there is no single road to power for Communism, that local Marxists may employ peaceful persuasion, violent means, or a combination of the *via pacifica* and direct action in the drive to power, and that the U.S. government and private financial institutions may be counted on to recognize diplomatically and support financially Latin American Marxist movements if handled properly.

The Kremlin seeks to wed Marxism to Latin American nationalism and anti-Americanism and to exploit the inability or unwillingness of the U.S. Government's policy makers to support alternatives to Marxist movements in the search for a progressive and stable Ibero-America. Having thus defined the intellectual parameter for clients, adversaries and targets, the Soviet Union has managed to expand its ties with Latin American governments, while simultaneously pursuing subversion and revolution as opportunities are fomented or arise. For Soviet foreign policy is based on creating chaos and exploiting opportunities, and the U.S. power base in Latin America is not immune.

The Castro regime has been providing direct support to urban and rural guerrillas throughout the hemisphere since 1959. When Castro activated OLAS (*Organización Latinoamericana de Solidaridad*—Organization of Latin American Solidarity) in 1967 he did so under the slogan, "it is the duty of the whole revolutionary army to make revolutions."

Cuban success in the Caribbean and Central America is striking. Guyana, under Prime Minister Linden Forbes Burnham, is a Marxist pro-Soviet state. Forbes Burnham applied for associate membership to COMECON in January 1977. Georgetown permitted Cuba to use Guyana's international airport for refueling purposes during the initial Cuban incursion into the Angolan Civil War in 1975. Moreover, when 70 delegates from 18 Caribbean countries attended a labor conference in Georgetown, they called for improved working conditions in the Caribbean by copying "the Cuban socialist model"; deplored the "capitalist and imperialist"exploitation of the peoples of the Caribbean; and praised Communist Cuba for having eliminated exploitation.

Jamaican Prime Minister Michael Norman Manley visited Cuba in July 1975. *Granma*, the Cuban Communist daily, called him "a sincere friend of the Cuban revolution." Manley's son studies in Havana. His government gave official approval to the Cuban Angolan adventure, and his police force, which is larger than the Jamaican army, is Cuban trained. On the theory that Manley's Labor Government was nationalistic, under no forced connection with Moscow, and pursuing ideological pluralism, Jamaica received $22 million in U.S. aid in 1978.

Maurice Bishop came to power in Grenada in March 1979. Bishop's new airport is being constructed by the Cubans. This air field commands the deep water channel alongside the island of Grenada through which flows 52 per cent of all imported U.S. oil. Tankers from Arabia, Africa and Latin America come into the Caribbean and deliver petroleum to refineries in the Bahamas and Virgin Islands, Trinidad, Aruba and Curaçao for processing and trans-shipment to the United States. In addition, over half of the aluminum the United States imports from the Caribbean comes from Jamaica.

The Panama Canal also plays a vital role in U.S. oil supply. Panama is under the control of a left wing military regime which, according to the CIA, was the intermediary in the transfer of Cuban and U.S. arms to the Sandinistas in the Marxist takeover of Nicaragua in July 1979. El Salvador and other Central American nations are now threatened with revolutionary guerrilla warfare. Meanwhile the U.S. Government continues an apparent attitude of strategic indifference while calling for social, economic, agrarian and human rights reforms as if even the most perfect resolution of these problems would arrest Castroite colonial expansion and subversion and thereby resolve strategic issues as a by-product.

The Committee of Santa Fe contends that U.S. foreign policy is in disarray; that the norms of conflict and social change adopted by the Carter Administration are those of the Soviet Union; that the area in contention is the sovereign territory of U.S. allies and Third World trading partners; that the sphere of the Soviet Union and its surrogates is expanding; and that the annual balance sheet of gains and losses favors the U.S.S.R.

The American response of camouflaged escapism to Soviet imperialism must be reversed. The United States must push for an inventive, creative and strategic solution to this situation. Ethical realism provides the underlying moral support to the foreign policy principles the United States has traditionally used to solve the problem of value and power in external affairs. U.S. intervention abroad was only justified for the security of the Republic and was not justified for the shaping of any particular order in any other country unless activities there were tied to an extracontinental threat to the United States. The

United States can grant this same nationalistic perspective to all Latin American nations which do not develop a semi-vassalage-like relationship with an extracontinental super power. Such a semi-colonial connection introduces a sterilizing internationalism into the culture and countries of the Western Hemisphere and undercuts a Latin American policy based on reciprocity.

The Committee of Santa Fe wishes to stress that the United States does not desire to pursue a policy of intervention in the foreign and domestic affairs of any Latin American nation unless Ibero-American states follow policies which aid and abet the intrusive imperialism of extracontinental powers. Such a U.S.-Latin American policy has the potential for substantial Latin American support, especially among the remaining independent regimes. Many years ago the well known Chilean international lawyer Alejandro Alvarez wrote:

> The Monroe Doctrine represents the interests of the entire continent and all the states of America have agreed to maintain it. Furthermore, although up to the present time the United States has been its sole defender, Latin States would now be found who are powerful to maintain it should the United States refuse.

A United States-Latin American policy which fosters American and Ibero-American security, based on mutual national independence and inter-American dependence, promotes autonomous economic and political development based on our cultural and religious heritages, accepts limits on U.S. impulses to promote internal reforms in Ibero-America, and recognizes and respects that the dignity and sensibilities of our neighbors should be pursued. In 1914 the Peruvian statesman Francisco García Calderón wrote about the importance of style in politics. His words should be our guide for the 1980s:

> Latins have a feeling for forms, and respect for the proprieties. . . .
> Nothing ruffles them more than the rudeness of Washington politicians.

Diplomacy, no matter how skillfully applied, is, however, merely a method of attaining foreign policy objectives. Foreign policy and national strategy are, in turn, instruments by which peoples seek to expand or defend their interests.

Defense of a nation's sovereignty and preservation of a people's cultural identity are basic to survival. Both of these elements are being suppressed and sterilized by international Communism. Only a U.S. policy aimed at preserving the peace, promoting production and achieving political stability can save the New World and salvage the U.S. global power position which rests upon a secure and sovereign Latin America. The Americas are under attack. Whither Washington?

•

PART ONE

External Military Threat

Proposal 1

Revitalize the hemispheric security system by supporting the Inter-American Treaty of Reciprocal Assistance (IATRA) and taking the lead in the Inter-American Defense Board (IADB) to support the long list of resolutions which would enhance security of the hemisphere against external and internal threats.

Politics change, but geography doesn't. This hemisphere is still one-half of the globe—our, the Americas', one-half. Our geostrategic, economic, social and political futures must be secured by a hemispheric security system. The dreams of Simón Bolívar and Thomas Jefferson are as valid today as they were in 1826. The IATRA (Inter-American Treaty of Reciprocal Assistance) or Rio Treaty is as vital today as it was in 1948 when signed in Bogotá.

The policy of the United States must be directed towards a rebuilding of the sense of community and mutual interests which are the essential elements of revitalization of this Treaty. The threat represented by the massive efforts of the Soviet-Cuban axis to subvert from within and attack from without the legitimate governments of this hemisphere can only be met within the framework of such a security arrangement. The Soviet bluewater navy, coupled with the massive Soviet presence on the island of Cuba, represent a clear and present danger to all the free nations of the hemisphere. The Rio Treaty is a measured and prudent response to this flagrant threat.

The organ of the Rio Treaty is the Inter-American Defense Board, which was established by the Rio Treaty to advise and recommend to the member governments those measures necessary for the security of this hemisphere. Present policies have been destructive of the expediency of the Treaty and the Board. The clearly stated resolutions of the IADB regarding the Soviet-Cuban threat have been eminently ignored and disregarded by recent administrations. The United States should fully support and assist the IADB in the proper discharge of its functions.

The security system of this hemisphere should consist of three elements or tiers. The first and basic tier is the Rio Treaty. The second should be a subset of the first—the regional security organizations. The third tier would consist of bilateral arrangements between the various members of the first two tiers.

Proposal 2

Encourage regional security arrangements which would contribute to both regional and hemispheric security against external and internal security threats.

As outlined in the first proposal, the basic security arrangement for this hemisphere should be the Rio Treaty. However, this represents only the first step in a three-tiered arrangement. Operating under the nuclear umbrella afforded all the Free World, the Rio Treaty represents a strategic arrangement of the first magnitude, on a level with NATO and our security arrangements with Japan, Australia and New Zealand.

Unfortunately, this arrangement is not sufficient. People do not easily relate on a hemispheric basis: the concept is abstract; and the ability of the average person in the street to relate to such an arrangement is difficult, if not impossible. Therefore, we need something to which they can relate.

The regional arrangement meets this requirement. An Argentine or Paraguayan can understand a regional arrangement for the security of the South Atlantic very easily. It secures his food, his imports and his exports. It is immediate and clear, while the concept of hemispheric security is difficult to visualize and hazy or fuzzy to his experience, and also interjects a heavy North American hand.

The policy of the United States must be to encourage and support these regional security arrangements. This is in clear contrast to the present policies, which have been to discourage such mechanisms. The failure of the regional security arrangement in Central America (CONDECA) illustrates the case in point. This regional security organization has been and is a major obstacle to Cuban-Panamanian-U.S. subversion [*sic*] of the governments under attack—El Salvador, Honduras and Guatemala.

Proposal 3

Reactivate as the third element of our hemispheric security system our traditional military ties within this hemisphere by offering military training and assistance to the armed forces of the Americas with particular emphasis on the younger officers and non-commissioned officers. Offer technical and psychological assistance to all countries of this hemisphere in the struggle against terrorism, regardless of the source.

The policies of the past decade regarding arms sales and security assistance are totally bankrupt and discredited at home and abroad. The only reason for arms sales and security assistance is to enhance the security and viability of the

United States and its allies in the broadest sense. Our leadership role and technology give us this onerous responsibility. Recent tragic failures in this area, particularly in this hemisphere, have encouraged our enemies and enraged and confused our friends.

We must now move to meet both the external and internal threat by using our security assistance to further our national interests. This assistance takes many forms and should be carefully orchestrated to meet the mutual needs of our allies and friends. Through careful assessments, conducted jointly with our allies, we can use the vast reservoir of talent and strength available in this hemisphere to meet the threat. Combining our arsenal of weaponry with the manpower of the Americas, we can create a free hemisphere of the Americas, that can withstand Soviet-Cuban aggression.

By utilizing our military training in this country, the United States can provide not only first class professional leadership, but also provide a moderate model for the rest of the military personnel of the Americas and their families. By living in the United States and observing our political process in action, the military leaders of this hemisphere can once again regain respect and admiration of [*sic*] the United States.

The strategic military advantages to be gained by common training, common equipment and common logistics is obvious. While striving heroically to achieve this in NATO, the Carter Administration has systematically destroyed all attempts at cooperation and commonality in this hemisphere with the single exception of the left wing and brutally aggressive dictatorship of Omar Torrijos. This policy must be reversed.

Proposal 4

> If the present treaties fail, place the Panama Canal under the protection of the Inter-American Defense Board to insure that the nations of this hemisphere have free and fair access to the Pacific and Atlantic Basins.

The Panama Canal Treaties, despite the best efforts of both the Carter Administration and certain elements of the Panamanian government, are in trouble. President Aristides Royo has formalized some of these problems in a recent letter to President Carter. The White House has failed to clarify the situation; indeed, President Carter is totally mum on the situation. Basically, the two countries have ratified and are talking about two different sets of treaties.

The problem now is how to cope with a potentially dangerous and explosive bilateral issue. Traditionally in inter-American affairs, when bilateral negotiations fail to resolve a major strategic issue, multilateral approaches are often found to solve otherwise intractable problems.

The Panama Canal is of major strategic value to most of the countries of this hemisphere. Its security and availability are a significant concern to the countries of North, Central and South America. By placing this responsibility on the signatories of the Rio Treaty, which in turn would designate the IADB as its agent, the problem would be put in proper strategic content and elevated to a position of international visibility which it so richly deserves.

By moving the IADB to the Canal, establishing a security zone under the nineteen flags of the IADB and conducting combined exercises, the free countries of the Americas will put the Soviets and their Communist allies in this hemisphere on notice that we are ready, willing and able to defend our vital interests.

The actual day to day operation and the required maintenance of the Canal could be accomplished by Panamanian and U.S. personnel or by private contract.

•

PART TWO

Internal Subversion

Proposal 1

U.S. policy in Latin America must recognize the integral linkage between internal subversion and external aggression.

The "Roldós Doctrine," named for Ecuador's president, must be condemned. It states that outside powers do not violate the traditional principle of non-intervention if their involvement in a nation's affairs is seen as a defense of human rights. An increasingly bold State Department policy of attacking anti-Communist governments for alleged human rights violations has provided a timely background for such intervention.

Given the Communist commitment to utilize every available means to overthrow the capitalist order and to transform the world, internal and external security become inseparable. Destabilization through misinformation and polarization is the first step. As the subverting assault proceeds into the terrorist and then the guerrilla phase, external (usually Cuban) support and involvement which was originally only ideological merges into logistical support and even recruitment of foreign volunteers to fight the war of national liberation.

The relationship between subversion and terrorism is the same as that between the whole and the part. A revolutionary war usually goes through several phases.

The war begins with the establishment of a subversive apparatus. The second phase consists of terrorism and anti-government activity in the name of human rights and liberation; the third phase is guerrilla war. The fourth phase is full-scale war leading to the final offensive, such as occurred in Nicaragua in 1979 and will very probably be the case in El Salvador in 1980. Throughout the entire campaign a mounting barrage of propaganda is directed at the United States.

The principal goals of the subversive and urban guerrilla who wage war against existing society are threefold:

1. to demonstrate to "the people" that the authorities are powerless to protect them, or even themselves, against the terror;

2. to finance escalating levels of violence, propaganda and terror by kidnapping, murder and robbery;

3. to provoke the authorities into overreacting; (The aim here is to radicalize individuals who might sympathize with the revolution but probably would not themselves assist if it were not for the overreaction which leads to hatred and polarization, and the loss of U.S. support.)

4. to overthrow the established government by combining the first three goals with "propaganda of the deed." As a major step to the ultimate goal, the terrorists create chaos.

The Sandinista triumph in Nicaragua clearly followed this pattern, but it also involved a new element—external aggression by troops with operational bases in Costa Rica that were equipped with arms imported via Panama from Cuba and the United States.

The Sandinistas included Communist cadres from other countries. In spite of all this international aid, when Somoza left the country, the insurgents had not even achieved their objective of liberating the town of Rivas, close across the Costa Rican border, where they intended to proclaim a provisional government. Somoza and the Nicaraguan Guard abandoned the fight because the United States had curtailed re-supply of ammunition.

The Nicaraguan base on the American continent will now facilitate a repeat of the new Nicaraguan revolutionary model. Already U.S. arms previously sold to Nicaragua have been sent to guerrillas in Guatemala. Guatemala is the strategic prize of Central America, adjoining as it does the vast Mexican oil fields.

Proposal 2

U.S. policy formulation must insulate itself from propaganda appearing in the general and specialized media which is inspired by forces explicitly hostile to the United States.

Coverage of Latin American political reality by the U.S. media is both inadequate and displays a substantial bias favoring proponents of radical socio-economic transformation of the less developed countries along collectivist lines. Reform and development are often not distinguished from Communist revolution, and insufficient news attention is devoted to the peculiar geophysical and sociological differences between Guatemala, for instance, and Costa Rica, or between Argentina and Peru. This results in fostering the misconception that the only alternatives are oligarchic, authoritarian regimes which profess anti-Communism and some form of left-populism or socialism.

Radical activists exploit shallowness of understanding about particular countries and the misconception concerning real political and economic alternatives by feeding a constant stream of misinformation which abuses our friends and glorifies our enemies.

Manipulation of the information media through church-affiliated groups and other so-called human rights lobbies has played an increasingly important role in overthrowing authoritarian, but pro-U.S., governments and replacing them with anti-U.S., Communist, or pro-Communist dictatorships of a totalitarian character.

Proposal 3

U.S. foreign policy must begin to counter (not react against) liberation theology as it is utilized in Latin America by the "liberation theology" clergy.

The role of the church in Latin America is vital to the concept of political freedom. Unfortunately, Marxist-Leninist forces have utilized the church as a political weapon against private property and productive capitalism by infiltrating the religious community with ideas that are less Christian than Communist.

Proposal 4

The United States must reject the mistaken assumption that one can easily locate and impose U.S. style democratic alternatives to authoritarian governments and the equally pervasive belief that change *per se* in such situa-

tions is inevitable, desirable, and in the American interest. This belief has induced the Carter Administration to participate actively in the toppling of non-Communist authoritarians while remaining passive in the face of Communist expansion.

Proposal 5

Human rights, which is a culturally and politically relative concept that the present Administration has used for
intervention for political change in countries of this
hemisphere, adversely affecting the peace, stability and
security of the region, must be abandoned and replaced by
a non-interventionist policy of political and ethical
realism.

The culturally and ethically relative nature of notions of human rights is clear from the fact that Argentines, Brazilians and Chileans find it repugnant that the United States, which legally sanctions the liquidation of more than 1,000,000 unborn children each year, exhibits moral outrage at the killing of a terrorist who bombs and machine guns innocent civilians. What, they ask, about the human rights of the victims of left wing terrorism? U.S. policy makers must discard the illusion that anyone who picks up a Molotov cocktail in the name of human rights is human-righteous. Likewise the loudest critics of a country's institutions and way of life do not necessarily articulate the popular aspirations of the majority.

An ideologically motivated and selectively applied policy of human rights is detrimental to human rights properly conceived. It has cost the United States friends and allies and lost us influence in important Latin American countries. It has even contributed to the destabilization and loss or prospective loss of countries like Nicaragua, El Salvador, Guatemala and Costa Rica.

Nowhere are the human rights of life and property and civil liberty more secure now than they were before the selective initiation of the human rights campaign in 1977. The reality of the situations confronted by Latin American governments that are under attack by domestic revolutionary groups assisted by the Soviet-Cuban axis, must be understood not just as a threat to some alleged oligarchy but as a threat to the security interests of the United States.

If the United States will content itself with a foreign policy that promotes peace and stability and the exclusion of Communism from the Americas, there will be ample opportunity to promote respect for concrete civil liberties and actual economic betterment for all the people of the Americas.

•

PART THREE

Economic and Social Policies

A. Energy

Proposal

The United States should encourage and aid the nations of the Western Hemisphere in developing their petroleum, nuclear, agricultural and industrial energy potential. The Eisenhower formula of "atoms for peace" and trading capital and technology for imported energy must be revived.

High energy consumption and advanced technology are the hallmarks of modern industrialized societies. Production is the password to progress. Since the advancement and modernization of Latin America is mutually advantageous to all of the Americas, the United States should seize the lead in exchanging capital and technology for energy imports.

Ibero-America is endowed with vast petroleum potential. Mexico, Venezuela, Ecuador and Argentina are among the world's major producers. Nevertheless, these reserves, although vital to the Free World as Middle Eastern supplies are endangered, are limited. Therefore, the United States should assist in the development of alternate energy sources such as nuclear, fusion, geothermal and solar power, for if Ibero-America is to assume its full role in the defense of the West, it must modernize.

The emerging industrialized nations of Latin America are already committed to the development of nuclear power. Energy needs for current and future development must be met. U.S. opposition by the Ford and Carter administrations to Ibero-American atomic installations failed to stop the projects and has only pushed Mexico, Brazil and Argentina into acquiring nuclear technology in Western Europe and Japan. Consequently, the United States lost not only revenue, but also any guidance over these nuclear programs. Fossil fuels are finite. America must assume the lead in an atoms for peace program which will accelerate industrial and even agricultural production.

Food is a weapon in a world at war. Four of the globe's seven surplus agricultural producers are in the Western Hemisphere—Canada, the United States, Brazil and Argentina. In league with the Pacific producers, Australia and New Zealand, the Americas could exert powerful pressure on potentially hostile states by holding their food imports as hostage, and thus redress the balance between the New World and the Old.

B. Agriculture

Proposal 1

U.S. agricultural trade policy with Latin American countries and U.S. assistance programs for their agricultural sector should seek to maximize comparative production advantages and encourage shifts to the production of cash crops for increased reciprocal trade.

The U.S. winter fresh fruit and vegetable markets are the most obvious examples of where a reduction of import barriers to U.S. markets for Latin American products could maximize comparative productive advantages for mutual gain.

Land, climate and relative labor/technology costs give the United States a production cost advantage in cereal grains and beans *vis à vis* Mexico, Central America and the Caribbean. Similarly, the Caribbean basin possesses advantages in the production of table fruits, vegetables and sugar. Yet, corn and beans are a staple in the diet of many of these countries. Small farmers in Guatemala or Nicaragua could receive greater return by converting to the production of such cash crops as asparagus, raspberries, etc., for sale to the United States and by buying corn imported from the United States.

Cognizant of the economic reality of comparative advantages, Chilean agriculture is rapidly moving away from grain production and expanding specialty crop production for export largely to the Orient, Europe and the United States. As a rule, wheat can be bought more cheaply from Argentina than it can be produced in Chile, while the specialty crops can be sold at high prices elsewhere.

Proposal 2

To the extent that the United States encourages diversification of Latin American agriculture in order to maximize comparative productive advantages, it must allow those products access to U.S. markets.

The United States should seek to expand U.S. market demand to traditional Caribbean basin sugar production through the development and purchasing of sugar-based alcohol fuels.

The price of OPEC oil and the balance of payment dislocation it has caused for countries of this hemisphere makes the rapid introduction of alternative fuel sources from renewable American resources highly desirable. At the same time, petroleum-short Brazil, Jamaica and other Caribbean nations mass produce sugar abundantly. Already Brazil is investing considerable attention and resources in its alcohol fuel program. The United States should join this effort, bringing to bear all feasible advanced technology.

Proposal 3

The U.S. Congress should establish through the Agency for Industrial Development [*sic*] (AID) a direct agricultural loan program for cooperative or communal-tribal enterprises.

Tribal community ownership of land is a centuries-old tradition of Indian cultures. Cooperatives are likewise a useful and efficient institution for collaborative action and joint ownership of productive capital for development and operation.

In Guatemala, where the government is opening enormous tracts of virgin land for settlement principally by Indians whose holdings in the highlands have been progressively fractionalized with each generation's population growth, the new lands are being assigned to community ownership; or if held privately, they are not subject to sale or mortgage foreclosure. Credit resource provision is critically important for these farmers, whose government is wisely encouraging them to shift to cash crops for export instead of growing the traditional corn and beans for their own consumption.

By providing capital funding for the founding of new lending institutions tailored to these unique ventures that possess no mortgageable land equity, the United States could encourage governments striving to help their poor farming population escape subsistence agriculture. Congressional action would publicize the U.S. assistance commitment and provide for oversight to insure that U.S. aid is directed to free and productive ventures instead of to uneconomical statist programs.

Proposal 4

Present U.S. emphasis on public rural infrastructure development should be augmented by stimulating small, creative for profit ventures that will reinvest a significant portion of their profits in technical training and assistance to local farmers both in the course of normal operations and through special community oriented projects.

Since 1974, the U.S. Agency for International Development has been mandated to focus its resources on helping improve the lot of the poorest segments of the population in less developed countries, who are in most cases the rural poor.

In continental Latin America, perhaps a majority of the very poor, rural agricultural population is non-europeanized indigenous Indians who maintain pre-colombian, traditional life styles and languages. Too frequently, efforts to improve these peoples' standards of living and to integrate them into the modern economy of their countries proceeds from a premise of either latent or explicit cultural imperialism—explicitly, that traditional culture patterns must be eradicated in order to improve the indigenous population's standard of living; or latently, through the introduction of development or assistance programs which are inappropriate to the extant cultural milieu, and which could succeed only to the extent that the people abandon their traditional ways and attitudes.

The construction of highways, hydro-electric plants or steel mills is not nearly so helpful to these people as is the installation of simple potable water systems, the introduction of new vegetable crops to improve their vitamin deficient diets and provide cash crops for sale, or teaching them to worm their sheep and thereby increase their meat and wool supply for consumption or sale. To help them now and to open the way for cultural transformation—if that is what they decide they want—these people need simple technology and techniques that show results which they can perceive and which are readily applicable to their immediate situation.

Innovative and adaptable personnel working and living with these indigenous people, not enormous sums of money, is the key to helping them. The existing delivery system for development assistance is not appropriate to helping people help themselves within their given situation, because it either operates through public institutional structures which are remote, overly sophisticated and impersonal, or because—as in the case of the Peace Corps—personnel are too temporary to be able to win the locals' confidence or inadequately skilled in the most appropriate technologies; whereas a long-term, localized and highly personalized approach is necessary.

Small, private, for profit ventures in a targeted area can be turned into a mechanism for assisting indigenous local populations, particularly small agricultural businesses that are committed to applying profits to field work with social impact for community development.

C. The Debt

Proposal

The U.S. Congress should conduct periodic reviews of the debt problems of the Latin American nations and should aim its developmental policy at the objective of creating an autonomous Latin American capital market.

> To complement and coordinate the effort to establish an autonomous Ibero-American capital market, the Congress should encourage direct foreign private investment.

Perhaps the most serious obstacle to economic development in Latin America today is the ever increasing debt burden. Domestic growth is and will continue to be reduced because of the increasing need to use scarce foreign exchange to service foreign debts. Peru's recent experience provides an example of this region-wide problem.

In June 1978 Peru was considered to be practically in default of its debts. Peruvian government debt totaled more than $5 billion, and if all the interest due for 1978 had been met, these payments would have exceeded 55 per cent of Peru's total export income. The general rule of thumb on proportion of debt to foreign exchange earnings is: debt service should not exceed 25 per cent of annual gross foreign exchange income. Peruvian private industrial debt added another $2 billion to Peru's external debt. Default on this seven billion dollar total debt was averted when private banks rescheduled debt payments and U.S. government aid was forthcoming.

U.S., European and Japanese private bankers postponed outright payments due them in the year 1978. Moreover, AID granted Peru a $15 million twenty year rural agricultural loan (at 2 per cent for the first seven years and 3 per cent thereafter). After the U.S. government loan, the private banks made a new loan in December 1978 with longer terms to cover the postponed payments.

Proposals regarding the Latin American debt problem made in the United States usually suggest increasing the flow of U.S. public funds to the multinational banks (MNB) and rescheduling or lengthening the private debt repayment. In addition, Congress is called on to expand its contribution to the multinational banks and to provide direct funds in case of default. The United States, under Congressional direction, needs to take a long look and develop a coherent policy to deal with debt problems in Latin America, within the context of a policy designed to stimulate development and promote an autonomous Latin American capital market.

D. The Free Labor Movement

Proposal

> The United States, working with and through the AFL-CIO and other independent workers' organizations, should foment the free labor movement in Latin America, for autonomous unions are essential to the economic advance and the defense of democratic institutions.

Productivity is the key to progress. Labor, management and capital all share in the responsibility for increasing industrial and agricultural output. Private enterprise and a free market economy have consistently proven to be superior to state capitalistic, controlled economies in delivering goods and services to the consumer.

A free labor movement, if it is based on choice and voluntary association, is basic to the philosophy of a free market economy. Moreover, the right of workers to organize in their own interests, not only to provide economic protection, but also political defense against monopolistic power, be it public or private, national or international, is in the interest of liberty. The United States, since it is one of the few countries that ever gave the working man a chance, is the ideal agent to shield and support the free labor movement, which for its own survival and self interest must stand strong against statism and centralism.

E. Technology Transfer

Proposal 1

The United States should undertake to transfer technology for the Americas as part of our strategic refurbishing of this hemisphere. The objectives would be to strengthen hemispheric ties and enhance security by building viable free enterprise political and economic systems, thereby alleviating poverty, hunger and disease, which are critical problems for many of the countries of the Americas.

Transfer of technology has over the past decade been a constant irritant in hemispheric relations. Particularly in the past three years, allies of the United States have observed the transfer of U.S. technology to the Soviets and the Eastern European nations while at the same time being denied this opportunity by the Carter Administration. As another and critical example of the cynical and hypocritical use of human rights as a political weapon, the United States' friends in the Western Hemisphere are confused and saddened by this outrageous and unwarranted discrimination in technology transfer.

The impact is total and devastating—dooming millions of people who are literate and resourceful to an existence of poverty or semi-poverty. For the Indian populations, the future is even more dismal. Left wing rhetoric concerning human rights and dignity is meaningless to starving families, whether in the Andes or on the island of Cuba.

By adopting a policy that would encourage transfer of technology as one of our strategic tools, the United States would not only enhance its own reputation as the responsible leader of the Free World, but would substantially contribute to the improvement of human rights in the Americas.

As a reciprocal contribution to our common culture, our common security and our common economic and social system, transfer of technology holds the greatest potential for the future of a free and strong Americas.

Proposal 2

As part of a new policy towards this hemisphere, the United States should adopt a strategy of technology transfer similar to that which is currently in effect with Israel. This policy would recognize the strategic importance of the Free World's combining human resources with U.S. technology to enhance the economic, political and social fabric of the individual countries. It would constitute a major and positive response to the problems of poverty, unemployment and economic distress which are the breeding grounds of Communism and urban terrorism. Obviously, this policy would be tailored to meet the needs of each individual country.

Historically, there has been a reluctance on the part of the United States to transfer technology to Latin America. The reasons for this are many and varied. Suffice it to say that this reluctance has produced frustration and hostility on the part of Latin Americans as they have witnessed the United States pouring technology into other areas of the world, including the Communist bloc. In the eyes of some, this was part and parcel of the "economic aggression" waged by the United States against the rest of the hemisphere. This theme was repeated and amplified by Communist movements throughout the Americas. The transfer of technology is a very complex and complicated problem which involves a number of areas, some of which are immediate and straightforward, such as the presence of scientists at various U.S. high technology facilities. Others are more difficult and time consuming, such as the training of managers and programmers in facilities in the United States and the recipient country. Still others are complicated by various laws governing royalties and patents. Examples are the technical aid packages that are transferred to a country to enable the recipient to manufacture the particular item. This latter case requires a high level of technical capacity or substantial assistance from another source.

It is high time that the United States, as a part of a new policy towards our neighbors in this hemisphere, adopt a more enlightened and strategically sensible policy regarding the transfer of technology.

F. Education

Proposal

The United States must seize the ideological initiative. Encouragement of an educational system in Latin America which emphasizes the common intellectual heritage of the Americas is essential. Education must instill the idealism that will serve as an instrument for survival.

The war is for the minds of mankind. Ideo-politics will prevail. The United States has singularly failed to project the ideals of political liberty, private initiative, dogmatic decentralism and prudent patriotism which the American people cherish. Regional differences notwithstanding, these same concepts, inherited from Greek culture, Roman law and Judeo-Christian morality are common to both Anglo and Latin America. Thus, while technical training is necessary to material progress, philosophical education is paramount. For the two great questions of every age—"Who am I?" and "What am I doing here?"—remain. Answers are many and varied and blend well with the diversity of the Americas. But, with the exception of the totalitarian Marxist states of the Western Hemisphere, the independent nations share a common tradition.

Education is the medium by which cultures retain, pass on and even pioneer their past. Thus, whoever controls the educational system determines the past—or how it is viewed—as well as the future. Tomorrow is in the hands and the heads of those who are being taught today.

The United States should not seek to impose its own image on Ibero-America. Neither liberal pluralism nor Wilsonian democracy has been successfully exported. We should, however, export ideas and images which will encourage individual liberty, political responsibility and respect for private property. A campaign to capture the Ibero-American intellectual elite through the media of radio, television, books, articles and pamphlets, plus grants, fellowships and prizes must be initiated. For consideration and recognition are what most intellectuals crave, and such a program would attract them. The U.S. effort must reflect the true sentiments of the American people not the narrow spectrum of New York and Hollywood: unless the image is genuine it will fail. The United States must provide the political will and philosophy behind the policy if the Americas are to survive and prosper.

G. Economic, Trade and Investment Policies

Proposal 1

The United States should promote a policy conducive to private capitalism, free trade and direct local and foreign investment in productive enterprises in Latin America.

Capitalism is concerned with production. Socialism is directed at distribution.

The immediate problem in Latin America is production, not distribution: one must have something to give away first. Of the two types of capitalism—private and state—private capitalism has consistently been the most productive. Hence the United States should, for the commonwealth of both Latin and Anglo America, promote private enterprise.

Both trade and aid are essential. The lowering of tariff barriers among the independent nations of the Americas will facilitate the exchange of goods and services. While the United States should give preferential tariff treatment to all Latin American agricultural and some industrial products, Ibero-America should reciprocate. Liberal importation into the United States of Latin American farm products and key industrial goods would steady the foreign exchange earnings of Ibero-America, thus helping their debt service dilemma and easing the need for U.S. government loans.

Proposal 2

The United States, in order to facilitate inter-American commerce, should not only seek a closer relationship with the Latin America Trade Association [sic] (LAFTA) and the Latin American Economic System (SELA), but also apply for associate status in those two organizations. Full U.S. partnership with LAFTA and SELA would be feasible after the establishment of an autonomous Latin American capital market.

Proposal 3

The economic foreign policy of the United States should be to influence multinational banks to cooperate with the United States in controlling inflation, supporting self financing schemes in productive sectors, encouraging energy development—hydro-electric, nuclear and gas—and financing such projects as rural electrification.

Proposal 4

The United States should support institutional reform of the multinational banks and direct Congressional grants to the Inter-American Development Bank for specific developmental programs, as Venezuela did in 1975; and Congress should consider a Latin American Monetary Fund, all to the purpose of assisting the development of autonomous capital formation capabilities within Latin America for productive purposes.

All the multinational corporations are important issues to those concerned with economic development. But the multi-lateral development banks are critical to a U.S. economic policy designed to stimulate autonomy and cooperation among the American nations. The World Bank offers a large amount of money to many countries. But it is not primarily concerned with Latin America. Congress should continue to use its influence and urge the World Bank to support Hispanic American nations seeking autonomy and cooperation with the United States.

Established in 1959 with an authorized capital of one billion dollars, the Inter-American Development Bank (IDB) was founded to respond to Latin American demands for a lending agency which would finance the Latin American states exclusively on a flexible basis. The bulk of IDB capital was designed to back regular banking operations, while 15 per cent went to Special Operations to make soft loans. The United States took 41 per cent of the regular stock and 66 per cent of the Special Operations Fund (SOF). IDB has operated on the principle of generating self-help among its recipients. In July 1976 nine non-American nations joined the IDB, and now IDB is a multi-regional bank.

Congress has evidenced increasing concern over the lack of oversight, the openness of operations and the accountability of the multinational banks. Congressional assertiveness in these areas would be welcomed, not merely because the U.S. taxpayer is called upon to provide substantial funds for these institutions, but also because the Congress needs to evaluate the over-all effectiveness of these programs and coordinate U.S. direct and indirect economic policies.

Proposal 5

The United States should help protect middle group Latin American industries from destruction by the multinational corporations.

Latin America is industrializing. Though most leaders have abandoned the Raùl Prebish thesis (that while industrial prices tend to increase, the prices of agricultural products tend to decrease) and consequently have launched an over-ambitious program of industrialization and abandoned the fields and farms for the factory, there are many middle group industries which are economically viable. These industries can compete in the open market if they are not stifled or swamped by dumping from MNCs which aspire to maintain a monopoly. Integration of the Amazon and Andean Pacts in December 1979 as well as the strengthening of SELA (Sistema Económico Latino Americano) indicate Ibero-American awareness of the problem. The United States, cooperating with LAFTA and SELA in the reduction of tariffs and establishing oversight of U.S. based MNCs, can contribute to salvaging these middle group industries.

●

PART FOUR

Human Rights and Ideological Pluralism

Proposal 1

The United States should cease targeting its allies with its present inequitably applied human rights program.

A vigorously and equitably applied human rights program is America's wonder weapon against the Soviet Union, its satellites and surrogates. Curiously, the current administration, in spite of the Helsinki Accords and the Basket Two Agreements, has not seriously attempted to apply its human rights doctrine against Castroite Cuba, Sandinista Nicaragua or other Soviet satellites in the Western Hemisphere. Argentina, Brazil, Chile, El Salvador, Guatemala, Somoza's Nicaragua and Paraguay—all old time allies—have, however, been harassed.

Faced with the choice of an occasionally deplorable ally and a consistently deplorable enemy, since 1977 the United States has aided its adversary and alienated its ally. The result, as covered in the section on internal subversion, has been the destabilization of friendly governments convinced that they are confronted with an internationally inspired and supported civil war, who have acted accordingly.

Proposal 2

The United States should apply the doctrine of ideological pluralism to the entire political spectrum, not just to leftist internationalist regimes.

Since 1977 the United States has practiced a one-sided policy of ideological pluralism. El Salvador is under siege by internationally supported insurgents. Seeking to stabilize the situation, the United States aided the installation of a military junta in San Salvador on October 14, 1979. Nevertheless, the country continues in chaos. Moreover, U.S. intervention to prevent a series of takeover attempts since November 1979 by nationalist elements in the Salvadoran Armed Forces has not only further destabilized the nation, but also made a mockery of ideological pluralism. For the State Department appears to equate ideological pluralism with leftist-internationalist regimes and automatically eliminates rightist-nationalist and, seemingly, even centralist parties. This uneven application of an essentially sound doctrine has only served to strengthen the stranglehold of the Soviet Union and its surrogates in the Caribbean and Central America.

●

PART FIVE

Inter-American Relations

A. Special Relations with Key Countries—Brazil, Mexico and Cuba

Proposal 1

The United States must devote particular attention to three nations—Brazil, Mexico and Cuba—because of their particular importance in the Western Hemisphere.

A new policy for the Americas involves more than the sum of its parts. The United States needs more than an assortment of satisfactory bilateral relationships with more than a score of countries ranging from Canada to Argentina. Yet the individual parts can hardly be neglected.

Three countries in particular need close attention because of their intrinsic importance and because the Carter Administration's efforts to improve relations with each have failed. The countries are Brazil, Mexico and Cuba. Brazil and Mexico are selected because in size and strength, they rank first and second in Latin America. Cuba, on the other hand, despite its small size and negligible resources, has become our most formidable adversary in the hemisphere—extending its influence, and the Soviet Union's, far beyond the Americas.

Proposal 2

The United States should publicly announce a policy of encouraging appropriate and reasonable acquisition and use of advanced technology by Brazil, including peaceful uses of nuclear energy. The United States must refrain from all public comment on human rights in Brazil, coupled with a rescinding of the congressionally imposed requirement to report on human rights conditions in friendly and allied countries.

The next president of the United States should extend an early invitation to the Brazilian president for a working meeting in Washington in order to prepare talks including trade, debt and energy issues. In addition, the United

States should actively encourage the Argentine-Brazilian
rapprochement that opens fresh possibilities for the
Southern Cone's rapid economic development, a development that will help stimulate growth in the Cone's
periphery countries—Bolivia, Paraguay and Uruguay.

BRAZIL. Brazil is the giant republic of South America. Its population (120
million); its size (larger than the continental U.S.A.); its economic strength
($200 billion GNP); and its fabled natural resources already make it a
formidable regional power. By the end of the century, Brazil should become a
world standard major power.

By luck, circumstance and rational policy, the United States has nearly
always enjoyed good relations with Brazil, in sharp contrast to our often tumultuous relations with the Spanish speaking republics. Brazil was, for example, the only country in this hemisphere besides the United States and
Canada that made a substantial contribution of blood and treasure toward the
Allied victory in World War II.

In 1976, during the last year of the Ford Administration, Brazilian-
American relations had probably reached their zenith. A working "special relationship" was cemented in a memorandum of understanding signed by the
American and Brazilian foreign ministers. That memorandum promised close
consultations between the two countries on all matters that closely concerned
them both.

The Carter Administration, however, put a quick end to the special relationship by placing heavy pressure on West Germany to cancel its nuclear
power deal with Brazil—a move the White House did not bother to mention to
the Brazilians beforehand.

The Carter Administration's attempts at South American nuclear non-
proliferation were both clumsy and unsuccessful. For Brasília, it meant that
Washington had engaged in unwarranted interference in its affairs. Worse, it
was felt that the United States was intent on denying high technology to a developing economy—a suspicion long held by Brazilian officials.

The United States' insensitivity on the nuclear power accord was equalled,
if not surpassed, by the Carter Administration's public criticism of Brazil's
human rights record—which, incidentally, applying even the Administration's
criteria, by the late 1970s was among the best in the region. Furthermore, Mr.
Carter compounded his Administration's error by adopting an aloof attitude
toward the Geisel government during his 1977 state visit to Brazil, an aloof-
ness complemented by warm talks with "human rights activists." On the next
stop of his trip, Mr. Carter added to Brazil's annoyance by embracing the military dictator of Nigeria, no paragon on human rights issues.

These twin policies of nuclear non-proliferation and human rights have
poisoned relations with our traditional friend and ally at a moment in history
when Brazil is beginning to fulfill its potential. In the near future, relations

can be repaired but not completely mended. The Brazilians have made it quite clear that the old relationship can never be wholly restored because future administrations might do what Mr. Carter did, namely, destroy old assumptions literally overnight.

In view of our recent misguided efforts to manipulate Brazil with scant regard for improving American-Brazilian relations and thus preserving American interests, the new Administration must take the initiative in bettering relations with this key country.

Proposal 3

The United States should immediately initiate high level, interrelated talks on energy, immigration and trade.

The special ambassadorship for Mexican affairs should be abolished, and the United States ambassador in Mexico City must be the chief of delegation in the negotiations. America should keep its markets open to Mexican products. The goal is not the establishment of a greater North American common market, but the U.S. market kept open to Mexican goods—particularly those that are from labor intensive industries.

The United States and Mexico must seek a solution to the flow of undocumented workers into the U.S.A. The goal is providing employment on a temporary basis for a fixed number of Mexican citizens. Strict enforcement of the quota will be carried out by both Mexican and American authorities.

The United States and Mexico must work out long term supply agreements on gas and oil. The goal for U.S. petroleum imports is some two million barrels per day by the early 1980s. Such an agreement could benefit both countries. For the United States, however, Mexican petroleum imports coupled with increased supplies from other Western Hemisphere suppliers would relieve the United States from its dependence on Persian Gulf oil by 1985.

MEXICO. Mexico must have the next Administration's highest priority. If for no other reason, this is so because U.S.-Mexican relations are at their lowest point since Woodrow Wilson's first term in office. The mistakes of the

Carter Administration are not all that is wrong in our relations with our neighbor to the south. Our relationship with Mexico is an inherently difficult one—among the most difficult the United States has in the world. But the sheer ineptness of the White House has brought this always difficult relationship to the point of rupture.

Mr. Carter's first mistake was promising too much and delivering too little. The initial promise in early 1977 suggested a special relationship could be worked out with Mexico. The newly elected López Portillo believed in this promise and desperately needed our help after the debacle of his predecessor's last two years in office.

Mexico's confidence in that special relationship was shaken early in the Carter Administration when the Department of Energy quashed a natural gas agreement worked out by Mexico and U.S. gas companies. It was shaken further by the appointment of an American ambassador generally viewed as incompetent. These initial mistakes were compounded by a presidential visit to Mexico City that involved no substantive negotiations but was marred by diplomatic gaffes committed by the American chief executive after he received a public rebuke from his Mexican counterpart. Finally, the Carter Administration made an attempt to cover up its feeble grasp of Mexican issues and appointed a second ambassador for Mexican affairs headquartered in Washington. That ambassador was supposed to coordinate negotiations on a number of issues, but succeeded only in adding to the confusion.

Three years had been wasted. Unfortunately, nearly all the issues that need resolution must now be settled by the end of 1981. The López Portillo government has one more year of effective power beyond 1980. During his last year in office (1982) power will slip from his hands as his successor develops a political following. Moreover, if a half-century pattern of Mexican politics holds, the next Mexican president will be further to the left politically and therefore more difficult to deal with. In any case, the Carter Administration's own instinct in dealing with regimes to the left of this country is to move to the left in a vain pursuit of mutual compatibility. Unfortunately, in the case of Mexico, such movement on the part of the United States results in the Mexican regime of the day's drifting even further to the left in order to preserve a much needed distance between the United States and Mexico.

Carlos Fuentes, the Mexican novelist, has criticized the United States for looking upon Mexico only as an oil well—ignoring the great civilization that Mexico surely is. Mr. Fuentes has a point. But men of letters too often forget that governments are expected to deal with such mundane matters as the price of gas and oil and tomatoes. The problem is that the United States has failed to deal with the mundane—but the mundane in this case is fundamental.

The next Administration must address critical questions involving trade, energy and immigration, and the negotiated agreements must be in place by 1982.

Proposal 4

The United States must launch a new positive policy for the greater Caribbean, including Central America. That policy will provide multi-faceted aid for all friendly countries under attack by armed minorities receiving assistance from hostile outside forces. The program will wed the most successful elements of the Truman Doctrine and the Alliance for Progress.

Concurrently, the United States will reaffirm the core principle of the Monroe Doctrine: namely, no hostile foreign power will be allowed bases or military and political allies in the region. A revitalized Monroe Doctrine will be made multilateral—a view long held by key Latin American republics.

The United States can no longer accept the status of Cuba as a Soviet vassal state. Cuban subversion must be clearly labelled as such and resisted. The price Havana must pay for such activities cannot be a small one. The United States can only restore its credibility by taking immediate action. The first steps must be frankly punitive. Cuban diplomats must leave Washington. Aerial reconnaissance must be resumed. American tourist dollars must be shut off. The 1977 fishing agreement, highly advantageous to the Cuban fishing fleet, must be reassessed.

The United States must offer the Cubans clear alternatives. First, it must be made absolutely clear to the Cuban government that if they continue as they have, other appropriate steps will be taken.

CUBA. Cuba has been a problem for American policymakers for more than two decades. The problem is no nearer solution today than it was in 1960—indeed, the problem has grown to truly dangerous proportions. Cuba is not only an effective weapon for the Soviet Union in Africa and the Middle East, it is also increasingly effective as a force for subversion of our southern flank—the Caribbean and Central America.

The next Administration must understand that Havana does not want normal relations except on its terms—terms which are inimical to the most basic security interests of the United States and our friends in the Western Hemisphere. Cuba will not accept any *modus vivendi* with this country that compromises its relationship with the Soviet Union.

For more than a decade, Havana's subordination to Moscow's foreign policy goals has lifted both Communist powers to new heights of influence around the world. In Africa and the Middle East, the Cubans have supplied the raw military force that keeps Marxist regimes in power in Angola, Ethiopia and South Yemen. These countries in turn supply Moscow and Havana still further opportunities in mineral rich south and central Africa and the oil rich Persian Gulf.

Meanwhile, Cuban aid to left wing movements in Nicaragua, El Salvador and Guatemala have in the last two years turned Central America into an area of great instability. That in turn presents great opportunities for both Cuba and the Soviet Union in Mexico with its oil and Panama with its canal.

Finally there remains the glaring problem of the Soviet Union's growing military and intelligence presence in Cuba itself. The Carter Administration has done nothing about Soviet pilots flying air defense missions for Cuba. It has done nothing about supersonic attack aircraft (MiG 23s) and submarines being transferred to the Cuban military. It has done nothing about military base improvements in Cienfuegos and San Antonio de los Baños. It has done nothing about Soviet intelligence facilities near Havana.

Cuba at some point must be held liable for working with the Soviets on a successful policy of subversion and destabilization in this hemisphere. At the same time, we must shore up our remaining friends in the area and carry out, for once, some preventive measures.

Havana must be held to account for its policies of aggression against its sister states in the Americas. Among those steps will be the establishment of a Radio Free Cuba, under open U.S. government sponsorship, which will beam objective information to the Cuban people that, among other things, details the costa [sic] of Havana's unholy alliance with Moscow. If propaganda fails, a war of national liberation against Castro must be launched.

The second alternative will be to encourage the Cubans to make a radical shift in their foreign policy. Although it is unlikely that the United States can win the Cubans away from the Soviet Union, we should make it clear that if the Cuban-Soviet alliance is ended, the United States will be generous. The Cuban economy is in ruins—demolished by twenty years of mismanagement and Soviet modeling. U.S. assistance should go well beyond what even the Castro regime is demanding as an American step toward normalization of relations. Thus Havana must be presented with two clear options. It is free to choose either, but the United States must carry out the threat or the promise with equal vigor.

B. Hemispheric Relations

Proposal

In view of the common problems we face in the Americas over the next two decades, the American states should establish an Energy Development Committee open to all countries in the hemisphere which will be dedicated to fostering cooperation on the rational development of gas and oil resources throughout the hemisphere; revitalize the Inter-American Defense Board, the Inter-American Continental Command and the Rio Treaty; and revitalize the OAS itself and relocate the Secretariat in Panama.

The idea of the Western Hemisphere as a special place politically distinct from the Old World—largely Europe—has both waxed and waned since that idea's inception in the Eighteenth Century. At times the idea has been exaggerated—too much expected from it, too soon. At other times, like the present, it is ignored, particularly in the United States. And still at other times, the idea has been used by one nation in pursuit of narrow self interest. The advancing of national self interest, of course, is not pathological behavior, but it is rarely sufficient to convince others that the hemispheric idea is of advantage to them as well.

Throughout this hemisphere's history, however, it can be said that the idea itself has never been completely and definitively repudiated. It has often enough served the interests of the American community, and the institutions and instruments created through common consent, though far from perfect, have been made more perfect through the trial and error of nearly two centuries. The hemisphere as an idea, then, is a process by which the members of this community have drawn together for common advantage.

The goal of this process is not clear, although no one proposes a hemispheric federation of states—a one America as opposed to a one world. The Americas are plural—in culture, history and political institutions. But the Americas are drawn together by similar aspirations, by the force of geography and shared historical experience. In the last decades of this century, they will also be pulled together by common needs, dangers and opportunities.

Two fundamental interests that merge the above three factors are paramount—first, national security; second, economic stability.

The first simply reflects the fact that most of the republics in the Americas have to a greater or lesser degree adopted the principles of representative and democratic government limited in its authority. There is no pretense that all regimes meet the test perfectly—but all regimes are measured against this test, and to a remarkable degree the idea of non-totalitarian forms of government still holds late in the Twentieth Century. Moreover, this principle is under attack by a hostile and alien ideology whose subscribers, principally the Soviet Union and Cuba, are supporting armed minorities bent on revolution—a revolution based on radically anti-democratic, anti-libertarian principles. Resistance to these attacks is vital and cannot be done on a bilateral basis alone. The counter-attack must be multilateral, as was the case during World War II.

An instrument is at hand for multinaturalization [*sic*]—the Organization of American States. The chief complaint against the OAS is that it serves only the interests of the United States. This has not always been the case, but dispersing OAS functions throughout the hemisphere might help overcome that suspicion. Moreover, we propose that the headquarters of the OAS be shifted from Washington to Panama by the end of the century.

Panama, of course, was the site of the first inter-American gathering in 1826, called to order by Simón Bolívar. Panama is centrally located in the hemisphere, and its service based economy could accommodate an Inter-American Secretariat within two decades. Moreover, locating the OAS Secretariat in Panama would further the inter-Americanization of the Trans-isthmian Canal and strengthen the Panamanian economy by the additional presence of the Inter-American Defense Board and its protective defense forces.

Another need is to provide economic stability in the hemisphere. No nation in the hemisphere is invulnerable to economic collapse. The U.S. economy has a major impact on the economies of the Latin American states. But the economy of Latin America—its larger economies especially—have an increasingly greater impact on the United States. That trend will continue for the balance of the century at the least. Thus, each part of the Americas has become dependent on the rest for trade and investment. U.S. policy has, however, not reflected this fact at all.

For the future prosperity of the entire hemisphere, national markets must remain relatively open. Technology must be allowed to flow freely on the basis of market principles. Investment should not be unduly restricted but made to work for the rational economic development of each country.

More importantly, it must be made clear that over the next two decades, the Americas must learn to depend on their own natural resources, especially energy, if the hemisphere is to remain economically healthy. The two largest nations in the Americas, Brazil and the United States, are dangerously dependent on foreign—that is, extrahemispheric—oil suppliers. These same suppliers are extremely unstable and too near the Soviet Union to be considered reliable in the future.

It is only a matter of prudence that our hemisphere become energy independent in the next decade. It can be done. Not only are Mexico and Venezuela presently energy-rich; virtually every nation in the hemisphere—including the United States—possesses as yet vast and untapped sources of gas and oil. This is especially the case in Argentina. What each producer nation needs is a rational energy development policy; unfortunately, the chief sinner in this regard is the United States. Already there is an awareness of the need for intrahemispheric energy market development. The Brazilians and Argentines are out in front. Mexico and Venezuela are not far behind. Only the United States and Canada among the major countries seem dimly aware of the possibilities.

C. Canada and the Americas

Proposal

Canada must be induced to assume greater responsibility in American defense and development by extending its influence into the former British West Indian colonies in and around the Caribbean.

The hemispheric idea at its maximum has always had its geographic limits extending from Cape Horn to the forty-ninth parallel. The great blank space, of course, is Canada, which for historic and cultural reasons has looked toward Britain and to a lesser degree France rather than to the Western Hemisphere.

Although Canada has remained generally aloof from the Inter-American community, it has been an observer at the OAS for many years and is a member of the Inter-American Development Bank. Canada's full participation in the OAS and its many instruments is for Canada to decide, and no pressure should be placed on it at any time in the near or distant future.

Nevertheless, Canada should be warmly encouraged to meet its responsibilities in the region by promoting the economic development and political civility of the English speaking Caribbean. Canada must do so in its own interest commensurate with its historic, cultural and economic ties with the island states. By doing so Canada would become a genuine partner in the hemisphere's security and growing prosperity. Indeed, this should only be a step in an evolutionary process in which the United States, Britain and Canada, the old ABC alliance, would work together in protecting the English speaking political heritage in the Caribbean.

•

Summary Statement

The Americas are under external and internal attack. Latin America, an integral part of the Western community, is being overrun by Soviet supported and supplied satellites and surrogates. The implosion of the U.S. presence in the Caribbean and Central America—America's maritime crossroad and petroleum refining center—continues. Meanwhile the remaining independent Ibero-American nations, doubting the United States' will and purpose, strive desperately to salvage their own strategic and economic situations.

America's wounds are self-inflicted. Decisive action, such as the occupation of the Dominican Republic in 1965, has been replaced by retrograde action, as exemplified by the Carter-Torrijos Treaties of 1978, and by anxious accommodation, as evidenced by the May 1980 cancellation of the sea-air exercise "Solid Shield '80" after a protest by the president of Panama about the provocative presence of U.S. forces in the Caribbean.

The Committee of Santa Fe, therefore, urges that the United States take the strategic and diplomatic initiative by revitalizing the Rio Treaty and the Organization of American States; reproclaiming the Monroe Doctrine; tightening ties with key countries; and, aiding independent nations to survive subversion.

The Committee of Santa Fe further proposes that the United States initiate an economic and ideological campaign by developing an energy plan for the Americas; easing the Latin American debt burden by encouraging Hispanic-American capital formation; assisting Ibero-American industry and agriculture through trade and technology; and, above all, providing the idea behind the instrument of foreign policy through educational programs designed to win the minds of mankind. For the belief behind the policy is essential to victory.

Latin America is vital to the United States: America's global power projection has always rested upon a cooperative Caribbean and a supportive South America. For the United States of America, isolationism is impossible. Containment of the Soviet Union is not enough. Detente is dead.

Only the United States can, as a partner, protect the independent nations of Latin America from Communist conquest and help preserve Hispanic-American culture from sterilization by international Marxist materialism. America must take the lead. For not only are U.S.-Latin American relations endangered, but the very survival of this republic is at stake.

The Committee of Santa Fe
May 1980

2

U.S. Security and Latin America

Jeane Kirkpatrick

While American attention in the past year has been focused on other matters, developments of great potential importance in Central America and the Caribbean have passed almost unnoticed. The deterioration of the U.S. position in the hemisphere has already created serious vulnerabilities where none previously existed, and threatens now to confront this country with the unprecedented need to defend itself against a ring of Soviet bases on and around our southern and eastern borders.

In the past four years, the Soviet Union has become a major military power within the Western hemisphere. In Cuba, the Soviets have full access to the naval facilities at Cienfuegos, nuclear submarines, airstrips that can accommodate Backfire bombers. From these, Soviet naval reconnaissance planes have on several occasions flown missions off the east coast of North America. They also have electronic-surveillance facilities that monitor American telephone and cable traffic and a network of intelligence activities under direct Soviet control. And, of course, a Soviet combat brigade.

During the same four-year period the Soviets have continued to finance, train, and staff a Cuban military establishment which has by now become a significant instrument of Soviet expansion in Africa, the Middle East, and South Asia as well as throughout the Caribbean and Central and South America. Today Cuba possesses a small navy; a sizable number of supersonic aircraft—including Il-14's and MIG 21's and 23's—that can be quickly armed with nuclear weapons; modern transport planes capable of airlifting Cuban troops anywhere in the area; a huge army; and an estimated 144 SAM-2 anti-aircraft missile sites. The presence of more than 50,000 Cuban troops and military advisers in Africa and the Middle East provides one measure of the size and utility of Cuba's armed forces. The Cuban role in training, supplying, and advising revolutionary groups throughout the Caribbean and Central America illustrates the hemispheric implications of this build-up.

"U.S. Security & Latin America" is reprinted from *Commentary*, January 1981, by permission; all rights reserved.

The first fruits of these efforts are the new governments of Grenada and Nicaragua, whose commitment to Marxist-Leninist principles and solidarity with Soviet/Cuban policies led Castro to brag on returning from Managua, "Now there are three of us." There may soon be four. El Salvador, having arrived now at the edge of anarchy, is threatened by progressively well-armed guerrillas whose fanaticism and violence remind some observers of Pol Pot. Meanwhile, the terrorism relied on by contemporary Leninists (and Castroites) to create a "revolutionary situation" has reappeared in Guatemala.

Slower but no less serious transformations are underway in Guyana, where ties to Castro have become extensive, tight, and complex, and in Martinique and Guadeloupe, where Castroite groups threaten existing governments. (In Dominica and Jamaica, the recent electoral victories of Eugenia Charles and Edward Seaga have for the moment reversed the Castroite tides there.) Fidel Castro is much clearer than we have been about his interests and intentions in the area, and frequently declares, as at last year's meeting of the nonaligned in Havana, "I will pursue to the end the anti-imperialist struggles of the Caribbean people and especially those of Puerto Rico, Belize, Guadeloupe, Martinique, and Guyana."

American policies have not only proved incapable of dealing with the problems of Soviet/Cuban expansion in the area, they have positively contributed to them and to the alienation of major nations, the growth of neutralism, the destabilization of friendly governments, the spread of Cuban influence, and the decline of U.S. power in the region. Hence one of the first and most urgent tasks of the Reagan administration will be to review and revise the U.S. approach to Latin America and the Caribbean.

Such a review should begin not just with the previous administration's policy in the hemisphere, but with the quiet process by which new theories of hemispheric relations came to preempt discussion within that somewhat amorphous but very real group known as the foreign-policy establishment. For to an extent unusual in government, Carter administration policies toward Latin America and the Caribbean (as in the world more broadly) were derived from an ideology rather than from tradition, habit, or improvisation.

Indeed, nothing is as important as understanding the relationship between the recent failures of American policy—in Latin America and elsewhere—and the philosophy of foreign affairs that inspired and informed that policy. Such an effort of understanding requires, first, that we disregard the notion that the failure of the Carter policy was the personal failure of a man unskilled in the ways of diplomacy; and, second, that we look beyond superficial day-to-day policy changes to the stable orientations that reasserted themselves after each discrete crisis in world affairs.

•

Those orientations had their roots in the Vietnam experience, less as it was fought in Southeast Asia than as it was interpreted in Washington and

New York. President Carter, after all, was not the only political leader in America to have lost his "inordinate" fear of Communism, lost his appetite for East-West competition, grown embarrassed by the uses of American power, become ashamed of past U.S. policies, and grown determined to make a fresh start. By the time Richard Nixon had left office, a large portion of the political elite in America, including a majority of the Congress, had drawn away not only from Vietnam but from what was more and more frequently called the cold war—the revisionists' preferred term for U.S. determination to resist the expansion of Soviet power.

From these feelings were inferred the famous "lessons" of Vietnam—that the cold war was over, that concern with Communists should no longer "overwhelm" other issues, that forceful intervention in the affairs of another nation is impractical and immoral, that we must never again put ourselves on the "wrong side of history" by supporting a foreign autocrat against a "popular movement," and that we must try to make amends for our deeply flawed national character by modesty and restraint in the arenas of power and the councils of the world. Underpinning these "lessons" was a new optimistic theory of historical development which came in the decade of the 70's to focus the discussion of the future within the dominant foreign-policy elite.

No one expressed the new spirit better than Zbigniew Brzezinski, whose book, *Between Two Ages* (sponsored by the Council on Foreign Relations), spelled out the implication of the new spirit for Latin American policy. Brzezinski argued that U.S. Latin American policies were inappropriate to the new realities of declining ideological competition, declining nationalism, increased global interdependence, and rising Third World expectations. The U.S. should therefore give up its historic hemispheric posture, which had postulated a "special relationship" with Latin America and emphasized hemispheric security and, since World War II, anti-Communism. We should, instead, make an explicit move to abandon the Monroe Doctrine, "concede that in the new global age, geographic or hemispheric contiguity no longer need be politically decisive," adopt a "more detached attitude toward revolutionary processes," demonstrate more "patience," and take an "increasingly depoliticized" approach to aid and trade.

The views of hemispheric policy expressed in *Between Two Ages* were further elaborated in two other documents born in the bosom of the foreign-policy establishment: the reports issued in the name of the Commission on United States-Latin American Relations headed by Sol Linowitz and composed of "an independent, bipartisan group of private citizens from different sectors of U.S. society" funded by the Ford, Rockefeller, and Clark foundations. The intellectual framework and most of the specific recommendations of the two Linowitz reports were identical. Both affirmed that economic and technological developments had created new international problems, and that interdependence had generated a pressing need for a new global approach to those problems. U.S. policy toward Latin America, "from the Monroe Doctrine through the

Good Neighbor Policy to the Alliance for Progress and its successor, the Mature Partnership," was outmoded because based on assumptions which had been overtaken by history. Earmarked for the dustbin were the beliefs that the United States should have a special policy for Latin America; that Latin America constituted a "sphere of interest" in which the U.S. could or should intervene (overtly or covertly) to prevent the establishment of unpalatable governments; and that national security should be an important determinant of U.S. policy toward that area. Now, the first Linowitz report counseled:

> It [U.S. policy] should be less concerned with security in the narrowly military sense than with shared interests and values that would be advanced by mutually satisfactory political relations.

The new approach was to be free of paternalism, "respectful of sovereignty," tolerant of political and economic diversity. Above all, it was to be set in a consistent global framework.

Most of the specific recommendations of the two Linowitz reports— negotiating the Panama Canal treaties, "normalizing" relations with Cuba, "liberalizing" trade and "internationalizing" aid, promoting human rights, and never, ever, intervening militarily—flowed from these new assumptions. Given detente, the U.S. could and should "keep local and regional conflicts outside the context of the superpower relationship" and no longer "automatically" see "revolutions in other countries and intraregional conflicts . . . as battlefields of the cold war." And given interdependence (manifested in global phenomena like inflation and multinational corporations), the U.S. should no longer hope for or seek "complete economic and political security . . . " but instead participate in the new international agenda.

Despite the commission's determined globalism, it recognized that Cuba constituted a special case. Both reports recommended U.S. initiatives toward "normalization" of relations with Cuba and some acts (removing restrictions on travel, increasing scientific and cultural exchanges) regardless of overall progress on normalization. But the second report also noted Cuba's military involvement in Africa and its support for "militant" and violence-prone Puerto Rican *independistas,* and concluded that full normalization of relations, however desirable, could take place only as Cuba gave assurances that its troops were being withdrawn from Angola and that it had no intention of intervening elsewhere.

●

The most striking characteristic of the Linowitz recommendations was their disinterested internationalist spirit. U.S. policy, it was assumed, should be based on an understanding of "changed realities" and guided by an enlightened confidence that what was good for the world was good for the United

States. Power was to be used to advance moral goals, not strategic or economic ones. Thus sanctions could be employed to punish human-rights violations, but not to aid American business; power could be used "to the full extent permitted by law" to prevent terrorist actions against Cuba, but not to protect U.S. corporations against expropriation. Nor was power to be a factor in designing or implementing economic aid or trade programs *except* where these were intended to promote human rights, disarmament, and nuclear nonproliferation.

Like Brzezinski's *Between Two Ages,* the Linowitz reports were, in the most fundamental sense, utopian. They assumed that technological change had so transformed human consciousness and behavior that it was no longer necessary for the United States to screen policies for their impact on national security. To be sure, neither argues that self-interest, conflict, or aggression had been entirely purged from the world. But Brzezinski asserted (and the Linowitz commission apparently believed) that only the Soviet Union was still engaged in truly "anachronistic" political behavior against which it was necessary to defend ourselves. Since no Latin American nation directly threatened the position of the United States, relations with them could be safely conducted without regard for national security.

Adopting the Linowitz commission's recommendations thus required abandoning the strategic perspective which had shaped U.S. policy from the Monroe Doctrine down to the eve of the Carter administration, and at the center of which was a conception of the national interest and a belief in the moral legitimacy of its defense. In the Brzezinski-Linowitz approach, morality was decoupled from the national interest, much as the future was divorced from the past. The goals recommended for U.S. policy were all abstract and supranational—"human rights," "development," "fairness."

Still, if the Linowitz reports redefined the national interest, they did not explicitly reject it as a guide to policy or name the U.S. as the enemy. This was left to the report of yet another self-appointed group whose recommendations bore an even closer resemblance to the actual policies of the Carter administration. This report, *The Southern Connection,* was issued by the Institute for Policy Studies Ad Hoc Working Group on Latin America. The group included key personnel of the Linowitz commission, and it endorsed most of the specific recommendations of the second Linowitz report—divestment of the Panama Canal, normalization of relations with Cuba, strict control of anti-Castro activists, aid through multilateral institutions, limitations on arms sales and nuclear proliferation, and systematic linkage of human-rights concerns to all other aspects of policy. But the IPS report went beyond these in various respects.

First, it not only proposed a break with the past, but contained a more sweeping indictment of past U.S. policy as reflecting an "unquestioned presumption of U.S. superiority" and an "official presumption of hegemony" which was not only outdated but also "morally unacceptable."

Second, it went beyond the call for normalization of relations with Cuba to a demand that the U.S. "*support* the ideologically diverse and experimental approaches to development" (emphasis added), recognizing that "both the need for change and the forces propelling such change in the developing areas are powerful and urgent." Latin America's "most challenging development experiments" were identified as Cuba, Jamaica, and Guyana.

Third, the IPS report located the ground of human-rights violations and "institutionalized repression" throughout Latin America in U.S. interests, "virulent anti-Communism," and "national development based on free play of market forces." The remedy: "practical steps to reduce [socio-economic] inequities are . . . steps toward the mitigation of the broader human-rights crisis of our times." That is, fight for human rights with socialism.

The ease with which the Linowitz recommendations were incorporated into the IPS analysis and report demonstrated how strong had become the affinity between the view of the foreign-policy establishment and the New Left, how readily the categories of the new liberalism could be translated into those of revolutionary "socialism," and how short a step it was from utopian globalism and the expectation of change to anti-American perspectives and revolutionary activism. And the impact of these ideas on the Carter administration was enhanced by the appointment of members and associates of the IPS group (such as Robert Pastor, Mark Schneider, and Guy Erb) to key Latin American policy positions. In the administration these officials joined others with like-minded approaches to the Third World, including Ambassador Andrew Young and his deputy Brady Tyson.

•

This whole cluster of ideas—of facing painful truths, making a fresh start, forswearing force, and pursuing universal moral goals—was enormously attractive to Jimmy Carter. No sooner was he elected than he set out to translate them into a new policy for dealing with the nations of the hemisphere.

The repudiation of our hegemonic past was symbolized by the Panama Canal Treaties, to which the Carter administration—from the President on down—attached great importance and of which it was inordinately proud. As Vice President Mondale put it in Panama City, the treaties symbolized "the commitment of the U.S. to the belief that fairness and not force should lie at the heart of our dealings with the nations of the world."

Anastasio Somoza's Nicaragua had the bad luck to become the second demonstration area for the "fresh start" in Latin America. Just because the regime had been so close and so loyal to the U.S., its elimination would, in exactly the same fashion as the Panama Canal Treaties, dramatize the passing of the old era of "hegemony" in Central America and the arrival of the new era of equity and justice. As the editor of *Foreign Affairs*, William Bundy noted,

"Somoza [was] as good a symbol as could have been found of past U.S. policies in Latin America."

The "global" approach adopted by the Carter administration constituted another sharp break with past U.S. practice. The "special relationship" with Latin America was gone. In speech after speech, the President, the Vice President, Secretary of State Vance, and Assistant Secretaries for Inter-American Affairs Terrance Todman and Viron Vaky explained that henceforth there would not *be* a U.S. policy toward Latin America. Instead, hemispheric policy would be incorporated into a global framework and Latin America would be treated in the context of the "North-South " dialogue. "What we do in Latin America," Vaky asserted, "must be a consistent part of our global policies."

Incorporating the nations of Latin America into a "global framework" meant deemphasizing U.S. relations with them. Especially, it meant reducing U.S. assistance to the area, since from the perspective of North-South relations, Latin America's claim to assistance was not nearly as impressive as that of most other nations of the so-called Third World. And, once the strategic perspective was abandoned, there was no reason at all for military assistance.

Not surprisingly, therefore, U.S. assistance to the countries of Latin America declined steadily during the Carter years. By 1980, the administration was requesting only half as much economic aid for Latin America as a decade earlier. Military assistance declined even more drastically—both quantitatively and qualitatively. Fewer countries were slated to receive military assistance and more strings were attached to how they could use the amounts received. No new weapons systems could be purchased; instead, everyone was to be encouraged to acquire non-lethal weapons. Assistance to military training (which had produced many personal and professional ties between U.S. and Latin American officers) was cut sharply.

The "global" approach also encouraged the imposition of unprecedented curbs on the sale of arms. By 1978, the U.S., long the most important supplier to Latin America, accounted for only 10 percent of arms sales. President Carter bragged to the OAS, "We have a better record in this hemisphere than is generally recognized. Four other nations of the world sell more weapons to Latin America than does the United States."

The impact of the global approach was felt beyond arms sales. Although the nations of Latin America are major trading partners of the United States, and in 1979 accounted for one-sixth of total U.S. exports, and 80 percent of U.S. private investment in the developing world, the Carter administration's manifest unconcern for hemispheric economic ties (as recommended in the Linowitz and IPS reports) resulted in a steady loss of ground to European and Asian competitors, all of whom enjoyed heavy support from their governments.

The global approach involved deemphasizing Latin American relations, not destabilizing governments. But other aspects of the Carter doctrine com mitted the administration to promoting "change." "Change," indeed, was the favorite word of the administration policy-makers. In speeches with titles like "Currents of Change in Latin America," Carter, Vance, and their associates reiterated their conviction that the world was in the grip of an extraordinary process of transformation which was deep, irresistible, systematic, and desirable. Administration spokesmen reiterated in the fashion of a credo that "our national interests align us naturally and inescapably with the forces of change, of democracy, of human rights, and of equitable development" (Philip Habib). And the belief that the whole world was caught up in a process of modernization moving it toward greater democracy and equality subtly transformed itself into an imperative: the U.S. should throw its power behind the "progressive" forces seeking change, even if they "seemed" anti-American or pro-Soviet.

•

If commitment to "change" was the rock on which Carter's Latin American policy was built, his human-rights policy was the lever to get change started. Two aspects of the Carter approach to human rights are noteworthy. First, concern was limited to violations of human rights by governments. By definition, activities of terrorists and guerrillas could not qualify as violations of human rights, whereas a government's efforts to repress terrorism would quickly run afoul of Carter human-rights standards.

Secondly, human rights were defined not in terms of personal and legal rights—freedom from torture, arbitrary imprisonment, and arrest, as in the usage of Amnesty International and the U.S. Foreign Assistance Acts of 1961 and 1975—but in accordance with a much broader conception which included the political "rights" available only in democracies and the economic "rights" promised by socialism (shelter, food, health, education). It may be that no country in the world meets these standards; certainly no country in the Third World does. The very broadness of the definition invited an arbitrary and capricious policy of implementation. Panama, for instance, was rather mysteriously exempt from meeting the expansive criteria of the State Department's human-rights office, while at the same time the other major nations of Central America were being censored (and undermined) for violations.

Why Panama, a dictatorship with a higher per-capita income than Nicaragua, El Salvador, or Guatemala, did not qualify as a gross violator of human rights while the latter countries did; why and how an administration committed to nonintervention in the internal affairs of nations could try to replace an unacceptable government in Nicaragua with one more palatable to it; why such an administration should attempt not only to "normalize" relations with Cuba but also to destabilize the governments of El Salvador and

Guatemala—to answer these questions required on the part of the policy-makers an intuitive understanding of which governments were outmoded and which reflected the wave of the future. What was *not* required was an ability to distinguish between which were Communist and which were non-Communist. The President and other members of his administration apparently believed with Brzezinski that in most of the world ideological thinking had already given way to pragmatism and problem-solving, and that a concern with Communist ideology was therefore just another artifact of a past epoch, "the era of the cold war."

Ignoring the role of ideology had powerful effects on the administration's perception of conflicts and on its ability to make accurate predictions. Although Fidel Castro has loudly and repeatedly proclaimed his revolutionary mission, and backed his stated intentions by training insurgents and providing weapons and advisers, Carter's Assistant Secretary for Inter-American Affairs, William Bowdler, described Cuba as "an inefficient and shabby dictatorship"— a description more appropriate to, say, Paraguay, than to an expansionist Soviet client state with troops scattered throughout the world. The refusal to take seriously, or even to take into account, the commitment of Fidel Castro or Nicaragua's Sandinista leadership to Marxist-Leninist goals and expansionist policies made it impossible to distinguish them either from traditional authoritarians or from democratic reformers, impossible to predict their likely attitudes toward the United States and the Soviet Union, impossible to understand why in their view Costa Rica and Mexico as well as Guatemala and Honduras constituted inviting targets. Ignoring the force of ideology—and its powerful contemporary embodiments—fatally distorted the Carter administration's view of politics in Central America and elsewhere.

●

The policies which grew out of these expectations have had a large impact on U.S. relations with most nations of South America. In Central America in particular, the direction of administration policy interacted with the presence there of weak regimes and Cuban-supported insurgents to transform the region into a battleground in an ideological war that the administration did not understand and could not acknowledge.

Except for Mexico, the nations of Central America are quite small, and, by North American standards, quite poor. There are significant social and economic differences among them. Guatemala's large traditionalist Indian population and multiple linguistic groups are unique in the region, and bring with them special problems of economic, social, and political integration. El Salvador's overcrowding places especially heavy strains on its institutions. Revenues from the Canal and the Canal Zone give Panama a higher per-capita in come than any of its neighbors except Costa Rica and about twice that of the sparse, scattered people of Honduras.

Despite their differences, these countries also share a good many social and economic characteristics. All are "modernizing" nations in the sense that in each, urban, industrial, mobile, "modern" sectors coexist with traditional patterns of life. In each, a large portion of the population is still engaged in agriculture—most often employed as landless laborers on large estates and plantations that have long since made the transition to commercial agriculture. Economic growth rates in Central America have been above the Latin American average and per-capita income is high enough to rank these nations among the "middle-income" countries of the world. But in all of them wealth is heavily concentrated in a small upper class and a thin but growing middle class, and large numbers live as they have always lived—in deep poverty, ill-nourished, ill-housed, illiterate. Things have been getting better for the people of Central America—infant mortality rates have dropped, years in school have increased—but they have been getting better slowly. It has been easier to break down the myths justifying the old distribution of values in society than to improve access to education, medical care, decent housing, good food, respect, and political power.

There are also *political* differences among the small nations of Central America. Costa Rica has managed to develop and maintain (since 1948) a genuine democracy. Honduran politics have been especially violent, while Nicaragua (under the Somozas) was the most stable political regime. But again despite differences, Guatemala, Honduras, El Salvador, Nicaragua, and Panama (like Costa Rica before 1948) share several characteristics with one another and with most of the nations of Latin America. These include a continuing disagreement about the legitimate ends and means of government, a pervasive distrust of authority, a broad ideological spectrum, a low level of participation in voluntary associations, a preference for hierarchical modes of association (church, bureaucracy, army), a history of military participation in politics, and a tradition of *personalismo*.

The boundaries between the political system, the economy, the military establishment, and the Church are often unclear and unreliable. Weak governments confront strong social groups, and no institution is able to establish its authority over the whole. Economic, ecclesiastical, and social groups influence but do not control the government; the government influences but does not control the economy, the military, the Church, and so on.

•

A democratic facade—elections, political parties, and fairly broad participation—is a feature of these systems. But the impact of democratic forms is modified by varying degrees of fraud, intimidation, and restrictions on who may participate. Corruption (the appropriation of public resources for private use) is endemic. Political institutions are not strong enough to channel and contain the claims of various groups to use public power to enforce preferred policies. No procedure is recognized as *the* legitimate route to power. Competition for influence proceeds by whatever means are at hand: the Church manipulates symbols of rectitude; workers resort to strikes; businessmen use bribery; political parties use campaigns and votes; politicians employ persuasion, organization, and demagoguery; military officers use force. Lack of consensus permits political competition of various kinds in various arenas, and gives the last word to those who dispose of the greatest force. That usually turns out to be the leaders of the armed forces; most rulers in the area are generals.

Violence or the threat of violence is an integral, regular, predictable part of these political systems—a fact which is obscured by our way of describing military "interventions" in Latin political systems as if the system were normally peaceable. Coups, demonstrations, political strikes, plots, and counterplots are, in fact, the norm.

Traditionally, however, actual violence has been limited by the need to draw support from diverse sectors of the society and by the fact that politics has not been viewed as involving ultimate stakes. The various competitors for power have sought control of government to increase their wealth and prestige, not for the "higher" and more dangerous purpose of restructuring society. In traditional Latin politics, competitors do not normally destroy each other. They suffer limited defeats and win limited victories. The habit of permitting opponents to survive to fight another day is reflected in the tendency of Latin regimes to instability. In such a system a government normally lasts as long as it is able to prevent a coalition from forming among its opponents. Because there is no consensus on what makes government itself legitimate, successive regimes remain vulnerable to attacks on their legitimacy. They are also especially vulnerable to attacks on public order, which tends to be tenuous and to lack a firm base in tradition, habit, and affection.

To these patterns of political interaction there has been added in recent years the unfamiliar guerrilla violence of revolutionaries linked to Cuba by ideology, training, and the need for support, and through Cuba to the Soviet Union. Such groups rely on terrorism to destroy public order, to disrupt the economy and make normal life impossible, to demoralize the police, and mortally wound the government by demonstrating its inability to protect personal security and maintain public authority. As Robert Chapman has emphasized, a revolutionary situation can be created in any country whose government is weak or whose economy is vulnerable or dependent, with or without the participation of the masses.[†]

[†] Other new participants in the traditional pattern of political competition include the Socialist International and the Catholic Left. A number of socialist leaders (Willy Brandt, Olof Palme, François Mitterand, Michael Manley), unable to win popular support for peaceful

The nations of Central America (including Mexico) and the Caribbean suffer from some form of institutional weakness—because significant portions of the population have not been incorporated into the political system, and/or because political action is not fully institutionalized, and/or because the legitimacy of the government is in doubt, and/or because the economy is vulnerable to shifts in the international market, and/or because regular infusions of aid are required, and/or because rising expectations have outstripped capacities. All are vulnerable to disruption, and must rely on force to put down challenges to authority.

It is at this point that the roles of Cuba on the one hand, and the U.S. on the other hand, become crucial. Cuba stands ready to succor, bolster, train, equip, and advise revolutionaries produced within these societies and to supply weapons for a general insurgency when that is created. The U.S. is important as a source of economic aid and moral and military support. Traditionally it has also exerted a veto power over governments in the area and reinforced acceptable governments with its tacit approval. Thus, to the objective economic and political dependency of nations in the area has been added a widespread sense of psychological dependency. When aid and comfort from the U.S. in the form of money, arms, logistical support, and the services of counterinsurgency experts are no longer available, governments like those of Nicaragua, El Salvador, and Guatemala are weakened. And when it finally sinks in that the U.S. desires their elimination and prefers insurgents to incumbents, the blow to the morale and confidence of such weak traditional regimes is devastating.

•

The case of Nicaragua illustrates to perfection what happens when "affirmative pressures for change" on the part of the U.S. interact with Cuban-backed insurgency and a government especially vulnerable to shifts in U.S. policy.

The Nicaraguan political tradition combined participatory and autocratic elements in a characteristic Latin mix. *Personalismo*, popular sovereignty, and brute force were present in the politics of Nicaragua from its founding as a separate nation in 1938 to the Sandinista triumph in July 1979. Throughout the 19th century and the first three decades of the 20th, geographically-based political factions representing a single, small ruling class competed under a

revolution in their own countries, have grown progressively enthusiastic about revolution elsewhere and less fastidious about the company they keep and the methods utilized. As for the Catholic Left, its interest in revolution on this earth has waxed as its concern with salvation in heaven has waned. Both the Socialist International and the radical Catholics conceive themselves as specialists in political rectitude, and their participation in Central American politics has enhanced its moralistic content at the same time that Cuban/Soviet participation has enhanced its violence.

symbolic two-party system in elections in which neither contender was willing to accept an unfavorable outcome. Frequently victory was obtained by enlisting the help of foreign governments and/or financial interests.

The United States was repeatedly called on by incumbent governments for assistance in maintaining peace. In 1910 it was the Conservatives who requested financial assistance and advice, and in 1912, again at their request, the U.S. posted a 100-man legation guard to Nicaragua. From then until 1933 an American military presence was a regular feature of the Nicaraguan political system. These U.S. troops (who at their height numbered about 2,700) supervised presidential elections and organized a National Guard which was conceived as a professional national police force that would remain aloof from politics. In 1936, less than three years after American military forces had withdrawn, the leader of this "non-political army," Colonel Anastasio Somoza Garcia, ousted the Liberal president, Juan B. Sacasa. In this manner began the more than four decades of Nicaraguan politics dominated by the Somoza family.

Somocismo was based in the first instance on the military power of the National Guard. Its durability, however, also owed much to the political skills of the successive Somozas who ruled the country and headed its armed forces. These skills were reflected in the construction of an organizational base to support their personal power, long-standing success in exploiting divisions among their opponents, and the ability to retain U.S. support. The organizational basis of the Somozas' power is the most interesting factor because, like that of Juan Peron, it was largely created rather than captured.

The Somoza organization rested on four pillars: a hierarchically structured national party forged on the base of the traditional Liberal party; an expanded bureaucracy whose members also served as party workers; a national federation of trade unions created by the Somozas; and the National Guard. The whole operated rather like an efficient urban political machine, oiled by jobs, pensions, profits, and status, and perquisites of various kinds. Most urban machines, however, do not have a private army. The loyalty of the National Guard is the most powerful testimony to the Somozas' political skill, for in Latin America armed forces are more easily won than retained. Nicaragua's National Guard remained loyal until after the last Somoza had fled.

Nicaraguan politics in the Somoza period featured limited repression and limited opposition. Criticism was permitted and, in fact, carried on day after day in the pages of *La Prensa* (whose editor was an opposition leader). Although the Somozas had large landholdings, the government enjoyed no monopoly of economic power, and made no serious effort to absorb or control the Church, education, or the culture. The government was moderately competent in encouraging economic development, moderately oppressive, and moderately corrupt. It was also an utter failure at delivering those social services American and Europeans have come since the Depression to regard as the responsibility of government.

Anastasio Somoza Debayle, a West Point graduate with an American wife and an expansive appetite for women and alcohol, had accommodated successive American administrations and received aid from successive Congresses. He had every reason to suppose that his regime would continue to enjoy U.S. favor, and no reason to suppose that his power could be brought down by the small group of Cuban-backed terrorists who periodically disturbed the peace with their violence.

Three things seem to have disturbed these calculations. One was the progressive alienation of certain members of the country's *oligarchia* and business class when, after the earthquake of 1973, Somocistas raked off too large a share of the international relief; a second factor was Somoza's heart attack; the third and most important factor was the election of Jimmy Carter and the adoption of an all-new Latin American policy.

•

At the time the Carter administration was inaugurated in January 1977, three groups of unequal strength competed for power in Nicaragua: the President and his loyal lieutenants—who enjoyed the advantages of incumbency, a degree of legitimacy, and nationwide organization, and the unwavering support of the National Guard; the legal opposition parties which had been gathered into a loose coalition headed by Joaquin Chamorro, editor of *La Prensa*; and several small revolutionary groups whose Cuban-trained leaders had finally forged a loose alliance, the FSLN (Sandinista National Liberation Front).

From the moment the FSLN adopted the tactics of a broad alliance, the offensive against Somoza was carried out on a variety of fronts. There was violence in the form of assassinations and assaults on army barracks. When the government reacted, the U.S. condemned it for violations of human rights. The legal opposition put forward demands for greater democracy which had the endorsement of the FSLN, thus making it appear that democracy was the goal of the insurgency.

Violence and counterviolence weakened the regime by demonstrating that it could not maintain order. The combination of impotence and repression in turn emboldened opponents in and out of the country, provoking more reprisals and more hostility in a vicious circle that culminated finally in the departure of Somoza and the collapse of the National Guard.

What did the Carter administration do in Nicaragua? *It brought down the Somoza regime.* The Carter administration did not "lose" Nicaragua in the sense in which it was once charged that Harry Truman had "lost" China, or Eisenhower Cuba, by failing to prevent a given outcome. In the case of Nicaragua, the State Department *acted* repeatedly and at critical junctures to weaken the government of Anastasio Somoza and to strengthen his opponents.

First, it declared "open season" on the Somoza regime. When in the spring of 1977 the State Department announced that shipments of U.S. arms would be halted for human-rights violations, and followed this with announcements in June and October that economic aid would be withheld, it not only deprived the Somoza regime of needed economic and military support but served notice that the regime no longer enjoyed the approval of the United States and could no longer count on its protection. This impression was strongly reinforced when after February 1978 Jimmy Carter treated the two sides in the conflict as more or less equally legitimate contenders —offering repeatedly to help "both sides" find a "peaceful solution."

Second, the Carter administration's policies inhibited the Somoza regime in dealing with its opponents while they were weak enough to be dealt with. Fearful of U.S. reproaches and reprisals, Somoza fluctuated between repression and indulgence in his response to FSLN violence. The rules of the Carter human-rights policy made it impossible for Somoza to resist his opponents effectively. As Viron Vaky remarked about the breakdown in negotiations between Somoza and the armed opposition: ". . . when the mediation was suspended we announced that the failure of the mediation had created a situation in which it was clear violence was going to continue, that it would result in repressive measures and therefore our relationships could not continue on the same basis as in the past." When the National Palace was attacked and hostages were taken, Somoza's capitulation to FSLN demands enhanced the impression that he could not control the situation and almost certainly stimulated the spread of resistance.

Third, by its "mediation" efforts and its initiatives in the Organization of American States (OAS), the Carter administration encouraged the internationalization of the opposition. Further, it demoralized Somoza and his supporters by insisting that Somoza's continuation in power was the principal obstacle to a viable, centrist, democratic government. Finally, the State Department deprived the Somoza regime of legitimacy not only by repeated condemnations for human-rights violations but also by publishing a demand for Somoza's resignation and by negotiating with the opposition.

Without these "affirmative pressures," William Bundy concluded in *Foreign Affairs*:

> It seems a safe bet that Tacho Somoza would still be in charge in Nicaragua and his amiable brother-in-law still extending abrazos to all and sundry in Washington as dean of the diplomatic corps.

•

Why did the Carter administration do these things? Because it thought the fall of Somoza would bring progress to Nicaragua. Viron Vaky put it this way:

Nicaragua's tragedy stems from dynastic rule. Times have changed. Nicaragua has changed, but the government of Nicaragua has not.

History was against Somoza. He was an obstacle to progress. He should relinquish power to make room for "change." When he declined to do so, the Carter administration accused him of "polarizing" the situation. When the National Guard responded to FSLN violence with violence, the State Department said that the National Guard had "radicalized the opposition."

On the other hand, the fact that Cubans were supplying arms to the FSLN was not regarded as being of much importance. Brandon Grove, Jr., Deputy Assistant Secretary for Inter-American Affairs, explained to the Committee of the House (June 7, 1979):

> The flow of such supplies is a symptom of the deeper problem in Nicaragua: polarization and its attendant violence that day by day are contributing to the growing alienation of the Nicaraguan government from its people . . . The real cause for concern today should be the breakdown . . . of trust between government and people essential for the democratic process to function.

Since the "real" problem was not Cuban arms but Somoza, obviously the U.S. should not act to reinforce the regime that had proved its political and moral failure by becoming the object of attack. Because the State Department desired not to "add to the partisan factionalism," it declined to supply arms to the regime. "The supplying of arms in a war situation we feel only adds to the suffering. We have urged others not to do that."

In the event, the Carter administration did a good deal more than "urge." In June 1979, after the U.S. and the OAS had called for Somoza's resignation, and U.S. representatives William Bowdler and Lawrence Pezzulo had met with the FSLN, the State Department undertook to apply the final squeeze to the Somoza regime—putting pressure on Israel to end the arms sales, and working out an oil embargo to speed the capitulation of Somoza's forces. They were so successful that for the second time in a decade an American ally ran out of gas and ammunition while confronting an opponent well armed by the Soviet bloc.

The FSLN were not the State Department's preferred replacement for Somoza. Nevertheless, from spring 1977, when the State Department announced that it was halting a promised arms shipment to Somoza's government, through the summer of 1980, when the administration secured congressional approval of a $75-million aid package for Nicaragua, U.S. policy under Jimmy Carter was vastly more supportive of the Sandinistas than it was of the Somoza regime, despite the fact that Somoza and his government were as doggedly friendly and responsive to U.S. interests and desires as the Sandinistas have been hostile and non-responsive.

The Carter administration expected that democracy would emerge in Nicaragua. Their scenario prescribed that the winds of change should blow the outmoded dictator out of office and replace him with a popular government. Even after it had become clear that the FSLN, which was known to harbor powerful anti-democratic tendencies, was the dominant force in the new regime, U.S. spokesmen continued to speak of the events in Nicaragua as a democratic revolution. In December 1979, for example, Warren Christopher attempted to reassure doubting members of the Senate Foreign Relations Committee that "the driving consensus among the Nicaraguans" was "to build a new Nicaragua through popular participation that is capable of meeting basic human needs."

The expectation that change would produce progress and that socialism equaled social justice made it difficult for Carter policy-makers to assess Nicaragua's new rulers realistically, even though grounds for concern about their intentions, already numerous before the triumph, continued to multiply in its aftermath.

•

Revolution begins with destruction. The first fruit of the destabilization of Somoza and the reinforcement of his opponents was a civil war in which some 40,000 Nicaraguans lost their most basic human right (life), another 100,000 were left homeless, and some $2-billion worth of destruction was wrought. Nicaragua was left in a shambles.

Where did the expectations, the hopes, the intentions of the Carter administration then lead us, and the Nicaraguans who took the consequences? Although the FSLN had solemnly committed itself to hold free elections, its leaders have shown no disposition to share the power they seized in July 1979. To the contrary, the consolidation and centralization of power have moved steadily forward. Despite the strenuous opposition of the two FSLN junta members, the Sandinista directorate which has effectively ruled Nicaragua since the fall of Somoza moved in the spring of 1980 to institutionalize its control of Nicaragua's Council of State by expanding and "restructuring" it to insure the Sandinistas a permanent majority. (Under the reform they would be assured of 24 of 47 seats where previously they had been entitled to only 13 of 33.)

Meanwhile, the election to which the FSLN had committed itself has been pushed further and further into a receding future, even though the new rulers, who need all the help they can get, have been under heavy pressure from the governments of Venezuela, Costa Rica, and the United States to set a date. Sandinista leaders have made no secret of their opinion that competitive elections are an unsatisfactory and unnecessary mechanism for choosing rulers. Junta members have asserted that the people spoke through the revolution— "with their blood and with the guns in their hands the people have cast their votes" (as a junta member told the *Economist*)—and that anyway, having been brainwashed by forty years of Somoza rule, they are not capable of choosing among candidates—at least not until they have been "reeducated."

In the last days of August 1980, the restructured Council of State announced that elections will not be held before 1985. And those elections, declared Humberto Ortega Saavedra (Minister of Defense), "will serve to reinforce and improve the revolution and not to give just anyone more power, which belongs to the people." Meanwhile, no "proselytizing activities" on behalf of any candidate will be permitted before candidates are officially designated by an electoral agency which itself will be created in 1984 (and violations will be punished by terms of three months to three years in jail).

Decrees accompanying these decisions have underscored the junta's distaste for criticism. Henceforth, dissemination of news concerning scarcities of food and other consumer goods is prohibited on pain of imprisonment (from two months to two years), as is "unconfirmed" information concerning armed encounters or attacks on government personnel.

These restrictions constitute one more significant step in the Sandinistas' gradual campaign to control the climate of opinion. The television and radios had already been brought under control. Among opposition newspapers, only *La Prensa* remains; it has already come under pressures more harsh than those applied to the media during the Somoza era, and its continuation as an independent critical voice is at best uncertain. The requirement that all professional journalists join a new government-sponsored union as a condition of employment represents yet another move to bring the press under control. The literacy campaign has extended the junta's reach further into the minds of Nicaragua's people as well as into the countryside. Every lesson in the literacy textbooks instructs students (and teachers) in the prescribed interpretation of Nicaragua's past, present, and future.

•

Parallel efforts to organize and coordinate other traditionally non-governmental associations reflect the characteristic totalitarian desire to absorb the society into the state, to transform social groups into agencies and instruments of the government. This has required taking over some existing institutions (banking, industries, television and radio, trade unions), coopting and/or intimidating others (the private sector, trade unions, the educational establishment, portions of the press), and forcibly eliminating still others—such as the National Guard, whose members have either fled into exile or remain in prison with little prospect of ever being tried, much less released.

When, in early November 1980, representatives of the private sector (COSEP) and the labor federation (CUS) withdrew from the State Council to protest the Sandinistas' ever-tightening grip on all aspects of the economy, no concessions were forthcoming. Instead, the offices of the leading opposition party, the social-democratic MND, were sacked, and an unarmed leader of the private sector, Jorge Salazar, was gunned down by Sandinista police.

Among the traditional pillars of Nicaraguan society only the Church remains relatively intact. While the presence of priests in prominent roles in the Sandinista Directorate has facilitated communications between the two groups, this has not been translated into political domination of the Church hierarchy.

But the Sandinistas do not rely on control of these agencies or rules to preserve their power. To accomplish that task new institutions have been forged, the most important of which are an enormous, all-new revolutionary army whose training (military and political) and equipment have been provided by Cubans, and a new internal police force which is already more extensive and effective than Somoza's.

Other institutions developed to support the new government include the "block" committees which were found to be so useful in Cuba (and in Nazi Germany), and the revolutionary brigades initially assigned to the literacy campaign.

The most telling indicator of Sandinista intentions and commitments is their unambiguous identification of Nicaragua with the foreign policy and perspectives of the Soviet Union. The first step was somewhat tentative: Nicaragua only "abstained" on the UN resolution condemning the Soviet invasion of Afghanistan. Subsequent moves have left less room for doubt. At the Havana conference for the nonaligned nations, Nicaragua became one of the few countries in the world to recognize Kampuchea (the regime imposed by North Vietnam on Cambodia), an act which Foreign Minister Miguel d'Escoto explained as "a consequence of our revolutionary responsibility as Sandinistas to recognize the right of the peoples of Kampuchea to be free." In Pyongyang, another Sandinista leader, Tomás Borge, assured the North Koreans of Nicaraguan solidarity, and promised, "The Nicaraguan Revolution will not be content until the imperialists have been overthrown in all parts of the world."

In March 1980 the Sandinista directorate offered a public demonstration that its ties extended beyond Cuba to the Socialist Fatherland itself when four top leaders—Moises Morales Hassan, Tomás Borge, Henry Hernandez Ruiz, and Humberto Ortega Saavedra—paid an official visit to the Soviet Union. A joint communiqué formalized the attachment of Nicaragua to Soviet global policy. In addition to signing multiple agreements concerning trade and cooperation, condemning South Africa and Chile, applauding Zimbabwe, Khomeini's Iran, and the "legitimate national rights of the Arab people of Palestine," the "two sides" strongly attacked the NATO decision to deploy medium-range nuclear missile weapons and condemned the "mounting international tension in connection with the events in Afghanistan, which has been launched by the imperialist and reactionary forces aimed at subverting the inalienable rights of the people of the Democratic Republic of Afghanistan and of other peoples . . . to follow a path of progressive transformation."

Since "Zionism's loss of a bastion in Nicaragua" (Moises Hassan), the ties with the "Palestinian people" have become not closer, but more public.

The PLO and the Sandinistas have long enjoyed a relationship of mutual support, we are now told. Sandinistas trained in Palestinian camps, and participated in PLO raids; the PLO reciprocated by ferrying arms to the Sandinistas in their hour of need. Yasir Arafat received high honors when in July 1980 he opened a PLO embassy in Managua where he assured the "workers" that "the triumph of the Nicaraguans is the PLO's triumph."

"We have emerged from one dictatorship and entered another," asserted MND leader Alfonso Robelo recently. "Nicaragua has become a satellite of a satellite of the Soviet Union."

•

Nothing that happened in Nicaragua seemed able to dampen the Carter people's enthusiasm for "change" in Central America. In El Salvador, Guatemala, Bolivia, and wherever else the opportunity presented itself, the administration aligned the United States with the "forces of change." "The fundamental problem we share with our neighbors," Deputy Secretary of State Warren Christopher explained, "is not that of defending stability in the face of revolution. Rather, it is to build a more stable, equitable, and pluralistic order. That is the challenge of Nicaragua in the present day and that is the challenge of the whole region."

To meet the challenge the administration welcomed with enthusiasm a military coup in El Salvador which, in October 1979, overthrew President Carlos Humberto Romero, an event the State Department described as a "watershed date" on which "young officers broke with the old repressive order" and along with "progressive civilians" formed a government committed to "profound social and economic reforms, respect for human rights and democracy."

Until the violent events of November-December 1980, which also saw the suspension of U.S. aid, the Carter administration backed the new Salvadoran junta in the only way it knew how: by helping it to bring about "profound social and economic reforms." In the effort to preempt the revolution and expedite the achievements of "social justice," the administration supplied experts who have planned the most thoroughgoing land reform in the Western hemisphere. To encourage and finance these and related reforms, the U.S. embassy provided nearly $20 million in long-term loans at very low interest. Under the direction of the American Institute for Free Labor Development, an AFL-CIO-sponsored group, a plan was drafted to transfer to some 250,000 of El Salvador's 300,000 peasants ownership of the land they work.

So far, not all the land has been transferred, and titles have not been delivered for much of what has been transferred. Few of the former owners have received any significant compensation. In theory, the reforms will vaccinate the masses against Communism by giving them a stake in the society. In practice, as was made dramatically clear by the murder of three American nuns and a social worker in early December, continuing violence from Communists, anti-Communists, and simple criminals has brought death and destruction to El Salvador. Under the pressure of that violence, the society has begun to come apart. "There is no name for what exists in my country," commented a Salvadoran, describing the almost random murder, intimidation, and looting. But there is a name; it is anarchy.

The U.S. under Carter was more eager to impose land reform than elections in El Salvador. Although claims and counterclaims have been exchanged, there is no way of knowing whether the junta (in any of its manifestations) has enjoyed much popular support. It combines Christian Democrats, committed to finding a middle way of "true democracy" between capitalism and Communism, with representatives of various tendencies within the armed forces. It is chronically threatened with schism from within and coup from without. Though its civilian members and their State Department supporters have consistently emphasized the danger from the Right—that is, from authoritarian, intensely anti-Communist defenders of the status quo—El Salvador is more likely in the long run to fall to a coalition of revolutionaries trained, armed, and advised by Cuba and others. The cycle of escalating terror and repression is already far advanced. By failing to offer the junta the arms and advice required to turn back the well-equipped insurgency, the Carter administration undermined the junta's ability to survive and encouraged the insurgents in their conviction of ultimate victory.

•

Central America was not the only target of the Carter administration's restless search for "constructive change" in the hemisphere. Pressures were applied, and resisted, in Argentina, Brazil, Uruguay, and Bolivia. In Bolivia, the State Department withdrew our ambassador, "drew down" the embassy staff to approximately half its normal size, cancelled U.S. aid, terminated the Drug Enforcement Agency's program that aimed at reducing the production of coca (and cocaine), and indicated in a dozen other ways its determination not to accept the military junta whose seizure of power prevented the inauguration of Hernán Siles Zuazo as President.

Why did the U.S. work so hard to undo a coup which had prevented the accession to power of a man whose vice president had strong Castroite leanings and ties, whose coalition included the Communist party of Bolivia and the Castroite MIR, and whose elevation had been strongly supported by the Soviet Union? When Siles Zuazo polled 38 percent of the vote in a race against moderate socialist Víctor Paz Estenssoro, and the more conservative Hugo Banzer Suarez, the selection of the President was left to the Congress. No legal or conventional niceties required that U.S. influence be exerted on behalf of the selection of Siles Zuazo rather than one of the other candidates.

Yet Siles Zuazo became "the American candidate" even though the military
had made clear that his selection would not be tolerated. After conversations
with the U.S. ambassador that included both threats and promises of aid, Paz
Estensorro withdrew and Siles's selection was insured. The predictable coup
occurred.

Even five years ago, the U.S. would have welcomed a coup that blocked a
government with a significant Communist/Castroite component. Ten years
ago the U.S. would have sponsored it, fifteen years ago we would have conducted it. This time, however, the U.S. ambassador to Bolivia and the State
Department lobbied hard in Washington and with the press against the new
military rulers, insisting that what had occurred was not a coup like the two
hundred previous ones, but a singularly objectionable coup marked by unique
violence, engineered by foreigners, and led by drug traffickers. The State Department's campaign coincided with a Soviet press offensive, resulting in a
sustained international campaign bent on bringing Siles to power.

One understands the desire to see constitutional democracy replace
authoritarian governments in Bolivia. Despite a good deal of recent myth-
making to the contrary, Americans have always believed that democracy is the
best government for everyone. What was unusual about the Carter policy was
the *intensity* of the expressed disapproval and of the administration's preference
for a government that included in its leadership persons effectively attached to
Soviet policies and hostile to the United States. The decision to throw its
weight behind Siles reflected the characteristic predilections of the Carter
administration in Latin America, including its indifference to strategic concerns and its tendency to believe that leftists were more likely than any other
group to bring democracy and social justice to the area. Supporting Siles
seemed to offer the Carter administration an opportunity to assume its preferred role: trying to "moderate," by its good will and friendship, the "extreme"
elements in a governing coalition committed to "basic" social change.

•

Because it failed to take account of basic characteristics of Latin political
systems, the Carter administration underestimated the fragility of order in these
societies and overestimated the ease with which authority, once undermined,
can be restored. Because it regarded revolutionaries as beneficent agents of
change, it mistook their goals and motives and could not grasp the problem of
governments which had become the object of revolutionary violence. Because
it misunderstood the relations between economics and politics, it wrongly assumed (as in El Salvador) that economic reforms would necessarily and
promptly produce positive political results. Because it misunderstood the relations between "social justice" and authority, it assumed that only "just"
governments can survive. Finally, because it misunderstood the relations between justice and violence, the Carter administration fell (and pushed its allies)

into an effort to fight howitzers with land reform and urban guerrillas with improved fertilizers.

Above all, the Carter administration failed to understand *politics*. Politics is conducted by persons who by various means, including propaganda and violence, seek to realize some vision of the public good. Those visions may be beneficent or diabolic. But they constitute the real motives of real political actors. When men are treated like "forces" (or the agents of forces), their intentions, values, and world view tend to be ignored. But in Nicaragua the intentions and ideology of the Sandinistas have *already* shaped the outcome of the revolution, as in El Salvador the intentions and ideology of the leading revolutionaries create intransigence where there might have been willingness to cooperate and compromise, nihilism where there might have been reform.

The first step in the reconstruction of U.S. policy for Latin America is intellectual. It requires thinking more realistically about the politics of Latin America, about the alternatives to existing governments, and about the amounts and kinds of aid and time that would be required to improve the lives and expand the liberties of the people of the area. The choices are frequently unattractive.

The second step toward a more adequate policy is to assess realistically the impact of various alternatives on the security of the United States and on the safety and autonomy of the other nations of the hemisphere.

The third step is to abandon the globalist approach which denies the realities of culture, character, geography, economics, and history in favor of a vague, abstract, universalism "stripped," in Edmund Burke's words, "of every relation," standing "in all the nakedness and solitude of metaphysical abstraction." What must replace it is a foreign policy that builds (again Burke) on the "concrete circumstances" which "give . . . to every political principle its distinguishing color and discriminating effect."

Once the intellectual debris has been cleared away, it should become possible to construct a Latin American policy that will protect U.S. security interests and make the actual lives of actual people in Latin American somewhat better and somewhat freer.

3

Geopolitics, Security, and U.S. Strategy in the Caribbean Basin

David Ronfeldt

We are entering a new historical phase of the Basin's importance to U.S. interests. For the 1980s there are good reasons—global, domestic, and regional—to revive and modernize traditional concepts that treat the Caribbean Basin as a geopolitical zone of unique importance to the United States. As in the past, this rising importance derives as much from fundamental changes in the global and domestic conditions of U.S. power as from changes and conflicts within the region itself.

UNSETTLING GLOBAL AND DOMESTIC U.S. TRENDS

The following global and domestic developments are once again creating the classic preconditions for both heightened insecurity and U.S. interest in the Basin:

Global balance of power patterns are in flux: The international system is becoming more multipolar, with the Western alliance system seeming especially loose. Patterns of conflict, competition, and cooperation are in flux in Europe, the Middle East, and around the Indian Ocean. Not only the Soviet Union, but also resurgent European powers, notably France and Germany, are expanding their involvement in Caribbean and Central American conflicts.[1]

Reprinted from pages 29-47 of *Geopolitics, Security, and U.S. Strategy in the Caribbean Basin (R-2997-AF/RC), November 1983*. The RAND Corporation, 1700 Main Street, P. O. Box 2138, Santa Monica, California 90406-2138.

[1]   In reviewing how global systemic change may affect the behavior of France and other states, Lyons (1982, p. 144) [Lyons, Gene M., "Expanding the Study of International Relations: The French Connection," *World Politics*, Fall 1982, pp. 135-149.] observes "that the choices actually made will largely be the result of the interplay of domestic political forces in the different countries."

A new naval power is on the rise: The growing blue-water capabilities of the Soviet Navy are enabling the USSR to challenge the U.S. presence around the globe. In the Caribbean, Soviet naval flotillas have steamed into Cuba at a rate of nearly two visits per year since 1969. Left unchecked, the Soviets may seek to acquire military facilities elsewhere in the Caribbean Basin, notably Nicaragua and Grenada.

Competition is mounting for scarce resources: Secure access to distant natural resources, especially petroleum and minerals, is a continuing strategic concern of the major industrialized powers. The vulnerability of Middle Eastern oil supplies to potential disruption and the critical importance of such supplies for the West magnify the value of Basin petroleum resources and production capabilities.

New technologies enhance the efficacy of overseas bases: For both the United States and the Soviet Union, the development of ever more sophisticated weapons, transportation, and electronic communications systems is increasing the geopolitical and military value of having overseas bases and other facilities in regions contiguous to their adversary. Such facilities enhance medium-range power projection, reconnaissance, and intelligence gathering.

The growing likelihood of confrontations in third-world regions: A NATO-Warsaw Pact war in Europe and a U.S.-Soviet confrontation over the Persian Gulf will remain the most dangerous threats. But they will also remain less likely ones. The combination of geopolitical trends and technological developments suggests that the Soviet Union and the United States are likely to test each other in far-flung locations where geographic positions, raw materials, or power perceptions are at stake. Both governments are having to face and are working to create "threats from the South," formerly their flanks of greatest security.

Extra-hemispheric actors are intruding into Basin affairs: Nonhemispheric governments and subnational actors—ranging from European Christian Democratic and Social Democratic movements to Arab and European terrorist groups—are seeking to extend their influence within the Basin. In general, they are contributing as much to destabilizing as to restabilizing its politics. Simultaneously, local governments and anti-government actors in the region are also soliciting support from outside the hemisphere, independent of the United States. Although West European involvement can contribute to the region's economic and political development, this general push-pull process is fostering the internationalization of local conflicts and eroding U.S. leverage.

Potential for domestic spillovers from regional unrest: Caribbean Basin politics intrude on domestic U.S. politics more than ever before and more so than for any other third-world area. Law, order, and security concerns within the United States and along its borders cannot be isolated from major events and trends in the Basin. The primary linkage is through massive immigration, refugee, and exile flows: The United States receives more immigrants and refugees than all the rest of the world combined, and most of these come from within the Basin. The extension of Central American conflicts into Mexico or Puerto Rico would thus have dangerous, uncontrollable, and unpredictable domestic consequences. In the meantime, the prognosis is for continued large immigration flows. Terrorism and low-level violence represent another domestic connection. This includes violence conducted within the United States by revolutionaries from the Basin (e.g., Puerto Rican FALN), by local right-wing exiles (e.g., Cubans, Nicaraguans, or El Salvadorans in Miami), by left-wing exiles or sympathizers supporting revolution abroad, and by narcotics smugglers.

In sum, we find ourselves in an evolving conflict environment that once again raises the ultimate concerns of U.S. security in the Basin: the effect on U.S. positions, responsibilities, and priorities around the world; and the exposure of the U.S. mainland to potential threats and domestic spillovers.

VIOLATIONS OF THE KEY PRINCIPLES
FOR REGIONAL STRATEGY

Within the Caribbean Basin, the central challenges for U.S. policymakers and strategists derive largely from neglecting interrelated "violations" of the four traditional principles. Trends within the Basin indicate that if these violations are altogether neglected and not contained, they will have increasingly detrimental consequences for broader U.S. interests and strategies.

Maintenance of the Basin as a stable, secure preserve for U.S. presence, power, and passage has not been as seriously violated as other principles. The United States still enjoys secure access to sea lanes and strategic resources in Venezuela, Mexico, and elsewhere. However, U.S. presence and influence have declined throughout the Basin over the past decade, to the detriment of security interests. Chronic underdevelopment, mounting population pressures, poor export prices, debt-and-devaluation crises, and for the Eastern Caribbean a proliferation of mini-sovereignties all bode ill for future political stability in many states. Regional security also continues to deteriorate through the transmission of political radicalism, guerrilla insurgency, international terrorism, and other forms of low-intensity conflict among the smaller countries. Even Mexico's stability and security are no longer assured. Meanwhile, Cuba, now heavily armed as an ally of the Soviet Union, has improved its ability to export revolution; but it does not pose a direct military threat to the United States and is unlikely to do so except possibly under wartime conditions.

Exclusion of hostile military powers must now be treated more seriously than at any time since the 1962 missile crisis. Soviet and related Cuban military capabilities have grown disturbingly strong on the island in recent years: The Soviets have long operated a large electronic monitoring station near Havana; they have stepped up their use of the island as a turnaround point for

Soviet TU-95 Bear long-range reconnaissance and antisubmarine aircraft; they dispatch Soviet naval flotillas and submarines to Cuba; and they retain a specialized 2500-3000 man combat brigade on the island. In addition, the offensive and defensive military capabilities of Cuba's Revolutionary Armed Forces (FAR) have expanded through the continued acquisition of MiG-23s, Osa and Komar guided-missile patrol boats, a Koni-class frigate, Foxtrot attack submarines, amphibious transport ships, AN-26 short-range military transport planes, and SAM antiaircraft missiles, all supplied by the Soviet Union.

This may be tolerable in peacetime as long as the Soviet and Cuban military expansion does not greatly exceed present levels and remains contained in Cuba. However, with the strategic and conventional balances shifting away from U.S. superiority, and with Cuba so heavily armed, U.S. policymakers can no longer assume that Soviet-Cuban military actions would be largely irrelevant or easily neutralized in the event of general war, a simultaneous crisis elsewhere, or a U.S.-Cuban confrontation. The possibility of a plausible military threat from Cuba could tie down a considerable number of USN and USAF units.

If Cuba's armed forces continue to modernize and expand at the present pace, the Castro regime will command a veritable "fortress Cuba" by the mid-1980s.[2] Furthermore, the possible availability of military facilities to the Cubans or Soviets elsewhere in the area, such as in Central America or in the Eastern Caribbean, could exacerbate vulnerabilities in the U.S. and NATO military postures as well as damage political perceptions of U.S. power. Thus the expansion of Soviet-Cuban military capabilities must be halted; otherwise the United States will have to make costly countervailing military investments in the not too distant future.

Exclusion of foreign balance-of-power struggles is inoperative at present. Not just one but three extra-regional struggles are contributing to the internationalization of local political conflicts in the Basin: Alongside the long-standing U.S.-Soviet competition, U.S.-European tensions have risen. European party rivalries between Social Democrats and Christian Democrats have intruded into Central America and served to compound its instability; this was partly the case in El Salvador when the insurgents enjoyed the support of the former, and the regime of former President Duarte was assisted by the latter.[3] The Arab-Israeli conflict has also extended to Central America, with Libya and the PLO supporting the Sandinistas and guerrilla groups elsewhere, and with

2   Recent press reports reveal that Cuba may next obtain variants of the TU-95 Bear bomber from the Soviets, probably for long-range reconnaissance, but adaptable for antisubmarine warfare and other missions.
3   This does not mean, of course, that European party rivalry was the whole story. It was also tangled up with the regionally more important rivalry between Venezuela and Mexico, with Venezuela supporting Duarte and the Christian Democratic line, and Mexico aiding the insurgents and the Socialist International.

Israel providing weapons and advice to Guatemala, Honduras, and earlier to Somoza's Nicaragua. The Basin, once considered an "American lake," is being fractured by more extra-regional struggles than any other third-world area of major strategic interest to the United States.

Analyzing West European political involvement as though it may pose an unwelcome foreign intrusion under a strategic principle that also covers Soviet and other extra-hemispheric forces requires some explanation. Since World War II, the friendly resurgence of West European involvement in the Basin has generally benefited U.S. interests. Britain, France, and the Netherlands still have colonial and post-colonial responsibilities in the Basin; if these are mismanaged or abandoned, the United States may face new risks and have to bear new costs (recently the case in Suriname, potentially the case in Belize). In addition to their usefulness as local trade and investment partners, the West European nations also contribute economic development financing and technical assistance through the international banks and their own bilateral assistance programs. West European political party philosophies and organizational activities, primarily Christian Democracy and Social Democracy, have enjoyed broad appeal in the region and helped strengthen democratic tendencies among moderate and center-left sectors.

The United States needs the Europeans to continue playing such constructive roles. It would be a mistake and a misunderstanding of the third principle[†] to suppose that this broad European involvement is detrimental to Basin security and that U.S. strategy should seek to exclude the West Europeans to the same general extent as the Soviets. Where European activity selectively supports U.S. interests, it is worth encouraging, as we have done in the past.

However, it would be a mistake and violation of the third principle to give the Europeans carte blanche for ever greater political involvement in the Basin. Contrary to U.S. security interests, major elements of their political involvement have served inadvertently to further internationalize local conflicts, link them to competitive global struggles, and disturb U.S.-European relations.

- The Europeans do not have vital security interests directly at stake in the Basin. Their most important stakes, largely ignored by the European public, are the security of sea lanes for reinforcing NATO or the Persian Gulf, and the general absence of threats to the south of the United States, a crucial requirement for preserving our forward posture abroad.

[†] The third principle is "Foreign balance-of-power struggles should be excluded and prevented from destabilizing the region." Ronfeldt, *Geopolitics, Security, and U.S. Strategy in the Caribbean Basin*, p. 7—Ed.

David Ronfeldt

- In the absence of vital interests, some European governments and political parties have responded to domestic political interests in placating left-wing sectors and displaying independence from the United States.[4] This has particularly been the case with Social Democracy in France and Germany.[5]

- Left-wing sectors within Social Democracy and the related Socialist International support revolutionary change in the Basin, argue that the United States could live with more Cubas, justify European involvement as a way to defuse U.S.-Soviet tensions, and advocate international negotiations to settle the conflict(s). This policy approach, exemplified by the Mitterand government and the Olaf Palme/Willy Brandt faction in the Socialist International, has compounded the internationalization of the region's instability.[6]

- The European Economic Community (EEC) has also become a platform for publicly criticizing U.S. policy and expressing support for alternatives.[7]

These elements do not constitute a major case against West European political involvement, but they indicate that it is increasingly undesirable in its

---

[4]   I have argued elsewhere (Ronfeldt and Sereseres, 1977) [Ronfeldt, David F., and Caesar D. Sereseres, "U.S. Arms Transfers, Diplomacy, and Security in Latin America and Beyond," The Rand Corporation, P-6005, October 1977] that politicians and intellectuals in the United States have sometimes used Latin America as a dumping ground for idealistic liberal principles (usually about democracy, arms transfers, or human rights) that are more seriously violated in other third-world regions but too difficult to apply there because of Soviet threats or other security interests. Perhaps a similar syndrome affects some European political behavior toward the Caribbean Basin.

[5]   The mainstream of Social Democracy in Germany is quite moderate and much more interested in matters other than Central America and the Caribbean, but it must contend with a left wing in the party that opposes U.S. policy in this region.

[6]   Some mainstream Social Democratic leaders in Germany have now recognized that their party should have coordinated and consulted better with Washington before becoming so outspokenly involved in Central America in the 1970s. They (like most Europeans) did not understand American sensitivities about the area and now see they erred in trusting the Sandinistas to remain democratic.

[7]   Recent meetings of its members' foreign ministers (responding to German and Dutch initiatives in particular) have thus approved the efforts of the Contadora group (Colombia, Mexico, Panama, Venezuela) to bring about political negotiations among all parties to the Central American conflict. For years the EEC has steadfastly supported Grenada's economy under the provisions of the Lomé Convention, and ignored Washington's warnings about Grenada's potential alignment with the Soviet Union and Cuba.

present form.[8]   Whereas the old bipolar international system presented the dangerous risk of U.S.-Soviet confrontation in the Basin, Europe's resurgence and the prospective evolution of a competitive multipolar system will not necessarily introduce greater harmony and less conflict there. Instead, this global systemic evolution, to the extent it molds political patterns in the Basin, may produce new difficulties for U.S. policy because European interests and objectives increasingly differ from those of the United States.[9]

There would be a powerful case for inviting expanded European political involvement if it could help accomplish the de-Sovietization of Cuba and elsewhere assure the denial of military access to the Soviet Union and other hostile powers, in keeping with the second key principle.[†]   To date, however, there is no clear evidence for this in Cuba, Nicaragua, or Grenada.[10]   Instead, it appears that the more internationalized the Basin becomes, the more likely are opportunities to arise for Soviet and Cuban exploitation and expansion.

There is another potentially reasonable argument for desiring a European politico-military presence: If faced with the necessity of choosing, U.S. interests should prefer to have nonaligned radical nationalist regimes in the Basin that look to European socialists for support and sustenance, than to have more Soviet-aligned Cuban types of regimes in the area.[11]   This argument looks sensible in theory, and it may have limited validity for U.S. interests

---

[8]   A useful German statement of the case *for* European involvement is by Grabendorff, 1983 [Grabendorff, Wolf, "The Role of Western Europe in the Caribbean Basin" (mimeo.), 1983], which further develops the ideas he presents in Grabendorff, 1982b, pp. 201-212 [Grabendorff, Wolf, "Western European Perceptions of the Turmoil in Central America," in Richard E. Feinberg (ed.), *Central America: The International Dimensions of the Crisis*, Holmes and Meier, New York, 1982].

[9]   To cite one handy example: "The Federal Republic of Germany will not be able to pursue any longer an official Latin American policy of 'low profile' by subordinating itself to the hemispheric interests of the US.   An independent German political, economic, and social interest in Latin America are [*sic*] a fact and, moreover, the Latin Americans themselves would gladly see European powers, such as the FRG, active in their countries as counterbalance to, and competitor with, the US.   On the other hand, it would be unrealistic to call for a common US-European or US-West Germany policy toward Latin America because of the highly uneven geopolitical, security-political, and economic interests and uneven hemispheric responsibility." Mols, 1982, pp. 115-116 [Mols, Manfred, "The Latin American Connection," in Peter H. Merkl (ed.), *West German Foreign Policy: Dilemmas and Directions*, The Chicago Council on Foreign Relations, Chicago, 1982].

[†]   The second key principle: "Potentially hostile foreign powers should be prevented from acquiring military bases and facilities in the area." Ronfeldt, *Geopolitics, Security, and U.S. Strategy in the Caribbean Basin*, p. 7—Ed.

[10]   France's weapon sales to the Sandinista government are unlikely to prevent further Soviet arms transfers and may instead embroil France in possible future US-Nicaraguan hostilities.

[11]   This preference is prominent in the views of US, European, and Latin American policy analysts who believe that radical nationalist and socialist regimes are the wave of the future and who have grave doubts about US abilities to respond constructively.

among the small Eastern Caribbean islands that were European colonies. For the Basin as a whole, however, the argument is too hypothetical to meet U.S. interests, least of all in Central America and among the larger Caribbean islands where the West Europeans have neither the vital interests nor the means for sustaining a constructive political, economic, and military presence. Inviting European involvement for the sake of blocking Soviet or Cuban expansion would thus probably give way to a Balkanization of the Basin and a new pattern of U.S.-Latin American and U.S.-European discord.

If European political involvement continues to expand in the Basin, the United States may have to dedicate increasing resources to channeling and constraining its influence (while we simultaneously strive to contain and counter Soviet involvement). European economic and political roles may at times complement and supplement U.S. roles in the Basin, especially if we lead the way as the strongest power. But they cannot substitute for U.S. roles in restoring stability and security, especially not if our policies are inadequate and our programs in decline. The United States cannot use Britain, France, West Germany, or Spain as subordinate instruments in the way that the Soviets use East Germany.

Minimal allocation of U.S. military assets to regional security, the fourth principle, remains in effect but not in a mode that positively enhances U.S. security interests. There is still no clear sense of why and how U.S. military power should play a role in the Basin's security and its political, economic, and military development. Instead, post-Vietnam antipathies have increased public, congressional, and bureaucratic constraints on U.S. military involvement in the area, however modest. The current U.S. force posture is having little effect on the prospects for continued low-level conflicts in the Basin. Planning estimates for potential major contingencies yield such large, costly numbers that hardly anyone wants to prepare for them in peacetime.

For the first time in almost a century, Basin security trends are headed toward a fundamental contradiction of the historical imperative that, despite contemporary global interdependence, still explains the Basin's place in U.S. global strategy and force posture: To greatly enhance U.S. abilities to act in a global balance-of-power system, extra-hemispheric threats and political struggles should be contained, if not altogether excluded from operating in the Basin. If current adverse trends continue unabated, we may find ourselves having to divert excessive U.S. military and other resources to deal with Basin insecurity, to the detriment of our strength and flexibility elsewhere.

SOURCES OF EMERGING THREATS TO U.S. SECURITY

Today's strife is not unusual for the Caribbean and Central American area. We have faced the pattern before; it combines the spread of low-level instability and the threat of involvement by extra-hemispheric powers. To give one historical example:

The Guatemalan coup was the last of a series of governmental turnovers . . . that installed new administrations in all five of the republics, completely changing the political atmosphere in the region. Most of the new governments were unsteady and had a common desire for external support against anticipated counterrevolution.

The situation in Central America worsened, and soon the entire Isthmus seemed on the verge of explosion—revolts threatened the regimes. . . . Many of the uprisings were launched from neighboring countries. . . . Border raids among Nicaragua, Honduras, and El Salvador brought these nations to the brink of war. . . . Bandits were operating between the states, taking refuge across the frontiers when pursued, keeping all three republics in turmoil. Exiles from each nation were attempting to organize invasions behind the sanctuary of borders.

The cruiser *Tacoma* was dispatched to the Gulf of Fonseca to provide an American "presence."

This reads like today's bad news, but it happened between 1919 and 1923.[12] In other times we were able to surmount such conflicts and help restore stability and security to the area. Nonetheless, the task this time does look more difficult, complex, and risky than ever before. Current and prospective trends raise two types of potential threat sources that may become increasingly serious in the years ahead: (a) the incremental expansion of a hostile force presence, and (b) the domino-like spread of low-intensity conflict.

HOSTILE FORCE EXPANSION: THE THREAT OF A HOSTILE AXIS

The assumption that the United States would not face any serious or time-consuming threat from the south has long been central to the international military posture of the United States. Indeed, the absence of hostile powers on our border has been a major asset for NATO, "since in a real sense it is the non-threatening environment close to home that permits the United States to concentrate so much manpower, equipment, and attention on Europe."[13]

Hostile-force presence in the Basin has for 20 years been limited to Cuba and related Soviet naval and air movements. However, the future may bring a further expansion of Soviet-Cuban military capabilities to where "fortress Cuba" is joined by new pro-Soviet and pro-Cuban military positions in Central America (e.g., Nicaragua) or the Eastern Caribbean (e.g., Grenada). This

---

[12] The quotations are from Grieb, 1976, pp. 42 and 50 [Grieb, Kenneth J., *The Latin American Policy of Warren G. Harding*, The Texas Christian University Press, Fort Worth, 1976].

[13] Fascell, 1981, pp. 26-33 [Fascell, Dante B., "Challenge in the Caribbean: The United States and Her Southern Neighbors," *Nato's Fifteen Nations*, August-September 1981, pp. 26-33].

could lay the foundation for a "hostile axis" that would transform the Basin into an air and naval theater for Soviet power projection.

Few analysts believe the development of a "hostile triangle" is likely, and the public seems to greet such speculations with doubt and lack of interest. Yet we should remind ourselves that in 1959 no one expected the Soviets would attempt to turn Cuba into a nuclear missile site in 1962, they would attempt to build a submarine base there by 1970, and Cuba would be so heavily armed by 1982 as to pose a potentially costly and time-consuming threat to NATO supply lines in wartime. It is not inevitable that Nicaragua or Grenada will become Soviet-Cuban military cohorts, but one lesson from the Cuban experience is that the possibility should not be dismissed.

The Soviet Navy and Air Force have had considerable success in penetrating the Caribbean Basin through an incremental process that has avoided major confrontations with the United States. The Soviets were forced to halt their construction of a base for nuclear submarines in Cienfuegos in the fall of 1970. Within months of that incident, however, a nuclear-powered November-class submarine was serviced at Cienfuegos; another Echo II nuclear submarine visited the port in May 1971; and a diesel-powered ballistic missile submarine put into another Cuban port in 1972. Soviet naval visits to Cuba continued during the remainder of the 1970s, and new naval basing and repair facilities were under construction at Cienfuegos and elsewhere on the island by the end of the decade. Meanwhile in the 1970s, unarmed Soviet TU-95 Bear reconnaissance bombers routinely used Cuba as their refueling and turnaround point, or as a way station into the South Atlantic. In 1983 variants of the Bear armed for antisubmarine warfare stopped at Cuba for the first time. MiG 23/27 fighter bombers were first shipped to Cuba in spring 1978, and some four years later the Cuban Air Force possessed over 40 of these combat planes (including the nonexport version) in its inventory of over 200 MiG aircraft. The Cubans, if not the Soviets, are thus acquiring a potential offensive (and defensive) capability. This arsenal is complemented by the construction of three (and possibly six) Cuban airfields that could handle the Soviet Backfire strategic bomber and that may require an expansion of NORAD's defensive deployment to the south.

In like manner, the creation of a "hostile axis" would probably come about slowly, incrementally, and ambiguously. It could take many forms in the location and manning of military hardware and the type of Soviet military access. For example, the type and number of MiGs in Nicaragua, if any, would make a difference; so would using Grenada (or Suriname) as a site for naval refueling facilities or, visibly more threatening, for stopover and stationing of tactical air and transports. Such developments could provide the Soviets and the Cubans with a routine Basin-wide military presence that could support rapid air, naval, and army movements and be used to pose threats, or at least worrisome problems, within the Basin and reaching into the Atlantic, the Pacific, South America, and to CONUS and its air and sea lanes. At the upper ends of the threat spectrum, the installation of a defensive, Basin-wide military infrastructure could augment potential Soviet capabilities for conducting a surprise nuclear decapitation strike against U.S. command, control, and communication centers, and for recovering post-attack bombers.

Soviet acquisition of naval and air position in the Atlantic reaches of the Eastern Caribbean and of a naval base on the Pacific side of Central America would be dramatic gains for Soviet strategists. Cuba already provides a good position from which to pose threats to NATO supply lines leaving the Gulf coast and for monitoring and gathering intelligence on U.S. military operations. But to command key sea and air lanes in the Basin and across the Atlantic, for surveillance and antisubmarine warfare operations, for locating tactical aircraft, and as a stopover site between the Caribbean Basin and Africa or South America, the islands of the Eastern Caribbean (e.g. Grenada) would provide much more useful positions—just as, for the United States, Puerto Rico has always been much more important for basing than Cuba (Guantanamo).[14] Military access to Nicaragua would certainly improve the Soviet position within the Basin but would not contribute much to the Soviet global position unless they developed a naval base on the Pacific side (they are currently building a fishing port) with which to expand and support Soviet operations in the Pacific Basin.[15]

Critics and opponents of the Reagan administration assail its warnings that the development of a "hostile axis" would threaten U.S. interests. In their view, only one development might pose a serious threat: the establishment of Soviet military bases, and then perhaps only if Soviet offensive weapons are emplaced. They doubt, however, that this would give the Soviet Union much advantage in the global struggle. They claim that the United States could readily (and immediately should) dispose of such a Soviet threat if it materialized. Thus they suppose that because the Soviet Union is averse to accepting high risks and high costs for marginal gains, it is unlikely to establish military bases in the Basin, especially if the United States tells it absolutely not to do so.[16]

---

[14] Guantanamo is mainly an excellent location from which to conduct deep-water training.
[15] A hostile foreign power has never gained a base on the Pacific side of Central America. The United States patrolled the area during World War II to keep German submarines away from such places as the Bay of Fonseca.
[16] For example, see Ullman, 1983, p. E21 [Ullman, Richard H., "Plain Talk on Central America," *New York Times*, July 10, 1983, p. E21]; and Maynes, 1983, p. IV-1 [Maynes, Charles William, "Reagan Is Wrong on Central America," *Los Angeles Times*, June 12, 1983, pp. IV-1]. Senator Christopher Dodd (D-Conn.) has voiced similar views, as have many academic specialists on Latin America.

This line of reasoning rationalizes tolerating the evolution of a militarized hostile axis in a Balkanized Basin so long as the Soviet Union does not pose an overt offensive threat. It neglects the political and politico-military advantages this would provide to the Soviet Union. It does not heed the ways in which defensive military infrastructures may suddenly be used to augment offensive threat capabilities. It ignores the enduring political and military importance of a secure, un-Balkanized Basin for U.S. global performance. It exaggerates the availability of U.S. military resources for disposing of a material Soviet (or Cuban) theat. If in the critics' view of the future the United States could, would, and should attack to eliminate the establishment of a Soviet base only after it is equipped with defensive and offensive weaponry, we may end up with neither the will nor the ability to do so if conditions deteriorate to the extent that these critics deem tolerable.[17]

In sum, the Soviet Union and related hostile axis would not have to develop as an overt offensive threat in order to jeopardize U.S. security interests and divert U.S. forces. The Soviets and their allies are skilled at incrementally building ambiguous capabilities, first for defending a revolutionary regime, then later for exploiting politico-military vulnerabilities and supporting military operations and power projection in its vicinity. In both political and military respects, tolerating the development of a "hostile axis" would reflect badly on U.S. power, foment political divisiveness at home and with our allies abroad, and require costly countermeasures in terms of air-defense and air and sea patrolling. Because of changes in the East-West military balance and the expansion of Cuba's armaments, neutralizing or defending against "fortress Cuba" alone would nowadays pose a temporarily troublesome task for the U.S. military, particularly if it were preoccupied with a crisis or war elsewhere.

---

[17] Soviet military expansion and the disruptive potential of a hostile axis would be dramatically enhanced if the Sandinista regime were to construct a sea-level trans-isthmian canal with Soviet assistance. Plans and surveys have long existed for a route through Nicaragua; it was originally preferred over Panama. Although Japan showed some interest in assisting the recent Somoza regime to build a sea-level canal, the United States agreed, in the Panama Canal treaties negotiated in 1976 with Gen. Omar Torrijos, that it would not build a sea-level canal anywhere but in Panama. Torrijos, still concerned about Nicaragua, aided the Sandinistas and abetted Somoza's downfall in 1979 partly to keep him from building a competitive canal. To nobody's particular concern, and perhaps only for propaganda purposes, the Soviet Union has now indicated some interest in assisting the Sandinistas to build it by early next century. The Soviet Union may now lack the capital for such a colossal undertaking, but with time and Western acquiescence, they might assemble a package for Nicaragua that includes Western capital and technology. Actual construction might solve the unemployment problems of Cuba and other grateful governments and introduce numerous Soviet bloc personnel into the area. The end result could be a strategic asset under Soviet military protection and the marginalization of the Panama Canal.

- Soviet military advances at new locations in the Basin could require the United States to make a large counter-investment, and in case of a local conflict, to divert or tie down scarce resources.
- As a result, USAF roles in the area would probably need to expand more than U.S. naval and army roles, including for tactical air defense of our ships at sea.
- NORAD and USAF capabilities for southern defense of CONUS, which have been insignificant but are expanding slowly, would be put in a bind.
- The operational importance and use of U.S. bases and facilities in Panama and Puerto Rico would need to be raised drastically, so that any "hostile triangle" may be countered by a U.S. posture that is also traditionally triangular (Panama, Puerto Rico, and Key West/Guantanamo).

LOW-INTENSITY CONFLICT AND ITS INTERNATIONALIZATION

The other potential source of threat is the domino-like spread of low-intensity conflicts to places where the United States has vital interests at stake: from Central American northward through Guatemala into Mexico or southward into Panama, or by island-hopping in the Caribbean to Puerto Rico.[18] This is a much more subtle and ambiguous source of threat than the Soviet Navy or Cuban Air Force. Nonetheless, such conflicts might create opportunities for the kind of hostile force expansion discussed above, lead to revolutionary instability in Mexico, Panama, or Puerto Rico, diminish the interests of key regional allies (especially Venezuela and Mexico) in cooperating with the United States, or put pressure on U.S. bases in Panama and Puerto Rico. Should local institutions and neighboring governments prove incapable of containing the instability, the results could provoke a costly, prolonged U.S. military intervention.

Revolutionary insurgency and terrorism have posed threatening problems for decades, especially in the mid- and late 1970s, following the Cuban Revolution, when the United States supported counterinsurgency programs throughout Latin America. In this earlier period the guerrillas failed in country after country, mainly because they were operating with a deficient strategy and did not have favorable conditions. But with the success of the Sandinistas against the Somoza regime in Nicaragua in 1979 and the recent growth of revolutionary warfare in El Salvador and Guatemala, it has become clear that the

---

[18] The term "low-intensity conflict" is used in contrast with conventional war and does not suggest that casualties are few. It includes revolutionary insurgency and terrorism, counterrevolutionary violence, forceful seizures of government, and border conflicts.

revolutionaries now are more sophisticated and enjoy more favorable conditions.

It would be a mistake to view this latest generation of revolutionary violence as though it were merely a more advanced version of the 1960s generation. The earlier strategies typically relied on the "foco theory" of small isolated units operating in the countryside, looked mainly to Cuba and the Soviet bloc for assistance, and treated the United States as a monolithic enemy where little sympathy could be generated. However, today's revolutionaries are refining orthodox Marxist-Leninist strategies, which emphasize broad-based armed organizations and popular-front coalitions. Moreover, they are seeking allies, resources, and volunteers from around the world (notably Western Europe). And they are building sympathetic support networks within the United States (for example, through some media, universities, and churches). Unable to garner majority domestic support, the revolutionaries (and also the counterrevolutionary extremists) have sought to promote polarization at home and internationalization abroad. Low-intensity conflict has come to depend on diplomatic as well as military expertise.

In many respects, we are witnessing a substantially new pattern of low-intensity conflict, whose main new characteristic is deliberate internationalization. More than ever before, the revolutionaries' strategy is to promote the internationalization of ostensibly local conflicts. They have turned Central America into the world's most internationalized laboratory for revolutionary (and counterrevolutionary) conflict.

This does not mean that the sources of the low-intensity conflict are strictly external to the region. There has been a prolonged and futile argument over whether the sources of violence in Central America are largely *external* to the area (Cuban and Soviet subversion) or essentially *internal* (chronic underdevelopment, indigenous poverty, exploitation, corruption).[19] In this area the internal and external sources of violence are virtually inseparable, and the current internationalization of conflict conforms to an often overlooked historical pattern: For almost two centuries Central American elites have fought their indigenous conflicts by seeking foreign allies and resources. It's the sensible thing for competing elites to do in small countries that have weak (mainly imported) political institutions and poor (mainly export-oriented) economies,

---

[19]   A recent political expression of this argument may be found in *The Americas at a Crossroads: Report of the Inter-American Dialogue*, chaired by Sol M. Linowitz and Galo Plaza, conducted under the auspices of the Woodrow Wilson International Center for Scholars, 1983, which concluded that "the sources of insecurity are mainly internal to each nation; external influences are secondary." Paradoxically, many scholars who now write editorial opinion pieces insisting that the revolutionary unrest in Central America is due primarily to internal causes and not to external Soviet-Cuban support, have earlier subscribed to dependency theories that treat US domination and other external factors as the major sources of economic underdevelopment and political dictatorship in Latin America.

where external support can be used to compensate for the absence of domestic majority support, and whose geopolitical position attracts foreign interests.[20]

In brief, even though Central America's elites respond mainly to local conditions, their struggles normally invite international connections. The weaker U.S. power and presence seem to be in the area, the more likely are local protagonists to entertain extra-hemispheric entanglements.

The relative decline of U.S. power and presence in the Basin during the mid- and late 1970s, although sometimes hailed as spelling an end to U.S. hegemonic presumptions, may have spurred the domestic and international destabilization of security conditions in Central America. The perceived U.S. decline seems to have prompted both extreme left- and right-wing elements to become aggressive. It simultaneously weakened and victimized "moderates" who were typically associated with European-oriented Christian Democracy and Social Democracy and not protected by U.S. human-rights advocacy.[21] The U.S. decline also created openings for foreign entry and incentives for local protagonists to seek foreign support either to compensate for or take advantage of the U.S. decline.

This latest pattern of low-intensity conflict first emerged in Nicaragua in the late 1970s. Within the Sandinista movement, the "tercerista tendency" deliberately sought to involve moderate Latin American and West European governments in supporting the revolutionary struggle to topple Somoza, to gain legitimacy and resources for the Sandinistas, and to isolate the United States.[22] The pattern is being repeated, with variations, in El Salvador and Guatemala. The communicability of conflict in Central America, where borders mean little and politico-military networks cut across national lines, increases the relevance of the "domino theory."

---

[20] For example, during the 19th century the United States often provided support to leaders and coalitions who campaigned to exclude Spanish, French, or British influence. In the mid and late 1800s, local struggles between Liberals and Conservatives overlaid the US-British rivalry for preeminence in the Isthmus. Since the early 20th century, when the United States established virtual hegemony and occupied several countries, local elite struggles have often depended on who gained most favor within the United States. (However, the last US intervention in Nicaragua, in 1927, was directed against Mexican-backed insurgents and thus at preventing the spread of Mexico's revolutionary influence in Central America.) In recent years, Western Europe's political and economic resurgence and the international activism of its Christian Democratic and Social Democratic parties have offered new sources of outside support for Central American nationalists.

[21] Indeed, it has been in the strategic interests of both the extreme right and extreme left to use violence to accentuate polarization and to destroy (or force into exile) moderate leaders, parties, and followers, leaving little choice but one extreme or the other.

[22] See Bosch, 1984 [Bosch, Adriana, "Nicaragua: The Internationalization of Conflict and Politics in Central America," The Rand Corporation, N-2119-AF, June 1984].

"Contagion" may not be contained, however, by the increasing complexity of elite and institutional structures north of Nicaragua, which affects how easily revolutionary insurgents may define the "enemy" and seek broad popular support. Nicaragua featured one dictator and one family ruling through a military identified with that family dynasty; El Salvador, however, is ruled by a somewhat broader, elected coalition backed by more than its so-called 14 families, while the military as an institution is breaking its ties with the traditional socioeconomic order. Guatemala's elite consists of numerous families who are not closely interrelated, its military is quite strong and professional for the region, and the recent coups still offer hope for the institutionalization of a politicoeconomic strategy to defeat the guerrillas.[23]   Mexico presents no clear oligarchy, has developed institutional and elite complexity to a degree that defies easy description or targeting, and its military is professionally integrated into the political system. The "dominoes" should be more difficult and complicated to topple northward from Nicaragua, and the same may hold true southward.

Further constraints on conflict transmission may extend from the expansion of U.S. military, economic, and diplomatic roles in the area. Unfortunately, the United States has had great difficulty dealing with low-intensity conflict and its multiple political, socioeconomic, and military causes. An important part of the problem in Central America is that terrorism and other forms of violence have had debilitating if not murderous consequences for the two pillars that U.S. policy prefers: the political and economic "moderates" and the professional military forces. Moderate elements are typically killed, forced into exile, or simply flee. Although many end up in the United States, the U.S. government has not developed a broad strategy or even much of an interest in working with exile and refugee groups that might reconstitute a moderate political force for their countries. Meanwhile, if the local armed forces can win the conflict, they normally end up much more politicized and repressive than is desirable for U.S. policy (even though U.S. interests are served by their winning). If the United States should become more resourceful as it becomes more active, moderate elements should stand a better chance of surviving and remaining in the area, and local military establishments should stand a better chance of conforming to higher standards of professional behavior. But this is far from assured. We are probably in for a prolonged, difficult struggle to understand the political, social, and economic change coursing through the area and to manage it in a way that leads to a mutually more secure and self-reliant region.

---

[23]   See Sereseres, 1984 [Sereseres, Caesar D., *Military Politics, Internal Warfare, and U.S. Policy in Guatemala*, The Rand Corporation, R-2996-AF, April 1984].

PRELIMINARY IMPLICATIONS FOR U.S. SECURITY

The two great threat sources feed on each other. If low-level conflict brings a revolutionary government to power, it may create new opportunities for hostile force expansion. In turn, the establishment of a new revolutionary government may create a new source from which to foment low-level conflict elsewhere. The past and present roles of Castro's Cuba and now the behavior of the Sandinistas' Nicaragua exemplify this synergy.

The structural linkages are not so strong and direct that it makes sense for U.S. strategy to treat them as a unified threat with a common central source. Although it is true that Castro's Cuba lies at the center of both threat sources, each has unique dynamics and raises separate requirements for U.S. response. Containing Cuba and Nicaragua would not necessarily prevent low-level leftist struggles elsewhere; and halting Nicaragua would not necessarily prevent Cuba and other nations from developing a fortified, hostile military axis.

The crucial factor behind hostile force expansion is the Soviet Union. Hence, the decisive requirement for U.S. strategy is to " de-Sovietize" Cuba, or at least to contain and diminish its close military collaboration with the USSR.[24] This could also help halt the spread of low-intensity leftist violence elsewhere in the region. At the same time, the broader requirement for U.S. strategy against low-intensity conflict is to "de-internationalize" conflict processes in the Basin—in part by working to diminish West European as well as Soviet involvement in local conflict processes while expanding U.S. influence.

Besides not identifying the threat sources as though they were unified, U.S. strategy must also guard against becoming susceptible to policy tradeoffs that would mean tolerating the advance of one for the sake of limiting the other. In particular, it would be foolhardy to allow "a very strong and continuing Cuban commitment to the defense of revolutionary Nicaragua and Grenada in tacit exchange for the tapering off of Cuban support for revolutionary movements in El Salvador and in other countries."[25] As long as Cuba maintains its present leadership and policy directions, this would not bring peace to the Basin or security to the United States but would instead ensure the

---

[24] See Gonzalez, 1982a and b [Gonzalez, Edward, *A Strategy for Dealing with Cuba in the 1980s*, The Rand Corporation, R-2954-DOS/AF, September 1982, and "U.S. Policy: Objectives and Opinions," in Jorge I. Dominguez, ed. *Cuba: Internal and International Affairs*, Sage Publications, Beverly Hills, California, 1982].

[25] An idea broached in Jorge I. Dominguez, 1982a, p. 47 [Dominguez, Jorge I., "Cuba's Relations with Caribbean and Central American Countries," paper prepared for the Center for International Affairs, Harvard University, August 1982], as an element in a moderate scenario for deterring the generalization of warfare and the polarization of regional relations by the mid-1980s.

foundations for enlarging Cuba's military presence and the gradual creation of a hostile axis in the Basin.

Additional boundaries to U.S. strategy are set by the fact that, under general peacetime conditions, there is no easy military formula for eliminating either threat source. Primarily military solutions would require very costly diversions of scarce U.S. military resources, thus violating the strategic principle of minimizing military allocations to the region so as not to degrade our global posture.

Soviet military objectives in this area remain quite unclear. Nevertheless, in addition to disrupting U.S.-hemispheric relations, Soviet strategists would benefit from exploiting revolutionary regimes and conflicts in the Basin if that led to expansion of the Soviet global presence and military power projection capabilities or U.S. political entrapment and military diversion.[26] Either of these outcomes would weaken U.S. military capabilities elsewhere, further shake the Western alliance system, and disrupt hemispheric solidarity and cooperation. Because the United States needs to avoid either outcome, events in the Caribbean Basin cannot and should not be assessed in isolation from the global East-West struggle. The nature of that struggle cannot, by itself, provide the sole basis for U.S. strategy in the Basin, but it does impose certain limits:

- U.S. policy and strategy must assure that the Soviets gain no military positions outside Cuba.
- They must also assure that U.S. military forces, already stretched thin, do not get entrapped in a sizable, untenable intervention.

Either extreme would violate at least one of the key strategic principles discussed in Sec. II* and seriously jeopardize U.S. national security.

The United States needs to develop a primarily nonmilitary strategy for the Basin, integrating political, economic, and military instruments for addressing threats, their sources, and other security challenges. The outlines of such a strategy are presented in the next section.† However, we must still prepare militarily for the possibility that either threat source may loom large (and that global security conditions may deteriorate) in the years ahead and thus oblige the United States to take stringent military action.

---

[26] As Edward Gonzalez has noted, the former may be preferred by the Soviet Air Force and Navy, and the latter by the Soviet Army and KGB.
* Not included in this excerpt.—Ed.
† Not included in this excerpt.—Ed.

4

East Confronts West in Central America

William Ratliff

It's little wonder most Americans don't understand the nature and extent of the Soviet-bloc challenge to the United States through Central America. Most seldom think about international affairs at all. Those who do may be easily bewildered by the complexity of the issues, by the confusing and often misleading statements of many presumed specialists, and by their own inability to think independently on strategic matters.

In this chapter, I will focus first on the problems of mindset, bias, and terminology that hamper discussions and understanding of strategic issues—and, specifically, the East-West conflict—in Central America. I will then take seven examples of muddled, sometimes simply propagandistic, "thinking" in this particular realm of foreign affairs, that is, seven of the dozens of myths of the day. Other contributors to this volume will dissect the political leaders who call upon their adversaries to "say uncle" and the superpatriots who brand all who disagree with their views communists. I will focus on a different group of elite activists, found mainly in the churches, media, and universities, and the widely circulated myths they promote, almost all of which are critical of the United States and sympathetic to the Sandinista National Liberation Front (FSLN). And I will conclude that as long as our debates and policies toward Central America are dominated by set minds and myths, satisfactory solutions to the almost overwhelming problems of the region will be extremely difficult to achieve, if not altogether beyond our grasp.

MINDSETS AND CONSTRUCTIVE CHANGE

There are many impediments to rational and productive analyses of Central American conditions today and to realistic and constructive U.S. policies toward individual countries and the region. These range from different and often incompatible ideas on how to confront the fundamental political, social, and economic needs of the individual countries to the varying national interests and involvement of foreign powers in the region, in the past, present, and future.

But more often than not these already formidable problems are aggravated by a secondary level of impediments: the inflexible mindsets of many of the parties involved and the seeming compulsion of so many Central and North Americans to revile and attack each other rather than to honestly confront problems, to criticize, compromise, and cooperate for constructive change.

The problems emerge as soon as one begins to discuss East-West involvement in Central America, U.S. policy in the region, or other related issues. Discussions are complicated or frustrated by the ignorance, ideologies, double standards, twisted terminology, and inflammatory rhetoric of the participants on all sides. Speakers prove unable to distinguish between alternate meanings of terms, or to tell reasoned argument from emotional tirade, fact from assertion, the possible from the impossible. And there is the conviction of moral superiority wielded by many participants and the resulting moral and ideological arrogance that precludes tolerance and flexibility, two essential qualities when operating in the always-imperfect real world beyond the luxuries of ideology and academe.

On the specific subject of this volume, most people do not understand geostrategic issues on more than a superficial level; many don't even recognize that there *are* such issues. And finally, but not least, most people have no grasp of comparative political, social, and institutional histories. The zealots of our day are forever comparing systems, and vigorously advocating some over others, without really understanding all, or sometimes any, of the systems they trot out to praise or condemn.

Ironically, constructive discourse often is most difficult in U.S. universities, where objectivity, rationality, and the open (but not empty) mind are supposed to be cultivated and exercised. But tragically, nowhere are prejudices more relentlessly pursued, pressures to conform more intense, acceptable and unacceptable political and other leaders more neatly lined up for adulation or abomination. And nowhere are the double standards more sanctimoniously intoned.[1]

Why is this so? Because in the universities and society at large people march into battle—for that is what discussion of Central American issues has become—laden with all manner of intellectual and emotional baggage, with perspectives that often reach far beyond U.S. relations with Central America. These perspectives—say, on the natures of entire social, political and economic systems throughout history—often become mindsets that determine, and often in advance, what one will make of and do with new information as it arrives, or whether new information will ever be acknowledged. The mindset usually is based in a religion or pseudoreligion, ranging from Orthodox

---

[1]   Two recent books dealing with this subject are the autobiography by Sidney Hook, *Out of Step* (New York: Harper and Row, 1987) and Allan Bloom, *The Closing of the American Mind* (New York: Simon and Schuster, 1987).

Christianity or liberation theology through militant relativism to any of the innumerable and often contradictory strands of Marxism-Leninism. Sometimes, but all too seldom, perspective is based to a degree on actual experience in and with the part of the world in question, though the experience may not in itself impart balanced understanding, and emotional ties to the area may hamper or preclude some rational judgments.

The problem with perspectives is not that they differ, but that some are so intolerant of others; some are neither open to revision in light of new developments nor are they flexible enough to meet what is perceived as a mortal enemy on middle ground for the common good. It's the problem of the rock and the hard place.

The highly emotional component of the current debate is understandable and, to a point, even desirable. It brings a long-overdue sense of urgency and commitment to the discussion and reminds people that Central America is not simply a chessboard where alabaster kings (or queens, knights and bishops) fight with and over stone pawns. On the contrary, the players are millions of people, many of whom live in appalling conditions which have become worse since the late 1970s when armed conflict began to engulf the area. Tens of thousands have died and hundreds of thousands have been driven from their homes and even their homelands.

But if Central America is not simply a chessboard with alabaster players, then it is all the more essential that ignorance and ideological pontificating be replaced by informed, reasoned discussion of what is going on. Ignorance, bias, fanaticism, and wishful thinking, however well motivated, often have a strong impact on the formation of foreign policy in the United States, Nicaragua, and other countries. And the impact almost always is negative, making real, long-term improvement in international relations and living conditions in that region infinitely more difficult to achieve.

As long as these antagonisms persist in such intense forms as they do today, it will be virtually impossible even to discuss constructive change, much less bring it about. Recognizing these roadblocks may be the first step to removing them, if the involved parties want to do so. The realist must recognize the unlikelihood of removing the roadblocks, however, without abandoning the effort to do so.

POLITICAL MYTHOLOGY

Traditionally, a myth was a simple story intended to convey, usually indirectly, an important truth. Over the past century Marxists and some others have depicted myths as stories of the ruling class that are used to keep the lower classes in servitude. That is, a myth is a lie or half-truth intended to serve the interests of the rulers at the expense of everyone else.

And in common discourse today, "myth" often means the accidental or deliberate distortion of facts which by chance or intent convey a partial truth or an untruth, the conveyance of which has practical impact on thinking and action in the real world. Such myths abound in the realm of international politics generally, but they are particularly common when political stakes are high and the facts alone do not advance the mythmaker's political cause. Not surprisingly, with stakes so high now in Central America, myths have become as common there as guerrillas, and they often are even more destructive.

The first step toward an honest discussion of the Central American situation must be a weeding out of myths. Retiring myths would seem self-evidently a good idea if one's objective is to deal honestly and realistically with people and the world. Indeed, few people would deny that if one's conclusions are based on falsehoods or distortions rather than facts and the truth, then one's "facts," and one's conclusions, should be reexamined. But one of the unfortunate realities of our day is that many in the activist intellectual elite, no less than the politicians they criticize, manipulate the facts and public opinion for their own purposes. And there is little evidence that they want to change.

SOME MYTHS OF THE DAY

MYTH 1: The United States Is the Rabid Enemy of Freedom.

Even before the Sandinista movement was born in 1961, its founders—then all members of the Nicaraguan Socialist Party (PSN), which was the country's Moscow-aligned Communist party—believed that the United States was the principal cause of pain and poverty in Central America and the Third World. Nicaraguan president Daniel Ortega reaffirmed this conviction when he told a congress of Latin American workers in late 1982 that the "hegemonistic policy" of the United States is "the principal cause of the economic problems that plague the world."[2] And this perspective, now a mindset, more than any other single factor, has fixed the direction of Sandinista analyses and policies in Nicaragua and the world beyond. And it hardened, by seeming to confirm, the worst suspicions and fears of many in the United States.

What is the fundamental Sandinista view of the United States? According to a Sandinista (FSLN) National Directorate document in September 1979, "American imperialism" is "the rabid enemy of all peoples who are struggling

---

[2] See Carlos Fonseca Amador's 1969 article "Nicaragua: Zero Hour," in A. C. Sandino, C. Fonseca, *Nicaragua: La estrategia de la victoria* (Mexico City: Editorial Nuestro Tiempo, 1980), p. 29, where the founder of the Sandinista movement argues that Nicaragua is not only exploited by US imperialism, but is a base for US aggression in the Americas; and Ortega's comments in Daniel Ortega, *El acero de guerra o el olivo de paz* (Managua: Editorial Nueva Nicaragua, 1983), p. 89.

to achieve their definitive liberation or who are in the process of achieving it."

In President Ortega's words in the same month, U.S. imperialism "cannot conceive of a free people, a sovereign people, an independent people." The Sandinista anthem asserts that the Nicaraguan people must "fight against the Yankee, the enemy of humanity." And, according to the FSLN's electoral platform in 1984, "the war policies of the North American administration threaten the survival of humankind."[3]

If this is in fact the U.S. attitude toward freedom and humanity, then the Sandinistas and all other decent people in the world would do well to devote their lives to fighting it. But the Sandinistas do not fight it simply because it is evil, but because they think they must do so to ensure their own survival. It follows from the Sandinista perspective that they and their government are in constant danger of being crushed so long as Nicaragua is surrounded by countries that are dominated by and subservient to this U.S. "imperialism." So, working from this perspective, it is hardly surprising that the FSLN's 1969 Program and other party documents and individual statements argue that the Sandinista revolution must combat imperialism everywhere in order to secure the Sandinista revolution. That is, it must support "liberation movements" throughout the region, for its own good and as international comrades, and indeed even unite all of Central America in a single nation.[4]

But does this perspective correspond to the facts? No. Nor does the other side of the Sandinista outlook, namely that their Soviet ally represents a higher level of humanity than the United States, as FSLN founder Carlos Fonseca Amador asserted as early as the late 1950s in his book *Un Nicaragüense en Moscú*, published while the author was still a member of the Nicaraguan Communist Party. Nor is it true that the Soviet Union, in contrast to the United States, is a great advocate of national independence and popular rights.

Only in a period of overpowering ideology, and extreme ignorance, cynicism and disillusionment, would people in the noncommunist world give these arguments any credence at all. But we are in such a period.

---

[3] FSLN National Directorate, "Analysis of the Situation and Tasks of the Sandinista People's Revolution" (*72-Hour Document*), translated by the US Department of State and published in Washington in 1986, available in Mark Falcoff and Robert Royal (eds.), *The Continuing Crisis: U.S. Policy in Central America and the Caribbean* (Lanham, Md.: Ethics and Public Policy Center, 1987), p. 504; Ortega's speech, at the Sixth Summit Conference of Nonaligned Countries, in Havana, in Ortega, *El acero de guerra*, p. 16, translated in Tomás Borge et al., *Sandinistas Speak* (New York: Pathfinder Press, 1982), edited by Bruce Marcus, p. 44; *Plataforma Electoral del FSLN* (Managua: Casa Nacional de Campana, 1984), p. 12.

[4] See "Programa del Frente Sandinista de Liberación Nacional," in its original form in *Tricontinental* (Havana), Marzo-Abril 1970, p. 68, and revised in *Sandinistas Speak*.

It is absurd, for example, to suggest that the United States favors oppression in Europe, where its allies are democracies, or that the Soviet Union supports democracy, when its allies are assorted despotisms, though most play games with words and call themselves "people's democracies." And while Europe is not the Third World, Europeans too are people and members of that "humanity" the Sandinistas claim the United States is out to destroy.

Outside of Europe, it also is difficult to admire Soviet over U.S. allies for their independence and regard for human rights. Contrast Afghanistan and Costa Rica, for example. But critics of the Sandinistas err in trying to overmake their case in the Third World. In Latin America, for example, U.S. "allies" have been more varied for many reasons, though not because the United States is bent on wiping out humankind, as President Ortega asserts. And although the U.S. record in the Third World is a great deal better than the Soviet record, U.S. political relationships were formed that have come back to haunt U.S. policymakers today.

The United States has had some unsavory friends in, and some bad policies toward, a number of Latin American countries, including Nicaragua. Many Nicaraguans, including some of the nine comandantes ruling in Managua today, had bitter personal and family experiences with the Somoza government and the National Guard, both of which the United States helped set up and supported in varying ways and degrees for many years. It is understandable that they can feel hostility toward "U.S. imperialism."

But the vast majority of Nicaraguans, who lived through the same national history, often with similar experiences, do not hate the United States with the same white-hot passion as the comandantes. And there is no evidence that this majority—who are not demonstrably intellectually or morally inferior to the comandantes—accept the Sandinista line that the U.S. system is a gigantic conspiracy which by its very nature bleeds and oppresses the people of Nicaragua and the entire Third World. Nor do most seem to believe that Nicaragua must do mortal battle against the United States in league with Cuba, the Soviet Union, and the Palestine Liberation Organization. In short, their perspective is not a mindset, frozen by ideology and hatred, and unreceptive to change in the United States and to the realities touched on in the following discussion.

The fact is that all Nicaraguans who look north see a giant superpower looming over them—beyond the Mexican mini-superpower, that is. But over the decades policymakers in Washington who looked south usually didn't see Nicaragua at all. Indeed, given the continuous international crises in Europe, Asia, and the Middle East that demanded their attention, most top U.S. policymakers rarely turned their faces to Latin America. Consequently U.S. policies toward Nicaragua, and often toward the entire region, tended to be nonpolicies of convenience reflecting an unfortunate "I've-got-more-important-things-to-think-about" indifference to the area.

Cuba to guarantee safe transport. And even if the additional forces to secure the Caribbean were available, and did their job, the securing itself would take time and materiel during a crisis when both probably would be in short supply.

This brings us to the small but important role—alluded to above—that Cuba, Nicaragua, Castroite guerrillas, and others can play in the big Soviet chess game, not only in an emergency but on a regular basis. While the Soviet Union, China, and many other countries know the great cost of having to maintain large standing armies on hostile or potentially hostile borders, the United States does not. But if a larger number of Central American countries, and perhaps Mexico as well, were allied to Cuba and the Soviet Union, this would force the expansion or redeployment of substantial U.S. forces. It would mean bringing home tens of thousands of Americans stationed in Europe and elsewhere to secure the home front, or greatly expanding U.S. military forces so as to be prepared for a potential crisis at home *and/or* abroad. Many Americans would prefer the former—just bringing troops home—because it would mean fewer men under arms. The Soviet Union would prefer that too, for the withdrawal of U.S. troops would make areas of the world, most importantly Europe and Asia, that are of *primary* importance to Moscow—which the Western Hemisphere is not—more vulnerable to Soviet power and influence.[6]

MYTH 3: The United States Brought the East-West Conflict to Central America.

We often hear that history means more to the people of Latin America than to those of North America, that the past continues to play a more obvious and immediate role in their lives. The old saw is partly true, for history lives in Latin America in many ways it does not in the north. But the saying can be very misleading if it is taken to mean history never matters to North Americans and widespread failure to recognize the importance of history has contributed to a misunderstanding of how the so-called East-West conflict was introduced into Central America.

One aspect of history that matters deeply to many North Americans is, in fact, the East-West Conflict, a rivalry and bitter hostility that spans most of the twentieth century. The conflict is essentially between those powers taken to be the chief representatives of the "East" (the Soviet Union) and the "West" (the United States), or in even broader terms the kinds of political systems they represent. Latin America, and particularly Central America, has *seemed* far removed from that conflict, until a quarter century ago.

6 See R. Bruce McColm, "Central America and the Caribbean: The Larger Scenario," *Strategic Review* (Summer 1983): 28-42; and *The Challenge to Democracy in Central America* (Washington: US Departments of State and Defense, October 1986).

MYTH 2: Nicaragua Is No Threat to the United States.

This is obviously true, so far as it goes. But like Niggle's leaf in the Tolkien story, Nicaragua is just a small part of a larger geostrategic picture, indeed of two larger pictures, and *these* pictures are of *great* strategic importance to the United States, to the Western Hemisphere generally, and to other parts of the world. And in the twentieth century international competition between the superpowers, these pictures are of equal interest to the Soviet Union. The pictures are of the world and the Caribbean Basin, the latter including Central America, Panama, and Mexico.

There is no evidence whatsoever that Soviet leaders have any great concern for the well-being of individual residents of Central America and the Caribbean, among them Cubans and Nicaraguans. Indeed, the Soviet Union is notoriously stingy when it comes to providing general developmental aid or assistance of any sort anywhere in the world, as is shown by its record of massively arming some African countries while refusing any but the most minimal economic or relief aid, even during such crises as the famine that hit its ally Ethiopia—much less other countries—in the mid-1980s.

How, then, do we account for Moscow's inordinate generosity in providing economic aid to Cuba: at least $4 billion annually for many years, more than half the economic aid the Soviet Union gives to the entire Third World? Anyone who has talked with Cuban or Soviet officials knows it is not because the two nationalities have any special fondness for each other. Nor is it because Soviet leaders particularly like Castro, for the bearded caudillo periodically has been almost as big a headache for Moscow as for Washington.

For Soviet strategists, it *is* a game of chess. Cuba, and to a lesser extent Nicaragua, are pawns on Moscow's chessboard of international politics. It is worth putting up a quarter of the Cuban GNP annually because Cuba is an ally in the heart of a region of critical strategic importance to the United States. Nicaragua is more of the same, in a related but separate area, and in early 1987 was worth Soviet investments of about $1 million per day. The difference between the two is that Nicaragua—like Grenada before it—is far more expendable, as the comandantes in Managua will find out if push ever really comes to shove with any administration in Washington.

Soviet policy increasingly has been to establish a strong presence in important areas of the world. Of particular interest are those that control critical sea lanes, for though much individual travel these days is by plane, most products, many essential goods are moved by sea. Just since the mid-1970s the Soviet Union has established a massive presence in Southeast Asia, in the South Pacific, in Ethiopia along the Red Sea, and in the backyard of the United States—in Central America and, more broadly, the Caribbean Basin.

These steps into the U.S. "backyard" have been in three main forms—general relations, unrest, and allies—which are important for several reasons.

Closer general political and economic ties in the region improve the climate of opinion toward the Soviet Union and increase both Moscow's physical presence and the region's dependency on Soviet-bloc ties. One manifestation of this increasing Soviet interest and involvement is Gorbachev's scheduled visit to Latin America in 1987.

Soviet gains also have been in the form of unrest in Central American countries. A Marxist-Leninist government or an active guerrilla movement can draw significant U.S. attention away from Europe, the Middle East, or Asia by making the United States feel threatened by the actual *and potential* spread of hostile forces in the Americas.

The Soviet Union has picked up allies in Cuba, Nicaragua, and for a while, Grenada; and perhaps in the future it will add El Salvador and/or other countries. In allied countries the Soviet Union may establish important intelligence outposts—the largest Soviet electronic intelligence facility outside the USSR is at Lourdes in Cuba—or gain other advantages. For example, partly in exchange for massive military aid to Cuba—more than $4 billion between 1980 and 1986 alone—Moscow gets support from tens of thousands of Cuban troops in Africa, and increasingly easy and frequent access to naval and air bases (and thus direct military presence) in the Caribbean Basin.

All of this matters to the United States because Central America and Mexico are close to its heartland and because it needs to have free sea travel through the Panama Canal and Caribbean Basin. On a regular basis, 45 percent of all U.S. imports and exports pass through the Straits of Florida between Cuba and the United States; 55 percent of all U.S. crude oil exports come through the Caribbean Basin; and 65 percent of all ships using the Panama Canal carry goods to and from the United States. Clearly, many other countries—in the Western Hemisphere, Europe, Africa, and Asia—benefit also from the transported materials represented by these percentages. And in the event of a European war, the United States would send 60 percent of its troop and supply ships to NATO through the Caribbean Basin.

As in their nature, strategic questions seem irrelevant to most observers until an emergency arrives, when the concern—if it comes even then—may be too late. Are the Cubans really going to harass ships carrying bananas to U.S. ports, some critics gibe? Of course not, under ordinary circumstances. But in an emergency they and their allies could intercept military and other ships with significant destructive force, as the Germans did at the beginning of World War II. To cut off the threat of Soviet/Cuban interdiction of sea transport, the United States might well have to invade the island. Defense Department estimates are that an invasion of Cuba would require some 100,000 troops, just about what the United States probably would be trying to send to NATO through the Caribbean Basin. That would mean the United States would always need a minimum of 100,000 more troops than currently available to allow for meeting not only NATO needs but those required for an invasion of

Cuba to guarantee safe transport. And even if the additional forces to secure the Caribbean were available, and did their job, the securing itself would take time and materiel during a crisis when both probably would be in short supply.

This brings us to the small but important role—alluded to above—that Cuba, Nicaragua, Castroite guerrillas, and others can play in the big Soviet chess game, not only in an emergency but on a regular basis. While the Soviet Union, China, and many other countries know the great cost of having to maintain large standing armies on hostile or potentially hostile borders, the United States does not. But if a larger number of Central American countries, and perhaps Mexico as well, were allied to Cuba and the Soviet Union, this would force the expansion or redeployment of substantial U.S. forces. It would mean bringing home tens of thousands of Americans stationed in Europe and elsewhere to secure the home front, or greatly expanding U.S. military forces so as to be prepared for a potential crisis at home *and/or* abroad. Many Americans would prefer the former—just bringing troops home—because it would mean fewer men under arms. The Soviet Union would prefer that too, for the withdrawal of U.S. troops would make areas of the world, most importantly Europe and Asia, that are of *primary* importance to Moscow—which the Western Hemisphere is not—more vulnerable to Soviet power and influence.[6]

MYTH 3: The United States Brought the East-West Conflict to Central America.

We often hear that history means more to the people of Latin America than to those of North America, that the past continues to play a more obvious and immediate role in their lives. The old saw is partly true, for history lives in Latin America in many ways it does not in the north. But the saying can be very misleading if it is taken to mean history never matters to North Americans and widespread failure to recognize the importance of history has contributed to a misunderstanding of how the so-called East-West conflict was introduced into Central America.

One aspect of history that matters deeply to many North Americans is, in fact, the East-West Conflict, a rivalry and bitter hostility that spans most of the twentieth century. The conflict is essentially between those powers taken to be the chief representatives of the "East" (the Soviet Union) and the "West" (the United States), or in even broader terms the kinds of political systems they represent. Latin America, and particularly Central America, has *seemed* far removed from that conflict, until a quarter century ago.

---

[6] See R. Bruce McColm, "Central America and the Caribbean: The Larger Scenario," *Strategic Review* (Summer 1983): 28-42; and *The Challenge to Democracy in Central America* (Washington: US Departments of State and Defense, October 1986).

Both U.S. and Soviet policies toward Central America, or any region of the world, must be seen in the broader context of those nations' policies generally and in the context of each power's allies. Officials in Washington, and even more so planners in Moscow, think in broad geostrategic terms, even when their rivals and critics do not. Whether one likes it or not, that is how international politics is played in the Big Leagues; to deny it is simply to affirm that one is aware only of the bush leagues of international affairs.

By its very nature the conflict between the superpowers spreads if one of the two upsets the status quo by winning a new ally, particularly if that ally is in a previously uncontested region of the world. This occurred in the Caribbean Basin after Fidel Castro's victory in Cuba in 1959.

For years some politicians, journalists, academics, and others argued that United States hostility to Castro in 1959 and 1960 had pushed Cuba into the Soviet camp. This argument flew in the face of Castro's own statement made during 1958 in a letter to his confidante Celia Sanchez, namely his pledge that once the war against Batista was over his "true destiny" would be to wage a "much wider and bigger war" against the United States. This letter reflected a militant hatred of and hostility toward the United States far beyond that of any but a very small number of other Cubans then or now.

But the ruler of a small Caribbean island in the shadow of the United States could not launch a crusade against a neighboring giant on his own. Castro quickly saw that he would need a shield against the United States, and to get it he would have to align himself with the powerful international enemy of his nemesis, that is with the Soviet Union. Thus,.ties to the Soviet Union and its bloc were necessary for Castro to achieve his own personal ambitions. His intention from the moment he took power was to cement this tie, as has been documented in great detail by former *New York Times* Latin American correspondent Tad Szulc in his *Fidel: A Critical Portrait*. This recognition of Castro's self-motivated turn to the Soviet Union is not a matter of moral judgment for or against Castro or the United States. It is simply a fact.[7]

Much the same chain of events occurred in Nicaragua twenty years later. Carlos Fonseca Amador and other lesser founders and early members of the Sandinista movement—among them the current interior minister, Tomás Borge—were frustrated comrades of the PSN when Castro took power in Cuba in 1959. Inspired by Castro's example, they broke from the PSN and, taking Castro's revolution as their model for Nicaragua, in 1961 they formed the Sandinista movement. The 1969 FSLN Program, the first major statement by the party as such, stated the group's determination to throw Somoza and the

---

[7] For the text of the letter to Sanchez see Hugh Thomas, *The Cuban Revolution* (New York: Harper Torchbooks, 1977), p. 278; the letter is on public display in Havana. For Castro's calculated move into the communist camp, see Szulc, *Fidel: A Critical Portrait* (New York: William Morrow and Co., 1986), pp. 463ff.

United States out of Nicaragua and establish a government of their own. But the program went further and pledged the Sandinistas' "combative solidarity" with and "active support" for the peoples in Latin America, Africa, and Asia who are "fighting against imperialism, colonialism and neo-colonialism." The movement sought to coordinate the popular forces in Central America seeking "national liberation" and a new social system free from "imperialist domination." And finally it looked to establish a "true union of the Central American peoples in a single homeland."[8]

Their determination to oppose "imperialism" wherever it was found, and particularly close to home, followed logically from their conviction that no true revolution could survive the presence of the United States or nearby U.S. allies. And given the size of Nicaragua, and the country's proximity to the United States, the Sandinistas' natural, indeed unavoidable, allies were the other powerful, like-minded nations of the world, above all those led by the Soviet Union. And one of those Soviet-bloc nations, hardly coincidentally, was their original and continuing inspiration—Castro's Cuba.

Thus, quite aside from whether the Sandinista analysis of the United States is correct, the incontrovertible fact is that by placing themselves alongside Cuba—a tie that has been asserted proudly, defiantly, and repeatedly in personal contacts as well as party documents and individual statements over more than a quarter century—and thus in the Soviet bloc, the Sandinistas dragged the East-West conflict into Central America.

MYTH 4: The United States Forced Nicaragua into Soviet Alignment.

This is just as false in the case of Nicaragua in 1979 as it was for Cuba two decades earlier, and for exactly the same reasons, as already discussed. Sandinista hostility toward the United States, and determination to help overthrow, or at least neutralize, "imperialism" throughout the region, dates from the beginning of the movement in 1961; and as long as the position is maintained—openly or otherwise—Soviet-bloc alignment is the only logical international alternative open to the comandantes.

The Carter administration bungled its effort to promote a non-Sandinista alternative before June 1979. Nevertheless, Carter had long since cut U.S. aid to the Somoza government, and the CIA made no efforts to subvert the Sandinista guerrillas in their military efforts, which it could easily have done. In June 1979 Carter cosponsored the OAS resolution that withdrew recognition from Somoza's seated government and called for its replacement. Carter's Agency for International Development (AID) director in Managua, Lawrence Harrison, recounts a luncheon in Managua in mid-1979 at which the Sandinistas hosted former Venezuelan president Carlos Andrés Pérez, whose support

8   "Programa de Frente Sandinista de Liberación Nacional," p. 68.

for the overthrow of Somoza had been a critical factor in the dictator's defeat. Pérez accepted the praise from the Sandinistas and then turned to the U.S. ambassador and said, "We must remember that were it not for the government represented by that ambassador, we would not be here today."[9]

And during the next eighteen months the United States gave more aid to Nicaragua than did any other country: $118 million in bilateral aid, which was far more than the United States had ever given Somoza during a comparable period, including the time after the 1972 earthquake. Also, the United States supported the refinancing of Nicaragua's debt to foreign banks and helped the Sandinistas get new loans of $1.6 billion from international financial institutions and democratic nations. While these actions have been attacked by some Sandinistas and their supporters as a plot to bind the new government to the capitalist world, no one forced the Sandinistas to betray their principles and accept the offers.

According to AID director Harrison, immediately after the war, as many as a quarter of all Nicaraguans were eating food aid from the United States. When seeds were short for agricultural planting, the United States sent more in; when an Atlantic flood threatened lives, the United States sent medical teams and boats; when there was a shortage of intravenous solutions, the United States provided more; when money was needed to buy materials for artificial limbs for war wounded, the United States provided it overnight. The United States sent in agrarian reform experts and university professors, provided scholarships to Nicaraguan students, funded activities of private volunteer agencies in the country, and supported the Sandinista literacy campaign even when teaching materials defamed the United States. U.S. offers of military aid did not go through because the Sandinistas insisted on using only Cuban military advisers, an impossible demand, as the Sandinistas very well knew, considering the state of U.S.-Cuban—and Cuban-Soviet—relations.[10]

The administration had a hard time getting some of this aid approved by Congress, but in large part this was because all the fears of Washington's hawks were repeatedly refueled by Sandinista statements and actions. An example was the September 1979 Sandinista National Directorate document describing "American imperialism" as "the rabid enemy" of all people seeking freedom. During that same month, even as the U.S. ambassador to Nicaragua and the head of the AID mission in Managua were in Washington lobbying for

---

9   Harrison, "The Confrontation with the Sandinistas" [note 5 above]. This was the same Pérez who was invited to Daniel Ortega's inauguration as president in early 1985 and publicly refused to go, charging that the Sandinistas had betrayed their promises to establish a democracy in Nicaragua; see Pérez's letter of January 1985 to Daniel Ortega in Robert Leiken and Barry Rubin, eds., *The Central American Crisis Reader* (New York: Summit Books, 1987), pp. 300-302.
10   Harrison, "The Confrontation with the Sandinistas" [note 5 above]. Also see Robert Matthews, "The Limits of Friendship," *NACLA Report on the Americas* (May-June 1985): 23.

more and quicker aid, Daniel Ortega addressed the Nonaligned summit in Havana and denounced the United States in terms indistinguishable from those of Fidel Castro.

But the actual break in U.S. relations with Nicaragua came over another, related, matter: the Sandinistas' determination to secure their own victory by assisting like-minded groups in other countries, specifically in the "final offensive" of the guerrillas in El Salvador. As Harrison explains it, U.S. Deputy Assistant Secretary of State James Cheek went to Managua in September 1980

> explicitly to warn the Sandinistas of the grave consequences for relationships between the United States and Nicaragua should the FSLN provide assistance to the guerrillas in El Salvador. Three months later, it became clear to the Carter administration that the warning had had no effect. The evidence of Sandinista involvement in El Salvador was sufficiently compelling to cause the president to consider suspending assistance to Nicaragua during his last few days in office. He chose to leave the decision to the incoming Reagan administration, but not because there was ambiguity in the evidence. . . .
>
> The Reagan administration inherited a confrontation that its predecessor had done all it could to avoid. For six months, until after the visit of then Assistant Secretary of State Enders to Managua in August of 1981, the new administration tried to avert a confrontation. For example, when it decided to respond to the Sandinista involvement in El Salvador, it did so in a very muted way, only partially suspending assistance and leaving the door open for additional assistance if the Sandinistas ceased aid to the Salvadoran guerrillas.[11]

Arturo Cruz, who was a member of the Sandinista Junta from May 1980 until March 1981—before, during and after the "final offensive" in El Salvador—wrote in 1984 that the Sandinistas'

> misguided and untimely involvement is perhaps one of the principal reasons leading to the difficulties which presently beset Nicaragua and hinder regional political stability and economic advancement. Their intrusion in El Salvador made Nicaragua a controversial actor on Central America's political stage and raised the suspicions of the United States, which started to see a threat coming from Nicaragua. Moreover, from that moment a correlation was established between the radicalization of the Sandinistas and economic deterioration in Central America.[12]

[11]   Harrison, "The Confrontation with the Sandinistas" [note 5 above]. Even Sandinista witnesses at the International Court of Justice hearings in 1985 acknowledged Sandinista involvement in supplying the Salvadoran guerrillas. See John Norton Moore, *The Secret War in Central America: Sandinista Assault on World Order* (Frederick, Md.: University Publications of America, 1987), passim, for evidence and quotations from the hearings.
[12]   Arturo Cruz, "Implications of an Orthodox Communist Political System in Nicaragua,"

Comandante Bayardo Arce has admitted that Carter played down the U.S.-Soviet conflict in 1979 and was inclined to view the Sandinista revolution as "basically a revolution indigenous to Central America." And Daniel Ortega has said that after the triumph of the revolution the Sandinistas decided "it was necessary to normalize relations with the United States within a new framework of respect and cooperation." Thus, he says, he met with President Carter in September 1980 and found that "it was possible to initiate an effective dialogue."

But there is a lot more here than meets the ear. Arce's comment was made on 20 February 1985, at the conclusion of the First Latin American Congress on Anti-imperialist Thought, long after Carter was out of office, in order to condemn the Reagan administration by contrasting it to something less aggressive, namely Carter's earlier policies. And Ortega's comment was made at the United Nations Security Council on 25 March 1982, also in the course of a long attack on the Reagan administration. But note that Ortega refers to possible dialogue in September 1980—*14 months* after Somoza was overthrown; and note that this was exactly the month Carter's representative openly confronted the Sandinistas with U.S. concerns over Managua's active involvement in the Salvadoran war. Arce's and Ortega's comments on how relatively reasonable Carter was are distinctly after-the-fact; when it really counted, when the Carter administration was in office and trying to establish a working relationship with the FSLN, the Sandinistas condemned the United States just as forcefully and rejected his policies, too.

If all these comments and events are seen in their historical context, the fact is that after July 1979, as Harrison concludes, the United States made many sincere efforts to convince the Sandinistas that the two governments could live together, but "it didn't work, and the principal reason that it didn't was that the Sandinistas wouldn't let it work."[13]

MYTH 5: The Sandinista Government Is Nonaligned.

In June 1979 the Sandinistas promised the Organization of American States that if in power they would maintain a nonaligned foreign policy. This promise was critical in getting the OAS to undertake the unprecedented act of withdrawing recognition from a seated government in preference for the rebel forces. It still claimed to be nonaligned in early 1987.

Occasional Paper, Institute of Interamerican Studies, University of Miami, 1984, pp. 22-23. Cruz was head of the Central Bank from the fall of Somoza until his appointment to the junta, and was Nicaraguan ambassador to the United States after leaving the junta until his defection in 1981.

[13] See Arce, *Política de la Revolución Sandinista: Una repuesta ante la política agresive de la Administración Reagan* (Managua: Edición del Centro de Comunicación Internacional, March 1985), p. 22; Ortega, *El acero de guerra*, p. 60; and Harrison, "The Confrontation with the Sandinistas" [note 5 above].

But if Nicaragua is nonaligned, what does nonaligned mean? In contemporary usage, the term was taken to designate those countries—which formed a "movement" of their own in the 1950s—that stood more or less aside from either of the superpowers in the East-West conflict. That is, they stood something like midway between the United States and the Soviet Union. Though some clearly were more completely nonaligned than others, the term and the movement represented a basically sincere effort to form a third force in international politics.

But with Cuba's increasing active participation, a portion of the movement veered far away from the original objectives, much to the concern of many conscientiously nonaligned members. This contradiction came to a head in 1979 when Castro, by then militantly pro-Soviet—with more than 30,000 Soviet-armed Cuban troops, pilots, and officers in Angola and Ethiopia, under Soviet commanders—hosted the movement's summit in Havana. His comments at the sessions were manifestly *not* nonaligned nor, as noted above, were those of Daniel Ortega, representing the recently triumphant FSLN. After 1979 Sandinista antagonism toward the United States continued to equal Cuba's, even as both rapidly expanded their dependence on the Soviet bloc.

Again, it is no moral judgment for or against any party involved to recognize that if a government is a close ally of one of the two superpowers and a mortal enemy of the other, then by definition that government can not be nonaligned in the East-West conflict.

MYTH 6: U.S. Support for the Contras *Provoked an Arms Race.*

The common explanation of the Sandinista military buildup is that it was necessary to meet the threat of U.S.-backed *contras* on the Honduran and Costa Rican borders, or that Nicaragua feared being invaded by the United States after the U.S.-led overthrow of the New Jewel Movement in Grenada. But this is not true. The real reason is something very different, though it followed logically from the broader Sandinista perception of, and hostility toward, the United States.

The National Directorate analysis of September 1979 said that with the Sandinista victory in July 1979 "the National Guard collapsed like a house of cards. . . . Nothing was left of that army but shame, smoke and ashes." And it continued:

> The kind of military victory achieved over the dictatorship makes it impossible for now, from the practical point of view, to organize aggression by the defeated National Guard . . . . At present there are no clear indications of an armed counterrevolution by Somocista forces from abroad which actually threatens our stability.[14]

---

[14] FSLN National Directorate, "Analysis of the Situation and Tasks of the Sandinista People's Revolution" [note 3 above], pp. 5, 7, 8.

When did the "U.S. aggression" through the *contras* begin, according to the Sandinistas? In his speech of 9 January 1987, announcing the new Nicaraguan Constitution, President Ortega traced the "aggression" back to January 1981. In March 1981 the Nicaraguan government had first accused the United States of setting up training camps for "counterrevolutionaries" on U.S. soil. Carlos Tunnermann, the Nicaraguan ambassador to the United States, said the United States decided to assist the armed resistance in November 1981. (Presidential authorization actually came in December 1981.) At that time—the end of 1981—Tunnermann added, "there were only a few hundred ex-National Guard soldiers staging sporadic raids on farms along the border. Their principal occupations were cattle-rustling and extortion."[15]

So if U.S. aid to the *contras* was the cause of the Sandinista military buildup, that buildup would have begun in January (or March?) 1981 at the earliest, or even at the end of 1981, when the Sandinista government says President Reagan approved military support for the exiled opponents of the Sandinista government.

But that isn't what happened. By the end of 1980—several months before Daniel Ortega says the aggression began, and a year before Tunnermann noted a few hundred cattle-rustlers on the border—Nicaragua had built a military force of about 25,000, the largest army in the history of Central America. In February 1981 the Sandinistas announced their plans to build a militia of 200,000 though, as the *New York Times* pointed out at the time—and the Sandinista statements confirm—there was "surprising little counter-revolutionary activity." When November 1981 came around, and Tunnermann noted the few hundred guardsman cattle-rustlers, the Sandinista army was almost 40,000 strong—three times larger than Somoza's army in 1979—and more than 10,000 larger than the next largest army in Central America. It was armed with Soviet-made tanks, artillery, and armored personnel carriers. By 1986 it was the third largest army in Latin America, behind only Cuba and Brazil.[16]

Thus the Sandinistas assembled the largest army in Central American history before the United States even *began* arming any *contras* and while the United States was still by far its main foreign source of economic aid. Why? Because they maintained the United States was their "rabid enemy" and, no matter what fronts of friendship it might put on, was by its very nature destined to try to overthrow them.

---

[15] Official transcript of Ortega's 9 January 1987 speech picked up at the Sandinista press office in Managua on 28 January 1987; Instituto Nicaragüense de Investigaciones Económicas y Sociales, *Crónica de Una Guerra no Imaginaria, 1979-84* (Managua: INIES, 1986), p. 17; and Tunnermann letter to *Washington Post*, 30 March 1985.

[16] See *New York Times*, 20 February 1981; *The Challenge to Democracy in Central America* [note 6 above], pp. 19-20.

The reality is that from the moment they took power the Sandinistas believed they needed a massive military force at the service of the FSLN. The National Directorate articulated this conviction in its September 1979 document when it spoke in detail of the need to "build, strengthen and educate the Sandinista People's Army while cultivating its loyalty to its people and its revolution, whose vanguard is the FSLN." The Directorate stated:

> The objective of the FSLN's foreign policy is to achieve the consolidation of the Nicaraguan revolution as this will help to strengthen the Central American, Latin American and world revolution. The consolidation must be achieved through the solution of the military and economic problems, principally because with the solution of the first we are strategically preparing to repel any aggression and with the second we can make headway in severing the ties of economic dependence on North American imperialism.[17]

Even more pointedly, an FSLN document on the Sandinista People's Army describes the nation's preparation for war, and then asks: "What war? Not the war against the counterrevolutionaries or Somocistas, but the war against North American imperialism." And this comment was made in 1983, almost two years after the United States *had* begun supporting the *contras*.[18]

Note that the point here is not whether the comandantes were right, that the United States is, by its very nature imperialistic, determined to overthrow any government that wants freedom, and the intractable "enemy of humanity." The point is that many journalists, academics, churchmen, and others have accused the United States, and particularly the Reagan administration, of provoking the arms race in Central America *by its arming of the contras*, and that accusation is without substance. Notwithstanding some propagandistic statements by Ortega, Arce, and others, the Sandinista conflict is not with the Reagan administration for arming the *contras*, or even with the Reagan administration for reviving the Monroe doctrine, but with the U.S. system as a whole, whether headed by Carter or Reagan or anyone else.

MYTH 7: The Contras *Are All Marauding Somocistas.*

Most critics of the United Nicaraguan Opposition (UNO) and the *contras* during 1986 charged that the Nicaraguan opposition abroad simply represents Somoza-ism without Somoza. But it is much more complicated than that: the

---

[17] FSLN National Directorate, "Analysis of the Situation and Tasks of the Sandinista People's Revolution" [note 3 above].
[18] FSLN National Directorate, "Analysis of the Situation and Tasks of the Sandinista People's Revolution" [note 3 above], p. 13; *El E.P.S. y la participación de las masas en la defense de la soberanía* (Managua: Departamento de Propaganda y Educación Política del FSLN, 1983), p. 11.

contras are not a band of blameless "freedom fighters," but neither are they a marauding mob of National Guard (GN) thugs.

The presence of former National Guardsmen, particularly in prominent positions, has been an issue of concern to critics of the *contras* in the United States, but also to some Nicaraguan officials of the *contra* movement abroad and Nicaraguans at home, many of whom oppose the Sandinistas but are uncertain about *contra* connections with the former GN.[19]

First it must be noted that there are former National Guardsmen in the rebel's National Democratic Force (FDN) army, as there are former guardsmen in the Sandinista army. As the FSLN National Directorate statement noted in September 1979, not all in the National Guard were bad men and some had skills that are still needed. There evidently are approximately 200 former guardsmen in the *contras*, and of the 53 top command and staff positions at the end of 1986, 27 percent were held by former guardsmen, 20 percent by former Sandinistas and 53 percent by civilians.[20]

From the beginning the FDN has been headed by former guardsman Enrique Bermudez, who from 1975 through the fall of Somoza was out of Nicaragua as his country's representative on the Interamerican Defense Board. Bermudez was so highly regarded by Americans that President Carter tried to get Somoza to put him in charge of cleaning up the guard, which Somoza refused to do.

But it is beyond dispute that some *contras*—like the Sandinistas—have committed human rights violations, as reported repeatedly in the world press and by human rights organizations, and efforts to curtail them reportedly are underway. Much more does need to be done to prevent violations whenever possible while recognizing that atrocities do occur in wars; U.S. soldiers committed some in Vietnam, but even critics of the war there seldom charge that the U.S. army was a band of marauding thugs.[21]

The level of *contra* violations almost certainly has been exaggerated, sometimes by a press that is overzealous, confused in a situation where the difference between civilian and military often is blurred, or simply hoodwinked.

---

[19] Some UNO leaders have been concerned about the guard from the beginning, and this proved to be one of the issues that came up repeatedly in the restructuring of the rebel movement that came into the open in early 1987. Nicaraguans of all social levels expressed concerns in interviews I conducted during January 1987 in Managua, Granada, Matagalpa, and Jinotega.

[20] See *The Challenge to Democracy in Central America* [note 6 above], p. 40.

[21] On Sandinista rights violations and atrocities, see the Sandinista organ *Barricada* (3 October 1986), cited in Michael Radu, "Nicaragua," in Richard Staar (ed.), *Yearbook on International Communist Affairs* (Stanford: Hoover Institution Press, 1987). On Sandinista harassment of human rights activists, see *Los Angeles Times*, 16 April 1987.

At the end of 1986 the Nicaraguan government claimed to have 300,000 people under arms, of whom about 70,000 are thought to be regular army. It often is very difficult to tell one from another—for *contras* and correspondents. A sign in a restaurant/bar in a small mountain town illustrates the ambiguity: "No liquor sold to soldiers, men in uniform or those with weapons."[22]

At times reporters have been able to uncover Sandinista efforts to discredit the *contras* by propaganda; how many times the propaganda goes undetected is an open question. In March 1987 the Sandinistas charged the *contras* had made a "terrorist attack" on civilians in the southeastern mountains, but when reporters talked with peasants in the area, and even survivors of the attack, they found that the *contras* had let pass unhindered one truck they found loaded with unarmed peasants but attacked a truck of rifle-bearing loggers, many wearing government uniforms. "I was dressed like a soldier," one survivor admitted, and another said, "I think they fired on us because they could see we were armed."[23]

Finally, according to Alvaro Baldizon, former chief rights investigator of Sandinista interior minister Borge, Sandinista units have been set up that wear FDN uniforms and commit atrocities to discredit the *contras*. Clearly the only ones to benefit from charges of *contra* atrocities are the Sandinistas.[24]

It is not even clear how many *contras* there are. In his speech on 9 January 1987 Daniel Ortega put the number of *contras* at 6,000, while a Nicaraguan diplomat in Washington a month later put the number at 9,000; independent media estimates range up from 12,000, the minimum figure being more than twice as many *contras* as there were Sandinistas on the day Somoza was overthrown.[25]

•

At the end of 1986, UNO consisted of a broad spectrum of Nicaraguans. Indeed, the breadth is both its greatest strength and one of its greatest weaknesses. It reunited a major portion of the anti-Somoza movement of 1978/1979, but it is not unified—whatever the acronym UNO suggests—just as the Sandinistas were not unified for many years prior to the final reuniting and successful offensive against Somoza.

There are two tendencies within UNO, one more militaristic and under more conservative influences, and one more political, with a stronger liberal democratic orientation. Many Nicaraguans I spoke with in January 1987 in widely scattered parts of the country were bitterly hostile toward the Sandinista

---

[22] See *Los Angeles Times*, 28 March 1987.
[23] See reports by Julia Preston, *Washington Post*, 28 March 1987 and Richard Boudreaux, *Los Angeles Times*, 28 March 1987.
[24] See Baldizon testimony in *Inside the Sandinista Regime: A Special Investigator's Perspective* (Washington: US Department of State, 1986).
[25] See *New York Times*, 22 January 1987; *Washington Post*, 29 January 1987.

government but nonetheless uneasy about the *contras*, not knowing what they would do if they were to take power. What is more, UNO evidently does not command strong support from many Nicaraguans in exile.

UNO's top political triumvirate was shaken up in early 1987. Two of the three original members, both of whom had been in the Sandinista junta during the early years of the new government—Arturo Cruz and Alfonso Robelo—forced the resignation of the more conservative third member, Adolfo Calero, who has the closest ties with the FDN guerrillas operating out of Honduras. Calero's place was taken in the triumvirate by Pedro Joaquín Chamorro, former editor of *La Prensa*, a paper that was in opposition to Somoza *and* then the Sandinistas, until it was closed down permanently in 1986. Chamorro also is director of a new *contra* radio station, Radio Liberación, which began broadcasting in January 1987 and is intended to build support for the opposition within Nicaragua. But it is not certain how FDN military commanders will respond to these changes and efforts to shift command structure.

In early 1987 the future of the *contras* remained uncertain. By this writing (April 1987), Cruz and Robelo also had resigned from UNO. Further U.S. funding seemed in doubt in the wake of the Iran/*contra* scandal—and its charges of the diversion of funds from Iran to the Nicaraguan rebels—and amidst continuing disunity in the opposition forces.[26]

CONCLUSIONS

Most of Central America is so desperately poor that even if everyone worked together in harmony, bringing significant and long-term improvements would be both time-consuming and problematical. And, of course, people do not always work in harmony. The irony is that to some degree a lack of harmony is for the better since the freest and most economically productive societies are those that recognize and make the most of creative diversity by allowing, in fact encouraging, a broad interplay of ideas and activities.

The objective of this essay is not to propose a policy, but to show that the East/West conflict has become a factor in Central America, and why. North Americans, Central Americans, Latin Americans, and others must recognize that the current military conflict in and around Nicaragua is political. This is not in any way to downplay the critical importance of economic and social problems in the country or region. It is to say that policies undertaken to overcome underlying problems in Nicaragua—notably domestic political structures and international ties—derive from political decisions Sandinista

---

[26] Author's interviews in Costa Rica, with Alfonso Robelo and Pedro Joaquín Chamorro, and in Nicaragua, during January 1987. Also see *Washington Post*, 29 January 1987, and *New York Times*, 22 February and 2 March 1987.

leaders have made in line with long-held nationalist and Marxist-Leninist convictions. These have set the direction of relations between Washington and Managua.

The political positions of the Sandinista leaders, which have so influenced the direction of Central American politics since 1979, are much more understandable than their critics usually acknowledge. But the Sandinista's policies also are far less well-founded in history and institutional reality, and more intractable, than they or their supporters acknowledge.

Both sides need to openly recognize the fundamental political barriers to the resolution of the existing conflict, barriers deriving from differing, and in many respects contradictory, interpretations of history, institutions, and domestic and international interests. And then to try to deal with them. To deny the basic differences and parrot the same old myths is simply to scratch the surface of problems and infect them; for most of the myths of the day, on both sides of the political spectrum, are at best simplistic statements and at worst propagandistic bags of half-truths and outright lies. This is not to say that all who spread these myths know them to be largely or completely untrue, though one must note that they seem to have made far too little effort to check on the validity of what they preach.

Perhaps the main practical, working conclusion of this essay is the rejection of another myth: that there is one easy, ideologically dictated answer to the crises in Nicaragua and the rest of Central America. The only road, in my judgment, is the one I have tried to initiate here: to put the basic differences and facts as you see them openly on the table; to discuss them rationally and honestly with others, of other perspectives, who have done the same; and to negotiate realistic responses to often almost overwhelming problems in a terribly imperfect world. It is a ridiculously simple, and yet perhaps impossibly difficult, proposition.[27] But it should appeal to all people of good will, for the alternative is peddling myths that will bring as yet untold destruction and grief to millions for many years to come.

---

[27] This has been tried periodically, without remarkable success. See, for example, a volume by Lord Lindsay of Birker, who spent some years with Mao Zedong in China during the Second World War: Michael Lindsay, *Is Peaceful Coexistence Possible?* (East Lansing: Michigan State University Press, 1980); more recently, Carmelo Mesa-Lago's effort to launch a debate with Cuban scholars on the nature of "Cubanology" in the United States, in Mesa-Lago (ed.), *Cuban Studies: 16* (Pittsburgh: University of Pittsburgh Press, 1987), pp. 211-236; also, Hook, *Out of Step*, pp. 398-399.

5

Central America and U.S. Security

Ronald Reagan

Following is President Reagan's address to the nation, Washington, D.C., March 16, 1986.

My fellow Americans, I must speak to you tonight about a mounting danger in Central America that threatens the security of the United States. This danger will not go away; it will grow worse, much worse, if we fail to take action now. I am speaking of Nicaragua, a Soviet ally on the American mainland only 2 hours flying time from our own borders. With over a billion dollars in Soviet-bloc aid, the communist Government of Nicaragua has launched a campaign to subvert and topple its democratic neighbors.

Using Nicaragua as a base, the Soviets and Cubans can become the dominant power in the crucial corridor between North and South America. Established there, they will be in a position to threaten the Panama Canal, interdict our vital Caribbean sealanes, and, ultimately, move against Mexico. Should that happen, desperate Latin peoples by the millions would begin fleeing north into the cities of the southern United States or to wherever some hope of freedom remained.

The U.S. Congress has before it a proposal to help stop this threat. The legislation is an aid package of $100 million for the more than 20,000 freedom fighters struggling to bring democracy to their country and eliminate this communist menace at its source. But this $100 million is not an additional $100 million. We are not asking for a single dime in new money. We are asking only to be permitted to switch a small part of our present defense budget—to the defense of our own southern frontier.

Gathered in Nicaragua already are thousands of Cuban military advisers, contingents of Soviets and East Germans, and all the elements of international terror—from the PLO [Palestine Liberation Organization] to Italy's Red Brigades. Why are they there? Because, as Colonel Qadhafi has publicly exulted: "Nicaragua means a great thing, it means fighting America near its borders—fighting America at its doorstep."

United States Department of State. Bureau of Public Affairs. Washington, D. C. *Current Policy* No. 805.

For our own security, the United States must deny the Soviet Union a beachhead in North America. But let me make one thing plain. I am not talking about American troops. They are not needed; they have not been requested. The democratic resistance fighting in Nicaragua is only asking America for the supplies and support to save their own country from communism.

The question the Congress of the United States will now answer is a simple one: will we give the Nicaraguan democratic resistance the means to recapture their betrayed revolution, or will we turn our backs and ignore the malignancy in Managua until it spreads and becomes a mortal threat to the entire New World? Will we permit the Soviet Union to put a second Cuba, a second Libya, right on the doorstep of the United States?

THE NICARAGUAN THREAT

How can such a small country pose such a great threat? Well, it is not Nicaragua alone that threatens us, but those using Nicaragua as a privileged sanctuary for their struggle against the United States.

Their first target is Nicaragua's neighbors. With an army and militia of 120,000 men, backed by more than 3,000 Cuban military advisers, Nicaragua's Armed Forces are the largest Central America has ever seen. The Nicaraguan military machine is more powerful than all its neighbors combined.

This map [see p. 2]* represents much of the Western Hemisphere. Now let me show you the countries in Central America where weapons supplied by Nicaraguan communists have been found: Honduras, Costa Rica, El Salvador, Guatemala. Radicals from Panama to the south have been trained in Nicaragua. But the Sandinista revolutionary reach extends well beyond their immediate neighbors. In South America and the Caribbean, the Nicaraguan communists have provided support in the form of military training, safe haven, communications, false documents, safe transit, and sometimes weapons to radicals from the following countries: Colombia, Ecuador, Brazil, Chile, Argentina, Uruguay, and the Dominican Republic. Even that is not all, for there was an old communist slogan that the Sandinistas have made clear they honor: the road to victory goes through Mexico.

If maps, statistics, and facts aren't persuasive enough, we have the words of the Sandinistas and Soviets themselves. One of the highest level Sandinista leaders was asked by an American magazine whether their communist revolution will—and I quote—"be exported to El Salvador, then Guatemala, then Honduras, and then Mexico?" He responded, "That is one historical prophecy of Ronald Reagan that is absolutely true."

---

*   Map omitted.—Ed.

Well, the Soviets have been no less candid. A few years ago, then Soviet Foreign Minister Gromyko noted that Central America was "boiling like a cauldron" and ripe for revolution. In a Moscow meeting in 1983, Soviet Chief of Staff Marshal Ogarkov declared: "Over two decades there was only Cuba in Latin America. Today there are Nicaragua, Grenada, and a serious battle is going on in El Salvador."

But we don't need their quotes; the American forces who liberated Grenada captured thousands of documents that demonstrated Soviet intent to bring communist revolution home to the Western Hemisphere.

THE NATURE OF THE SANDINISTA REGIME

So, we're clear on the intentions of the Sandinistas and those who back them. Let us be equally clear about the nature of their regime. To begin with, the Sandinistas have revoked the civil liberties of the Nicaraguan people, depriving them of any legal right to speak, to publish, to assemble, or to worship freely. Independent newspapers have been shut down. There is no longer any independent labor movement in Nicaragua or any right to strike. As AFL-CIO [American Federation of Labor and Congress of Industrial Organizations] leader Lane Kirkland has said, "Nicaragua's headlong rush into the totalitarian camp cannot be denied—by anyone who has eyes to see."

Well, like communist governments everywhere, the Sandinistas have launched assaults against ethnic and religious groups. The capital's only synagogue was desecrated and firebombed—the entire Jewish community forced to flee Nicaragua. Protestant Bible meetings have been broken up by raids, by mob violence, by machineguns. The Catholic Church has been singled out—priests have been expelled from the country, Catholics beaten in the streets after attending Mass. The Catholic primate of Nicaragua, Cardinal Obando y Bravo, has put the matter forthrightly. "We want to state clearly," he says, "that this government is totalitarian. We are dealing with an enemy of the Church."

Evangelical pastor Prudencio Baltodano found out he was on a Sandinista hit list when an army patrol asked his name. "You don't know what we do to the evangelical pastors. We don't believe in God," they told him. Pastor Baltodano was tied to a tree, struck in the forehead with a rifle butt, stabbed in the neck with a bayonet—finally, his ears were cut off, and he was left for dead. "See if your God will save you," they mocked. Well, God did have other plans for Pastor Baltodano. He lived to tell the world his story—to tell it, among other places, right here in the White House.

I could go on about this nightmare—the blacklists, the secret prisons, the Sandinista-directed mob violence. But, as if all this brutality at home were not enough, the Sandinistas are transforming their nation into a safe house, a command post for international terror.

The Sandinistas not only sponsor terror in El Salvador, Costa Rica, Guatemala, and Honduras—terror that led last summer to the murder of four U.S. marines in a cafe in San Salvador—they provide a sanctuary for terror. Italy has charged Nicaragua with harboring their worst terrorists, the Red Brigades.

The Sandinistas have even involved themselves in the international drug trade. I know every American parent concerned with the drug problem will be outraged to hear that top Nicaraguan Government officials are deeply involved in drug trafficking. This picture, secretly taken at a military airfield outside Managua, shows Frederico Vaughn, a top aide to one of the nine commandantes who rule Nicaragua, loading an aircraft with illegal narcotics bound for the United States.* No, there seems to be no crime to which the Sandinistas will not stoop—this is an outlaw regime.

U.S. SECURITY INTERESTS AND THE NICARAGUAN DEMOCRATIC RESISTANCE

If we return to a moment to our map, it becomes clear why having this regime in Central America imperils our vital security interests.†

Through this crucial part of the Western Hemisphere passes almost half our foreign trade, more than half our imports of crude oil, and a significant portion of the military supplies we would have to send to the NATO alliance in the event of a crisis. These are the chokepoints where the sealanes could be closed.

Central America is strategic to our Western alliance, a fact always understood by foreign enemies. In World War II, only a few German U-boats, operating from bases 4,000 miles away in Germany and occupied Europe, inflicted crippling losses on U.S. shipping right off our southern coast.

Today, Warsaw Pact engineers are building a deep water port on Nicaragua's Caribbean coast, similar to the naval base in Cuba for Soviet-built submarines. They are also constructing, outside Managua, the largest military airfield in Central America—similar to those in Cuba, from which Russian Bear bombers patrol the U.S. east coast from Maine to Florida.

How did this menace to the peace and security of our Latin neighbors and, ultimately, ourselves suddenly emerge? Let me give you a brief history.

In 1979, the people of Nicaragua rose up and overthrew a corrupt dictatorship. At first, the revolutionary leaders promised free elections and respect for human rights. But among them was an organization called the Sandinistas.

---

*   Photograph omitted.—Ed.

†   Map omitted.—Ed.

Theirs was a communist organization, and their support of the revolutionary goals was sheer deceit. Quickly and ruthlessly, they took complete control.

Two months after the revolution, the Sandinista leadership met in secret and, in what came to be known as the "72-Hour Document," described themselves as the "vanguard" of a revolution that would sweep Central America, Latin America, and, finally, the world. Their true enemy, they declared: the United States.

Rather than make this document public, they followed the advice of Fidel Castro, who told them to put on a facade of democracy. While Castro viewed the democratic elements in Nicaragua with contempt, he urged his Nicaraguan friends to keep some of them in their coalition, in minor posts, as window dressing to deceive the West. And that way, Castro said, you can have your revolution, and the Americans will pay for it.

And we did pay for it. More aid flowed to Nicaragua from the United States in the first 18 months under the Sandinistas than from any other country. Only when the mask fell, and the face of totalitarianism became visible to the world, did the aid stop.

Confronted with this emerging threat, early in our Administration I went to Congress and, with bipartisan support, managed to get help for the nations surrounding Nicaragua. Some of you may remember the inspiring scene when the people of El Salvador braved the threats and gunfire of the communist guerrillas—guerrillas directed and supplied from Nicaragua—and went to the polls to vote decisively for democracy. For the communists in El Salvador it was a humiliating defeat.

But there was another factor the communists never counted on, a factor that now promises to give freedom a second chance—the freedom fighters of Nicaragua.

You see, when the Sandinistas betrayed the revolution, many who had fought the old Somoza dictatorship literally took to the hills and, like the French Resistance that fought the Nazis, began fighting the Soviet-bloc communists and their Nicaraguan collaborators. These few have now been joined by thousands.

With their blood and courage, the freedom fighters of Nicaragua have pinned down the Sandinista army and bought the people of Central America precious time. We Americans owe them a debt of gratitude. In helping to thwart the Sandinistas and their Soviet mentors, the resistance has contributed directly to the security of the United States.

Since its inception in 1982, the democratic resistance has grown dramatically in strength. Today, it numbers more than 20,000 volunteers, and more come every day. But now the freedom fighters' supplies are running short, and they are virtually defenseless against the helicopter gunships Moscow has sent to Managua.

A CRUCIAL TEST

Now comes the crucial test for the Congress of the United States. Will they provide the assistance the freedom fighters need to deal with Russian tanks and gunships, or will they abandon the democratic resistance to its communist enemy?

In answering that question, I hope Congress will reflect deeply upon what it is the resistance is fighting against in Nicaragua. Ask yourselves, what in the world are Soviets, East Germans, Bulgarians, North Koreas, Cubans, and terrorists from the PLO and the Red Brigades doing in our hemisphere, camped on our own doorstep? Is that for peace?

Why have the Soviets invested $600 million to build Nicaragua into an armed force almost the size of Mexico's—a country 15 times as large and 25 times as populous. Is that for peace?

Why did Nicaragua's dictator, Daniel Ortega, go to the Communist Party Congress in Havana and endorse Castro's call for the worldwide triumph of communism? Was that for peace?

Some Members of Congress ask me, why not negotiate? That's a good question, and let me answer it directly. We have sought, and still seek, a negotiated peace and a democratic future in a free Nicaragua. Ten times we have met and tried to reason with the Sandinistas. Ten times we were rebuffed. Last year, we endorsed church-mediated negotiations between the regime and the resistance. The Soviets and the Sandinistas responded with a rapid arms buildup of mortars, tanks, artillery, and helicopter gunships.

Clearly, the Soviet Union and the Warsaw Pact have grasped the great stakes involved, the strategic importance of Nicaragua. The Soviets have made their decision—to support the communists. Fidel Castro has made his decision—to support the communists. Arafat, Qadhafi, and the Ayatollah Khomeini have made their decision—to support the communists. Now, we must make our decision. With Congress' help, we can prevent an outcome deeply injurious to the national security of the United States. If we fail, there will be no evading responsibility—history will hold us accountable. This is not some narrow partisan issue; it's a national security issue, an issue on which we must act not as Republicans, not as Democrats, but as Americans.

Forty years ago, Republicans and Democrats joined together behind the Truman Doctrine. It must be our policy, Harry Truman declared, to support peoples struggling to preserve their freedom. Under that doctrine, Congress sent aid to Greece just in time to save that country from the closing grip of a communist tyranny. We saved freedom in Greece then—and with that same bipartisan spirit, we can save freedom in Nicaragua today.

Over the coming days, I will continue the dialogue with Members of Congress, talking to them, listening to them, hearing out their concerns. Senator Scoop Jackson, who led the fight on Capitol Hill for an awareness of the danger in Central America, said it best: on matters of national security, the best politics is no politics.

You know, recently one of our most distinguished Americans, Clare Boothe Luce, had this to say about the coming vote. "In considering this crisis," Mrs. Luce said, "my mind goes back to a similar moment in our history—back to the first years after Cuba had fallen to Fidel. One day during those years, I had lunch at the White House with a man I had known since he was a boy—John F. Kennedy. 'Mr. President,' I said, 'no matter how exalted or great a man may be, history will have time to give him no more than one sentence. George Washington—he founded our country. Abraham Lincoln—he freed the slaves and preserved the Union. Winston Churchill—he saved Europe.' 'And what, Clare,' John Kennedy said, 'did you believe—or do you believe my sentence will be?' 'Mr. President,' she answered, 'your sentence will be that you stopped the communists—or that you did not.'"

Well, tragically, John Kennedy never had the chance to decide which that would be. Now, leaders of our own time must do so. My fellow Americans, you know where I stand. The Soviets and Sandinistas must not be permitted to crush freedom in Central America and threaten our own security on our own doorstep.

Now the Congress must decide where it stands. Mrs. Luce ended by saying: "Only this is certain. Through all time to come, this, the 99th Congress of the United States, will be remembered as that body of men and women that either stopped the communists before it was too late—or did not."

So tonight I ask you to do what you've done so often in the past. Get in touch with your Representative and Senators and urge them to vote yes; tell them to help the freedom fighters—help us prevent a communist takeover of Central America.

I have only 3 years left to serve my country, 3 years to carry out the responsibilities you entrusted to me, 3 years to work for peace. Could there be any greater tragedy than for us to sit back and permit this cancer to spread, leaving my successor to face far more agonizing decisions in the years ahead? The freedom fighters seek a political solution. They are willing to lay down their arms and negotiate to restore the original goals of the revolution, a democracy in which the people of Nicaragua choose their own government. That is our goal also, but it can only come about if the democratic resistance is able to bring pressure to bear on those who have seized power.

We still have time to do what must be done so history will say of us, we had the vision, the courage, and good sense to come together and act—Republicans and Democrats—when the price was not high and the risks were not great. We left America safe, we left America secure, we left America free— still a beacon of hope to mankind, still a light unto the nations.

6

Why Democracy Matters in Central America

Ronald Reagan

Following is President Reagan's address to the nation from the White House, Washington, D.C., June 24, 1986.

My fellow citizens, the matter that brings me before you today is a grave one and concerns my most solemn duty as President. It is the cause of freedom in Central America and the national security of the United States. Tomorrow, the House of Representatives will debate and vote on this issue. I had hoped to speak directly and at this very hour to Members of the House of Representatives on this subject but was unable to do so. Because I feel so strongly about what I have to say, I've asked for this time to share with you—and Members of the House—the message I would have otherwise given.

Nearly 40 years ago a Democratic President, Harry Truman, went before the Congress to warn of another danger to democracy, a civil war in a faraway country in which many Americans could perceive no national security interest.

Some of you can remember the world then. Europe lay devastated. One by one, the nations of Eastern Europe had fallen into Stalin's grip. The democratic Government of Czechoslovakia would soon be overthrown. Turkey was threatened, and in Greece, the home of democracy, communist guerrillas, backed by the Soviet Union, battled democratic forces to decide the nation's fate.

Most Americans did not perceive this distant danger, so the opinion polls reflected little of the concern that brought Harry Truman to the well of the House that day. But go he did. And it is worth a moment to reflect on what he said.

In a hushed chamber, Mr. Truman said that we had come to a time in history when every nation would have to choose between two opposing ways of life. One way was based on the will of the majority—on free institutions and human rights. "The second way of life," he said, "is based upon the will of a minority forcibly imposed upon the majority. It relies upon terror and oppres-

United States Department of State. Bureau of Public Affairs. Washington, D. C. *Current Policy* No. 850.

sion, a controlled press and radio, fixed elections and the suppression of personal freedoms. I believe," President Truman said, "that it must be the policy of the United States to support free peoples who are resisting attempted subjugation by armed minorities or by outside pressures."

When Harry Truman spoke, Congress was controlled by the Republican Party. But that Congress put America's interest first and supported Truman's request for military aid to Greece and Turkey—just as 4 years ago Congress put America's interest first by supporting my request for military aid to defend democracy in El Salvador.

THE THREAT TO DEMOCRACY

I speak today in that same spirit of bipartisanship. My fellow Americans and Members of the House, I need your help. I ask first for your help in remembering—remembering our history in Central America so we can learn from the mistakes of the past. Too often in the past the United States failed to identify with the aspirations of the people of Central America for freedom and a better life. Too often our government appeared indifferent when democratic values were at risk. So we took this path of least resistance and did nothing.

Today, however, with American support, the tide is turning in Central America. In El Salvador, Honduras, Costa Rica—and now in Guatemala—freely elected governments offer their people the chance for a better future, a future the United States must support.

But there's one tragic, glaring exception to that democratic tide—the communist Sandinista government in Nicaragua. It is tragic because the United States extended a generous hand of friendship to the new revolutionary government when it came to power in 1979. Congress voted $75 million in economic aid. The United States helped renegotiate Nicaragua's foreign debt. America offered teachers, doctors, and Peace Corps volunteers to help rebuild the country. But the Sandinistas had a different agenda.

From the very first day, a small clique of communists worked steadily to consolidate power and squeeze out their democratic allies. The democratic trade unionists who had fought Somoza's National Guard in the streets were now told by the Sandinistas that the right to strike was illegal and that their revolutionary duty was to produce more for the state.

The newspaper *La Prensa*, whose courage and determination had inspired so much of the Nicaraguan revolution, found its pages censored and suppressed. Violeta Chamorro, widow of the assassinated editor, soon quit the revolutionary government to take up the struggle for democracy again in the pages of her newspaper.

The leader of the Catholic Church in Nicaragua, Archbishop—now Cardinal—Obando y Bravo, who had negotiated the release of the Sandinista leaders from prison during the revolution, was now vilified as a traitor by very men he helped to free.

Soviet arms and bloc personnel began arriving in Nicaragua. With Cuban, East German, and Bulgarian advisers at their side, the Sandinistas began to build the largest standing army in Central American history and to erect all the odious apparatus of the modern police state.

Under the Somoza dictatorship, a single facility held all political prisoners. Today, there are eleven—11 prisons in place of one.

The Sandinistas claim to defend Nicaraguan independence. But you and I know the truth. The proud people of Nicaragua did not rise up against Somoza—and struggle, fight, and die—to have Cubans, Russians, Bulgarians, East Germans, and North Koreans running their prisons, organizing their army, censoring their newspapers, and suppressing their religious faith. One Nicaraguan nationalist, who fought in the revolution, says: "We are an occupied country today."

I could go on, but I know that even the Administration's harshest critics in Congress hold no brief for Sandinista repression. Indeed, the final verdict has already been written by Cardinal Obando himself in the *Washington Post*. Listen carefully to the Cardinal's words. He says: that the Sandinista regime "is a democratic government, legitimately constituted, which seeks the welfare and peace of the people and enjoys the support of the overwhelming majority" is not true. To accept this as true, the Cardinal says, "is to ignore the mass exodus of the Miskito Indians, the departure of tens of thousands of Nicaraguan men and women of every age, profession, economic status, and political persuasion. It is to ignore the most terrible violation of freedom of the press and of speech in the history of our country, the expulsion of priests and the mass exodus of young people eligible for military service." As for the Catholic Church in Nicaragua, we have been "gagged and bound," the Cardinal says.

Many brave Nicaraguans have stayed in their country despite mounting repression—defying the security policy, defying the Sandinista mobs that attack and deface their homes. Thousands—peasants, Indians, devout Christians, draftees from the Sandinista army—have concluded that they must take up arms again to fight for the freedom they thought they had won in 1979.

The young men and women of the democratic resistance fight inside Nicaragua today in grueling mountain and jungle warfare. They confront a Soviet-equipped army, trained and led by Cuban officers. They face murderous helicopter gunships without any means of defense. And still they volunteer. And still their numbers grow.

Who among us would tell these brave young men and women: "Your dream is dead; your democratic revolution is over; you will never live in the free Nicaragua you fought so hard to build"?

all these freedom fighters *contras*—for "counterrevo-
real counterrevolutionaries are the Sandinista *coman-*
the hopes of the Nicaraguan revolution and sold out their
empire.

es even betrayed the memory of the Nicaraguan rebel leader
Sanduⅼⅼ.,　　　　ⅼacy they falsely claim. For the real Sandino —because he
was a genuine nationalist—was opposed to communism. In fact, Sandino
broke with the Salvadoran communist leader, Farabundo Marti, over this very
issue.

The true Nicaraguan nationalists are the leaders of the United Nicaraguan
Opposition: Arturo Cruz—jailed by Somoza, a former member of the Sandinista government; Adolfo Calero—who helped organize a strike of businessmen to bring Somoza down; and Alfonso Robelo—a social democrat and
once a leader of the revolutionary government.

These good men refused to make any accommodation with the Somoza
dictatorship. Who among us can doubt their commitment to bring democracy
to Nicaragua?

U.S. VITAL INTERESTS

So, the Nicaraguan people have chosen to fight for their freedom. Now we
Americans must also choose. For you and I and every American have a stake
in this struggle.

Central America is vital to our own national security, and the Soviet
Union knows it. The Soviets take the long view, but their strategy is clear:
to dominate the strategic sealanes and vital chokepoints around the world.

Half of America's imports and exports, including oil, travels through the
area today. In a crisis, over half of NATO's supplies would pass through this
region. And Nicaragua, just 277 miles from the Panama Canal, offers the Soviet Union ports on both the Atlantic and Pacific Oceans.

The Soviet Union already uses Cuba as an air and submarine base in the
Caribbean. It hopes to turn Nicaragua into the first Soviet base on the mainland of North America. If you doubt it, ask yourself: why have the last four
Soviet leaders—with a mounting economic crisis at home—already invested
over $1 billion and dispatched thousands of Soviet-bloc advisers into a tiny
country in Central America?

I know that no one in Congress wants to see Nicaragua become a Soviet
military base. My friends, I must tell you in all seriousness, Nicaragua is becoming a Soviet base every day that we debate and debate and debate—and do
nothing.

In the 3 months since I last asked for the House to aid the democratic resistance, four military cargo ships have arrived at Nicaraguan ports, this time
directly from the Soviet Union. Recently we have learned that Russian pilots

are flying a Soviet AN-30 reconnaissance plane for the Sandinistas.

Now, the Sandinistas claim this is just for making civilian maps. Well, our intelligence services believe this could be the first time Soviet personnel have taken a direct role in support of military operations on the mainland of North America.

Think again how Cuba became a Soviet air and naval base. You'll see what Nicaragua will look like if we continue to do nothing. Cuba became a Soviet base gradually over many years. There was no single dramatic event— once the missile crisis passed—that captured the nation's attention. And so it will be with Nicaragua.

The Sandinistas will widen and deepen another port while we debate: is it for commercial vessels or Soviet submarines? The Sandinistas will complete another airstrip while we argue: is it for 707s or Backfire bombers? A Soviet training brigade will come to Nicaragua; half will leave and half will stay. And we will debate: are they soldiers or engineers?

Eventually, we Americans have to stop arguing among ourselves. We will have to confront the reality of a Soviet military beachhead inside our defense perimeters—about 500 miles from Mexico. A future President and Congress will then face nothing but bad choices, followed by worse choices.

My friends in the House, for over 200 years the security of the United States has depended on the safety of unthreatened borders, north and south. Do we want to be the first elected leaders in U.S. history to put our borders at risk?

Some of you may say, well, this is fearmongering. Such a danger to our security will never come to pass. Well, perhaps it won't. But in making your decisions on my request for aid tomorrow, consider this: what are the consequences for our country if you're wrong?

THE DEMOCRATIC RESISTANCE: POPULAR SUPPORT AND THE NEED FOR U.S. AID

I know some Members of Congress who share my concern about Nicaragua have honest questions about my request for aid to the democratic resistance. Let me try to address them. Do the freedom fighters have the support of the Nicaraguan people? I urge Members of the House to ask their colleague, the Chairman [Les Aspin] of the House Armed Services Committee, who recently visited a town in Nicaragua that was a Sandinista stronghold during the revolution. He heard peasants, trade unionists, farmers, workers, students, and shopkeepers all call on the United States to aid the armed resistance.

Or listen to the report from *Time* magazine of Central American scholar Robert Leiken, who once had hopes for the Sandinista revolution. He says, "I have gone to a number of towns in Nicaragua where I have found that the youth are simply not there. I ask the parents where they've gone, and they say, they've gone off to join the *contras*." In Managua, Leiken reports 250 Nicaraguans stood on a breadline for 3 hours. "Who is responsible for this?" he asked. "The Sandinistas are responsible. The Sandinistas." That's what the people said. "The Sandinistas," Leiken concluded, "have not only lost support, I think they are detested by the population."

Can the democratic forces win? Consider there are 20 times as many Nicaraguans fighting the Sandinista dictatorship today as there were Sandinista fighters a year before Somoza fell. This is the largest peasant army raised in Latin America in more than 50 years. And thousands more are waiting to volunteer if American support comes through.

Some Members of Congress—and I know some of you—fear that military aid to the democratic resistance will be only the first step down the slippery slope toward another Vietnam. Now, I know those fears are honest. But think where we heard them before. Just a few years ago, some argued in Congress that U.S. military aid to El Salvador would lead inevitably to the involvement of U.S. combat troops. But the opposite turned out to be true.

Had the United States failed to provide aid then, we might well be facing the final communist takeover of El Salvador and mounting pressures to intervene. Instead, with our aid, the Government of El Salvador is winning the war, and there is no prospect whatever of American military involvement.

El Salvador still faces serious problems that require our attention. But democracy there is stronger, and both the communist guerrillas and the right-wing death squads are weaker. And Congress shares credit for that accomplishment. American aid and training are helping the Salvadoran Army become a professional fighting force, more respectful of human rights. With our aid we can help the Nicaraguan resistance accomplish the same goal.

I stress this point because I know many Members of Congress and many Americans are deeply troubled by allegations of abuses by elements of the armed resistance. I share your concerns. Even though some of those charges are Sandinista propaganda, I believe such abuses have occurred in the past, and they are intolerable.

As President, I repeat to you the commitments I made to Senator Sam Nunn. As a condition of our aid, I will insist on civilian control over all military forces; that no human rights abuses are tolerated; that any financial corruption be rooted out; that American aid go only to those committed to democratic principles. The United States will not permit this democratic revolution to be betrayed nor allow a return to the hated repression of the Somoza dictatorship.

The leadership of the United Nicaraguan Opposition shares these commitments, and I welcome the appointment of a bipartisan congressional commission to help us see that they are carried out.

U.S. POLICY GOALS

Some ask: what are the goals of our policy toward Nicaragua? They are the goals the Nicaraguan people set for themselves in 1979: democracy, a free economy, and national self-determination. Clearly the best way to achieve these goals is through a negotiated settlement. No humane person wants to see suffering and war.

The leaders of the internal opposition and the Catholic Church have asked for dialogue with the Sandinistas. The leaders of the armed resistance have called for a cease-fire and negotiations at any time, in any place. We urge the Sandinistas to heed the pleas of the Nicaraguan people for a peaceful settlement.

The United States will support any negotiated settlement or Contadora treaty that will bring real democracy to Nicaragua. What we will not support is a paper agreement that sells out the Nicaraguan people's right to be free. That kind of agreement would be unworthy of us as a people. And it would be a false bargain. For internal freedom in Nicaragua and the security of Central America are indivisible. A free and democratic Nicaragua will pose no threat to its neighbors or to the United States. A communist Nicaragua, allied with the Soviet Union, is a permanent threat to us all.

President Azcona of Honduras emphasized this point in a recent nationwide address:

> As long as there is a totalitarian regime in Central America that has expansionist ambitions and is supported by an enormous military apparatus . . . the neighboring countries sharing common borders with the country that is the source of the problem will be under constant threat.

If you doubt his warning, consider this: the Sandinistas have already sent two groups of communist guerrillas into Honduras. Costa Rican revolutionaries are already fighting alongside Sandinista troops.

My friends in the Congress, with democracy still a fragile root in Central America—with Mexico undergoing an economic crisis—can we responsibly ignore the long-term danger to American interests posed by a communist Nicaragua, backed by the Soviet Union, and dedicated—in the words of its own leaders—to a "revolution without borders"?

KEEPING FAITH WITH A COMMITMENT TO FREEDOM

My friends, the only way to bring true peace and security to Central America is to bring democracy to Nicaragua. And the only way to get the Sandinistas to negotiate seriously about democracy is to give them no other alternative. Seven years of broken pledges, betrayals, and lies have taught us that.

And that's why the measure the House will consider tomorrow—offered, I know, in good faith—which prohibits military aid for at least another 3 months, and perhaps forever, would be a tragic mistake. It would not bring the Sandinistas to the bargaining table—just the opposite.

The bill, unless amended, would give the Sandinistas and the Soviet Union what they seek most—time: time to crush the democratic resistance, time to consolidate power. And it would send a demoralizing message to the democratic resistance: that the United States is too divided and paralyzed to come to their aid in time.

Recently, I read the words of a leader of the internal democratic opposition. What he said made me feel ashamed. This man has been jailed, his property confiscated, and his life threatened by the security police. Still he continues to fight. And he said:

> You Americans have the strength, the opportunity, but not the will. We want to struggle, but it is dangerous to have friends like you—to be left stranded on the landing beaches of the Bay of Pigs. Either help us or leave us alone.

My friends, in the House of Representatives, I urge you to send a message tomorrow to this brave Nicaraguan and thousands like him. Tell them it is not dangerous to have friends like us. Tell them America stands with those who stand in defense of freedom.

When the Senate voted earlier this year for military aid, Republicans were joined by many Democratic leaders: Bill Bradley of New Jersey, Sam Nunn of Georgia, David Boren of Oklahoma, Howell Heflin of Alabama, Lloyd Bentsen of Texas, Bennett Johnston and Russell Long of Louisiana, Fritz Hollings of South Carolina, John Stennis of Mississippi, and Alan Dixon of Illinois.

Today, I ask the House for that kind of bipartisan support for the amendment to be offered tomorrow by Democrats Ike Skelton of Missouri and Richard Ray of Georgia and Republicans Mickey Edwards of Oklahoma and Rod Chandler of Washington. This bipartisan amendment will provide the freedom fighters with what they need—now.

With that amendment, you also send another message to Central America. For democracy there faces many enemies: poverty, illiteracy, hunger, and despair. And the United States must also stand with the people of Central America against these enemies of democracy.

And that's why—just as Harry Truman followed his request for military aid to Greece and Turkey with the Marshall Plan—I urge Congress to support $300 million in new economic aid to the Central American democracies.

The question before the House is not only about the freedom of Nicaragua and the security of the United States but who we are as a people. President Kennedy wrote on the day of his death that history had called this generation of Americans to be "watchmen on the walls of world freedom." A Republican President, Abraham Lincoln, said much the same thing on the way to his inauguration in 1861. Stopping in Philadelphia, Lincoln spoke in Independence Hall, where our Declaration of Independence had been signed. He said far more had been achieved in that hall than just American independence from Britain. Something permanent—something unalterable—had happened. He called it: "Hope to the world for all future time."

Hope to the world for all future time—in some way, every man, woman, and child in our world is tied to those events at Independence Hall, to the universal claim to dignity, to the belief that all human beings are created equal, that all people have a right to be free.

We Americans have not forgotten our revolutionary heritage. But sometimes it takes others to remind us of what we ourselves believe. Recently, I read the words of a Nicaraguan bishop, Pablo Vega, who visited Washington a few weeks ago. Somoza called Pablo Vega the "communist bishop." Now, the Sandinistas revile him as "the *contra* bishop." But Pablo Vega is really a humble man of God. "I am saddened," the good bishop said, "that so many North Americans have a vision of democracy that has only to do with materialism." The Sandinistas "speak of human rights as if they were talking of the rights of a child—the right to receive from the bountifulness of the state—but even the humblest *campesino* knows what it means to have the right to act. We are defending," Pablo Vega said, "the right of man to be."

Well, Reverend Father, we hear you. For we Americans believe with you that even the humblest *campesino* has the right to be free. My fellow citizens, Members of the House, let us not take the path of least resistance in Central America again. Let us keep faith with these brave people struggling for their freedom. Give them, give me, your support; and together, let us send this message to the world: that America is still a beacon of hope, still a light unto the nations. A light that casts its glow across the land and our continent and even back across the centuries—keeping faith with a dream of long ago.

7

Nicaragua and the Future of Central America

George Shultz

Following is an address by Secretary Shultz before the Veterans of Foreign Wars, Washington, D.C., March 3, 1986.

In recent years, around the world, we have seen the yearning for freedom take extraordinary forms. Last week, the world watched as the people of the Philippines rose up to claim their democratic rights and recapture their democratic heritage.

We saw in the Philippines a government increasingly at odds with its own people. We saw a Catholic Church, a middle class, moderate opposition parties, the business community, the media, and other segments of society increasingly disaffected from their government. We saw an election in which the government was shaken by the vigor of the opposition's campaign and sought by fraud to perpetuate itself in power. We can be thankful that as his moral authority slipped away, President Marcos had the wisdom and courage to step down peacefully.

Today, we see similar phenomena in a country much closer to home—Nicaragua. But with a striking difference: it's *far worse* in Nicaragua. There, opposition parties have been systematically harassed and intimidated, including by violence or threat of violence; independent media are not merely hampered but censored or shut down; the Catholic Church has been stifled or abused for being a voice of democratic conscience. The secret police have rounded up leaders of private sector, labor, and church organizations, subjecting them to interrogations and threats. A massive military buildup by the Soviet Union and Cuba threatens not only the regime's internal opponents but all neighboring countries as well. And the regime—after a manipulated election over a year ago—is clearly determined to maintain itself in power by whatever brute force is necessary.

In the Philippines, the forces of democracy were able to rally, organize, compete for and, eventually, win power peacefully, despite the flawed election,

United States Department of State. Bureau of Public Affairs. Washington, D. C. *Current Policy* No. 803.

because it was, at bottom, a pluralist democratic political system. In Nicaragua, once the communist regime consolidates its power, the forces of democracy will have no such hope. A Leninist regime seeks a monopoly of power and the strangulation of all independent institutions. The church, the independent media, the business community, the middle class, and democratic parties are all severely beleaguered and struggling for their very survival. Thousands of the regime's opponents—estimated at as many as 20,000—have been driven to take up arms to resist the communist attempt to consolidate a totalitarian system.

For historical, moral, and strategic reasons, the United States took a direct interest in the progress of Filipino democracy. For similar reasons, we are deeply concerned with the hopes for democracy in Nicaragua. After 6½ years, it is clear that, without our help in strengthening the Nicaraguan democratic opposition, hope for democracy in Nicaragua is doomed and progress elsewhere in Central America could be undone.

SUBVERSION ABROAD

Despite our efforts to coexist with, and even aid, the revolutionary leadership that overthrew the dictator Somoza in 1979, the strategic threat posed by the Nicaraguan communists has grown steadily. Today, the country is home to some 200 Soviet advisers, some 7,500 Cubans, and assorted personnel from East Germany, Bulgaria, Libya, and the Palestine Liberation Organization (PLO). You can see who its friends are.

Nicaragua's military machine has no parallel in the history of Central America. Since 1981, the country has received more than half a billion dollars in Soviet arms shipments, including tanks and other heavy armaments that, in the context of Central America, are clearly not defensive. By the end of 1980, Nicaragua's Armed Forces were twice as large as the Somoza National Guard at its height. By the end of 1982, the army of the Nicaraguan communists had doubled again. Today, Nicaragua has some 60,000 troops on active duty and 60,000 more in reserves. Honduras, by contrast, has 21,000 troops; Costa Rica, the oldest democracy in Latin America, has no army. No other country in Central America has as many tanks and armored vehicles as Nicaragua. Only Nicaragua has one of the most sophisticated attack helicopters in the world, the Soviet-built Mi-24 HIND.

Why such a formidable buildup? [Interior Minister] Tomás Borge gave the answer in 1981. "This revolution," he said, "goes beyond our borders."

What do these words mean? Look at the record. Almost immediately, the communists in Nicaragua joined with Salvadoran communists to prevent democratic reforms in El Salvador. They armed guerrillas who maintained their central headquarters in Managua until late 1983. (Incidentally, they moved not long after our liberation of Grenada.) And they still maintain radio transmitters, training facilities, R&R camps, and major logistics support facilities in Nicaragua.

But for the Nicaraguan communists, subverting El Salvador has not been enough. Nicaragua has also been equipping, training, organizing, and infiltrating guerrillas and agents into Honduras. It has launched direct attacks into that country using its regular armed forces.

Costa Rica is another target. The Nicaraguan communists have used their diplomatic presence in Costa Rica to conduct bombings and assassinations; they have financed, equipped, and trained Costa Ricans for subversive activities; and they have conducted cross-border incursions almost at will.

They are also involved in Colombia. Many of the arms with which the M-19 terrorists attacked the National Palace of Justice have been traced to Nicaragua. And what were the M-19 terrorists after? Just those Justices trying drug traffickers. It should be no surprise to find that the Nicaraguan communists are involved in this criminal activity.

Think about the pattern that emerges from this record. It is violent. It is indiscriminate, aimed at democracies and even Contadora peacemakers. And it is intimately tied to Cuban and Soviet military power. These efforts at subversion and infiltration are facilitated by the regime's close relations with terrorists from across the globe. It has issued Nicaraguan passports to radicals and terrorists from the Middle East, Latin America, and Europe. Groups with a known presence in Nicaragua include the Basque ETA terrorists, the German Baader-Meinhof gang, the Italian Red Brigades, and the Argentine Montoneros. Alvaro Baldizon, a high-ranking Sandinista who defected in 1985, reported that Interior Minister Borge is personally involved in cocaine smuggling from Colombia to the United States. Videotapes by a DEA [Drug Enforcement Administration] informer on the ground in Nicaragua show at least one other regime official personally supervising the loading of a narcotics shipment for the United States.

Agents of the PLO working in Central America and Panama use Nicaragua as their base of operations. Their ties to the PLO are particularly strong. Some were trained in PLO camps in the 1960s and 1970s. Some have even participated in PLO hijackings.

The Nicaraguan communists have another benefactor in the Middle East: Libya. By the time they took power in 1979, they had developed a direct relationship with Qadhafi. And Qadhafi has obligingly sent them arms. One shipment labeled "medicines" was intercepted by accident in Brazil in April 1983; authorities found about 84 tons of arms, explosives, and other military equipment.

REPRESSION AT HOME

By betraying their promises of pluralism, the Nicaraguan communists have forced the citizens of Nicaragua to take up arms once again. Like Somoza, they don't seem to listen to anyone who isn't armed. And, like Somoza, they seek to blame outside forces for the resistance of their own people to their policies.

The Nicaraguan communists like to say that covert U.S. support created the resistance; that their opponents are all agents of the CIA [Central Intelligence Agency] and heirs of Somoza. This is nonsense. It was their repression that in 1979, 1980, and 1981 destroyed the coalition that overthrew Somoza and sparked the resistance. In 1979, 1980, and 1981, the United States was providing aid to the Government of Nicaragua, not to the resistance.

From mid-1984 until late in 1985—well over a year—the U.S. Government provided no aid to Nicaraguan resistance forces. During that time, the resistance grew by 50%, roughly from 10,000 to 15,000. So much for the theory that the resistance is a creature of U.S. cash.

Who are these Nicaraguans who are willing to risk their lives against the communist security apparatus? The resistance fighters are overwhelmingly rural youths. Most are between 18 and 22 years old. They are fighting to defend their small plots of land, their churches and, in some cases, their indigenous cultures. Some joined the resistance rather than be forced by the Nicaraguan communists to fight against their friends and neighbors. In defending their families and communities, these young Nicaraguans are fighting for self-determination above all else.

Their leaders are more likely to come from urban areas and have more diverse occupations and backgrounds. They include both former National Guardsmen and former Sandinista fighters, but most are civilians from the very groups the communists claim to represent: peasants, small farmers, urban professionals, and students. One was a primary school teacher; another, an evangelical pastor.

An analysis of the backgrounds of the 153 most senior military leaders of the largest resistance group last November shows that 53% were civilians, 27% served in the National Guard, and a full 20% were former comrades-in-arms of the communists themselves.

The evidence irrefutably confirms that the Nicaraguan resistance is the product of a popular, pervasive, and democratic revolt.

A TIDE OF DEMOCRACY

Historians will detect an irony in the changing course of Latin American tyranny throughout these years. While Nicaragua was trading one dictatorship for another, strongmen elsewhere in the region were falling in rapid succession. In the past decade, elected civilian governments have replaced authoritarian regimes in Argentina, Bolivia, Brazil, Ecuador, El Salvador, Grenada, Guatemala, Honduras, Peru, and Uruguay. Over 90% of the people of Latin America now enjoy self-government, as opposed to less than one-third 10 years ago.

The contrast between communist rule in Nicaragua and the political trend in the rest of Latin America could not be more dramatic. After centuries of struggle, self-government has taken root. Now, Nicaragua is not only the odd man out; its policies of militarism and subversion place all the region's hopes for democracy at risk.

No one is more aware of that risk than the leaders of Latin America. For years, they have been searching for a way of defusing the threat from Nicaragua. Indeed, the central purpose of the Contadora negotiations is to ensure that military tensions created by the Nicaraguan regime's behavior can be overcome peacefully and democratically without the widening conflict the Nicaraguan communists seem bent on provoking.

Not surprisingly, the communists have consistently torpedoed these negotiations. In 1984, the United States pursued direct negotiations with Managua in an attempt to help the Contadora nations negotiate a settlement. Nine rounds of talks were held over 5 months. But the Nicaraguan communists proved mainly interested in manipulating the bilateral talks to short-circuit the Contadora process.

They have also refused the proposal of the country's Roman Catholic bishops, made in their 1984 Good Friday pastoral letter, to negotiate with all Nicaraguans—armed and unarmed, inside Nicaragua and outside of it. The democratic resistance called for a cease-fire and agreed to negotiations mediated by the Catholic Church. The regime refused. So the dialogue that counts the most—the internal dialogue between the regime and its opponents—is stymied by the regime's intransigence. The communists know what they want and have no intention of changing.

Nicaragua's neighbors are well aware of the regime's intentions. So are we. And we are profoundly concerned with the threat Nicaragua poses to the security and well-being of other Latin American nations. We have been deeply involved with encouraging democracy throughout Central and South America, supporting free elections and giving moral and economic support to democratic governments and democratic forces. And like our democratic neighbors, we don't want to see these gains rolled back by Nicaraguan subversion.

Just 2 weeks ago, I met with representatives from the eight nations involved in the Contadora negotiations. They are committed, as we are, to political solutions. But there is no mistaking their grave concern about Soviet and Cuban support for Nicaragua's attempts to undermine regional stability.

U.S. POLICY

Our objectives in Nicaragua, and the objectives of our friends and allies, are straightforward. We want the Nicaraguan regime to reverse its military buildup, to send its foreign advisers home, and to stop oppressing its citizens and subverting its neighbors. We want it to keep the promises of the coalition government that followed Somoza's fall: democratic pluralism at home and peaceful relations abroad.

The United States and its friends have sought these objectives through diplomacy. We continue to believe that a negotiated settlement represents the ultimate hope for peaceful change in Nicaragua. But all serious efforts at negotiation have been blocked by the Nicaraguan communists. They believe that they can continue their domestic oppression and foreign aggression with impunity, and they continue to regard their military might as their guarantee of success. The United States has the power to help Nicaraguan freedom fighters convince the communists that their course is disastrous. We must give them help before it is too late. And when we do that, we increase our leverage in support of our diplomatic objectives.

Our goals are limited and reasonable. They are also essential for our values and our security and those of our neighbors. We must consider many options. Some are so stern that we hope never to resort to them. The United States does not want its own military directly involved in Nicaragua. So far, we have not had to consider this option, because we know there is another way of discouraging the regime from its destructive course. That is why we support the democratic resistance.

Military help for the democratic resistance will give the Nicaraguan communists an incentive to negotiate seriously—something they have yet to do. They did not negotiate with the Carter Administration when the United States was Nicaragua's largest supplier of aid. And they did not negotiate seriously either with us or with their neighbors when the Congress suspended all aid to the resistance 2 years ago. On the contrary, in the fall of 1984, instead of bringing their political opponents back into the political process through competitive elections, they imported assault helicopters from the Soviet Union.

The resistance finds itself at a critical juncture. They have proven themselves by their extraordinary growth and by the desperate measures to which the regime has been driven to combat them. But the Soviet, Cuban, and Eastern-bloc military buildup confronts them with unfair odds. If *we* fail to help the forces of democracy, these forces will suffer severely—not because their cause lacks merit but because the communists will have shown more determination than we.

A strengthened democratic resistance is the only way to force the Nicaraguan communists to halt subversion in this hemisphere; it is the only way to counter their stifling tyranny at home.

Power and diplomacy must go hand in hand. That is a lesson we should have learned by now. Diplomacy without leverage is impotent. Whether in arms control negotiations with the Soviet Union or in the resolution of regional conflicts, diplomacy works best when our opponents realize they cannot win military victory or unilateral advantage. Sometimes we have forgotten that lesson and paid the price.

That is the lesson we are seeking to apply in Nicaragua today: we are trying to convince the communist regime that a military option does not exist. Only stout internal resistance by the Nicaraguan people can pressure the regime into seeking national reconciliation and fulfilling the democratic promise of 1979.

CONSEQUENCES OF INACTION

If we do not strengthen the resistance, our worry in the future will be a very different one—a far more serious one. Our worry will then be a Soviet and Cuban base on the mainland of Latin America, a regime whose consolidated power will allow it to spread subversion and terrorism throughout the hemisphere.

Nor is that all. If the Nicaraguan communists succeed in consolidating their power and in destroying the democratic resistance, their victory would immediately boost radical forces everywhere that rely on violence, militarism, and terrorism to achieve their ends—particularly in Latin America. Radicalism will seem irresistible; the forces of moderation and democracy will be disheartened. *All* the countries in Latin America, who *all* face serious internal economic problems, will see radical forces emboldened to exploit these problems for their own destructive ends.

A communist victory in Nicaragua would also have global repercussions for U.S. policy. It would severely damage our credibility with adversaries who would test our mettle and with those around the world who rely on us for support in their battles against tyranny. If democratic aspiration is snuffed out in Nicaragua, then where can we claim to nurture it or protect it? If an armed aggressor on our own doorstep is allowed to have its way, despite enormous opposition inside the country and out, then how can our reputation for deterring aggression be credible in places farther removed?

The bipartisan Kissinger commission put it starkly in its 1984 report, listing the possible consequences of a failure to contain the present conflict in Central America. The consequences included:

- A series of developments which might require us to devote large resources to defend the southern approaches to the United States, thus reducing our capacity to defend our interests elsewhere.

- A proliferation of Marxist-Leninist states that would increase violence, dislocation, and political repression in the region.

- The erosion of our power to influence events worldwide that would flow from the perception that we were unable to influence vital events close to home.

WHOSE VISION?

This brings me to my final point. In the long run, the debate over military aid to the Nicaraguan resistance is no partisan affair. It is a debate over what moral and political principles shall inspire the future of this hemisphere, over whose vision will be allowed to prevail. One vision—the vision of democrats throughout the Americas—calls for economic progress, free institutions, and the rule of law. The other is a vision of two, three, many Nicaraguas—a hemisphere of burning churches, suppressed newspapers, and crushed opposition.

The Nicaraguan dictatorship may soon have the power to dog the resistance to its death. The United States *now* has the power to prevent that tragic outcome. Will we allow this hemisphere to be taken hostage by totalitarians? That is the question that the Congress faces. For the security of our own country and of the young democracies who turn to us for support, we should give the Nicaraguan people what they need to struggle for the freedoms that were denied them by Somoza and then snatched from them by an armed communist minority.

PART 2

CRITIQUES AND ASSESSMENTS OF THE CLAIM

8

Soviet-Cuban Involvement in Central America: A Critique of Recent Writings

Marc Edelman

INTRODUCTION

This essay discusses conceptual and methodological problems in recent writing about Soviet-Cuban involvement in Central America, including the Kissinger Commission *Report*,[1] recent Reagan Administration white papers,[2] and a number of other works by authors whose views have done much to shape both public discourse and Administration thinking.[3] With virtually unlimited access to the major news media, administration spokespeople have bombarded the Congress and public with a barrage of half-truths and outright distortions which, however well debunked by administration critics,[4] has successfully

Social Text: Theory, Culture, Ideology 15, v. 5 n. 3, Fall 1986, pp. 99-125. Copyright © 1986 Social Text. Reprinted by permission.

[1] *Report of the President's National Bipartisan Commission on Central America* (New York: Macmillan, 1984).

[2] For example, U.S. Department of State, *"Revolution Beyond Our Borders": Sandinista Intervention in Central America* (Report 132, September 1985); and *The Soviet-Cuban Connection in Central America and the Caribbean* (March 1985).

[3] This genre is rapidly growing. Representative works include: Thomas O. Enders, "Revolution, Reform, and Reconciliation in Central America," SAIS *Review* 3, 2 (Summer-Fall 1983), pp. 1-10; William H. Luers, "The Soviets and Latin America: A Three Decade U.S. Policy Tangle," *The Washington Quarterly* 7, 1 (Winter 1984), pp. 3-32; Thomas H. Moorer and George A. Fauriol, *Caribbean Basin Security* (New York: Washington Papers—Praeger, 1984); Morris Rothenberg, "Latin America in Soviet Eyes," *Problems of Communism* 32, 5 (September-October 1983), pp. 1-18; Pedro Ramet and Fernando López-Alves, "Moscow and the Revolutionary Left in Latin America," *Orbis* 28, 2 (Summer 1984), pp. 341-63; Robert Leiken, "Nicaragua's Untold Stories," *The New Republic* 191, 5 (October 8, 1984), pp. 16-22; Jiri and Virginia Valenta, "Soviet Strategy in the Caribbean Basin," in Alan Adelman and Reid Reading, eds., *Confrontation in the Caribbean Basin* (Pittsburgh: University of Pittsburgh, 1984); Max Singer, *Nicaragua: The Stolen Revolution* (Washington: U.S. Information Agency, 1984).

[4] This genre too has grown, but with less impact. See, for example, Ted C. Lewellen, "Human Rights as Propaganda: The Political Manipulation of Central American Human Rights Data," Paper presented at the International Studies Association, Washington, DC,

narrowed the spectrum of acceptable discourse about Central America. A co-
terie of analysts writing in prestigious foreign policy journals has contributed
significantly to the Reagan Administration's efforts to shape a consensus
around its Central America policies by lending what otherwise would be
transparently tendentious arguments an appearance of scholarly legitimacy.
Errors of fact, once having found their way into print in this literature, become
elevated to the status of unquestioned reality. More fundamental mis-
conceptions about historical processes, shaped by an almost exclusively globalist and geopolitical outlook, lead to more basic problems.

The deficiencies of this literature on Soviet-Cuban involvement in
Central America include an unusually large number of inadvertent errors—
"howlers," as E. Bradford Burns appropriately termed them—that are indicative
perhaps of some authors' unfamiliarity with the region;[5] distortions and
omissions which in some cases are unintended, but which in others may be
deliberate efforts to justify viewpoints or policies decided upon for other reasons; frequent considerations of "facts" isolated from their contexts; a remarkably uncritical use of sources; and, in some cases, the use of highly ideological, value-laden language. Underlying much of the literature is a conception of
history that gives inadequate attention to the real processes which have shaped
nations, movements and events in Central America and that is only rarely accompanied by any serious consideration of the full weight of past and present
US activities in the region. In studies of Soviet-Cuban activities in Central
America, to ignore or downplay the history of US involvement is to employ a

March 6-9, 1985; Abraham Brumberg, "Reagan's Untruths About Managua," *The New York
Times*, June 18, 1985. One thorough study which, although commissioned by the State De-
partment, ends up questioning the basic premises of U.S. policy is Carl G. Jacobsen, *Soviet
Attitudes Towards Aid to and Contacts with Central American Revolutionaries* (Washington:
DOS, 1984). See also the excellent annotated edition of the Kissinger *Report* by Gregorio
Delser, *Informe Kissinger Contra Centroamérica* (Mexico: El Día, 1984).

5   E. Bradford Burns, "The Kissinger Report: Visions of History Through Alice's Looking
Glass," LASA *Forum* 15, 1 (Spring 1984). The Kissinger Commission, after all, spent only
six days in Central America and three in Mexico and Venezuela. It did, however, hear testimony from over 300 individuals on this trip and nearly 200 others in the United States. The
Commission itself was composed entirely of non-experts. The fact that Carlos Díaz-Alejan-
dro, one of the two liberal Commission members and an authority on South (but not Central)
America, was appointed by mistake is a sorry if humorous comment on the level of knowledge
among Administration policy makers. See *The New York Times*, September 6, 1983; also
William M. LeoGrande, "Through the Looking Glass: The Kissinger Report on Central America," *World Policy Journal* 1, 2 (Winter 1984), p. 253. It is noteworthy that apart from Cole
Blasier and perhaps Robert Leiken, there are simply no US scholars who can claim to have
any real expertise on both Latin America and the Soviet Union. Sovietologist Jerry Hough has
made an interesting effort to explore the views of Soviet Latin Americanists. See "The
Evolving Soviet Debate on Latin America," *Latin American Research Review* 16, 1 (1981),
pp. 107-123. In the specific case of Central America, the dearth of knowledge among Soviet
specialists is even more pronounced than is the case for the continent as a whole.

conceptual framework fraught with faulty assumptions and guaranteed to produce highly dubious conclusions, as many of the examples discussed below indicate. Until students of Soviet-Cuban policy toward Central America examine empirically the origins of the phenomena they study and dispense with the fundamentally deductive premises which have guided their research, North Americans will be poorly equipped to understand whatever geopolitical aspects Central American conflicts actually may have.

LANGUAGE, BALANCE, AND UNCRITICAL USE OF SOURCES

Stephen Cohen, one of the foremost US historians of the Soviet Union, remarked on how language influences perceptions of Soviet Policy:

> Objective political analysis requires language that is value free. But much American commentary on Soviet affairs employs special political terms that are inherently biased and laden with double standards. . . . The United States has a government, security organizations and allies. The Soviet Union, however, has a regime, secret police and satellites. Our leaders are consummate politicians; theirs are wily, cunning or worse. We give the world information and seek influence; they disseminate propaganda and disinformation while seeking expansion and domination.[6]

Many might argue that there is an *a priori* element in social science research that makes "value free" terminology (and analysis) an impossibility. In writing about Soviet-Cuban involvement in Central America, however, the use of biased language frequently conceals premises which should be the subject of explicit discussion and poses as fact assertions which might be better viewed as research hypotheses. Psychologist Joel Kovel, commenting on the labels ("Communist," "totalitarian," etc.) the media apply to Nicaragua, makes a point which could serve as well to describe much of the foreign policy literature:

> The keywords insert themselves in a chain of reasoning and fix discourse at the level of automatism. They obviate both the need to look at what is really happening and to evaluate just what it really means.[7]

Here a few citations from the literature should suffice to indicate the kind of terminology that is sometimes used. Moorer and Fauriol write that

> to underestimate Havana's genuine strategy of armed aggression, political intimidation, deception, subversion, sabotage, and propaganda is

---

6   "Sovieticus," *The Nation* 238, 18 (May 12, 1985), p. 568.
7   Joel Kovel, "The Eagle Hovers Over Nicaragua," *Old Westbury Review* 1, 1 (1985).

144 *Marc Edelman*

folly. . . . Past activities and present trends in Central America and elsewhere leave no doubt as to the Cuban regime's single-minded intentions.[8]

Leiken declares that:

The Soviets move cautiously in Latin America, out of cunning, not restraint. While Soviet probes in the region do not signify an independent threat to U.S. security, they are more serious precisely because they are components of and subordinate to Soviet global strategy.[9]

Regarding the question of armed struggle, an issue examined in more detail below, Luers writes that "Moscow has now instructed its toady parties in such places as El Salvador not to be on the sidelines."[10] Kissinger Commission member and Boston University President John Silber asks:

Did observers understand what is meant when Castro spoke for three hours at Daniel Ortega's inauguration? President Ortega disappeared in the shadow cast by the architect of Cuba's cruel and increasingly discredited revolution.[11]

In fact, *pace* Silber, Castro did not speak *at all* at Ortega's inauguration, although he did deliver a long address later that week at a sugar mill the Cubans had donated to Nicaragua. Nor was he the only foreign head of state to attend the inauguration, as *The New York Times* erroneously reported for the historical records. Heads of state from Surinam and Yugoslavia also were present.

What these quotations reflect on a more fundamental level is a lack of balance derived from devoting attention primarily to the Soviet (or Cuban) factor at the expense of other elements. This lack of balance has two dimensions, reflecting analysts' weighing of internal vs. external factors and of US vs. Soviet involvement in the region. Virtually all writers on Soviet-Cuban involvement in Central America concede that internal factors, such as poverty and injustice, are important in understanding the current situation. A few recapitulate the mixed economic results of post-World War II modernization, in which Central America experienced extremely rapid growth but increasing inequalities in income distribution and rising absolute poverty for large numbers of the rural poor. They then discuss the crisis of the 1970s, characterized by

[8] Moorer and Fauriol, p. 74.
[9] *Soviet Strategy in Latin America* (New York: Washington Papers-Praeger, 1982), pp. 41-42.
[10] Luers, p. 23.
[11] John Silber, "Plain Talk Behind Closed Doors in Central America," *The Wall Street Journal*, February 8, 1985, p. 21.

declining terms of trade, worsening balance of payments problems, difficulties with import substitution industries, fiscal crises and mounting foreign debts.[12] Much of the literature mentions the way in which pressures for reform in the 1960s and 1970s were repressed through state terror.

Then, however, comes a peculiar shift in emphasis. Rather than systematically examining how such conditions favored the development of revolutionary movements, many analysts shift from examining the internal conditions of Central America to focusing almost exclusively on the Soviet Union and Cuba (and, as we shall indicate below, this analysis is often faulty on its own terms).[13] The underlying fallacy of this approach, as William LeoGrande points out in his trenchant critique of the Kissinger *Report*,

> is that when guerrillas in Nicaragua, El Salvador and Guatemala were developing into serious contenders for power during the mid-1970s, the Cubans were not engaged in Central America. The hiatus in Cuban involvement in Latin America, between 1968 and 1978, is too well established to deny. . . .[14]

Most of the literature on Soviet-Cuban involvement is also largely devoid of any realistic assessment of the relative strength of the Soviet Union and the United States in the Central American area or of the comparative weights of different foreign interventions. Frequent references are made, for example, to the aggressive intentions and the large size of the Nicaraguan armed forces and militias. One cannot help but wonder why such writings, which include works by Leiken and Rothenberg, downplay the repeated *contra* attacks on Nicaragua, the superiority of Honduras' air force, and the major US buildup in Honduras.[15] Similarly, while it may be true that Nicaragua and Cuba

---

[12] For example, Leiken, *Soviet Strategy*, chap. 1; Kissinger *Report*, chaps. 3-4; Jiri and Virginia Valenta, "Sandinistas in Power," *Problems of Communism* 34, 5 (Sept.-Oct. 1985), pp. 1-3. Even Cole Blasier's *The Giant's Rival: The USSR and Latin America* (Pittsburgh: University of Pittsburgh, 1983), which has much to recommend it in other respects, barely mentions this essential background to the crisis.

[13] Leiken does note that repression gave rise to "left-led popular organizations and guerrilla movements." Rather than analyzing this, however, he switches almost immediately to considering the "Soviet presence." See "Overview: Can the Cycle be Broken?" in Leiken, ed., *Central America: Anatomy of a Conflict* (New York: Pergamon, 1984). Similarly, his essay on "The Salvadoran Left" in the same volume considers in detail the issues separating the different left organizations. The emphasis is not, however, on the long, hard years of organizing and repression these groups experienced, but rather on genealogies of splits and coalitions which are defined primarily in relation to different factions' views of the USSR and Cuba.

[14] LeoGrande, "Looking Glass," p. 256.

[15] Leiken, *Soviet Strategy*, pp. 84-86; Rothenberg, "The Soviets and Central America," in Leiken, ed., *Central America*. Blasier notes that the "large Nicaraguan military buildup [is] not surprising in view of the armed opposition to the regime at home and abroad." *Giant's Rival*,

provided limited training and support for guerrillas in El Salvador (discussed in more detail below), even the most outlandish allegations pale in comparison with the support lent by the United States to the *contras*.

Even those analysts whose basic stance is opposed to US intervention in the region sometimes fall into this mode of thought. To argue, as Blasier does, that pro-Moscow Communist parties give the Soviet Union "an entree into the local politics of these countries not available to any Western power,"[16] is problematical, given the tiny size and lack of influence of the Central American Communist parties. Such assertions reflect both questionable assumptions about the relative significance of US and Soviet interventions and a tendency to confuse what might be the Soviets' desires with their actual capabilities. In fact, in these nations (with the exception of post-1979 Nicaragua) US organizations (such as the Agency for International Development, the American Institute for Free Labor Development, US Information Agency, the Military Assistance Groups, etc.) undeniably carry considerable weight and exercise great influence on local politics.[17]

Revelations that the US Central Intelligence Agency provided $1.4 million to two political parties during the 1984 election campaign in El Salvador are but one recent example.[18] In Central America today, where US-sponsored escalation of local conflicts is widely documented, it seems rather one-sided to point, as Luers does, to the danger of a *Soviet* "miscalculation" in the region.[19] If anything, the danger of "miscalculation" is perhaps greater on the other side, as the US-directed mining of Nicaraguan waters and the subsequent damaging of a Soviet tanker suggest. These events seem to indicate that addressing the danger of sea lane interdiction, a theme much emphasized in the

---

p. 46. Elsewhere Robert Matthews and I have analyzed how the Nicaraguan buildup occurred *in response to*, and not prior to, specific threats and acts of real or potential aggression. See Robert Matthews, "The Limits of Friendship: Nicaragua and the West" and Marc Edelman, "Lifelines: Nicaragua and the Socialist Countries," *Report on the Americas* 19, 3 (May-June 1985).

[16] *Giant's Rival*, p. 144.

[17] In mass communications, where many analysts think the Russians and Cubans are gaining the upper hand, this lack of balance is also evident. With respect to Costa Rica, for example, a 1982 US Embassy handout notes that "USIS San José feeds portions of VOA's 'BUENOS DIAS AMERICA' daily to seven local stations, including top-ranking Radio Reloj and Radio Monumental . . . .[on television] USIS materials are not subject to censorship." USIS-authored articles, some based on impossible to corroborate anonymous sources, appear with frequency in the country's main newspaper. See for example Luis Bertrand, "Sufrimiento," *La Nación Internacional*, March 19-25, 1984, p. 13. Former Costa Rican Security Minister Juan Echeverría has charged that the editors of the major communications media meet with USIA officials to discuss how to handle news questions. See "Costa Rica: Interview With Juan Echeverría Brealey," *Mesoamerica* [Costa Rica], 1, 11 (November 1983), pp. 8-9.

[18] *The New York Times*, May 12, 1984.

[19] Luers, pp. 24-25.

alarmist literature, requires attention to US and not only Soviet or Cuban "behavior."

The use of sources is a major problem in much of the literature that seeks to establish external forces as an important cause of social upheaval in Central America.[20] There is widespread and uncritical use of State Department and defector reports. There are even references to published Soviet sources which "prove"—not surprisingly—that pro-Moscow Communist parties play a leading role in the region's revolutionary movements.[21] At times the most fantastic charges find their way into print and become "facts" of record. An article in the widely read journal *Orbis*, for example, declares that Nicaragua has already "received some eighty MIG fighters" and is involved in gun-running, "with at least fifty helicopters reaching Salvadoran guerrillas each month from Managua."[22]

The footnote for this bizarre claim about helicopter arms shipments (which to my knowledge has never been made elsewhere) refers to three articles, none of which mention anything similar, and to a speech by Colonel John Waghelstein, head of the US Military Group in El Salvador—probably not the most disinterested source on the matter. One cannot help but wonder, however, how many readers of *Orbis* will ever stop to consider the weak empirical foundation for such claims. More importantly the unchallenged repetition of this kind of charge in prestigious journals has done much to shape the current foreign policy consensus.

RECENT HISTORY—ARMED STRUGGLE IN EL SALVADOR

The literature on Soviet-Cuban involvement in Central America devotes much attention to the civil war in El Salvador, although except for the Kissinger *Report*, very little consideration is given to the country's political institutions or history. The treatment of Salvadoran political life in the *Report* is predictable and not worth examining in detail. The scarcely credible paeans to

---

[20] Methodological concerns of this type are virtually never discussed in the literature. Blasier's comment on the Valentas' article in Adelman and Reading's anthology is an exception.

[21] Rothenberg, "The Soviets and Central America," p. 138. The most widely cited defector's report involves the allegations by Miguel Bolaños Hunter, a former Nicaraguan intelligence operative, about Cuban direction of the Nicaraguan Interior Ministry. Never reported in the literature is the fact that Bolaños, who stole a plane in Nicaragua and flew to Costa Rica in 1983, left Costa Rica shortly afterwards travelling on a US passport and in the company of an American who used a diplomatic passport. Costa Rican government documents which describe this affair were obtained and published in 1984 by the Costa Rican Socialist Party in Costa Rica: *Entre la neutralidad y la guerra,* pp. 42-44. The documents, the authenticity of which was not subsequently denied by the government, would seem to suggest that Bolaños had (or quickly established) some sort of connection with American intelligence.

[22] Ramet and López-Alves, pp. 356, 358.

an ongoing process of reform, to the creation of durable democratic institutions and to government efforts to control the military and the ultra-right have all been extensively criticized, even by those sympathetic to US goals in the region.[23] More relevant here is the basis of the analysis which accompanies these unfounded assertions.

In February, 1981, shortly after Reagan's inauguration, the US State Department issued its White Paper, entitled *Communist Interference in El Salvador*, which was said to be based on documents captured from People's Revolutionary Army [ERP] and Salvadoran Communist Party [PCS] guerrillas. According to the White Paper, over 200 tons of arms were shipped to Salvadoran guerrillas following a 1980 arms purchasing mission by PCS Secretary General Schafik Handal to the USSR, Eastern Europe, Vietnam and Ethiopia. The White Paper charged that Cuba played a key role in unifying the Salvadoran guerrilla organizations, first in the Unified Revolutionary Directorate [DRU] and subsequently in the Farabundo Martí National Liberation Front [FMLN] (the members of which now include the PCS, the ERP, the National Resistance [RN], the Popular Liberation Forces Farabundo Martí [FPL] and the Revolutionary Party of the Central American Workers [PRTC]). It also pointed to Nicaraguan logistical support in transferring arms to El Salvador by air, sea and land.

On June 8, 1981, an exclusive story in *The Wall Street Journal* detailed numerous errors and distortions in the White Paper and suggested that there were good reasons to doubt many of its claims. *The Washington Post* followed with a similar article the next day. Both reports pointed to inconsistencies in the documents and in the government's analysis. Several of the most important documents were attributed to guerrilla leaders who did not write them. Statistics regarding arms shipments were not found in the documents, but were "extrapolated." Much of the other information in the White Paper did not appear in the documents at all. The key document about a supposed arms purchasing mission to the East bloc by PCS leader Handal was written in the third person and could not, on the basis of internal evidence, have been authored by Handal or by the other PCS representative in Cuba, as the White Paper suggested. No mention occurs in the documents of unity as a condition for receiving Cuban aid. Finally, the *Journal* reported that then-U.S. Ambassador to El Salvador Robert White heard nothing about the documents when they were captured, even though they were supposedly seized along with the entire ERP propaganda commission. This would have been a major success that clearly would have come to his attention. John Glassman, the principal

---

[23]   See, for example, the criticism of the agrarian reform by the individual recognized as its main architect. Roy Prosterman, "The Unmaking of a Land Reform," *The New Republic* 187, 6 (August 9, 1982). For a discussion of the current conjuncture see the articles by Ignacio Ellacuria and Ricardo Stein in *Report on the Americas* 20, 1 (Jan.-Feb. 1986).

State Department author of the White Paper, acknowledged it contained "mistakes" and was "misleading" and "over-embellished." The *Journal* concluded, "if anything, Mr. Glassman may be understating the case in his concession that the White Paper contains mistakes and guessing."

The media critiques of the White Paper received widespread attention.[24] This, however, seems to have escaped both globalist and regionalist analysts of Soviet-Cuban involvement in Central America, many of whom continue to cite the 1981 White Paper (or initial news reports about it) as if it were a completely reputable source, even in works published in 1983 and 1984.[25]

This reliance on the 1981 White Paper, aside from being dubious in methodological terms, sometimes leads to serious errors of analysis. Moorer and Fauriol, for example, declare that "in the Spring of 1980, the three small non-Communist groups constituting the Democratic Front [FD] joined the Marxist leadership to create the FDR [Democratic Revolutionary Front]."[26] This is apparently paraphrased from the White Paper's "Long Analysis" and simply bears no relation to historical reality. In fact, the FD included the social democratic and social Christian political parties, an organization of professionals and technicians, six unions, and observers from two universities and the Catholic Church. Five days after its formation it merged with five mass organizations (that had only recently staged a demonstration attended by some 100,000 people) to form the FDR, the leaders of which are not Marxists, but social democrats and dissident Christian Democrats.[27]

The White Paper also claimed a major Cuban role in the unification of the five Salvadoran guerrilla groups in late 1979 and 1980, arranged at meetings in Havana attended by Fidel Castro. While there are inconsistencies in the documents which cast doubt on whether some of these meetings occurred, questions of perhaps equal or greater importance are whether Cuban tutelage was necessary to achieve unity and whether the unified structures were actually effective. Leiken, commenting on the Havana meetings and on an article by PCS leader Handal on the unification process, conceded that:

> Whatever the Soviet-Cuban role in this, it remains true, as Handal affirms in his *Kommunist* article, that "the situation in the country demanded unification of all revolutionary and democratic forces."[28]

[24]   Barry Rubin notes that "The White Paper did not sway public opinion . . . since several critiques which challenged its interpretation of the source documents received wide publicity." See "Reagan Administration Policymaking and Central America," in Leiken, *Central America*, p. 309.

[25]   Rothenberg, "The Soviets and Central America," p. 137 and "Latin America in Soviet Eyes," p. 12; Leiken, *Soviet Strategy*, pp. 78-80; Blasier, *Giant's Rival*, pp. 116-17; Valenta, "Soviet Strategy," pp. 258, 267.

[26]   Moorer and Fauriol, p. 76.

[27]   Tommie Sue Montgomery, *Revolution in El Salvador* (Boulder: Westview, 1982), pp. 133ff; Leiken, "The Salvadoran Left," pp. 117, 128.

[28]   *Soviet Strategy*, p. 80.

This assessment is largely accurate and uncontroversial. As we shall indicate shortly in discussing the literature's treatment of the Salvadoran left, unity and armed struggle were widely perceived at the time as obvious steps in a context where other alternatives were nonexistent.

The effectiveness of the unification of the guerrilla organizations is a more interesting issue. Even though most analysts point to the Cubans' tutelage in the unity process as being part of their desire to expand influence and power, few mention just how unsuccessful unification (and by implication Cuban tutelage) was in its initial phases. Even Leiken's 1984 article on the Salvadoran left, which focuses primarily on the five FMLN guerrilla groups' analyses of Salvadoran society and their attitudes toward the Soviet Union, says little about the effect of having maintained distinct military (and organizational) structures. After the achievement of formal unity, serious divisions persisted. Until 1983, the radios of the main organizations rarely reported actions by other groups, and joint military efforts were few.

The decision of the PCS (and the Soviet Union) to adopt an armed struggle line is a major focus of much of the literature. The change in line is attributed to lessons learned from the overthrow of the Allende government in Chile and to raised hopes after the Sandinista victory in Nicaragua. Some analysts maintain that the decision was also influenced by shame at the late participation of the pro-Moscow Nicaraguan Socialist Party [PSN] in the revolution.[29] Others cite orders from Moscow and Havana.[30]

Characteristically, little or no attention is devoted to conditions within El Salvador in the 1979-80 period when this important change in PCS strategy took place. Among those learning lessons from the Nicaraguan revolution were the reformist young army officers who led the October 1979 coup. They ushered in a government that has been described as "El Salvador's last chance for peaceful social change."[31] Although the literature on Soviet-Cuban involvement in Central America rarely mentions it,[32] the PCS participated in the post-coup government, abandoning or at the very least suspending its still untested armed struggle strategy and trying to give peaceful change a chance. The intensification of repression in this period, however, prompted the government's resignation in early January. In the following months, the murder of FDR leaders and sympathizers at public meetings and demonstrations led the PCS, as well as a significant number of social democrats and Christian Democrats, to conclude that armed struggle and unity with the guerrillas were

[29]   Mark Katz, "The Soviet-Cuban Connection," *International Security* 8, 1 (Summer 1983), p. 92; Leiken, *Soviet Strategy*, pp. 33-35; Luers, p. 13.
[30]   Luers, p. 23.
[31]   Montgomery, p. xi.
[32]   The only exception among works considered here is Leiken, "The Salvadoran Left," p. 117.

the only alternatives to annihilation at the hands of the army, security forces and death squads. In this context, it is very dubious to assert, as Luers does, that a

> Soviet-Cuban agreement in early 1980 not to press for an immediate espousal of a Marxist-Leninist revolutionary victory was key to enabling the Salvadoran guerrilla groups and their external supporters to place the Social Democratic leader Guillermo Ungo at the head of the political front organization.[33]

After all, Ungo, who was junta president Duarte's running mate in the fraudulent 1972 elections, only became president of the FDR in November 1980 after the previous president and five other leaders were seized at a public meeting in San Salvador and assassinated. The previous FDR president, Enrique Alvarez, was not a Marxist-Leninist, but a millionaire dairy farmer and member of the oligarchy. A reformist, he served as a minister of agriculture in the October junta and in two previous governments. When he resigned from the reformist junta to protest the growing repression, other members of the oligarchy denounced him as a traitor to his class.[34]

There are indications that the PCS began to favor armed struggle, at least in theoretical terms, as early as its clandestine Seventh Congress of April 1979.[35] Surprisingly, none of the analysts of Soviet-Cuban involvement in Central America mention this, perhaps because they are accustomed to seeking answers in Soviet and Cuban party pronouncements, not in those of local parties. The PCS Seventh Congress, however, was held before the Sandinista victory in Nicaragua and, more importantly, before the publication of the Soviet literature which is continually cited as marking the emergence of an armed

---

[33]   Luers, p. 24.

[34]   Robert Armstrong and Janet Shenk, *El Salvador: The Face of Revolution* (Boston: South End Press, 1982), pp. 121-22; Montgomery, pp. 206-07.

[35]   William Bollinger, "Revolutionary Strategy in Latin America," *Monthly Review* 34, 9 (February 1983), p. 30. Leiken's claim that the PCS may have formed its armed force [FAL] as early as 1977 is based on an ambiguous quote from a *World Marxist Review* article by PCS leader Handal, which probably reflects as much as anything Handal's desire not to appear late in joining the armed struggle. See Leiken, "The Salvadoran Left," pp. 115, 127. Handal's most detailed statement on the shift to an armed struggle line is replete with *ex post facto* attempts to rationalize the PCS's lateness in joining the guerrilla movement. He does claim that the decision was made in 1977, but then describes various ideological and practical obstacles which kept this from occurring. Handal does not claim that the PCS had created the FAL in 1977. Even the FAL's precursor, the self defense "revolutionary action groups" [GAR] were, he says, only beginning to be formed in 1978. See Schafik Jorge Handal, "Consideraciones acerca del viraje del Partido Comunista de El Salvador hacia la lucha armada." *Fundamentos y Perspectivas* 5 (1983), pp. 15-54. Alan Riding reported in 1982 that the PCS had "virtually no guerrilla force of its own." See "The Central American Quagmire." *Foreign Affairs* 61, 3 (1982), p. 646.

struggle line.[36] This does not mean necessarily that pro-Moscow parties had not decided already on a change in line which was first manifested at the PCS Congress. It does, however, suggest that the prevailing explanations of this shift require substantial qualification.

The reasons why the PCS chose the route of armed struggle may, of course, have something to do with pressures, orders or suggestions from Cuba and/or the Soviet Union. It is also important to keep in mind, however, that as early as 1975

> both the FPL and RN vanguards, through their respective mass organizations, had begun to surpass the PCS in influence within the working class and the peasantry.[37]

A declining base of support was certainly one factor which prompted a reevaluation of the PCS's political line, as Handal admits,[38] but the severe repression of the post-1978 period was clearly of paramount importance.

AN EXPORTED REVOLUTION

The assertion that arms are flowing from Nicaragua to other countries, especially El Salvador, has become a *sine qua non* of the "Soviet threat" argument and a major justification for US policy in the region. Remarkably little evidence exists, however, to support this article of faith.[39] There is general agreement that the Sandinistas did ship arms, some of which were obtained from Cuba, up to early 1981 in preparation for the FMLN's failed "final" offensive.[40]

Former Secretary of State Enders presents the most evidence of post-1981 arms flows. Nevertheless, all he is able to point to are statements by guerrilla leaders captured in a Tegucigalpa safe house that the insurgents receive arms from Nicaragua and to an incident in which Honduran authorities surprised a

---

[36] Some Soviet analysts apparently were sympathetic to armed struggle by the mid-1970s, although this has rarely, if ever, been noted by U.S. analysts and was not reflected in official policy until 1979-80. See Nikolai Sergeevich Leonov, *Ocherki novoi i noveishei istorii stran TSentral' noi Ameriki* (Moscow: Mysl', 1975). Typically, however, little attention is paid in the U.S. literature to the debates which probably occurred in the USSR itself around this issue. See Hough, and Edmé Dominguez, "Los debates académicos soviéticos sobre América Latina durante la década de los setenta," *Cuadernos Semestrales* 12 (1982).

[37] Bollinger, p. 29.

[38] Handal, pp. 29, 33, 47.

[39] A thorough treatment of this is Raymond Bonner, *Weakness and Deceit* (New York: New York Times Books, 1984), chap. 13.

[40] Laurence Whitehead, "Explaining Washington's Central American Policies," *Journal of Latin American Studies* 15 (1983), pp. 331-32; Wayne Smith, "U.S. Central American Policy: The Worst-Alternative Syndrome," SAIS *Review* 3, 2 (Summer-Fall 1983), pp. 12-13.

group of guerrillas in transit from Nicaragua who "escaped after a firefight but left behind documents identifying infiltration routes."[41]

This scanty (albeit documentary) evidence has never been released for public scrutiny. More revealing is the 1982 Senate testimony of former US Ambassador to El Salvador Deane Hinton. Replying to a query about how many arms had been seized since Congress allotted the CIA $19 million for that purpose, Hinton conceded, "Not a pistola, Senator."[42] In 1982 and again in 1983 the Reagan administration attempted to convince skeptics that arms from Nicaragua were continuing to flow to the FMLN. Some critics were apparently convinced, but the administration refused to release the evidence, which it considered highly sensitive.[43] More recently, administration claims have focused on the large percentage of captured guerrilla M-16 rifles traceable to US stockpiles in Vietnam and to the capture of a Costa Rican jeep in Honduras that contained cash and munitions for the FMLN.[44] Beyond displaying a map with arrows, however, the latest White Paper provides no new evidence of continued arms trafficking by the Sandinistas.

Why did the Nicaraguans apparently stop sending significant quantities of arms to the Salvadoran guerrillas? Partly as a result of the failure of the guerrillas' "final offensive," the FMLN, Nicaragua and Cuba expressed interest in reaching political settlements with the United States and probably chose to make good faith gestures wherever possible. In April 1981 the Reagan Administration even conceded that arms trafficking had declined. But seeing the calls for discussions as a sign of weakness, the US government pressed ahead with plans for creating a *contra* army and for increasing aid to the Salvadoran military.[45] This US effort to achieve a military solution involved the construction in Honduras, beginning in 1982, of a sizeable network of bases and radar installations which would surely complicate any cross border traffic not meeting with US approval. One radar base is in the Gulf of Fonseca, where it can effectively monitor El Salvador's coastline.[46] Most importantly,

---

[41] Enders, p. 2. A later report in *The New York Times* (April 23, 1984) indicated that this firefight took place near El Salvador, only two and one-half miles inside Honduras.

[42] Quoted in Policy Alternatives for the Caribbean and Central America. *Changing Course* (Washington: Institute for Policy Studies, 1984), p. 27 (see also pp. 38-39).

[43] Whitehead, p. 332.

[44] *The New York Times*, December 20, 1985; DOS, *Soviet-Cuban Connection*, pp. 33-34. See also Julia Preston, "What Duarte Won," *The New York Review of Books* 32, 13 (August 15, 1985), p. 33.

[45] Smith, "U.S. Central America Policy," p. 16 and "The Grenada Complex in Central America," *Caribbean Review* 12, 4 (Fall 1983), p. 64.

[46] The idea that, with this massive presence and improved surveillance capacity, there could still be any significant arms traffic from Nicaragua through Honduras to Guatemala, much less El Salvador, is hardly plausible, although Leiken, citing State Department sources, claims this. See *Soviet Strategy*, p. 82. Guatemala's remaining guerrillas operate in that part of the country most distant from Honduras and even the Guatemalan military claims that if any

however, the Salvadoran guerrillas were capturing large quantities of arms from the military. Indeed,

> it is reliably estimated that 40% of the equipment the United States gives the Salvadoran army passes to the FMLN. Inasmuch as the army outnumbers the rebels by a factor of four to one, Washington apparently is doing a better job of arming each guerrilla than it is each soldier.[47]

Even US Under-Secretary of Defense Fred Iklé conceded in 1984 that previously undisclosed official estimates were that half of the guerrillas' arms were captured from the army, although he insisted that 80 percent of their ammunition came from the Soviet Union and Cuba via Nicaragua.[48] Salvadoran Army commander Domingo Monterrosa, undeniably closer to the situation than Iklé and probably less attuned to the public relations value of his remarks, stated not long before his death in combat that although the guerrillas were getting some ammunition from abroad, they were not receiving any weapons.[49]

NICARAGUA IN ADMINISTRATION EYES

The effort to damn Nicaragua as a Soviet outpost begins with the emphasis many writers give to the Cubans' support for unity among the three factions of the Sandinista Front [FSLN] during the war against Somoza.[50] A key role in the unification of the FSLN was also played, however, by the leaders of Panama and Venezuela.[51] The military and political support lent by Venezuela, Costa Rica and Panama to the FSLN, if mentioned at all, is either distorted or downplayed. The fact that virtually all forces allied with the Sandinistas in 1979, including present-day *contra* leader Alfonso Robelo, favored close relations with Cuba has been conveniently forgotten in the interest of rewriting history to suit current policy.[52] Similarly, Luers' (and others')

arms flow across the border they come from Mexico. See "Situación general Operación Ixil," *Revista Militar* (Sept.-Dec. 1982), p. 31. The State Department's Luers, hoping to explain how all those arms get to the Salvadoran guerrillas, simply redraws the map, stating that "now Nicaragua, with borders on three [sic] countries, is directly engaged in support for guerrillas." Nicaragua, of course, borders only on Costa Rica and Honduras. See any map of Central America and Luers, p. 30.

[47] Eldon Kenworthy, "Central America: Beyond the Credibility Trap," *World Policy Journal* 1, 1 (Fall 1983), p. 189.

[48] *The New York Times*, March 28, 1984.

[49] *The New York Times*, April 18, 1984.

[50] For example, *Report*, p. 32; Enders, p. 2.

[51] Arturo Cruz, "The Origins of Sandinista Foreign Policy," in Leiken, *Central America*, p. 102.

[52] On Robelo's praise for Cuba see Edelman, p. 38. Shirley Christian, in her tendentious

mention of Cuban "volunteers" sent to fight for the FSLN is misleading. Few Cubans fought with the FSLN, although hundreds of Central Americans, Panamanians, Mexicans, and South Americans did risk their lives to bring down Somoza. Luers' identification of the Ortega brothers as heads of "the two northern Sandinista factions" is simply wrong; they were members of the *tercerista* faction which fought primarily in the south (and to which Luers elsewhere refers incorrectly as the "Terciarios").[53]

Another recurring theme in the literature is that the Sandinistas faced no real security problems when they came to power in 1979 and therefore had no need to build up their armed forces.[54] In fact, the Sandinista "army" at the time of the revolution was a motley unorganized crew unable to deal effectively with the snipers that were plaguing Managua or the bands of regrouping National Guards along the Honduran and Costa Rican borders. Since fleeing Somoza supporters had looted the treasury, leaving the country with virtually no reserves, the question of which countries would give security and military aid on favorable terms became of immediate paramount importance. It is from this starting point that one must analyze the future course of the Nicaraguan revolution's foreign relations, rather than from any supposed predispositions on the part of the Sandinista leadership.[55]

Typically, the literature on Soviet-Cuban involvement in Central America devotes little or no attention to this question of initial alternatives; to Sandinista efforts to maintain a mixed economy; to the actual organization of the government; to the elections which, while universally disparaged by the administration and its allies, received a clean bill of health from numerous international observers;[56] to the continued existence of opposition political par-

yet influential book *Nicaragua: Revolution in the Family* (New York: Random House, 1985), does provide some discussion of the Venezuelan and Panamanian roles in overthrowing Somoza. A comparison with Robert Matthews' article, cited above, suggests that Christian's interpretation is severely deficient, since it provides almost no analysis of the external constraints which, right from the beginning, circumscribed the Nicaraguan revolution. For a discussion of Christian's book see George Black, "The Christian Network," *The Nation* (September 7, 1985).

[53] Luers may have picked this up during his diplomatic service, since declassified CIA documents from 1978 also employ this term. See Document #81(281B) on microfiches published by the Declassified Documents Reference System, Research Publications, Inc.

[54] For example, Singer, p. 4.

[55] On this issue see the previously cited articles by Matthews and by Edelman. The main source of the charge is the "72 Hour Document," cited by Singer (p. 4) and by the DOS, *Soviet-Cuban Connection* (p. 21), among others. This document, a report of a high-level FSLN meeting held in September 1979, actually says that the National Guard could not organize attacks *"since it would have to have strong backing from a bordering or neighboring country"* (p. 14 of manuscript translation provided to author by Max Singer). Obviously, the FSLN underestimated the danger from Honduras, but their statement was much more equivocal than the selective quotations repeatedly used in the literature suggest.

[56] Lithuanian emigré Abraham Brumberg provides an interesting evaluation of the elec-

ties; to the fact that elections were announced in 1980, before the beginning of
the so-called "covert" war; to Nicaraguan assurances that they will consider
United States security needs; or to the ways in which US pressures and *contra*
attacks have radicalized FSLN policies and led broad sectors of Nicaraguan
society to view dissent as unpatriotic.

The issue of press censorship has also been distorted with charges, such as
those by Ramet and López-Alves in *Orbis*, that the FSLN has driven "the once
vigorous   independent   newspaper   *La   Prensa*,   into   a   corner
. . . proscrib[ing] publication of any articles critical of the Soviet
Union or any of its bloc allies."[57]   While the rhythm of censorship clearly
rises and falls with the intensity of the *contra* war, a few headlines from recent
issues should suffice to make the point that the vision of a silenced *La Prensa*
is far from accurate: "Dissident Explains Life in Soviet Prison," (*La Prensa*
January 7, 1985), "Cuban Poetry in Exile," (*La Prensa* February 24, 1985),
"Ex-Prisoners Tell of Horror at UN, Ask Investigation of Cuban Prisons," (*La
Prensa* February 26, 1985). With the intensification of the administration
campaign to aid the *contras* and the reimposition of the state of emergency,
however, it is unlikely that many such headlines will continue to appear.

That some Nicaraguan officials remain critical of the Soviet Union and
Cuba is suggested by the recently published manual on Marxism used to train
FSLN cadres.[58] Describing itself as offering "an open, creative and revolutionary Marxism, grounded in the soil and roots of the struggle of the
Nicaraguan people," fully one-third of the manual is devoted to the history of
the struggle against Somoza. The manual's authors refer to the Cuban revolution as being characterized by "successes but also by errors" and have particularly harsh words for the pro-Moscow Nicaraguan Socialist Party [PSN] which
they describe as being "stupidly retarded [*tarado*] from its beginnings because
of its links with the Communist Party of the United States."[59]

They note with disdain that the founding of the PSN was announced at a
1944 labor meeting called to support the Somoza government.[60] More re-

---

tions in "'Sham' and 'Farce' in Nicaragua?" *Dissent*, 32, 2 (Spring 1985). Allegations by
Administration allies such as Leiken about FSLN-sponsored election violence are discussed in
detail by Alexander Cockburn in "The Case of Robert Leiken," *The Nation* 241, 22 (December
28, 1985), pp. 702-03.
[57]   Ramet and López-Alves, p. 356.
[58]   Equipo Interdisciplinario Latinoamericano, *Teoría y práctica revolucionarias en
Nicaragua* (Managua: Ediciones Contemporáneas, 1983).
[59]   Equipo, p. 42. It is difficult to convey in translation the strength of the opprobrium
conveyed by the epithet *tarado*. Incidentally, the use of this term is one of several pieces of
internal linguistic evidence which suggest that the manual's authors are South Americans from
the southern cone, as the introduction claims, rather than Cubans or Soviets. The term is
common in Argentine Spanish and infrequent, although not unknown, in the Spanish of
Central America and the Caribbean.
[60]   Equipo, p. 45.

cently, the marginal role of the pro-Moscow PSN has been reported by one conservative Central American newspaper that frequently criticizes the Sandinistas' Marxist orientation. In an article on the Nicaraguan elections, it points out that "the Socialist Party . . . has never been taken into account in the important decisions that the [Sandinista] Front has taken."[61]

Nicaragua's adoption of "pro-Soviet" positions at the UN or in foreign policy is often cited in the literature which emphasizes the "Soviet threat," but the explanations offered usually ignore the military and economic pressures of the United States and stress instead the long-term marxist commitment of the FSLN leaders. The signing of a party-to-party agreement between the FSLN and the Soviet Communist Party is certainly an indication of the sympathies of some Sandinistas, as several analysts suggest, but these same authors systematically overlook the fact that the FSLN also maintains links, strained at times, with the Socialist International and with the Mexican-sponsored Conference of Latin American Political Parties. Rarely in the literature is it mentioned that Nicaragua, like India, has abstained in UN General Assembly votes on the question of Afghanistan, repeatedly refusing to vote with the Soviet Union;[62] has voted differently from the Soviet Union on the Iran-Iraq conflict; voted for the suspension of nuclear testing when the USSR abstained; voted for sending reconstruction relief to Chad, which the USSR opposed; and— with China, Zimbabwe and Guyana—abstained in the Security Council vote on the Soviet downing of the Korean airplane. Even Arturo Cruz, Jr., who ascribes Sandinista "pro-Soviet" foreign policy positions to the poverty of "political culture" in Nicaragua (a position echoed at times by leftist Central Americans from elsewhere on the isthmus), does not link this legacy of the Somoza dynasty to US support for the Somoza regime.[63] The waging of an open "covert" war under US auspices has been a major factor in breaking off constructive diplomatic initiatives and in increasing the reliance of the Nicaraguans on the USSR, as key State Department functionaries who served in the region in the crucial years 1979-81 repeatedly emphasize.[64] Similarly, after US reductions in Nicaragua's sugar quota, the cutoff of economic assis-

---

[61] *La Nación Internacional*, March 1-7, 1984.
[62] Sometimes it is falsely charged that Nicaragua "faithfully followed the Cuban and Soviet line on . . . . the Soviet invasion of Afghanistan." See David Nolan, *The Ideology of the Sandinistas and the Nicaraguan Revolution* (Coral Gables: University of Miami, 1984), p. 117. One peculiar mention of Nicaragua's actual position is by Juan del Aguila, who states "Nicaragua's relationship with the Soviet Union is dramatically reflected in its voting record at the United Nations." He then notes in a footnote, without mentioning the word "abstention," that Nicaragua "failed to condemn the Soviet invasion of Afghanistan." See "Central American Vulnerability to Soviet-Cuban Penetration," *Journal of Interamerican Studies and World Affairs* 27, 2 (Summer 1985), pp. 81, 95. For official Nicaraguan statements critical of the Soviet position on Afghanistan see Edelman, p. 40.
[63] Cruz, passim.
[64] Smith, "U.S. Central American Policy."

tance, the vetoing of loan requests to international lending agencies and the imposition of a trade embargo, it is difficult to accept the prevailing view that Nicaragua's ills are due simply to Sandinista mismanagement. This is a major theme, for example in Leiken's work, especially his widely read 1984 essay in *The New Republic*, which was based primarily on unnamed sources and marred by serious errors of fact which, when exposed, received—as is usually the case—less attention than the original article.[65] The political significance of those economic restrictions (which undeniably *have* been taken) for Nicaragua's international stance is somehow not analyzed.

The nature of the *contra* movement is also distorted in much of the literature on Soviet-Cuban involvement in Central America. The Kissinger *Report* refers to rebels "who *reportedly* receive US support,"[66] as if this were not an established fact. Enders, who devoted considerable attention to this theme, claimed that the Nicaraguan Democratic Force [FDN], the main Honduras-based *contra* group, "repudiate[s] the Somocista past and affirm[s] the nationalistic and patriotic principles of Sandino."[67] While the FDN may claim to "repudiate the past," something dubious at best considering the large number of ex-Somoza Guard members in its ranks, it has not shown any interest in claiming the mantle of Sandino. This has, however, been true of the Costa Rica-based Democratic Revolutionary Alliance [ARDE], which claims to be true to Sandinismo, even though they too have taken ex-Somoza Guards into their ranks.[68]

In an apparent effort to downplay *somocista* influence in the FDN, Enders states that "the one former National Guard officer in the [FDN] directorate is Enrique Bermúdez, whom Somoza removed from Nicaragua by naming him military attaché in Washington from 1975 to 1979."[69] While this is technically true, it suggests incorrectly that Bermúdez, the main FDN military leader, is of little importance and that pro-Somoza elements are not a significant force in the FDN.[70] Probably no more credible witnesses may be found

---

[65]   Robert Leiken, "Nicaragua's Untold Stories," *The New Republic* 191, 15 (October 8, 1984). For a critique see Peter Marchetti, "The Disenchanted Liberal Stereotype," *In These Times* 9, 15 (March 13-19, 1985), p. 15. The respected British *Latin America Weekly Report* commented in its edition of February 15, 1985, that Leiken's article "seems to say more about domestic politics than realities in Nicaragua." Nevertheless, this "Sandinista-bashing," as the *Weekly Report* terms it, seems to have made Leiken something of a darling of the Administration's Central American policy team, in spite of his protestations that he favors a "third way" between the hardline Reaganites and the Sandinistas. On at least one occasion, Leiken's trips to the region are reported to have been sponsored directly by the State Department. See *La Nación*, October 23, 1985.

[66]   *Report*, p. 37, emphasis added.

[67]   Enders, p. 5.

[68]   *Mesoamerica* 3, 2 (February 1984), pp. 8-9.

[69]   Enders, pp. 4-5.

[70]   In 1983, Sandinista sources claimed that the eight members of the FDN high command

on this point than the brothers Fernando "El Negro" and Edmundo Chamorro, the leaders of a minor *contra* faction (the Nicaraguan Democratic Union [UDN]) that was first part of ARDE, then moved to Honduras to join the FDN, then rejoined ARDE and is currently part of the FDN-dominated "UNO" coalition. When the UDN rejoined ARDE in March 1984, the Chamorros charged that while in Honduras there had been efforts to manipulate them by "sectors which seek a return to the past and which still exercise too much influence in certain organizations"—a clear reference to the *somocista* presence in the FDN.[71]

Like the arms traffic issue, the question of whether Nicaragua poses a security threat to the United States is of major concern to foreign policy analysts and indeed to many critics of the Reagan Administration's Central America policy (see conclusion below). Analysts who emphasize the "Soviet threat" seem oblivious, however, to a long series of Nicaraguan initiatives intended to reassure the United States about its national security interests. In fact, "Nicaragua has shown no interest in allowing itself to be used as a Soviet forward base, and . . . the Soviet Union has shown no interest in paying the economic price of obtaining one."[72]

In the Kissinger *Report*, an individual note by San Antonio Mayor Henry Cisneros gives the only detailed consideration to the Nicaraguan initiatives.[73] Cisneros argues that:

> The Sandinista regime should be encouraged to intensify dialogue with the hierarchy of the Nicaraguan Catholic Church, the private sector, and the opposition parties; expand its offer of amnesty for anti-Sandinista rebels; introduce details of legislation to permit the free functioning of political parties and the promise of elections in 1985; eliminate censorship of the press; fulfill its recent promises to the opposition newspaper *La Prensa* to acquire newsprint; and reduce the numbers of Cuban advisers and Salvadoran rebel elements from Nicaragua.

Ironically, within a few months of the *Report's* appearance, many of these objectives had been fully or partially accomplished. While relations with the Church hierarchy remained tense, press censorship was relaxed around the November 1984 elections. Only after renewed Administration efforts on behalf

were all former Somoza Guard officers. See *Barricada Internacional*, March 8-14, 1983. This is substantially supported by the later revelations of ex-*contra* Edgar Chamorro, see "How the U.S. Should Handle Nicaragua." *The New York Times*, June 25, 1985, and by the reportage of *Washington Post* reporter Christopher Dickey in *With the Contras* (New York: Simon and Schuster, 1985).

[71] *La Nación Internacional*, March 8-14, 1984, p. 5.

[72] LeoGrande, "Through the Looking Glass," p. 269.

[73] *Report*, p. 154. Leiken, in "Overview" (pp. 19-20) also mentions these early diplomatic efforts.

of the *contras* was press censorship again reimposed. Many Salvadorans and Cubans departed. In late 1984 Nicaragua offered to sign the draft Contadora accord and opened talks with the Miskitu Indian opposition. The tentative conciliatory gestures of the Nicaraguan government may, of course, be reversed if conditions worsen and *contra* attacks intensify. Indeed, with the prospect of increased US aid for the *contras*, the "covert" war may in fact further polarization within Nicaraguan society and endanger regional peace.

It is clearly beyond the scope of this article to enumerate the distortions about Nicaragua emanating from Washington officials and their allied scholarly community. Nevertheless, it is important to note that certain canards have a way of repeating themselves, such as the story that the Soviets recognized the Sandinistas diplomatically only a day after the July 1979 revolution (in fact they did so in October). The allegation that the Sandinistas called for "a revolution without borders," repeated over and over by Administration spokesmen and used as the title for a September 1985 White Paper, was shown to be false by *The New York Times* in March 1985.[74] The *Times* also found that there was no basis for the statement, frequently attributed by President Reagan and other Administration spokespeople to Tomás Borge, that democratic Costa Rica would be "the dessert" in Nicaragua's foreign conquests.

COSTA RICA: THE DESSERT?

Costa Rica is often portrayed in the literature on Soviet-Cuban involvement in Central America as a defenseless country under direct assault by Cuban- or Nicaraguan-sponsored terrorism. The Kissinger *Report* states that

> Costa Rica has no armed force, only a small civil guard and a rural constabulary. These police forces must patrol a dangerous border and guard a democracy threatened by Central America's turbulent political currents. The provisions of U.S. law under which no aid can be provided to police organizations create a particularly absurd situation for Costa Rica. Because of these provisions, we are unable to furnish badly needed assistance to forces dedicated to the safeguarding of democracy.[75]

Although the *Report* is correct in noting the legal limitations on aid for foreign police, it is simply wrong when it suggests that this technicality has kept the United States from providing military aid to Costa Rica. In fact, since fiscal year 1982, the United States has provided $2 million annually to Costa Rica under the Military Assistance Program plus additional funds for training.

---

[74]   DOS, *Revolution Beyond Our Borders: Sandinista Intervention in Central America* (Washington: DOS, 1985); *The New York Times*, March 30, 1985. See also Saul Landau and Daniel Siegel, "Reagan's Penchant for 'Stretchers,'" *Los Angeles Times*, April 23, 1985.
[75]   *Report*, p. 120 (see also pp. 39, 115).

In fiscal years 1984 and 1985, the Reagan Administration provided $9 million annually in military aid for Costa Rica.[76] Moreover, in addition to the "small civil guard and rural constabulary," Costa Rica now has a 10,000 member militia, a highly efficient judicial police, several other specialized police bodies and a growing number of right-wing private paramilitary groups.[77]

The worst case interpretation of facts considered out of context is a major problem in the literature's treatment of Costa Rica. Leiken, for example, notes ominously that the leaders of the Costa Rican Popular Vanguard (Communist) Party [PVP] are among those endorsing "guerrilla warfare as a method," that they are among the parties for which "coordination or integration with organizations pursuing armed struggle . . . is now the order of the day," and that at the PVP's 13th congress "a special call was made for 'strengthening unity with other parties which have adopted Marxism-Leninism as their doctrine'"[78] The source on which the guerrilla war advocacy charge is based is one paragraph (not quoted by Leiken) from an interview with a PVP leader in *World Marxist Review* and it is actually quite equivocal:

> The communists are doing their utmost to win power with a minimum of violence and without bloodshed. To be sure, the circumstances may change abruptly and that would inevitably necessitate a different road and non-peaceful forms and methods of struggle.[79]

Clearly this is something less than a call to arms. Similarly, the unity plan to which Leiken refers was intended to establish an electoral coalition with the Costa Rican Socialist Party [PCS] and the Revolutionary People's Movement [MRP], not any sort of armed movement. All three parties in this coalition were emphatic in their condemnations of the ultra-left violence which briefly shook Costa Rica in 1981-1982.[80] Although some captured ultra-leftists had earlier belonged to these organizations, no evidence ever emerged linking the legal organizations of the Costa Rican left to violent acts.[81]

[76] See data cited in Marc Edelman, "Back from the Brink: How Washington Bailed Out Costa Rica," *Report on the Americas* 19, 6 (Nov.-Dec. 1985), p. 41. The Kissinger *Report* also claims (p. 119) erroneously that in Guatemala, the "armed forces have been able so far to contain the insurgency without assistance from abroad." In fact, Guatemala has received substantial aid from Israel since 1975. See George Black, "Israeli Connection: Not Just Guns for Guatemala," *Report on the Americas* 17, 3 (May-June 1983), pp. 43-45.
[77] Marc Edelman and Jayne Hutchcroft, "Costa Rica: Modernizing the non-Army," *Report on the Americas* 18, 2 (March-April 1984), pp. 9-11; *The Tico Times* [Costa Rica], March 18, 1983.
[78] *Soviet Strategy*, pp. 35-37.
[79] Comments of Arnoldo Ferreto in "Revolution: The Ways to Do It," *World Marxist Review* 22, 10 (October 1979), p. 63.
[80] *Libertad*, June 19-15, 1981; *La Nación*, July 3, 1981; Alvaro Montero, *Terrorismo y revolución* (San José: Ediciones Pensamiento Revolucionario, 1982).
[81] The Valentas nevertheless claim that those arrested belonged to the MRP. See "Soviet

Moreover, when a major factional split occurred in the Communist PVP in late 1983, the main issues in dispute were not guerrilla warfare and violence, but whether or not to break the PVP's implicit pact with the ruling social democrats by helping to organize more militant strikes and demonstrations against deteriorating living conditions.[82]

Much has also been made in the literature of supposed Nicaraguan involvement in terrorism in Costa Rica. The main source of this charge is another White Paper issued by the State and Defense Departments on May 27, 1983.[83] The paper asserts that "Cuba funded a new leftist political party designed to unify various leftist elements and attract broad popular support" and that "the Cubans and Sandinistas provided weapons and training for Costa Rican leftist terrorists." Costa Rica's three major newspapers are all quite conservative[84] and are generally eager to publish accusations like these. Yet few such allegations have appeared in the press and none have been substantiated.

The 1983 White Paper's treatment of supposed Nicaraguan complicity in the July 1982 bombing of the Honduran airlines office in San José is frequently seized upon uncritically by the writers concerned about the "Soviet threat" and was mentioned by President Reagan in a major 1984 policy speech.[85]

It is a revealing case, because it illustrates the extent to which events are manipulated and then selectively publicized or ignored in both the media and the scholarly literature. Germán Pinzón, a Colombian M-19 member, arrested for the bombing was acquitted of all charges on April 20, 1983, over a month before the White Paper was issued.[86] The prosecution presented no evidence other than a confession implicating Nicaraguan diplomats in the attack. Three diplomats were expelled from the country immediately after Pinzón's arrest. But shortly after the arrest, Pinzón retracted his confession, claiming it had been made under duress. Later a three-judge court ruled the confession inadmissible as evidence. It turned out that the suspect was a deserter from the Colombian army and may have been threatened with deportation at the time of his arrest. A former Costa Rican ambassador to Colombia, who was acquainted with Pinzón, described him in a telegram quoted in the press as having a "fantasizing and unreliable personality."[87] Nevertheless, in spite of the

---

Strategy," p. 256. This is untrue. The MRP, in fact, has since renamed itself the Movement for a New Republic and has moved ever closer to the country's ruling social democratic party.

[82]   *Libertad Revolucionaria,* January 21-28, 1984; Eduardo Mora, *Autocrítica y perspectiva revolucionaria en la construcción del Partido* (San José: XIV Congress PVP, 1984).

[83]   *Background Paper: Central America.* The end of Enders' tenure in the State Department was reportedly related to his doubts about the political efficacy of issuing this document, given the poor reception accorded the faulty 1981 White Paper.

[84]   Indeed, they are less diverse politically than the three major papers in Nicaragua.

[85]   Enders, p. 3; Leiken, "Overview," p. 11; *The New York Times,* May 10, 1984.

[86]   *La Prensa Libre* [Costa Rica], April 21, 1983.

[87]   *Semanario Universidad* [Costa Rica], September 10-16, 1982.

court acquittal and the questionable circumstances in which the suspect was brought to trial, the 1983 White Paper and subsequent Administration statements point to this case as an example of Nicaraguan perfidy and political analysts (and politicians) are quick to cite the White Paper, just as they did its 1981 predecessor.

Other cases of violence in Costa Rica might conceivably provide better ammunition for those wishing to demonstrate Nicaraguan support for terrorism. Such incidents include a 1982 grenade attack against the family of *contra* leader Fernando Chamorro, the 1983 explosion of a bomb—which may have been intended for ARDE leaders—that killed one Nicaraguan and wounded another, and the attack on *contra* leader Alfonso Robelo in November 1984. While efforts were made to link these cases to Nicaraguan espionage, no hard evidence emerged. In the 1983 incident, initial news reports cited ARDE spokesmen who claimed that those wounded while carrying the bomb were ARDE members, thus raising the possibility that the explosion was due to *contra* efforts.[88] Similarly, the 1984 attack on Robelo took place at a time of serious feuding among the Costa Rican-based *contra* organizations.

The assertion in some of the literature that Costa Rica's 1981 break with Cuba was due to meddling and diplomatic differences also requires some qualification. Leiken, who makes this claim, says nothing about the real context of the events (in which domestic factors were almost certainly of key importance).[89] Prior to the break in relations, there had been several violent incidents involving a small band of Costa Rican ultra-leftists. The group's lack of sophistication as guerrillas, as well as subsequent judicial investigations and trial testimony, revealed that they were domestically spawned and had no foreign ties. During the period, however, the extreme right Free Costa Rica Movement [MCRL] waged a major petition and publicity campaign blaming Cuba and the Soviet Union for fomenting subversion. The pretext for cutting relations was a harshly worded Cuban note (which Leiken mentions) responding to Costa Rica's intervention on behalf of Cuban exiles seeking an investigation of prison conditions on the island. Inexplicably (and unmentioned by Leiken), the Costa Rican government claimed the note was not received until May (which happened to be at the height of the MCRL campaign) even though it had supposedly been sent the previous January. The abrogation of Costa Rica's technical assistance treaty with the Soviet Union also occurred in May. Influential business leaders were quoted in the press at the time as saying that "now all that's lacking is to break [diplomatically] with the Soviet Union."[90]

---

88 Panama City ACAN, June 29, 1983 in *Foreign Broadcast Information Service-Latin America*, June 30, 1983, p. P1.
89 Leiken, *Soviet Strategy*, p. 97.
90 *The Tico Times*, May 15, 1981.

The fact that many Latin American students study in Moscow at Lumumba University is another element frequently cited as evidence of Soviet "penetration" in the region. It has been suggested that Costa Rica, in particular, is at risk because of the 675 students (in 1981) that were studying in the Soviet Union.[91] Yet the meaning of this fact is by no means self-evident, as the descriptions by returning Lumumba students of their experiences in the Soviet Union suggest. Many, if not most, Lumumba graduates probably go on to become Communist Party functionaries or enter academic or professional life with their pro-Soviet beliefs intact.

For a significant minority, however, the experience of life in the Soviet Union is disillusioning. Plutarco Hernández, a Costa Rican who studied at Lumumba University from 1965 to 1969 and who was in the Sandinista leadership prior to the overthrow of Somoza, describes the atmosphere among the Central Americans in Moscow:

> Little by little we developed a highly critical attitude which tended to question the old traditional values which constituted the theoretical arsenal of the communist parties of our countries. . . . This inevitably brought us ideological clashes and conflicts with the more orthodox *compañeros* in our party organizations and, to some degree, signified a challenge in the face of the pseudo-Marxist dogmatism of many *compañeros* and Soviet professors. The ideological struggle was in the open and we were disposed to fight the battle. . . . On one side were the traditional groups, the orthodox, those faithful to the Soviet foreign and domestic policy line, members of what was called the Latin American Students Federation. We dissidents were on the other side. We maintained a critical spirit in the face of the facts and rebelled at being treated and manipulated like simple sheep accustomed to a good ideological pastor.[92]

Hernández goes on to describe the violent repression of solidarity demonstrations by the Soviet militia, the convocation by the university rector of "a virtual political trial in which we had no right to defend ourselves," and various other experiences which, if they did not at first lead him away from being a revolutionary, certainly disabused him of many illusions about the Soviet Union.[93]

---

[91] For example, Rothenberg, "The Soviet and Central America," p. 145; Kissinger *Report*, p. 86; Leiken, *Soviet Strategy*, p. 71; Blasier, *Giant's Revival*, pp. 12-13.
[92] Plutarco Hernández, *El FSLN por dentro* (San José: Trejos hermanos, 1982), pp. 28-31. Similar experiences have been described by other third world students in the USSR. See Sergius Yakobson, "Russia and Africa," in Ivo Lederer, ed., *Russian Foreign Policy (New Haven: Yale University Press, 1962)*, p. 481.
[93] Hernández, who was identified with an ultra-left faction asked to leave Nicaragua shortly after the Sandinista victory, had by 1982 joined the ARDE *contras*.

From these descriptions, as well as from conversations with other Lumumba graduates, one cannot help but be skeptical of the reductionist view that the 675 Costa Ricans (or the many others) studying in Moscow will necessarily become simple pawns of a "foreign penetration" of their country.

CONCLUSION: ALTERNATIVE METHODOLOGIES, ALTERNATIVE POLICIES

The first conclusion that emerges from analyzing the literature on Soviet-Cuban involvement in Central America is that US policy makers and analysts frequently are abysmally ignorant of the Central American region. Many are given to assertions that rely on very questionable evidence. To the extent that these assertions underly current discussions about US policy, either as the "scientific" basis of that policy or as props intended to garner political legitimacy, they clearly must be viewed and evaluated not only on their own terms, but as products of a particular climate in the policy making and research communities—one in which scholarly integrity sometimes takes second place to ideologically motivated concerns. The largely deductive approach and the simplistic textual exegeses, which form the basis for much of the literature, are too often isolated from the study of other events and processes and consequently lead to a sterile and distorted vision of reality. Moreover, the methods appropriate for studying the Soviet Union itself are not necessarily sufficient for understanding Central America, where different types of sources are available and other kinds or processes have been taking place.[94] Similarly, to ignore or neglect the history of US intervention is to employ a methodology fraught with faulty assumptions and guaranteed to produce highly dubious conclusions.

Second, the questionable understandings derived from flawed conceptual and methodological premises often lead to alarmist views of the policy issues confronting the United States. Anti-interventionist, "regionalist" scholars implicitly downplay the importance of local political forces by defining Soviet-Cuban involvement as their object of study. They thus sometimes contribute (albeit unwittingly) to this alarmism. The alarmist approach is epitomized in the literature's discussion of the threat Marxist states and movements potentially or actually pose to US sea lanes.[95] Proponents of this argument rarely

---

[94] The "Kremlinological" emphasis of much of the literature is often so pronounced that efforts to measure Soviet commitment to Nicaragua, for example, are made on the basis of the frequency of certain buzz words (the main one being "socialist orientation") in Soviet publications, rather than on the basis of publically available data about, say, trade and aid packages.

[95] Joseph Cirincione and Leslie Hunter, "Military Threats, Actual and Potential," in Leiken, ed., *Central America*; Kissinger *Report* ,pp. 111, 145, 147; Leiken, *Soviet Strategy,*

note that in this age of supertankers and extra-wide aircraft carriers and battle-ships, the relatively narrow Panama canal, while still of major significance, is probably declining in economic and military importance;[96] that political in-surgency per se does not threaten sea lanes in the same way that, say, a Soviet base on Pacific Central America might;[97] or that sea lane interdiction has very low priority in Soviet strategic doctrine.[98]

Finally, as one critic suggests, the sea lanes argument is based on a series of increasingly unlikely assumptions: that Central American revolutionary regimes would adopt an anti-US and pro-Soviet national security stance and grant the Soviet Union bases; that such a regime would be able to weather the cut-off of all economic relations with the United States implied by such a posture and would be able to extract economic concessions from the Soviet Union like those now granted Cuba; that in a situation of war between the United States and the Soviet Union, the only context in which it is possible to conceive an attack on US shipping, there would not be the nuclear escala-tion which would make sea lanes largely irrelevant strategically; and finally, given overwhelming US conventional superiority in the region, it must be assumed "that a Central American government would be prepared to commit suicide in order to give the Soviet Union a marginal and fleeting advantage in a global war."[99]

As Wayne Smith reminds the panicked worst-case enthusiasts,

> There hasn't been a Soviet missile or nuclear submarine in a Cuban port since 1974. There have not been any Soviet bombers flying out of Cuban airfields since 1962. . . . The Cubans don't have a navy that could

---

pp. 42, 62; Moorer and Fauriol, passim. The most extreme statement of SLOC (sea lanes of communication) fear is Wesley McDonald, "Atlantic Security—The Cuban Factor," *Jane's Defence Weekly*, 2, 24 (December 22, 1984), pp. 1107-11.

[96]   Robert Henriques and Luis Goldring, "U.S. Strategic Interests in Central America," in Stanford Network, eds., *Revolution in Central America*.

[97]   Viron Vaky, a career diplomat with long experience in Latin America, includes the sea lanes argument among the "'kitchen sink' arguments . . . [which] are adduced to rally every possible justification for courses of action already chosen for other reasons." See "Reagan's Central American Policy: An Isthmus Restored," in Leiken, ed., *Central America*, p. 240.

[98]   Cirincione and Hunter, pp. 176ff.

[99]   LeoGrande, "Through the Looking Glass," pp. 268-69. It is too often forgotten, as R.W. Johnson points out with respect to Africa, that "the whole idea of Russian submarines starving the West into submission by a strategy of protracted interdiction or blockage was . . . absurdly nineteenth century in its conception. The very first ship sinking, after all, would constitute a major act of war and the nuclear bombers and missiles would be in the air only a few minutes later." *How Long Will South Africa Survive?* (New York: Oxford University Press, 1977), p. 213.

threaten our sea-lanes in any serious way. They have two diesel-powered submarines, perhaps they'll acquire more.[100]

The real issues, which link the realms of both social science methodology and policy making, are whether the United States (and by extension, US policy analysts) are willing to accept that in Central America decades of poverty and despotism (for which US policies are in some measure responsible) often give rise to revolutionary movements; that these movements, even if they receive moral encouragement and small amounts of material assistance from abroad, would occur whether or not there existed a state of global confrontation between the United States and the Soviet Union; that, given past US actions, these movements are unlikely to express friendship for or trust in the US government, but that they are generally willing to adapt to what the US government considers its basic national security interests as long as this does not threaten their own national sovereignty and independence; and that the political institutions which emerge in post-revolutionary Central America will be greatly affected by the postures assumed by the US government today.

Every instance of US intransigence toward Central America both confirms what many in the region have long suspected about the United States and limits the options available to revolutionary movements and goverments. The emergence of armed struggle reflects the fact that these options have already been narrowed by years of reactionary despotism. To restrict these options further still compounds the tremendous responsibility the United States already bears for contributing to this historical legacy and for having been largely silent during Central America's long years of suffering.

[100] "The Failure of Statecraft," in Joseph Cirincione, ed., *Central America and the Western Alliance* (New York: Holmes & Meier, 1985), p. 185.

9

The Dual Strategy Myth in Central American Policy

Mary Vanderlaan

The Reagan administration is sending mixed messages on its policy in Central America, leading some observers to label the policy "schizoid" and influencing yet others to give the president the benefit of the doubt until policy implications become clearer or unavoidable. Commenting in July on White House policy as it has been iterated in the first half of 1983, Senator Christopher Dodd (1983), a leading administration critic, asserted that "there is total confusion in Washington as to what the administration's policies are, and there is a total confusion in Central America as to what U.S. intentions are." Similar charges have been made from both sides of the aisle in Congress.

Almost sadly, these charges are not part of an opposition's political ploy, but in fact are rooted in speeches, position papers, and actions formulated by the president and his Central America policy team.[1] My own experiences attest to the source of the confusion. In August 1983, I made my second trip in a year to Central America. Visiting Nicaragua and Honduras, I interviewed a broad range of people in and out of government and across socioeconomic classes in an effort both to assess the political mood in each country in this tense period, and to witness firsthand the working and impact of U.S. policy in the region. If there is one condition that could tie together succinctly my observations, it would be this: Not only does U.S. policy bear little resemblance to Central American realities and needs, but the enunciated policy also bears little relationship to foreign policy activities.

From the *Journal of Interamerican Studies and World Affairs*, v 26 n 2, May 1984, pp. 199-244. © 1984 Sage Publications, Inc. Reprinted by permission of the Institute of Interamerican Studies, University of Miami.

† Author's Note: I would like to thank Professor John O. Lindell and three anonymous reviewers for their comments on an earlier draft of this article.

1 I will focus primarily on policy positions and actions taken during 1983.

Indeed there is a rather large and growing discrepancy between verbal policy statements or descriptions and U.S. foreign policy moves in the region—a discrepancy between words and actions. The purpose of this article is to consider one aspect of the confusion about Central American policy. Putting aside for now the issue of pertinence or suitability of U.S. policy, here the task will be to juxtapose the words and actions in an effort to assess which speak louder. To this end I first will review U.S. policy as it is outlined by administration officials—our word politics—and second, examine major U.S. foreign policy activity in the same period.

THE WORDS

Administration public policy pronouncements essentially focus on the theme that the United States has a dual strategy in Central America. The first strategy, the provision of military assistance, exists to make a second one possible, that is, support for reform, human rights, and democratic institutions. After being advised by his aides in February 1983 to take his case to the American public, President Reagan in the following months outlined the dual strategy in several major speeches. In his March 10 speech before the National Association of Manufacturers, the president argued that in Central America "the strategic stakes are too high for us to ignore the danger of governments seizing power there with ideological and military ties to the Soviet Union," and that "the Communist agenda" is to "strike at the heart of the Western Hemisphere." The president continued by highlighting a dual strategy (Reagan, 1983e):

> We will be submitting a comprehensive, integrated, economic and military assistance plan for Central America. First we will bridge the existing gap in military assistance. . . . Second, we will work to support reform, human right and democracy. . . . By acting responsibly and avoiding illusory shortcuts, we can be both loyal to our friends and true to our peaceful, democratic principles.

Again in his April 27, 1983, speech before a joint session of Congress, the president presented a policy of giving military assistance not "as an end in itself, but as a shield for democratization, economic development and diplomacy," where "with better training and material help, our neighbors can hold off the guerrillas and give democratic reform time to take root." As the president explained, "This means using our assistance, our powers of persuasion, and our legitimate leverage to bolster humane democratic systems."

It is also in this speech that the president for the first time claims U.S. security interests worldwide are threatened by unrest in Central America, thereby upping the stakes for policy in the region, while presenting a near-crisis atmosphere (Reagan, 1983d):

> In summation, I say to you that tonight there can be no question: the national security of all the Americas is at stake in Central America. If we cannot defend ourselves there, we cannot expect to prevail elsewhere. Our credibility would collapse, our alliances would crumble, and the safety of our homeland would be put in jeopardy. We have a vital interest, a moral duty and a solemn responsibility.

Echoing the dual strategy policy that our purpose is to move on two fronts, Secretary of State Shultz in April presented the administration's case for increased military aid to Salvador. In a letter to Representative Long of the House Appropriations Subcommittee on Foreign Operations, Shultz (*New York Times*, 1983b) argued:

> Without military assistance to provide security for the people of Salvador, there can be no progress in achieving social justice and improving human rights. The military effort is essential to provide the shield we need to succeed in our broader efforts. We do not seek a military solution. But we do seek enough military assistance to make possible a longer-term and more meaningful peace in Central America.

President Reagan (1983c) returned to this theme in his June 28 news conference and in the July 18 speech to the International Longshoremen. Denying any plans for sending U.S. troops to the region, but insisting that presidents can "never say never," he continued as follows:

> They need us to help them with training to provide arms and munitions so that they can defend themselves while they're instituting these democratic reforms.

And in July (Reagan, 1983b):

> Of all the words I've spoken today, let me underline these especially: America's emphasis in Central America is on economic and social progress, not on a purely military solution. But to give democracy and development a chance to work in the face of increasing attacks, we are providing a shield of military training and assistance to help our neighbors protect themselves.

As presented, U.S. policy seeks to use military means to buy time and present a protective shield so that democratic institution building and socio-economic reform can take place in an atmosphere where the reforms can take root. A variation of the two-strategy theme presents the military shield paving the way for economic aid from the United States to spur regional growth and development. Yet another variation suggests that a military strategy makes possible a strategy of negotiation. In his April letter requesting additional military assistance for Salvador, Secretary Shultz says it is the U.S. purpose to "find a basis for dialogue" (although "the U.S. will not support negotiations for power sharing") and that "we favor a negotiating process which would lead the way to a political solution." Likewise, the president in his March address defended his policy as one seeking not a military solution, but where "negotiations are already a key part of our policy. We support negotiations among all the nations of the region to strengthen democracy."

The consistent and central public theme then is that the United States does not seek a military solution through military victory over insurgents who challenge regional governments. But a military strategy of aid, training, and advice is necessary to make other things possible—socioeconomic reform, economic growth, diplomacy, and so forth. The military strategy is justified as creating an atmosphere of stability or guaranteeing the maintenance of current ruling groups that can meanwhile sponsor change.

THE PHILOSOPHY

That U.S. policy has been characterized carefully by officials in the last year as one in pursuit of a dual strategy is no accident. Clearly, the emphasis on a military response and what is seen as an intrusion into the hemisphere by Eastern bloc forces grows out of a wider administration world view. But the rejection of a policy stressing military activity by important sectors within and outside the White House has caused administration spokespersons and the president to react by playing down military aspects of U.S. presence in the region. A concerted, high-level effort has been made to highlight nonmilitary aspects of U.S. policy. The dual strategy policy has evolved in reaction to domestic politics.

Since 1981 Reagan's administration has placed conflicts in Central America into the context of an East-West struggle, pursuing a regional policy that disregards not only individual sociopolitical and historical realities of these states, but also largely ignores indigenous root causes of civil unrest.[2] For example, in his July 26, 1983 news conference the president again insisted that "the trouble that is going on down there comes from outside the area, is revolution exported from the Soviet Union and from Cuba and from others of their allies." Moreover, it increasingly has become evident in the last year

2   Leslie Gelb reported in the *New York Times* on April 22, 1982, that some State Department policy "doubters" would prefer to emphasize the specific situations in each Central American country and that these same people question the communist "contagion" image presented by the administration. Other critics have been charging the administration with perpetuating Cold War containment and brinksmanship strategies in the region.

that the administration sees the situations in El Salvador, Nicaragua, and Honduras in particular as inextricably linked, as part of the same problem for the United States. Indicative of this philosophical approach is the president's charge that "an aggressive minority has thrown in its lot with the Communists, looking to the Soviets and their own Cuban henchmen to help them pursue political changes through violence. Nicaragua has become their base."[3] Likewise, speeches by Enders, Kirkpatrick, Sanchez, Shultz, Bush and others raised the specter of dominoes falling in the direction of Mexico and Texas. A June 1983 U.S. State Department (1983) release asserts: "The new form of dictatorship is that of a command economy and a self-appointed elitist vanguard, imposed by guerrilla war. Nicaragua has become its base and Central America is its target."

Moreover, the U.S. military buildup of Honduras, the training of Salvadorans there and the support of anti-Sandinist *"contras"* all grow out of this regional perspective as does the position that a strong military response is needed. The stress on the military strategy is invigorated by concerns over losses by the Salvadoran army and the reported failure of counter-revolutionary efforts in Nicaragua in the last year.

Running even deeper as a philosophical foundation for a military strategy, however, is the dictum elaborated by Ambassador Kirkpatrick in 1979 that dictatorships have potential for evolving democratically, whereas totalitarianism (read communism) leaves no room for such an event. Following from her argument, the United States should support friendly authoritarian governments, however bloody, when "Marxist" elements attempt to overthrow the traditional order (Kirkpatrick, 1979).[4] The administration long has labeled Nicaragua a communist, totalitarian regime that "wages war on its own people," while praising Salvadoran and Honduran democracy and Ríos Montt's moderation (Montt was overthrown by General Mejia on August 8, 1983). That the personal dictatorships of Latin America that Kirkpatrick uses in her model are mostly a thing of 20 years past has not kept this position from becoming administration credo. The old style dictatorships have been replaced by institutionalized, bureaucratic ruling groups (often technocratic armies) that are supported by business, church, and professional interest groups hoping to mediate policy. Such regimes ultimately work against democratic openings.

But the insistence that the United States indeed is following a dual strategy also comes in response to growing congressional and Pentagon discontent with administration policy and the public's concern about eventual American troop deployments, all of which came to a head in spring and summer of 1983. As congressional committees threatened military assistance cutoffs and

---

[3] This particular charge is repeated in President Reagan's March 10, April 27, June 28, July 18, and July 26 speeches.
[4] For a cogent critique of this work, see Farer (1981).

opinion polls registered public disapproval, the administration redoubled efforts to stress nonmilitary aspects of U.S. policy and what it said were movements toward social and democratic reforms in Salvador and Honduras.

The State Department's public information bureau was ordered to beef up its attempts to educate the public due to the president's belief that discontent exists because "we haven't adequately explained our policy," and because there had been a negative "drumbeat" sounded by the press that had induced public "suspicion that somehow there is an ulterior purpose in this."

Pressure from Congress resulted in the president giving more attention to the issues of negotiation as evidenced by his appointment of a roving negotiator for the region and his measured praise for the Contadora process. That these efforts came in direct response to recent domestic politics is clear from a statement by an unnamed high administration official (Gelb, 1983):

> The feeling was that we could negotiate an agreement on El Salvador or Nicaragua. Notwithstanding, we decided in February that we needed to move on the diplomatic side to deflect the perception of our policy going for a military solution.

Interestingly, some Pentagon and Defense Department personnel have joined in pressuring the Reagan team to back away from a large military involvement. Arguing that the issues are mainly internal, political, and economic and that the president has not evinced a commitment to military action from the American people or Congress, the Joint Chiefs and lower-level officers have advised the president against military solutions. Bearing scars from the Vietnam experience, military officers contend that unless a government is willing and able to promote fundamental economic and political reform while providing internal security, there is little a U.S. effort could accomplish (Halloran, 1983a). This attitude and the fact that public opinion has limited U.S. military options is reflected in the Defense Department position that it would be better for long-term U.S. interests to pull out of Central America now, that if U.S. efforts are "hobbled and trimmed back" by opposition, "the chances of failure are high."[5]

These domestic forces together have necessitated the public portrayal of U.S. Central America policy as pursuing a dual strategy where a military shield protects processes of reforms and negotiation. Pressed to produce a foreign policy victory for his administration in a context of apparent failures to date in Central America, the Middle East, and Southern Africa, and to have something to show for Shultz's first anniversary as Secretary of State, President Reagan on July 26 sought to convince Americans that the United States was on a steady course for peace in Central America. He contended that the

---

[5] The Department of Defense position is outlined in an administration working paper dated July 8 and reported on by Philip Taubman (1983c).

various elements of U.S. policy are "being pursued simultaneously in a carefully balanced manner" (Reagan, 1983a).

CONFUSION, IMBALANCE

But a wary public and Congress continues to voice confusion about U.S. intentions in Central America. Concern over how balanced the policy was increased considerably, moreover, with the administration's sudden announcement in mid-June of major military exercises in the region that would continue into 1984. The announcement surprised even U.S. diplomats in the region. Press accounts of administration intentions to seek a 40% increase in military funds for Latin allies added to the inquietude. The apprehensions of critics at home and abroad in fact prompted the president to hold a special press conference in an attempt to allay fears of an impending war or a Vietnam-like involvement.

Yet as I argued earlier, the confusion over Central American policy is rooted in actual gaps between public words and policy actions and between public statements and private policy descriptions leaked to the press by foreign policy administrators critical of current policy. In effect, despite all their words, the administration in practice is implementing a military solution in Central America, or more to the point given domestic restraints, is attempting a military solution. To that end, the United States is maneuvering to manipulate and control as much as possible political events in Central America.

Although there is much evidence pointing to this conclusion, I will focus on several major policy actions and revelations during 1983. These involve regional strategy and policy directions outlined in National Security Council options papers, recent military and diplomatic personnel shifts in the region, the militarization of Honduras, U.S. support for Somocista counter-revolutionaries (*contras*), and the events surrounding the U.S. invasion of Grenada.

Two recently leaked working documents give insight into the administration's thinking on Central American policy. The first document, dated April 1982, is a National Security Council (NSC) report entitled "U.S. Policy in Central America and Cuba Through F.Y. '84, Summary Paper," and summarized NSC projections for regional policy. The second document is a working paper prepared for the White House by a NSC task force and dated July 8, 1983.[6] Neither document suggests the dual strategy approach presented in public speeches nor emphasizes a balanced approach to regional issues. Indeed the focus of both documents is to highlight military and intelligence issues and U.S. options, while stressing an active Cuban-Soviet influence in the region. In one telling section the 1982 document states, "Strategically, we have

---

[6]   Texts and synopses of these documents were printed in the *New York Times*, April 7 and July 17, 1983.

a vital interest in not allowing the proliferation of Cuban-model states.
. . . In the short run we must work to eliminate Cuban/Soviet influence
in the region and in the long run we must build politically stable governments."

The April 1982 policy summary targets what decision makers perceived as
problems weakening U.S. policy efforts and therefore recommits the United
States to strengthening counterinsurgency capabilities in El Salvador and
Guatemala, improving military capacities, policy coordination, and collective
security among ally states, increasing covert pressure on Nicaragua and Cuba,
and improving intelligence collection in ally and other Central American
states.

A major policy problem addressed in this document concerns congressional and public opinion on U.S. policy, which the NSC concluded
"jeopardizes our ability to stay the course." The document outlines public relations efforts to woo or to neutralize Congress and the public. Among the efforts would be campaigns to "build up public pressure against Cuba" and to
"turn around" Mexico and Social Democrats in Europe from their support of
leftists, while disseminating more State Department materials defining the issues. Central to the effort is a commitment to "step up efforts to co-opt the
negotiations issue to avoid Congressionally mandated negotiations which
would work against our interests." The document makes clear the NSC intention for eventual "negotiations and compromise on our terms."

U.S. economic aid to the region, moreover, is discussed not in a context
of concern for the objective life conditions of the majority poor, but in the
context of "our efforts to stabilize the situation" and the contribution of such
aid: "[to] achieving domestic political support," to "correcting severe social
dislocations which foment and aid insurgency," and to avoiding "political dis-
integration in Salvador and Guatemala" ultimately, to moving toward U.S.
objectives for these states. Characteristic of the Reagan approach to the region,
economic aid is discussed jointly with plans to increase intelligence activity
and military training.

In sum, the April 1982 document presents a picture of decision makers
intent on policy "constance," despite increasing skepticism at home and abroad
about the direction, purpose, and implications of U.S. policy, and despite the
realization that the U.S.-supported Salvadoran and Guatemalan governments
are politically weak and disintegrating. Their policy intent—to work
consistently overtly and covertly against any "Cuban-modeled" and non-U.S.
aligned states emerging in the area—is clear.

A reading of the July 1983 document suggests that there had been little
attitudinal change in the intervening 15 months. Yet the continued and growing domestic opposition to administration policy is reflected in the language
of urgency, exemplified by the claim that issues "are nearing a critical point."
Again policymakers recognize congressional opposition. But the strategy now

is to co-opt dissent by stressing a need for bipartisan support in a near-crisis period and for improved military-political performance in Salvador. Reflecting another reality, the document discusses policy disagreements between the State and Defense Departments.

The stress remains, however, on security-military issues, the "communist threat" to the Caribbean and "the political structure in Mexico." The central theme of the paper is the need to take "timely and effective action" now, as there is still opportunity to limit Soviet/Cuban influence without introducing U.S. troops. The assumption, reiterated by Henry Kissinger in July, is that the United States can and should manage Central America.[7] To that end and arguing that "the United States has the power and the resources to prevent such outcomes," policymakers urge a "sizable" increase (in the 40% range) in military aid to Salvador, Guatemala, and Honduras; an upgrading of the Salvadoran army; prepositioning of military equipment in Honduras; building air and sea forces in Honduras; intensifying covert action against the Sandinista government; CIA planning for Salvadoran army hits against rebel camps in Honduras, and the like. Meanwhile, PR efforts would highlight U.S. support for peace efforts in order to shape congressional policy and "to surmount even greater opposition."

Both private administration documents in sum fail to project commitment to policy balance between military-intelligence actions and activity in areas of socioeconomic and political reform. Nor is much energy given to developing strategies for negotiation or other nonmilitary initiatives. In fact where the creation of a blue-ribbon bipartisan commission on long-term Central American policy is discussed in the second document, it also is asserted that such a body would not have veto powers over nor "impinge" on presidential powers. In short, the documents yield little evidence of a dual strategy.

PERSONNEL SHIFTS

Another series of events suggests that current policy opts for military solutions. Since February and March 1983, and with interagency disputes over policy tactics (not goals), decision-making momentum moved from Thomas Enders and the State Department to become consolidated under more ideological and action-oriented White House, military, and intelligence officials. According to administration officials, regional policy has been shaped by National Security Advisor William Clark (who left the Department), U.N. Ambassador Jeane Kirkpatrick, and CIA Director William Casey, notwithstanding

---

[7] Just after being appointed to head the President's Commission, Kissinger stated that (Gwertzman, 1983a), "If we cannot manage Central America, it will be impossible to convince threatened nations in the Persian Gulf and in other places that we know how to manage global equilibrium. We will face a series of upheavals."

Secretary Shultz's attempts to regain policy control for the State Department's experienced diplomats. Policy disputes and fighting for turf between the White House team and State Department officials flared several times during 1983.

The transferral of policy authority away from State reflects a struggle among competing foreign policy decision-making bodies—White House and NSC staff, the State Department, Defense and Pentagon personnel, and the intelligence community—at a time when policy is being challenged rigorously and when U.S.-supported operations in Salvador and Nicaragua at best are stalemated. Assistant Secretary of State for Inter-American Affairs Enders had dominated regional policymaking up until May 1983. In the latter part of that month, both Enders and Hinton, U.S. Ambassador to Salvador, were replaced. The reasons for their removal illuminate the nature of U.S. policy in Central America.

In congressional and other forums during the first half of 1983 and demonstrating a sensitivity to congressional concern over policy practicability, Enders promoted a 2-track policy. In this conception, military aid to Salvador would continue while the United States also sought negotiations with the FMLN and among other contending forces in the region. As Enders posed the main question for U.S. policy, the administration had to choose between emphasizing this dual approach or stressing military successes in Central America. When the CIA later produced a White Paper reiterating Soviet and Cuban support for subversives, Enders sat on it, labeling it "tendentious" and without new information, and thus angered CIA and Pentagon officials. At the same time he responded to Richard Stone's appointment as Special Envoy with complaints that the State Department was being circumvented and shorn of its policy authority.

Enders's support for Deane Hinton in Salvador also contributed to his decline. Although Hinton was rebuked by a White House official for his speech before Salvador businessmen in which he equated the guilt of right-wing death squads ("gorillas") and leftist guerrillas in destroying Salvador (quoted in Weintraub, 1983), Enders earlier had approved the text. Enders supported Hinton's attempts to keep rightist politicians from dominating Salvadoran politics after the March 1982 election, an effort designed to move Salvador toward democratic development, thereby gaining congressional support for administration policy. Such support was crucial especially as it was becoming clearer to the Reagan team that a long-term regional commitment was necessary to prevent a leftist victory. Both Enders and Hinton were committed to military success over the guerrillas, a basic policy objective. The disagreement that was emerging in the administration, however, was over tactics.

As domestic turmoil over policy grew, so did White House resentment of Enders's domination over policy. When U.S. military support appeared to be producing little payoff in reduced guerrilla strength, touching off administration fear of "losing" Salvador, the president and his NSC policy team moved to take control over policymaking. Clark and Kirkpatrick's contention that Enders was letting the region "slip away" by not working hard enough to win increased military aid and political support from Congress reflected the harder ideological line at the White House. Although the president had verbalized a commitment on April 27 to a dual approach, administration officials revealed that others at the White House were urging a more dramatic initiative by the president to turn the tide. Clark, moreover, was said to be angered by Enders's emphasis on negotiations. In this scenario Enders, a staunch anticommunist who had built his career on this reputation, was presented as a policy moderate.[8]

Even more illuminating of policy, however, is a consideration of the team of White House, military, and intelligence officials of the NSC who moved to take over policy in Central America. While Clark, Kirkpatrick, and Casey appear as the Big Three of policy in 1983, Defense Secretary Weinberger, Envoy Stone, Ambassador-at-large General Vernon Walters, Deputy Assistant Secretary of Defense for Inter-American Affairs Nestor Sanchez and Undersecretary of Defense for Policy Fred C. Iklé also influenced policy direction and had easy access to the president. Each of these officers has a solid reputation for ideological rigidity, an East-West world view, and conservative politics. Sanchez, for instance, who recently was characterized as being "the soul of the Reagan Administration's policy toward Central America," earlier worked for the CIA in Latin America and is "fervent about defeating the spread of communism" there. As the Pentagon's man on Central America, he approved the Defense Department's involvement in CIA operations in the region (Taubman, 1983d).

Military and intelligence communities, action-oriented bodies, figure squarely in current U.S. policy. Enders's replacement at State, Langhorne Motley, fits nicely into the mold. Named ambassador to Brazil in 1981, his only diplomatic experience, Motley is a former Air Force officer who served in Panama in the 1960s and worked with U.S. counterinsurgency programs throughout Latin America. But CIA Director Casey, who reportedly has bypassed senior aides to direct personally U.S. covert actions against Nicaragua (the largest such action since Vietnam), also gives daily intelligence briefs to the president as a member of the NSC. Commenting on this, a CIA official recently remarked, "How can you run an invasion and at the same time provide objective reports about the country you're invading?"

A major shake-up and upgrading of military leadership in Central America during 1983 points to further efforts at greater preparedness in the Caribbean. Four veterans of leadership positions in Vietnam, all generals, have been placed in influential posts in Central America. General John Wickam replaces

---

[8]   This led Representative Michael Barnes, Chair of the House Foreign Affairs Subcommittee on Latin America, to comment (Gwertzman, 1983b), "For anyone to imagine that Tom Enders is some kind of a left-leaner is a pretty strange argument to make."

General Edward Meyer as new Army Chief of Staff. General Paul Gorman, promoted to a 4-star general, replaces General Wallace Nutting as head of the U.S. Southern Command in Panama, while Nutting has been promoted to command the Green Berets based in Florida. Lt. General Robert Schweitzer is the new chair of the Inter-American Defense Board (Inter-Religious Task Force, 1983). General Nutting in particular has been vocal in the last year about a military role in Central America. In March 1981, he told Honduran army commander Alverez that the United States will support Honduras in any conflict with Nicaragua. In 1982 he sounded warning about nickel and diming in Salvador, arguing for a long-term U.S. presence in Central America where Guatemala was the big prize. More recently he has argued for an open-ended commitment in the region with a "national consensus behind a free presidential hand."[9]

In short, personnel and power shifts in decision circles belie the public claim that the United States pursues a balanced approach in the region and suggest instead the consolidation of a hard-line and military stance.

THE MILITARIZATION OF HONDURAS

A more concrete example of the high priority given to a strong military posture and preparedness exists in Honduras, the poorest state in Central America and the site of 1983-1984 joint U.S. maneuvers, unprecedented in the region for their magnitude.[10] During the last two years, Honduras has been built with U.S. aid into a formidable regional military power, prompting politicians across a broad political spectrum there to charge not only that Honduras is the "pawn" of the United States, but also that Honduran democracy has been subverted by General Gustavo Alverez Martinez and his attempts to build a national security state there (on the model of Argentina). In such a state, an all-encompassing role for the armed forces is envisioned where they are the guarantors of internal and external peace. Pointing to evidence of such a trend

---

[9]   Vietnam-era military men recently have been reflecting on lessons from that war. Col. Harry Sumner in *On Strategy* (1983), for example, argues that a major strategic failure in that war was the failure to invoke the national will and that Johnson failed to rally the nation and Congress for war by creating a prowar psychology. Other military leaders have advised President Reagan to stay away from committing troops to battle in Central America without first forging domestic political support for such action. But they have also expressed the opinion that the United States must be ready and willing to "confront the main adversaries" in Central America, the Soviets and Cuba (see Taubman, 1983d).

[10]   In congressional testimony on August 4, Secretary of State Shultz confirmed what many observers were saying about the large maneuvers in Honduras and the fleets sent at the same time to patrol off Nicaragua's Atlantic and Pacific shores—that they were much more than routine. Relinquishing earlier contentions by administration officials that the large presence in the region should be seen as routine and defending the administration's policy stance, Shultz (Taubman, 1983b) said the military moves were "designed to make a point."

in Honduras, an opposition spokesman charged, "They require internal control of the politics and the economy. Whoever is against them is wrong and must be neutralized."[11] Supporting that view, Adolfo León Gómez, respected Honduran law professor, commented, "The army is isolating itself from the central government, is converting itself into an independent entity of public administration." (U.S.-El Salvador Research Group, l983a).

This reality is only too obvious to the visitor. In Tegucigalpa, uniformed, armed men are posted on every corner, outside banks and government offices, and at major intersections.[12] As an opposition Congress member in Honduras outlined to me in a recent interview, the new antisubversion law Decree 33 is being used to jail peasant and labor leaders, to evict peasants from land they have reclaimed, and to intimidate unions into accepting management's terms. The decree's effectiveness is reflected in a dramatic decline in the number of strikes in Honduras in the last two years.

That Reagan's aid to Honduras focuses on creating a military bulwark— Honduras borders Nicaragua, El Salvador and Guatemala—no matter the domestic effects of such aid, also is reflected in aid figures and Honduras' socioeconomic position. While total economic assistance to Honduras decreased by 50% from previous levels in fiscal year 1981, total security assistance that year zoomed upward 300% over the previous year to $8.94 million. By the end of 1982 total military assistance had jumped to $68 million and economic aid totalled $82 million, down from $127.6 million in 1980. For 1983 Reagan requested an additional $17 million over the $20.3 million allocated by Congress for military aid. The president's request for 1984 is $41 million in military aid and $40 million in economic support funds (Morrell and Biddle, 1983; Instituto Histórico Centroamericano, 1983b).

Meanwhile, during his trip to Washington in June 1983, General Alverez told the administration that Honduras needed $400 million in military aid over the next three years. He also revealed that the Defense Department has agreed to ask Congress for a large increase in assistance (Institute for Central American Studies, 1983b). Alverez's argument, one also made by the U.S. embassy

---

[11] Similar charges were made August 18-22, 1983, by a number of Honduran congressmen and politicians during interviews with them in Tegucigalpa. Among them: Manuel Acosta Bonilla of the National Party, former minister of finance; Efraín Díaz Arrivillaga, an economist who holds the only Christian Democratic seat in Congress; Jorge Arturo Reina, secretary general of the ALIPO faction of the Liberal Party, and Carlos Montoya, vice president of Congress (see also the *Miami Herald*, August 21, 1983).

[12] Across the street from the hotel I used on my recent trip stands the headquarters of the DIN, Honduras' secret police, which is said to have 80,000 "ears" (informers) among the four million Hondurans. In my five days there I witnessed a steady stream of prisoners being led inside, thumbs tied behind their backs with string or wire, by pistol-carrying men in Daytona Beach and other assorted T-shirts. The family members hovering outside this building around the clock bore a sad witness to the liberality with which the new antisubversion law Decree 33 is being enforced in Honduras today.

in Tegucigalpa, is that Honduras' security is the United States' security and that Honduras is holding the line against communist advance in Central America. At a news conference in Tegucigalpa on August 17, General Alverez made his position clear: What happens now in Central America "is going to depend on the decisions that the U.S. government takes. If the United States helps us now, we will not need help later." Otherwise, "the United States will have to intervene directly or lose Central America" (Gugliotta, 1983). By late November, Alverez's position took on the tone of a challenge (*New York Times*, 1983a):

> I've always said that we are in business with the United States. There's an important interest for the United States, which is regional security. For us it's a vital security. All this implies a price. With aid we can maintain peace. If you don't want to help us now, you'll have to pay a higher cost politically, logistically, and in lives.

Indeed, emboldened by and exuberant over U.S. military commitments in 1981-1983, Alverez and the Honduran government presented a document to the United States in October requesting: $10 billion in aid over 12 years, a continuing U.S. presence and a special bilateral defense treaty (on the model of the U.S.-South Korean treaty). It was revealed later by a member of the ruling Liberal Party's ALIPO faction, Jorge Arturo Reina, that the document also asked the United States to consider Honduras for Free Associated State Status (Institute for Central American Studies, 1983a).

The new and reinvigorated air force, navy and radar bases, the miles of newly paved roads, the army training centers, and the large number of U.S. military advisers (240-300 by mid-1983) in Honduras in fact have led to speculation recently that Honduras may become the new headquarters of the Southern Command as well as the new site for the School of the Americas, scheduled to leave Panama by 1984 pursuant to Carter-Trujillo treaties.

The impact on Honduras of this buildup and of the role Honduras is being given to play in U.S. military strategy for the region reflects the urgency the U.S. administration puts on the militarization of the area. It reflects the U.S. embassy view that Honduras is the "ham in the sandwich" in Central America.[13] Not only is Honduras the poorest country in Latin America, but the U.S. embassy economic report for that country warns that "the outlook for an improved economic picture . . . is not bright." The report's opening sentences read (Cohen, 1983), "The sharp economic downturn Honduras has suffered

---

[13] I attended a briefing and question-and-answer period at the U.S. Embassy in Teguci-galpa on August 17, 1983, given by Christopher Arcos, the Public Affairs Officer; Al Barr, the Political-Military Officer; Larry Cohen, the Economic Officer; Col. James Strachan, a highly decorated veteran of the Vietnam war and coordinator of the 1983-1984 U.S.-Honduran joint military maneuvers; and others.

since mid-1980 continued during 1982 and into mid-1983. Little improvement is expected in the near term." Unemployment and underemployment together stand at 75%, illiteracy hovers at 43%, and only 12% of the economically active population has full-time work. While 80% of the population is rural and without land ownership, 90% of all children 5 years and younger are malnourished (Agence Latinaméricaine d'Information Alternative, 1983). Reports of growing repression, detentions, and disappearances as well as of circumventions of the Honduran Congress and president by the army in decision making regarding U.S. activities there round out a picture of a troubled ally.

THE UNITED STATES AND THE CONTRAS

The emphasis on a military solution in Central America is exemplified further by the U.S.-trained, -equipped, and logistically supported attack force of 10,000 to 12,000 men stationed in Honduras and dubbed "freedom fighters" by President Reagan. This force of ex-Somoza former National Guardia, Nicaraguan exiles, and mercenaries is directed by U.S. Ambassador to Honduras John Dmitri Negroponte and General Gustavo Alverez in Tegucigalpa, by William Casey in Washington, and by Somoza's former Guardia head in the field. While the CIA chooses the targets of attack inside Nicaragua, it also provides the equipment, instruction, and along with the U.S. air force, the intelligence. In October CIA personnel themselves led the most successful-to-date sabotage attack—on Nicaragua's main oil facility at Corinto. The operations, financed from several CIA and U.S. military funds, have grown fourfold from an original budget of $20 million (U.S.-El Salvador Research Center, 1983b).[14] The administration has requested an additional $80 million allotment and announced in early August 1983 that it intended to increase the force to 15,000 men. This came after the House vote in July to cut off funds for the *contras*.

The administration's continued commitment to this force is illuminating, given the controversy that surrounds its existence. For one thing, the CIA's role in these efforts is demonstrably illegal, standing in violation of the Boland Amendment, U.S. Law, Title 18, sections 96 and 960, international law, and numerous American treaty obligations prohibiting intervention in the internal affairs of other states. But the behavior and stated goals of the *contras* are also an embarrassment to a country supposedly pursuing democracy in Central America. According to FDN leaders, who make up the political wing of the fighting force, their purpose is to overthrow the Sandinistas, to return the land to the owners of Somoza's time, and to punish the FSLN by creating a "bloodbath" in Managua. Their fighting tactics give testimony to a similar

---

[14] These revelations were first made by the *New York Times* in April 1983 and were confirmed by two Senate Intelligence Committee members.

brutality. Substantiated reports from Nicaragua tell of the mutilation, decapitation, and dismemberment of victims, many of them unarmed peasants. These devices of terror are employed as warnings to the living. Shouting the battlecry, "For God and against communism," the forces had taken 1100 lives by the end of 1983.[15]

Claims by the United States that the *contras* have broad support inside Nicaragua do not hold up. Based on my own experience in Nicaragua in 1982 and 1983, reports from independent research groups inside Nicaragua, and Ambassador Quainton's assertion that if elections were held in Nicaragua, the FSLN would win "hands down," there is little evidence of such support. In contrast, a number of accounts put the support rate for the Sandinistas at the 75-80% mark. By the end of 1983 and after two years of fighting, the *contras* had not taken over one village inside Nicaragua. Nor interestingly had they interdicted one weapon from the flow of weapons the administration claims Nicaragua is supplying to the FMLN in Salvador.

But U.S. support for the *contras* is also interesting in light of Ambassador to Nicaragua Anthony Quainton's remarks in an August 1983 interview. Quainton argued both that U.S. intentions in supporting the *contras* were to influence behavior changes by the FSLN and that a military solution in Nicaragua was not possible. Although he argued that "internal affairs are internal. We have no right, nor do we attempt to dictate," he went on to comment, "We do say there should be institutions with real choice for the people." Although Quainton maintained that "there's lots of participation here in all sorts of aspects; the revolution brought participation," he discounted it, charging "the overall political orientation, context is defined by one political party; choice is circumscribed over time."

Earlier, in referring to the *contras* and other regional efforts, the Ambassador commented: "The U.S. finds itself tied to those concerned with democratic goals in the region." Given the power it wields, the U.S. government "cannot stand away from the world; there is growing feeling that the U.S. must speak out on human rights and use resources in terms of human rights." When asked about the seeming inconsistencies in the way the United States pursues "real choice for the people" through its relations with forces in Guatemala, Salvador and Nicaragua, Quainton responded that "in each case the question must be asked, will supporting them produce the effect? In each case

[15]   In an August interview, Ambassador Quainton put the number dead at 700. By mid-November, *Barricadas* (1983), the official Nicaraguan government newspaper, put the death toll at 1000. Instituto Histórico Centroamericano and major U.S. media also regularly report *contra* activities and casualty figures.

we must make a choice."[16] The implication to be drawn from his comments is that in the case of support for the *contras*, the answer to the question is yes.

However, putting these statements together with the fact that the *contras'* only clearly stated program to date is anticommunism yields a picture of U.S. policy with confused and unrealistic goals and purpose. One goal pursued by the Reagan team in late 1983, for example, was to present the *contras* to the public as a united indigenous and legitimate political front to be reckoned with by the Sandinista government in any negotiation process. This effort was increasingly important as the administration faced the overwhelming ineffectiveness of the *contras* in establishing a beachhead inside Nicaragua or in undermining support for the FSLN. Yet the cracks in the administration's image were all too apparent when Ambassador Stone, set to convince the *contras* to develop a coherent political program, was forced to meet separately in Panama on December 1 with each of the five factions that make up the body. Needless to say, the FDN, split by leadership and intracorps squabbles and bearing some resentment toward CIA control, will not easily accommodate to the role assigned it in current policy.

CONDECA, GRENADA

Finally, events and policy statements of late 1983 manifested the administration's emphasis in Central America on the use of military force and drawing battle lines. Although there are important differences of politics and history between Grenada and Nicaragua, the intervention into Grenada by 6000 U.S. troops in October underlined the administration's decision to use military pressure in the region in attempts to eliminate selected "thugs."[17] Setting aside the debate over the legitimacy of the reasons cited by the president for the invasion, it is clear that the message to Nicaragua and other leftists in the region was that President Reagan was prepared and willing to employ military might against governments not to his liking.[18]

Concerned that U.S. public opinion and Congress would not support a direct or long-term American military presence in Central America, however, the administration hurried in September and October to ready regional proxy forces to hold the battle lines set by the policy team. Meanwhile, the Pentagon ordered regular U.S. forces in the area to prepare for a larger and perma-

[16] I (and several colleagues) interviewed Ambassador Quainton in his office at the U.S. Embassy in Managua on August 16, 1983.

[17] It is not my purpose here to consider the Grenada situation in detail, but to place it in the broader context of Central American policy. The circumstances surrounding the use of force against the post-Bishop government can be seen as a natural outgrowth of President Reagan's stance toward leftist governments and socioeconomic change in the Western hemisphere.

[18] The repeated rejection of Sandinista negotiation offers by the administration during this period highlights the preference for a military solution (also see Smith, 1983).

nent role in Central America and the Caribbean (McCormick, 1983; Halloran, 1983a). As administration officials revealed, the White House had decided to abandon its efforts to seek accommodation with Congress on policy. Instead, policymakers would go on the attack against congressional opposition.

The "get tough" policy stance was outlined in a public address on September 12 by the third ranking Pentagon officer, Fred C. Iklé. Notable for its harsh criticism of Congressional opposition to military spending in Central America (including the votes to cut funds for the *contras*), the speech is more important for the insight it gives into administration thinking on broader or longer-term regional policy. Arguing that U.S.-supported forces in Salvador must be victorious over the FMLN guerrillas, he further stated (Taubman, 1983a):

> We must prevent consolidation of a Sandinista regime in Nicaragua that would become an arsenal for insurgency. If we cannot prevent that, we have to anticipate the partition of Central America. Such a development would then force us to man a new military front line of the East-West conflict, right here on our own continent.

The revitalization of the U.S.-sponsored Central American Defense Council (CONDECA) on October 1, 1983 provided the administration its regional proxy force. An anticommunist military alliance, CONDECA establishes mechanisms for the coordination of the forces of Guatemala, Panama, Honduras and Salvador in the case of regional threats. (Nicaragua was excluded from membership, while Costa Rica refused observer status in the body.)[19] As Honduran General Alverez put it, CONDECA is "an alternative in case the Contadora negotiations fail" (Institute for Central American Studies, 1983a).

That the CONDECA members were not sitting by idly, however, became clear from reports of their October meetings in Guatemala City and Tegucigalpa. The (secret) final report of the 14 top military leaders from the four countries recommended among other things: that the group should study whether or not "legal instruments" existed that would allow "the security and armed forces of Panama and the other Central American countries to participate in the action for the pacification of Nicaragua"; and that in such a move the United States should be called on to provide logistical support, or if needed, direct participation "with all its resources." The report expressed the group's feelings that "a war situation is predictable" and that there is an "urgent need to join forces and take actions aimed at guaranteeing the security and stability of

---

[19]   Guatemala's membership in a regional military alliance under U.S. tutelage only became possible with the overthrow of Ríos Montt in August. Montt in November 1982 had informed President Reagan that he would not be part of such an organization, which, as he saw it, pursued U.S. policy interests. Immediately on coming into office on August 8, General Mejia announced his support for U.S. policy objectives in Central America.

the region." It envisions a scenario for an invasion into Nicaragua at the invitation of U.S.-backed "*contra*" forces (Gerth, 1983).

The U.S. role in the reinvigoration of CONDECA (which has been reported by Gerth, 1983; Instituto Histórico Centroamericano, 1983; Institute for Central American Studies, 1983a, and elsewhere) came as Honduras was taking on the look of a permanent U.S. base, as U.S. spokespersons were drawing East-West battle lines in the region and as U.S. forces were "mopping up" in Grenada. Again the message to the Sandinistas was clear.[20] As the earlier NSC memorandum revealed, it was the United States' intention to create the atmosphere for "negotiations on our terms."

CONCLUSION

At present, the administration's own failure to match words and actions contributes to the growing distrust of Central American policy. Criticisms of U.S. policy in Central America are being raised not only because conflicting statements of purpose emanate from sectors within the administration and from U.S. officials and allies in the region, but also because recent U.S. activity has not followed verbal policy. The process is spurred by news reports that present pictures of the region that contrast with images the administration has created. Given the discrepancies between words and actions and the growing attention being given these issues by the public, the questioning of U.S. policy is bound to accelerate. Moreover, the actual emphasis on preparing for a military solution heightens tensions and makes an outbreak of fighting likely. Baseless rhetoric suggesting, for example, that there can be no solution or negotiation with the FSLN in power in Nicaragua, that Nicaragua has aggressive designs on Honduras, or that the *contras* are freedom fighters works to encourage continued reliance on military means. Such spiraling activity is easy to start but very difficult to stop.

In foreign policy, words are as important as actions, and when the two contradict, actions speak louder than words in the short term. The net result is a general loss of confidence in the policy and its owners.

---

[20] In this same period, the administration gave little active or verbal support to the Contadora process, it turned away four draft treaties delivered by Nicaraguan Foreign Minister d'Escoto, and it instructed *contra* forces to show some results in Nicaragua.

REFERENCES

Agence Latinaméricaine d'Information Alternative
1983   Quebec. (February 25). Cited in *U.S.-El Salvador Research* (1983b).

Barricadas Internacional
1983   Managua, November 21:3,20.

Cohen, L.
1983   "Foreign Economic Trends: Honduras." U.S. Embassy, Tegucigalpa, Honduras.

Dodd, C.J.
1983   Interview with David Brinkley, "This week with David Brinkley," American Broadcasting Co., July 23.

Farer, T.
1981   "Reagan's Latin America." *New York Review of Books*, March 19.

Gelb, L.H.
1983   "U.S. officials see need for big effort in Salvador." *New York Times* (April 22).

Gerth, J.
1983   "Latin bloc studies Nicaragua action." *New York Times* (November 11).

Gugliotta, G.
1983   "Honduras: U.S. should provide and now, or prepare to intervene." *Miami Herald*, International Edition (August 18).

Gwertzman, B.
1983a   "Kissinger on Central America: a call for firmness." *New York Times* (July 19).
1983b   "Ousting Enders, President signals a tougher commitment." *New York Times* (May 29).

Halloran, R.
1983a   "Planning memos stress U.S. show of armed force." *New York Times* (May 29).
1983b   "Vietnam consequence: guilt from the military." *New York Times* (May 2).

Institute for Central American Studies
1983a   "Nicaragua" and "Honduras." *Mesoamerica* (November): 2,11.
1983b   "Honduras." *Mesoamerica* (July): 2,7.

Instituto Histórico Centroamericano
1983a   "A las puertas de la invasión." *Envio* (November): 2, 11.
1983b   "Las cañoneras Norteamericanas aputan contra la paz Centroamericana." *Envio* (Agosto): 3, 26.

Inter-Religious Task Force on El Salvador and Central America
  1983   "July update." New York: author.
Kirkpatrick, J.
  1979   "Dictatorships and double standards." *Commentary* (Fall).
McCormick, P. R.
  1983   "U.S. will continue military role in Honduras, pentagon aide says." *New York Times* (October 5).
Miami Herald
  1983   "U.S. role in Honduras is large, growing steadily." (August 21).
Mohr, C.
  1983   "Bill on Salvador killed by Reagan." *New York Times* (November 31).
Morrell, J. and W. J. Biddle
  1983   "Central America: the financial way." *International Policy Report* (March). Washington, D.C.: Center for International Policy.
New York Times
  1983a   "Honduras wants U.S. commitment." (November 27).
  1983b   "Text of Shultz's letter to Long on El Salvador." (April 27).
  1983c   "National Security council document on policy in Central America and Cuba." (April 7).
Reagan, R.
  1983a   President's news conference on foreign and domestic matters (July 28).
  1983b   "Saving freedom in Central America." Current Policy 499, Bureau of Public Affairs. Washington, D.C.: U.S. Department of State.
  1983c   "President's news conference on foreign and domestic matters." *New York Times* (June 29).
  1983d   "Central America: defending our vital interests." Current Policy 482, Bureau of Public Affairs. Washington, D.C.: U.S. Department of State.
  1983e   "Strategic importance of El Salvador and Central America." Current Policy 464, Bureau of Public Affairs. Washington D.C.: U.S. Department of State.
Smith, H.
  1983   "U.S. policy on Nicaragua: keep the pressure on." *New York Times* (November 31).
Sumner, H.
  1983   *On Strategy: The Vietnam War in Context*. Strategic Studies Institute, U.S. Army War College. Washington, D.C.: U.S. Government Printing Office.

Taubman, P.
  1983a   "Pentagon gets tough on Latin policy." *New York Times*
                   (September 12).
  1983b   "Shultz says fleet does not pursue Latin showdown." *New York
                   Times* (August 5).
  1983c   "U.S. says to weight 40% increase in military funds for Latin
                   allies." *New York Times* (July 17).
  1983d   "Point man speaks out about Central America. *New York Times*
                   (May 2).
U.S. Department of State
  1983   "Central America: U.S. Policy." Bureau of Public Affairs. Wash-
                   ington, D.C.: U.S. Department of State.
U.S.-El Salvador Research and Information Center
  1983a   "From bananas to bombers: the development of U.S.-Honduran
                   relations." *El Salvador Bull.* 2 (June).
  1983b   "Banana diplomacy: the development of U.S.-Honduran rela-
                   tions." *El Salvador Bull.* 2 (May).
Weintraub, B.
  1983   "U.S. envoy warns Salvador of cut in military aid." *New York
                   Times* (November 3).

10

Reagan Administration Policymakers

Barbara Epstein

I have made several trips to Washington to talk with members of the Reagan administration, and others in close touch with the administration, about US foreign policy. In January and February of 1985 I conducted interviews about a broad range of issues, including policy toward Central America. I returned in October 1985 and May 1986 to conduct interviews about policy toward Central America. Through these interviews, I learned that there has been an ongoing debate within the administration between those who oppose negotiations and those who, at least on occasion, favor them. However, those who favor negotiations do so not because they believe that the United States should reach a settlement with Nicaragua that would leave the Sandinista government intact, but because they believe that the aims of the United States, which include the ultimate overthrow of the Sandinistas, can be better achieved through a process that includes negotiations than through one that excludes them.

From its inception, the Reagan administration has been sharply divided over issues of foreign policy. The divisions have been well aired in the press. On the one hand there are those on the far right, mostly political appointees of this administration, many of them centered in Washington's right-wing think tanks. They have been labelled "ideologues" by their detractors, and the term has caught on throughout the administration (except among those to whom the label is applied). Their main opponents are those who call themselves the "pragmatists," centered in the State Department. This term is also used throughout the administration. In general, the ideologues have argued for harsh policies toward the Soviets and towards nations, such as Nicaragua, that are regarded as aligned with the Soviets. In general, the pragmatists have argued for greater caution. The administration cannot be neatly divided into these two camps: there are many shadings of opinion in each grouping, there are people who move in between the two, and there are major groupings, such as the military, that play an independent role. Nevertheless, it is the ideologue and pragmatist positions that set the framework for debate within the administration.

Many observers of the administration believe that the ideologues were in a strong position during, say, Reagan's first year in office, but that since that time they have been driven away from any real power, and it is the pragmatists who have been in charge of US foreign policy. My interviews have led me to believe that, whatever may be the distribution of power between these two groupings, there is a basic consensus within the administration on the aims of foreign policy, and that the terms of that consensus are those expressed most clearly by the ideologues. In the case of Central America at least, the policies that have been followed have adhered to the values of the administration's right wing.

EARLY 1985: NEGOTIATIONS?

In January and February of 1985, I found a sharp debate under way in Washington, over the question of whether the United States should negotiate with Nicaragua and, if it should, what the content of those negotiations should be. On 25 February 1985 I interviewed Craig Johnstone, who at the time was deputy assistant secretary of state for Latin American Affairs, under Langhorne Motley. Johnstone told me [paraphrase] that

- the debate was between those who were on principle opposed to negotiations, and those who believed that the interests of the United States would be best served by negotiations;
- the differences were based on each side's understanding of the constraints that are imposed upon foreign policy in a democratic nation, and of what policies are possible, given those constraints;
- the ideologues argue that when a democratic nation negotiates with a totalitarian nation, the democratic nation is automatically at a disadvantage, for the democratic nation must respond to public opinion;
- in negotiating with Nicaragua the United States may come under pressure to moderate its position, so as to arrive at an agreement; it is also under pressure to abide by its promises; and
- the Sandinistas are under no such pressures.

Johnstone told me that he agrees with these views but found them incomplete. "All of this is true," he said. "We do suffer in negotiations, because we are committed to our agreements while our opponents are not. But [the ideologues] have only half analyzed the problem. They talk about the weaknesses of democracy, but not its strengths."

The pragmatists, Johnstone said, do not see public opinion as presenting a permanent obstacle to the achievement of the aims of the national security community; often, he argued, Congress can be brought to support the policies that the administration favors. He offered an episode in the Contadora process as an example. On 7 September 1984 the Sandinistas offered to sign the Contadora Act that was then being discussed. If the United States had indicated its approval of this document, it is very likely that the agreement would have gone through. But the administration was able to persuade Congress that the document should not receive US approval.

Furthermore, Johnstone argued, attempting to ignore public opinion, as the ideologues would do, could end by undermining administration policies. "If we were not making a good faith effort to achieve a settlement with the Soviets [in the area of arms control], we could be undermined," he said. "The Freeze movement could grow to twice its size." Johnstone claimed that the ideologues tend to see both the Soviet Union and Nicaragua as much stronger than they are in fact, and also to lack understanding of the US political system and how it can be manipulated. Many of the ideologues are from Eastern Europe and tend to be obsessed, he said, by the "Soviet evil." He pointed out that the debate about negotiations with Nicaragua is closely parallel to the debate about arms control with the Soviet Union. But the real issue, he said, is not the nature of the Soviet Union, or Nicaragua; it is over the extent to which the US political system hinders the conduct of foreign policy, and to what extent the United States can derive advantage from conducting negotiations, given the constraints of the democratic process.

Johnstone also insisted that the difference between the ideologues and the pragmatists is not between "hardliners" and "softliners," which he rejected as spurious terms. Johnstone claimed that the ideologues call the pragmatists "softliners" merely in order to undermine their argument for negotiations. "I was a strong proponent of the use of the paramilitary in Central America, and of [the invasion of] Grenada," he said; "I'm also a strong proponent of negotiations. Am I hardline or softline? Without Shultz there would have been no Grenada. Which category would you put him in?"

I asked Johnstone what sort of negotiated settlement he saw as a possibility in Nicaragua. He said that such a settlement would have to be a "time limited *modus vivendi*," meaning that the United States would be ready to move back, at any time, to a military posture toward Nicaragua. The settlement itself, he said, would be based on changes in Nicaragua: the unification of the internal opposition and the *contras*, the granting of "political space" in Nicaragua to this unified grouping, and agreements on the part of the Nicaraguans that they would not accept Soviet military aid, or provide aid to insurgents in El Salvador. In short, the prerequisite for Johnstone's negotiated settlement would have been Sandinista acceptance of the legitimacy of the *contras*.

On 26 February 1985, I interviewed Constantin Menges, a CIA official on the staff of the National Security Council, and at the time the leading advisor to Reagan on Central America. I repeated to him Johnstone's formula for a negotiated settlement with the Sandinistas. Menges became livid. "That has nothing to do with US policy, with the President's policy," he said. "'Political space'—that could mean anything, it could mean that the *contras* can write an editorial once a week." Describing himself as a "realist" (and naming Jeane Kirkpatrick, Fred Iklé, William Casey, and Ronald Reagan as fellow "realists"), Menges argued that power-sharing would not be a viable option in Central America, either in Nicaragua or in El Salvador. "What we want," he said, "is democracy, complete democracy." In administration lingo, "democracy" means the sway of the forces the United States supports: in the case of Nicaragua, the deposition of the Sandinistas, and the accession to power of the *contras* and their internal supporters. At this time, no one that I interviewed advocated US armed intervention in Nicaragua, but Menges certainly verged on this. He said that he could not tell me exactly what would happen, but that a Congressional vote for aid to the *contras* would be the turning point in the war.

OCTOBER 1985: THE "MIDDLE WAY"

When I returned to Washington in October, 1985, I learned that Johnstone had become ambassador to Algeria, Langhorne Motley had left the administration, and that Menges had been demoted. One interviewee said that I could regard this as an indication that the two clear-cut alternatives, getting rid of the Sandinistas or negotiating a settlement with them, had both been put aside, at least for the time. Consensus had been formed around an intermediate position. Asked what this "middle way" consisted of, an official in the State Department Bureau of Latin American Affairs, Luigi Einaudi, said, "you grind 'em down." (22 October 1985). The pragmatists were no longer advocating negotiations with the Sandinistas. I was told that prior to Reagan's second election, and prior to the Congressional vote for aid to the *contras*, it had been deemed wise to press for negotiations so as to demonstrate the administration's reasonableness. Now that both of those aims had been achieved there was no longer any need to raise the issue of negotiations with the Sandinistas. Instead, I was told by Einaudi, the policy was to do everything possible to undermine the Sandinistas, short of invasion, and to provide aid to the Salvadoran army and wait for it to defeat the FMLN.

I asked how long it might be before the United States would achieve its objectives in Central America. One official in the Latin American Bureau told me that if the Sandinistas didn't make any major mistakes, they might be in power for ten or twelve years. This official and others told me that in El Salvador, the government is winning. When I pointed to the continuing strength of the FMLN, Einaudi said that in societies like these, there are always bandits in the bush. Asked how long it would be before the FMLN ceased to be a serious factor in El Salvador, he said, perhaps two and a half years, adding that, of course, anything could happen in that time. I pointed out that already a third of the Salvadoran population has either been killed or displaced, and I asked

Einaudi how long he thought civil war could go on in El Salvador without destroying the fabric of Salvadoran society. "You underestimate the resilience of Salvadoran society," he said. "These people can take this better than we could."

Some State Department officials, and former officials, seemed prepared to accept what they regarded as defeat in Nicaragua, that is, the continued presence of the Sandinista government. One former Reagan administration State Department official said, "We've won in El Salvador, not in Nicaragua." Asked whether the ongoing civil war in El Salvador could be regarded as a US victory, he said,

> You could see it as a stalemate, or you could say, we've accomplished our objective. Ten to fifteen years from now, they'll see it as a major accomplishment, a place where revolution did not take place even though all the preconditions were present. This is a major event, the objective of two administrations. If the question is the spread of revolutionary governments, the record now shows that it can be dealt with. It is possible to prevent the spread of revolution.

In many of my interviews I raised the possibility that the United States had no strategy in Central America, but was hoping that with time and luck the Salvadoran army and the Nicaraguan opposition would both win. One State Department official, recently returned from several years of service in Central America, agreed emphatically. "There are two possibilities," he said, "either you negotiate with the Sandinistas, or you bomb them. Everyone knows we can't invade. And this administration doesn't want to negotiate for its own ideological reasons." He went on to argue that it is the extreme right that has set the terms for policy toward Central America. "The extreme right," he said,

> needed a stage in which to act out its views. In domestic politics, it got the abortion issue. In foreign policy, it got Central America. You can't give these people a place like the Middle East, it would be too dangerous. But Central America keeps them happy. The problem is, they don't have a solution either. Their aim is not to have an agreement, but even they know we can't invade. But they've got an investment in the place by now, so they run around raising money for the *contras*.

What is the underlying aim of US policy in Central America? One answer to this question came from Elliott Abrams, Assistant Secretary of State for Human Rights when I interviewed him on 25 February 1985. Abrams was later to become Assistant Secretary of State for Latin American Affairs. Abrams told me that the United States has no significant tangible interests in

Central America; the issue, he said, was one of psychology. "If people see that the Americans are not going to move against the Sandinistas in their own backyard, what will they do ten thousand miles away?"

DEMOCRATS AND TOTALITARIANS

This is one of the purposes of US policy: to demonstrate the hegemony of the United States in what it regards as its own sphere, so as to discourage others elsewhere from asserting their independence. The second purpose of US policy in Central America relates to US internal politics. Reagan came to office promising to conduct a worldwide campaign against Soviet communism. He needed examples of the Soviet threat, preferably in areas where he could demonstrate strength with a low risk of actual confrontation with the Soviet Union. Central America seemed perfect for the role; there had recently been a revolution in Nicaragua, there was the possibility of a revolution in El Salvador, and there was the ongoing "problem" of Cuba in the background.

Reagan, however, underestimated the ability of the Sandinistas to withstand US pressure; he also underestimated the strength of domestic and international opposition to his policies. Moreover, he could not find any easy retreat from his confrontational stance. Having described the Sandinistas as a major threat to the United States, he could not say that Nicaragua had ceased to be an important issue. So the administration is caught: on the one hand it has proclaimed the overthrow of the Sandinistas to be a major goal, on the other hand, the political cost of a US intervention has thus far precluded such action.

The Reagan administration perceives the world as a battlefield between the forces of democracy, consisting of the United States and its allies, and the forces of totalitarianism, consisting of the Soviet Union and other nations that the United States opposes. Fitting Central America into this schema can be difficult, but the officials whom I interviewed made valiant efforts. I asked many of my interviewees what they made of the fact that while in El Salvador, if one engages in public dissent, one's body may be found on the street the next morning, this does not happen in Nicaragua. Charles Lichenstein, former deputy ambassador to the United Nations under Jeane Kirkpatrick, interviewed on 11 February 1985, responded by telling me that there were death squads in both countries. "The only difference," he said, "is that in Nicaragua they're publicly sanctioned." Pressed for evidence, he mentioned the fact that some Miskito Indians have been killed, and he claimed that "all of the Jews have left Managua, and some of them have disappeared."

In fact, there is no evidence of death squads in Nicaragua, or of "disappearances," at least not in the usual Latin American sense, that is, kidnapping followed by torture and often assassination. Some Miskito Indians were killed in the course of armed conflict between Sandinistas and opposition groups. Many Jews left Managua at the time of the Sandinista revolution, as did other Nicaraguans, especially members of the upper and middle classes. Some Jews, however, chose to remain; these people have not disappeared. There have been violations of human rights under the Sandinistas, such as the forced removal of the Miskitos from their villages, and the imprisonment of some Miskitos without sufficient charges. But these violations are not evidence that death squads operate in Nicaragua.

In a later interview with Lichenstein, on 26 February 1985, I asked if he could tell me more about the Nicaraguan death squads to which he had referred. "Did I mention death squads?" he asked. "I must have been speaking loosely. What I meant is that Nicaragua is a repressive society. Dissent is at least equally dangerous in Nicaragua as in El Salvador, though up to now most people haven't been killed for it. The repression is unpredictable; that's one of their techniques. These societies work on the probability of terrible things happening to those who dissent."

Other administration officials agreed that there is more repression in El Salvador than in Nicaragua, but argued that this is not the most important measure of democracy or the lack of it. Elliott Abrams, for instance, readily conceded this point, but argued that US policy should not be based on a "body count" but rather on an estimate of whether the regime in question is following a "democratic" or a "totalitarian" path. Despite the greater level of violence in El Salvador than in Nicaragua, Abrams argued that "El Salvador is a freer society. An established Leninist society doesn't have to do a lot of killing. All of the organs of repression are in place. People respect the limits that the state draws up. If you violate them you go to jail. What is happening in Nicaragua is the beginning of a Leninist system. This is not happening in El Salvador; there, there is an embryonic effort to establish democracy."

Bruce Weinrod, the Director of Foreign Affairs at the Heritage Foundation, explained to me, in an interview on 29 January 1985, that the way he distinguishes between a nation that is on the democratic path and one that is on the totalitarian path is by looking at the foreign friends and the internal forces that the nation cultivates. If the nation in question allies itself with the United States and encourages private enterprise internally, then it is on the democratic path; if it allies itself with the Soviets and discourages private enterprise, it is on the totalitarian path. While Weinrod is not part of the administration, his thinking on this question seems entirely consonant with the thinking of administration officials.

CONSENSUS TO OVERTHROW

My interviews persuaded me that while there are disagreements within the Reagan administration over whether or not to negotiate with the Sandinistas at particular moments, there is consensus on the aim of US policy, which is to undermine the Sandinista government, and, if possible, to bring about its overthrow.

Fundamentally, there are two ways in which international relations can be conducted: diplomacy or war. Diplomacy, ideally, entails negotiations between two nations, each of which recognizes the sovereignty and the legitimacy of the security concerns of the other. The differences between the ideologues and the pragmatists over policy toward Central America are important: the pragmatists' at least occasional interest in negotiations opens up some possibility of a peaceful solution to the tensions between the United States and Nicaragua. But even the pragmatists are interested in negotiations as a strategy for accomplishing other ends (gaining support for the administration's positions on Central America, inducing the Sandinistas to include the *contras* in their government) rather than as a way of finding some basis for agreement between the two nations. The administration's unwillingness to engage in genuine negotiations has brought turmoil and violence to Central America and has damaged the reputation of the United States in many areas of the world.

11

Explaining Washington's Central American Policies

Laurence Whitehead

Why have the Washington authorities under both Democrat and Republican administrations chosen to devote so much time, money, and political capital to the pursuit of a policy in Central America that most international opinion, and a substantial proportion of domestic U.S. opinion, considers to be unwarranted interference? The standard answers to this question fall into two main groups, each with strong ideological connotations. The official American position, most forcefully expressed in speeches by such prominent figures as former secretary of state Alexander Haig, UN ambassador Jeane Kirkpatrick, and President Ronald Reagan himself, judges events in Central America as yet another example of worldwide Soviet expansionism, in this case channelled through Cuba. On this view, it is not possible for America to stand back from the struggles of this small and apparently unimportant region, for unless the Russian cause is decisively rebuffed there is a real risk of "falling dominoes," to the Panama Canal and beyond in one direction, and even northward into Mexico. Improbable though it may seem, these spokesmen also invoke the cause of democracy, claiming that revolutionary totalitarianism threatens to destroy budding hopes for freedom and reform under American sponsorship. Thus, U.S. policy is explained by the magnitude of the strategic and geopolitical issues at stake, and by America's traditional morality in international affairs.

The alternative explanation starts with a total disbelief in the morality and sincerity of Washington's policymakers, and heavily discounts the threat of Soviet expansionism. Like the official view, it also appeals to the morality of the American people, but identifies a different source of evil, one located in Washington rather than Moscow. A typical recent example of this approach reviewed the evidence of Salvadoran official involvement in many political crimes and highlighted the reluctance of American spokesmen to acknowledge the true scope of this involvement.

The original version of this article appeared in the *Journal of Latin American Studies* 15(2):321-361. © 1983 Cambridge University Press. The version published here has appeared in *Politica Internazionale* [Rome], #10/11, 984.

> The deeper meaning of U.S. complicity is to be found in the profound commitment on the part of both Carter and Reagan to the reconstruction of a network of stable and unconditional allies linked to American global and regional military-corporate and financial interests. In this context the lives of missionaries and archbishops and social democratic leaders counted for little.[1]

A complete evaluation of these two opposed explanations would require an assessment of various complex questions of international politics concerning the purposes of Soviet behavior, the local sources of the conflict in Central America, and the homogeneity of American "military-corporate and financial interests" around the world. This paper, however, is confined to exploring the ways that American internal politics have helped to shape Washington's stance toward the crisis in Central America. Nevertheless, this restricted focus may shed some light on the adequacy of the two approaches sketched above. For both the suggested explanations would relegate domestic American politics to a secondary role, and would present Washington as a "unitary actor," pursuing long-range objectives (either good or evil) with a large degree of coherence and consistency. Consideration of the domestic sources of U.S. Central American policy brings such assumptions into question and draws attention to a number of other important factors.

Indeed, too much attention to international or Central American realities might mislead, rather than assist the task of explaining Washington's behavior. For what counts is not so much the actual complexities of the local situation, but the extremely selective way that these are perceived and presented within the American bureaucracy, where the decision-making process only permits the development of "stylized facts" about the outside world. No doubt the rational pursuit of some kind of interest (not necessarily the collective interest) plays an important role in the policy-making process, yet this is a very bounded rationality (i.e., many ways of thinking about a problem are excluded from consideration *a priori*), and a surprising amount of mythology and misinformation also enters into the system.[2]

---

[1]   James F. Petras and Morris H. Morley, "Supporting Repression: US Policy and the Demise of Human Rights in El Salvador, 1979-81," *The Socialist Register 1981* (London), p. 56. George Black sees more of a contrast between Carter and Reagan, and attributes the Central American policies of the latter to an "unstable right-wing coalition . . . responsive to the ascendant Sunbelt and West Coast bourgeoisie," which allegedly has a substantial economic stake in the Isthmus. Black's interpretation is that "this powerful and overlapping set of corporate, political and religious interests have helped place Central America high on Reagan's agenda." "Central America: Crisis in the Backyard," *New Left Review* (London) 135 (September-October 1982):28/9.

[2]   Wayne S. Smith, the top American diplomat in Cuba until his resignation in 1982, used a striking phrase to underline the undercurrents of emotion and irrationality that are also present: "Central America now exercises the same influence on American foreign policy as the full moon does on werewolves." See also note 16.

The limited rationality of Washington's policies in Central America can be illustrated by a simple mental experiment. Suppose that Washington's sole purpose was, indeed, to combat Soviet expansionism around the world; would it so clearly serve that end to make Central America into a test case? After all, this involves drawing attention to the region's historic subordination to the United States, and disregarding the good offices of allies who are as concerned as Washington to stem any Soviet advance. Or, alternatively, suppose that Washington's sole purpose was to reconstruct a network of stable and unconditional allies subordinate to America's military-corporate interests. Once again, how rational would it be to concentrate so heavily on Central America, which has relatively little to offer to corporate America or even to the defense establishment? Surely the strategists for military-corporate power would weigh in the balance the risks of diverting attention from more valuable allies, and the cost of aiding the weak, unattractive, and dependent client regimes that Central America would have to offer. In fact, neither of the dominant explanations provides a very convincing rationale for recent American policies in Central America.

BEFORE 1979

Although the Central American crisis has only been overt and critical since 1979, it has extremely deep roots. Washington has an exceptionally long history of interest in Central America because, throughout the nineteenth century, the Isthmus promised to provide the most economical trade route linking the Atlantic and Pacific coasts of North America. This interest was accompanied by a series of very crude political interventions undertaken by such adventurers as William Walker (who briefly conquered the Nicaraguan presidency in 1855), "General" Lee Christmas (organizer of a successful revolution in Honduras in 1908), and E. Howard Hunt (political and propaganda chief of the CIA's covert operation to overthrow the Guatemalan government in 1954, and subsequently a key organizer of the Watergate break-in).[3]

America's economic power in the region was also expressed in a rather crude manner over much of the period. J. P. Morgan acquired direct control over Nicaraguan and Honduran customs houses before the First World War, and thanks to the United Fruit Company the region became known for a distinctive form of political organization—the "banana republic."[4] The creation

---

[3] Hunt and Liddy directed and supervised the Watergate operation. Hunt's plan was that if anything went wrong, both families could take temporary refuge "among the Cuban community in Florida long enough for a Nicaraguan National Guard transport aircraft to slip in quietly and fly us all out to sanctuary on Corn Island, courtesy of the Somoza family. . . . Later, in the D.C. jail, Hunt tried to interest me in a joint venture with him and the Somozas, after we were free, to develop Corn Island in the Caribbean Sea." G. Gordon Liddy, *Will* (New York: St. Martin's, 1980), p. 272.

[4] Mira Wilkins, *The Maturing of Multinational Enterprise: American Business Abroad*

in 1903 of the Republic of Panama and the importance of the Canal Treaty, the occupation in the 1920s of Nicaragua and Honduras by U.S. Marines, and the training of military establishments throughout Central America since the 1940s all exemplify a history of unequal relations that have shaped the psychological attitudes of both sides to this day.

The 1954 covert operation that brought down the Arbenz government in Guatemala was a very formative experience, both in Washington and on the Isthmus. It made the U.S. government overconfident about the efficacy of this method of intervention, thus contributing to the abortive Bay of Pigs invasion in 1961. On the Latin American left, it was used to demonstrate the futility of temporization and half measures, and the unavoidable necessity for armed struggle. The events of June 1954 lend support to the interpretation of Petras and Morley sketched above: none of the supposedly countervailing forces of American democracy played any part in restraining the administration; the media misinformed the people; America's allies (with the honorable exception of France) fell into line; and *perhaps*—although here there is still some scope for disagreement—the essential cause of Washington's wrath may have been the indignation of the United Fruit Company over Arbenz's land reform.[5] There are some remarkable parallels between the events of 1954 and the covert operation against Nicaragua that was approved in November 1981. For example, the U.S. ambassadors to the United Nations and Honduras had surprisingly similar roles to perform in the two cases, and State Department White Papers display the same lack of veracity. However, at a deeper level, the conditions favoring the 1954 operation no longer exist. Washington may have enjoyed an uncritical consensus over Guatemala at the height of the McCarthy period, but the domestic debate over foreign policy objectives has become far more open since then, above all with regard to Central America. One reason for this is that the 1954 and 1961 precedents have alerted many U.S. citizens to the possibility of being deceived by their own government. The *New York*

---

from 1914 to 1970 (Cambridge: Harvard University Press, 1974), pp. 96-98, illustrates the political power of United Fruit in Guatemala, Honduras, and Costa Rica in the 1920s. A former senior official of the company, Thomas McCann has provided some insights into its more recent activities in *An American Company: The Tragedy of United Fruit* (New York: Crown, 1976).

[5]   For a recent well-researched statement of this case, see Stephen Schlesinger and Stephen Kinzer, *Bitter Fruit—The Untold Story of the American Coup in Guatemala* 2d ed. (New York: Doubleday, 1983). They show that the company "deployed a platoon of lobbyists and publicists at a cost of over half a million dollars a year . . . worked both the left and the right of the American political leadership and won the backing of both liberals and conservatives for its policies in Guatemala. This campaign . . . had a remarkable impact on the American government" (p. 67). They do admit that Washington also had other reasons for overthrowing Arbenz, but their crucial judgment is that "the takeover of United Fruit land was *probably* the decisive factor pushing the Americans into action. Without United Fruit's troubles, it seems *probable* that the Dulles brothers might not have paid such intense attention to the few Communists in Guatemala" (p. 106—my italics).

Times was manipulated in 1954, and is taking care to avoid similar complicity on this occasion. (Indeed, one of the authors of *Bitter Fruit* now reports for that paper from Central America.) There is another reason why Washington now finds it hard to raise a domestic consensus on Central America. Richard Nixon, when vice-president, visited Guatemala after the overthrow of Arbenz and declared "This is the first instance in history where a Communist government has been replaced by a free one. The whole world is watching to see which does a better job."[6] Twenty-eight years later, it is quite widely known how Guatemala's "free" governments have used the opportunity that Washington provided.

During the 1970s, long-postponed grievances came to the fore as Washington grappled first with Panamanian demands for sovereignty over the Canal Zone, and then with the aftermath of the Nicaraguan revolution. Remarkably, Zbigniew Brzezinski's 600-page memoir covering his term as National Security Adviser (1977-1981) contains no mention of El Salvador, and only the most passing allusions to Nicaragua. The only Central American country that does receive attention is Panama. Thus, he is able to judge his policy to be both enlightened and successful. He quotes President Carter's declaration in Panama on 16 June 1978, "I believe we have set in motion a different pattern of relations with Latin America," and comments "Indeed we had. Ratifying the treaty was seen by us as a necessary precondition for a more mature and historically more just relationship with Central America, a region which we had never understood too well and which we occasionally dominated the way the Soviets have dominated Eastern Europe."[7] Although the treaties were indeed a "necessary precondition," they were in fact far from sufficient to produce a mature and just relationship with Central America. However, even this first step was such a sharp break with past American practice that it provoked a strong challenge from the Republican right, particularly among followers of the former governor of California, Ronald Reagan, who denied that America's record in Central America required any apology or rectification.

Ronald Reagan had long taken a direct personal interest in Central America. Competing for the Republican presidential nomination of 1976, he came out strongly against the Panama Canal treaties then under negotiation by

---

6   Schlesinger and Kinzer, *Bitter Fruit*, p. 234.

7   Zbigniew Brzezinski, *Power and Principle* (New York: Farrar, Straus, Giroux, 1983), p. 139. It seems the author always had difficulty in reaching a stable combination between the two elements invoked in his title. On Panama, for example, notwithstanding the principles quoted above, he also records a White House briefing at which he was asked "But what if after the year 2000 the Panamanian government simply and suddenly announced that it is closing down the canal for repairs?" Without a moment's hesitation I [*sic*] replied, "In that case, according to the provisions of the Neutrality Treaty, we will move in and close down the Panamanian government for repairs" (p. 136). Less flippantly, he also states that when it seemed that the Senate might fail to produce the required two-thirds majority for ratification he "expected massive violence in Panama and I had ordered that military contingency plans be drawn up" (p. 138).

President Gerald Ford and Secretary of State Henry Kissinger. After setbacks in several primaries, Reagan's fortunes picked up after he denounced President Omar Torrijos in May 1976 as a "petty dictator," and declared that the Canal Zone "is ours and we intend to keep it." One of his campaign strategists commented that "people see in this issue some way, after Vietnam, and Watergate, and Angola, of reasserting the glory of the country."[8] In its first two years, the Carter administration used up much of its political capital in pushing for the ratification of the treaties against a well-financed opposition in which the ideological right tested out their new techniques of political opposition. The latter saw "the Canal issue as a lever for regaining the White House in 1980. Their most effective publicist was Ronald Reagan." The Conservative caucus raised nearly $1 million by direct-mail fund-raising to fight the pact. "The new names collected through the Panama campaign could later be sold to conservatives running for office in 1978 and 1980."[9]

Initially, there was an influential human rights lobby within the Carter administration that took a clear line against the Somoza dynasty in Nicaragua. In 1977, the House Appropriations Committee was even persuaded to cut off $3.1 million in military aid to Nicaragua because of Somoza's human rights abuses. But on this, as on so many issues, the Carter administration was in two minds—many influential voices in the State Department warned against actions that might play into the hands of the armed Sandinista opposition. Moreover, the Somoza government was not lacking friends in Washington. It mounted an expensive lobbying campaign and persuaded the full House of Representatives to reinstate the military aid. Hearing of this victory "Somoza claimed he has more friends in Congress than Carter," and, indeed, at the height of the civil war in September 1978, seventy-eight members of Congress wrote to Carter expressing their support for the Somoza regime.[10] Up to the end of the civil war (June 1979), the Carter administration was still casting around for some political regrouping in Nicaragua that would avert an outright Sandinista victory ("Somozismo without Somoza," said the critics).

JULY 1979-JANUARY 1981

The Carter administration's failure to prevent an outright victory by the Sandinista revolutionaries gave the ideological right a promising new issue. The generalizations in Jeane J. Kirkpatrick's November 1979 article on "Dictatorships and Double Standards" were drawn quite explicitly from the Iranian and Nicaraguan revolutions of the preceding year. The opening sentence won Reagan's approval by condemning Carter's proposed "transfer of the Panama Canal from the U.S. to a swaggering Latin Dictator of Castroite

---

8   Walter LaFeber, *The Panama Canal* (New York: Oxford, expanded edition 1979), p. 190.
9   LaFeber, *The Panama Canal*, pp. 232-233.
10   Penny Lernoux, *Cry of the People* (New York: Doubleday, 1980), pp. 96-107.

bent." This bizarre characterization of President Torrijos was immediately followed by descriptions of the recently deposed rulers of Iran and Nicaragua as follows:

> Both Somoza and the Shah were, in central ways, traditional rulers of semi-traditional societies . . . neither sought to reform his society in the light of any abstract idea of social justice or political virtue. . . Both did tolerate limited opposition . . . but both were also confronted by radical, violent opponents . . . Both rulers, therefore, sometimes invoked martial law to arrest, imprison, exile, and *occasionally, it was alleged*, torture their opponents. The Shah and Somoza were not only anti-Communist, they were positively friendly to the U.S., sending their sons and others to be educated in our Universities, voting with us in the United Nations and regularly supporting American interests and positions . . . In each of these countries the American effort to impose liberalization and democratization on a government confronted with violent internal opposition not only failed, but *actually assisted the coming to power* of new regimes in which ordinary people enjoy fewer freedoms, and less personal security than under the previous autocracy—regimes, moreover, hostile to American interests and policies.[11]

Thus, the celebrated distinction between "moderately repressive" autocracies and totalitarians was evidently founded on a highly subjective assessment of pre- and postrevolutionary Nicaragua. Kirkpatrick suggests, for example, that Somoza "tolerated limited opposition," whereas the murder of Chamorro was widely considered proof to the contrary and so united all shades of opinion against the autocrat. Similarly, her view that the Carter administration "actually assisted the coming to power" of the Sandinistas ignores all Washington's vain efforts to promote what became known as "Somozismo without Somoza." However that may be, her article struck a chord, perhaps because of its comforting oversimplifications. It provided a frame of interpretation that was narrowly to constrain American policies towards the Central American crisis.

This constraint, most pronounced under the Reagan administration, was already present during the last year of Carter's presidency. Virtually no official in Washington was prepared to be exposed to the charge (however exaggerated) of "assisting" an anti-American revolution in El Salvador, least of all after the Iranian hostage crisis had inflamed the public mood in the United States, and when a presidential election was looming. Central American events contributed little to the sharp change of mood in the United States, but the region was destined to experience a disproportionate share of the effects. Inflation was overwhelming Carter's economic policy achievements, the Iranian revolution had overshadowed the Camp David agreement, and the mood of public opinion

---

[11] Jeane J. Kirkpatrick, "Dictatorships and Double Standards", *Commentary* (November 1979). My italics.

was hardening against what were seen as well-intended but naive liberals in the White House. The last fifteen months of the Carter administration were dominated by the Iranian hostage crisis which began in November 1979. Two related side effects of this national humiliation were the virtual paralysis of the human rights lobby that might otherwise have exercised some restraining influence over American policy toward El Salvador and at the same time the magnification of the indignation of American conservatives against any sign of weakness in the face of yet another anti-American revolution. But for the misfortune of Iran, could the Carter administration have handled the aftermath of the Nicaraguan revolution with calm and moderation? Probably not, considering that already in July 1979 (well before the hostages were taken) the National Security Council began overreacting to the Sandinista revolution. Brzezinski's memoirs record his exaggerated alarm at suddenly "discovering" in July 1979 the existence of a Soviet brigade in Cuba. Not until two months later did he correct his information to recognize that the brigade had been there since the 1960s. He admits that the issue was mishandled so that it shook public confidence in the administration, heightened public hostility toward the Soviet Union, and intensified the conflict between Carter's foreign policy advisers.[12]

There is uncertainty over the precise extent of U.S. involvement in the October 1979 military coup that brought a "reformist" junta to power in San Salvador.[13] What is clear is that, in the wake of the Nicaraguan revolution, oligarchic control in El Salvador rapidly weakened, creating a vacuum that necessarily drew in both Managua and Washington. The unquestioned American objective was to ensure that, whatever else might take place in El Salvador, there would be no second armed revolution. The Sandinistas were unpalatable enough (Carter was offering aid to Nicaragua in order to strengthen the "pluralists" against the "Marxist-Leninists" within the revolutionary coalition), but the FMLN were considered even worse—i.e., more explicitly communist and committed to class conflict. Even had this not been so, from Washington's viewpoint, two revolutions in Central America would be much more than twice as bad as one. A revolution against Somoza might be dismissed as an exceptional (and containable) reaction to an exceptionally tyrannous and incompetent dynasty; but a second revolution in El Salvador would show that something of far more general significance was afoot. It would greatly increase the threat to other reactionary military regimes (most notably, Guatemala), and it would give comfort both to America's enemies abroad, and to the administration's critics at home. For all these reasons, Carter's advisers saw no choice but to endorse whatever emerged from the October 1979 coup in

---

[12] Brzezinski, *Power and Principle*, pp. 346-353 and pp. 565-566.
[13] Philip Wheaton, "Agrarian Reform in El Salvador: A Program of Rural Pacification," EPICA Task Force (Washington, 1980) makes the case for direct US control of the process, but I have been unable to confirm this interpretation.

El Salvador. Characterizations of the various juntas differ according to the political perspective of the observer. Carter's Washington tried strenuously to persuade itself that this had produced a regime dedicated to genuine reform, and that gross and systematic repression was committed, if at all, not by the junta but by uncontrolled elements whom it was trying to restrain. The Petras and Morley interpretation[14] may be a more accurate reflection of Salvadoran realities but, if so, this would be something that Carter's Washington simply could not have afforded to recognize. Consequently, notwithstanding individual protests and acts of contrition by U.S. ambassador White, Carter's Salvadoran policy simply paved the way for the course to be subsequently adopted by the Reagan administration.

Reagan was better placed than other presidential challengers to capitalize on the national mood of frustration at Carter's alleged foreign policy weakness. The Caribbean Basin provided an inevitable focus of attention. Early in his campaign, Reagan spoke lightly of imposing a naval blockade of Cuba until the Soviets withdrew from Afghanistan. Reportedly, the U.S. navy hastily contacted his team to point out the impracticality of this proposal, and it faded from view, but what mattered was the general tone. Throughout 1980, Washington prepared the way for tough counterinsurgency measures in El Salvador. A few weeks before his murder, Archbishop Oscar Romero wrote a personal appeal to President Carter not to send more arms.[15] By the time Reagan won the election, the mold of U.S. policy towards El Salvador was set. Only the third party candidate, John Anderson, raised any real demur. He advocated Latin American policies similar to those promised by Carter in 1976. In electoral terms he was a complete outsider, but his policy on Central America did have some private following within the Washington bureaucracy, as became clear after the election results.

JANUARY 1981-JUNE 1984

Two days after Reagan's victory, a "Dissent Paper on El Salvador and Central America" began to circulate. Not surprisingly, the authors concealed their

---

[14] See note 1.

[15] One month before his assassination, Archbishop Romero wrote to President Carter as follows: "if you really want to defend human rights I beg you: to veto plans for the provision of military aid to the Salvadorean government; to guarantee that your government will not intervene directly or indirectly, with military, economic, or diplomatic pressure, to shape the destiny of the Salvadorean people." He argued that "political power in El Salvador is in the hands of unscrupulous military men who only know how to repress the populace and promote the interests of the oligarchy," so that the planned military aid "would undoubtedly intensify the injustice and aggression against the organized populace who generally have been struggling to secure respect for their most fundamental human rights." The day before his death he urged soldiers to disobey genocidal orders. President Carter disregarded this appeal, and some American commentators suggested that the Left might have caused the Archbishop's death. In Catholic and Latin American circles very few people believe this.

identities, but the paper claimed to give the private views of "current and former analysts and officials at the National Security Council, the Department of State, the Department of Defense, and the CIA," together with members of Congress and their staff. It described Reagan's plans for Central America and the Caribbean as "deeply disturbing," but added that "should President Reagan choose to use military force in El Salvador, historians will be able to show that the setting for such actions had been prepared in the last year of the Carter Administration." The paper recommended U.S. recognition of the FDR/DRU coalition as "a legitimate and representative political force in El Salvador" (a step actually taken by the French and Mexican governments a year later); disengagement from "those sectors inside and outside the armed forces responsible for gross excesses"; and encouragement for "other regional actors" to increase their involvement as the United States disengaged. Clearly, the authors of this document did not expect their advice to be taken by the incoming administration, but they were making the point that an alternative to the Carter/Reagan approach did have respectable credentials. The effect was to deny a consensus to the Reagan team (although Carter personally made every effort to smooth the transition and to achieve continuity of policy on Central America) and to encourage those in Congress and the news media who would seek to curb the belligerence of the new administration.

From the outset, Reagan's team tried to put as much distance as possible between themselves and their predecessors. Carter's ambassadors to Nicaragua and El Salvador were dismissed, economic aid to Managua was suspended, and the new appointees refused even to consult with their counterparts to ensure a continuity. Secretary of State Haig appointed a series of Vietnam associates with no prior Latin American experience to handle Central American affairs. Within a month of the inauguration, the State Department issued a White Paper entitled "Communist Interference in El Salvador," which concluded that "in short, over the past year, the insurgency in El Salvador has been progressively transformed into a textbook case of indirect armed aggression by Communist powers through Cuba."[16]   This was followed on 9 March 1981 by a

---

[16]   *White Paper Whitewash* ed. by Warner Poelchau (New York: Deep Cover Books, 1981) p. A-8. This source reprints the White Paper and the captured documents on which it is allegedly based and provides a lengthy critique of the evidence. Two issues were involved: were the captured documents genuine? (The English translations contained some remarkable errors of transcription and some unwarranted interpolations); and, even if they were, did they support the sweeping conclusions of the White Paper? Congressman Barnes, Chairman of the Western Hemisphere Subcommittee, concluded that the State Department had failed "to lay to rest doubts about the White Paper" (*Washington Post*, 19 June 1981). The alternative view is that at this time most rebel arms were obtained locally or on the black market. Castro states that the Cubans initially sent some arms, without Soviet involvement, but claims that in April 1981 these flows ceased. Wayne S. Smith, chief of the US interests section in Havana 1979-1982, has criticized the White Paper for "shoddy research, and a fierce determination to advocate the new policy, whether or not the evidence sustained it." "Dateline Havana: Myopic Diplomacy", *Foreign Policy* 48 (Fall 1982):162. He states that very shortly after

"Presidential Finding" on Central America that authorized large-scale intelligence gathering and arms interdiction activities throughout the Isthmus. In Haig's words, the administration would "go to the source" of the trouble, by which he meant cut off supplies and support coming from Cuba. In August 1981 Managua was offered a "separate peace," whereby the United States would hold back from hostile measures against the Sandinistas if they in turn would cease cooperating with Cuba and would stop supporting the rebels in El Salvador. The Nicaraguan response to this (possibly cosmetic) offer was not judged acceptable in Washington, and so on 17 November 1981, the President authorized $19.5 million for CIA covert operations to interdict arms flows to El Salvador. These operations involved the establishment of counter-revolutionary base camps in Honduras to harass the Nicaraguan regime, and the training of paramilitary forces (the *contras*). Argentina and Israel were enlisted in this undertaking, which had authorization of the relevant congressional committees meeting *in camera*. Although these measures were authorized by the president, he apparently rejected additional proposals from Secretary Haig, involving the early use of U.S. forces against Cuba and Nicaragua. At that time, these ideas were considered to be too dangerous and to lack support either from the U.S. public or from U.S. military leaders.

The March 1982 elections in El Salvador and the "reformist" coup in Guatemala that came shortly thereafter were taken as vindications of administration strategy. In April 1982 the National Security Council (NSC) made a fairly optimistic evaluation of Central America. The most likely prospect was thought to be that by 1984 Nicaragua would be isolated; that the Salvadoran guerillas would be thrown on to the defensive, and would be suffering increased internal divisions; and that "democratic structures would be 'strengthened' in a number of countries." According to this view, there might be an incremental increase in Cuban and Nicaraguan efforts, and substantial flows of arms would continue to get through, but there would be no major qualitative change in types of external support being supplied. On the other side, no U.S. troops would be introduced to the Isthmus. This last point was evidently considered of real importance, since the NSC appraisal expressed worry about the resistance still to be encountered by Congress, U.S. public opinion, and from allies of the United States.[17]

Reagan's inauguration, arms shipments from Cuba and Nicaragua to El Salvador declined (p. 161) and that since then "while some arms have been sent from Cuba to El Salvador, the quantities are almost certainly far less than alleged. If the guerrillas had received all the arms reported by US intelligence, the Salvadorean army would be outgunned 20 to 1" (p. 169). However, after secret congressional hearings held in May 1983, various critics of the Reagan administration accepted that arms from Nicaragua had become vital for the insurgents.

[17]   *New York Times* (7 April 1983):16. Although this was considered the most probable outcome, the NSC document also contained an annex discussing a variety of other "less likely" developments. These included the introduction of Soviet MIGs into Nicaragua, or of Cuban ground troops. Either of these developments would give Washington favorable opportunities for escalation. On the other hand, Congress could inflict a "perhaps irre-

The mid-1982 replacement of Alexander Haig by George Shultz apparently had little effect on Central American policy, which remained firmly under the control of Assistant Secretary of State Thomas Enders, at least until the spring of 1983. By then, various of the hopes expressed in the NSC's April 1982 "most likely outcomes" were proving decidedly overoptimistic. The Salvadoran insurgents were evidently stronger than before, and the U.S.-backed regime was suffering severe problems in the areas of military leadership, supplies, morale, economic management, and political cohesion. The Nicaraguan regime was also facing severe problems, but many of these could be attributed to U.S. clandestine operations that had become far from covert as the U.S. news media pursued their investigative reports. These press revelations had stirred up such unease in the U.S. Congress that funds for military assistance seemed in jeopardy (these points will be developed more fully below). The administration still may seem dedicated to the pursuit of a mainly military solution, but the proxy forces at its disposition may well prove inadequate.

Since the optimistic forecast of April 1982 has not been borne out by events, the predictable inclination in Washington has been to escalate, increasing the pressure on Nicaragua (now to be formally classified as a "communist" country ineligible for various trade benefits) to the point where the logical next step would be the overthrow of the Managua government. Within the U.S. administration, the only admissible explanation for a failure to achieve its goals in Central America is that the external backers on the "other side" have expanded their military commitment. Thus, an NSC appraisal of July 1982 argued that "the Soviets may already have decided to raise the ante" by sending MIG aircraft to Nicaragua, in which case Washington should consider "actions to destroy the planes and/or a blockade quarantine." Over the ensuing nine months, the United States intensified air and sea surveillance of Nicaragua, including the AWACs and naval patrols. In April 1983 the Nicaraguans responded to a U.S.-backed incursion from Honduras by threatening various forms of retaliation. But, to the apparent disappointment of the U.S. administration, there is as yet no hard evidence of either Soviet fighters or Cuban combat troops. Indeed in the wake of the U.S. invasion of Grenada (in October 1983) the Cuban government rather clearly indicated its inability to defend the Nicaraguans from direct attack. The Soviet Union has probably stepped up its supply of weaponry since then but also seems reluctant to get overcommitted.[18] The Nicaraguan government has stepped up conscription and military preparedness on the assumption that it is

---

trievable setback" on the administration if it either cut off military aid to El Salvador or required negotiations as a condition for the semiannual certification of progress on human rights. (The *Washington Post* of 17 April 1983 summarized this annex.)

[18]   For the reasons for this Soviet reluctance see Nikki Miller and Laurence Whitehead, "The Soviet Union and Latin America: an Economic Perspective," in Robert Cassen (ed.), *Soviet Interests in the Third World* (London: Royal Institute of International Affairs, 1985).

their own nationals who must provide the main defense against U.S.-directed harassment.

The nature of that harassment has become progressively clearer, thanks to a series of revelations published in the U.S. news media. A cover story in *Newsweek* on 8 November 1982 detailed allegations of a covert operation to interdict the flow of arms through Honduras to El Salvador that had supposedly "escalated far beyond Washington's original intentions." It added that attempts to harass and undermine the government of Nicaragua might instead provoke a Nicaraguan-Honduran war and thus a direct American intervention. The report stated that the U.S. ambassador in Honduras was directing covert military operations that were "just about out of control." This lengthy report in a mass circulation weekly contained little that was surprising to informed readers, but it reawakened a public concern that had lain dormant since the Salvadoran elections. It was followed, in March and April of 1983, by a long series of reports in the *New York Times* casting doubt on the veracity of official statements about covert activities in Central America, and even questioning the legality of the operations. As we shall discuss below, these reports found a receptive audience in Congress (where the Democrats had made substantial gains in the midterm elections of November 1982).

In July 1983 President Reagan appointed a twelve-person "bipartisan" commission chaired by Henry Kissinger, to "study the nature of U.S. interests in the Central American region and the threats now posed to those interests" and to advise on "elements of a long-term U.S. policy" and on "means of building a national consensus" around that policy. By this means the White House succeeded in blunting congressional criticism and in buying time during which its strong stand against the Nicaraguans could be extended. However, in the six months until the commission issued its report, administration policy toward Central America was by no means always characterized by a search for bipartisan consensus, or by an emphasis on sophisticated and comprehensive regional policy making. On the contrary, perhaps buoyed by the success of the "invasion" of Grenada in October 1983 and the appearance of an improved political and military situation in El Salvador, the Pentagon took an increasingly heavy-handed and militaristic approach to the consolidation of the U.S. position in Honduras, while the CIA was authorized to undertake increasingly provocative and indeed piratical measures against Nicaragua. It seems that with the dismissal of Enders as Assistant Secretary of State in May 1983, operational control over such matters shifted further away from the State Department and into the hands of the National Security Council. The key decisionmakers became McFarlane (National Security Adviser), Casey (Director of the CIA) and perhaps also Weinberger (Secretary of Defense) and Kirkpatrick (UN Ambassador). As we shall see, the President seems to have played an active part in directing and reinforcing the activities of this group.

According to official sources quoted, without attribution, by the *Washington Post* on 10 October 1983, CIA officers aboard a ship off the coast

of Nicaragua directly supervised commando raids involving speedboats that
heavily damaged the Pacific port of Corinto. It was not until early the following year that the House Intelligence Committee discovered the direct
involvement of the CIA in this port raid. Initially those responsible for congressional oversight were told that this operation was carried out by Nicaragua
counter-revolutionaries, and it was only after persistent questioning that the
direct involvement of agency officers was revealed. Then, starting in January
1984, the CIA began mining Nicaraguan harbors inflicting damage on merchant ships in Nicaraguan territorial waters. In March 1984 CIA Director
Casey testified to the Senate Select Committee on Intelligence that the mines
had been placed by U.S.-supported groups, but he gave no indication that this
was an operation controlled by U.S. agents operating from a ship in international waters, or that about 600 mines had been laid. The following month the
Chairman of the Senate Select Committee, Senator Goldwater, published a
letter he had written to Casey on April 19 to express his

> feelings about the discovery of the President having approved mining
> some of the harbors of Central America. . . . During the important
> debate we had last week . . . on whether we would increase funds for
> the Nicaragua program, we were doing all right until a member of the
> committee charged that the President had approved the mining. I strongly
> denied that because I had never heard of it. I found out the next day that the
> CIA had, with the written approval of the President, engaged in such
> mining and the approval came in February; . . . mine the harbors of
> Nicaragua? This is an act violating international law. It is an act of war.
> For the life of me I don't see how we are going to explain it.

The following day the Senate voted by 84-12 for a non-binding resolution
reading:

> It is the sense of Congress that no funds heretofore or hereafter appro-
> priated in any act of Congress shall be obligated or expended for the
> purpose of planning, executing or supporting the mining of the ports or
> territorial waters of Nicaragua.

Forty-one Republican senators voted for this, and only one Democrat voted
against, eliciting the comment from Senator Byrd that "the President asked for
bipartisanship in foreign policy and he got it."
     This was undoubtedly a significant setback for hardliners in the Reagan
administration, and indeed the mining of Nicaraguan harbors has apparently
been suspended since April 1984. However political forces within the United
States remain very finely balanced on the appropriate policy for "containing"
or "rolling back" what is still widely viewed as a communist threat in Central
America. The administration still has the initiative in devising and
implementing foreign policy, and its critics in Congress can only obstruct,

not impose an alternative strategy. Moreover, the Kissinger Commission report did take on board some of the arguments of these critics, challenging Congress to provide more funds so that a "political" as well as a "military" approach could be pursued. The spring 1984 elections in El Salvador were viewed by many U.S. moderates as evidence that a pro-American democratic and reformist alternative to the extremes of right and left might still offer an honorable way forward. Consequently, in June 1984 the two houses of Congress struck a compromise on budgetary policy toward Central America for fiscal year 1984. The administration's proposals for El Salvador were scaled down and then approved, but funding for the 10,000 or so counterrevolutionaries waging "covert" war against Nicaragua was rejected. However it remains to be seen whether the administration is willing to live within these constraints. President Reagan continues to use language that suggests a higher duty (saying, for example, that the "strategic balance of the world" is at stake), and he will interpret reelection as a mandate for more forceful and decisive action in Central America. By contrast, a future Democratic president would be under quite a strong obligation to seek a phased disengagement from the regional conflict.

We now turn to an evaluation of the various forces at play within the United States, and the ways in which they interact to shape Washington's Central American policies. The NSC appraisal of April 1982 made it clear that the administration regarded Congress as its major obstacle, but to understand legislative resistance it is first necessary to consider the attitudes of the American churches, the news media, and the electorate in the United States.

THE AMERICAN CHURCHES

On the one hand, there are many Roman Catholics among the architects of present U.S. policies (including Zbigniew Brzezinski, Alexander Haig, Richard Allen, and Ambassador Jeane Kirkpatrick). And the pope—perhaps influenced by his background in Poland—has resisted attempts by some Central American clergy to reconcile Christianity with Marxism. During his visit to Nicaragua in March 1983, Pope John Paul II warned that church unity was threatened "by unacceptable ideological commitments and temporal options." On the other hand, the March 1980 assassination of the archbishop of El Salvador, and later of three American nuns, produced a profound effect within the U.S. Catholic church. The pope reinforced this position during his visit to El Salvador. He expressed strong support for churchmen who have condemned human rights violations by the U.S.-supported military, and he made an appeal for political rather than military solutions (which can be taken as an indirect criticism of the Reagan administration). A few weeks after the pope's visit, a former Christian Democrat member of congress and president of the El Salvador Human Rights Commission was killed by government troops. The press office of the Salvadoran High Command described her as "a terrorist and subversive," but the archbishop (newly appointed by the pope to replace the murdered Romero) called her "a courageous humanitarian worker."

Not surprisingly, therefore, members of the U.S. Congress from Catholic areas (particularly in the Northeast) report opposition to administration policies from sources not normally associated with the traditional left. Catholic organizations and channels of communication represent a powerful resource for those opposing further U.S. intervention or escalation. In November 1981, U.S. bishops appealed for "a U.S. policy that would engage Nicaragua diplomatically, not isolate it," and called for a restoration of U.S. economic aid to Managua. Then, in March 1983, Archbishop Hickey of Washington told Congress that the U.S. Catholic Conference believed that "the primary issue in El Salvador is the domestic economic and political structure of the country, not the role of the Soviet Union or Cuba in Central America," and that military assistance should be provided (if at all) only "with stringent conditions requiring the pursuit of dialogue and cease-fire."

Although the Protestant churches are less directly involved, and more divided on the issue, their activities are also significant. About 5% of the population of El Salvador are Protestant, as are about 10% of Nicaraguans (including the Miskito Indians on the frontier with Honduras), and perhaps 20% of Guatemalans (including, since March 1982, the president). The leading Protestant organization in the United States, the National Council of Churches (which claims to represent some forty million churchgoers) has contributed funds for the literacy campaign in Nicaragua, and has condemned human rights violations in Central America. But some evangelical and fundamentalist organizations—e.g., those associated with the so-called Moral Majority—have taken a very strong cold war stance. The Moravian church in Nicaragua, and the Protestant sects in Guatemala, have become identified with U.S. policies, and their reports are far more conservative than the Catholic ones. Nevertheless, in general, religious opinion presents a substantial obstacle to administration policies.

THE NEWS MEDIA

In its first year the Reagan administration enjoyed the usual honeymoon with the news media. In particular, establishment publications with a reputation for liberalism offered a series of olive branches. Significantly, it was the news staff of the conservative *Wall Street Journal*, rather than of the liberal *Washington Post* or the *New York Times*, that in early June 1981 first exposed deficiencies in the White Paper on El Salvador and that made damaging revelations about the first presidential nominee to direct the CIA. The liberal press continued to take an editorial line quite sympathetic to the administration's viewpoint until about the middle of 1982. But the balance of news reporting soon became quite adverse, as foreign correspondents have found administration claims to be inaccurate.[19]

The March 1982 elections in El Salvador were warmly welcomed by nearly all the U.S. media as evidence that, after all, the administration did have a constructive political strategy, and that, contrary to the claims made by the insurgents, the Salvadoran electorate was eager to participate in the new constitutional process. This coverage clearly reflected a sense of hope that at last a foreign policy success might prove attainable in Central America. During this temporary phase, few critical voices were heard; the special nature of an election campaign held in civil war conditions was little analysed; and the worrying implications of the strong right-wing showing for U.S. policy were lightly treated. For the American media, it was enough that the elections had been held at all, and that the claims made by the insurgents had proved inflated. Thereafter (with help from the South Atlantic conflict), the administration experienced a significant respite from press criticism over Central America, so much so that the public could be excused for supposing that the Isthmian crisis was gradually fading away.

However, following the *Newsweek* exclusive of November 1982, editorials in the liberal press became quite critical in tone, and the discrepancy between reportage and proprietorial commentary was narrowed. But only a small minority of the population is reached by these establishment newspapers, and even fewer readers notice such nuances.

Television reporting has a far greater mass impact, as the Vietnam War demonstrated so clearly. Indeed, it could be argued that what finally ensured the acquiescence of the Carter administration in the Sandinista victory of June 1979 was a brief sequence broadcast on prime-time news, in which one of Somoza's men forced an unarmed U.S. reporter to lie down, and then shot him in the head. Subsequent footage from El Salvador has been equally repellent, but without the same catalyzing effect, perhaps because U.S. citizens were not involved.[20] However, a news item showing U.S. military advisers carrying

---

[19] Consider, for example, a *Washington Post* report (10 March 1982) on the testimony by Assistant Secretary of State Thomas Enders, who at the beginning of February 1982 told Congress that "we sent two embassy officers to investigate recent reports of a massacre in the Morazan village of El Mozote. They reported that . . . no evidence could be found to confirm that government forces systematically massacred civilians." Strictly speaking, this was true, but what the *Post* report stressed was that the two officers in question were not able to get closer than three miles to the scene.

On Mozote, see also Joan Didion's *Salvador* (London: 1983) pp. 37-40. More generally, Didion dwells on the near impossibility of communicating Salvadorean realities to a US mass public, and on the great difficulties of verifying even the most basic facts (the episode on pp. 67-69 is especially telling). Her observations on the role played by the US media (e.g. pp. 29, 49-51, 86) are extremely revealing, as is her discussion (pp. 85-96) of the official US preoccupation with "the appearance of things, how the situation might be made to look better" rather than with the sordid reality.

[20] The television critic of the *New York Times* offered this assessment of network reporting

weapons that infringed official assurances of their noncombatant status forced a flurry of rectifications. U.S. camera teams have sent extensive reports from behind guerrilla lines, presenting the insurgents in a neutral, or perhaps even a favorable light.[21]

THE ELECTORATE

During 1981, letters reaching the State Department were running twenty to one against the administration's El Salvador policy. A Gallup poll taken in February 1982 found 89% opposed to the despatch of U.S. troops to that country, and only 8% in favor. (In April 1983 the proportions were almost unchanged.) Whereas in March 1981, 43% had approved Reagan's handling of the El Salvador situation to 41% who disapproved, eleven months later the approval rating fell to 33%, and disapproval rose to 49%. Three-quarters of those polled believed that the United States' deepening involvement resembled the experience in Vietnam. Only 37% favored sending military supplies (60% against). The only comfort that the administration might draw from this survey was the fact that 80% accepted their view of El Salvador as a domino, and 62% favored the provision of economic aid. In the face of this public disenchantment, Secretary Haig called it "fallacious" to base foreign-policy decisions on "the lowest common denominator of the national mood." The Salvadoran elections of March 1982 provided some comfort to administration supporters, and for a while reduced pressure from the critics, but Democratic gains in the November 1982 midterm elections strengthened the hand of the opposition in the lower house, and weakened (without eliminating) the administration's majority in the Senate. By April 1982, the administration's strenuous efforts to rally opinion to its side had made a little headway, but not much. Immediately following President Reagan's televised appeal to the joint houses of Congress, the approval rating for his handling of the situation in El Salvador was 44% for, 42% against (compared with 33% to 49% a year earlier), and the proportion favoring the provision of U.S. military advisers had risen from 42% to 55%. However, many of the specific claims made by the administration still met with deep skepticism. Asked whether the United States should aid anti-Sandinista forces in Nicaragua, the replies were 25%

in February/March 1983: "Sometimes the programs present the news about El Salvador tardily, sometimes they get it confused and sometimes they focus on the rhetoric rather than the reality. . . . The evening news programs are better at reporting what the Administration says it is doing, rather than what it does. Rhetoric is skimmed off the top; the substance is untouched." *New York Times* 22 March 1983:C19.

21   The TV programs seen by Hispanic audiences in various parts of the United States give far more detailed and sensitive coverage than those seen by English-speaking viewers. Many Hispanics see news reports originating in Mexico City that to some extent reflect the relatively proinsurgent perspective of the Mexican authorities. By contrast, the US Spanish language press is, in general, extremely hostile to the insurgents.

yes, 56% no. Asked to rank the cause of the conflict, only 29% gave preference to external subversion, compared with 50% who cited poverty and injustice; 56% believed that there had "not been much improvement at all" in El
Salvador's human rights record over the previous year. According to a separate
poll taken two weeks earlier, the claim that El Salvador is vital to U.S.
defense was rejected by 45% to 33%; the claim that the U.S. role there is
morally justified was rejected by 49% to 26%. This poll also asked what may
well be the most fundamental question influencing public attitudes—"will
U.S. involvement end in victory?"—to which 40% said no, and only 23% said
yes. It is probably on this last point, rather than on any of the others, that the
Reagan administration has pinned its hopes of eventually swaying public
opinion over to its side.

CONGRESS

Many Democrats in Congress have reacted warily to the various indicators of
public opinion about Central America, perhaps from consideration of the inherent fickleness of the public, but more probably from consciousness that the
president can create a *fait accompli* and then appeal for patriotic unity.
Alternatively, there are some signs that if the Central American situation de-
teriorated further, the Republicans might gain a party advantage by taking a
strong line, forcing the Democrats to cut off funding, and then blaming their
opponents for "losing" another domino. Representatives from the South and
West are apparently more reluctant to challenge the president than those from
the North and East. A nonpartisan motive may be the belief that presidential
strength is a prerequisite for the national success so widely desired after a succession of foreign policy setbacks. Finally, of course, legislators may be more
inclined than many of their voters to judge Central American developments in
the light of national security doctrines.

HOUSE OF REPRESENTATIVES

Traditionally the House of Representatives has less interest in foreign policy
than the Senate, but since 1980 the Democrats have possessed a majority only
in the lower house. Consequently, the House has become a main forum for
expressing opposition to administration policies. To counteract the influence
of Helms in the Senate, a Vietnam veteran who is also a liberal Democrat
(Barnes, from Maryland) was appointed to chair the House Subcommittee on
Inter-American Affairs. In 1981, liberals in Congress succeeded in attaching a
rider to the law authorizing disbursement of foreign aid funds to El Salvador,
requiring the administration periodically to certify approval of the human
rights record of the Duarte government. When Reagan issued such a certification at the beginning of February 1982, fifty members of Congress wrote to

Democrat from New York) stated that "this assessment simply flies in the face of reality," and House Speaker O'Neill (Democrat, Massachusetts) expressed rising dissatisfaction in the Democrat party, prompted by heavy lobbying from Catholic areas. Similar opposition was expressed during the August 1982 certification exercise, and following Republican losses in the midterm elections, the February 1983 certification became, if anything, even more controversial.

On 2 March 1982, House Democrats proposed a resolution calling for unconditional discussions among the major political factions in El Salvador. This resolution might well be considered a direct challenge to administration policies but, even so, House Republicans decided it would be impolitic to oppose it. The resolution was carried by 393 to 3. Also in March 1982, Barnes introduced a bill to ban the use of foreign aid funds for covert action against Nicaragua. The chairman of the House Foreign Aid Subcommittee (Long, Democrat from Maryland) has also proposed legislation banning the despatch of U.S. troops to El Salvador and has pressed strongly for a "political" rather than a military solution there. In all these respects the lower house was more restive than the Senate and began imposing its restrictions earlier. However, the most important constraints concerned the so-called "Boland Amendment," and the power of the purse.

THE BOLAND AMENDMENT

Since the *Newsweek* article of November 1982, attention has shifted to the activities of the CIA and, therefore, to the House Intelligence Subcommittee. The House counterpart to Senator Goldwater (Republican, Arizona) is Representative Boland (Democrat, Massachusetts) who, in December 1982, proposed an amendment to an appropriations bill stipulating that "none of the funds provided in this act may be used by the CIA or the Department of Defense to furnish military equipment, military training or advice, or other support for military activities, to any group or individual, not part of the country's armed forces, *for the purpose* of overthrowing the Government of Nicaragua or provoking a military exchange between Nicaragua and Honduras" (my emphasis). This is the "Boland amendment" which was carried by 411 votes to zero in the House and subsequently adopted by the Senate as well, on a bipartisan vote. (A straight prohibition on covert operations would have been far more divisive.) In March and April 1983, the *New York Times* published testimony that, notwithstanding this law, the CIA was funding anti-Sandinista paramilitary forces, whose avowed aim was not just to interdict arms supplies, but also to overthrow the Managua government. Moreover, in the words of one key informant quoted in these reports "the brains behind the operation" was U.S. ambassador to Honduras John D. Negroponte, and "the decision to shift the operation from one of harassment to one of trying to overthrow the Sandinistas was made jointly by Honduran and U.S. officials in

Tegucigalpa."[22] Confronted with this evidence, the administration (and President Reagan personally) denied that there was any breach of the law, a position accepted by Senator Goldwater. The essence of the denial was that the Boland amendment just specified expenditures "for the purpose" of overthrowing the Sandinistas, and the official purpose of CIA activities was only to interdict supplies. The administration offered no guarantee that the *intentions* of the paramilitary forces, or the *results* of their actions, would conform to the *purpose* of the funders. Representative Boland commented that "the evidence is very strong" that the administration was violating the law. He therefore resolved to invite top administration officials to closed hearings.[23]

In these hearings, the Congress was startled to learn the size of the force recruited by the U.S.-backed *contras*. Initially, there had only been about 500 men under arms, but by the spring of 1983 the numbers were reliably reported to have risen to 7,000, and President Reagan was publicly defending their activities as "freedom fighters." Whereas the CIA's initial budget for these activities in fiscal year 1983 was about $20 million, by April 1983 the estimated cost had risen to $31 million. This was not what the authors of the Boland amendment had expected, and so the House Intelligence Subcommittee voted to cut off funding for covert operationsagainst Nicaragua. After that, Congress would still provide funds to block the flow of arms from Nicaragua, but no longer using covert means. However, the Republican-controlled Senate was not willing to go along with this, and it was not until June 1984 (under great pressure to reduce the federal deficit) that both houses of Congress agreed to cut off funds for the counter-revolutionaries from 1 October 1984.

THE POWER OF THE PURSE

It is only by denying administration requests for funds, by attaching clearly verifiable conditions to appropriate bills, that Congress can exercise control over the executive. Therefore, the legislative record on foreign aid to Central America deserves attention (see Table 1).

A confidential NSC document dated April 1982, and leaked to the *New York Times* a year later, estimated that about one billion 1982 dollars per year would be required from fiscal year 1982 to fiscal year 1984 (and probably beyond) to cover all security and economic assistance in Central America and the Caribbean Basin Initiative. Since only $700 million was (at that time) being requested for fiscal year 1983, the NSC document foresaw that "early in 1983 the funding shortfall will have to be addressed." The initial $700 million

[22] *New York Times*, 3 April 1983. The source of this report was an unnamed Honduran directly involved in planning US covert activities, but it was also "confirmed in large measure by two senators on the Senate Intelligence Committee and by a highly placed Reagan official." About 5,000 paramilitary were reported to have entered Nicaragua from Honduras at this time.
[23] *New York Times*, 14 April 1983.

request included $63 million for military aid to El Salvador, but Congress authorized only $26 million because of El Salvador's continuing failure to prosecute the assassins of the American nuns and of the U.S. aid officials.

In the spring of 1983, the administration orchestrated a sudden alarm about the gravity of the security threat in El Salvador. For example, Enders testified that the Salvadoran army might run out of ammunition within thirty days; later, however, an under secretary conceded that it would take something like a Nicaraguan invasion to burn up ammunition that fast. (Nicaragua shares no border with El Salvador.) The administration hoped to stampede Congress into supplying the additional funds for Central American operations anticipated a year earlier. In particular, it requested an additional $50 million in fiscal year 1983 of military aid for El Salvador, to be voted as a supplementary expenditure, together with the "reprogramming" of $60 million already allocated that year as military aid to Morocco but to be diverted to El Salvador.

The funds would be used to increase the size of the Salvadoran army, to train additional battalions in counterinsurgency warfare, and to implement a "civic action" program in the areas of guerrilla strength. The press revelation that, far from being a response to a sudden emergency, this was a budget initiative that had been planned by the administration

TABLE 1. U.S. AID TO CENTRAL AMERICA 1981-1983
($ MILLION)

Fiscal Years	COSTA RICA		GUATEMALA		HONDURAS	
	Military	Economic	Military	Economic	Military	Economic
1981	0.04	13.3	..	16.7	8.9	33.1
1982	2.06	50.7	..	13.5	31.3	78.1
1983	1.13	160.4	0.2	38.1	20.3	58.9

Fiscal Years	NICARAGUA		EL SALVADOR	
	Military	Economic	Military	Economic
1981	..	59.6	35.5	104.5
1982	..	6.2	82.0	186.2
1983	..	0.3	26.3	205.0

Note
Fiscal years begin three months before calendar years. The figures for FY83 refer to amounts approved by March 1983. The Reagan administration has since requested $110 million in military aid for El Salvador in FY83 but will obtain far less. The funding of covert operations is not included. The CIA has presidential authorization to spend at least $22 million— probably from its Reserve for Contingencies—on Central American operations. According to some reports, a total of $55 million was spent from contingency reserves (i.e., without congressional authorization) in FY82. Congress is likely to prohibit the President from drawing on such funds thereafter.
Source. Various issues of New York Times (April 1983).

a year earlier, added to congressional resistance. Moreover, the simultaneous press revelations of covert operations tending to subvert the Nicaraguan government, in defiance of the Boland amendment, stiffened the resolve of members of Congress (particularly in the now more strongly Democrat lower house) to use the power of the purse to enforce a political rather than a military solution in Central America. On Barnes's initiative, the Western Hemisphere Subcommittee recommended the $50 million increase in aid to El Salvador, but stipulated that the funds be used for economic rather than for military assistance. This proposal was upheld by the House Foreign Affairs Committee in a nineteen to sixteen vote. As for the $60 million "reprogramming" of military aid, even the Republican-controlled Senate cut this figure to $30 million. The House Appropriations Subcommittee on Foreign Operations (chaired by Representative Long) refused to consider the proposal unless the State Department agreed to appoint a high-level envoy to El Salvador, to promote a negotiated settlement, and to report on the judicial and prison systems. Looking further ahead to fiscal years 1984 and 1985, the subcommittee voted to prohibit military assistance and arms sales to Guatemala, to limit El Salvador's total military aid to $50 million per year (about $2,000 per soldier) for the next three years, and to uphold a legal maximum of fifty-five U.S. military advisers in El Salvador at any one time.

Clearly, Congress was trying to alter the direction of administration policy, without actually resorting to the destructive last recourse of a financial veto. In response, President Reagan made an unusual televised appearance before both houses in an appeal to reverse these decisions. He received a standing ovation for his reiteration that no U.S. troops would be sent to Central America, and the Congress also listened respectfully to his vehement defense of the administration's position. To some extent, he may have gained ground by appealing over the heads of Congress to his television audience, and certainly there were signs of division within the Democrat party over how strongly to react. But the widespread unease about the administration's view of Central America was not assuaged, especially when it emerged that his choice for special envoy to El Salvador was someone who would lack the confidence of congressional skeptics. Nor did the president diminish their fears of further military escalation in the region. Consequently, the possibility of a congressional cut-off of all military funds still loomed very close.

The Kissinger Commission was appointed in July 1983 with this funding problem in mind. The Democrats were well represented on this bipartisan Commission which was invited to consider both the security and the development needs of Central America, and to propose a strategy that could be sustained over a number of years without the constant funding crises and partisan disputes that had hampered U.S. policy toward the region since 1979. It recommended a five-year (fiscal years 1985-1990) program of economic assistance costing $24 billion, of which the U.S. government was asked to provide $8 billion. This would mean roughly doubling the scale of economic assistance that had been provided in fiscal year 1983. The success of this proposal is still in some doubt but at least for fiscal year 1985 the two houses have agreed on a total outlay for Central America of $1.4 billion of which about $900 million would be economic aid and about $500 million would be military assistance. There is a genuine element of bipartisanship in this outcome in that critics of the administration's priorities (strongest in the House) have been obliged to accept a greater level of military spending and to concede more discretion to the executive than they had intended; on the other hand, supporters of the administration (strongest in the Senate) have acquiesced in the termination of authorization and funding for the CIA's "covert" war and in a scaling down of the magnitude and the stridency of the U.S. commitment in the region. Some hardliners fear that the net effect is to keep the U.S. presence in place, but without a sufficient show of determination and consistency to overcome the enemy. On balance, however, the "bipartisan" outcome must be regarded as surprisingly close to the Reagan administration's initial position, a remarkable achievement in an election year, especially considering the strength of voter and congressional opposition to those positions when the commission was appointed. To explain why that opposition was not more effective we must turn next to the Republican-dominated Senate, and then to the various agencies of the administration.

THE SENATE

In 1980 the Republicans captured not only the presidency but also the Senate, and they maintained control of the upper house (traditionally most active on foreign policy matters) in the 1982 elections. Moreover, in 1980 some prominent Democrats known for their liberalism on foreign policy issues (e.g., Church and McGovern) lost their seats, and the Republicans, having secured a majority, placed the pro-Somoza Senator Helms in charge of the Western Hemisphere Subcommittee of the Senate Foreign Relations Committee, from which position he attempted to veto all but the most intransigent Latin American nominations at the State Department. When covert operations against Nicaragua were reported to the Senate Intelligence Committee in November 1981, it was a fairly hawkish body of legislators, even on the Democrat side, who had oversight of the proposals. Nevertheless by early 1984, as I indicated above, the "secret war" had become so public, and it was so clear that the CIA had escaped effective Senate oversight, that Select Committee chairman Goldwater issued a remarkable public reproof to CIA director Casey. Pro-administration senators probably objected more to the manner in which the policy was being conducted than to the substance of the policy itself. And indeed after that, Republicans still held out in favor of continued funding for the Nicaraguan counter-revolutionaries until a House-Senate compromise on the 1985 budget required them to drop this item. However mixed the motives of some individuals, the fact remains that a Republican-dominated Senate has ended up exercising more vigilance and restraint over the foreign policy excesses of a Republican president than the Democratic Senate ever practiced in relation to Presidents Kennedy and Johnson. In June 1984 Senator Goldwater attempted to compensate for this criticism of the CIA by declaring that "the President of our country, the Commander-in-Chief, has made the decision [to back the counter-revolutionaries] and I intend to follow orders"; but this was no longer a typical view. The memory of Vietnam, and public fears that the administration might create another such crisis for itself, has compelled most senators to cross-examine the executive rather closely on its Central American priorities and purposes.

An important stage was reached in early 1982, when the Senate minority leader Byrd (Democrat, West Virginia) proposed an amendment to the 1974 War Powers Act that would bar the president from sending U.S. troops to El Salvador without first obtaining congressional authorization. However this approach tended to divide the Senate along partisan lines, since it could be interpreted not so much as an assertion of the congressional right to declare war, but as a vote of nonconfidence in the president, and an invitation to America's enemies to mount military challenges without fear of retaliation. Thus, for example, when the Democrat-controlled House voted a ban on the deployment of U.S. combat troops anywhere in Central America without specific approval (May 1984), the Senate voted down a similar measure with the solons dividing essentially on party lines. No doubt partisanship was intensified by the approach of another round of elections, during which the Republicans would face a serious challenge to their majority in the upper house. The one third of Senate seats that they had contested—rather unsuccessfully—in 1978 are up for renewal in 1984, and even if they fight off this challenge they will be hard-pressed to retain a majority in 1986. Overall then, the Senate has acted as a significant restraint on the Reagan administration's Central American policies and might well become even more troublesome to the president in the event of a second term. In order to assess the effects of congressional oversight on the administration's Central American policies we must distinguish between the major components of the policy-making apparatus.

THE PENTAGON

At the beginning of February 1982, Secretary of Defense Caspar Weinberger appears to have deliberately leaked to the press his opposition to either the sending of U.S. troops, or the despatch of naval forces, to blockade Cuba and/or Nicaragua. Pentagon opposition helped persuade the president to veto proposals along these lines that had been formulated in November 1981 by Secretary of State Haig. In November 1981 the well-connected defense correspondent of the *New York Times*, Leslie Gelb, quoted a Pentagon source as asking the State Department: "Tell us whether the problem [in Central America] is one of social and internal upheaval or Communist-inspired subversion: whether the problem is military or broader and deeper and much more intractable." Three months later, the head of the Panama-based U.S. Southern Command, Lt. General Wallace Nutting, commented after a visit to El Salvador that he had "absolutely no idea" how much aid might be needed for the Salvadoran regime to defeat the guerrillas. With reference to State Department proposals to cut off international supply lines to the guerrillas, he warned that past efforts to cut off supply routes, in Italy during World War II, for example, had not been very successful. In a similar vein, a highly confidential report by one of the Pentagon's leading experts on the Isthmus, Brigadier-General Frederick Woerner, began to circulate on Capitol Hill in April 1983. Contrary to one of the most central tenets of the administration's policy, it reportedly concluded that increased U.S. aid would do little to ensure a victory by the Salvadoran government.

It seems that defense planners have disagreed over the importance of arms flows from Nicaragua in sustaining the Salvadoran rebellion. No one doubts that this route is in operation, but some official claims on the scale of the traffic passing through it appear highly speculative, and little attempt has apparently been made to assess how much material the guerrillas may be obtaining from other sources, such as seizures or purchases from the Salvadoran military itself. Through kidnappings and ransoms the Salvadoran guerrillas accumulated perhaps $100 million with which arms could be purchased from corrupt officers, e.g., in Honduras or in the efficient black market for arms that has operated in Costa Rica since the Nicaraguan insurrection.

In the end, of course, military officers will try to obey whatever orders they are given, and those who express too many reservations risk being passed over for promotion. But, in view of these rather public expressions of unease at the Pentagon, and the senior levels from which they emanate, it is hardly surprising that the administration has tried to make do with irregular and proxy forces only. The main consideration seems to be a fear that U.S. military involvement in this controversial and unrewarding theatre of operations could create domestic opposition that would interfere with the deeply desired program of accelerated defense expenditure. The Defense Department evidently considers that America's military capacities are already overstretched and that, in any case, the highest Third World priority is to build up a Rapid Deployment Force capable of acting in the Middle East. Direct Defense Department involvement to date has officially been limited to the provision of some fifty-five "advisers" within El Salvador (and probably hundreds more in Honduras and other areas, where congressional vigilance is less sharp),[24] plus the

---

[24]   However, on 24 June 1984 Representative William V. Alexander (Democrat from Arkansas) obtained a report from the General Accounting Office (GAO) which concluded that much of the Pentagon's military construction and training in Honduras over the previous two years had involved "improper" use of federal funds. Defense Secretary Weinberger called this a "bookkeeping" dispute, but according to Congressman Alexander "this report says that the President has bypassed Congress in order to militarize Honduras. . . . The Constitu-

accelerated training of a few thousand Salvadoran counterinsurgency forces in the United States and Panama. However, it is also reported that owing to Pentagon dissatisfaction with the intelligence being received from the CIA, the Defense Department set up its own rival unit which began operating in El Salvador in early 1982. This Army Intelligence Support Activity group not only collects intelligence but engages in its own covert operations, apparently without informing the CIA. Whether there is effective congressional oversight remains unclear.[25]

THE STATE DEPARTMENT

On taking office, the Reagan administration dismissed several State Department officials (notably Ambassadors White and Pezzullo, the Carter administration's emissaries to El Salvador and Nicaragua, respectively), who were regarded as "soft" on Central America. This almost certainly had a salutary effect on any like-minded career officers. In practice, there was probably not very much strong resistance within the State Department to the administration's hard line. At any rate, Secretary of State Alexander Haig, and his Assistant Secretary for Inter-American Affairs, Thomas O. Enders, immediately took firm control over U.S. policy toward Central America. Neither of them had any previous experience of Latin America. Compared with the insular nationalists on the White House staff, Haig and Enders have a much stronger grasp of the realities of alliance politics. But when dealing with Central America they rely for precedent upon their experience in Southeast Asia.

There is lengthy description of the collaboration between Haig and Enders in Cambodia in *Sideshow*, a well-researched study by William Shawcross. It recounts the 1969 recruitment to the NSC of Colonel Alexander Haig and his direct involvement in the April 1970 invasion of Cambodia from South Vietnam. Enders was appointed deputy chief of the U.S. Mission in Phnom Penh at the end of 1971 and "soon became Haig's favorite diplomat at the Embassy."[26] In February 1973, control of American bombing raids on Cambodia "was shifted secretly into the Embassy," and "an Embassy panel, chaired by Enders . . . became responsible for bombing strikes in all parts of the country except the east . . . targets could be proposed by the Embassy."[27] Despite the alleged efforts of Enders to disguise from Senate investigators the extent of his involvement (and perhaps even from the Secretary of State), at

---

tion says that is illegal. The GAO, in observing all the facts, has stated that the President is acting outside the law."

[25]   *New York Times*, 12 May 1983.

[26]   William Shawcross, *Sideshow: Kissinger, Nixon and the Destruction of Cambodia* (New York: Simon and Schuster, 1979), p. 270. The topics of Korea and Vietnam occupy a substantial portion of Haig's chapter entitled "On Central America" in his memoir *Caveat* (London: Macmillan, 1984), pp. 117-140)

[27]   Shawcross, *Sideshow*, p. 271.

the end of April Senator Symington of the Senate Foreign Relations Committee concluded that the embassy's activities were "illegal."[28]

This antecedent had probably not been forgotten when liberal members of Congress came to evaluate Enders's testimony, on Central America, ten years later. He stated that covert operations against Nicaragua (under his overall direction) are not a violation of the OAS Charter, and do not conflict with a December 1982 congressional prohibition on expenditures "for the purpose" of overthrowing the Nicaraguan government. However, according to the *Newsweek* cover story on the covert operations against Nicaragua, "The driving forces behind this operation were Haig and Enders . . . both the agency (CIA) and the Pentagon had qualms."[29] The same report adds that local command of the operation is in the hands of U.S. ambassador to Honduras John Negroponte who "was handpicked for the job" and "sent down there by Haig and Enders to carry out the operation without any qualms of conscience."[30] "Negroponte, under pressure from Haig and Enders to produce some successes against the Sandinistas, turned to the only promising group available—the Somocistas . . . that wasn't the original plan. . . . It was Negroponte who began dealing with the guardsmen and the Somocistas."[31] Here, too, the Vietnam connection resurfaces, for Negroponte had served as political officer in Saigon.[32] Congressman Torricelli (Democrat, New Jersey) states that when, in April 1983, he reproached Ambassador Negroponte with violating a December 1982 law against attempting to overthrow the Nicaraguan government, the ambassador told him this was "a legal triviality" that should not stand in the way of U.S. objectives.[33]

For career officials with this background, Central America seems to offer the chance of purging the "Vietnam syndrome" by reenacting that drama, but this time on territory they judge to be more favorable to the American cause. The crucial point, however, is that Haig chose career officials known for this approach to Southeast Asia, and gave them full powers to conduct Central American policy, a decision confirmed by Haig's successor. They can be under

---

[28] Shawcross, *Sideshow*. As Shawcross explains it: "The justification for bombing Cambodia had been to protect Americans in Vietnam. Since October 1970 the Congress had included in every military appropriation bill a proviso expressly forbidding bombing in Cambodia except for that purpose. By the end of March 1973 there were no American troops left in Cambodia. Still the bombing of Cambodia increased" (p. 277). In 1974 the Senate Foreign Relations Committee "issued an unusual rebuke in which it called Enders's original description of the embassy role 'grossly misleading' and concluded that the embassy had made 'a conscious effort' to conceal its role in the bombing."

[29] *Newsweek* (8 November 1982):10.

[30] *Ibid.*, p. 11.

[31] *Ibid.*, p. 12.

[32] He is quoted by Shawcross as follows: "I am a Vietnam expert, and I always thought of Cambodia as just an adjunct to the whole damn thing. I knew what I had to do but I didn't get involved in the gory details." Shawcross, *Sideshow*, p. 269.

[33] *Washington Post*, 14 April 1983.

little doubt what their superiors expect of them. Consequently, the State Department has for the most part acted to sharpen the regional confrontation and to insist on the kind of U.S. victory that would leave no compensations to the losing side. Intermittent expressions of interest in various Latin American and European proposals for a compromise settlement have been rather obviously cosmetic. Although there are various tactical advantages to taking such plans seriously (throwing critics on the defensive, possibly splitting moderates away from the far left) the administration has seemed unwilling to make any real concessions in order to obtain genuine settlement. Indeed, the one occasion (in February 1983) when Enders showed some small signs of flexibility (seeking the good offices of Felipe González) his freedom of action was promptly curtailed on orders from the NSC. In May 1983 Enders was dismissed and State Department control over Central American policy was sharply reduced. Over the ensuing year the main initiative seems to have passed to the National Security Council, with the CIA and the ideological right exercising a decisive role. [At the time of writing (June 1984), with a presidential election looming, there are some signs that the State Department may once again be taking a more active role, prompted no doubt by the cutoff of funds for the Nicaraguan counter-revolutionaries. Certainly Secretary of State Shultz's unexpected decision to meet that month with the Nicaraguan leadership indicates some change of emphasis, though whether this is cosmetic or substantial remains to be established.]

THE SECURITY AGENCIES

The National Security Council operates from inside the White House, and the NSC adviser (like the director of the CIA) reports directly to the president. Under Nixon, both these agencies enjoyed great authority and encroached on the prerogatives of rival bureaucratic and legislative agencies that lacked such direct sponsorship from the presidency. In the aftermath of Watergate and the American withdrawal from Vietnam, both these agencies were somewhat curbed. But the spectacle of executive impotence during the Iranian hostage crisis created a strong demand for a more forceful presidency.

Already before the 1981 election, President Carter had somewhat strengthened the CIA's defenses against what was considered excessive public and congressional supervision, and had tilted toward the NSC, rather than the State Department, as a major source of foreign policy advice. The Reagan administration set out with the intention of revitalizing the CIA and freeing it from burdensome restraints. As regards the NSC, however, Reagan's initial intention was to give it a more subordinate role, leaving the main responsibility for foreign policy in the hands of the secretary of state. In general, that is how Reagan's Central American policy has been managed, but as this subject became an object of great public and congressional controversy during

1982 and early in 1983, more initiative passed to those agencies closest to the White House, and least subject to congressional control.

Reagan's first appointees to head both the CIA and the National Security Council proved controversial, and unsettling for the agencies. This made it easier for Haig and Enders to establish their preeminence as managers of administration policies in Central America. One possible motive for the State Department's subsequent inflexibility on the regional crisis may have been to outflank the security agencies, and to ensure that the President reposes full confidence in a unified foreign-policy-making establishment at the State Department.

A March 1981 Presidential Finding on Central America authorized a major program of intelligence gathering by the CIA, and in November of the same year authorization was granted for covert operations to interdict arms flows from Nicaragua to El Salvador. Until late 1982 it was believed that these operations were all under tight control from Washington, and that they conformed to the various congressional restrictions and reporting requirements introduced in the mid-1970s to guard against abuses of power by the CIA. However, as noted above, the information reaching Congress in the spring of 1983 suggested that either these operations were slipping out of control from Washington or some executive agencies were misleading the legislature. There has, however, been no suggestion that the CIA has acted contrary to the instructions of the National Security Council, or without the knowledge of the Departments of State and Defense. All the evidence suggests that these agencies have been effectively coordinating their activities in Central America. By April 1983 some $50 million had been spent on CIA intelligence-gathering activities that feed information to the U.S. embassies in Honduras and El Salvador. In addition to a limited number of U.S. military advisers, there are several hundred intelligence personnel stationed in Central America (150 in El Salvador alone), including some agents engaged in counterinsurgency operations in Guatemala.[34]

The administration denies that these officials are engaged in unauthorized subversion against the government of Nicaragua. The evidence presented to closed hearings of congressional committees has given rise to considerable alarm. Perhaps the best summary available to the general public has been provided by Stansfield Turner, who served as President Carter's director of the CIA, and who comments that:

> CIA people can get carried away with the dedication to getting the job done. There is no question that, as in the case of Nicaragua, controls make the task of covert action more difficult. It was my observation, as head of the CIA, that quite a few of the "old hands" in the Agency found it very difficult to accept these impediments. I forced several dozens of them into

[34] The *New York Times, 20 March* 1983 gave a fairly full description of the US intelligence network in Central America.

retirement because the controls were the law of the land. . . . A large number of CIA retirees have apparently been called back into service to direct the Nicaraguan operation.

Turner believes that CIA activities in Nicaragua probably do tend to subvert the Managua government. He explains that "the people the CIA enlists to do the covert work will not always have the same purpose as the United States. . . . In most cases the people working for us gain sufficient momentum of their own at some point to go on without us if necessary." Moreover, in this case "the CIA may have started out deliberately to undermine the government of Nicaragua only to have the Congress prohibit that purpose."[35]

Although the CIA may have been "carried away" in its enthusiasm for the covert war against Nicaragua, the agency is not entirely beyond congressional restraint, as the June 1984 cutoff of the funds for that war makes clear. Senator Moynihan expressed the fear that the CIA would try to get around this by obtaining money from third parties such as Israel or Saudi Arabia, or might use funds from other programs; indeed such devices are probable at the margin. However, according to Bob Woodward in the *Washington Post*, when the White House asked the CIA if it could divert money from other operations, or "slush funds," to Central America, the agency replied with a legal opinion advising against any attempt to skirt the letter or spirit of congressional oversight. It seems that the memory of Watergate lives on.

At least since 1981, and probably since 1979, the NSC has provided the framework for coordinating Washington's responses to the revolutionary challenge in Central America. This is not to deny the leading role of the State Department in initiating the implementing policy, but it underlines the close and continuing concern of the White House in this aspect of foreign policy making. The NSC deals only with crises and with issues of pressing concern to the president. It selects certain issues for priority attention and provides a means of resolving deadlocks and overcoming inertia in the major government departments. Any issue that comes before the NSC will certainly be evaluated with an eye to America's global rivalry with the Soviet Union. Other facets of the issue may often not receive such thorough attention.

These general characteristics of the NSC are of course much accentuated under the Reagan administration, all the more so in the case of the Central American crisis. In response to opposition from much of the press, U.S. and international opinion, major currents within Congress, and even important sections of the Washington bureaucracy, the NSC has acquired an increasingly prominent role in asserting and enforcing the official viewpoint. According to the *New York Times*, in 1981 President Reagan established a new committee, the National Security Planning Committee, with membership restricted to a very few senior White House and cabinet officials. The paper quotes one

[35]   As quoted in *The Guardian* (London) 25 April 1983.

informant as saying that the people "are fascinated with covert operations and find it easier to approve them than to discuss complicated diplomatic matters."[36]

William Clark, national security adviser from 1981 to 1983, took especial care to ensure that President Reagan's views on Central America were faithfully reflected in NSC documents, and used his considerable influence with the president to ensure that any slight deviations of line (e.g., by the State Department) were quickly corrected. As controversy mounted in the spring of 1983, Clark also encouraged the president to personalize his endorsement of the administration's approval. Clark's successor as adviser, Robert C. McFarlane, has scrupulously continued this tradition. Clearly President Reagan's personal convictions have contributed significantly to shaping the policy of his administration on Central America. But equally clearly these policies are not the personal whim of a single individual. They stem from a worldview that is strongly entrenched in U.S. public life and that is promoted by many active exponents, fundraisers, and organizers. These may be called the "ideological right."

THE IDEOLOGICAL RIGHT

The Reagan campaign naturally attracted support from the many U.S. political commentators and analysts who consider that over the past decade the United States has been too weak in its response to Soviet challenges. From the White House, Reagan has favored those who express this view with the greatest intransigence and ideological purity. A widespread U.S. reaction to the frustrations of Vietnam and Iran, and to Soviet actions in Poland and Afghanistan, has facilitated this stance for which UN ambassador Jeane J. Kirkpatrick has become a representative figure. In speeches to the UN, she has compared the Sandinista regime in Nicaragua unfavorably with the preceding Somoza dictatorship, and she has taken a correspondingly charitable view of human rights violations in El Salvador, a country she describes as an imperfect democracy. She has expressed shock that there is so little support within the UN for this method of classification or for the policy prescriptions that it serves. Nevertheless, her convictions remain unshakeable.

Indeed, disregard for contrary opinion is a hallmark of the ideological right. In general, they view Soviet expansionism as the theme that unifies all the United States' apparently disparate international difficulties. They also regard the Soviet Union as incorrigible and therefore advocate more or less indiscriminate confrontation with the USSR's allies, and almost equally indiscriminate reconciliation with those political forces around the world that share their anti-Sovietism. They regard critics who seek to qualify the simplicity of this formula as self-deluded and lacking in clarity about the true condition of

[36] *New York Times*, 11 June 1984.

the world. Opinions of this kind are strongly represented within the security agencies and in the entourage of the president. Those in charge of the State Department may not fully share all these beliefs but, having borrowed from this rhetoric, they must operate within its framework of assumptions if they are to retain the confidence of the White House. (Thus, statements on Central America by Secretary of State Shultz have come increasingly to resemble the terms used by his predecessor.) The key assumption shared by the president's most trusted advisers is that nothing must deflect the administration from its resolve to crush the "pro-Soviet" challenge in Central America. It would be a logical application of this worldview to authorize the mining of Nicaragua's harbors and to back the ex-Somocistas in a war to the finish against the Sandinista government. After Congress had rejected these two measures, in the spring of 1984, Kirkpatrick announced that she would be returning to academic life at the end of that year. It should not be supposed however that this current of opinion has definitively lost its influence. On the contrary, a reelected President Reagan would have no further elections to contest and might therefore feel freer to do what he believes to be "right."

PRESIDENT REAGAN

Clearly, Ronald Reagan's vehement anticommunism, and his opposition on patriotic grounds to the Panama Canal treaties, made him a figure particularly unlikely to show flexibility in response to the revolutionary challenge in Central America. Thus, over the course of his presidency, as the U.S. position in the Isthmus came under increasing challenge, and as pressure mounted within the United States for a more conciliatory approach to the conflict, responsibility for Washington's decisions was increasingly—and rightly—attributed to the president personally. Against the advice of some of his political strategists, Reagan has proved willing to publicize his personal involvement on behalf of this unpopular cause.

It would, however, be an error to conclude from this that Washington's policy in Central America is explicable mainly in terms of an individual political biography. Every U.S. president elected since 1945 can claim to have "saved" some foreign country from communism (at least temporarily). Truman "saved" Greece; Eisenhower "saved" Guatemala; Kennedy "saved" South Vietnam; Johnson "saved" the Dominican Republic; Nixon "saved" Cambodia; and Carter "saved" El Salvador. These are not all equivalent cases but, equally well, Reagan can point to a long succession of precedents for his stance. However, on further examination this historical record is less reassuring to the present incumbent, because all but one of the above-mentioned Presidents also "lost" some foreign country to the Soviet sphere of influence (China, North Korea, Cuba, South Vietnam, and Nicaragua). The only exception was Lyndon Johnson, hardly a very heartening precedent considering the associated consequences. Of course, this way of classifying events is quite crude and misleading in terms of international politics, but it is a fairly accurate representation of U.S. domestic perceptions.

Consequently, the civil war in El Salvador would present *any* U.S. president with some politically difficult decisions, regardless of whether the United States had any vital strategic or material interest at stake in that particular country. For Reagan it would be particularly costly. He has presented himself as a strong leader dedicated to restoring his country's old self-confidence and international authority. Thus he can hardly acquiesce in the "loss" of any allied country, however minor, especially if he has no offsetting success that he could demonstrate. Powerful backers on the right of Republican politics would be bitterly alienated by such an outcome, whatever the excuses. A broad swathe of public opinion would be disillusioned because there is a widespread desire in the United States to believe that the country's former greatness can be restored by a suitable display of leadership and principle.

President Reagan has not hesitated to throw his personal authority behind the administration's hard line on Central America. In the spring of 1983, when his critics in Congress seemed on the point of forcing a change of course, he addressed a special joint session and appealed over the heads of the members of Congress to the wider American public. On several occasions since then he has made national appeals stressing the administration's view of what is at stake in Central America. In April 1984, for example, he invited Hispanic-American leaders to the White House to tell them that the "strategic balance of the world" was at stake, and that "if Central America is lost then our own borders will be threatened." These appeals have undoubtedly strengthened his hand domestically, although they have also raised the stakes internationally. His own merits as a "communicator" are well known, and he always poses the issues in terms that are readily intelligible to a relatively ill-informed public opinion. In addition, and perhaps of decisive importance, most shades of opinion in the United States are tired of foreign policy failures and discredited presidencies. They give Ronald Reagan the benefit of the doubt because they want him to succeed when Johnson, Nixon, and Carter are all felt to have failed. Nevertheless, the substance of his message must cause quite widespread skepticism and unease. To "lose" China might be a tragedy—even to "lose" Cuba—but it requires a suspension of disbelief to argue that El Salvador is in the same league. If Mexico were really in jeopardy would the Mexican government be begging for U.S. restraint? If the Panama Canal and the security of the West was at risk, would all U.S. allies (and most members of the U.S. Congress) hold back from presidential initiatives? Finally, if the security threat in Central America were as grave as the president claims, why has he ruled out the despatch of U.S. forces? In fact, the greatest source of unease is the fear that eventually his domino analysis will force him to send U.S. troops to the region.

In April 1984 the *Washington Post* quoted a senior administration official to the effect that, if Mr. Reagan wins reelection in November 1984, "the

President is determined to go all out to gain the upper hand" over leftist forces in Central America. (However this would probably take the form of increased funding for U.S.-supported forces, rather than the introduction of U.S. troops, according to this informant.) On 12 April the administration responded to this report with an unusual three-page joint statement signed by Shultz, Weinberger, Casey, and McFarlane: "We state emphatically that we have not considered, nor have we developed plans to use military forces to invade Nicaragua or any other Central American country." They denied plans for a "post-election military enterprise in Central America" and stressed their determination to work with Congress and to stay within the law. Notwithstanding this striking declaration, well-informed critics assert that since the summer of 1983 U.S. forces have been practicing amphibious landings in Honduras and have pre-positioned ammunition and other equipment there. Skeptics have also seized on the word "invasion" in this statement, pointing out that a troop landing invited by a friendly government would not receive that designation.

In the last analysis it is hard to doubt that any U.S. president who was presented with a suitable justification would possess the legal, political, and military means to despatch U.S. troops. "Difficulties" with Congress, and with public opinion would develop *after* that decision had been taken, if general assent for the president's interpretation of the local situation could not be won. A reelected President Reagan is more likely than most to run such a risk, since he has committed so much personal prestige to the presentation of pro-American regimes in the area, since he strongly believes in the hard-line analysis of what is at stake, and since after reelection he will be in a stronger position to hold out for his views, even against widespread domestic skepticism.

CONCLUSION

This article deals only with the domestic factors affecting Washington's policies towards the Isthmus. It cannot fully assess the validity of administration claims that Soviet-Cuban expansion in the area threatens vital national interests of the United States. There is a vast and unresolved debate on this question. That discussion is based upon scraps of hard evidence embedded in large chunks of mis- or disinformation. There is at least some element of self-fulfilling prophecy involved, as the Reagan administration has pushed the Nicaraguans into the Soviet camp. Of course, there is no doubt that the Cubans and the Nicaraguans have supported the insurgents in El Salvador with the aim of extending revolution through Central America, a development that would certainly cause a substantial loss of American prestige and that might also put some strategic interests at risk. But the administration has misrepresented this support, magnifying its importance out of all proportion to the other causes of conflict and even provoking the authorities in Havana and Managua by giving no credit to their gestures of restraint.[37]

The above account of U.S. policy making argues that the initiative in Reagan's Washington lies with the "ideological right" who propose a far more Manichean view. They would see retreat in Central America as involving not just a loss of U.S. prestige but a major moral defeat for the cause of freedom; not just a limited strategic advantage to Havana, but a major advance in the Soviet scheme of worldwide aggression. They talk quite literally of Soviet-inspired civil war in Mexico, with millions of refugees pouring across the Rio Grande. They answer those who cannot share their sometimes apocalyptic visions by charging them with either naïveté or complicity. In its extreme this is a closed system of belief responsive neither to counterargument nor to contrary evidence.

Consequently, arguments over the persuasiveness of such claims are something of a false trail, unlikely to explain very much about the real motives for Washington's decisions. It would be a different matter if the arguments put by the ideological right had persuaded the Pentagon, Congress, the press, or America's leading allies. But they have persuaded only the president, his immediate entourage, and some predisposed sectors of U.S. opinion. As we have seen above, there *was* a consensus on such views at an earlier time (Guatemala in 1954) when the shock of Korea was still vivid. That precedent undoubtedly encourages members of the ideological right to believe that their past successes can be repeated, but it also serves to alert their critics to where such an analysis may lead.

It is, of course, possible to visualize Soviet initiatives that would transform the climate of American opinion and vindicate the administration. However, it is not necessary to hold a benevolent view of Soviet intentions to predict that Moscow is likely to exercise a degree of restraint. The costs of overinvolvement in Central America would be higher for the USSR than for the United States. In any case, Soviet interests are so well served by the present intransigent posture of the Reagan administration that they would be foolish, indeed, to provide the justification that would rally a skeptical nation around its president.

The introduction also sketched an alternative explanation that views Washington's policies as the product of a worldwide network of "military-corporate" interests. Here, too, the article can only be indicative, and not conclusive, but it lends little support to any interpretation resting on economic determinism or the hypothesis of a unified power elite.

On the military side, we have presented evidence of bureaucratic dissension between the Defense Department and the CIA, with the latter organization seeking to restore its funding after a period of austerity and to escape from the restraints on it imposed during the 1970s. Central America has been an area of

---

[37] See note 16.

special interest to the CIA ever since its "success" there in 1954, but many in the Pentagon are evidently dissatisfied by the CIA's amateurism and lack of perspective on Isthmian matters. If America's "military-corporate interests" do, in fact, act in a unified way to promote their vital interests, this would be expressed through the Defense Department and crystallized in support for its plans massively to increase U.S. military spending. Viewed from this perspective, Reagan's Central American involvement is an irritating distraction that threatens to jeopardize public support for a much wider defense buildup.

On the corporate side it is not easy, since the decline of the United Fruit Company, to identify major U.S. business interests that would be deeply affected by anything that could happen in Central America. Among the many active groups of lobbyists seeking to influence Washington's Isthmian policies, the main business organizations are conspicuous by their absence. Thus, to vindicate the "military-corporate" interpretation one would either need to demonstrate that the "ideological right" is the true vanguard of the U.S. ruling class, or to invoke some more concealed bias in the system causing it to serve military-corporate interests without any visible exercise of direction on their part. This article has not explored these alternatives very far, but, even so, it indicates the difficulty of sustaining such an interpretation. Undoubtedly the "ideological right" has been well funded, and its network of wealthy and powerful supporters would constitute a significant element of any putative U.S. ruling class. However, this group is far from being hegemonic. Its frustration with the press and television is one indication of its minority status. Even in the case of privately funded foundations and lobbying organizations, the right is far from dominating the field. Its hold at the national level is demonstrably quite contingent and precarious. Therefore, the "military-corporate" explanation would have to rely on some more intangible counter-revolutionary bias in the U.S. political system.

The existence in U.S. politics of a strong slant in favor of private enterprise and against all but the tamest variants of socialism hardly requires elaborate demonstration. Nor is it surprising that Washington takes a systematically unfavorable view of those Third World governments and political movements that are closely aligned with the archrivals in Moscow.

However, to explain U.S. policy in Central America would require identifying a far more specific source of bias than this. From these starting points it does not obviously follow that Central America should receive priority attention in Washington; or that America need identify itself so closely with the kind of protégés it has acquired in the Isthmus; or that allied proposals for a resolution of regional conflicts on the basis of compromise should be shunned; or that the United States need promote a polarization within the region that necessarily expands the numbers willing to take help even from Moscow. Far from that, these biases in U.S. politics would be perfectly compatible with a policy of disengagement in Central America and could even provide a rationale for indifference at the prospect of "Cuba model states" (NSC jargon) throughout the Isthmus. On these premises, a corporate-military strategist might perfectly well argue that these countries are unlikely to provide showcases for central economic planning that would dim the appeal of the private enterprise system. Moreover, the strategist might argue, if Moscow were unwise enough to underwrite the experiment, so much the better for Washington (rid of an unpopular and unrewarding encumbrance) and so much the worse for the rival power. In short, unless the ideological right can be shown to be the true vanguard of America's "corporate-military" power structure, this type of analysis becomes far too imprecise to explain in even the broadest outline the kind of response Washington has made to the Central American crisis.

To explain the pattern of Washington's response requires far more attention to the uncertain balance of forces within the United States on this issue and to the idiosyncratic concerns of U.S. domestic politics. The rationalizations outlined above are a facade. As far as the United States is concerned, the real significance of Central America is as a focus for the reenactment of unresolved internal disputes about the nature of U.S. society and the purpose of U.S. power. It is just the accident of the Nicaraguan revolution that has caused these internal U.S. preoccupations to be projected with such intensity on to Central America, when they could just as well be played out in Africa, Southeast Asia (or, indeed, in outer space).

Perceptions in Washington of the Central American situation are what shape the United States' Isthmian policies; and those perceptions have a surprisingly loose relationship to local realities. This point has been argued with particular reference to the official "definition of the situation" presented by the Reagan administration, and undoubtedly that definition presents a rather clear-cut example of oversimplification, distortion, and disregard for inconvenient evidence. But the point is, in fact, far more general. Washington policy debates are, in general, conducted on the basis of capsule statements about complex and unfamiliar foreign conditions. This tendency is most pronounced when dealing with what are defined as crisis situations requiring urgent high-level attention and when dealing with minor countries that elicit little interest except in times of tension. In order for the affairs of a country like El Salvador or Honduras to "get on the agenda" of senior officials, members of Congress, powerful lobbyists, or even influential news reporters, some way must be found to demonstrate their "relevance" to more general Washington concerns. (The continual effort to present Central America in terms of "another Vietnam" exemplifies this need—felt as strongly by critics of the administration as by supporters—to place the Isthmus within some frame of reference that will command more general recognition and interest.) Joan Didion's perceptive essay *Salvador* underlines the unimportance of any local reality except what can be packaged into familiar U.S. categories and assumptions.

The March 1982 elections in El Salvador provide one illustration. It would require considerable familiarity with Salvadoran society and politics, and an unusual combination of both empathy and detachment, to grasp what such an electoral test might signify to those caught in the middle of that country's turmoil. However, U.S. interpretations of the event detached the familiar fact of voting from its real context, so that it could be more readily fitted into the categories of the Washington debate.

It is the enormous disproportion between the pressure that the United States can bring to bear on Central America and U.S. knowledge of, or accountability to, the people who live there, that explains why the fit between Washington's perceptions and local realities can be so loose. Latin Americans (and Latin Americanists) have difficulty in appreciating the importance, and the inevitability, of the filtering process at work here. It is natural for them to assume that when Washington adopts a forceful policy towards some government in the region, the essential explanation must be found in something that has happened, or might happen, or is imagined to be possible in the country in question. However, it is equally plausible to argue that Washington's hard line against Arbenz was a reaction to the Korean War, and that Carter's policy towards El Salvador was determined by events in Teheran. Certainly an essential element of the Washington response to Central America's turmoil has been the deep-felt wish by most U.S. leaders (and much U.S. public opinion) for some kind of "victory" that would restore national morale after the humiliations of Watergate, Vietnam, and Iran. It happens that Washington has turned to Central America as the location for a prospective victory, but the location is almost accidental.

However, Central America might seem a particularly promising choice of arena in which to restore U.S. prestige and morale. Yet, from another vantage point, it seems highly unsuitable. The historical role of the United States in the region has been the object of much criticism, and in any case local conditions offer little prospect of any "victory" in which the United States could really take pride. Indeed, a plausible case can be made that if the Reagan administration were finally to prevail in Central America, this would be a worse outcome for America's international prestige, and even for domestic self-esteem, than any setback that could follow from "losing," say, El Salvador. However, as suggested in the introduction to this paper, it would be unwise to seek explanations of U.S. policy that rely too heavily on an assumed calculus of national interest. U.S. power is still so great in relation to many of her neighbors that U.S. foreign policy can afford to disregard the usual limitations imposed by reciprocity. The heart of the matter is that U.S. opinion is deeply divided (and not always entirely rational) about what kind of national prestige it would like to see reestablished and about what type of foreign policy would restore domestic morale. It is Central America's misfortune to have become the arena for working out these internal U.S. disagreements.

The animus behind what I have called the "ideological right" comes from the belief, forcefully articulated in many of Reagan's speeches, that the United States was justified in fighting the Vietnam War, and that Washington should have taken the measures necessary to prevail in that conflict. The cause was righteous, the means were at hand, the diagnosis was accurate—all that failed was the resolve of the nation's leaders. On this view, the main obstacles to reestablishing U.S. prestige and morale are the liberal media, the unpatriotic or misguided critics of the war, and those sectors of public opinion who were misled by these influences. The conflict in Central America was seen as providing the Reagan administration with the opportunity to reengage and defeat these domestic opponents, in a debate that existed quite independently of any Isthmian developments. Opponents of the administration are also engaged in reenacting old conflicts, largely unrelated to Central American conditions. They see what they consider the errors of Vietnam being repeated with the same damaging effects as before on U.S. prestige and on domestic morale. Opposition to the administration is only secondarily concerned with the consequences that are following for the inhabitants of Central America or for the strategic balance; the consequences within the United States, and the implications for the country's sense of national purpose and identity, concern them rather more. The progress of this far-reaching and still unresolved internal debate, not really about Central America at all, is what really shapes Washington's policies toward that region.

An explanation pitched at this level of generality must not overlook some rather concrete observations. In reality, the contrasts between U.S. involvement in Southeast Asia and in Central America are very large; in practice, many top Washington policymakers are aware of the inaccuracies of the ideological posture they have been adopting; and critics of the administration also realize that this is no mechanical repetition of an earlier experience.

One clear contrast with Vietnam concerns the economic cost to the United States. In April 1982 the NSC estimated that the administration policy would probably "succeed" without the deployment of any regular troops, if Washington was prepared to spend about one billion dollars a year for, say, four or five years. By 1984 the Kissinger Commission had increased this to $8 billion over five years, by adding broader socioeconomic objectives. By Southeast Asian standards this is a negligible sum. Of course, cost overruns are predictable in such cases, and, contrary to NSC calculations, the administration faces a real risk of ever-deepening involvement, to the point where regular forces might have to be deployed. But Congress has made clear that, in contrast to Vietnam, it will not approve increased appropriations or approval for the despatch of troops. The administration must try, therefore, to make do with proxy forces and a very limited budget (less, for example, than London is devoting to the annual cost of garrisoning the Falkland Islands).

Despite the ideological rhetoric cloaking administration policy, many senior advisers (if not the president himself) almost certainly have private reservations about the administration's wilder claims. For example, they probably have access to sober assessments of Soviet motivations, and these almost certainly indicate caution in Moscow. The Soviet Union will not wish to overextend itself but would view the despatch of U.S. troops as an opportunity for anti-American propaganda and would hope that the cost of suppressing dissent in Central America would weaken the U.S. defense effort. Senior officials in the State Department and the Pentagon (e.g., those responsible for reacting to the Polish crisis of 1981) are most unlikely to misunderstand this point. Nor are they likely to take at face value the moral invocations used to justify administration policy. The truth about "human rights" must be as well known inside the administration as outside; it is simply not possible to say so. The nature of Salvadoran democracy must also be quite well understood by experienced officials. After deploying massive firepower to destroy the Khmer Rouge (presented as puppets of Hanoi who, in turn, were taking orders from Moscow and Peking), the Vietnam hawks now serve in an administration that indirectly encourages the Khmer Rouge and that even presses their claims for recognition at the UN. Knowledge of this must breed some skepticism in official circles about allegations of any monolithic conspiracy running from Moscow through Havana and Managua to El Salvador and Guatemala. Such allegations may not be credible among the better informed. They are propagated, nonetheless, at least in part because, in their absence, it would be necessary to debate seriously the United States' historical role on the Isthmus, not a topic on which the administration wishes to dwell.

The more thoughtful critics of the administration also understand that the Vietnam analogy is neither so direct nor so unambiguous as it might seem. For instance, they know that what followed the U.S. withdrawal from Indochina (and subsequently from Iran) is impossible to explain or justify to the American people. That fact has given the ideological right much of its impetus. Critics of the administration must, therefore, be very wary of overidentification with the Central American insurgents. U.S. withdrawal may be the least of evils, but those who think so need a way of withdrawing in good order and without rashly endorsing the "other side." The Reagan administration's strongest card is that it may force the closure of this option, knowing that, whatever doubts the American people may have about U.S. involvement in Central America, the U.S. public does not want another national humiliation. Critics who explain U.S. policy in terms of a conspiracy by "military-corporate interests" tend to bypass these awkward realities and thereby deceive themselves.

Although the underlying debate about U.S. identity and purpose was crystallized by the Vietnam War, its origins go back much further, as do the origins of Washington's present dilemma in Central America. Indeed, the weight of history bears more heavily on this aspect of U.S. foreign policy than perhaps on any other. Reagan achieved distinction within the Republican party at least in part because of his intransigence over the Panama Canal, a far earlier episode of national history on which the liberal intelligentsia (together with the entire spectrum of Latin American opinion) are quite out of touch with much popular nationalist sentiment in the United States. It is startling to recall the lurid rhetoric used by opponents of the Canal treaties before they were ratified. Although none of their dire predictions came to pass they remain unabashed. Now even more lurid predictions emanate from the same quarters about the possible consequences of an insurgent victory in El Salvador. If, by any chance, such predictions were shown to have even a grain of truth, their authors could expect a high reward. Their careers would suffer little harm, on the other hand, if their predictions proved groundless. This is a reflection of what has traditionally been America's enormous power in relation to her near neighbors, which leaves her free to pursue a regional policy of over-insurance, a luxury almost unknown to the foreign-policy makers of other nations. This disproportionate power has also enabled Washington to reassert old-fashioned forms of domination (e.g., by the present ambassador in Honduras). It also explains why Central America can be used as a screen on which to project U.S. internal debates. Friends and allies of the United States in Europe and in Latin America have attempted to interpose themselves and thus to facilitate a U.S. disengagement from a region where its historically established reflexes are so atavistic. But that is unacceptable to the ideological right because it would undercut their position in the internal U.S. debate.

This article has focused attention on the interplay between a variety of domestic institutions, interests, and influences. The final outcome for Central America still seems very hard to predict. This approach suggests that much can depend upon accidents of timing (the electoral timetable, the side effects of other controversies) and on rather specific questions of institutional detail (for example, the composition and susceptibilities of various congressional subcommittees, the way in which rivalries within the administration are resolved). Beyond these inherent uncertainties of the decision-making process in Washington, this article has also drawn attention to the complex and uncertain role played by public opinion in general, and by certain specific lobbies in particular. Although the polls have shown opinion to be strongly adverse to the administration viewpoint, this has not proved sufficient to impede the implementation of a highly intransigent policy. The relationship between opinion and policy is far from direct or unilineal and, although hostile opinion has greatly constrained the administration's freedom of maneuvre, there are ambiguities in the public attitude that may still be exploited in favor of the Reagan administration's stance. In contrast to the 1950s, the news media have played a fairly independent and critical role—in part, no doubt, because Vietnam and Watergate gave encouragement to dissenters, and perhaps also because Central America is so geographically and linguistically accessible to U.S. reporters.

In view of all these competing influences and the institutional complexities, one might expect that Washington's Central American policy would be vacillating and centrist, but this has not been so. The additional ingredient that has caused such polarization and intransigence, and that makes the eventual outcome still so uncertain, is a factor supposedly abolished from pluralist politics long ago: ideology (or perhaps less grandly one might call it hurt national pride). The outcome in Central America may not in practical terms be that important to the United States, but it has now become highly charged in symbolic terms. U.S. citizens are once again debating the nature of their society, and what use to make of their nation's still very considerable relative power. Central America provides them with a touchstone for this internal debate.

12

The Nicaraguan Conflict: Politics and Propaganda

George Philip

The conflicts now taking place in Central America are being fought at several levels. The military conflict is low-intensity and at present seems roughly stalemated. No Central American government is in imminent danger of collapse and no insurgent group currently faces elimination. The future of Central America will be affected, however, not only by the balance of force within the area but also by the ways in which the protagonists seek to win the sympathies of the outside world and by their success in doing so. For example, Washington's commitment to democratisation within the area—genuine enough, it seems, if somewhat belated—has played an important part in the political evolution of El Salvador and may yet have its effect upon Guatemala. It has also greatly helped rally opinion within the United States round President Reagan's policies and has also helped attract support for these policies in western Europe and elsewhere. The propaganda war has obvious implications for the way in which Central America is perceived in other parts of the world. These perceptions may ultimately matter far more than events within the region itself.

Nicaragua is a case in point. Here, the propaganda conflict is particularly acute because the Sandinista government is seeking international support with at least as much energy as is Washington. For Nicaragua, a good international reputation is necessary to produce the aid needed for economic survival. The United States faces a particularly hard task in Nicaragua. Its aid to the anti-Sandinista *contras* is a far more difficult project to sell than support for President Duarte in El Salvador. Moreover, if there is to be a major escalation of the military conflict in Central America, this is most likely to occur in Nicaragua. Certainly if Washington were to step up its pressure upon Managua to the point of direct military involvement, the international repercussions would be very great indeed.

"The Nicaraguan Conflict: Politics and Propaganda," *The World Today* (London), December 1985, pp. 222-224. Copyright © 1985 The Royal Institute of International Affairs. Reprinted by permission.

POLICY AND PROPAGANDA IN NICARAGUA

The importance to the Sandinista government of maintaining a favourable international image can virtually be summed up in a single statistic. In every year from 1980 to 1984, Nicaragua's trade deficit has approached the value of its exports (actually exceeding it in 1984). In 1984 its exports totalled $374m and its imports $790m. If allowance is made for some repayment of debt, it seems clear that Nicaragua "earns" at least as much from foreign aid as it does from trade.

Some of this aid does indeed come from the Soviet Union, including such vital elements as guaranteed oil supplies and weaponry. The east European countries have also been increasing their involvement. Indeed, as aid to Nicaragua from Latin America and international agencies supported by the United States has declined, so the proportion of aid provided by the Soviet bloc has increased.

Nevertheless, it does not seem possible for the Nicaraguan government to try to follow the "Cuban model" of socialising the domestic economy, aligning itself with Moscow and then relying on a heavily increased aid inflow from the Soviet Union. One obvious difficulty here is that the Soviet Union is already too heavily involved financially in Cuba, Afghanistan and elsewhere to want to embark on a major new commitment. Even though the absolute sums involved in shoring up Nicaragua may not be large, it is only one of a number of potential client states which Moscow feels unable fully to satisfy. In any case, its geographical location hardly makes it a crucial factor in Soviet thinking. Another major difficulty, probably even more serious, is that a high-profile Soviet involvement in Nicaragua would almost certainly lead to the stepping up of military pressure from the other side—both from Nicaraguans decisively alienated from the government and from Washington which can ultimately always put more resources into Central America than can the Soviet Union.

There are some indications, however, that Soviet policy toward Nicaragua may be both more subtle and more active than this essentially negative calculation might suggest. Fundamentally, the Soviet strategy is a propaganda one. In a situation somewhat analogous to that of the 1936-9 Spanish Civil War, Soviet support for Nicaragua is given with a sharp eye to its effect upon the European democracies. That is to say, the aim is to use Nicaragua to divide, as far as possible, the United States from its west European allies. This strategy has the merit of being effective whether or not the Sandinistas survive in power. A Sandinista government has a powerfully irritating effect in Washington, whereas an American invasion—or even a limited military action—would obviously intensify anti-American feeling in Europe and Latin America. The obvious middle strategy open to Washington—a mixture of financial squeeze and indirect military pressure—can be countered by the present Soviet policy of guaranteeing oil and counter-insurgency weapons to Managua while encouraging the Sandinistas to seek the less essential aid in precisely those European countries which Moscow hopes to alienate, as far as possible, from Washington.

This Soviet strategy seems relatively new. Indeed, in 1981 the Cubans and the Russians were hoping that a revolutionary tide would sweep Central America and pose major problems to any American government. By last year this hope was temporarily, though not necessarily definitively, abandoned. The Salvadorean rebels, dropping their earlier objective of an early seizure of state power, ended their use of large military units and switched to the use of smaller sabotage squads. They also sought to rebuild their urban political strength, which was largely eliminated by the "dirty war" in and after 1980, and began exploratory peace negotiations with the Duarte government. In July 1985, moreover, President Castro told an international conference in Havana that it was more important for all Latin American countries to agree to a debt repudiation than for there to be "three or four isolated revolutions" in Latin America. Castro's outspokenness on the debt may have helped men like President García of Peru to appear moderate. It may also have helped persuade Washington of the need for some kind of new initiative on the debt issue. The other side of the message, however, clearly understood in Managua, was that "isolated revolutions" needed broad diplomatic support from the Latin American mainstream if they were to survive. Cuba alone could not protect the Sandinistas from Reagan. It was a call for consolidation, which was later re-echoed in Managua itself.

An important part of this strategy is precisely for the Soviet Union not to enthuse too much over the Nicaraguan government. Publicly, Soviet spokesmen state their belief that the Nicaraguan question is a north-south issue rather than an east-west one and, however great their contribution may be to sustaining what is admittedly a very small Central American country, the "headline aid" comes above all from western Europe. The aim is to capitalise on errors and failures on the part of Washington while giving Reagan himself as little as possible to win at.

All of this may give the impression that the Reagan Administration's diagnosis of Nicaragua—a hardline Marxist state with an unsuspected talent for disguise—is essentially the correct one. Such a conclusion would, however, be misleading in a number of ways. For one thing, the character of the Nicaraguan system is not so well defined. During 1985, for example, some major changes of direction have been announced. There has been a marked (though so far incomplete) shift of economic emphasis in the direction of giving incentives to agriculture and a real, if more limited, shift toward offering material incentives to private export interests; the government has also shifted emphasis away from large agricultural units to a policy of permitting land distribution and support for peasant agriculture. Autonomy has been promised to the peoples of the Atlantic Coast, although the situation in this area remains highly complex. The final role of the opposition parties is not yet assured, but this is another area where the government may make changes. The Sandinista government's enforced responsiveness to international opinion has had far more than a marginal effect on the policies pursued; nor, in the best of circumstances, is it likely that the Sandinistas will become autonomous of opinion in the developed democracies for many more years by which time the system may have evolved in some unexpected ways.

Moreover, Nicaragua's international situation plays a major part in determining the balance of forces within the government. Specifically, the Sandinistas are at present advised by a small number of well-known international figures (many of whom have links to Catholic radicals). While there is undoubtedly some resentment at these "foreigners" among native-born Nicaraguans, these advisers have proved their usefulness to the Sandinista leadership by their effectiveness at international public relations ("telling the truth about Nicaragua", as one of them put it). This effectiveness has a direct financial return. It is this which gives these advisers influence with the Sandinistas themselves. Since these advisers tend, almost without exception, to be on the moderate *blando* side of discussions their collective influence is considerable. But it is so mainly because there is a sympathetic and financially generous sector of international opinion to which it can relate. A corollary is that the Sandinistas have been able to rely on a highly sophisticated set of advisers (by no means all of them foreigners, of course) and have, at times, shown political cunning which has taken their opponents by surprise.

This is not to say that the Sandinistas have avoided clumsy errors in their handling of international issues (examples include the poor reception given to the Pope on his 1983 visit, President Ortega's notorious visit to Moscow in the spring of this year, and, in all probability, the recent re-introduction of a state of emergency within Nicaragua). Nor is it to deny that hardliners are to be found in the Sandinista hierarchy. These are *duros* rather than just left-wingers. It is, after all, true that the Sandinistas began as a military organisation and, in any case, a continuing civil war—even though "low-intensity" in the eyes of Washington—presents a real test for the capacities of a small state such as Nicaragua. The need to enforce conscription is obviously a sore point here although this has obvious advantages as well as disadvantages for the government. For example, it removes any threat of unemployment, presents opportunities for indoctrination of troops and disciplines some of the Sandinistas' own formerly wild supporters. If the war goes badly, the Sandinistas will retain the capacity (and, assuredly, the motivation) to return to the hills and offer military opposition to any new government in Managua. If only for these reasons, there are authoritarian tendencies within the Nicaraguan regime which must be set against the moderate public image which the Sandinistas seek to cultivate. It would nevertheless be misleading to identify the hardliners too closely with the Soviet Union and Cuba.

Indeed, the conventional American interpretation of the Sandinistas gives insufficient weight to another of their important characteristics—their generation. By no means all of the leading Sandinistas have been educated abroad, but almost all have been sensitive to the contemporary intellectual currents of their youth. Thus, whereas Reagan's mind seems to have been set in the days of the Second World War and the early Cold War, the Sandinistas are the first Latin American government—and one of the first in the world—to be generationally a part of the student radicalism of the 1960s. (Alan García in Peru is another such figure as, in a different way, is Felipe González in Spain. Daniel Ortega's very warm welcome in Madrid earlier this year was surely no coincidence. Nor is the degree of esteem felt for the Sandinistas on the left wing of the British Labour Party.) The Sandinista heroes are Castro and Guevara rather than Stalin. Many leading Sandinistas spent years of exile in Havana and became critical of the excessive Sovietisation of Cuban society. Their "third-worldism" and dislike of orthodox bureaucratic structures is real. So is their attachment to the radical trend within the Roman Catholic church. They claim to represent "the people" rather than "the proletariat" (a tiny fragment of Nicaraguan society, in any case) and prefer to retain a quasi-military structure rather than seeking to transform themselves into an orthodox Communist Party. Many outsiders find these characteristics attractive. The emergence of the Sandinistas as one of the preferred causes of the no-longer-so-new Left in north America and western Europe should not be a matter for surprise.

THE LATIN AMERICAN DIMENSION

Another obstacle to the Reagan Administration's efforts to present the Nicaraguan conflict as an east-west issue is the attitude of several Latin American governments. The Mexican government, in particular, has an interpretation of the Central American conflicts which is very different from that held in Washington. During the oil-boom years of the López Portillo presidency, Mexico was quite aggressively opposed to American policy in the area. In August 1981, Mexico, together with France, where President Mitterand had just come to power, called for a negotiated solution to the civil war in El Salvador. Under López Portillo's successor, Miguel de la Madrid, a financially strapped Mexico has been far less sympathetic toward Managua; earlier this year Mexican oil exports to Nicaragua were drastically scaled down owing to Nicaraguan non-payment for previous supplies.

Nevertheless, no Mexican government can avoid viewing Central America in quite a different perspective than that of the east-west conflict. There is the traditional "safety valve" interpretation of Mexican politics: that a left-wing foreign policy is used to co-opt potential opponents of far more conservative internal policies and is, therefore, an important component of internal security. But, quite apart from this, there is the additional point that the Mexican Foreign Ministry is largely composed of nationalists who will find ways of seeking to help Nicaragua which are not specifically forbidden by the Mexican President.

Moreover, recent political changes in South America have tended to help the Nicaraguan position. The emergence of García in Peru and of a civilian government in Brazil—to add to earlier changes in foreign policy orientation in Colombia and Argentina—have virtually ensured that the United States cannot find a majority in the Organisation of American States (OAS) or a similar international body for an intensification of diplomatic pressure against Managua. Instead, the addition of the so-called Lima countries (Peru, Brazil, Argentina and Uruguay) to the Contadora countries (Mexico, Venezuela, Panama and Colombia) at the end of July has been a considerable source of comfort to the Nicaraguan authorities. The fact that Costa Rica and, very recently also, Ecuador have taken positions which are openly hostile towards Nicaragua only emphasises Washington's inability to swing Latin American opinion as a whole. The United States' position would have been much stronger had it not been for the South Atlantic conflict in 1982 in which the United States supported Britain rather than Argentina. Meanwhile Costa Rica, whose hostility to Managua has been increasing, has found itself increasingly isolated diplomatically within Latin America.

Space here does not permit a detailed survey of recent diplomatic maneuvring around the question of Nicaragua. Nonetheless, this is an important issue particularly as the original Contadora initiative came to its conclusion at the end of November. Of even greater potential importance will be the composition and outlook of the new governments in Honduras, Guatemala and Costa Rica which will be formed after elections scheduled between November 1985 and February 1986. It may be that Washington will finally succeed in welding together its allies in Central America into an effective united front, but there are still powerful obstacles in the way. No Honduran government, in particular, will want to face an outright confrontation with Nicaragua. All Central American politicians will be aware, moreover, that even the successful destruction of the Sandinista government would not end the civil conflicts in the region. The Sandinistas would survive as a military force even if the *contras* took Managua. Moreover, if the Nicaraguan government did fall, Cuba would have an incentive to abandon its present stance of studied moderation and to supply left-wing insurgents with higher-calibre weapons. An armed Left, working as much against the American presence as against domestic governments, might well spring up in countries such as Honduras which have so far had relatively few internal conflicts. Other Central American governments, therefore, face a tradeoff; their ability to control their own internal situations will be greater if the international status quo is allowed to remain—however unwelcome they may find the prospect of sharing the region with a Sandinista government. The public unwillingness of the Honduran military leaders to become too closely involved with the *contras* shows that this perception is widely shared.

CONCLUSIONS

All of this highlights some of the dilemmas which Washington now faces in its dealings with Nicaragua. It could, of course, try to negotiate a status quo agreement with the Sandinistas. Nicaragua would certainly negotiate on international military matters with Washington—the number of foreign military advisers, the avoidance of foreign bases and so on. It has already offered an amnesty to the *contras*, except the *Somocistas*, and might accept international observers to check that its terms were not violated. Nevertheless, the Sandinistas would not agree to make fundamental political changes. Nicaragua would remain essentially a "Socialist" state. Daniel Ortega recently defined the ruling Sandinista party (the FSLN) as "a political party like the others, but not exactly like the others." This is more of a Leninist concept of a vanguard party than a liberal concept of one party in free competition with others—although one quite far removed from orthodox bureaucratic Stalinism. Such an outcome would not be in line with the aims and objectives of the present American Administration although Washington may later find it has little choice but to accept it.

Alternatively, the United States could choose a military escalation. While an invasion of Nicaragua by American troops would probably still be prohibitively costly in terms of men and reputation, a slightly softer option might involve the selective targeting of Nicaraguan installations (bridges, the oil refinery and so on) for air attacks. Some Sandinistas fear that Washington is now looking for an excuse, possibly a staged border incident with Costa Rica, to launch precisely such an attack. Yet even if the political and diplomatic opposition to this tactic from western Europe and Latin America could be contained, there would remain a Sandinista military movement and possibly still a Sandinista government. The military conflicts in Central America would only intensify.

The present direction of American policy, steering between these two extremes, is not free of difficulty and embarrassment either. Above all, despite the optimistic pronouncements of some American spokesmen, the demise of the Sandinistas does not seem imminent—a fact which Washington may soon have to face. The ability of Daniel Ortega to draw a massive crowd in Madrid, the twinning of Labour-controlled British cities with Nicaraguan towns, the obvious sympathy expressed for Nicaragua in smaller European countries such as Sweden and Holland—will all help the Sandinistas survive and add to friction within the Atlantic alliance.

13

A West European View: Walking a Tightrope Between Self-Assertion and Alliance Loyalty

Peter W. Schulze

In one sense, a West European policy exists only for those subjects on which European institutions hold a discernible policy. We could confine our inquiry to those institutions. In that case we would consider, for example, the European Economic Community (EEC) Council of Ministers, or the Council for European Political Cooperation, the European Parliament (Strasbourg), or the still-dormant West European Union. In foreign policy matters this European record is very slim.

Although European institutions have only a limited mandate to deal with external affairs—mainly economic matters of interest to all member states—there is another sense, paradoxically, in which a "European policy" exists. We find this in the policies of the several European states. European supranational organizations may have issued no guidelines, and there may be no body of priorities, goals and designated policy instruments; but foreign policy issues have always generated "European positions." Of course, the states differ in the priority and intensity of their engagement with any given issue, but their policies—taken together—reflect a European interest.

European political leaderships are mindful that Europe remains a pivotal center of the East-West and North-South conflicts. It is a focal point of emerging superpower rivalry. The focus initially rested on superpower conflict in Eastern Europe; anticolonial struggles—the first form of North-South conflict—excited little interest. Nonetheless, the crises in Berlin, Korea, and Indochina, and political change in China and Southeast Asia, evidenced global political dimensions in which both conflict structures were intertwined. In a way, despite the European losses of "middle-power" status after 1945, Europe never left the international scene solely to the superpowers.

Similar and shared history has led to common norms and interests among European states, a post-World War II "policy consensus." They have achieved this despite remaining at a distance from some international conflicts, or having been unwilling to formulate precise policy options, and despite real differences of interests among them.[1]

"West European policy" is an amalgam of (1) interests of some dominant national states, (2) institutionalized supranational compromises and requirements, and sometimes even (3) interests of specific internal social groups. In the strict sense, then, there is no such thing as a "West European policy," or a West European "Central American policy." If we kept to this strict understanding, we would find national interpretations of Central American issues as elements in national policies, but no defined West European policy.

But if there is a policy in the less strict sense, we would find it by looking at France, Britain, Spain, and Germany, the main contributors to a "West European policy consensus" on foreign policy issues. We would find that we also had to consider domestic political forces. Even if they are outside the government, domestic parties and movements influence, enforce, or bend by some sort of "veto power" the political decisions of governing coalitions. Of special moment are the broad alliances of antinuclear, pro-peace, antimilitarist, antiracist, and ecological groups and Third World solidarity initiatives, for they have become an increasingly consequential political factor in European policies.

Unlikely though it may seem, Central America—less importantly only than South Africa and the Middle East—has motivated the EEC to political activities and statements that assume the texture of a "policy."

EUROPE AND CENTRAL AMERICA

Europe's interests in Central America, even if marginal, are not of recent origin. Spain and Portugal lived a colonial past in Latin America, and England, France, and The Netherlands retain a colonial presence, especially in the Caribbean, Belize, and French Guyana. While old interests were subdued by more pressing facts after World War II—rebuilding European economies and strengthening democratic political systems—from the mid-1960s onward Latin America attracted Europe's attention once more.

Five changes in international politics and the world market created favorable conditions for Europe's renewed interest in Central America:

1. In foreign affairs, *the United States*, although the dominant power of the hemisphere, *was absorbed with the war in Indochina*, and coping with its effects on American society. It had also shifted considerable attention to other

---

[1] For a detailed discussion on European self assertiveness, the emerging correlations between the "Europeanization of security" and its enhanced role in the international system, see: Volker Rittberger, "Europa zwischen den weltpolitischen Interessen der USA und der Sowjetunion," in Arbeitsgruppe Friedensforschung Tübingen: *Atomwaffenfreiheit und Europäische Sicherheit*. Verein für Friedenspädogogik (Argumente 7), Tübingen 1983.

crisis areas, like the Middle East. The result, defined then as political and military *global overcommitment*, changed the economic and political constellation of international forces.

2. This period coincided with *the end of European economic reconstruction, and the beginning of Europe's gradual ascendance in the international system* as an active economic and political factor. Especially in the 1970s, fueled by the internationalization of production, commerce, and financial transactions, Europe's search for new markets unleashed an economic offensive in the Third World that dwarfed "Soviet expansionism."

3. *Latin America*, with a relatively developed infrastructure, educated work force, and cultural and political traditions akin to Europe's own, *became a favored terrain for European capital investments and trade*. European capital investments are concentrated in Argentina, Brazil, Mexico, and to a lesser degree in Venezuela, Colombia, and the Central American states. The EEC has become the second most important export market for Central American goods (coffee, bananas, cotton). To widen and intensify relations with European countries and with the EEC (to reduce dependence on the North American market, and to diversify trade partners) was in the economic interest of Latin America.

Furthermore, the very distance between Europe and the Isthmus, and Europe's not interpreting the region as one of vital security or geostrategic interest, positioned Europe as an ideal potential mediator in conflicts between the United States and countries of the region. Such expectations remain widespread in Latin America.

4. Because of cultural and political similarities and common historical experiences, *a growing network of contacts between nongovernmental organizations, churches, parties, and trade unions developed on both sides*. This realm was not only that of emerging "international solidarity movements of the New Left." Traditional parties, like the Social Democrats and the Christian Democrats, became aware of new ideas and concepts in development (dependency theory, for example) and strengthened contacts with their counterparts through international organizations (for example, the Socialist International).

5. During the 1970s, *Latin America became a focus of attention of Europe's political elite, left and right alike*. Key experiences for the European Left were (a) the rise of the democratically elected Socialist Government of Allende in 1970, and its bloody oppression through a military putsch, aided by the CIA, in 1973 and (b) the emergence of nationalist-oriented military officers and parties in Peru, Panama, Ecuador, and elsewhere. They initiated economic reform programs, often with problematic results, but nevertheless opened social and political avenues for further reform and democratization. Without any doubt, since the successful completion of the Nicaraguan revolution in 1979, the focus of attention and critical support, aggravated by the policies of

the Reagan administration, has shifted toward the Sandinistas and the crisis in Central America.

EUROPEAN-CENTRAL AMERICAN RELATIONS

Central America is a subject of the EEC's Latin America policy. Its main aims were to develop trade relations, strengthen the interregional cooperation of Central American and Caribbean countries and render economic aid and technical support to the region. During the 1970s, there was little European political intervention. Expectations, on the part of the political and cultural elite in some Latin American countries, that Western Europe could position itself as an arbitrator and mediate conflicts with the United States, were not shared by European governments.

Since the deepening of the Central American crisis, some European governments, especially the socialist government of Spain under Felipe Gonzáles, were repeatedly asked either to mediate between the United States and Nicaragua (to renew dialogue) or between the *contras* and the Sandinista government (a proposal of the Reagan administration). The Gonzáles government declined to mediate. But active European support for a comprehensive, collective, and peaceful settlement of the crisis, and help to reduce the economic, social, and political tensions in the region, has been explicitly expressed in declarations of the EEC since 1981.

Despite the fact that most European governments were and still are quite reluctant to get too deeply drawn into a conflict that could eventually expose them to criticism and reprisals from the United States, the EEC has come up with an interpretation and approach to solve the crisis, an approach that differs fundamentally from policies pursued by Washington.

CRISIS DEFINITION, CONFLICT-SOLVING STRATEGIES AND THE LINK TO EUROPEAN INTERESTS

The Central American crisis does not touch upon vital essentials of European policies. The crisis is widely perceived as an interregional conflict in which, because of geographical closeness, the traditional U.S. role in the region, and interrelated global security factors, the United States has immediate and over-ruling interests. And it is further conceded that the United States must be part of any future conflict resolution, and among its guarantors. But at this point the Atlantic consensus on Central America encounters its limits.

In interpreting origins, aims, and perspectives of crises in the Third World, and particularly in the case of the Sandinista revolution or the ongoing struggle in El Salvador, European positions—even those held by my conservative compatriots—seem to differ widely from the Reagan administration's point of view, and even more from its plan of action: the Reagan doctrine.[2] To put it simply—and for the moment disregarding for reasons of analytical clarity different views among the foreign policy elite of the Reagan administration—Washington views Nicaragua and El Salvador as zones of the East-West conflict. In its view, the Soviet Union undertakes there one part of its program of global subversive activity, a first spark in a prairie fire on the American continent which could eventually unleash effects similar to those predicted for Indochina. It is interesting to note the internal contradiction of the conservatives' line of argument. On the one hand, they deny the similarity to Vietnam and its consequences. On the other hand, they evoke the image of the Vietnam disaster, as a catastrophic eventuality for the chain of events in the region of the Isthmus.

Based on what I term "theories of linear apocalypsis," conservative protagonists are obsessed with the following scenario: A revolutionary wave, originating in Nicaragua, will ripple through neighboring countries, topple their US-friendly governments, and transform them into communist puppet states. Picking up momentum and strength, it will set afire the powder keg of Mexico. Mexico will fall in no time at all, and then the Red Hordes will jump across the Rio Grande and link arms with marginalist and fifth column groups already operating in the United States. Consequently, and along the lines of such self-supporting logic, the political, social, and economic order of the United States is defended best by either going to the source (USSR, Cuba), or by stamping out the origins of subversion in Nicaragua. Going to the source (as envisioned in the arcane "Santa Fé" document, the master plan of the American Right for containment and rollback in Latin America) was given up in the light of international force constellations. What remained was to shift the strategy of containment and rollback, now directed against the Sandinistas and Salvador.

Neither West European states, regardless of their political persuasion, nor the EEC would object to the containment of military conflicts in Central America. Furthermore, most European governments, including those led by social democratic or socialist parties, would welcome changes and improvements in Nicaragua's domestic policies, especially the strengthening, granting, and protecting of civil and participatory political rights. Even the establishment of a coalition government between the present Sandinista junta and opposition parties, in a way reestablishing the original political composition of the Sandinista revolution of 1979, would be most welcomed and supported by all political ideological elite groups in Europe.

The European critique of U.S. policies in Central America stresses its reductionist and one-sided interpretation of the conflict as part of the East-West

---

[2]   See Robert F.Tucker, "Intervention and The Reagan Doctrine," in *Ethics and Foreign Policy* Lecture Series, CRIA, 1985.

power struggle, and deplores the instruments and concepts used so far in dealing with the crisis.

SOCIOSTRUCTURAL ORIGINS OF THE CRISIS AND THE HISTORIC FAILURE OF U.S. POLICIES IN CENTRAL AMERICA

According to the European critique[3] the primary cause of the Central American crisis does not lie in the East-West conflict. Its deeper causes—and the sources of the specific form of its present revolutionary solution in Nicaragua and El Salvador—are sociocultural factors. This is true of any other Third World country which was ruled by repressive forces, by a coalition of oligarchic landholding cliques and the military. Underdevelopment in all its aspects and revolutionary, emancipatory social movements seem to be the corollaries of oligarchic and repressive rule.

Any solution to the Central American crisis must include (or even be based on) strategies to change the social and economic structure. Change must extend to agrarian reform and reform of industrial relations, establishing an enforceable judicial system, altering the pattern of distribution of social wealth, and opening education to a broader public. Only by such changes can more democratic and pluralist political systems, able to survive, be established.

Political democracy is a product of socioeconomic changes which often result, in turn, from violent revolutionary processes and civil war, in which the old political repressive order is destroyed. Integrating such an emerging society into a supporting international framework seems the only kind of "acceptable interventionism" for the realization of democratic goals. The new society still carries all the marks of the past. The duration of former dictatorial rule and its ruthlessness of oppression determine whether such a society possesses embryonic democratic political institutions or traditions. One of the obligations of the international community is to render support, to help integrate the new society into the international community. International solidarity and material support are neither illusionary nor futile but are, as recent European experience shows, the only legitimate means to strengthen a democratic perspective. Europe's own policy was substantially successful: it helped to bring about the peaceful transformation of authoritarian and repressive states in Portugal, Spain, and Greece.

While Europe never questioned fundamental strategic interests of the United States, it developed at the same time a clear understanding of the historical failure of U.S. policies in the region. War with Mexico (1846-1848)

---

[3] Here, of course, we have to distinguish various government positions along lines of ideological affiliations.

and victory over Spain (1898) established the United States as the hegemonic power of the Americas, a position uncontested until 1959. The historic failure of U.S. policies can be characterized by the simple fact that despite a hundred years of dominance the "backyard" was never economically cultivated or developed, nor was the groundwork laid for establishment of civil societies and hence democratic institutions. The United States relied on repressive regimes up to the last minute, and even intervened actively to protect private commercial interests. By doing so, Washington often reestablished or reintroduced authoritarian regimes, which had no other social legitimacy than rule by brute force.

The Cuban revolution was the first challenge to U.S. policies in the region. And again, the history of U.S. relations to revolutionary Cuba (failed intervention, counterproductive embargos, CIA plots to murder Castro) rarely convinces Europeans of the U.S. way to contain communism and win the hearts of the people.

The Spanish foreign minister, Fernando Morán,[4] has pointed out this puzzling paradox of the post-World War II order: In the 1940s and 1950s, the United States ideologically supported anticolonial struggles of the colonies against France, Britain, and The Netherlands. But astonishingly, Europe was quite successful in adapting to the changing forces in world politics and gradually mastered withdrawal from its colonial possessions. In contrast, there was very little change in the relationship between the United States and its Central American and Caribbean neighbors.

Even if we witness momentarily a change in the conduct and instruments of U.S. foreign policy in other crisis regions of the world (the Philippines, Haiti, cautiously hinted in South Africa, even possibly a change in policy toward the archenemy of democracy, the Chilean military junta), change does not apply to the conduct of U.S. policy in Central America.

EUROPE'S POSITION ON CENTRAL AMERICA

Most European governments and political elites would agree with one proclaimed goal of American policies, that of pressuring the Sandinistas for swift and broader democratic and pluralist reforms in the political system. But all—even post-Malvinas Britain—deplore and condemn the use of military force (external intervention, logistic support for counterrevolutionaries, the mining of harbors, economic embargo). Even isolating Nicaragua politically is opposed by most European countries. There are several reasons why such a consistent view is taken among the European states, even though the issue invites

---

[4]   Fernando Morán, "Europe's Role in Central America: A Spanish Socialist View", in Andrew J. Pierre (ed.), *Third World Instability. Central America as a European-American Issue* (New York: Council on Foreign Relations, 1985), EuropeAmerica 3, p. 10.

U.S. retaliation. The caveat should be borne in mind, of course, that these factors weigh differrently in the several EEC member states.

1. Neither the EEC nor any member state with interests in Latin America isolates Central America from Latin America as a whole. The many attempts to create regional economic and political bodies, however temporary and feeble they may be, indicate a growing wish among Latin American elites to transcend national boundaries and establish hemispheric networks and contacts. Argentina and Brazil, which in the 1970s (and in the case of Argentina up to the Malvinas disaster) were staunch allies of the United States, have grown more independent and critical of U.S. hemispheric policies. Policies to diversify economic, political and cultural contacts signal *the continent's trend towards self-affirmation, wishing to stay clear of superpower rivalry and to reduce the hegemonic position of the United States.* European contact has been a prime object of this policy since the middle of the 1970s. Another sign of this trend is the increasing readiness of governments to seek regional or hemispheric solutions of economic and political conflicts. Contadora itself (and its wider support group), the support given Argentina in the Malvinas affair, and the November 1986 Brazilian-Argentinian agreement on economic and technological cooperation (open to other Cono Sur countries) exemplify an emerging tendency to integration. This must be taken into consideration when dealing with Latin American states and regions.

2. *The leading European powers,* having shed colonialism and found themselves needing to reach some *modus vivendi* with the socialist countries, *have discovered common principles that are now essentials of a European policy: (1) the right of peoples to self-determination, to choose their own form and nature of government and their preferred models of economic accumulation, and (2) respect for other countries' social and political sovereignty.*

Force, including economic sanctions, embargos, and the like, as an instrument of foreign policy to influence or change other states' behavior, has practically vanished from the arsenals of European states. In its place has been substituted an art in which Europe excelled: patient diplomacy. Only on occasion have colonial powers like France and Britain intervened militarily in Third World conflicts in which their former colonies or protectorates were involved.

From this perspective it is understandable that modern versions of "gunboat diplomacy" and adventurous "search-and-destroy missions" introduced into U.S. foreign policy, indicating a profound lack of coherent concepts for conflict resolution, are criticized acidly in Europe.

3. *Europe's outspokenness against the use of force and its intercession for a comprehensive, negotiated solution of the crisis reflects very specific security interests.* First, acknowledgment that the United States has a special and decisive commitment in the region cannot be arrogated to a claim to a *carte blanche* for the use of force. The historic failure of U.S. policies in general and

the specific disaster of its policies towards Cuba are well remembered . To prevent the United States from continuing on such a path, and in the light of special commercial interests, Europe cannot keep silent if obviously wrong policies are presented as "common Western interests."[5]

Second, any European acquiescence, tacit or open, in a policy that might escalate and widen the conflict to other Central American countries would have disastrous repercussions throughout Latin America. And it could undermine the normalization process between Eastern and Western Europe.

Third, such an unfortunate development would not only reestablish U.S. security hegemony over Western Europe, but also reduce efforts for European self-assertiveness to zero. It would weaken West European security, because lasting instabilities in the Central American region would require a continuing active, military U.S. involvement and presence.[6]

ECONOMIC AND POLITICAL INITIATIVES OF WESTERN EUROPE, THE CONFERENCES OF FOREIGN MINISTERS OF SAN JOSÉ, AND BRUSSELS: LIMITS OF EUROPEAN ENGAGEMENT

Since the middle of the 1970s, economic contacts between member states of the EEC and Central American institutions have intensified. European states maintain contact with the Permanent Secretariat of Economic Integration in Central America (SIECA) of the Central American Common Market (MCCA), and with the Central American Economic Council (CEC). In November 1981, the Commission of the EEC produced a catalogue of guidelines for EEC-Central American cooperation which stressed (a) additional economic aid and assistance for development, technical and financial aid, food aid, preferential trade treatments and trade promotion, (b) promotion of selected agricultural and food commodities for trade, and (c) multi- and bilateral consultations and coordination on aspects of cooperation.

As a result, economic aid to the region and trade relations increased substantially in the following years. In light of further economic cooperation, and in accordance with the EEC's general strategy—to stabilize democratic systems, to promote democratic solutions in nondemocratic societies, to support structural reforms, and to aid interregional economic cooperation—there were efforts on both sides to conclude a general economic agreement. Modeled on the experiences of the EEC's agreement with the five ASEAN states, it should

[5] Michael D. Barnes, "U.S. Policy in Central America: The Challenge of Revolutionary Change," in A. J. Pierre (ed.), *Third World Instability*, p. 98.

[6] For a European conservative perspective, which generally resembles more Washington's preoccupation with the East-West element of the Central American crisis, but takes issue at its military solutions, see the late Alois Mertes, "Europe's Role in Central America: A West German Christian Democratic View," in A. J. Pierre, *Third World Instability*, p. 117.

specify (a) the region's and the EEC's interests at strengthening regional cooperation and development, (b) provisions for long term cooperation, and (c)
requirements for integrating different policies of the EEC vis-à-vis Central
America.[7] The aggravation of the crisis since 1982—which has led to the
near-breakdown of the MCCA, and to the deplorable state of human rights in
Salvador and Guatemala—has rendered conclusion of such an agreement impossible.

Until 1984 various initiatives (originating from the EEC Commission, or
the European Parliament in Strasbourg) stressed concepts like tripartite cooperation by including Mexico, or special aid programs for the region. Apart
from special monetary aid to Central America in 1982 and 1984, which excluded Salvador and Guatemala because of their dismaying human rights
records, all of these proposals ran aground, either obstructed by European
governments or victimized by immanent EEC problems.

Ironically, a breakthrough since 1983 in European-Central American relations was provoked by Washington's policies of conflict escalation. The initiative for a joint European-Central American foreign policy meeting rested
with German Foreign Minister Genscher.[8] It was first hinted in Genscher's
speech at the United Nations in September 1983, and then pursued at a meeting of German ambassadors in San José, Costa Rica. In keeping with the low
profile policy of the FRG—abstaining from direct involvement in conflictive
issues which could arouse an unwelcome U.S. response, even threats because
of the FRG's vulnerable security position—the Foreign Ministry followed a
double track strategy: it played the traditional European card of strengthening
interregional economic, financial, and technical cooperation as the fundamental
approach for crisis resolution. But regional cooperation, from which no
country should be excluded, and which would be aided by European programs,
was seen as an integral part, even prerequisite, of any regional peace and conflict resolution initiatives, like the Contadora process. The economic proposal
carried a strong but hidden political message.

It intended to prevent a further escalation of the US-Nicaraguan crisis by
dissociating Europe's position distinctively from U.S. Central American policies. But the FRG and the EEC wanted to avoid taking issue openly with the
United States. Nevertheless, the U.S. Department of State was at no stage of
the conference's planning and convening either consulted or invited. But, of
course, the State Department was eager to influence the conference outcome. It
was later apparent that the United States had failed to influence the conference.

---

7   See Hans J.Petersen (ed.), *Die Beziehungen zwischen der Europäischen Gemeinschaft und
Lateinamerika*. (Baden/Baden: Bestandsaufnahme und Perspektiven, 1984).
8   For a detailed discussion see Klaus Bodemer, "Westeuropas Engagement in Zen-
tralamerika, Politisches Schattenboxen oder Ausdruck einer neuen Qualität im trilateralen
Verhältnis Europa-USA-Lateinamerika," *Analysen*, Bonn (Mai 1986):43-44.

In the wake of the conference, but for different reasons, both the Europeans and the Central Americans hurried to declare repeatedly that neither the noninvitation of the United States nor the thrust of the conference was directed against U.S. interests. To no one's surprise, but in drastic contrast to courteous bows to the North, discussion and analysis of causes of the present crisis and tensions in regional affairs differed substantially from Washington's simplistic reliance on the East-West conflict.

Let me summarize the main lines of argument evident at the first conference (San José, Costa Rica, 28-29 September 1984). It was an economic conference with political aspects, as one commentator correctly observed. New was the political or diplomatic perspective of the conference, because it implicitly commented on U.S. policy in Central America. The conference was politically important as a symbolic act of joint European foreign policy formulation, despite its meager results which disappointed high Latin American expectations, expectations additionally fueled by the economic recommendations of the then recently released "Kissinger Report" The results were interpreted as the beginning of a new era of cooperation, which would become even more intense with the entry of Portugal and Spain into the EEC.

Europe's principal motive in Central American affairs was to prevent a further military escalation of the conflict, and to create conditions for a peaceful settlement, even if it meant taking issue with U.S. policies. The EEC could convincingly argue that European efforts were not linked to power objectives in the region. The EEC policy was neither directed against the United States nor intended to thrust the EEC into the role of a mediator. Europe was concerned over the conduct of U.S. policy in general. Central America served as something of a litmus test to evaluate U.S. leadership in the Atlantic Alliance and as a test of its ability to learn how to cope with societies based on different models of politics and accumulation.

European analysis of the present crisis focused on historically rooted sociostructural factors. Latin America was described as being in the middle of a process of socioeconomic and political transformation in which old oligarchic groups or power coalitions of landholders, the military caste, and corrupt elements of the bourgeoisie, which were fully dependent on outside military support, are being supplanted by new professional elites. These elites, educated in the United States, Western Europe, or in the East, are becoming the nucleus of a group holding populist, nationalist development concepts. But their search for national identification and development, for the establishment of more pluralistic and efficient systems, transcends at the same time national boundaries and reinforces regional cooperation. Conflicts, then, are a resultant corollary of trends for national emancipation and regional cooperation, because the intermeshing power interests of the old oligarchic groups and their foreign supporters obstruct the quest for modernity.

For this reason, the social movements that spearheaded socioeconomic and political changes in Central America, as elsewhere in Latin America, were both (a) anti-American in ideology and (b) directed against the dependent, corrupt bourgeoisie of their countries. This does not imply, even if their rhetoric resembles socialist doctrine, that these liberation movements have been dominated by communist forces. The nationalist, populist elements of the movements are stronger by far than any communist disposition.

In effect, the best policy of Western industrialized countries would be to leave the region's conflicts to its own forces and to limit intervention to diplomatic and economic means.

The final conference resolution underlined European support for Contadora efforts and refused to support the U.S. strategy of isolating Nicaragua. One may even argue that the conference isolated the United States.

Economically, the results of the conference were rather disappointing. They certainly yielded no "European Marshall Plan" for Central America on the scale foreseen by the Kissinger Commission—$500 million distributed over ten years. The foreign ministers did agree to assist the region in ongoing and future deliberations on the debt problem. Promises of the EEC to support intraregional economic cooperation were renewed and an economic general agreement was again held out as a prospect. Economic and financial aid was linked to concrete and successful steps in regional economic cooperation. As an incentive for improved domestic relations, those steps should help to strengthen civil rights, build democratic institutions, and increase respect for human rights.

•

The following years saw a dramatic escalation and aggravation of the crisis as the Reagan doctrine was put into practice against Nicaragua. Some of the steps were: the funding of the *contras*; disrespect for the decision of the World Court; cancellation of direct talks with the Sandinista government; a trade embargo against Nicaragua; direct political and economic pressures on neighboring countries like Costa Rica and Honduras to block unwanted developments within the Contadora peace process by raising the stakes for Nicaragua; the implicit use of the Mexican debt situation to limit Mexico's active support for Nicaragua; and the constant military buildup and maneuvering of U.S. troops in neighboring Honduras.

The escalation of U.S. policies against Nicaragua produced ambiguous results in Europe and in Central America. The United States was successful in steps to weaken, even to destabilize, the economic and social situation in Nicaragua; constant harassments from the US-financed *contras* and their raids into the country, and uncertainties about a potential U.S. intervention have contributed to the transformation of Nicaragua's economy to "war production," to gearing for "survival." The intention, to destroy the people's confidence in the revolution, to mobilize them against the Sandinista government, has not so far been achieved, but these methods of economic strangulation and terrorist activities have created a society in a permanent state of siege.

The Contadora peace process, which had enjoyed a certain importance and momentum, was immobilized by U.S. disrespect for a regional, peaceful, and collective settlement. The Reagan administration's double policy, to heighten demands through its allies within the Contadora group (conference of Panama 1985) and render them unacceptable to Nicaragua, has further undermined the importance of the wider Contadora support group. The Contadora peace proposal of 1984 was rejected by the United States.

In Europe, changes in the political landscape (end of the Social Democratic-Liberal coalition under Chancellor H. Schmidt in the FRG, and increasing difficulties of the French socialists followed by their loss of power) and spinoffs of the U.S. conservative onslaught, left their mark on societies and the media. Governments held back in their critique, or talked tongue in cheek. In the German case, because of the influence of an aggressive faction within the Christian Democrats—its Bavarian wing, the CSU—tensions arose in the new Christian Democrat-Liberal government coalition over the conduct of policies towards Nicaragua. Among the Christian Democrats, a political current to follow Washington and subscribe to a policy of isolating the Sandinistas grew stronger and caused problems with the Liberals who controlled the Foreign Office. Even Spain's Socialist prime minister, Felipe Gonzáles, while becoming more critical of the Sandinistas, held back from open attacks on the United States because of domestic reasons in order not to jeopardize Spain's membership in NATO. During this period the focus of critique shifted to European political institutions, such as the European Parliament and the EEC, but which held at most a limited political mandate for action.

When the follow-up conference of Central American and European foreign ministers convened in Brussels (11 November 1985), it met under changed international and national conditions.

A general economic agreement between both regions was finally signed. It included preferential trade treatment clauses and favored intraregional projects. But politically, the conference reflected the changes in government of some member states. The wording and flow of discussions was more cautiously scrutinized and any open attack on U.S. policy in Central America was avoided. In a way, the Reagan administration's aggressive policy towards Nicaragua had paid off by silencing opposition voices in Europe. The political changes noted above in the FRG, in France, and in Spain (the move of the Spanish Socialists towards NATO and the center), as well as towering economic and social problems in some EEC countries, and finally the beginning of a long-awaited and longed-for dialogue between both superpowers, combined to restrain European critique.

But in essence the final declaration of Brussels followed the declaration of San José. The EEC refused to isolate Nicaragua from the rest of the region or to exclude it from European aid and economic assistance, despite some very hard lobbying from conservatives, including the FRG representatives.

Since 1985 the situation has not changed in EEC policies. On the national level, some countries, among them the FRG, have become more receptive to persuasion by the Reagan administration to isolate Nicaragua. Economic aid to Managua has been frozen and diplomatic contacts to El Salvador reestablished. The Spanish government under Gonzáles has not introduced European initiatives and has continued to pursue a policy of critical support for the Contadora process and the Sandinistas. The change in government in France has not led to dramatic alterations of the French position, which began with the Mexican-French declaration under the Socialists in 1981 and has evolved since then into a pragmatic maintenance of the *status quo*. Cautious criticism of Washington and admonishment of the Sandinistas, but support for Contadora and the peace proposal of Costa Rica's president Arias, adds no new elements to the French position.

On the EEC level and in European institutions, support for a political solution is still dominant. *With changes in Soviet policy since Gorbachev, the threats perceived by Washington and its moves against Nicaragua are seen as even more insensitive and dangerous.*

CONCLUSIONS

To explain why the EEC (or some of its member states) took such an interest in Central America, going to pains to defend its own assessment of the "crisis" against dominant U.S. positions, is no easy task. If Central America were just a side issue, in which no essential interests of EEC countries were at stake, why confront the hegemonic power of the Atlantic Alliance with which Western Europe shares such ideologic, economic, and political affinities, and on which it appears to be militarily dependent? Given existing problems, which torment the Alliance and especially Atlantic trade relations, protracted opposition against the Reagan administration on an issue which it accords high or even top priority would seem to be a luxury.

However, as sketched above, Europe's Central American policy evolved out of an economic dialogue, which started early in the 1970s and gradually moved, challenged by political changes in the region, into the political arena. In a way, Western Europe was drawn into the conflict, and was forced to take issue, by its very successful economic penetration of Central America and the far more important South America. Again, Central America as a single issue is of very little economic or political importance to Western Europe. But clarification of the European position was demanded by the regional elites with which it conducts relations.

Even the most unlikely possibility that some of the Central American countries would be transformed overnight into "Soviet puppet states" and would arm themselves to the teeth is taken in the Old World with a certain cold detachment. The very experience of a divided Europe, where about 50% of the world's weapon systems are deployed, usually does not cause sleepless nights on either side of the still-dividing curtain.

However, in an era of extremely chilled superpower relations, every additional crisis adds to the general and potential threat of global or regional war. *It was not in Europe's interest to project an alternative policy, but to break the vicious circle of mutual obsession in which both superpowers seemed to be locked.*

Europe's main interest was to voice caution about Washington's claims of crisis and its call for urgent action. Washington's crisis policies, if put into practice without restraint, could have a disastrous impact on political relations in Europe as a whole. In this regard the European position on Central America, especially its efforts to restrain militarization of the conflict, is a policy complementary to that of the United States—and not a policy alternative, as the European Left would prefer. It reflects its essential and overriding interest in maintaining the *status quo* of détente between East and West in Europe. Central America became a case for evaluation of the leadership qualities of the Atlantic hegemonic power. At the same time the crisis offered a legitimate case for Europeans to demonstrate the changes of forces in the international system, that the post-World War II order of Yalta is in a process of decomposition. New actors—and even former actors—have entered or reentered the international arena.

We may find that, because of the balancing stalemate in superpower relations and their parity in strategic nuclear arms, the United States and the USSR may loosen their grips on the spheres they once controlled. Discussions in Europe on a post-Yalta order, on a genuine peace order for the old continent overcoming its division, as well as expressions of European self-assertiveness, have flourished among the political and academic elites everywhere, including Britain. The erosion of U.S. leadership in advanced sectors of high technology and difficulty in keeping pace with international competition have added oil to the flame of such discussions. To put this positively, there is very little evidence today in Europe of anxiety about the scarecrow of "Europessism" or "Eurosclerosis," invented by conservative ideologues enthralled by the Reagan era. Views of more autonomy or room for political latitude are shared by conservative and liberal forces in Europe: a new period of increasing autonomy and international political participation for middle powers like the EEC and Japan, or even for newly industrialized Asian and South American states may be in the making.

The independent position of the EEC and its member states on Central America seems to point in such a direction.

PART 3

SOVIET AND CUBAN ACTIVITIES IN CENTRAL AMERICA

14

Perspectives on the Soviet Presence in Central America

Russell H. Bartley

A serious discussion of the thorny subject of Soviet interests and objectives in Central America is long overdue. Given the level of rhetoric surrounding the issue, I have wondered for some time why such a discussion was not taking place—why the Reagan administration's claims were not being subjected to closer scrutiny by those with experience and expertise to do so. In my own case I confess to having been intimidated by the pitfalls of such an effort. Until recently I have focused my own scholarship on the history of tsarist relations with Latin America; and it is in the pre-Soviet period that I continue to feel most comfortable.[1] The growing severity of the crisis in Central America and the grave threat to peace posed by the administration's insistence on defining that crisis in terms of East-West confrontation have, however, convinced me of the need to tread the treacherous ground.

Let me state at the outset that I am not a Kremlinologist nor do I possess a complete familiarity with the particulars of Soviet-Latin American relations. Rather, I am an historian of Latin America with a specialized interest in the history of Russo-Latin American ties. Pursuit of this interest has afforded me direct experience in the USSR and in Soviet Latin Americanist circles, as well as in several areas of this hemisphere where the Soviet presence has become an issue. It is from this background that I formulate my thoughts on the subject before us.

In seeking to clarify the Soviet role in current Central American affairs—and I do not dispute that there is a Soviet role—I believe it necessary to consider three separate, albeit interrelated, aspects of the problem: first, how the problem is being defined in the United States and why; second, the historical

---

[1] See, for example, Russell H. Bartley, *Imperial Russia and the Struggle for Latin American Independence, 1808-1828* (Austin: Institute of Latin American Studies, University of Texas Press, 1978); *idem*, "G.I. Langsdorf i russko-brazil'skie otnosheniia v pervoi treti XIX v.," *Latinskaia Amerika*, 3 (May-June 1976): 164-169; *idem*, "The Inception of Russo-Brazilian Relations (1808-1828)," *The Hispanic American Historical Review* 56, 2 (May 1976): 217-240.

and geopolitical bases of Soviet relations with Latin America as a whole; and third, the objective particulars of Soviet involvement in Central America. In an effort to suggest ways of thinking about this problem, I shall focus on the first two aspects, that is, on the contextual backdrop. Others can no doubt provide the specifics of current Soviet involvement in the region.

The first observation to be made, it seems to me, is that the issue of Soviet involvement in Central America during the 1980s has not been raised in response to any qualitative change in established Soviet policy toward that region. Nothing has happened that is even remotely analogous to the attempted installation of medium-range ballistic missiles in Cuba during the fall of 1962. The fact that Jeane Kirkpatrick and other voices of the Reagan administration have suggested that the USSR may seek to repeat Khrushchev's nuclear brinkmanship in Nicaragua says more about their view of the world that it does about Soviet behavior or Soviet policy. Indeed, the one statement that can be made with certainty about Soviet intentions in Central America is that the USSR seeks neither military bases nor the emplacement of nuclear weapons anywhere in the region. Those who suggest otherwise do so with a view to manipulating public opinion, for as any disciplined observer of Soviet affairs can attest, Kremlin policymakers reject such hypothetical objectives as self-defeating and counter to the larger interests of the USSR in the long run of history.

The very notion of a patterned Soviet "behavior," I would add, is a specious concept introduced into the propaganda arena by cold warriors. The attribution of behavior patterns to societies, like the attribution of comportment to "human nature," is an empirically discredited practice long ago abandoned by the social sciences. What we are witnessing today is the propagation of a "red legend" of Soviet expansionism in America which, like the "black legend" that once legitimized the plunder of Catholic Spain's New World dominions by Protestant Europe, seeks to mobilize the legions of capitalism for profitable war against an "evil empire." Whenever the guardians of power begin to speak of their adversaries' behavior in terms of moral absolutes—good and evil, civilized and uncivilized—it is a sure sign that they are doing violence to truth in preparation for doing violence against other nations. But the Soviet Union does have a policy towards Central America, an involvement there, and a set of perceived interests to be advanced and defended. In order to understand that relationship, it will be useful to review briefly the history of Russian and Soviet involvement with Latin America as a whole.[2]

---

[2]   The following review of historical background is taken from an earlier paper, "Soviet-Latin American Relations: The Historical Parameters," delivered at the 29th annual meeting of the Pacific Coast Council on Latin American Studies, 13-15 October 1983, in Portland, Oregon.

TSARIST INTEREST

Russian interest in the Americas antedates the American Revolution. As a matter of state concern, it was first articulated during the reign of Tsar Peter the Great and developed gradually throughout the eighteenth century and into the nineteenth as a logical outgrowth of Russian imperial and maritime expansion. Efforts to promote the autonomous development of the Russian Far East by integrating economic intercourse across the Pacific led to direct maritime contacts with Mexico, Peru, and Chile, as well as with Brazil, which became the key link in early nineteenth century communications between St. Petersburg and the far-flung settlements of the Siberian littoral and Russian America. With the transfer of the Portuguese court to Brazil in 1808, Rio de Janeiro would become the seat of Russia's first diplomatic mission in Latin America. Russo-Brazilian diplomatic relations, established *de facto* in 1812, continued unbroken throughout the remainder of the nineteenth century and were interrupted only with the triumph of the Bolsheviks in the fall of 1917.[3]

Tsarist relations with the Spanish American republics, on the other hand, developed unevenly. Compared to those of the West European nations and the United States, they were in fact quite insignificant. Yet there were contacts and ties between these two geographically removed regions of the globe and they did evolve gradually, incrementally, in accord with the geopolitical imperatives of the times.

In the early decades of the nineteenth century, tsarist interest in Spanish America related primarily to the development of Russian settlements and outposts around the northern Pacific rim. During the tumultuous years of struggle for independence in Spain's New World colonies the Russian court sought actively to gain access to the products and foodstuffs of Chile, Peru, and New Spain. In the 1830s, despite continued tsarist adherence to the principle of legitimacy and the resultant refusal of the Russian court to recognize the newly independent Spanish American republics, efforts were made to ease tensions with Mexico over the Russian presence in Alta California. The subsequent Russian withdrawal from California in 1841, coupled with the collapse of the fur trade and the parallel abandonment of earlier pan-Pacific ambitions, all but ended Russian interest in the Pacific coast republics until the 1870s, when guano and nitrates again moved Russia to seek relations with the area.

Peru was the first Spanish American republic to establish formal diplomatic ties with tsarist Russia. This occurred in October 1873 and was followed

---

[3]   On nineteenth century Russo-Latin American relations, see Bartley, *Imperial Russia and the Struggle for Latin American Independence*; N. V. Korolëv, *Strany Yshnoi Ameriki i Rossiia, 1890-1917 gg.* (Kishinëv: Shtiintsa, 1972); L. A. Shur, *Rossiia i Latinskaia Amerika: ocherki politicheskikh ekonomicheskiki i kul'turnykh otnoshenii* (Moscow: Mysl', 1964); A. I. Sizonenko, "Stanovlenie diplomaticheskikh otnoshenii Rossii so stranami Yushnoi Ameriki i Meksikoi," *Latinskaia Amerika*, 5 (May 1983):61-73.

eight months later by the signing in St. Petersburg of a Treaty of Peace, Friendship, Commerce, and Navigation between Imperial Russia and the Republic of Peru. The treaty was officially ratified in January 1875.[4] As a practical matter, the subsequent development of commercial and diplomatic relations between Russia and Peru were frustrated by the outbreak of the War of the Pacific and that conflict's devastating consequences for Peru.[5] These developments, however, do not detract from the significance of those relations as a logical object of Russian foreign policy in an age of expanding global intercourse among nations.

In the latter part of the nineteenth century, the tsarist government formalized diplomatic ties with other Spanish American republics as well: Argentina in 1885; Uruguay in 1887; and Mexico in 1890.[6] These ties were motivated in large measure by commercial interests, as well as by a growing outmigration of Russian subjects to Latin America. By the turn of the century, for example, Russians constituted the fourth largest immigrant group in Argentina, after the Italians, Spanish and French; in Brazil they occupied sixth place, surpassed additionally by German and Austrian immigrants.[7]

Russian emigration to Latin America in the tsarist period established patterns that would, with some modification, continue into the Soviet era. Thus, for example, a majority of Russians who settled in Argentina, Brazil, and other countries of the region represented religious minorities—in the main, Roman Catholics, Lutherans, and Jews. Relatively few members of Russian Orthodoxy emigrated to Latin America.[8]

In addition to ethnic Russians there were also Ukrainians and other nationality groups of the Russian empire. With the October Revolution and the bitter civil war that followed, refugees and ideological emigrés added their numbers as well to the previous emigrant flows from tsarist Russia. Their presence remains visible today in the crevices and interstices of Buenos Aires, Asunción, São Paulo, and innumerable other cities and towns throughout the region.

RUSSIAN AND SOVIET RELATIONS WITH LATIN AMERICA

It should be stressed here that it is the pattern of Russian ties with Latin

4   Ministerio de Relaciones Exteriores de la República del Perú, Archivo General, Servicio Diplomático, Año 1873: Legación en Rusia, nos. 1-2; Año 1874: Legación en Rusia y Alemania, nos. 5-33. See also Luis Humerto Delgado, Perú y Rusia. Documentos para la historia (Lima: Latino-América, 1973); Sizonenko, "Stanovlenie diplomaticheskikh otnoshenii," pp. 62-64.
5   Sizonenko, "Stanovlenie diplomaticheskikh otnoshenii," p. 64.
6   Sizonenko, "Stanovlenie diplomaticheskikh otnoshenii," p. 66.
7   Korolëv, *Strany Ushnoi Ameriki i Rossiia* [note 3], pp. 48-49.
8   Korolëv, *Strany Ushnoi Ameriki i Rossiia* [note 3], pp. 48-49.

America that warrants our attention, not the relative weakness of those ties; for while in the nineteenth century they hardly indicate a Russian "opening" to the countries of the region, they do, as I have suggested elsewhere, evidence a continuity of interests in the hemisphere "consonant with the global perspectives of a major world power."[9] If active economic exchange, regular maritime communications, and major political relationships failed to materialize in the pre-Soviet period, it was not for want of interest or disposition. Indeed, efforts were made in all of these areas but were frustrated, by and large, by more pressing priorities in spheres of greater concern to the Russian national interest.

This, in turn, is the key thread of historical continuity one must weave into any evaluation of current Soviet objectives in the hemisphere. This is not, of course, to imply no interaction at all, rather the pursuit of normal international relations between two world areas that have remained essentially outside each other's respective areas of vital concern. In the nineteenth century this made Brazil the natural focus of Russian New World interest and the Latin American country that experienced the most significant Russian presence. Brazil was described suggestively by a contemporary tsarist diplomat as "the largest, most accessible and most productive part of South America's Atlantic seaboard."[10] Accordingly, it became the locus of tsarist activity on the South American continent. Contacts between the two imperial states even included a visit to Russia in 1876 by Dom Pedro II, whose extended travels took him to St. Petersburg, Kiev, Odessa, and the Crimea, where he was received by Tsar Alexander II and the Russian imperial family.[11]

By the 1890s, Mexico was occupying an increasingly prominent place in Russia's expanding relations with Latin America, eventually surpassing Brazil in the Soviet period as a prime focus of Russian New World interest.[12] By the First World War, in addition to its embassy and regular diplomatic staff, the tsarist government maintained a consulate general in Mexico City, as well as vice consulates in Veracruz, Monterrey, and Ciudad del Carmen in the state of Campeche.[13] With the emergence of the USSR in 1917, Mexico came to occupy a critical place in Soviet foreign policy as a counterbalance to U.S. hostility and Washington's concerted efforts to isolate the nascent revolutionary state internationally.

[9]   Bartley, *Imperial Russia* [note 9], p. 159.
[10]   Fëdor Smirnov, *Yuzhnaia pri-atlanticheskaia Amerika* (St. Petersburg: Obshchestvennaia pol'za, 1872), p. 1.
[11]   Sizonenko, "Stanovlenie diplomaticheskikh otnoshenii," [note 5], p. 67.
[12]   See, for example, Héctor Cárdenas, *Las Relaciones mexicano-soviéticas. Antecedentes y primeros contactos diplomáticos, 1789-1927* (México, D. F.: Secretaría de Relaciones Exteriores, 1974).
[13]   Mexico, Secretaría de Relaciones Exteriores, Archivo General, 42-19-131, Año 1919: Wladimir Wendhausen. Su expediente personal.

In addition to diplomatic, trade, and migration ties and periodic scientific and cultural contacts between tsarist Russia and Latin America, Russia also played a role in the diplomacy and international politics of the region. Successive U.S. perceptions of Russia, in this regard, are likewise illuminating. It is worth recalling, for example, that the administration of President James Monroe first invoked the specter of "Russian expansionism" in 1823 as a rationale for enunciating the exclusionist Monroe Doctrine, with its unstated corollary of U.S. hegemony in the Western Hemisphere. It is equally instructive to recall that this was done essentially for public consumption, inasmuch as Monroe and his secretary of state, John Quincy Adams, understood perfectly well that there was in fact no expansionist threat whatsoever from tsarist Russia.[14]

Later on, at mid-century, when tsarist interests could no longer be portrayed as a challenge to U.S. expansionism, Washington did an about-face and actually sought Russian endorsement of the 1850 Clayton-Bulwer Treaty, to which the United States and Great Britain were the principal parties and whose ultimate objective (from the American point of view) was to ensure U.S. dominion over an interoceanic canal route across Central America. Russia's "mighty name," declared the U.S. ambassador to St. Petersburg, would strengthen the Anglo-American treaty and, in so doing, help "guarantee to the entire world" the great advantages of a future Isthmian waterway. The Russian government, for its part, deemed its interests were best served by not adhering to the Clayton-Bulwer Treaty and accordingly rebuffed the U.S. invitation.[15]

In time, the United States would come to view Soviet influence as inimical to U.S. interests and once more would portray Russia as an "alien extra-hemispheric" power with no legitimate business in the Americas. Yet, in point of fact, by the advent of the Soviet state Russia had indisputably established itself as a power with perfectly legitimate interests in the Western Hemisphere and its right to pursue those interests had been duly recognized by the international community, including the United States. Moreover, Russia had been deemed a proper arbiter of hemispheric disputes, as in the Venezuelan crisis of 1902-1903,[16] and a legitimate party to international accords governing hemispheric affairs, as in the case of the Clayton-Bulwer Treaty. As a principle of historical analysis, this legitimacy cannot be arbitrarily negated at

14   Bartley, *Imperial Russia* [note 1], pp. 141-142; N. N. Bolkhovitinov, "On the Threat of Intervention in Latin America by the Holy Alliance," in Russell H. Bartley (trans. and ed.), *Soviet Historians on Latin America. Recent Scholarly Contributions* (Madison and London: University of Wisconsin Press, for the Conference on Latin American History, 1978), pp. 132-157.
15   A. M. Zorina, "The Clayton-Bulwer Treaty of 1850 and Russian Diplomacy," in Bartley, *Soviet Historians on Latin America* [note 14], pp. 209-220.
16   Korolëv, *Strany Yuzhnoi Ameriki i Rossiia* [note 3], pp. 119-124.

a later date when a change of political order in the tsarist realm renders the emergent Soviet state unpalatable to U.S. interests.

Soviet policy toward Latin America, in its turn, reflects the imperatives of each successive stage in the USSR's determined struggle to survive as history's first socialist state.[17] These stages have evolved from an initial period of consolidation, in which the new Soviet state sought recognition and the essential material conditions of survival, through the forced industrialization/Comintern years, the Second World War and postwar quest for defensible frontiers, to the cold war and, finally, the attainment of superpower status and military parity with the capitalist West. In each of these stages the USSR has sought to enhance its position by securing diplomatic recognition and establishing aid and trade ties wherever feasible.

With the exception of the war years when the USSR's decisive contribution to the Allied cause won Moscow the recognition of a majority of Latin American governments, the United States has pursued a deliberate policy of seeking to undermine Soviet ties with Latin America. In the early years of the Soviet state, Mexico and Uruguay alone chose to defy U.S. pressure against recognition.[18] The establishment of Soviet-Mexican diplomatic ties in 1924 was especially significant, for it offered Moscow a not inconsiderable measure of international legitimation, in effect aiding the USSR in breaking the iron ring of isolation imposed on it by Washington and other Western governments. Recognition of the new Soviet state was also a pointed expression of Mexico's own independence vis-à-vis its traditional overlord to the north. Uruguay's recognition of the USSR two years later was likewise an expression of independence and neutrality.

The creation of the Comintern as a de facto instrument of Soviet foreign policy in what, historically, might be viewed as the USSR's "adolescent period" greatly facilitated U.S. efforts to undermine Soviet relations with Western Hemisphere governments. Mexico, for example, was moved to sever its diplomatic ties with Moscow in 1930, charging interference in its internal affairs. Uruguay followed suit in 1935. Both countries had yielded to Washington's insistent protestations of Soviet subversion, perceiving Comintern ties to local Communist parties as evidence of just such a threat.

The year 1935 was the low point in Soviet-Latin American relations. Only Colombia continued to maintain formal diplomatic relations with

[17] For an overview of Soviet-Latin American relations, see Cole Blasier, *The Giant's Rival, the USSR and Latin America* (Pittsburgh: University of Pittsburgh Press, 1983); A. I. Sizinenko, *Ocherki istorii sovetsko-latinoamerikanskikh otnoshenii, 1924-1970 gg.* (Moscow: Nauka, 1971); *idem, Stanovlenie otnoshenii SSSR so stranami Latinskoi Ameriki, 1917-1945 gg.* (Moscow: Nauka, 1981).

[18] For a chronology of Soviet-Latin American relations, see "SSSR-Latinskaia Amerika: khronika mezhgosudarstvennykh otnoshenii," *Latinskaia Amerika*, no. 12 (December 1982):119-141.

Moscow, having established them in June of that same year only six months before Uruguay would break its ties. From this perspective, 1935 can also be viewed as a turning point in Soviet-Latin American relations, since from that year on those relations would steadily expand, with only passing setbacks, to the point where today they are desired and perceived as advantageous by a decisive majority of the hemisphere's governments.

The Second World War removed the Comintern as a conflictive element in Soviet foreign relations. That, together with the USSR's dramatically enhanced image as one of the Allies, gave impetus to a process of rapprochement between the USSR and Latin America. By 1946, fifteen Latin American governments had established diplomatic relations with Moscow.

The onset of the cold war moved five countries again to sever diplomatic ties with the USSR: Brazil and Chile in 1947; Colombia in 1948; and Cuba and Venezuela in 1952. Remarkably, that was the major extent of the cold war's impact on Moscow's developing relationship with the region. Already by the 1950s, trade, parliamentary, technical, and official state delegations were being exchanged between Latin America and the USSR. Trade and cultural agreements were signed. And, gradually, relations were reestablished with those governments that had broken their ties at the height of the cold war, while new ties were established with a growing number of the region's countries.[19]

ANTI-SOVIETISM

It is impossible to make sense of the current Central American imbroglio without having grasped the nature and significance of anti-Sovietism as a dynamic of U.S. foreign policy closely linked to the mechanisms of a popular culture that supports it. This linkage is hard to trace; but it is not less influential than the link between government and the corporate world. No student of international affairs can ignore the vital connection between current U.S. policy objectives in Central America—or in the world at large, for that matter—and the relentless deluge of anti-Soviet messages that is directed at American public opinion through the multiple media of popular culture. These messages combine to portray an inherently expansionist and morally reprehensible Soviet empire which seeks to establish worldwide hegemony at the expense of legitimate Western interests. And they make it difficult for the ordinary citizen to see clearly that on the one hand the experience of the past quarter century tends to invalidate the thesis of creeping Soviet hegemony, and on the other hand the legitimacy of Western interests is itself open to serious question. This is of course part of the larger question of the manipulation of "free" information, which has so severely handicapped the citizens of the

[19] Chronology [note 18].

advanced capitalist countries in thinking historically and for comprehending the role of social conflict and social transformation in world affairs.[20]

For example, the mass fiction market has been inundated with a veritable plethora of anti-Soviet pulp. In 1984, for example, a major effort was mounted to promote the adroitly contrived, sensationalist best seller, *Monimbo*, by Robert Moss and Arnaud de Borchgrave.[21] The coincidence of this novel's story line with the Reagan administration's notion of world affairs is unmistakable, for it targets at one and the same time Cuba, , and the USSR as enemies of the American people. The "Monimbo" of the title is Fidel Castro's code name for a "final solution" to the "American problem." "The terror is paid for with blood-drenched profits from Miami, drug capital of the world." The plot is diabolical: "First, flood the U.S. with Caribbean scum—terrorists and Cuban secret agents. Next, spill American blood—race riots, blackouts, a wildfire of murder that will bring America to its knees—and into the Soviet orbit." Moss and De Borchgrave have been linked to the CIA and other western intelligence services, and earlier wrote *The Spike,* a controversial novel about Soviet disinformation.[22]

A variation of this theme runs through *The Third World War: August 1985* and its sequel, *The Third World War: The Untold Story,* by the former commander of NATO's Northern Army Group, Gen. Sir John Hackett, and an anonymous group of ranking NATO generals and other military and intelligence advisers.[23] Already in 1980, runs the story line,

> Cuba's leaders had held a secret meeting with Central American Marxist leaders up country in Nicaragua to discuss their intended polarization of the region. They could by then celebrate a considerable triumph.
>
> This triumph had been the military victory of the Sandinista movement in Nicaragua and the overthrow of the Somoza dynasty.
>
>   .   .   .
>
> At the 1980 meeting in Nicaragua of rising Marxists the voice was that of Fidel Castro, but the hand belonged to the Soviet Union's President Brezhnev, who was already propping up Cuba's ineffective economy to the tune of forty million dollars a week. The Soviets had become attracted during 1980 by the possibility of drawing the United States into a deep trap just outside its southern backdoor, where it could

---

[20]   See, for example, Georgi Arbatov, *The War of Ideas in Contemporary International Relations* (Moscow: Progress, 1973); William A. Dorman, "Peripheral Vision: U. S. Journalism and the Third World," *World Policy Journal* III, 3 (Summer 1986):419-445; Michael Parenti, *Inventing Reality. The Politics of the Mass Media* (New York: St. Martin's Press, 1986).

[21]   Robert Moss and Arnaud de Borchgrave, *Monimbo* (New York: Pocket Books, 1984).

[22]   Robert Moss and Arnaud de Borchgrave, *The Spike* (New York: Avon, 1981).

[23]   Gen. Sir John Hackett, et al., *The Third World War: August 1985* (New York: Macmillan, 1978); *idem, The Third World War: The Untold Story* (New York: Macmillan, 1982).

flounder ineffectively while critical events beyond its control unrolled elsewhere.[24]

As in Moss and De Borchgrave's *Monimbo*, where the threads of conspiracy are moved by a "tall, fair-skinned" agent of the KGB, in Hackett's account, too, the prime mover of turmoil in Central America and the Caribbean is the USSR.

The theme is repeated in a popular fiction series entitled *Countdown World War III*, authored by "W.X. Davies" and the so-called "Strategic Operations Group." Davies, according to a preliminary blurb, is the pseudonym of a "well-known writer who took on this new series both to entertain and to argue for a more sophisticated espionage capability for the U.S." The Strategic Operations Group, for its part, is described as "an informal advisory council whose military, intelligence and security experience provides much of the background for the series." *Countdown World War III* has been distributed through bookstores, supermarkets, and other paperback outlets across the country. Volume three in the series is subtitled *Operation Choke Point* and revolves around Soviet penetration of Latin America.[25]

This list goes on—books, articles, films. Our popular market is being saturated with such material. The assumptions are always the same, and repeated over and over again: the USSR is a global menace; it seeks, with increasing success, to subvert governments on every continent; it has penetrated Latin America where, through Cuba, Nicaragua, and other revolutionary proxies, it is embarked on an all-out offensive against US vital interests and, ultimately, the United States itself. These are the premises of John Milius's *Red Dawn*, of the American Security Council Foundation's equally contrived film, *Attack on the Americas*,[26] of the commercial motion picture *Invasion USA*, a pathetic fantasy about Soviet takeover which was shown at movies houses across the country, and of the planned ABC extravaganza, *Amerika*, a $40 million, sixteen-hour miniseries about a Soviet occupation of the United States recently announced as the "centerpiece" of the network's 1986/87 prime time programming.[27]

"Suppose all Central America fell and the Communist regimes formed an alliance," Milius commented to a *San Francisco Chronicle* interviewer. "They

[24] Gen. Sir John Hackett, et al., *The Third World War: The Untold Story*, pp. 288-289.
[25] W. X. Davies, with the Strategic Operations Group, *Countdown WW III: Operation Choke Point* (New York: Berkeley, 1984).
[26] *Attack on the Americas* (copyrighted by the American Security Council Foundation, Boston, Virginia, 1982). A 25-minute, 16-mm color film documentary produced by the ASCF for the Coalition for Peace Through Strength.
[27] On the ABC *Amerika* series, see "Details at 11 O'Clock," *The Nation* (19 October 1985): 361; and Sally Bedell Smith, "ABC Film to Depict US After Soviet Takeover," *New York Times* (7 October 1985):12.

could field a significant force. Cuba has an army of half-a-million, including reserves. Nicaragua aims to create a standing army of 300,000. If Mexico has a revolution—and it's close—we'll see a vast influx of refugees to the American Southwest. Among them could be agents who could prepare the way for an armed incursion."[28]

This scenario is preposterous. Yet it is deeply rooted in the popular American psyche. "When I was growing up," Milius recalls, "the favorite kid's fantasy was to think about what we'd do when the Russians came."[29] That was in Colorado. It was also a favorite kid's fantasy when I was growing up on the East Coast. It was probably the same all over the country in the late 1940s and 1950s. What is distressing is that though we have grown up, the fantasy is now more widespread than ever—among kids and adults alike. This is disturbingly reflected in the camouflage clothing fad, the mercenary cult, the survivalist craze, the so-called National Survival Game, in which American adults play at guerilla war.[30]

There is, however, a political purpose for these fantasies. They are cultivated. They serve a purpose, to reinforce a particular foreign policy agenda. The lengths to which the proponents of that agenda are willing to go to promote the fantasy in other countries have been dramatically documented by the disclosure last year of the much-commented CIA manual, *Psychological Operations in Guerrilla Warfare*, prepared by the Reagan administration for Nicaraguan counter-revolutionaries operating out of Honduras and Costa Rica.[31] *Contra* propaganda teams, the manual states, should seek to persuade Nicaraguan citizens through discussions of local and national history "that the Sandinista regime is *foreignizing*, *repressive*, and that even though there are some Nicaraguans within the Government, they are *puppets* of the Soviets and Cubans." The people should be convinced, the manual stresses, "that they have become slaves, that they are being exploited by privileged military and political groups." They must be persuaded that "the foreign advisers and their counseling programs are in reality *interventionists* . . . who direct the exploitation of the nation in accordance with the objectives of the Russian and Cuban imperialists in order to turn [the Nicaraguans] into slaves of the hammer and sickle"[32] (emphasis added).

---

[28] Quoted by Bart Mills in "When the Commies Invade, Will America Be Ready?", *San Francisco Chronicle Datebook* (12 August 1984): 24.

[29] *Ibid.*

[30] See, for example, Lionel Atwill, *The Official Survival Game Manual* (New York: Pocket Books, 1983).

[31] Tayacan (nom de guerre), *Operaciones sicológicas en guerra de guerrillas* (US Central Intelligence Agency, 1984).

[32] *Ibid.*, pp. 15, 67. See also "Excerpts From C.I.A. Primer," *New York Times* (17 October 1984):6.

While this CIA manual on guerrilla psychological operations techniques targets Nicaragua, it reveals the degree of calculated deception employed by the US political establishment, in concert with associated strata of the private sector, in dealing with domestic as well as foreign public opinion. "Objectivity," "forthrightness," "honesty," and other such notions of the democratic tradition have become inoperative values in this context. This is nothing new, certainly, but it is an empirically verifiable reality that we live with and which hobbles the practicing democracy among us. The popular American mythology tends to mystify and obscure the real world of politics; those of us who wish to comprehend the real world cannot afford to take it at face value.

Turning now to underlying administration assumptions about Central America, at least as they have been articulated to the public, we see that they correspond in all essentials to those of the media and mass market publishing industry. The conclusions of the Bipartisan Commission on Central America, chaired by former National Security Advisor and Secretary of State Henry Kissinger, serve to illustrate the point.

ASSUMPTIONS UNDERLYING
REAGAN ADMINISTRATION POLICY

While recognizing that many of the conditions producing social unrest in Central America are indigenous to the region, the Bipartisan Commission is quick to assert that "these conditions have been exploited by hostile outside forces—specifically by Cuba, backed by the Soviet Union and now operating through Nicaragua—which will turn any revolution they capture into a totalitarian state, threatening the region and robbing the people of their hopes for liberty."[33]

Emphasizing that Central America's troubles are "to an important degree" the product of both internal and external conditions, including soaring energy costs, fluctuating market prices, recession, and rising interest rates, the commission repeats the familiar theme that "international terrorism, imported revolutionary ideologies, the ambitions of the Soviet Union, and the example and engagement of a Marxist Cuba are threatening the hopes of political progress."[34]

The United States, declares the report, "can have no quarrel with democratic decisions, as long as they are not the result of foreign pressure and external machinations." Here the text is strikingly reminiscent of the odious Platt Amendment and its implied assumption that, in matters of Cuba's

---

[33] Henry A. Kissinger et al., *Report of the National Bipartisan Commission on Central America* (Washington, D.C.: US Government Printing Office, 1984), p. 4.
[34] Report [note 33], p. 7.

domestic affairs, the United States was not to be considered a foreign power. "The Soviet-Cuban thrust to make Central America part of their geostrategic challenge," the report continues, "is what has turned the struggle in Central America into a security and political problem for the United States and for the hemisphere."[35] "The Soviet and Cuban threat is real," the Commission concluded. "No nation is immune from terrorism and the threat of armed revolution supported by Moscow and Havana with imported arms and imported ideology."[36]

The rhetorical devices employed by the Bipartisan Commission are themselves revealing, e.g. "imported ideology," "expanded Soviet influence," the "example and engagement" of a Marxist Cuba. (The historian recalls the "examples and engagement" of the French and American revolutions for Latin American insurgents of an earlier era—imported ideology and foreign influence if ever they have existed.) While the problem in Central America and the Caribbean is presented as a military problem, that is, as a direct threat to the national security of the United States, the real issue is the threatened restructuring of the region's social order in ways that would condition future US access to the area.

The challenge is not, in its essence, military. John Milius's fancy notwithstanding, Calumet, Colorado need never fear an invasion of Cuban and Nicaraguan armies, nor will US shipping ever have to run a gauntlet of Soviet and Cuban submarines along vital sea lanes connecting Gulf Coast ports to the Atlantic and the Panama Canal. To entertain the first scenario seriously, I should think, would constitute grounds for prompt commitment to a psychiatric institution. The second, of course, is a scenario for all-out war between the superpowers, in which case the issue would be moot.

A third world war will resemble neither of the two preceding world wars. To observe, as the Bipartisan Commission does, that the Soviets "have already achieved a greater capability to interdict shipping than the Nazis had during World War II," that the Soviets "now have a two-to-one edge overall in submarines," and that the Soviets "can operate and receive aircover from Cuba, a point from which all 13 Caribbean sea lanes passing through four choke points are vulnerable to interdiction" is to disregard the advance of history and to play on the public's ignorance.[37]

---

[35] Report [note 33], p. 12.

[36] Report [note 33], p. 14.

[37] Report [note 33], p. 92. Wayne Smith, former Chief of the US Interests Section in Havana adds the following insights into the military significance of Cuba for US interests in the Caribbean Basin: "There hasn't been a Soviet missile or nuclear submarine in a Cuban port since 1974. There have not been any Soviet bombers flying out of Cuban airfields since 1962. The Cubans do have MIG-23s—the United States could take out Cuban airfields and every MiG-23 on them within two hours if any international conflict occurred. The Cubans don't have a navy that could threaten our sea-lanes in any serious way . . . The idea that the

Again, the challenge is not military. It is instead a political, and ultimately economic, challenge. Moreover, it is a challenge that the Bipartisan
Commission, and the administration, feel compelled to portray as "alien" to
the Western Hemisphere—putting in contemporary clothes the earlier notion
that Marxism was "alien" to the Americas, an exotic European transplant for
which there was no fertile soil in the New World. Hence, the very idea of socialist transformation in Latin American society is attacked as "imported ideology" and "Soviet expansionism." The purported Soviet military threat in
the region is a subterfuge to justify US intervention against "imported ideology" and the real threat of structural change that it portends. When the Reagan
administration and its local partisans in Central America call for "political
pluralism" they of course mean a pluralism that excludes Marx.

"What clearly makes the Central American problem much more difficult
for us," affirms another former national security advisor, Zbigniew Brzezinski, "is its relationship, whether we like it or not, to the American-Soviet rivalry. The existence of Cuba, in fact, the Marxist cast of much of the Central
American revolution, automatically makes the Central American problem part
of the larger American-Soviet confrontation." And that, he states with telling
candor, "complicates not only the political ramifications of the problem, but
indeed even ultimately moral judgments regarding that problem."[38]

Brzezinski was addressing a major conference on "The Central American
Crisis and the Western Alliance," held in the spring of 1984 in Washington,
D.C., under the auspices of the Carnegie Endowment for International Peace
and the International Institute for Strategic Studies. Much of the discussion at
that conference revolved around the Soviet role in Central America, with con-
siderable divergence of views on the particulars of Soviet involvement.
Brzezinski, for his part, seemed to summarize the consensus not only of the
Washington conference, but of the US foreign policy establishment as well.

From a Soviet perspective, Brzezinski observed, "the Central American
issue is at best a secondary front. It is a relatively minor objective at this
stage; it does not constitute a central area of competition with the United
States."[39] There is, however, "a fundamental asymmetry between the American and the Soviet stakes in the region." Without defining precisely victory or
defeat, Brzezinski noted, "for the Soviet Union something amounting to historical victory in this region would be a genuine strategic triumph." Whereas
a Soviet defeat "would be only a tactical setback," a US victory in Central

problem we have in Central America is a threat to our sea-lanes is simply absurd. It is a threat
that could be so simply dealt with as not to be worth the discussion." See Wayne Smith, "The
Failure of Statecraft," in Joseph Cirincione (ed.), *Central America and the Western Alliance*
(New York & London: Holmes & Meier, 1985), pp. 185-186.
[38]   Zbigniew Brzezinski, "Strategic Implications of the Central American Crisis," in
Cirincione (ed.), *Central America and the Western Alliance*, p. 105.
[39]   *Ibid.*, p. 106.

America would amount at best "to a tactical success," while defeat for the United States would be "a strategic calamity." Which means, Brzezinski continued, that "Central America is a serious problem for us—a very complicated problem—but it is essentially a low-risk opportunity for the Soviet Union."[40]

And that brings us back to the nub of the matter: the "East-West issue" in Central America has to do with internal political change, with a restructuring of local societies, and not with competing hegemonies. Indeed, what is ultimately at issue is the breaking of an existing hegemony over the region, that of the United States, but not for the purpose of replacing it with Soviet hegemony, which is neither sought by the forces of revolutionary change in the area nor pursued by the USSR itself.

S. A. Mikoyan, a leading Soviet specialist on Latin America, once remarked that to comprehend Soviet objectives in Latin America one must view the region through the prism of Soviet security interests. Asia, the Near East, the Arab world, and Europe are of vital concern to the USSR, while "Latin America, and maybe Australia and New Zealand," Mikoyan stressed, "are the parts of the world that least matter for our security and where it is least possible for us to have economic contacts or to have any influence."[41]

This is not to say, of course, that the Soviets have no interests in Latin America. Those interests, however, lie in what Brzezinski refers to obliquely as a potential "historical victory," by which he apparently understands a collapse of US hegemony in Central America and the Caribbean that would signify a grave blow to US primacy in the world at large and, in turn, further the advance of socialism on a global scale.

Socialism, after all, is what the conflict is ultimately about. For socialism threatens US power, US primacy, US hegemony. It threatens the world capitalist order, and even, some would argue, Western civilization itself. Not Soviet-imposed socialism; not Soviet-style socialism, but any of countless possible variants that deny the private sector a decisive role in the determination of societal priorities—which is precisely why the Reagan administration has not been moved by protestations of nonalignment on the part of Salvadoran rebels or the Sandinistas. A socialist order of any stripe, whether or not it is aligned with Moscow, undermines US hegemony.

By the same token, the emergence of socialist-inclined regimes in Central America, and the resultant weakening of US hegemony in the region, necessarily serves Soviet interests. This is the basic asymmetry of US and Soviet stakes noted by Brzezinski. The Soviets, for their part, have no need to foment or control the revolutionary processes in Central America, only to provide aid and support in those limited instances where that can make a decisive

---

40   *Ibid.*

41   S.A. Mikoyan, interview, Moscow, 20 June 1981.

difference, as is the case of Nicaragua. Whatever the particular cast of an emergent revolutionary regime, it will further Soviet objectives by eroding the US hegemony. Just as a weakening of the Soviet sphere of influence would further the global agenda of the United States, so too any diminution of US influence in the world enhances the international position of the USSR.

The distinction that I wish to make here between influence and intrusion, between support and control, between presence and penetration, is a crucial one for our understanding not only of the Soviet role in Central America, but also of how the Reagan administration seeks to distort that role in the popular mind. For if the Soviets in fact do not seek to create revolutions where local conditions have not already done so, if they do not seek to control and direct existing revolutionary movements—as to date they have not, and if they do not seek to be where they have no legitimate business, then the basic assumptions around which the administration seeks to rally public support for its Central American policies are simply false. Which is, I believe, the case.

There is, it seems to me, a conscious effort by the present administration to obfuscate the issues in the public mind, to blur the distinction between a Soviet presence in Central America—a legitimate and historically logical presence—and Soviet penetration of the region. As was again apparent this past week* in New York, where the president took the occasion of the fortieth anniversary of the United Nations to launch a pre-Geneva public opinion offensive, there is a concerted effort to equate revolutionary ideology in Central America with the USSR and thus to delegitimate the Soviet presence in the area. "Over the past 10 years," the President stated in an interview with *The Times of India*, "a growing source of instability and war in the developing world has been the imposition of new regimes—Marxist-Leninist ones—that are, almost from the day they take over, at war with their own people, and then, before very long, at war with their neighbors."[42] "All of these conflicts," he told the UN General Assembly the following day, "are the consequence of an ideology imposed from without." And in each case, he added, "Marxism-Leninism's war with the people becomes war with their neighbors."[43]

This is insidiously effective propaganda. It is also historical bunk, for it assumes that rational people, left to their own devices, will not voluntarily embrace the postulates of Marxism-Leninism. It assumes that only through outside coercion can they be moved to espouse Marxist-Leninist ideology, an

---

*   October 1975.—Ed.

42   Quoted by Bernard Weinraub in "Reagan Asks to End Rivalry With Soviet in Third World," *The New York Times* (24 October 1985): 8.

43   "Transcript of the President's Address to the General Assembly," *The New York Times* (25 October 1985): 9.

ideology that not only is *alien*, we are told, but historically obsolete as well.[44]

Whether or not the president himself believes this vacuous formulation of contemporary human affairs is really beside the point. His policy advisers do not. No one with even a minimal understanding of today's world could take such views seriously. Again, their purpose is rather to manipulate and deceive a profoundly uninformed public. Once Marxists, or Marxist-Leninists (most people, including the President, have no idea what these terms actually signify) are equated in the public mind with an expansionist Soviet Union, it becomes more feasible to conduct military intervention anywhere in the world for the purpose of suppressing popular revolutionary movements.

Finally, this whole house of cards rests precariously on the untenable assumption that the Soviet Union really has no legitimate business in the region anyway. The pursuit of renewed US hegemony in Central America and the Caribbean has regenerated the old notions of hemispheric exclusivity, notions now invoked to deny the so-called Soviet bloc access to Latin America as a whole and thus to frustrate the development of normal relationships between Latin America and the socialist countries. The USSR, the Reagan administration implies, has no historical ties to Latin America and therefore no legitimate interests in the region.

In today's world, however, where interdependence is universal, arguments of geopolitical exclusivity are untenable. Certainly, no such arguments have been accepted by recent US administrations with respect to this country's interests abroad. The Soviet Union, for its part, is no more an "alien extrahemispheric" power, historically speaking, than are Japan, or the People's Republic of China. To the contrary, the Russian presence in the Western Hemisphere is older, more continuous, and more firmly established than any of these latter-day allies of US administrations—extrahemispheric allies whose own presence in the region not only is not questioned but is actually encouraged as a means of countering the perceived drift toward socialist experiments inimical to continued US dominion and the maintenance of capitalist relations.

What is more, Latin American governments themselves have come to view relations with the USSR as beneficial to their own interests. At the present time, sixteen governments of the region formally recognize and maintain diplomatic ties with Moscow. Indeed, perhaps the most eloquent indictment of the "evil empire" view of Soviet behavior in Latin America has been precisely

---

[44] "It is the Soviet Union that runs against the tide of history," Reagan bombastically declared to the British Parliament following the Malvinas/Falklands conflict of 1982. The revolutionary crisis in today's world, he proclaimed, "is happening not in the free, non-Marxist West, but in the home of Marxism-Leninism, the Soviet Union." Marxism-Leninism, he announced, will be left "on the ash heap of history." See "Text of President Reagan's Address to Parliament," *New York Times* (9 June 1982):8.

the readiness of so many governments, representing such diversity of political stripe, to maintain formal diplomatic and other ties with that very superpower that successive US administrations have portrayed as a threat to the hemisphere and humanity itself.

Neither the advent of socialist Cuba, nor the missile crisis of October 1962, nor the current turmoil in Central America has moved a single Latin American government to sever its ties with Moscow—even while several regimes in the region have been persuaded to terminate their relations with Cuba or otherwise follow Washington's lead in pursuing provocative policies toward the hemisphere's first socialist state. The expulsion of Soviet diplomats and other personnel from Grenada, it is worth noting, does not constitute an exception inasmuch as that extraordinary event was engineered and, in effect, implemented by the government of the United States.

There is, in sum, an historical logic to Soviet policy toward Central America, a logic based on the observable decentralization of power in the world and the corresponding breakdown of imperial hegemonies. Accordingly, the USSR seeks above all to develop the widest range of normal relations with governments of the region and to maintain correct relations with those governments. That is, the USSR does not attempt to subvert the governments with whom it maintains formal ties, nor is it perceived by those governments as a threat to their internal security. Were it otherwise, it is safe to assume that Moscow's ties with the region would not reflect the stability and scope that they in fact do. Even vulnerable Costa Rica, swept unceremoniously into the anti-Sandinista tide by Washington and its local allies, has shown no inclination to sever ties with the USSR.

AND SPHERES OF INFLUENCE

In conclusion, a major objective of Soviet policy toward Latin America, including Central America and the Caribbean, is to offer viable trade, aid and political options in the arena of international relations—in a word, to facilitate increased maneuverability to Latin American governments in dealing with the hemisphere's traditional locus of power, the United States. If this, in turn, is seen as a "chess move" designed to undermine long-standing US interests in the region, then the most one can say is that the game is legitimate, the United States plays it too, and if the USSR seems to play it particularly well, that does not signify an attempt to seize the hemisphere or anything of the sort. As our colleague Jacques Levesque reminds us in his thoughtful volume, *L'URRS et la révolution cubaine:* "There is no reason to think that a reduction in the US 'sphere of influence' and the appearance of new socialist states, even with Soviet support, necessarily means an expansion of the 'Soviet sphere'. There are simply too many examples to the contrary."[45]

[45] Jacques Levesque, *L'URSS et la révolution cubaine* (Montréal: Presses de l'Université de Montréal, 1976), p. 211.

15

Soviet Attitudes Towards, Aid to and Contacts with Central American Revolutionaries

C. G. Jacobsen

This is a report on Moscow's presence in Central America. Early chapters attempt to convey the political-ideological setting in that region as seen from Moscow, and in Western analyses critical of U.S. policy. Such views permeate Moscow's public posture; and their propagation is crucial to Soviet imagemaking. Washington is experiencing in Central America its most controversial foreign entanglement since Vietnam; this affords Moscow major advantages, allowing her to cloak her ambitions in larger ideals and to provide them with respectability by association. U.S. actions against Managua, for example, have clearly been hampered by Allied support for the Sandinistas. Yet Moscow's attempts to depict and exploit discrepancies between U.S. policy and American ideals inadvertently serve also to expose and highlight the inconsistencies and contradictions that bedevil her own position.

A number of peculiar problems attended this study. Sandinista reports on aid levels are prone to "double-counting"; media coverage occasionally suggests that deliveries on past agreements in fact constitute new accords. Dollar accounting of other currency transactions also often obfuscates the issue (e.g., the dollar figure affixed to France's original arms agreement with Managua has varied enormously, because of the wide fluctuations of the franc-dollar exchange rate). Finally, time and funding limitations precluded the full utilization of Appendix data; and follow-up studies are needed. The report has, moreover, relied exclusively on open sources; and it must be judged accordingly.

This is a minimally adapted version of the main text of the Jacobsen Report; it excludes its voluminous appendices. It is reproduced here with the permission of Dr. Jacobsen, who acknowledges the research assistance of David R. Jones, Mohiaddin Mesbahi, and Robin Rosenberg. The original report, *Soviet Attitudes Towards, Aid to and Contacts with Central American Revolutionaries*, carried the following disclaimer when issued in June 1984: "This report was funded by the US Department of State under the auspices of its external research program. Views and conclusions contained in this report should not be interpreted as representing the opinion or policy of the United States Government."

WHAT FUELS THE CENTRAL AMERICAN CAULDRON?

The root causes of crisis in Central America are extraordinarily complex. *Sui generis*, they lie outside the scope of this study. Conflicting perceptions as to what they are have, however, become central to the purpose of this investigation.

The extraordinary range and scope of Soviet policy interests and involvement in Central America is amply documented in this report, and elsewhere in what has become a substantial body of literature. Past U.S. government representations on the subject may, however, have gone beyond identifying the problem to actually exaggerating or even to exacerbating it. Their conclusions, which sometimes appear to outrun the data (perhaps because of the classified nature of supporting evidence), have allowed critics to impute to the government a disregard for the traditional rules of evidence. Skepticism has ensued, both within the U.S. body politic and among U.S. allies. This skepticism has in turn become a cornerstone of Soviet policy, and a central element of Soviet propaganda. That is perhaps the price of democracy.

The problem was highlighted in early 1981 by the *Wall Street Journal*'s treatment of the internal contradictions and information gaps of the State Department's White Paper on "Communist Interference in El Salvador,"[1] whose principal author, Jon Glassman, was compelled to concede: "we completely screwed it up,"[2] though continuing to defend the report's message. In the view of Wayne Smith, director of the State Department's Office of Cuban Affairs from 1977 to 1979 and chief of the U.S. interest section in Havana from 1979 to 1982, now a leading administration critic:

[The White Paper] became a source of acute embarrassment to the administration, primarily revealing shoddy research and a fierce determination to advocate the new policy, whether or not the evidence sustained it. Some of the supporting documents turned out to be forgeries. Others were of such vague origin as to be worthless. None of the documents linked the USSR to the supply of guerrilla forces in El Salvador or demonstrated that the violence there was a case of external aggression rather than an internal conflict.

The State Department's Special Report on "Cuban and Nicaraguan Support for the Salvadorean Insurgency (March 20, 1982)," invited the same kind of doubt,[3] as did other analyses.

Skepticism as to the causes of Central American insurgency appeared to

---

[1] *State Department Bulletin*, No. 2048.
[2] *Wall Street Journal*, 8 June 1981.
[3] *Miami Herald Viewpoint*, 27 March 1982.

reach into the highest circles of the armed forces. General Edward C. Meyer, then retiring Army Chief of Staff, observed in June of 1983: "Guerrilla warfare is based on the legitimate concerns of the people." General Wallace C. Nutting, then completing his tour as chief of the Southern Command in Panama, apparently concurred: "The fundamental causes of dissatisfaction are the existing social, political and economic inequities." In fact, the general attitude of top army officers was said to be: "Guerrilla uprisings, no matter how anti-American or how dependent on Soviet assistance, spring largely from genuine economic and political grievances that can't be swept away by U.S. troops."[4] Army concern that administration perceptions of Central America might be skewed seemed in fact to date back at least to General Omar Bradley's unsuccessful attempt as chairman of the Joint Chiefs to veto U.S. involvement in Guatemala 30 years ago.[5] The difference this time lies in the degree of publicity generated, which is a matter of some political importance.

The administration is no doubt correct that there was a "decision by Cuba with Soviet-bloc support to organize and arm guerrilla forces under Marxist-Leninist control" after the Sandinistas' victory in Nicaragua, and that "El Salvador became a target, with the expectation that Communist-bloc training and supplies would bring a quick victory to Cuban-backed extremists."[6] But many observers are unwilling to accord Moscow-Havana either a causal or a determining role in the events of Central America. They consider dynamics indigenous to the region to be the crucial factors.[7] Two thirds of the laity of the Catholic church in El Salvador has, for example, become predisposed towards "radical liberation theology," and this more radical laity has in fact forced church hierarchies in both Nicaragua and El Salvador to incorporate Marxism into what was originally pure "liberation theology."[8] Marxism incorporated does not equate with Marxism-Leninism. But if not granted independent respectability, it may come to serve the latter's interests.[9]

The perception that Washington's policy fixation on Moscow was too extreme, and too undiscriminatingly tolerant of dictatorial activities cloaked in the anti-Communist mantle, jarred the susceptibilities of otherwise friendly observers. With the exception of Britain all allied NATO governments disassociated themselves from the "fraud" of El Salvador's elections in 1982. Anti-Sandinista leader Eden Pastora expostulated that "gringos" caused the problems

---

4   *Wall Street Journal*, 20 July 1983.
5   *Miami Herald*, 20 January 1984.
6   *State Department Current Policy*, No. 468, 16 March 1983.
7   See, for example, "Extermination in Guatemala . . . Creating a Desolation and Calling it Peace," in *The New York Review*, 2 June 1983.
8   T. S. Montgomery, "Cross and Rifle," *Columbia Journal of International Affairs*, (Winter 1982).
9   Note Luis Serra's fascinating analysis of Christianity's revolutionary roots, in *El Nuevo Diario* (29 May 1983), and Stefan Mamuntov's article in *Latinskaya Amerika* 2 (1982).

with Nicaragua: "From the beginning there has been pressure from them . . . first the economic and political blockade, then the military escalation"; as did others, he feared that Washington's policy had become counterproductive, driving third-option advocates into opposition, and inadvertently legitimizing the Soviet presence.[10]

Moscow gave full publicity to "Discrepancies in the governing circles of the United States with respect to Latin American Policy."[11] Senator Moynihan, for example, was quoted to the effect that "in the Kissinger Commission Report he did not find a single thing proving that Soviet and Cuban policy regarding Central America posed a threat to the interests of the United States' national security. There was, he felt, no evidence of that."[12] Differences between the U.S. administration and West European leaders were given equal play.[13]

U.S. references to El Salvador's Christian Democratic party as "on the left"[14] stirred consternation in Europe, where Christian Democracy was seen to constitute the right wing of the legitimate political spectrum. Moscow reacted by sponsoring analysis and debate on the potentially crucial and positive role that Central America's "bourgeois" Christian Democrats might play in the "first step of National Liberation."[15]

There is little question that "socioeconomic factors not of its own making have created opportunities for the Soviet Union to project its power into the Western hemisphere."[16] Yet, as one scholar on the Left observed about U.S. countermeasures: "Recent Reagan administration assaults have galvanized and radicalized the mass movement."[17] Moscow may not be able to take direct advantage of this assistance; but she is appreciative of the potential it provides for increased propaganda and manipulation.

Again and again the assertions of U.S. officials have provided grist to their opponents' mills: on the subject of aid to Salvadoran rebels, for example, intelligence officials who claim that they can "hear a toilet flush in Managua" have not been able or free to produce a captured van, or a downed airplane. "U.S. officials in fact acknowledge that most of the arms in the guerrillas' arsenal are captured, stolen or bought within El Salvador itself."[18] Representative Clarence Long, chairman of the House Appropriations Subcommittee that screens aid requests, weighed in: "We are the principal

---

10   *L'Expresso*, Rome, 24 August 1983.
11   *America Latina*, No. 5, 1983.
12   Moscow Radio, 23 January 1984.
13   See, e.g., TASS, 26 January 1984; and Radio Sandino, 14 February 1983.
14   Most recently by Secretary of State Shultz; *State Department Current Policy*, No. 468.
15   *Latinskaya Amerika*, Nos. 3, 4, and 5, 1982.
16   Morris Rothenberg, *Problems of Communism* (September-October 1983).
17   George Black, in the *New Left Review* (September-October 1982).
18   *New York Times*, 22 April 1983.

suppliers now to the rebels."[19] Rebel tabulations of captured arms, heavy and light, buttressed the point.[20]

The legacy of discrepancies between U.S. claims and U.S. evidence may even have served Moscow's interests with regard to the Marine landing in Grenada, the more so when initial U.S. assertions of Soviet involvement there proved exaggerated. Both Moscow and Havana had adopted a public posture of dissatisfaction at General Austin's coup against, and killing of Prime Minister Bishop. They later went much further, asserting that the CIA was directly responsible for the coup, and that the action had been undertaken to establish a pretext for invasion,[21] and the return of former dictator Gairy; Gairy's return also served as reminder of U.S. support for others of the same ilk, "Batista, Somoza, Stroessner, Pinochet and Duvalier."[22] The assertion of CIA complicity paralleled a report that circulated in Miami after the intervention; it purported to detail the shadowy trail, and named an Israeli-associated Venezuelan businessman as the conduit who arranged for Soviet-bloc arms captured in Southern Lebanon to appear in Granadian warehouses. The tale drew sustenance from the climate of general skepticism regarding U.S. claims both in Central America and in Western Europe, and it was sustained when reporters were initially excluded from coverage of the Grenada invasion.[23] The unprecedented initial exclusion of reporters in fact provided a perfect backdrop for the propagation of conspiracy theories.

Moscow's appreciation of the long-term propaganda impact of developments such as these, perhaps even more in Western Europe and South America than in Central America, cannot be overestimated. Soviet investment in Central America is substantial and multifaceted. Yet Moscow appears ready to concede President Reagan's point that "the U.S. image is at stake,"[24] that this is America's backyard, and that Washington's bottom-line "right" to intervene in Nicaragua is the same as hers in Afghanistan.[25] Andropov put the case "in reverse," so to speak, though he thought America's case was more tenuous, since Nicaragua is 1,000 kilometres from U.S. soil; nevertheless, the parallel was drawn, and parallels work both ways. Soviet leaders appear to calculate that even if worse comes to worst and Washington decides to exercise

19   *Newsweek*, 16 January 1984.
20   Radio Farabundo Marti, 28 December 1983.
21   TASS, 24 January 1984.
22   Moscow Radio, 25 January 1984.
23   *Miami Herald*, 6 November 1983.
24   *New York Times*, 21 May 1983.
25   General Secretary Andropov's 19 April 1983 *Der Spiegel* interview; TASS, 24 April 1983.

its "right" to the fullest, the larger propaganda harvest may yet justify the cost of her investments.

One prong of Soviet policy revolves around the Nicaraguan investment—military, economic and political aid to the Sandinistas. In revolutionary circles Moscow wants to be seen to have done everything possible to ensure that regime's ability to survive and defend itself. But the bottom line, that the regime must ultimately defend itself, is nevertheless explicit. While Havana declares that Cuban internationalists working in Nicaragua have volunteered "to stay at their posts despite the threats of direct imperialist military intervention,"[26] Moscow promises only "political" support and "solidarity" in the event of a full-scale U.S. invasion.[27]

The other prong of Soviet policy addresses itself to the task of defusing Latin American elite perceptions of a possible Soviet threat, while at the same time encouraging national assertiveness vis-à-vis U.S. policy dictates, by means of normalizing state-to-state relations and significantly increasing trade. The quite startling de-emphasis of previously publicized contacts with Central American revolutionaries in the Soviet media during 1983 and early 1984 may in large part result from this strategy. Assertions such as "Andropov strongly supports Contadora proposals for regional settlement" serve a similar purpose.[28] Soviet media focused increasingly on Brazil and Argentina, juxtaposing Soviet and Soviet-allied support for "mutual security [and] genuine relaxation in the region" with an uncompromising U.S. hegemonism and militarism.[29]

As concerns the relationship between assertion and evidence, Moscow clearly suffers a credibility gap of its own, fully equal to that of Washington. But Washington has more to lose. Equal opprobrium benefits Moscow, not Washington.

SOVIET ATTITUDES TOWARDS LATIN AMERICA

The Nicaraguan Revolution caught Moscow off-guard. The Moscow-line Socialist party had judged that the situation in that country was not ripe for revolution, and had consequently condemned the Sandinistas' insurrectionary strategy as adventurist. The "sad experience" of the bypassed Socialist party was to have major consequences in El Salvador and Guatemala. In these countries also the Moscow-aligned parties had stayed aloof from the armed struggle; but now they scrambled to join Cuban-engineered coalitions with armed groups that they had previously castigated as ultra-leftist or petit-bourgeois—

---

[26]   Havana Radio, 26 November 1983.
[27]   Managua Radio, 4 November 1983.
[28]   *Pravda*, 19 August 1983.
[29]   Moscow TV, 20 and 21 January 1984.

and which in turn had sneered at the Communists' unofficial dealings with officialdom. These were to be uneasy marriages: elements within the Communist parties remained nostalgic for the ideological purity of old; some of their new partners remained skeptical about the sincerity of their conversion.[30]

Moscow's ambivalence towards the Sandinista revolution was manifest. Sergei Mikoyan, son of Anastas and editor of *Latinskaya Amerika,* acknowledged that the Sandinistas' alliance with the bourgeoisie constituted a "new and unexplored" phenomenon, but that nevertheless their experiment with economic and political pluralism was of "colossal importance"; and their "less centralized socialism could offer . . . a new model for the Third World."[31] Kiva Maydanik, of the Institute for World Economy and International Affairs, was, however, dubious. She saw the alliance as internally contradictory, inherently unstable, and unlikely to endure, and she noted furthermore Nicaragua's "unfavorable" geographic location near the powerful United States and "the practical knowledge of domination of the exploiter classes."[32]

Having underestimated revolutionary potentials in Nicaragua, Moscow at first overestimated them in El Salvador.[33] Then the failure of the FMLN "final offensive," whose timetable was later said to have been accelerated in anticipation of increased U.S. involvement, led to more sobering appraisals.[34] In Guatemala also, rosy visions of an easy emulation of the Sandinistas came up against harsh reality, and were followed by recrimination and reassessment.[35]

Washington's view of the area, as "vitally significant" for U.S. security, was given full recognition;[36] 1983 brought flares of optimism and reports of guerrilla successes, amid signs of the disarray in U.S. policy.[37] But the dominant Soviet attitude was that reflected by V. Kristianov: "complete victory . . . demands a long and difficult struggle."[38]

Moscow's caution was reflected during 1983 in a marked decline in media references to Soviet contacts with guerrilla individuals and groups. This de-emphasis may in part have been a reaction to America's grand-scale Big Pine "exercises" in Honduras. It may also have reflected Eastern Europe's ambivalence about a "junior partner" role in Central America; the choice of Cuban-

---

[30] On Nicaragua and El Salvador, see T. Y. Vorozheinkina, in *Latinskaya Amerika* (July 1982); on Guatemala, Managua International Radio, 13 October 1983; and Radio Cadena YSU report, 4 November 1983.

[31] See Richard E. Feinberg's report on Moscow talks, in the *Washington Quarterly* (Spring 1982).

[32] Maydanik, in *Mirovaya Ekonimika i Mezhdunarodnaya Otnoshenia* (June 1981).

[33] *Izvestia,* 6 January 1981.

[34] N. S. Leonov, in *Latinskaya Amerika* (August 1981).

[35] *Nepszabadsag,* Budapest, 27 November 1983.

[36] Antiasov and Vasiliev, *Mezhdunarodnaya Zhizn,* 9 July 1983.

[37] *Pravda,* 28 April 1983; *Krasnaya Zvezda,* 9 July 1983.

[38] *Mezhdunarodnaya Zhizn,* June 1983.

backed Joaquín Villalobos as overall commander of El Salvador's FMLN, rather than CP leader Jorge Shafik Handal, provided telling evidence of realities on the ground.

Soviet caution, uncertainty, and consequent desire not to make too great a commitment may also be reflected in Moscow's (and Havana's) advice to Managua to cultivate economic and other ties with Western Europe, Canada, and Japan. The level of Soviet-bloc aid to Nicaragua was kept below aid from other quarters in order to counter U.S. allegations of satellite status. Yet this point merely emphasizes the element of caution. From mid-1982 onwards, Moscow placed increasing stress on support for Contadora and other regional settlement proposals.[39] The Russians insist that this posture should not be misconstrued to mean "loss of revolutionary spirit," or "betrayal . . . of the revolutionary cause," interpretations attributed to bourgeois ideologists and ultra-leftists. "Lenin rejected outright the leftist opportunist idea of the 'export of revolution'." Western ideologists have always tried to smear his concept of peaceful coexistence as purely "tactical," but Soviet political literature has viewed this as a verbal juggling and quoting out of context. Lenin's contradictory exhortations belonged to the immediate postrevolutionary era of capitalist assault against the young Soviet state, of interventions opposed by "mass revolutionary action" at home: "In the face of the armed confrontation imposed on them by the world bourgeoisie, the Bolsheviks were duty-bound to render support to the fighting proletariat abroad."[40] Soviet ideologists have of course also quoted Lenin at times for purposes of the moment, choosing often questionable excerpts from his prolific legacy of writings.

Notwithstanding increased Soviet aid to and involvement in Nicaragua, Moscow seems generally content to leave Havana in the driver's seat for involvement in Central America, while she concentrates on state-to-state prospects to the south. The Central American countries may be important, but Moscow appears to share the allegedly U.S. sentiment that "the outcome of the opposition between the forces of progress and reaction, on the soil of Latin America, is being decided in key countries—Brazil, Mexico and Argentina"; next in importance are "the countries of the so-called 'second echelon': Colombia, Venezuela, Peru."[41]

Soviet-Latin American trade, excluding Cuba, grew from 116.5 million rubles in 1969 to 595 million in 1979, then shot up to 3,124.4 million rubles, or 4.6 billion dollars in 1981, from which figure it has continued to grow.[42] The Falklands/Malvinas war spurred a further significant increase in

---

[39]   M. F. Gornov, in *Latinskaya Amerika* (July 1982); *Pravda*, 19 August 1983; and note Robert Pastor's testimony to the Senate Foreign Relations Committee, 5 August 1982.
[40]   *International Affairs*, Moscow, January 1983.
[41]   Morris Rothenberg, in *Problems of Communism* (September-October 1983), quoting Glinkin and Yakovlev, *Mirovaya Ekonimika i Mizhdunarodnaya Otnoshenia*, October 1982.
[42]   Rothenberg, *ibid*.

Soviet-Argentinian trade.[43] Joint venture agreements have been signed with a number of countries.[44] "There has unfolded a stable and constantly increasing subsystem of ties between socialist states and Latin America . . . economic, political, scientific-technical and cultural ties."[45] There are now twenty-three Communist parties in Latin America,[46] though in South America their activities tend to be de-emphasized. Twenty-five years ago Soviet diplomatic recognition in South America was limited to Argentina, Brazil, and Uruguay; today Moscow enjoys diplomatic relations with all countries south of Panama except Chile and Paraguay.

Soviet authors still talk of Latin America in terms of dependence theory, as do most Latin American intellectuals. But the extent of the theory's relevance is now open to debate; there is general agreement that Latin American countries have acquired "a more important role in world affairs," and that their foreign policies have an "anti-imperialist element" that may serve to restrict imperialism's "freedom of manoeuver."[47] In the Falklands/Malvinas conflict, for example, "the imperialist essence of Washington's policy vis-à-vis Latin American countries [was] graphically pointed out."[48] The Soviet Union may be critical of national chauvinism in other areas of the world, but the Latin American variety receives very good press.

THE IDEOLOGICAL PERSPECTIVE

At the 1966 Tricontinental conference of African, Asian, and Latin American revolutionaries in Havana, Cuba accused Moscow of being "unrevolutionary," and called for armed struggle in Latin America whether Soviet-aligned Communist parties supported it or not. Cuba then proceeded to increase military assistance to insurgents in Venezuela, , and Bolivia. Soviet-Cuban relations became so strained that Moscow cut back on economic assistance and oil deliveries, while demonstratively increasing sales to other nations in the hemisphere. Then Cuba's "ultra leftist adventures" failed, as Moscow had predicted, and Havana was forced to mute its flamboyant independence.[49] "Ultra-leftists" remained objects of Soviet scorn through the 1970s,[50] and it was only after the Sandinista victory that Moscow for the first time praised

43 *Financial Times* (London), 28 February 1983.
44 *Soviet Shipping*, No. 2, 1982, discusses Soviet-Brazilian and Soviet-Mexican Joint Shipping Commissions.
45 A. N. Glinkin, *Latinskaya Amerika* (August 1981).
46 V. Burmistrov, *Foreign Trade* (January 1982).
47 *Latinskaya Amerika* discussion, August, September and October 1981.
48 *Pravda*, 5 May 1982.
49 D. Bruce Jackson, *Castro, the Kremlin and Communism in Latin America* (Baltimore: Johns Hopkins University Press, 1969).
50 Note, for example, General Secretary Brezhnev's harsh attack in his speech to the 25th Congress of the CPSU.

Castro's revolutionary model. In this model, it was recognized, a Marxist-oriented guerrilla army rather than a Communist party serves as the "vanguard force" of revolution: "As yet only the armed path has led to the victory of revolutions in Latin America. And the Nicaraguan experience affirms what had been considered refuted by some after the death of Che Guevara and the defeat of a number of other guerrilla movements."[51] The reversal was not total, however: the Cuban model was not the only armed path to socialism; and what might be a vanguard force at one point could conceivably become a reactionary force at a later point.

Both the extent and the limits of this volte-face are reflected in the following statements by a leading Soviet Latin Americanist. The first is quite startling: "The agricultural proletariat is not just part of the working class, but constitutes the principal force of social revolution, the base of a broad front battling for national independence, and profound social, political and economic transformation." The other comes in the last paragraph of the same article: "The leaders of the vanguard of the urban working class" organize and educate rural workers, conquer indifference, passivity, and mistrust, and lead "the country folk" to the "radical transformation of society."[52]

A much-publicized roundtable discussion after the Sandinista victory explicitly approved Che's previously rejected views on the primacy of armed struggle; one Soviet participant saw the event as "the beginning of a new stage in the struggle of the entire continent."[53] Although this momentary enthusiasm was soon tempered, Moscow did join Havana in declaring the Sandinista formula a "correct" revolutionary model for other Central American nations, in supporting armed struggle in El Salvador, and in calling for the unification of revolutionary forces in Guatemala.[54] Salvadorean party leader Handal acknowledged that Moscow-aligned CPs had been "tailing after events,"[55] and explained two years later: "We thought the first revolution could be achieved by leaving the 'progressive and anti-imperialist' sectors of the middle class . . . and even the bourgeoisie in the forefront of the action. . . . We saw the Cuban experience as the exceptional anomaly."[56]

Henceforth, Moscow conceded that "political-military fronts" might play the primary role in the creation of united fronts, displacing the CP as instigator, though not as inheritor, of revolutions. This in Central America, defined as an area where "socialist states" are emerging.[57] In countries where "political-military" fronts were inappropriate, such as Mexico, Argentina, and

51 S. A. Mikoyan, *Latinskaya Amerika* 3 (1980).
52 A. Galkina, *Latinskaya Amerika* 4 (1982).
53 *Latinskaya Amerika* 1, 2 and 3 (1980); and see *New Times* (Moscow), 19 March 1982.
54 Moscow Radio, in Spanish, 12 February 1982.
55 *Pravda*, 30 August 1980.
56 *El Nuevo Diario*, Managua, 7 October 1982.
57 R. Wyanowsky, *Kommunist* 11 (July 1979).

Brazil, "united" fronts were advocated instead.[58] This change in tune in Moscow was of course partly opportunistic, a scrambling to catch up with the crest of the revolutionary wave. But there was also a suggestion of something more—of a revival of the strategy of "Dimitrov uniform fronts against reaction." The reference is to the Bulgarian Bolshevik George Dimitrov, leader and spokesman of the Comintern during the mid- and late 1930s, and his campaign for united fronts against National Socialist and Fascist regimes. That strategy had been conceived at a time when Moscow saw herself facing an extreme danger, one against which other enmities had to be submerged. From Moscow, as from the pages of the *Bulletin of the Atomic Scientists*, the world of the early 1980s looked similarly ominous.

WORDS OF CAUTION AND AMBIVALENCE

Moscow has always been acutely aware of Central America's geopolitical position, as the "strategic rear" of the United States.[59] Even after the Sandinistas consolidated their power, there were signs that Moscow expected the covert U.S. destabilization effort to escalate into an overt and decisive intervention (e.g., Andropov's 1983 interview with *Der Spiegel*), an eventuality which, it was believed, might well rebound to Soviet advantage. The initial Soviet ambivalence was reflected in a longer than average pause between censor and print in newspaper coverage. The *Latinskaya Amerika* issue that contained the first brief note on the Sandinista revolution, published in January 1979, had been submitted to the censors on 11 August 1978.[60]

The ambivalence was in part geopolitical, a recognition of U.S. power; but it was also partly ideological. The Sandinistas' successes were focusing attention on a continent-wide problem: Communist parties were not the acknowledged leaders of the revolutionary movement in most countries. Moscow-line Communists of Peru, for example, had been obliged ruefully to acknowledge: "On the left we have two large blocs. One is the ultra-leftist, the Popular Democratic Unity (UDR), the Unity of the Revolutionary Left (UNIR) and the Revolutionary Communist Party or Red Fatherland, the Trotskyite Party. A strong sector of workers and the poor people in the barrios support this bloc." And, even more startling, and brutally frank: " . . . there are three fairly ignored sectors for the Communist Party. They are the campesinos, the young people and women. The laxity of the CP has permitted other forces to secure their positions. For example, not one Student Federation in the Universities is directed by a Communist. They are all ultra-leftist

[58] S. Mikoyan, *Latinskaya Amerika* 3 (1980).
[59] P. Vasiliev, *International Affairs* 6 (1971).
[60] I. M. Bulychev, "On Events in Nicaragua," *Latinskaya Amerika* (January 1979); the normal interval between submittal and publication for this journal is two months.

leaders!"[61] Similar soul-searchings and recriminations were wracking every Communist party in the region at that time. In Guatemala, for example, it was acknowledged that "arduous debate over the correlation of the forms and methods of peaceful or armed struggle" within the Moscow-aligned group, the PGT, "put obstacles in the way of unified action."[62] The failure of Salvadoran party chief Shafik Handal to assume leadership of the FMLN after the death of Cayetano Carpio in 1983, and the selection of the ultra-leftist Villalobos, was yet another sign of this difficulty.

The tenuousness of Moscow's ability to control or direct events in Latin America may well have contributed to the Soviet media phase-out of references to revolutionary individuals and groups. But the crucial consideration was probably the fact that the threat of U.S. intervention loomed ever larger. As Soviet analysts saw it "the geo-political factor is being moved more persistently to center stage" in the Latin American policy of the United States; and the area's "vital significance for the security of the United States" was being "frankly emphasized."[63]

Nicaragua was originally said merely to have "embarked on a road of independent development."[64] By 1982 she acquired the status of "People's Democracy" in Soviet eyes; she had corrected Allende's mistakes by avoiding antagonizing the middle classes, securing control of the armed forces, taking control of all the main levers of power, and creating instruments of mass mobilization.[65] But then, except for one lone reference to a "socialist orientation,"[66] Nicaragua returned in 1983 to the rubrics "democratic" and "progressive." This contrasts with Moscow's view of Cuba as "an inseparable part of the community of socialist states. . . . The Soviet Union firmly and invariably supports and will continue to support the fraternal Cuban people."[67]

Moscow has been frank with the Nicaraguans about the extent of her commitment to support them. When asked how the Soviet Union would react if the United States intervened directly, Moscow's ambassador to Managua replied: "we have, are and will always show our solidarity with the Nicaraguan people."[68] Yuri Fokin, secretary-general of the Soviet Foreign Ministry, had already spelled out the meaning and limits of "solidarity": "we will support

[61]   Caballero Mendez, *Latinskaya Amerika* 7 (1981).
[62]   N. Leonov, *Latinskaya Amerika* 8 (1982).
[63]   Antiasov and Vasiliev, *Mezhdunarodnaya Zhizn* (July 1983).
[64]   *Pravda*, 7 November 1979.
[65]   Rothenberg, *Problems of Communism* (September-October 1983); *Latinskaya Amerika* 1 and 2 (1980), and 3 and 7 (1983).
[66]   *Pravda*, 13 June 1983.
[67]   *Pravda*, 8 April 1981.
[68]   *Managua Radio*, 3 November 1983.

Nicaragua politically in every way."[69] With regard to military eventualities, Moscow pointedly stressed Nicaragua's own military capability.[70] The "Leninist" path might demand aid to revolutionary aspirations abroad, but the bottom line "truth" was that revolution could not be exported; it must be indigenous and "genuine," and must in the final analysis be ready to defend itself![71]

Cuba had warned the Sandinistas in 1980 not to rely too much on military aid from Moscow—and to keep the state sector of their economy small.[72] Subsequently, Soviet-Nicaraguan ties did of course solidify and grow. The Sandinistas, however, appreciated what could be and had been gained, and what could not. "The Soviets are talking about helping us dam rivers in the 21st century, but we are in trouble now. . . . We are responsible for our revolution and the Cubans are responsible first of all for their revolution."[73]

Notwithstanding insistent incursions by the U.S.-sponsored *contra* armies based in Honduras and supported by Salvadoran Air Force attacks on Nicaraguan installations,[74] Managua appeared fairly confident: "We are technically prepared to take on the Honduran Army, and even all Central American armies together . . . we have superior firepower and military capability as far as infantry, armoured cars and artillery are concerned in Central America."[75] Havana's announcement that Cuban civilians serving Nicaragua had volunteered to stay and fight in the event of an all-out U.S. invasion also bolstered confidence.[76] The fact that Cuba's small contingent on Grenada had fought well against overwhelming odds imparted credibility to this claim.[77] Similarly, El Salvador's FMLN rebels asserted equal confidence in their ability to deal with any U.S. "proxies": "If the Hondurans and Guatemalans are sent in, they will become dangerously bogged down . . . they don't have the military capability to effect a substantial change in the correlation of forces."[78]

It was recognized of course that a determined U.S. assault could not be faced directly. But "any intervention in El Salvador or Nicaragua would regionalize the war . . . we have the capability to regionalize the war."[79] Managua declared: "We are preparing ever more thoroughly for a people's

69 *Havana Radio*, 3 August 1983.
70 Andropov, *Pravda*, 26 March 1983; and Gromyko, *Pravda*, 17 June 1983.
71 *International Affairs* (January 1983).
72 *Latin America Report*, 5 December 1980.
73 "Salvador Rebels Urged by Allies to seek Accord," *New York Times*, 5 August 1983.
74 Moscow TV, 26 January 1984; *New York Times*, 11 February 1984.
75 T. Borge interview *Cosas*, Santiago de Chile, 6 October 1983.
76 Havana Radio, 26 November 1983.
77 *New Times* 3 (January 1984).
78 *El Día*, Mexico, 17 November 1983.
79 *El Día*, ibid.

national war in the event of any attempt to impose an alien will upon us."[80] These preparations accelerated late in 1983 and early in 1984, as the FMLN conducted its "nation-wide" campaign to build air defense shelters.[81] Meanwhile the Sandinistas confirmed their maneuvering to avert war: even withdrawal of Cuban advisors was said to be "negotiable."[82] By this time the danger of war was so great that other policy aims had to be set aside: "An immediate transition to socialism is not today on the agenda in Central America . . . ; objective conditions . . . do not yet exist."[83]

SOVIET MILITARY AID TO CUBA

The year 1962 saw the delivery of a record 250,000 tons of Soviet military equipment to Cuba. From 1963 to 1980 Soviet military aid averaged 15,000 tons per year.[84] But after President Reagan took office, Soviet aid to Cuba increased. Military aid rose to 63,000 tons in 1981 and 68,000 tons in 1982; the number of Soviet military advisers rose 20 percent, to 2,500; they joined 6,000-8,000 civilian advisers, and a 1,700-man combat brigade.[85] Cuban Vice President Carlos R. Rodriguez confirmed that Cuba had "almost doubled" its military capabilities in 1981.[86] By 1982 Cuba boasted 200 Mig fighters, 650 tanks, and 90 helicopters.[87] In October 1983 Castro asked Moscow to further "accelerate" weapons deliveries, to counter the Reagan administration's "growing hostility."[88] The response was: three new Mig 23s, bringing Cuba's Mig 23 total to thirty-five; a second 2,300-ton Koni-class frigate, joining one delivered in 1981; and a third 2,100-ton Foxtrot sub, joining those delivered, respectively, in 1979 and 1980.[89] Cuban naval strength totalled 100 vessels, including guided missile destroyers and high speed hydrofoils.[90] According to U.S. analysts this made Cuba's military capabilities "impressive in the Central American context"; but "by Western standards, Cuba's ability to intervene is modest."[91]

Soviet aid extended beyond the military sphere. From 1960 to 1979 she provided $16.6 billion worth of aid: 35 percent was in the form of low-inter-est deferred-payment loans for balance-of-payment support and developmental

80   *New Times* 3 (January 1984).
81   Radio Venceremos, 24 December 1983.
82   *EFEU*, 29 November 1983.
83   Cuban Vice President Rodriguez, in *New Times* 3 (January 1984).
84   *State Department Special Report* No. 103, August 1982.
85   Under Secretary of Defense Fred Iklé, *Miami Herald*, 29 July 1983.
86   United Nations speech, 16 June 1982.
87   Deputy Secretary of Defense Frank Carlucci, *Speech File Service*, DA No. 23, July 1982.
88   *Miami Herald*, "Around the Americas," 27 January 1984.
89   *Ibid.*
90   Defense Department's 1983 *Defense and Foreign Affairs Handbook*.
91   *State Department Special Report* No. 103, August 1982.

aid; 65 percent was in the form of subsidized prices for sugar and nickel from Cuba, and below-market price differentials on oil to Cuba.[92]

SOVIET MILITARY AID TO NICARAGUA

Soviet military aid to Nicaragua is unobtrusive and elusive to track. Former U.S. Assistant Secretary of State Thomas Enders, testifying to the Senate Foreign Relations Committee in 1983, declared that there were currently "no less than 2,000 Cubans, 50 Soviets, 35 East Germans and 50 PLO and Libyan personnel" in Nicaragua on security missions; a senior U.S. military official at about this same time placed the Cuban number at between one and two thousand, and the PLO number at "no more than 25."[93] Soviet Ambassador Shlypnikov claimed that there were no Soviet military advisers in the country, only twenty "officials," twenty "doctors" and fifteen "professors."[94]

Often U.S. claims of Soviet involvement proved open to question. In May 1983 the White House announced that reconnaissance photos proved the Soviet ships *Novovolynsk* and *Polotosk* were steaming towards Nicaragua loaded with heavy military equipment; American reporters present at the unloading saw only field kitchens from East Germany, and 12,000 tons of fertilizer.[95] President Reagan later declared that the ship *Ulyanov* was "loaded with weaponry"; yet a respected British Conservative observer saw "no sign of offensive weaponry or armoured vehicles," only two hundred transport vehicles, eighty jeeps, five ambulances, and assorted civilian equipment.[96]

Deliveries from Soviet allies and "friends" are also difficult to trace. The Libyan planes detained in Brazil in April of 1983 were said to carry "grenades" and offensive arms.[97] The Brazilian government later released a detailed listing of the planes' cargo, together with the Brazilian Air Force's formal report: the equipment was defensive and obsolete; "nothing of what was found is capable of changing the balance of forces in Central America."[98]

According to State Department-published data, Soviet military aid from 1979 to 1982 totalled $125 million.[99] Then in early 1983, "Soviet deliveries speeded up": they "recently shipped eight to ten Mi8 troop carrying helicopters and more appear to be en route. . . . In May a Soviet vessel unloaded about 350 trucks . . . a one-third increase in the roughly 1000 trucks

---

92 Lawrence H. Theriot, *Cuba Faces the Economic Relations of the 80s*, US Department of Commerce, 22 March 1982; *Washington Post*, 1 May 1982.
93 *New York Times*, 27 April 1983.
94 *ACAN-EFE*, 29 November 1983.
95 *Christian Science Monitor*, 1 June 1983.
96 *The Daily Telegraph*, 30 July 1983; see also Radio Sandino, 12 August 1983.
97 *New York Times*, 27 April 1983.
98 *O Estado de São Paulo*, 3 May 1983.
99 *Current Policy* No. 476, April 1983.

from East Germany previously delivered"; in addition, "20 to 25 Soviet-built BRDM 2 armoured fighting vehicles and BTR armoured personnel carriers have arrived in recent months, along with BM 21 multiple rocket launchers, ZIS 2 57mm anti-tank guns and a handful of additional tanks to boost the Sandinista total to about 60."[100] By August Nicaragua was able to constitute a second tank brigade.[101]

Still, the heavier equipment, epitomized by T-54 and T-55 tanks, was limited in quantity, and outdated. The trend was towards small arms, to equip the 22,000-man army, the 25,000-reservist force, and the 30,000 militia.[102] Much of what did come in came via Soviet allies. And the limited amounts of truly modern equipment acquired by the Sandinistas came from Western Europe, not the Eastern bloc. Outside observers might be forgiven for concluding that "the scope and nature of the Kremlin's intrusion are far short of justifying the President's exaggerated alarms."[103]

Soviet-bloc caution is evidenced in the following figures.[104] In 1981 the USSR signed military agreements totalling $6,060 million (U.S.) with Less Developed Countries (LDCs), of which only $105 million, well under 2 percent, was with Latin America as a whole. East European nations signed agreements totalling $2,030 million with LDCs, of which only $10 million, less than half a percent, was with Latin America. That same year saw 16,280 Soviet "military technicians" in LDCs, of which only 165, or 1 percent, were in Latin America. East Europe had 1,925 military technicians in LDCs, of which sixty, that is 3 percent, were in Latin America. Cuba had 39,175 stationed in LDCs, of whom 1,715, just over 4 percent, were in Latin America. The combined Soviet and East European total in Nicaragua was 125, just over .5 percent of the number abroad; Cuba, on the other hand, had 1,700, practically all of her Latin American contingent, in Nicaragua.

The Soviet Union and East European countries also provided training to 57,795 "military personnel" from LDCs during 1955-1981; only 1,050, less than 2 percent, came from Latin America; and, of these, only 260, less than 0.5 percent, came from Nicaragua. One must note, however, that this is misleading as a measure of more recent trends, since the Nicaraguan relationship is strictly post-Somoza. It appears that the share of Nicaraguan trainees in 1980/81 may have reached over 5 percent (a supporter of official U.S. policy places the figure at "closer to 10 percent" than to the sub-half percent suggested by the twenty-five-year survey). Overall, the Soviet Union itself has,

100   *Washington Post*, 2 July 1983; see also *Miami Herald*, 31 July 1983.
101   Radio Sandino, 18 August 1983.
102   *New York Times*, 27 April 1983; State Department numbers are 20,000 regulars and 80,000 total reservists and militia.
103   *Boston Globe* editorial, 7 July 1983.
104   From US Department of State, *Soviet and East European Aid to the Third World, 1981*, released February 1983.

since 1949, provided military training to "no more than 100,000 soldiers from the Third World," excluding China, while the United States trained 370,000 between 1948 and 1981.[105]

In fact, Soviet military sales to the Third World dropped in 1981, from $14 billion the year before down to $6 billion; new Warsaw Pact military sales agreements fell from $15 billion in 1980 to $8 billion in 1981. This downturn may have been a cyclical phenomenon, as suggested by one source.[106] Certainly, the trend since 1980 has been towards a "decidedly more discreet approach."[107]

CUBAN MILITARY AID TO NICARAGUA AND SALVADORAN REBELS

Cuban aid to Central American revolutionaries is as difficult to quantify as Soviet aid. Thus the U.S. claims that all Salvadoran rebels have been trained by Cuba or Nicaragua, yet captured rebels assert that only specialists such as sappers and communications people have been trained by these nations.[108] A joint Pentagon and State Department *Background Paper* on Central America which claimed that Cuba had trained twenty Honduran rebels and was training sixteen more was judged to contain "little new information"; "that, and the vagueness of the accusations was said to have caused Assistant Secretary of State Thomas Enders to have opposed the report's release."[109] The numbers involved were in any case less than impressive, when set beside the fact that "525 Salvadoran officers will be trained at Fort Benning this year" and "2,400 Salvadorans will be trained in Honduras over the next 6 months . . . by a 100 member American training team."[110]

El Salvador rebels say that each of the FMLN's five constituent groups used to have its own supply networks, but now only one remains, supervised by Joaquín Villalobos; Nicaragua says large quantities of aid were sent to El Salvador's rebels during 1980 and 1981 but that none has been sent since; Cuba's Vice President Rodriguez claims Havana ended its regular supply to

---

105 *Communist Aid Activities in Non-Communist Less-Developed Countries, 1979 and 1954-79*, US Central Intelligence Agency, 1980; and *Foreign Military Sales, Foreign Military Construction Sales and Military Assistance Facts as of September 1981*, US Department of Defense Security Assistance Agency, Washington, 1982.
106 US Department of State, *Soviet and East European Aid to the Third World, 1981*, released February 1983.
107 J. Krause, "Soviet Military Aid to the Third World," *Aussenpolitik*, English edition, No. 4, 1983.
108 *Miami Herald*, Viewpoint Special, 5 June 1983.
109 *New York Times*, 30 May 1983.
110 *Ibid.*

Salvadoran rebels about two years ago, and invites Washington to prove otherwise.[111]

"U.S. evidence of arms shipments . . . has never been solid . . . the quantities are almost certainly far less than alleged."[112] By early 1984 Representative Clarence Long, chairman of the House Appropriations Sub-committee responsible for U.S. aid programs, concluded that "we are the principal suppliers to the rebels."[113] That has long been a rebel claim.[114] It is supported by independent evidence that rebel seizures from the armed forces extend to heavy artillery and entire arsenals and is confirmed by reports from Western journalists in the field that the rebels request boots and clothing, but not arms.[115] The rebels' formal breakdown of the 3,393 heavy and light weapons seized during 1983 drove the point home.[116]

The U.S. administration asserts that Cuba has built or is building a total of thirty-six new military bases in Nicaragua.[117] One of the sites mentioned, Tipitapa, has been visited by a number of Western journalists; the construction in question is that of a very large sugar plant—among the workers are 100 Cuban technicians.[118]

As concerns Cuban "advisers" the United States has announced that 100 Cuban security and military advisers arrived in Managua within a week of the Sandinista victory; by October 1979 the number had risen to 200;[119] and, by early 1981, to 600-800.[120] The 1983 U.S. count was 2,000 Cuban military advisers plus 6,000-8,000 civilian advisors.[121]

Latin American governments friendly to the United States estimated in 1983 that there were then 1,000 Cuban military advisers in Nicaragua.[122]

Cuban Vice President Rodriguez said in June that "there are several dozen (though) not many dozen" Cuban military, intelligence, and security advisers in Nicaragua; and "much fewer" than 8,000 teachers, doctors, and other civilians.[123] In August, Castro stated that there were 200 Cuban military advisers in Nicaragua.[124] In September, Cuba declared that 628 of its health

111   *Miami Herald*, 5 June 1983.
112   Wayne Smith, *Foreign Policy* (Fall 1982).
113   *Newsweek*, 19 January 1984.
114   *Latinskaya Amerika* 7 (1983).
115   *Expresso*, Lisbon, 19 February 1983.
116   Radio Farabundo Marti, 28 December 1983.
117   *New York Times*, 15 March 1983.
118   *Granma*, 11 July 1983.
119   US Department of Defense and Department of State, *Background Paper*, May 1983, *op. cit.*
120   US Department of State, *Current Policy*, No. 282, 3 June 1981.
121   *Miami Herald*, "Around the Americas," 26 November 1983.
122   EFE, Madrid, 31 August 1983.
123   *Miami Herald*, 5 June 1983.
124   EFE, Madrid, 31 August 1983.

professionals were working in Nicaragua, and that they would be joined by 100 more.[125]

Cuba's tally was given added credibility by the fact that Washington's original dramatic claim with regard to the number of Cubans on Grenada at the time of the Marine landing later had to be slashed, until the final official U.S. figure agreed with Havana's.[126]

The impressively large-scale U.S. training programs for the Salvadoran and Honduran armed forces have been mentioned. To place the Cuban effort in perspective one must keep in mind the fact that the CIA was "responsible for financing and managing 10,000 Nicaraguan rebels" in 1983,[127] and that this number was scheduled to rise to 15,000 by spring, 1984.[128] In March 1984, there were reports that the figure had in fact already mushroomed to 18,000. The anti-Sandinista effort was by then apparently also able to call on help from the Salvadoran Air Force.[129] The formidable off-shore presence of the U.S. Navy had a political and military impact.[130] Finally, some 42,000 Latin American soldiers, many of them Nicaraguan National Guardsmen, had been trained earlier by the U.S. Army School of the Americas in Panama.[131] In the face of these figures, the Sandinista assertion that the withdrawal of Cuban military advisers was "negotiable" was understandable. [132]

The arrival in Nicaragua of "Cuba's top combat General,"[133] on the other hand, presumably reflected Havana's and Managua's conclusion that mutually acceptable negotiations with Washington were unlikely. In January 1984 Castro announced that Cuba was training Nicaraguan "military officers and noncommissioned officers."[134] Cuban advisers began accompanying Nicaraguan soldiers into battle.[135] Havana also let it be known that youth and increased exposure to militia training would henceforth distinguish civilian personnel sent to Managua; the related teacher rotation was soon completed.[136]

[125] Havana International Radio, 4 September 1983.
[126] *Miami Herald*, 6 November 1983.
[127] *New York Times*, 5 August 1983.
[128] *Miami Herald*, 7 August 1983, citing House of Representatives Intelligence Committee sources.
[129] *New York Times*, 11 February 1984.
[130] *Miami Herald*, 6 August 1983.
[131] *Washington Post*, 23 May 1983.
[132] *EFE*, Madrid, 31 August 1981.
[133] *New York Times*, 19 June 1983.
[134] Havana Radio, 4 January 1984.
[135] *New York Times*, 20 March 1984.
[136] *Washington Post*, 12 March 1984; Radio Sandino, 27 March 1984.

COMPARISON SUMMARY:
WESTERN MILITARY AID TO NICARAGUA

France provided the Sandinistas with $15 million to purchase 2 coastal patrol boats, 2 Alouette helicopters, 45 troop transports, 100 missile launchers and 7,000 missiles;[137] most of these items were delivered during 1982 and 1983;[138] but the missiles and the boats' armament appeared still outstanding. *Contra* port mining efforts, seen by Managua as a cornerstone of Washington's intensifying "policy of terrorism", brought a French commitment to participate in minesweeping operations.[139] Washington acknowledged, confidentially, that the mine-layers were "non-Nicaraguan . . . commandos, who operate from the CIA-controlled vessel," and proceeded to issue a sharp public warning to Paris to desist. The peremptory tone of this exchange bespoke discord within the Atlantic Alliance— and American impatience with Mitterand.[140] The Netherlands, in the meantime, provided $5.5 million to help with port defense improvements at Corinto;[141] and a Panamanian ship stopping in Costa Rica en route for Nicaragua was found to be loaded with explosives,[142] though these may have been intended to serve civilian rather than military ends.

SOVIET NON-MILITARY AID TO NICARAGUA

After the Sandinista revolution Moscow urged the new regime to seek economic aid from the West.[143] Thereafter, Soviet-Nicaraguan economic ties developed slowly. The first agreement was signed in March 1980: Moscow would give a $50 million credit for machinery, including trucks, Ladas, motorcycles and tractors, and a $30 million credit for small industries; the two sides pledged to cooperate in the development of fishing and marine resources, water power, mining and geological surveys, health care, small industry, communications, air traffic, and agriculture.[144] Planning ministers Ruiz and Baibakov agreed, at the same time, to cooperate and exchange planning information. In 1981 deliveries covered by the $50 million in credits were made,

---

137 *New York Times*, 27 April 1983, provides general coverage.
138 Radio Sandino, 17 September 1983, for example, reported the launching of the two boats.
139 *El Nuevo Diario*, 4 April 1984, quotes French Foreign Minister Cheysson; see also *Miami Herald* "Around the Americas" coverage, 22 March 1984.
140 *Miami Herald*, 7 April 1984.
141 *Central America Report*, 19 August 1983; Managua Radio, 21 June 1983.
142 *EFE*, Madrid, 26 April 1983.
143 Mikoyan, *Latinskaya Amerika* (March 1980).
144 US Department of State, *Soviet and East European Aid to the Third World, 1981*, February 1983.

and agreements were reached covering technical cooperation in radio, television, and fisheries.[145]

In May 1982 Moscow agreed to $50 million in credits for health care support, $16.8 million for an Inter-Sputnik satellite hookup and $100 million over three years for heavy machinery purchases.[146] The Soviet Union also contracted to expand ship repair facilities at the Pacific port of San Juan del Sur.[147] November brought $30 million in emergency aid for victims of the recent floods and the announcement of scholarships to Moscow for Nicaraguan students.[148] Nicaragua purchased a quantity of Soviet loaders, wagons, and mining equipment.[149] At the beginning of 1983, 15,000 tons of Soviet wheat arrived.[150] Another 7,000 tons arrived in November.[151] This made the total, "so far," 40,000 tons.[152]

In May Moscow sent 6,000 tons of urea; and the fertilizer donation was said to be "enough for the 83/84 harvests."[153] Eleven million dollars was given for laboratory equipment.[154] That same month saw an announced follow-up to the May 1982 pact: "A 7,000 ton Soviet drydock and a 60 foot long pier are scheduled to be anchored" in San Juan del Sur "in three months, to service Russian tuna vessels. . . . The Soviet Union will pay Nicaragua $200,000 a year as rental fee."[155]

In June, Bayardo Arce, head of the Sandinista political commission, arrived in Moscow to discuss implementation of an agreement for CPSUFSLN (Frente Sandinista de Liberación Nacional)-Sandinista party-to-party exchanges. In the same month a $50 million loan for heavy equipment was granted in partial fulfillment of the 1982 accord, and $30 million was provided in credits to buy raw materials.[156] In July it was announced that Soviet personnel manning the Soviet-Nicaraguan Friendship Field Hospital, which had treated 65,000 Nicaraguans, so far, had agreed to extend their contracts one more year.[157] Agrarian Reform Minister Jaime Wheelock also signed an agricultural agreement in July, and this was followed up by a "technical-agricultural agreement" in December.[158]

145   TASS, 4 September 1981.
146   *New York Times*, 11 May 1982.
147   Managua Radio, 10 May 1982.
148   Radio Sandino, 1 November 1982.
149   *Foreign Trade*, Moscow, 11 November 1982.
150   Havana Radio, 8 January 1983.
151   Radio Sandino, 17 November 1983.
152   Havana Radio, 23 November 1983.
153   *El Nuevo Diario*, 20 May 1983; *Barricada*, 10 June 1983.
154   Radio Sandino, 23 May 1983.
155   *New York Times*, 15 May 1983.
156   *El Nuevo Diario*, 11 June 1983.
157   Radio Sandino, 20 June 1983.
158   Sistema Sandinista TV, 19 December 1983.

The USSR All-Union Central Council of Trade Unions donated unspecified electronic and communications equipment for civilian projects in November.[159] December brought 200 tons of powdered milk;[160] 3,300 kilograms of medicine;[161] and the offer of Soviet participation in a $20 million yarn factory project.[162]

The year 1984 began as had 1983, with the Soviet ship *Kapitan Kushnarenko* delivering a gift of 14,000 tons of maize.[163] This was followed by the signing of a new two-year cooperative agreement covering science, education, culture, and sports,[164] and the opening of a new Soviet-supplied Fisheries Resources School.[165] Sandinista leader Ortega opined: "Soviet-Nicaraguan economic links represent a striking contrast to those inequitable relations within the international economic system to which Nicaragua was previously accustomed."[166] Moscow agreed: "Lasting ties of friendship and cooperation link the peoples of the two countries. While the Reagan administration is spending millions of dollars in financing and training the Somozist gangs, and is pursuing a course of destabilizing the situation in the country, the USSR is helping to implement a program of socioeconomic changes that the government of the country adopted in the interests of the majority of Nicaraguans."[167]

Panegyrics aside, there is little question that Soviet aid has had a major impact in Nicaragua. In view of the CIA-sponsored *contra* raids against Nicaragua's Pacific oil terminals, for example, it is worth noting that Soviet technical aid appears to have helped the Sandinistas initiate development of new geothermal and hydroelectric energy sources, and thus gradually begin to lessen Managua's dependence on costly and vulnerable oil imports.[168] When *contra* raids and complementary pressure from Washington led to cutbacks in Venezuelan and Mexican oil deliveries to Managua, Moscow also stepped in more directly. Early 1984 saw the arrival of two Soviet tankers carrying 242,000 barrels of crude oil and 25,000 barrels of jet and aviation fuel; a third tanker was reported to be on its way.[169] Next came oil storage tanks and oil distribution pipelines.[170]

---

[159]   *El Nuevo Diario*, 25 November 1983.
[160]   Radio Noticias, 3 December 1983.
[161]   Radio Sandino, 23 December 1983.
[162]   Managua International Radio, 24 December 1983.
[163]   TASS, 26 January 1984.
[164]   Details were unspecified; *El Nuevo Diario*, 11 February 1984.
[165]   Radio Sandino, 27 March 1984.
[166]   Moscow TV, 21 January 1984.
[167]   TASS, 26 January 1984.
[168]   R. Rosenberg, "Soviet Support for Central American Guerrilla Movements as a Strategic Initiative," *SAFRA* 1984.
[169]   *New York Times*, 6 February 1984.
[170]   Radio Sandino, 24 March 1984.

On the other hand, aid from Western Europe and UN agencies has been even greater than Soviet and Eastern European aid combined. Furthermore, it must also be said that, seen in the context of her overall aid to Third World nations, Moscow's commitment to Nicaragua is quite modest. The figures that follow are taken from the State Department's 1983 report, *Soviet and East European Aid to the Third World, 1981*. From 1954 to 1981 Moscow directed 22,355 credit grants to the Third World, of which 1,420, or just over 6 percent, went to Latin America. During the same period, Eastern Europe extended 11,885 credits, of which 2,135, less than 18 percent, went to Latin America. Of 2,070 Soviet Third World credits in 1980, Latin America received 250, 12 percent; of 1,330 1980 East European Third World credits, Latin America received 195, 14.6 percent (of this number, 150 went to Brazil). In 1981 Moscow granted only 445 new credits, with 17, or 38 percent, going to Latin America (of which 55, or 12.3 percent, went to Brazil, while 80, or 17.9 percent, went to Nicaragua). There were also fewer East European credits: 665, of which 50, 7.5 percent, went to Latin America; of these, 10, or 1.5 percent, went to Brazil, and 40, or 6 percent, to Nicaragua.

A total of 95,685 Soviet and East European "economic technicians" were in LDCs in 1981; of these, only 930, less than 1 percent, were in Latin America. Nicaragua hosted 200, barely over one fifth of the Latin American number, and one five hundredth of the overall total; Brazil hosted 100.

CUBAN NON-MILITARY AID TO NICARAGUA

Cuba's 1984 Cooperation and Economic Exchange Agreement with Nicaragua calls for only $40 million worth of trade.[171] But Cuba's economic aid cannot really be measured in dollars and cents. Cuban workers are playing a major role in Nicaragua's $200 million railway extension and improvement project;[172] they are also helping to construct sugar plants, roads, and military installations.[173]

In December 1982 Cuba and Nicaragua formed a joint shipping company, "Servicio Caribe," connecting Mariel and Cienfuegos in Cuba with Corinto, Sandino, and Arlen Siu.[174] Interestingly, Nicaraguan ships will dock only at Nicaragua's Atlantic ports, Arlen Siu, and later also El Bluff, while Cuban ships will carry the trade going to and from the Pacific ports of Corinto and Puerto Sandino. This means that only Cuban, Soviet, and other foreign vessels bound for Nicaragua will pass through the Panama Canalz. The fact that such vessels would be less prone to seizure was presumably considered.

---

171 Havana TV and Radio Sandino, 27 December 1983.
172 Havana TV, 11 July 1983.
173 Radio Sandino, 30 July 1982.
174 *Granma*, 28 December 1982.

By mid-1983 Cuba was engaged in 1,003 economic and social projects in Nicaragua.[175] U.S. figures for 1981 showed 23,075 Cuban citizens abroad, and 4,000 of these, 86.5 percent of the Latin American number and 17 percent of the overall total, were in Nicaragua.[176] The figures would appear to have increased since, but there is no agreement on exact numbers (see also section on Cuban military aid).

EAST EUROPEAN AND OTHER SOVIET-ALLIED AID TO NICARAGUA

Bulgaria and the German Democratic Republic (GDR) have been the Sandinistas' main East European benefactors. In March 1983 Bulgaria agreed to extend $165 million in credits for the construction of a deep-water port in Bluefields Bay, on the Atlantic. The agreement furthermore called for $38 million worth of financial aid to twelve industrial and agricultural development projects, and credits for Nicaragua's purchase of Bulgarian medical supplies, busses, electronics, mining equipment, and other machinery.[177] Bulgaria committed herself to participate in eighty-nine projects over the next three years,[178] and to provide 1984 training for 5,000 Nicaraguan construction workers assigned to the Bluefields Bay development.[179] Bulgaria also gave technical aid for training in agronomy;[180] "donated" support equipment, including blankets, food, business machines, and clothing, to the Ejercito Popular Sandinista;[181] and set aside $900,000 in credits for forestry developments[182]—a sum later increased to $1 million.[183]

The GDR donated $1 million for education in mid-1983.[184] Then came a more comprehensive agreement: East Berlin agreed to provide $148 million in credits, subdivided into eighty-three distinct packages: $120 million was to be used to purchase farm machinery, trucks, fertilizers, and chemicals; $28 million would be allocated to raw material purchases. The GDR also committed an initial $27 million credit for 1984, while agreeing to import food, cof-

---

175   Havana Radio, 8 June 1983.
176   US Department of State, *Soviet and East European Aid to the Third World, 1981*, released February 1983.
177   *New York Times*, 14 March 1983; the latter credits, because unspecified, do in fact most likely constitute integral parts of the $165 million Bluefields Bay sum; see also *Barricada*, 13 March 1983.
178   *Barricada, ibid.*
179   *El Nuevo Diario*, 3 December 1983.
180   *El Nuevo Diario*, 18 May 1983.
181   Sistema Sandinista TV, 17 June 1983.
182   Sistema Sandinista TV, 22 November 1983.
183   Radio Noticias, 6 January 1984.
184   Radio Sandino, 23 May 1983.

fee, and tobacco from Nicaragua.[185] The two sides furthermore signed a long-term scientific cooperation accord.[186]

Czechoslovakia gave $40 million in credits in 1983, for truck, machinery, and equipment purchases.[187] Hungary donated an unspecified amount of food, clothing, and medical supplies in May of 1983;[188] medical donations in 1983 totalled $30 million.[189] Hungary and Nicaragua have also signed a communications accord.[190]

North Korea gave emergency flood aid in 1982[191] and in mid-1983 donated 2,000 tons of corn and an unspecified number of light weapons.[192] This was followed by a pledge to meet all of Managua's steel requirements.[193] In October it was revealed that North Korea had given $30 million worth of credits "thus far."[194] A laundry list announced in November included most of the above information and noted that 5,000 tons of steel and 5,000 tons of urea had also been delivered during the preceding six months. A Center for Seed Research was promised for 1984.[195] And it appeared that the North Koreans might also be willing to provide some additional weapons.[196]

Vietnam signed a trade agreement with Nicaragua in September 1983, the details of which have not been made public.[197] After the stepping up of *contra* attacks in early 1984 Hanoi offered military and technical assistance, and "complete military solidarity."[198]

Libya extended a $100 million loan in 1981, sent sixty-four technicians,[199] and later donated a Falcon 20 plane.[200] Spring 1984 brought announcement of a joint Nicaraguan-Libyan agricultural investment project designed to increase corn production.[201] Yugoslavia has similarly engaged in agricultural cooperation with Nicaragua and provided loans for agriculture and

185   Radio Sandino, 5 December 1983.
186   GDR Radio, 4 December 1983.
187   Radio Sandino, 3 June 1983; Sistema Sandinista TV, 7 July 1983; *Barricada*, 6 October 1983, and *El Nuevo Diario*, 6 December 1983 for reported deliveries.
188   Radio Sandino, 17 and 23 May 1983.
189   *El Nuevo Diario*, 6 December 1983.
190   Radio Sandino, 19 September 1983.
191   Radio Sandino, 16 July 1982.
192   Sistema Sandinista TV, 17 June 1983; *El Nuevo Diario*, 21 June 1983.
193   Radio Sandino, 19 September 1983.
194   Sistema Sandinista TV, 20 October 1983.
195   Radio Sandino, 24 November 1983.
196   *New York Times*, 4 April 1984.
197   Radio Sandino, 7 September 1983.
198   *El Nuevo Diario*, 23 March 1984.
199   *New York Times*, 21 April 1981.
200   Managua Radio, 23 November 1983.
201   Managua Radio, 17 March 1984.

irrigation;[202] Yugoslavia has also given $10 million in credits.[203] Algeria signed a trade pact with Nicaragua in May 1983 and stepped in to pick up all of the 50,000 tons of sugar quota dropped by the United States.[204]

COMPARISON SUMMARY: SOVIET AND WESTERN ECONOMIC AID TO NICARAGUA

From July 1979 to June 1982 only $208 million of a total of $769 million in bilateral credits to Nicaragua came from socialist countries including Cuba.[205] If we count credits, grants, and donations, the total of "official" aid to Nicaragua during the first two years after the Sandinista victory came to $1 billion,[206] of which the United States contributed $125 million. American policy was then set on a radically different course; but few of the NATO allies followed suit. Of the seventeen OECD members only the U.S. and British governments have withheld aid from Nicaragua for political reasons, although West German aid was suspended after the election of Helmut Kohl's conservative coalition. As Tomás Borge has noted: this U.S. policy is opposed by the presidents of Panama, Venezuela, Colombia, Costa Rica, and Mexico, the SPD of Germany, Britain's Labour party, and the governments of most Western European countries.[207] Even Guatemala, Honduras, and El Salvador, the latter two intimately involved with Washington in *contra* support, continued their low-level trade with Managua. Nicaragua's biggest textile factory, Texnicsa, for example, uses yarn imported from El Salvador.[208] Even U.S. policy was not unidimensional: notwithstanding Washington's "economic warfare" against Managua, trade was not cut off completely until May of 1985. The United Nations Development Program granted Nicaragua over $600 million in technical assistance and $119,040,000 in financial assistance during the first years of Sandinista government.[209]

France gave Nicaragua a $15 million credit to purchase French military equipment.[210] She gave 200 million francs in nonmilitary credits for 1981/82, and promised to quadruple this figure for 1982/83.[211] France also donated 7,300 tons of flour during 1983; Radio Sandino, on 17 August 1983, referred to a shipment which may have represented an additional 7,000 tons,

---

202   Radio Sandino, 17 and 19 October 1983.
203   *Barricada*, 10 October 1983.
204   *El Nuevo Diario*, 1 July 1983.
205   *Le Monde*, 23 and 24 January 1983.
206   F. E. Feinberg, *The Washington Quarterly* (Spring 1982).
207   *Miami Herald*, 7 August 1983.
208   Radio Sandino, 26 March 1984.
209   Managua Radio, 10 October 1983.
210   *New York Times*, 27 April 1983.
211   *Barricada*, 24 July 1983.

bringing the total since 1979 to 24,000 tons of flour.[212] In September, Paris increased its aid by 20 million francs.[213] In December, President Mitterrand extended present-level aid through 1985, promised to increase the aid still further, and authorized donations of medical supplies;[214] of the latter, thirty tons had been transferred by 7 March 1984.

West Germany (FRG) provided food donations, food processing aid, and credits for the purchase of commercial ships in 1982.[215] In September 1983, Nicaragua and the FRG signed cooperation agreements in the areas of education, agriculture, and mapping; financing for the programs was said to be about $6 million; the FRG also promised to help prepare a topographic map of Nicaragua and give Nicaragua a complete aerial photography laboratory.[216] November brought "donation of equipment and rooms for natural science, chemistry, physics and biology laboratories," FRG agreement to train "180 teachers . . . of chemistry, biology and physics,"[217] and an FRG Committee of Solidarity donation of 353 kilograms of medical equipment.[218] Spring 1984 saw Social Democratic party leaders donate 100,000 DM to the Augusto C. Sandino Foundation, for the building of a rural children's center in Jinotega,[219] and for the arrival in Managua of a West German "brigade of volunteer physicians and health technicians."[220]

The Netherlands gave $5.5 million in 1983 to help with defense improvements at Corinto,[221] just weeks before the CIA and *contras* began mining that port. Italy provided food donations, and helped finance a $70 million geothermal plant;[222] and the Socialist-led Italian government, elected in 1983, also arranged a special EEC credit to Nicaragua for export promotion. The EEC included Nicaragua in its $35 million 1983 aid plan for Central America,[223] and donated 4,000 tons of wheat.[224] Spain donated wheat, and credits totalling $90 million.[225] Austria donated 9,000 tons of wheat in 1983,[226]

212   Radio Sandino, 17 June 1983.
213   Radio Sandino, 17 September 1983.
214   *El Nuevo Diario*, 19 December 1983.
215   *El Nuevo Diario*, 28 September 1982; Sistema Sandinista TV, 2 April 1982; Managua International Radio, 17 September 1982.
216   Managua Radio, 1 September 1983.
217   *El Nuevo Diario*, 23 November 1983.
218   Radio Sandino, 30 November 1983.
219   Managua Radio, 7 March 1984.
220   Sistema Sandinista TV, 15 March 1984.
221   *Central America Report*, 19 August 1983; Managua Radio, 21 June 1983.
222   *Central America Report*, 26 August 1983.
223   *Central America Report*, 15 April 1983.
224   Radio Noticias, 3 December 1983.
225   Managua Radio, 10 August 1982; *Central America Report*, 20 May 1983; *ACAN-EFE*, Madrid, 27 September 1983; Managua Radio, 12 March 1984.
226   *El Nuevo Diario*, 27 December 1983.

and extended credits for development and for the purchase of equipment and spare parts.[227]

Sweden donated $250,000 for rural transportation in 1983,[228] and gave $3.4 million in credits for a sugar processing project.[229] In November Stockholm acceded to an urgent request for an increase in her Agency for International Cooperation aid to Nicaragua.[230] and in December followed this up with $1.2 million in emergency food aid.[231] Swedish Prime Minister Palme's visit early in 1984 was preceded by the announcement of a donation of 7,000 metric tons of wheat; and the visit itself featured the dedication in Managua of a hospital financed by the Swedish government.[232] Finland provided farm and energy aid, as well as emergency food donations.[233]

Canada provided $34 million in credits and $7.1 million in food aid, and nongovernmental Canadian organizations added $7.4 million for developmental projects during the first three years of the Sandinista regime; another $13.4 million was granted in January 1984.[234] The long-term credit accord signed with Ottowa in 1982 was said to be worth an ultimate $180 million.[235] During 1982 Canada also donated 11,000 tons of wheat worth $2.2 million,[236] and agreed to help with sewage and water supply projects.[237]

Japan increased her trade with Nicaragua in direct proportion to America's decrease.[238] Even Taiwan donated research equipment and personnel, and supplied bat traps—to protect cattle from vampire bats.[239]

Mexico and Venezuela extended soft credits for oil purchases, in accordance with the San José Pact, although American pressure led to a significant fall-off in deliveries beginning in the fall of 1983. Colombia, Peru, Brazil, and Argentina provided Nicaragua with $105 million in trade credits during 1983.[240]

The Inter-American Development Bank, defying U.S. pressure, loaned $30 million to help develop Nicaragua's fishing industry.[241]

---

227   *El Nuevo Diario*, 14 June 1983; Radio Sandino referred on 13 September 1983 to a $17 million loan.
228   Managua International Radio, 24 September 1983.
229   Managua Radio, 15 November 1983.
230   *Central America Report*, 2 December 1983.
231   Radio Sandino, 23 December 1983.
232   Managua Radio, 10 February 1984.
233   *Central America Report*, 20 May 1983.
234   *Miami Herald*, 15 January 1984.
235   *El Nuevo Diario*, 29 April 1982.
236   *Central America Report*, 2 December 1983; Radio Noticias, 2 December 1983.
237   Radio Sandino, 12 December 1983.
238   *Barricada*, 23 May 1983.
239   *Central America Report*, 20 May 1983.
240   *Central America Report*, 15 April 1983; *Barricada*, 6 October 1983.
241   Managua Radio, 28 September 1983.

Seven hundred foreigners, mostly Western Europeans, arrived in Nicaragua in late 1983 to do volunteer work;[242] the arrival of the West German "health brigade" in March of 1984 signalled the continuation of this phenomenon. A mid-1983 analysis concluded that about half of Nicaragua's economic assistance came from Western Europe and Latin America and only 20 percent from communist countries, including Cuba.[243]

SOVIET CULTURAL AND EDUCATIONAL TIES
WITH LATIN AMERICA

The number of Soviet scholarships to Central American students rose dramatically during the early 1980s. More Central American students still attended U.S. colleges, but those tended to be self-financing, nonscholarship students from the thin and unrepresentative upper financial caste of their home countries. Soviet scholarships, on the other hand, were aimed at individuals and groups likely to exercise greater influence in more representative movements and governments.

Between 1972 and 1982 Soviet scholarships for a handful of Central American and Caribbean countries rose over 500 percent, to nearly 4,000.[244] By 1983 the Soviet Union and Cuba provided 7,500 scholarships to Central American students.[245] The end of the preceding year had seen 1,000 Nicaraguan students attending Soviet institutions.[246] By mid-1983 2,000 Nicaraguans were studying in Cuba;[247] of these, 1,200 were on the famous Isle of Youth.[248] Central American efforts probably constitute the second largest Soviet scholarship program aimed at Latin America, though the total of South American students is difficult to compute. (The U.S. Department of State Survey of Soviet and East European Aid to the Third World placed the 1981 number of Colombians in the USSR at 1,015.) The largest program, of course, is directed at Cuba. About 9,000 Cuban students attended Soviet institutes of higher learning during 1983/84.[249]

Publication and media trends are also suggestive. Moscow published just fifty-three Spanish language titles from 1949 to 1959, with a combined copy total of half a million. By 1975 the Soviets were publishing 353 Spanish titles, with a total of 13 million copies. The 1980 tally was 370 titles, with

---

242 Havana Radio, 20 November 1983.
243 *New York Times*, 17 July 1983.
244 Deputy Secretary of State Kenneth W. Dam, *Miami Herald*, 31 December 1983.
245 John R. Silber, elaborating on the Kissinger Commission Report, *Miami Herald*, 15 January 1984.
246 Radio Sandino, 1 November 1982.
247 *El Nuevo Diario*, 6 July 1983.
248 Radio Sandino, 6 July 1983.
249 *Granma*, 26 September 1983.

10.6 million copies. In 1958 there were only seven Soviet Spanish language serial titles; by 1980 the number had increased nearly five-fold. The crucial *Latinskaya Amerika* journal had an initial 1969 run of 3,000; after peaking at 9,000 after the Sandinista revolution, the number settled back to a steady 7,500 during 1982/83. In 1972, Communist countries, including Cuba, broadcast 708.5 hours per week to Latin America; the 1979 figure was 793, of which Cuba was responsible for 241.5.[250]

Another forum for contacts, and for massaging fears that U.S. policies might have generated among liberals and moderates, was provided by international peace councils and peace congresses. Latin American representatives were generally non-Communist, but they did tend to be critical of Washington.[251]

Professional ties, such as could be established through civil aviation activities and merchant shipping associations, were stressed.[252] Similarly, trade union contacts sometimes served as conduits.[253] Scientific exchanges, conferences, and cooperation were encouraged.[254]

"International" youth festivals provided yet other points of contact.[255] Russian language teaching in the region has expanded, though it remains at a very modest level;[256] at the same time, Moscow is devoting more resources to expanding indigeneous Latin American expertise. Fine arts exchanges also take place.[257]

The "Tournaments of Friendly Armies" in Havana are worth noting. The 1977 games involved over 1,000 sportsmen from eighteen nations, including Mexico, Guyana, and Jamaica.[258] The 1981 games attracted twenty nations; participants included Panamanian "soldier-sportsmen" then training in Cuba.[259] The immediate political impact of such events might be slight, but over the longer term they could have considerable impact on the armies and nations involved.

Moscow encourages exchanges of legislators and parliamentarians. Mexican National Congress delegations have visited Moscow, as have similar

[250]   Figures collated by Morris Rothenberg, in *Problems of Communism* (September-October 1983).
[251]   *Latinskaya Amerika* 10 (1981) and 11 (1983).
[252]   *Grazhdanskaya Aviatsia* 9 (1981); *Soviet Shipping* 4 (1982).
[253]   *EFE*, 18 December 1979, reported on Nicaraguan trade unionists studying in Moscow.
[254]   *Izvestia*, 18 April 1981, reported on a typical scientific-technical cooperation agreement with Brazil.
[255]   *Pravda*, 28 and 29 July 1978, reported on one held in Havana.
[256]   Radio Sandino, 18 November 1983.
[257]   *Pravda*, 15 April 1981.
[258]   *Soviet Military Review* 2 (1978).
[259]   *Soviet Military Review* 1 (1981).

delegations from Brazil, Peru, and other Latin American nations.[260] Supreme Soviet delegations go in the opposite direction.[261]

Political and military leaders also interact with their opposite numbers. During recent years Soviet leaders have, for example, met personally with the presidents of Mexico, Venezuela, Colombia, Panama, and Brazil,[262] and the then prime minister of Jamaica,[263] as well as with many of their ministers, and ministers from other Latin American nations. Soviet military leaders have similarly met with many of their Latin American counterparts.[264] Two meetings stand out: in 1978 then KGB chief Andropov received an award in Moscow from Peru's security chief;[265] in 1980 Army General Pavlovsky represented the USSR at Mexico's Anniversary celebrations, at which time he also conducted a number of meetings with Mexican leaders.[266]

CONCLUSIONS

1. Extensive and Varied Soviet Presence

Moscow's presence in Central America emerges as both more extensive and more multifaceted than generally appreciated. Soviet military and economic involvement is complemented by other contact points—political, cultural, and professional.

2. But Ability to Control Events is Limited

Yet Moscow's ability to control events may be less than it seems. The counterweights to Soviet influence are more far-reaching and varied than is sometimes appreciated. Extensive West European presence is often commented on, as is pervasive Church influence. Other actors have also moved in: UN agencies fund a large number of Nicaraguan development projects; Japan's trade with Nicaragua has risen; Algeria picked up the sugar quota that America cancelled; the larger South American states have given Nicaragua significant support; even the United States and *contra*-aligned Honduras, El Salvador, and Guatemala maintain trade with Managua.

---

[260] See, e.g., *Pravda*, 31 July 1981; *Izvestia*, 23 December 1983; and *Pravda*, 27 June 1981.

[261] See *Pravda*, 16 April 1980, for reports on a visit to Brasilia.

[262] *Pravda*, 18 and 20 May, and 9 August 1978; TASS, 8 August 1978; and *Pravda*, 13 and 17 March 1979, and 12, 17 and 20 April 1980.

[263] *Pravda*, 11 and 12 April 1979.

[264] See, e.g., *Krasnaya Zvezda*, 6 April 1978; 7, 22, 25 and 26 September 1979; and 12 March 1980.

[265] *Pravda*, 28 June 1978.

[266] *Krasnaya Zvezda*, 14 September 1980; *Pravda*, 18 September 1980.

Moscow's authority among revolutionary individuals and groups is also more limited than generally realized (the FMLN's 1983 choice of Villalobos was illustrative). In its scramble not to be outflanked by the resurgent ultra-leftists Moscow embraced the once vilified Cuban concept of foco. But while conceding that the Party had lost its role as the necessary instigator of revolution, she insisted that the Party must be the designated inheritor.

3. Moscow Cited Contacts with Revolutionaries Much Less Often in 1983

Moscow's ideological ambivalence, and her realization of the limits of influence, may have been a major reason for 1983's dramatic drop-off in Soviet media references to contacts with revolutionary movements and leaders. The more forceful U.S. presence, epitomized by the grand-scale Pine Tree maneuvers in Honduras and the CIA's rapidly-growing *contra* armies, provided another major reason.

4. Moscow Focused on State-to-State Support for Nicaragua and Deferred to Havana

Moscow's focus in Central America switched to state-to-state support for the Sandinista regime, and the need to give sufficient aid to ward off future accusations that the Soviets might have betrayed the revolutionary cause. But Moscow was increasingly deferring to Havana, allowing Cuba to carry the ball, so to speak, in Central America—while Moscow reverted to its traditional and preferred focus on improved relations with South American establishments and regimes; Soviet trade and other ties with South American officialdom expanded quite dramatically.

5. The Sandinistas Would Have to Defend Themselves If the United States Invaded

Moscow conceded that Washington's "right" to intervene in Nicaragua was analogous to the Soviets' "right" to intervene in Afghanistan. And Moscow clearly half-expected that the United States would intervene ever-more forcefully. The Soviets openly stated that, in the event of a full-scale U.S. invasion, the Soviet response would be restricted to "solidarity" and "full political support." Moscow had striven to give Managua the means, but the bottom line was that the Sandinistas would indeed have to defend themselves. Finally, one must note that the Soviets apparently expect to benefit whatever the course of events. Moscow appears to calculate that the political-ideological public relations harvest that would accrue from an all-out U.S. invasion would outweigh the loss of immediate advantage.

16

The USSR, Cuba, and the Crisis in Central America

Jiri Valenta

With the victory of the Sandinistas in Nicaragua in July 1979 and the ongoing civil war in El Salvador, Soviet and Cuban strategy and tactics in Central America are being analyzed with new seriousness. According to some observers, the revolution in Nicaragua is transforming that country into a "second Cuba." Meanwhile, the Reagan administration has presented an array of evidence of cautious yet active support (armaments, and military instruction) to left-leaning guerrillas in El Salvador. This support is relayed by the Cubans by way of Nicaragua.

These recent developments not only are significant within the context of the Caribbean basin, but they also shed new light on the more crucial issue of Soviet-Cuban strategy in the Third World in general.[1] The Soviet-backed, Cuban-orchestrated support to left-leaning allies in Central America follows a decade of limited Soviet-Cuban military and security assistance to other Third

Reprinted from *Orbis* (Philadelphia) Fall 1981, pp. 715-746. © 1981 Foreign Policy Research Institute. Reprinted by permission. The original contained the following author's note: "This article is an adaptation of a chapter from *Central America: The International Dimensions of the Crisis,* edited by Richard E. Feinberg, to be published by Holmes & Meier in spring 1982. Parts of this study were prepared for the Office of the Secretary of Defense. I am indebted to Andrew Marshall, director of Net Assessment, for his and his staff's encouragement. I am also indebted to Virginia Valenta, Mike Clough, Richard Feinberg, Jerry Hough, Robert Looney, and William LeoGrande (who disagrees with me on some basic points) for their comments, and to Linda Jenkins for her help with research."

[1]   See my earlier work on Soviet-Cuban alliance in the Third World: "The Soviet-Cuban Intervention in Angola, 1975," *Studies in Comparative Communism*, Spring-Summer 1978, pp. 3-33; "Soviet Decision-Making on the Intervention in Angola," in David Albright, ed., *Communism in Africa* (Bloomington, Ind.: Indiana University Press, 1980); "The Communist States and the Conflict in the Horn of Africa," in J. Valenta and D. Albright, eds., *Communist Countries and Africa* (Bloomington, Ind.: Indiana University Press, forthcoming); "Comment: The Soviet-Cuban Alliance in Africa and Future Prospects in the Third World," *Cuban Studies/Estudios Cubanos*, July 1980, pp. 36-43; and "The Soviet-Cuban Intervention in Angola," *U.S. Naval Proceedings*, April 1980, pp. 51-57. For an expanded version of the last article, see Steven Rosefielde, ed., *World Communism at the Crossroads: Military Ascendancy, Political Economy and Human Welfare* (Boston: Martinus Nijhoff, 1980).

World countries—to Mozambique, Guinea, and Zambia in Africa, to Syria and South Yemen in the Middle East—and comes on the heels of two Soviet-Cuban military interventions on behalf of revolutionary and government forces: in Angola in 1975-1976 and in Ethiopia in 1977-1978. Along with Soviet support for the 1978 intervention in Kampuchea (Cambodia) conducted by the North Vietnamese (the "Cubans of the Orient" as the Chinese call them) and the Soviets' own military intervention in Afghanistan in 1979, these activities are perceived by many U.S. policymakers as fitting into an overall Soviet plan.

Secretary of State Alexander Haig views developments in Central America as part of "a very clearly delineated Soviet-Cuban strategy," the clear objective of which is "to create Marxist-Leninist regimes in Central America—Nicaragua, El Salvador, Guatemala, and Honduras."[2] In Haig's view, the Soviet-sponsored interventions in Central America are "an extension of the 'Brezhnev doctrine' [once applying only to Eastern Europe] outside the area of Soviet hegemony." This school of thought was echoed by President Reagan himself, who explained that "the terrorists aren't just aiming at El Salvador," but "at the whole of Central and possibly later South America [and], I'm sure, eventually North America."[3] The Reagan administration has apparently decided to counter what it sees as Soviet implementation of the Brezhnev doctrine by acting on the principle of the Monroe Doctrine, whereby the U.S. government announced its intention to oppose outside interference in the Americas. Thus, the crises in Central America in general and El Salvador in particular have become crucial tests of this administration's determination to challenge Soviet-Cuban designs in the Western Hemisphere and perhaps in other areas of the Third World.

The present analysis will be limited to Cuban and Soviet perceptions of and strategies toward Central America and the Caribbean region, and will emphasize the specific tactics employed in Nicaragua and El Salvador. First, however, something should be said about the complex beginnings of the ongoing conflict in the region and the reasons for the revolutionary transformation occurring there. The present crises in Central America cannot be attributed solely to Cuban and Soviet interference. What is happening in El Salvador and to varying degrees in other Central American countries is the rapid decay of long-entrenched and autocratic power.[4] This process has been witnessed already in other Third World countries, such as Ethiopia. The decay of outmoded political, economic, and social orders is the result of a number of factors internal to the countries themselves. The societies of Central America are polarized by antagonism between a very small upper class and a very poor

---

2   *Time*, March 16, 1981, pp. 24-25.
3   *Ibid.*, p. 10.
4   For a more detailed discussion, see R. Feinberg's forthcoming volume, *Central America: The International Dimensions of the Crisis* (New York: Holmes & Meier, 1982).

majority; in most of these countries, the middle class remains weak and underdeveloped. Socioeconomic polarization and past and existing oppressive regimes have contributed significantly to the rise of internal and interregional conflicts in these countries.

Moreover, several decades of U.S. hegemony and short-sighted policies, ranging from intervention to benign neglect, have also contributed to the development of nationalist reaction in the region. The prevailing feeling of many nationalists and radicals south of the Rio Grande regarding the United States resembles the traditional attitude of the Poles and Hungarians toward the Soviets. This view was well articulated by prerevolutionary Mexican President Porfirio Díaz, who once lamented "Poor Mexico: so far from God, so near the United States." More recently, the tensions have been exacerbated by Cuba, the U.S.S.R., and some other communist and Third World states that have sought to exploit radical currents and capitalize on the tides of revolution.

In this examination of Soviet-Cuban strategies and tactics in Central America, the following questions will guide the discussion: How and why did the Soviets and Cubans become involved in Central America? What are their ties both with the more traditional communist parties and with the guerrilla groups of the region? How does Central America fit into Soviet global strategy? To what degree does Cuba exercise its own strategy in the region? Are Cuba, the U.S.S.R., and their allies competing with the United States for influence in Nicaragua and El Salvador, as they have done for several years in Africa, particularly in Angola and Ethiopia? If so, are they prepared to risk further deterioration of U.S.-Soviet relations to accomplish this? Are the Soviets motivated merely by the desire to cause problems for the United States, or by more complex aims? Do Soviet and Cuban commitments in Angola, Ethiopia, and South Yemen and the Soviet preoccupation with the war in Afghanistan, the crisis in Poland, and the Iran-Iraqi war limit their ability to become heavily involved in Nicaragua and El Salvador?

A HISTORICAL PERSPECTIVE

Unlike Cuba, which is an integral part of the Caribbean basin (defined here as the area including the Caribbean archipelago and the littoral nations of Central America), the Soviet Union has no long-standing cultural, political, or commercial ties with the countries of Central America. It began to develop such ties only as recently as the 1960s. In contrast to those with Europe and Asia, Soviet interactions with Central and South America have until recently been modest. This is chiefly because of the area's geographic remoteness and therefore marginal importance to the U.S.S.R., and the traditional hegemony there of the United States.

The element of geographic remoteness, it should be noted, has been an asset to the Soviet Union in its efforts from the 1960s onward to become involved in the region. Like the United States in Eastern Europe, the U.S.S.R.

does not have a strong imperial record in Central and South America. Like the American image in Eastern Europe, the Soviet image in some Central American countries has been a conspicuously favorable one. As "enemies of American imperialism," early Bolsheviks were viewed as natural allies by revolutionary and patriotic circles in Mexico. Despite U.S. intervention in favor of revolutionary forces in 1916, two years later the military boss of a Mexican region said, "I don't know what socialism is but I am a Bolshevik, like all patriotic Mexicans—the Yankees do not like the Bolsheviks. They are our enemies; therefore the Bolsheviks must be our friends and we must be their friends. We are all Bolsheviks."[5]

Although revolutionary elements were sympathetic to the Bolshevik revolution and the Soviet regime, the Soviets were ostracized for several decades by the ruling elites of Central America and handicapped by the absence of diplomatic relations. Soviet relations with the countries of the Caribbean basin, with the exception of Mexico, were limited up to the 1960s to relations with their respective communist parties. In fact, until the Cuban revolution, Mexico, Uruguay, and Argentina were the only Latin American countries with which the U.S.S.R. had diplomatic relations. Thus, first-hand Soviet knowledge of the Caribbean basin was effectively limited to Mexico.

Before World War II, Mexico was the principal center for the dissemination of Comintern publications to Spanish-speaking countries in the region. With the help of Mexican Communist party officials, the Comintern was able to supervise the founding of the Communist party of Guatemala and assist with the founding of other communist parties in the region. The communist parties of Central America were illegal, their memberships ranging from several dozen to a few hundred. In Cuba, with Soviet encouragement, the party even entered into a coalition with the government of Fulgencio Batista during the Popular Front era of the 1930s and again briefly in the 1940s. On the other hand, with the notable exception of the Communist party of Costa Rica, the Central American parties have traditionally operated in a conspiratorial or semilegal fashion. Even in Costa Rica the Communist party is weak and has participated in only a limited manner in the politics of the nation.

Comintern officials had traditionally discounted the prospects for communism in Central and South America, displaying, like Marx and Engels, a certain Eurocentric disdain for Latin peoples and viewing the countries within a colonial framework in which the United States was firmly in command. Until the victorious Cuban revolution, the Communist Party of the Soviet Union (CPSU) had had only sporadic contacts with the Latin American communist parties through individual party and Comintern officials. Soviet financial subsidies to these parties had been small, though regular.[6]

---

5   M. N. Roy, *Memoirs* (London: Allen & Unwin, 1964), p. 154.
6   For studies dealing with early Soviet relations with Latin American communist parties, see Rollie E. Poppino, *International Communism in Latin America: A History of the*

Local communist parties have been involved in several unsuccessful insurrections in Central America's past. In 1932 there was an uprising in El Salvador that was crushed by government forces. In Guatemala in 1953-54, the nationalistic regime of President Jacobo Arbenz attempted a swing toward radicalism with the backing of the Communist party of Guatemala, a small but influential party that was in control of the labor movement. Available evidence suggests that the Soviets provided Arbenz's regime with financial and political support and even shipped 2,000 tons of Czech-manufactured weapons to Arbenz and his supporters. This support was marginal, however, and there is little evidence pointing to direct Soviet involvement. The meager level of support was determined in part by the Soviets' then-limited capabilities and in part by the fact that the United States treated Guatemala as a major issue, thus warding off further Soviet involvement. With covert support from the U.S. CIA, anti-Arbenz forces launched an invasion from Honduras and soon overthrew the regime.[7]

The turning point in Soviet relations with Central America came in 1959-1960 after the Cuban revolution. When U.S.-Cuban differences became unbridgeable and the United States withdrew from Cuba, the Soviets, after a period of hesitation, tried to fill the political and economic vacuum thus created. After the Bay of Pigs invasion attempt, Nikita Khrushchev and his colleagues painstakingly went about building a major alliance with Cuba. Despite ups and downs and disagreements about strategies in the Third World and in Latin America, the alliance begun at this time has remained solid.

Initially—at least until the Cuban missile crisis in 1962—the Soviets were exuberant about the success of the Cuban revolution. The revolution spurred Soviet research into Latin American affairs, and in 1961 the Soviet leadership established a new Institute for the Study of Latin America.. For a brief time during this period of euphoria, Moscow seemed to believe that the Cuban style of revolution could be exported, with Soviet backing, to Central America. Thus in 1959 and 1960, respectively, the communist parties of Nicaragua and El Salvador tried to overthrow their countries' regimes. The Cuban missile crisis, however, which the Chinese describe as the "Caribbean Munich," soon reminded the Soviets of the limits of their power in the area.

Not surprisingly, Khrushchev's decision to remove the Soviet missiles had some repercussions for U.S.S.R.-Cuban relationships. In the aftermath of the Soviet capitulation, marching militia in Havana chanted "*Nikita mariquita,*

(cont)

Movement, 1917-1963 (Glencoe, Ill.: The Free Press, 1964); Robert J. Alexander, *Communism in Latin America* (New Brunswick, N.J.: Rutgers University Press, 1957); Karl M. Schmidt, *Communism in Mexico: A Study in Political Frustration* (Austin, Tex.: University of Texas Press, 1965); Ronald M. Schneider, *Communism in Guatemala, 1944-1954* (New York: Praeger, 1959); and Robert J. Alexander, "The Communist Parties of Latin America," *Problems of Communism*, July-August 1970, pp. 37-46.
[7] Cole Blasier, *The Hovering Giant: U.S. Responses to Revolutionary Change in Latin America* (Pittsburgh, Pa.: Pittsburgh University Press, 1976).

lo que se da no se quita (Nikita, you little braggart—what one gives, one doesn't take away)."[8] Fidel Castro was naturally worried at this time about the degree of Soviet commitment to protecting Cuba against the United States. Like many others, he did not realize what would become clear only in the 1970s: though humiliated, Khrushchev achieved at least one of his objectives during the missile crisis—while agreeing to remove the missiles from Cuba, he was able to extract an American pledge not to topple the revolutionary Cuban regime. In retrospect, considering the success of joint Soviet-Cuban operations in the Third World in the 1970s, it appears that Khrushchev and not John Kennedy may have been the winner in the 1962 confrontation.

The resolution of the Cuban missile crisis had a sobering effect on Soviet perceptions of the potential for revolution in the Caribbean basin. So did U.S. intervention in the Dominican Republic in 1965, when the motto "Never a second Cuba" became the imperative for U.S. policy in Latin America. The failure of Cuban-backed guerrilla revolutionaries in the 1960s in Guatemala, Nicaragua, and in South America (Bolivia, Peru, and Venezuela) further ingrained this Soviet attitude, which Castro did not (at least not immediately) share.

In the 1960s the Soviets and the Cubans had profound disagreements about which strategies to pursue in Latin America. As a result of doctrinal differences, Soviet-Cuban relations in 1966-1967 were strained almost to the breaking point. It was not only their pessimistic assessment regarding "revolutionary potential" in the Caribbean basin nor the realistic appraisal of the U.S. response to Soviet-Cuban-supported guerrilla revolution that re-strained the Soviets; there were other internal and external factors as well. Be-cause of their preoccupation with the power struggle after Khrushchev's dis-missal in 1964, the course of the Vietnam War, and the deepening of the Sino-Soviet dispute, the Soviets in the late 1960s were unwilling and unable to sponsor Castro's call to create "two or three" and even "four or five more Vietnams" for the United States in Latin America. Castro, who was in favor of a "genuine revolutionary road," criticized the U.S.S.R. for dealing with capitalist governments in Latin America. He even clashed over the issue with pro-Soviet leaders in some Central American parties, such as those of Guatemala and Venezuela, where young, pro-Castroist elements resisted Soviet advice to proceed gradually and with caution.

After the death of Ernesto "Che" Guevara in 1967, however, when most of the guerrillas were wiped out, the Cubans soon came to realize the need for overcoming their differences with Moscow and coordinating their policies with those of the Soviets. As Castro saw it, there were no immediate revolutionary opportunities in Latin America in the 1970s (the case was otherwise in

---

[8]   K. S. Karol, *Guerrillas in Power: The Course of the Cuban Revolution* (New York: Hill & Wang, 1970), p. 272.

Africa). Thus, he grudgingly approved the Soviet policy of employing diplomatic, commercial, and cultural channels (in addition to revolutionary tactics where feasible) in order to expand relations with "progressive forces" in Latin America. Until very recently, the Soviets and Cubans have been less successful in dispelling traditional anticommunist hostilities from the Caribbean basin than from the South American continent. Besides those in Mexico and Jamaica, prior to the revolution in Nicaragua the U.S.S.R. had only one other ambassador in the Caribbean region, stationed in Costa Rica. In some other countries of the area, however, the Soviets were able to accredit nonresident ambassadors (Panama and Honduras) and to negotiate trade representation (El Salvador).[9] The Soviets were also able to promote better economic cooperation with a friendly Mexico by helping to bring about a new cooperation treaty between Mexico and COMECON in 1975.

Soviet diplomatic initiatives in Latin America in the 1970s yielded some political payoffs, among other things helping to invalidate the political and economic blockage of Cuba. Subsequently, Cuba was able to normalize relations with many Latin American countries. It exchanged consuls with Costa Rica, established diplomatic relations with Panama, and extended its influence to the Caribbean countries of Jamaica, Guyana, Barbados, and Trinidad-Tobago.

It is misleading to suggest that because of these trends the U.S.S.R. and Cuba had given up the notion of supporting revolutionary movements in the region. Although their posture was realistic, it was not one of acquiescence. Neither the Soviets nor the Cubans entirely renounced the efficacy of revolution as a means for overthrowing unfriendly, anticommunist governments. In the mid 1970s, when conditions were not ripe for revolution in Latin America, the Soviets and Cubans were busy supporting their allies elsewhere, particularly in Africa. This situation changed dramatically with the successful revolution in Nicaragua in 1979 and the upswing in guerrilla warfare in El Salvador in 1980.

THE U.S.S.R. AND CENTRAL AMERICA

The behavior of the Soviets and Cubans in the Third World is not, of course, motivated solely by historical ties and opportunism. Both the U.S.S.R. and Cuba have developed a coherent strategic vision with regard to the Third World. Theirs is an integrated, though flexible, plan of action aimed at achieving specific long-term objectives. What are these objectives and how does Central America figure in them? I discern in Soviet strategy four distinct components that can be verified from Soviet sources: ideology, politics, security, and economics.

---

[9]   Blasier, *Soviet Relations with Latin America in the 1970s* (Washington: The National Council for Soviet and East European Research, 1980).

Ideology

With respect to ideology, the Soviet objective is to create Marxist-Leninist regimes in the Third World (although in the long run this does not always work to the benefit of the U.S.S.R., as was the case with China's conversion to communism). While it is misleading to assume that the Soviets support revolutionary political movements in the Third World chiefly because of an ideological affinity with such movements, ideology cannot be discounted. The Soviets belive that some radical Third World nations will someday embark on a path toward a truly socialist development, as Cuba did in the 1970s. Meanwhile, because of Moscow's bad experience in the 1960s and 1970s—when revolutionary or radical regimes were overthrown, when more moderate regimes substantially reduced Soviet presence and influence in the countries in question—they feel impelled to exercise caution in making commitments to socialist and would-be socialist regimes in developing countries.

Indeed, with the probable exception of Cuba, in the early 1980s the Soviets hardly view the radical regimes of the Third World as truly Marxist-Leninist in the Soviet understanding of the term. Thus, Soviet officials in the Central Committee responsible for dealing with Third World revolutionary regimes refer to them as being "progressive," "anti-imperialist," and "revolutionary-democratic," and at most (when referring to Angola and Ethiopia) as having a "socialist orientation" and pursuing "noncapitalist" (but *not* "socialist") development. Soviet experts on Latin America such as M. F. Kudachkin, who is responsible for the Latin American section of the Central Committee of the CPSU, appreciate the diversity and unevenness of economic and political development in Latin America. They recognize that the region holds a special place in the Third World because of its success in throwing off the Spanish colonial yoke in the nineteenth century, and because, unlike Africa and most of Asia, capitalism has reached a high state of development in part of Latin America—particularly in Argentina and Chile, and to a certain degree in Mexico.[10] These countries also possess a significant working class and, in Mexico and Chile (before the anti-Allende coup), large communist parties. In the Soviet view, the situation in the Caribbean basin is different, not only because of a lower level of capitalist development, but also, as stressed, because of a weak communist movement and a more pervasive U.S. hegemony. The Marxist inclination of new regimes in such countries as Nicaragua and Grenada, however, cannot but be appreciated and applauded by the Soviets. Because of it, the Soviets are better able to justify to their

[10]　M. F. Kudachkin, *Velikii Oktiabr' i kommunisticheskie partii Latinskoi Ameriki* [The Great October and Communist Parties of Latin America] (Moscow: Progress Publishers, 1978). The "anti-imperialist" strategy has also been argued for in many articles published in *Latinskaia Amerika* in the 1960s and the 1970s. There were, of course, some significant disagreements in formulating this strategy. These are well analyzed in a forthcoming book by Jerry Hough, to whom I am indebted for his comment.

domestic constituencies the aid extended to these countries. By the same token, as demonstrated by Jerry Hough, a debate is evolving among Soviet experts over the prospects for revolution in Latin America.[11]

Politics

The U.S.S.R. also has political objectives in the Third World. These appear to center on the fermentation and furtherance of "progressive" anti-American and anti-Chinese regimes. By exploiting growing anti-American currents, the Soviets hope to win influence at U.S. expense without directly projecting military power. Moreover, they hope to counter the activity of their other major rival, China, in such areas of the Third World as Asia, East Africa, and the Middle East; China's influence in Latin America is minimal. Although some Marxist groups in the region have sided with Maoism, most communist parties have taken a pro-Soviet position in the Sino-Soviet conflict, identifying Maoism with Trotskyism and adventurism.

Because the Soviets view Central America as the "strategic rear" of the United States,[12] they have until recently exercised caution in forming policy toward the region. From the Cuban revolution onward, however, they have challenged the Monroe Doctrine. As early as 1960, Khrushchev declared that "the Monroe Doctrine has outlived its times." U.S. acceptance of the Cuban revolution was proof that it had died "a natural death."[13] In spite of this new attitude, Soviet strategy in Central America during the past two decades has been refined and subtle. It provides for a revolutionary transformation that can use violent methods while following a "peaceful road" (that is, a prolonged political process during which anti-American "progressive forces" build national coalitions to challenge U.S. hegemony). As pointed out in the Havana Declaration adopted at the 1975 regional conference of Latin American and Caribbean communist parties:

> The utilization of all legal possibilities is an indispensable obligation of the anti-imperialist forces . . . Revolutionaries are not the first to resort to violence. But it is the right and duty of all revolutionary forces to be ready to answer counter-revolutionary violence with revolutionary violence.[14]

[11] For a very perceptive analysis, see Jerry F. Hough, "The Evolving Soviet Debate in Latin America," *Latin American Research Review*, vol. 10, no. 1, pp. 124-143.
[12] S. Mishin, "Latin America: Two Trends of Development," *International Affairs* (Moscow), July 1976, p. 450; Leon Gouré and Morris Rothenberg, *Soviet Penetration of Latin America* (Miami, Fla.: Miami Center for Advanced International Studies, 1973).
[13] Tass (Moscow), July 12, 1960.
[14] *Declaration of the Conference of Communist Parties of Latin America and the Caribbean* (Havana: 1975), p. 42.

The formulation of Soviet strategy in the 1960s was affected significantly by the Soviet-Cuban dialogue and even by Soviet-Cuban disputes. In this period, the Cubans decided to promote revolution when the Organization of American States levied sanctions against them. They favored and at first even insisted on Soviet-Cuban support of revolutionary guerrilla movements in Latin American countries, with the exception of such friendly states as Mexico. By adhering to Che's and Regis Debray's concept of guerrilla-peasantry insurgency (see Debray's *Revolution in the Revolution?*), Castro's strategy in Central America in the 1960s contradicted and even challenged the Soviet doctrine allowing for diversified roads to socialism. Yet, as Herbert Dinerstein notes, in the late 1960s the Soviets and Cubans arrived at a kind of compromise strategy by making mutual concessions. Thus, the Soviets approved support for guerrilla activities in some Latin American countries with extremely pro-American and anticommunist regimes, while the Cubans gave their blessing to the pursuit of diplomacy with other, friendlier nations.[15] Overall, the Cubans basically accepted the Soviets' more gradual and realistic "anti-imperialist" strategy.

Thus, in the 1970s diplomatic channels were pursued in Panama (where the late Omar Torrijos's dictatorial yet "progressive" regime was avidly courted by the Cubans and the Soviets), in Costa Rica to a certain degree, and rather more intensely in Mexico—both the latter being (in the Soviet view) liberal-democratic regimes. In the Caribbean proper, the Cubans courted the "progressive" Jamaican regime of Michael Manley. Available evidence suggests that the Soviets and Cubans have dissuaded the local communist parties and other leftist groups from trying to overthrow these regimes, encouraging them rather to expand their influence and work toward the greater goal of building "anti-imperialist" coalitions.

The Soviet and Cuban strategy in Central American countries having pro-American, anticommunist regimes—that is, Nicaragua, El Salvador, Guatemala, and Honduras—has been to encourage revolutionary struggle, although not necessarily by fostering terrorism. In the late 1970s more emphasis was placed on revolutionary struggle than on peaceful coexistence. Yet even at that time the party's role was designated as one of gradual coalition-building among all revolutionary forces and of leadership of their struggle (insofar as possible). In the Soviet view, the "correlation of forces" in the 1970s was shifting worldwide because of the U.S. defeat in Vietnam. In Central America, this shift manifested itself in a growing wave of radical anti-U.S. sentiment. This and the Soviets' greater military and economic capabilities paved the way for a more mature, assertive globalism in the Third World. Moreover, the 1973 ouster of Allende in Chile seems to have increased Soviet

---

[15] For an excellent analysis, see Herbert S. Dinerstein, *Soviet Policy in Latin America* (Santa Monica, Calif.: Rand, May 1966), pp. 28-30.

doubts about the feasibility of a "peaceful path" toward socialism in Latin America.[16]

Security

Another important component of the Soviet strategic vision regarding Central America and the Caribbean is concern over security. Soviet security objectives in the region fit into the overall "anti-imperialist" strategy of the U.S.S.R. in the Third World. This strategy includes gradually securing access to and maintaining naval and air facilities in the Caribbean basin to improve the projection of Soviet influence, while undermining the influence of the West— particularly of the United States and its allies. The basin—a geopolitical concept—constitutes a key transit zone for oil and vital raw materials from Guatemala, Venezuela, and the Caribbean islands to the United States, as well as for all seagoing vessels approaching the Panama Canal. In an extreme case, such as wartime, a substantial Soviet military presence in the basin would endanger logistics support for U.S. allies in Europe and the delivery of oil and other strategic materials to the United States. During such times, Cuba, though highly vulnerable, might nevertheless serve as a forward base for submarines and aircraft carriers. In general the Soviets recognize the strategic importance of Latin America as an area of special security concern for the United States (much as Eastern Europe is for them). They see it as a sort of hinterland on whose stability freedom of U.S. action in other parts of the globe depends.[17] Thus, Moscow remained passive throughout the U.S. intervention in the Dominican Republic in 1965 and the U.S.-supported anti-Allende coup in Chile in 1973. Likewise, Washington took no action during the Soviet interventions in Hungary in 1956 and in Czechoslovakia in 1968. Thus far, the Soviet military presence in the region is limited by a lack of facilities necessary for permanent deployment. At present, the Soviets do not have sufficient strength in the region to disrupt the flow of oil to the United States, a scenario feared by some analysts. Moreover, they would probably attempt such action only in case of an all-out war.

Despite these limitations, the Soviets were able to establish a military presence in Cuba after 1961, one that has grown considerably in the past two decades. In return for Soviet financial and advanced technical assistance, the Soviets are today permitted to use modern docking facilities, potential submarine facilities in Cienfuegos, air facilities for reconnaissance aircraft, satellite stations, and sophisticated intelligence facilities for monitoring U.S. satellite and microwave conversations as well as NATO advanced weapons testing in

---

[16] Kudachkin, "The Experience of the Struggle of the Communist Party of Chile for Unity Among Leftist Forces and for Revolutionary Transformation," *Voprosy istorii KPSS*, no. 5, May 1976, pp. 72-76.

[17] L. I. Kamynin, *International Affairs*, no. 3, 1967, pp. 27-33.

the Atlantic. Since 1978, Soviet pilots have been flying MiG-27s on patrol missions in Cuba while Cuban pilots serve in Africa. Meanwhile, Soviet TU-95s conduct regular missions to monitor U.S. naval activities in the Atlantic. Thus, Cuba is a center for close Soviet-Cuban coordination in gathering intelligence information in the basin itself.

Although proceeding with caution, the Soviets would undoubtedly like to see their military presence in the Caribbean basin expanded. Witness the increasing number of Soviet submarine visits to Cuba since 1969, an indication of Soviet plans to make permanent use of the facilities at Cienfuegos, which were partly shelved in 1970 because of vociferous U.S. protests. The Soviets are trying to establish other strategic footholds in the area. In revolutionary Grenada, for instance, Soviet equipment and financial assistance from the U.S.S.R. and Libya have enabled the Cubans to start building a new international airport capable of handling all types of jet aircraft, including the Soviet Backfire bomber. As the Cubans work to build a revolutionary army, the Soviets assist in developing and promoting a fishing industry on the island. After Sergei Gorshkov, commander-in-chief of the Soviet navy fleet, visited the island in 1980, there were unconfirmed reports about the Soviet intention to build naval facilities there as well.[18] The Soviets may be seeking similar facilities in Nicaragua.

Up to the present, in view of the Soviets' awareness of the basin's paramount importance to the United States, Soviet naval activities in the area, including regular visits by warships, seem to have been designed to establish the legitimacy of a Soviet naval presence. There have been twenty such visits by warships to the Caribbean in the past twelve years. During the most recent visit, in April 1981, the force included a cruiser equipped to carry small nuclear weapons. Besides warships, the Soviets deploy intelligence, fishing, and merchant vessels. They have also sponsored joint Soviet-Cuban marine cruises for the purpose of conducting fishery and oceanographic research, as well as for gathering and establishing future channels of information. Soviet naval deployment is designed to help encourage long-term political and economic transformation of the area along the lines of what Gorshkov refers to as "progressive changes" offshore. In this respect, the security, political, and economic aspects of Soviet strategy in the region are mutually complementary, for Soviet naval visits to the Caribbean are facilitated by the establishment of diplomatic and economic relations. As the Soviets see it, "progressive changes" offshore make the environment more amenable to Soviet interests in the region.

---

[18] Radio Paris, January 21, 1981, in Foreign Broadcast Information Service (FBIS), Daily Report (Latin America), January 21, 1981.

Economics

Economic calculations also play a role in Soviet strategies in Central America. Soviet trade and investment in the region, although growing, are limited chiefly to Costa Rica, where the Soviets are apparently running a large deficit (like everyone else in Latin America). Since they generally have to pay for imports in hard currency, the Soviets would not be expected to view Central America as a priority interest in strictly economic terms. Soon, however, one may look for the Soviets to establish regular trade relations with the new regime in Nicaragua.

The discovery of natural resources—particularly in Guatemala, Mexico, and the Caribbean proper—have doubtless spurred increasing interest in the basin. Thus, the Soviets are working with the Mexicans on long-term cooperation in oil matters and may be interested in similar cooperation with other oil producers in the region. (Mexico has also agreed to supply crude oil to Cuba, to assist with Cuba's oil exploration efforts, and to help expand Cuban oil-refining facilities.) Soviet bloc trade and economic aid to such "progressive regimes" as the one in Nicaragua encourage the Soviet's overall "anti-imperialist" strategy in the area. The Soviets may calculate that in the long run Central America will offer a more lucrative opportunity for COMECON trade than do many of the much-courted African and Asian countries. A full COMECON member since 1972, Cuba can play a key role in this effort. The Soviets view Cuba as a useful instrument in restructuring the economic base of the Caribbean basin by reducing the preponderance of U.S.-based multinational corporations. Thus, the Soviets applauded Cuba's important role in founding the Caribbean Free Trade Association (CARIFTA) and the Latin American Economic System (SELA), cosponsored by Mexico and Venezuela. With Cuban help, COMECON was able in 1975 to work out a special arrangement with Mexico that may soon be followed by a similar agreement with Nicaragua.

CUBA AND CENTRAL AMERICA

Two extreme views are current regarding the Soviet-Cuban alliance in the Third World. The first portrays Cuba as a surrogate of the U.S.S.R., merely carrying out Soviet orders. The second pictures Cuba as an almost totally unconstrained, autonomous actor, having its own independent strategic vision. As I have argued elsewhere, Cuba is neither of these.[19] The view that Cuban policy is necessarily subservient to that of the U.S.S.R. is unsophisticated and obscures the existence of mutual constraint and leverage in the alliance. While the U.S.S.R. plays the dominant role and exercises great influence over Cuban foreign policy, Cuba in turn provides certain inputs into Soviet decision-

[19]   See my "Comment: The Soviet-Cuban Alliance in Africa."

making regarding the Third World. The degree of Cuban autonomy in the Third World seems to vary with the area of involvement. In Africa, Cuba appears to exercise little autonomy; in the Caribbean basin, Cuba's autonomy seems to be significant.

Even Soviet African policy, however, has been dependent to some extent on the willingness of Castro and his colleagues to provide ground forces for joint enterprises in Africa. In Angola and Ethiopia, unlike Afghanistan, the Soviets were cautious about committing their own troops in direct military fashion. The use of Soviet combat units might have elicited a firmer response from the United States, with resulting detrimental consequences for the U.S.S.R.. Furthermore, the similarity of the physical environment of Africa, particularly in Angola, to that of Cuba and the presence of a substantial number of blacks and mulattos in the Cuban forces, who share a racial and cultural affinity with the black Africans, make the Cubans much more suitable for the task than the Soviets. Soviet strategic decisions regarding the Third World thus reflect, at least marginally, Cuba's desire to support revolutionary operations there and its willingness to supply the necessary manpower. Castro, who is currently president of the Nonaligned Movement, has exercised some influence on the U.S.S.R. both directly (by consulting with Soviet leaders) and indirectly (by serving as a broker between Soviet and Third World leaders, many of whom admire Castro's courage, self-confidence, and personal charm). As in Africa, Castro can serve as a useful mediator between the U.S.S.R. and Central American leaders because he is viewed by many radicals and revolutionaries in the region as a new type of leader, one signally worthy of being emulated and followed—if not as a second Bolivar, as a modern continental liberator.[20]

Although Castro's foreign policy cannot be viewed as totally subservient to that of the U.S.S.R., it would be far-fetched to think of Cuba as an independent or even a semi-independent actor. The basic subordination of Cuban foreign policy to that of the Soviet Union seemed to be acknowledged at the First Cuban Party Congress of December 1975.[21] Cuba's emergence as a major player in the Third World in the 1970s and early 1980s has been possible mainly because of growing Soviet military and economic power and Soviet willingness to exploit changes in the international system. More specifically, Cuban ascendancy in the Third World—particularly in Africa and the Middle East—in the 1970s and more recently in the Caribbean basin has been possible because of Soviet military-strategic cover and Cuba's expectation that Soviet support and protection will be forthcoming in the event of an attack on the island. Moreover, the Soviets subsidize the Cuban

---

[20] Edward Gonzalez, *Cuba Under Castro: The Limits of Charisma* (Boston: Houghton Mifflin, 1974), p. 220.
[21] Jorge I. Dominguez, *Cuba: Order and Revolution* (Cambridge, Mass.: Harvard University Press, Belknap, 1978), p. 149.

economy with an estimated $7 million a day. Without this help, Cuba's faltering economy could never have absorbed the cost of the military intervention in Africa. Certainly in Africa the major portion of these expenses has been picked up by the Soviets or by the recipient countries, who in turn have received the money from the U.S.S.R..

Another important factor suggesting Soviet preponderance in the Soviet-Cuban alliance is the growing Soviet military and economic presence in Cuba of the 1970s. At present there are some 2,700 Soviet soldiers in Cuba as well as several thousand intelligence personnel, technicians, and other specialists. In addition to protecting sophisticated communications facilities, the Soviets train the Cuban armed forces.

Cuba's dependence on the U.S.S.R. in carrying out military operations in Africa was first demonstrated during the Angolan crisis of 1975-1976. The view that the Soviet role was confined chiefly to the supply of weaponry is mistaken. It is true that because of initial uncertainties regarding the U.S. response, the Soviets were cautious about committing themselves in a direct military fashion in Angola. Nevertheless, in early November 1975 they took over the Cuban air- and sealift, transforming the Angolan campaign into a massive operation during which both the Soviet air force and navy were operationally active. A small yet effective Soviet naval task force provided physical and psychological support to the Cuban combat troops, protected the Cuban staging areas against local threats, served as a strategic cover for established sea and air communications, and worked as a deterrent against possible U.S. naval deployment. It is quite possible that if Moscow had not become so involved in Angola and if the South Africans had been encouraged actively by the United States to continue their blitz campaigns, the Cubans would have been defeated.

The alliance between the Soviets and the Cubans was even tighter in the case of the intervention in Ethiopia in 1977. While the Cubans initially functioned independently in Angola, four Soviet generals in Ethiopia ran the entire operation from start to finish. Cuba functioned as a very subordinate actor, if not a Soviet proxy, during the conflict between Somalia and Ethiopia in the Ogaden. Clearly, the Soviet leadership determines the limits of Cuban options in Africa. Although Cuba could choose not to become involved in a large-scale military operation with the U.S.S.R. (the war in Eritrea), it could not undertake a substantial military operation without Soviet approval or support. Also, Cuba is highly vulnerable to Soviet politicoeconomic coercion, which the Soviet leaders used to their advantage in the late 1960s when they slowed down the supply of oil and arms in order to encourage Castro to appreciate the subtleties of Soviet "anti-imperialist" strategy. The Soviets are likely to use this leverage again should the need arise.

Cuba and the U.S.S.R. basically agree regarding the joint coordination and implementation of strategy in the promotion of Soviet global interests and policies. Cuban strategic priorities, of course, are not necessarily identical to those of the Soviets. As a result, subtle and not so subtle differences tend to distinguish Soviet from Cuban policies. This is more the case in the Caribbean basin than in Africa. Although the basin is of marginal geopolitical importance to the U.S.S.R., it is of paramount importance to Cuba. The U.S.S.R. is a superpower with global interests, responsibilities, and capabilities; Cuba, notwithstanding its abundant rhetoric, is basically a regional power, culturally and historically a part of the Latin American community. Nevertheless, Cuba's strategic vision extends beyond Latin America to the broader spectrum of the Third World, with emphasis on the countries of Africa.

What ideological, political, security, and economic payoffs does Cuba expect for helping to promote a joint "anti-imperialist" strategy? Although Castro has never been renowned for his theoretical conceptualization of Marxism-Leninism, his ideological commitment to the revolutionaries in Africa and Central America would seem to be more genuine than that of the U.S.S.R.. The Cuban revolution is young in comparison with the Soviets' 1917 October Revolution. Soviet strategic priorities are now forged under the close scrutiny of Central Committee bureaucrats, whereas a Cuban strategic vision arose out of the revolutionary war against Batista. Cuba maintains a strong ideological affinity with the Third World nations, one conditioned by common Latin and African ancestries, colonial legacies, and exploitation by outside powers. Thus, in Castro's words, Cuban support of revolution comes as a natural "result of our principles, our convictions, and our own blood."[22] Castro, himself a sort of Red Robin Hood, has been a vehement and long-standing supporter of various revolutionary movements and a close friend of their leaders. Cuban support of revolutionary groups in Africa and Latin America has in most cases been consistent since 1960, without the ups and downs characteristic of Soviet support for some of these organizations.

The joint strategies pursued in Central America are important to Castro's regime for reasons other than ideology and cultural affinity. Although more ideologically motivated than the Soviets, Cuba has already witnessed the passing of an initial revolutionary exuberance and enthusiasm (aptly dubbed by Che Guevara "socialism with the *pachanga* [a Cuban dance]"). Today Castro has strong pragmatic security, political, and economic interests in pursuing a joint "anti-imperialist" strategy with the U.S.S.R.. His objective in this close association is to ensure the survival of the Cuban revolution and to obtain further security guarantees for his state in the face of continuous U.S. hostility. Further, Castro's regime hopes to rebuild bridges to Central American countries, all of which supported the expulsion of Cuba from the Organization of American States in 1962.

---

[22] Castro's speech at the Congress of the Cuban Communist Party, Radio Havana, December 22, 1975.

In political terms, Castro wants now more than ever to increase the prestige and influence of his regime in the Third World. Since the unpopular Soviet invasion of Afghanistan, many Third World countries have become less willing to accept Castro as leader of the nonaligned world and defender of progressive Third World regimes. They realize that a "natural alliance" with the U.S.S.R., as advocated by Castro, can also lead to an "unnatural death," as in the case of Afghan President H. Amin. Indeed, the situation in Afghanistan has had a detrimental political effect on Cuba's standing in the Third World and on Castro's ambitions for refurbishing the prestige of his regime and his personal image as the recognized leader of the Nonaligned Movement. Proof of this was the withdrawal of support by the nonaligned nations for the election of Cuba as Latin America's nonpermanent representative to the UN Security Council in 1980. It is not surprising, given this turn of events, that although Cuba voted against the UN resolution condemning the U.S.S.R., it made little effort to support or defend the Soviet rationale for the invasion, thereby signaling its frustration over Soviet policies there. Obviously displeased with the invasion, the Cuban leadership decided to give only qualified support to the U.S.S.R. (as in the case of the Czechoslovak invasion of 1968). Unlike other Soviet allies, the Cubans did not object to the UN's right to deal with the Afghan question. This is a good illustration of Cuba's dilemma as both titular leader of the Nonaligned Movement and Soviet ally. Cuban aid to Nicaragua and support of the rebels in El Salvador in 1980-1981 have provided Castro with new opportunities for improving his image as an independent and fearless defender of revolution in the Third World.

Cuba also receives some economic payoffs in the Caribbean basin itself for its pursuit of an "anti-imperialist" strategy. Although economic relations with the Caribbean and Central American countries are modest, Cuban leaders, like their Soviet counterparts, may hope for more substantial relations in the future, perhaps similar to those now in effect with Mexico.

More important than the promise of future dividends are the actual economic payoffs to Cuba for its support of "anti-imperialist" strategies. Because Cuban willingness to deploy regular troops in Africa and to support the revolutionary forces in Nicaragua and El Salvador became indispensable to the implementation of Soviet "anti-imperialist" strategy in these regions, Cuba gained the status of a privileged ally and was able to insist on adjustments in Soviet-Cuban economic relations, although these are difficult to specify. Thus, in the aftermath of the invasion of Angola in 1975 and again after the intervention in Ethiopia in 1978, the Cubans obtained even more favorable agreements from the U.S.S.R.. These operations and Cuban support for the Nicaraguan revolution and the guerrillas in El Salvador may have ensured continuation into the 1980s of Soviet subsidies of Cuban sugar and nickel production and of prices paid for petroleum. One source estimates that the U.S.S.R. paid $0.44 a pound for Cuban sugar when the world market price for this commodity was about $0.10. (In 1979 alone Cuba sold four million tons of sugar to the U.S.S.R..) The price that Cuba pays for oil is estimated to be about half that prevailing on the world market.[23]

Castro may also expect to be rewarded by increased economic aid from the U.S.S.R., such as a rescheduling of repayment terms for the enormous Cuban debt, new credits, and an increase in commerce with the U.S.S.R.. In addition, as indicated above, the U.S.S.R. ensures a continuously stable market for a large part of Cuban output. The trade agreement signed in Moscow during the Cuban-orchestrated arms transfer to El Salvador provides for trade between Cuba and the U.S.S.R. in 1980-1985 amounting to thirty billion rubles—a significant increase over the trade level of 1976-1980. The U.S.S.R. has apparently pledged to supply all Cuba's oil during this period. To further facilitate the solution to Cuba's energy problems, the Soviets plan to build a nuclear power plant in Cuba from 1981 to 1985.

Another payoff for Cuban assistance in implementing the U.S.S.R.'s Third World policies has been the Soviet modernization of Cuba's armed forces with sophisticated weaponry. The Cuban forces (190,000 active-duty troops, 60,000 reservists) are now more formidable than any others in the basin, including those of Mexico. In the whole of Latin America they are second in size only to the armed forces of Brazil. Of the U.S.S.R.'s Warsaw Pact allies, only Poland, which is four times the size of Cuba, has greater forces. Thanks to Soviet-supplied MiG-21s and MiG-23s, Cuba has the best-equipped air force in Latin America. Moreover, the Soviets have helped to build a small but modern and efficient Cuban coastal navy and merchant fleet. In the past few years, they have equipped the Cubans with seven guided-missile patrol boats, more than a dozen Turya-class patrol boats, several landing craft, and one Foxtrot- and one Whiskey-class submarine, with another expected. The Cuban army, meanwhile, has been equipped with T-62 tanks of Soviet origin. The Soviet arms transfer to Cuba is relatively advanced in the overall context of the Soviet arms aid program.

In spite of past disagreements and existing differences, the Soviets and Cubans in the 1970s discovered that their strategies in the Third World, a subject of disagreement in the 1960s, were inexorably linked. Moscow has made enormous ideological, political, security, and economic investments in Cuba. To turn its back on Castro's regime now would seriously undermine Soviet strategies in Africa and in Central America. Likewise, Soviet strategic, economic and political support is essential to Cuba. Cuba is too dependent on the U.S.S.R. to try to alter the relationship, and it is still too committed to revolutionary change to do so.

---

[23] "Failure of the Cuban Economy" (editorial), *La Prensa* (Buenos Aires), January 15, 1981.

SOVIET AND CUBAN TACTICS

The Nicaraguan Revolution

For the jubilant Soviets and Cubans, the triumph of the Sandinistas in Nicaragua in 1979 signaled an important juncture in the revolutionary trans-formation of the Caribbean basin, equal in importance only to the victory of the Fidelistas in Cuba twenty years earlier. In both cases, the United States was perceived by the Soviets as suffering a humiliating political defeat. In the view of such Soviet officials as V. Zagladin, deputy head of the international department of the Central Committee, the Nicaraguan revolution was one of the "starlets" of the "anti-imperialist" movement in Latin America. Zagladin has tried, at least implicitly, to link the "victory of Nicaragua" with Soviet-Cuban-supported "anti-imperialist" strategy, and has expressed the hope that Nicaragua will "have its continuators."[24] As during the Allende period (1971-1973), revolutionary change in Latin America has become a favorite topic in Moscow.

Was the triumph in Nicaragua indeed the result of coordinated Soviet-Cuban strategies and tactics in Central America, or of a complex interplay of internal and regional as well as external forces? Like the Cuban revolution in 1959, the revolution in Nicaragua was conditioned by various internal forces: the unpopularity of the Somoza regime among all classes, underdevelopment, unequal distribution of wealth, enormous poverty, and other deep social and economic cleavages. Nicaragua has long been dominated by dictators such as Anastasio "Tacho" Somoza (1936-1956) and his son .i.Anastasio "Tachito" Somoza (1967-1979). Also, the great powers have traditionally played a role in national policymaking.[25] The fact that Nicaragua contains a promising site for an interocean canal and lies in close proximity to the existing Panama Canal has caused its foreign policy to be of some concern to the United States. Thus, U.S. strategic interests were largely the motivating force behind the U.S. intervention in 1912 and in 1927, when, except for a brief interlude from 1926-1927 until 1933, Nicaragua was virtually a U.S. protectorate.

U.S. interventionism in Nicaragua gave rise to a "Yankeephobia" charac-terized by resentment of and even violent resistance to the United States. The human symbol of this resistance in 1927-1933 was Augusto César Sandino, who, like Castro in the 1950s, was a staunch radical nationalist and opposed both the corrupt dictatorship in his country and what he saw as U.S. interfer-ence. Although the Soviet press exalted him in the early 1980s as an "anti-imperialist" hero, in the 1930s, the Soviets and the Comintern had denounced

---

[24] Vadim Zagladin, "On the Threshold of the Eighties," *New Times*, January 1, 1980, pp. 5-7.

[25] Charles W. Anderson, "Nicaragua: The Somoza Dynasty," in Martin C. Needler, ed., *Political Systems of Latin America* (New York: Litton Educational Publishing, 1978), pp. 108-131.

Sandino and his "rebel bands." The Soviets had condemned the U.S. intervention of 1927, but they had failed to display much admiration for the original Sandinistas; while Sandino had cooperated with the communists in the 1920s, he then denounced their activities in 1936. After the withdrawal of U.S. troops from Nicaragua, Sandino actually made peace with the Nicaraguan government. The Comintern meanwhile accused him of "capitulation . . . over to the side of the counter-revolutionary government."[26]

Communism in Nicaragua, as elsewhere in Central America, has traditionally been a weak movement. In the past two decades, three Marxist parties have existed in Nicaragua—all of them illegal and clandestine, or semiclandestine: a very small Maoist group, the anti-Soviet Communist party of Nicaragua, and the pro-Soviet Socialist party of Nicaragua (PSN), a semiclandestine organization founded in 1937 and never boasting more than 250 members. Some members of the PSN had links with the Sandinistas in the 1960s and 1970s, but the PSN was not the main force behind the revolution. The Sandinista National Liberation Front (FSLN) was founded in 1961 by radical, left-leaning nationalists led by the late Carlos Fonseca Amador, who, though not a communist, had visited the U.S.S.R. in 1957. The Sandinistas, inspired and supported from the very beginning by Castro, tried to overthrow the Somoza regime but were soon crushed by the National Guard. In time, the FSLN evolved into a conglomerate of Marxist and non-Marxist elements united under an anti-Somoza banner, yet still separate from the PSN. Although Amador later died while fighting Somoza, the Sandinistas continued their struggle in the 1970s, with only limited support from the U.S.S.R. and Cuba. (Cuba actually sent material aid to the Somoza regime following the earthquake in 1972.) Despite the fact that the revolutionary struggle in Nicaragua coincided with Soviet-Cuban "anti-imperialist" strategy, geographic remoteness and general pessimism about the prospects for revolution in Latin America following the anti-Allende coup of 1973 caused the Cubans and Soviets to be rather pessimistic about the prospects of the Sandinista struggle. An additional, probable reason for the Soviets' low-keyed support up to 1979 was Soviet and Cuban military involvement in Angola, Ethiopia, and elsewhere in the Third World, as well as events in Afghanistan—all of which occupied the greater part of Soviet attention from 1975 to 1979. Soviet support of the FSLN continued to be modest even as late as 1978, when a unified FSLN directorate brought together in one coalition all the guerrilla factions, whose struggle had begun to assume a genuinely revolutionary character. Even during this high point, the role of the PSN was limited mainly to propaganda support, clandestine radio broadcasts, and some financial aid.

---

[26] Compare "U.S.S.R.-Nicaragua: Building Cooperation," *New Times*, March 1980, pp. 13-14, with "Struggles of the Communist Parties of South and Caribbean America," *The Communist International*, vol. 12, no. 10, May 20, 1935, pp. 564-576. See also, Alexander, *Communism in Latin America*, pp. 347-378.

Although by 1978 the Soviets probably knew of Somoza's critical situation, they may have thought that President Carter, despite his human rights rhetoric, would not let Somoza fall. Nevertheless, in the 1970s the Cubans, with Soviet blessings and perhaps even financial help, were training the FSLN in Cuba and providing them with arms (primarily rifles) and money.[27] However, the FSLN was securing weapons from elsewhere as well. Evidence at this time is insufficient to suggest that the Soviets and Cubans coordinated arms transfers for the Sandinistas as they were to do for the guerrillas in El Salvador in 1980; still, we do know that some weapons flowed from Cuba to the FSLN by way of such Third World countries as Costa Rica and Panama. We also know that the FSLN used weapons from Venezuela, Panama, the Middle East, and, as the Sandinistas maintain, from Mafia sources in the United States and Europe. Although many guerrillas were trained in Cuba, there is no evidence that Cubans were involved in command and control functions for the Sandinistas before early 1979. The Cuban factor was important but it was not crucial.

The Sandinistas also received active political, economic, and moral support from various groups in Venezuela, Panama, and Mexico, and found sanctuaries and a place to train on the territory of democratic Costa Rica. The Costa Rican capital of San José was the site of the FSLN government in exile. Leftists from other Central American countries, such as the Victoriano Lorenzo Brigade from Panama and various groups from Costa Rica, fought alongside FSLN forces in Nicaragua.[28]

The Cubans and particularly the Soviets exercised considerable caution prior to the Sandinista victory of 1979. Indeed, the Soviets published few analyses of the Nicaraguan struggle, and only in 1978 did the Soviets and Cubans begin to reassess the chances for a successful revolution. In early 1979 the Cubans finally set up intelligence headquarters in Costa Rica to monitor the anti-Somoza struggle and sent military personnel to advise the Sandinistas. Within months of the Sandinistas' assumption of power on July 19, 1979, Castro sent Cuban specialists in significant numbers to help with the reconstruction of Nicaragua: 1,200 teachers, 250 doctors and health personnel, technicians, some security and propaganda experts, and forces of construction workers to build a road uniting Nicaragua's east and west. At the same time, Castro reportedly cautioned the Sandinistas not to push their socialist program too far or too fast. The Cubans perceived the victory of the Sandinistas as an opportunity for them to pursue their own strategic objectives in Nicaragua as well as elsewhere in the region. Unlike the case in the 1960s, the risks of

---

[27] See statement of W. H. Duncan, a vice-president with the American Chamber of Commerce of Latin America in Nicaragua, in U.S. House, Committee on Foreign Affairs, *Central America at the Crossroads,* Hearing Before the Subcommittee on American Affairs, September 11-12, 1979, p. 47.

[28] James N. Goodsell, "Nicaragua," in R. F. Starr, ed., *Yearbook on International Communist Affairs, 1979* (Stanford, Calif.: Hoover Institution Press, 1980), pp. 369-371.

Cuban involvement seemed to be low both because of apparent U.S. inability to intervene and because the United States basically opposed Somoza and recognized the Sandinistas.

In contrast to the Cubans, the Soviets were typically guarded in their willingness to make commitments to the new Sandinista regime, as they had been in 1959 to Cuba. The only Soviet initiative at this time was the provision of emergency donations in the weeks following the overthrow of Somoza. These were much smaller, however, than U.S., Mexican, and Venezuelan donations during the period. Only after a gradual reassessment of their options did the Soviets decide to become more assertive in Nicaragua. This "new chapter," as the Soviets called it, opened in March 1980 during the first high-level visit of Sandinistas to the U.S.S.R. since the overthrow of Somoza.[29] Subsequently, the Soviets concluded various economic, technical, and trade agreements, mainly in the areas of fishing and marine affairs, water-power resources, mining and geological surveys, communications, and air traffic. The FSLN and the CPSU also agreed on future party-to-party contracts [*sic*], apparently along the same lines pursued by the Soviets with other revolutionary organizations whom they consider to be reliable, long-term partners, such as the regimes in Angola and Ethiopia. By the spring of 1981 the Soviets, Cubans, and East Europeans (particularly the East Germans and Bulgarians) had concluded several other related agreements with Nicaragua for economic aid (including the donation of 20,000 tons of wheat), scientific and cultural cooperation, and technical assistance in telecommunications, agriculture, and transportation. There were also signs of future military cooperation, as evidenced by the Soviet loan of a few helicopters to the FSLN and by East Germany's credit sale to the FSLN of 800 military trucks. As the crisis in neighboring El Salvador began to mount in late 1980, there were also unconfirmed reports of the influx of additional Cuban military officials into Nicaragua (officials who were supposedly running training camps) and of the transfer of tanks and helicopters, possibly for use in El Salvador. Western reports that the Soviets were building naval facilities in Nicaragua were denied by the Soviet ambassador to Nicaragua, G. Schlyapnikov. The Nicaraguan government, however, has confirmed that a Soviet floating workshop, designed for repairing ships, will be operating off the Pacific coast of Nicaragua.[30]

El Salvador

How do Soviet and Cuban perceptions of the crisis in Nicaragua (before the overthrow of Somoza) compare with their perceptions of the ongoing crisis in

[29] See "U.S.S.R.-Nicaragua: Building Cooperation."
[30] *Baltimore Sun*, February 26, 1981; *La Prensa* (Managua), July 30, 1980; *The News Gazette* (San Salvador), February 1-7, 1981; *Prela* (Havana), April 26, 1981, in FBIS, *Daily Report* (Latin America), March 30, 1981.

El Salvador? What similarities and differences can be seen in Soviet and Cuban tactics with regard to these two countries? The victory of the Sandinistas in Nicaragua prompted the Soviets to anticipate a chain reaction of leftist upheavals and revolutions throughout Central America. Thus, in an important speech on October 20, 1980, B. Ponomarev, candidate Politburo member and secretary of the Central Committee of the CPSU, added the countries of Central America to the list of states in Africa and Asia that could be expected to undergo revolutionary changes of "a socialist orientation." Ponomarev described the revolution in Nicaragua as a "major success" and compared it with the revolution in Angola and Ethiopia.[31] Professor Viktor Volskii, president of the Soviet Association of Friendship with Latin American Countries, assessed the Nicaraguan revolution as a "triumph for the people of Latin America and the Caribbean" and a "model for all peoples fighting for liberation."[32]

After Nicaragua, the Central American country singled out by Soviet writers as being most pregnant with revolutionary opportunities was, of course, El Salvador, which the Soviets see as occupying "an important strategic position in the region."[33] Like Nicaragua, El Salvador has a strong heritage of instability caused by a rigid class structure, unequal distribution of wealth, and 30 per cent unemployment. In El Salvador—the smallest yet most densely populated country in Latin America (400 people per square mile)—the socioeconomic life has been dominated by an oligarchy of wealthy families while military strongmen have controlled the country's politics.

In El Salvador, as in Nicaragua, the communist movement has been very weak. The pro-Soviet Communist party in El Salvador (PCES), founded in 1930, was actively involved in a massive peasant insurrection in 1932, which was crushed by the military and resulted in 30,000 deaths. Since that time, the PCES has been an illegal, clandestine organization. As late as 1979, it had only 225 members. In the 1960s and 1970s, however, the PCES, like the PSN, had to compete with more radical and relatively larger groups such as the Maoist-leaning People's Revolutionary Army (ERP) and the Trotskyite Popular Liberation Force (FPL). The latter organizations, and not the miniscule PCES, were responsible for the organized terrorism and guerrilla activities of the 1970s. In fact, the well-known General Secretary of the PCES Schafik Jorge Handal published a severe critique of these groups in the Soviet journal *Latinskaia amerika* in early 1979, before the fall of Somoza. He accused them of violence and nihilism.[34]

---

[31] Ponomarev's report can be found in *Kommunist*, no. 6, November 1970, pp. 30-44.
[32] Moscow Radio, July 17, 1980.
[33] V. Korionov, "El Salvador: The Struggle Sharpens," *Pravda*, December 30, 1980; and Ruslan Tuchnin, "Reign of Terror," *New Times*, April 1980, pp. 9-11.
[34] Thomas P. Anderson, "El Salvador," in Starr, ed., *Yearbook on International Communist Affairs, 1979*, pp. 347-348. See, also, Anderson's analysis in Starr, ed., *Yearbook on International Communist Affairs, 1980*, pp. 354-355.

Unlike those in Nicaragua, the various guerrilla factions in El Salvador have not yet united, in spite of rhetoric to the contrary. In El Salvador there is no Sandinista legacy. In contrast to the meager support given the Nicaraguan party, Soviet public support of the PCES has been strong, particularly of its leader Handal, who seems to be following the Soviets' tactical advice. With the Sandinista victory in Nicaragua and the increase in political violence in El Salvador, the PCES. and the Soviets have become more optimistic about the revolutionary potential of the region, especially in El Salvador. These changing perceptions are certainly shared by the Cubans. Although in their public reports the Cubans continue to be somewhat more cautious than the Soviets, they nevertheless have begun to increase their direct support to the various competing guerrilla factions. In addition, they have played an important role in minimizing factional differences and in trying to unite the various groups.[35]

The Soviets, for their part, have proceeded with deliberation. Although they promised initially, during a meeting organized by Castro in Havana in December 1979, to supply weapons to the guerrillas, only in the spring and summer of 1980 did they switch completely to the new support tactics, agreeing to provide the military training of a few dozen Salvadoran youths. This change in tactics was reflected by the pro-Soviet PCES endorsement of violent revolution at its Seventh National Congress in May 1980. As noted above, up to that time the PCES. opposed armed struggle and terrorism as revolutionary means in El Salvador. In the fall of 1979, though jubilant over the victory in Nicaragua, Handal was cautious about commenting on prospects for revolution in El Salvador. In April 1980, however, he became much more optimistic and, according to Soviet sources, expressed "confidence" in the "defeat of internal reaction, despite the fact that the latter is backed by imperialist forces."[36]

The example of Nicaragua, however important, was not the only motive for the changing perceptions and tactics of the PCES and the Soviets in the spring of 1980. Both the Soviets and the Cubans probably feared that if the PCES did not use violence to implement its "anti-imperialist" strategy it would soon be overtaken by its more radical rivals, who were quickly gaining popular strength. The PCES, they reasoned, should not be suddenly surprised by successes of the noncommunist guerrillas and deprived thereby of responsibility for the victory, as happened in Nicaragua to the PSN, who were outshone by the Sandinistas. Thus, Cuban and Soviet tactics since the spring of 1980 have been directed at transforming the numerically small PCES into a leading force in the guerrilla struggle in El Salvador..

[35] "Communist Interference in El Salvador," *Special Report*, no. 80 (Washington: U.S. Department of State, Bureau of Public Affairs, February 23, 1981).
[36] Interview with Handal, Tass (Moscow), October 22, 1980; V. Dolgov, "Mounting Struggle," *New Times*, April 1980, p. 11. In November of the same year, the leading theoretical journal of the CPSU published a lengthy article by Handal in praise of the guerrilla struggle. (See "Na puti k svobode" [On the Road to Liberty], *Kommunist*, no. 17, November 1980, pp. 94-103.

Soviet assessment of the U.S. ability to maintain hegemony in the region also seems to have changed. Despite the examples of the Cuban revolution, as noted, the Soviets continued to believe throughout the 1960s and 1970s that the United States had the ability and will to challenge outright revolution in Central America. In Nicaragua, however, the U.S. administration made one mistake after another. It failed to break completely with Somoza, and it tried too late to modify the outcome of a Sandinistan victory. A Soviet analyst, quoting an anonymous official in Washington, wrote in July 1980 that the Carter administration was "too late and too indecisive" with its intervention in the Nicaraguan crisis, that it therefore could not prevent the complete victory of the Sandinistas, and that "a different course of action" must be taken by the United States in El Salvador.[37] According to this analyst, the situation in El Salvador, which was arousing the "anxiety" of American strategists, was even more "tense" than in Nicaragua before the fall of Somoza.

The main Soviet reason for fomenting turmoil in El Salvador is probably to pin down the United States in its "strategic rear," as the opportunity presents itself. Developments in El Salvador may also be linked to Soviet-perceived changes in Soviet-American relations in the wake of the Iranian and Afghan crises in late 1979. In the Soviet view, as I have argued elsewhere, the U.S. administration was veering toward a dangerous new cold war by encouraging a semialliance with China, threatening Iran, and sabotaging SALT II negotiations.[38] Most grievous in the Soviet view was U.S., Chinese, and Egyptian "allied" support of the Afghan rebels with Soviet-made weapons. (Whether or not this was true in 1979 is still a matter of speculation; the Soviets profess to have believed that it was, and sometimes the perceptions of policymakers are more important than the facts.) The Soviet invasion of Afghanistan, a matter of necessity as the Soviets saw it, was met with retaliatory policies by the zigzagging Carter administration aimed at further punishing the U.S.S.R.. After Nicaragua, the Soviets may have thought that El Salvador provided an easily exploitable opportunity in the same geographic proximity to the United States as Afghanistan is to the U.S.S.R.. The idea of making El Salvador an "American Afghanistan" in retaliation for perceived U.S.-Chinese-Egyptian support for the Afghan rebels, and using the issue as a bargaining chip in future negotiations, may have played a part in the Soviet decision to back the Cuban orchestration of support for the guerrilla struggle.

One can only speculate, of course, on the motives for the Soviet decision. Nevertheless, the facts of the story are well known. Unlike the case in Nicaragua, the Cuban orchestration of the supply of armaments from Soviet allied countries has been significant. It appears that the Soviet-backed involvement of Cuba has significantly strengthened the guerrillas in El Sal-

---

[37]   Ye. V. Mityayeva, "The United States Interference in El Salvador," *SShA: ekonomika, politika, ideologiia,* no. 7, July 1980, pp. 60-64.
[38]   See J. Valenta, "From Prague to Kabul," *International Security,* Fall 1980, pp. 114-141.

vador. Handal's search for arms in the East, which seems to be well documented by the U.S. administration, began around the time of the Seventh Congress of the PCES., during which a passive line was exchanged for one of organized violence intended to topple a government. After the congress, the Cubans took charge of clandestine operations in El Salvador and Castro actively assumed the role of broker in attempting to unify the various revolutionary groups. In June and July, with the assistance of Soviet officials responsible for Third World affairs in the Soviet Secretariat (such as K. Brutens and his deputy Kudachkin), Handal visited the U.S.S.R. and certain East European countries, and obtained American-made weapons (M-14 and M-16 rifles, M-79 grenades) from Vietnam and Ethiopia, countries with large stocks of U.S. weapons. Thus, the U.S.S.R. could, by proceeding with caution, deny its involvement if accused. East European allies (minus Poland and Rumania) promised to provide communications equipment, uniforms, and medial supplies, while the Soviets helped to arrange for the transport of the weapons to Cuba in the fall of 1980. From Cuba, the weapons were conveyed to Nicaragua, and from there directly by ship or air, or by land through Honduras, to El Salvador. Following the U.S. presidential elections, Cuban experts, with cautious yet active Soviet backing, played a key role in the arms transfer and the preparation of the "final" guerrilla offensive. A U.S. State Department report concludes: "The political direction, organization, and arming of the insurgency is coordinated and heavily influenced by Cuba—with active support of the Soviet Union, East Germany, Vietnam, and other Communist states."[39]

CONCLUSION

The joint strategy for dealing with Third World countries worked out by the U.S.S.R. and Cuba in the late 1960s and 1970s is not necessarily designed to create Marxist-Leninist regimes in these countries but rather to achieve a variety of "anti-imperialist" ideological, political, security, and economic objectives. Soviet and Cuban strategic visions have not always been identical, particularly in the 1960s when there were serious disagreements regarding doctrine and tactics. As recent Soviet-Cuban policies in Africa and Central America attest, however, most of these differences have now been overcome. Although Cuba is not subservient to the U.S.S.R., for a variety of reasons its foreign policies are basically dependent upon Soviet support (Africa) or linked to Soviet foreign policy (Central America). The Soviets and the Cubans seem to have linked strategic visions regarding Central America. Although the Soviets

[39] "Communist Interference in El Salvador," *Special Report*, no. 80. Although several critics have rightly pointed out inconsistencies in this report, none has proved that it is a forgery or that the U.S.S.R. and other communist countries did not actively support Cuban assistance to the guerrillas of El Salvador. For a critique of the report, see T. Segel, *Washington Star*, May 18, 1981, and James Petras, *The Nation*, March 28, 1981.

are newcomers there, with Cuban help they have been able to exploit the socioeconomic malaise and anti-U.S. sentiment characteristic of the region. In doing so, they have employed a variety of tactics: peaceful and legal, violent, or often combinations of both.

Undoubtedly, deep socioeconomic cleavages are the main cause of the ongoing crisis in Central America, particularly in the countries located in the northern tier: Nicaragua, El Salvador, Guatemala, and, to a certain degree, Honduras. The more southern countries of Costa Rica and Panama do not have such pronounced social problems, but they face severe economic difficulties (particularly Costa Rica) and are by no means immune to revolutionary change. The civil war in El Salvador could escalate into a regional war, perhaps even leading to the involvement of Mexico and Venezuela, with Guatemala and Honduras assisting the regime, and Nicaragua and Cuba assisting the guerrillas.

Internal forces were the main impetus for local insurgency and revolution in Nicaragua in 1979; the Soviets and Cubans were deeply involved in Africa prior to 1978-1979, when the insurgency peaked, and their involvement in Nicaragua was marginal. Afterward, however, the Nicaraguan revolution became an inspiration to other revolutionaries in the region and a catalyst in changing the perceptions and tactics of the U.S.S.R. and Cuba. Both countries seem to have believed that the Nicaraguan "example" could be repeated soon in "strategically located" El Salvador. The dramatic change in Soviet and Cuban tactics in the spring of 1980, *after* the Nicaraguan revolution, is proof of their flexibility in the implementation of "anti-imperialist" strategy.

Although the socioeconomic problems in Nicaragua and El Salvador are similar, there are profound differences between the political situations in the two countries. Nicaragua's revolution was more genuine, in that it expressed the will of a majority of the people in overthrowing the hated dictatorship of Somoza, while El Salvador's revolution is less genuine, having significant Cuban support with cautious backing from the Soviets. Both Cuba and the Soviet Union supported, if not encouraged beforehand, a dramatic change in the tactics of El Salvador's Communist party in May 1980 and facilitated an impressive arms transfer in the fall of the same year. In late 1980 the guerrillas in El Salvador announced the creation of a united liberation front—the Farabundo Marti People's Liberation Front—whose general command includes Handal. Although the so-called final offensive in early 1981 failed, El Salvador may still develop into a "second Nicaragua." Up to now, however, the guerrilla offensive in El Salvador has failed to spark a popular insurrection of the Nicaraguan kind; the majority of the people do not appear to support the leftist guerrillas. One can "spur" revolutionary struggles,[40] but one cannot

---

[40] One is reminded of the eloquent words of José Marti, Cuba's national hero: "The Russians are the ship of reform. But these impatient and generous men, darkened as they are by anger, are not the ones who are going to lay the foundation for the new world! They are the

sustain them without genuine popular support.

The vigorous Soviet and Cuban support of Salvadoran leftists, and the new closer relationship with Nicaragua since last year are the result of more than a preconceived strategy. They also illustrate Soviet and Cuban tactical skill in exploiting opportunities. In the case of Nicaragua, such an opportunity was furnished by the hesitancy of the U.S. Congress in providing aid to that country and U.S. failure to assume a more active role.

The Soviets' position in El Salvador may go beyond the desire to exploit revolutionary opportunities. It may be that by taking a tough stand concerning that country, Moscow is trying to pin Washington down and eventually place itself in a position to bargain on other issues, such as Afghanistan and Poland. The internal situations in both of these border countries are causing the Soviet Union serious problems, which it has attributed to outside provocation and assistance. In may be, as suggested by some Central American observers, that Soviet tactics in El Salvador are being used to divert Western attention from Soviet domestic failures and the problems faced in Poland and Afghanistan, in order to prepare a hardening of Soviet policies in these countries, perhaps including some kind of intervention in Poland. In exchange for U.S. acquiescence to such hard-line policies, Moscow would change its tactics in El Salvador. The Soviet leadership appears to link the crises in Poland and Central America. Indeed, while delivering an important speech on the Polish crisis on April 7, 1981, Brezhnev unexpectedly concluded his remarks by stressing the Soviets' role as protector of Cuba's security.[41]

As of the fall of 1981, any firm conclusions about the outcome of the struggle in El Salvador are, of course, premature. Indeed, a number of internal and external constraints could mitigate assertive Cuban and Soviet implementation of "anti-imperialist" strategy in the Caribbean basin. The Cuban economic situation has reached its lowest level since the revolution, despite massive Soviet economic support. The economic malaise, to which the costly African adventures have certainly contributed, led in early 1980 to a radical reorganization of the Cuban government and the rationing of essentials. Public resentment was further fed by the soaring cost of living, culminating in open dissent in the spring of 1980: more than 10,000 Cuban dissidents sought asylum in the Peruvian embassy in Havana and subsequently emigrated to the United States. Cuban economic difficulties, however, failed to elicit any major antiwar movement, or, for that matter, any visible opposition or even political debate. Despite the difficulties arising from its alliance with the Soviet Union, Cuba in 1980-1981 has succeeded in maintaining its overseas commitments and even in expanding them, as seen in Nicaragua and El Salvador.

---

spur, and they come in time as the voice of man's conscience. But the steel that makes a good spur will not do for the builder's hammer." (1883)

[41] See Brezhnev's speech delivered at the Sixteenth Party Congress of the Czechoslovak Communist Party, in *Pravda*, April 8, 1981.

Furthermore, local conditions in the Caribbean basin may not always favor revolutionary upheaval and its exploitation by the Cubans and the Soviets. A crucial setback for them was the October 1980 defeat of the left-leaning regime of Manley in Jamaica by the more pro-Western Edward Seaga. In recent years, Soviet economic backing had allowed the Cubans to expand their influence in Jamaica. Like Nicaragua and Grenada, Jamaica was offered financial credits by Cuba (perhaps with Soviet help) and the assistance of several hundred Cuban civilian teachers, technicians, and construction workers, as well as some security officials to train the Jamaican security forces. Additional setbacks in the region include the electoral defeats of other parties with close Cuban ties on the small Caribbean islands of St. Vincent, Dominica, and Antigua.

Vigorous Cuban involvement in Africa and the Caribbean basin can also be constrained by the Soviets themselves, whose support determines the limits of Cuban assertiveness in the Third World. Given Soviet preoccupation with the Polish crisis, the continuing resistance of Muslim rebels in Afghanistan, and the ongoing war between Iran and Iraq, Soviet concerns in the next year may be directed toward Eastern Europe and the strategic "arc of instability" to the south of the Soviet borders in Asia (that is, Afghanistan and Iran). A significant shift in Soviet priorities could have a significant effect on Cuban foreign policy. Hence, Castro reportedly believes that Moscow is being too "patient" with Poland; he has repeatedly assaulted the Polish free trade unions, whose activities, he says, are prompted by "imperialistic provocation."[42] This should come as no surprise. Continuous Soviet preoccupation with Poland and Afghanistan could impose hard choices on the Soviet leadership with regard to its strategy in the Third World, including Cuba. What effect will all this have on Soviet-Cuban commitments in other parts of the Third World, particularly Angola and Ethiopia, but also in Central America? How long can Soviet-backed Cuban deployment in Angola and Ethiopia be maintained, and how effectively? These questions, for which there are no pat answers, are probably being posed now by foreign policy experts in the Soviet Union who may feel that Caribbean and Central American anti-U.S. nationalism simply cannot be exploited as vigorously as the Cuban leaders believe, at least not in the foreseeable future.

The most important factor affecting Soviet-Cuban strategy in Central America is the future course of U.S. policy vis-à-vis the U.S.S.R. and Cuba. In the wake of the Vietnam debacle, Cuban and Soviet activities seemed hardly constrained by the United States, because of the unwillingness of the American public and Congress to support a forceful response to such assertive behavior. This point was well demonstrated during the Angolan and Ethiopian

---

[42]   Radio Madrid, December 5, 1980, in FBIS, *Daily Report* (Latin America, December 5, 1980, and Castro's Speech at the Twenty-sixth Party Congress of the CPSU, Moscow, in FBIS, *Daily Report* (Latin America), February 24, 1981.

interventions. It seems that the political mood in the United States is now changing, as demonstrated in some degree by the election of Reagan, who back in 1980 suggested a naval blockade of Cuba as a response to the invasion of Afghanistan. In early 1981 Reagan and his advisers repeatedly warned that the United States would take all measures necessary to stop the arms transfer to El Salvador, not excluding actions against Cuba. These threats were taken seriously by the Cubans, who in late 1980 had decided to organize a territorial militia defense system. One thing is almost certain: the Soviets themselves are not going to undertake a direct military intervention in Central America. They still do not have the capability to do so effectively, in spite of what they see as a "weakening of U.S. hegemony" in the region.

Although U.S. emergency military aid to El Salvador is justifiable in the light of Soviet-Cuban involvement, the Reagan administration would be well advised to follow military aid to El Salvador with immediate comprehensive economic, financial, and technical assistance not only there but also to several other Central American nations. The roots of the problems in the region are socioeconomic. They call for a kind of "new Marshall Plan" in support of profound structural reforms. The United States should take the initiative in protecting its interests by a variety of means that include—but go beyond—the emergency first-aid measures needed to arrest Soviet-Cuban "anti-imperialist" strategy in Central America.

17

Soviet-Nicaraguan Relations and the Contra War

Marc Edelman

Seven years after the triumph of the Sandinista revolution and five years after the serious escalation of the *contra* war, events in retrospect appear to have had a certain inexorable quality. It was to be expected that a radical, nationalist movement such as that led by the FSLN would harbor deep suspicions of the United States, especially given the history of U.S. intervention in Nicaragua, with fourteen official or filibuster invasions between 1853 and 1926 (Schoultz 1984:122), two decades of direct occupation in this century, four decades of support for the Somoza dictatorship, and the Carter administration's last-minute efforts to deny power to the FSLN by supporting "provisional president" Francisco Urcuyo. In Central America, where of five countries only Costa Rica had durable democratic institutions and where earlier experiments in social change, such as that of Jacobo Arbenz in Guatemala, had been crushed by U.S.-supported mercenaries, it was perhaps not unreasonable for the victorious Sandinistas to expect eventual efforts to organize a counter-revolution. In Nicaragua, where the vast majority was politically and economically disenfranchised and where proponents of liberal democracy had historically been unable to mount meaningful opposition to the dictatorship, it should not be surprising that anti-Somoza youths turned to armed struggle and dreamed of socialism and resurrecting Sandino. Nor was it peculiar that Nicaraguans seeking to overthrow Somoza would seek support and refuge where it was to be had. In the early years of the Sandinistas' existence this meant Cuba and, to a lesser degree, the Soviet Union (Blandón 1981).

In the United States, on the other hand, the Sandinistas' victory coincided with a conservative shift in the political mood. The Iranian hostage crisis and the sudden attention given a Soviet army brigade in Cuba that had actually been detected long before, contributed to hardening attitudes towards groups

© 1988 *International Journal on World Peace*. An earlier version of this paper was presented to the Latin American Studies Association (Boston), October 1986. Research in the Soviet Union was supported by a fellowship from the International Research and Exchanges Board of the American Council of Learned Societies.

that seized power by violent means, even if they did so against others who had *held* power by violent means. The December 1979 Soviet invasion of Afghanistan marked the end of détente and provided ammunition for those who sought to place all Third World conflicts in an East-West context.

These mutual perceptions are important because to a large degree policies are shaped by these historically and ideologically influenced constructs. As U.S.-Nicaraguan relations worsened, these initial views contributed to polarizing a situation that already contained ample structural reasons for generating conflict. For Nicaragua, there was the real threat of U.S.-supported counter-revolution, anticipated for sound historical reasons almost from the first days after July 1979. For the United States, there was the sudden uncertainty brought about by the Sandinista victory in a region that had long been a stable and unquestioned U.S. preserve. For the more alarmist elements in Washington, the FSLN's historic relations with Cuba meant that what happened in Nicaragua could only be seen through the prism of U.S.-Soviet geopolitical competition.

While ultimately the Nicaraguan revolution may have set off alarm bells in Washington because it challenged the legitimacy of capitalism (Fagen et al. 1986:14), immediate security fears related to loss of U.S. control and a changing East-West balance were almost certainly more important. It is therefore key to examine the ways in which the military aid Nicaragua has received from the Eastern bloc developed in the context of its relations with the United States. This paper first considers the ways in which the Sandinistas and Soviets viewed each other in the period prior to July 1979. It then considers the development of one aspect of post-1979 Soviet-Nicaraguan relations: the course of the *contra* war and the expansion of Nicaragua's military, carried out primarily with Soviet assistance. As in the case of Nicaragua's economic relations with the socialist countries, which have grown as other possibilities were blocked (Berríos and Edelman 1985), much of the military assistance Nicaragua has received has been in response to concrete threats. Because security in conflict situations necessarily involves preparation for worst-case scenarios, Nicaragua has also been required to prepare for defense against eventual escalations of the *contra* war and direct U.S. intervention.

PRE-1979 SOVIET-NICARAGUAN RELATIONS

In late 1944, the U.S.S.R. and Nicaragua, then under the rule of Anastasio Somoza García, exchanged notes establishing diplomatic relations. There was not subsequently, however, an actual exchange of missions (Sizonenko 1971:196). Nicaragua's recognition of the U.S.S.R., like that of a number of other Latin American countries that established links with the Soviets in this period, occurred in a context of reduced U.S.-Soviet tensions growing out of both the wartime collaboration against the Nazis and the 1943 abolition of the

Comintern, a measure specifically intended to reassure the U.S.S.R.'s allies. These early Soviet-Nicaraguan diplomatic links had little real importance, however. Apart from some minor trade deals in the 1960s and 1970s (Acciaris 1984:107), there was virtually no contact between the Soviet and Nicaraguan governments prior to the 1979 triumph of the Sandinistas.

In Nicaragua, the World War II period was also the time of a brief political thaw that witnessed the creation of the pro-Moscow Nicaraguan Socialist Party (PSN) in 1944. Founded from the remnants of the more politically heterogeneous Nicaraguan Workers Party (PTN), the leaders of which had been forced to seek refuge in Costa Rica during the late 1930s, the PSN developed some presence in the small union movement and helped secure passage of the country's first labor code before being driven underground in 1948. In its brief legal life, the PSN lent support to the Somoza regime, refusing to participate, for example, in the 1944 general strike organized by the Conservative opposition (Barahona 1981:390-394; Pérez and Guevara 1980).

The PSN was always among the weakest of the small Central American Communist parties. Formed after the dissolution of the Comintern, its militants in all likelihood never experienced the close Soviet ideological and organizational supervision bestowed on other Latin American parties founded in the 1920s and 1930s. Strongly influenced by the larger Costa Rica Popular Vanguard (Communist) Party (PVP), under whose tutelege exiled Nicaraguan Communists had first organized in the late 1930s, the PSN absorbed much of the gradualist, reformist orientation that characterized PVP ideology in Costa Rica's more open political environment. According to one authoritative Soviet source, it only established "strong" links with the international Communist movement in 1959 and the "definitive formation" of the PSN "as a Marxist-Leninist party" occurred in 1967, when "a group of opportunists and conservatives entrenched in the party was routed" (Leonov 1975:201-202). Following the failures of the diverse guerrilla movements that sought to overthrow the Somoza dictatorship in the late 1950s (Blandón 1981), the PSN decided at a 1960 congress to "prepare for an armed uprising and the formation and strengthening of a single, anti-imperialist people's front" (Leshchiner 1965:60). But this call appears to have been only one in a series of resolutions that were never carried out due to infighting and weakness of the PSN organization.

In the 1950s, the future founders of the Sandinista National Liberation Front (FSLN)—Carlos Fonseca, Silvio Mayorga, and Tomás Borge—were recruited by the PSN, but it was, as Borge was later to remark, "a halfway recuitment" (Borge 1980:20). These young Nicaraguans' acquaintance with Marxism was superficial, in part because Marxist literature was difficult to come by in the Somozas' Nicaragua. Fonseca, the FSLN's principal theoretician, recalled that his study of Marxism was based on Mao Tse-tung's *New Democracy*, Lenin's *Left Wing Communism: An Infantile Disorder* and a few works by Marx and Engels (Fonseca 1982a:167). The young revolutionaries were also irked by the PSN's failure to pursue armed struggle against the Somoza regime. Sandinista reminiscences are replete with accusations of PSN perfidy, including charges of collaboration with the Somozas, failure to support strikes, betrayals of peasant organizers, and, on one occasion, betrayal of Fonseca himself (Arias 1980:31, 80, 86; Cabezas 1982:27; Randall 1980:50-51; Fonseca 1982a:183; Ortega 1980:143).

The FSLN's dislike of the PSN was coupled with some acrimonious feuds with the Costa Rican PVP. Shortly after Fonseca's abortive 1969 break from a Costa Rican prison, the PVP newspaper sarcastically charged that he was an amateurish "Boy Scout" and, calling him "Charles," implied that he was possibly even connected to the North Americans (Porras 1970). Fonseca responded with a long polemic lambasting the PVP for a 1934 attack on Sandino and its "very long policy of scorn for the revolutionary values of the Nicaraguan people and its encouragement of conciliation with the enemies of the Nicaraguan people" (Fonseca 1984).

Sandinista disdain for the pro-Moscow parties did not in most cases extend to the U.S.S.R. itself. Fonseca, who travelled to the Soviet Union and Eastern Europe in 1957 as the lone Nicaraguan delegate to the World Youth Festival, later wrote a short book, *Un nicaragüense en Moscú*, which praised Soviet economic development and achievements in social welfare (Fonseca 1980). Like numerous other Third World visitors to Moscow, Fonseca viewed the Soviet Union with the eyes of someone with little other travel experience, from an impoverished country that had suffered frequent U.S. military interventions and a U.S.-supported right-wing dictatorship. A similar impression was surely made on Gladys Báez, later a Sandinista, who in 1962 "went to the U.S.S.R. without knowing Managua" (Randall 1980:222). But not all Sandinistas shared Fonseca's rosy view of the Soviet Union. In the mid- and late 1960s, FSLN sympathizers studying at Moscow's Patrice Lumumba University were reported to have clashed frequently with the Soviets over issues of ideological control, armed struggle, the Sino-Soviet dispute and the Soviet occupation of Czechoslovakia (Hernández 1982:27-33; Christian 1986:32).

The few Soviet writings that mention the FSLN prior to July 1979 are largely uncritical, although occasional PSN statements published in the U.S.S.R. tend to be somewhat less accepting (Sánchez 1976:107-108). Leonov (Leonov 1975:293), without mentioning the FSLN by name, describes the founding by Fonseca of a "patriotic front for struggle with the Somoza dictatorship," but notes that Fonseca's capture in Costa Rica "confirms once again the uselessness and frequent harmfulness of an adventurist policy of 'direct action.'" Significantly, however, Leonov's criticisms of the PSN (Leonov 1975:293) are considerably more severe, even in 1975. Merin, who condemns the Guatemalan guerrilla movement and the ultra-left group that tried to split the PSN around 1970, is noncommital on the FSLN (Merin 1973:91, 119), although some obvious errors of fact in his description suggest that he was rather unfamiliar with this subject. Chumakova, in contrast, refers to the "development of guerrilla movements in Guatemala and Nicaragua" as being one of the factors threatening U.S. domination in the region (Chumakova 1970:3). She refers to Fonseca's detention in Costa Rica as the result of recommendations of the U.S.-sponsored ODECA military pact (Chumakova 1972:109). For the most part, Soviet analysts writing before 1979 believed Nicaragua to be one of the places in Latin America (if not *the* place) where U.S. domination was strongest (Leshchiner 1965:6; Merin 1973:103; Semenov et al. 1976:13). Only Leonov (Leonov 1972:34) presciently referred to Central America as "one of the weak links in the system of American domination in the western hemisphere."

Perhaps because of the PSN's weakness, Soviet analysts appear to have had at least some hopes for the FSLN, even in the early 1970s when the organization probably had only a few dozen full-time militants. In 1971, for example, *Pravda* published a greeting from Fonseca to the 24th CPSU Congress (Fonseca 1971). At this congress efforts were explicitly made to strengthen "ties with the revolutionary democratic parties of the developing countries" (Brutents 1977:II, 215), a category that presumably included the FSLN. There was no published repetition of this FSLN greeting on the occasion of the 25th CPSU Congress five years later (CPSU 1976). Nevertheless, such gestures are likely to have smoothed the way within the Soviet party for approaches to the FSLN after 1979. This was especially true in light of the chronic organizational and ideological problems of the "fraternal" PSN, which included a 1977 split in which a significant portion of the membership opted to collaborate with the FSLN.

Even as the Sandinista-led insurrection against the Somoza dictatorship gathered steam in late 1978 and early 1979, Soviet press coverage and analysis was sparse, suggesting a lack of in-depth knowledge of the FSLN. In October 1978, for example, *Komsomol'skaia Pravda* printed a sympathetic interview with Tomás Borge, who had recently arrived in Havana after being freed from prison in return for FSLN hostages seized in the National Palace, but it misidentified him as Tomás Jorge Martínez (Vesenskii 1978). Several months later *Pravda* published an interview with Luis Guzmán, another Sandinista prisoner who had been released as a result of the palace takeover (Serbin 1979). But until the final weeks of the insurrection in mid-1979, this was virtually all that the Soviet press reported about the FSLN.

Cuba, of course, provided inspiration, sanctuary, and training to the FSLN during its long struggle against Somoza, in part no doubt because of the latter's granting of bases to anti-Castro Cuban exiles during and after the 1961 Bay of Pigs invasion. In the final months of the 1979 insurrection, Cuba also provided substantial arms aid, as did Venezuela and Panama

(LeoGrande 1983:46). What has been frequently obscured in the subsequent fragmentation of the FSLN-led anti-Somoza coalition, however, is that virtually all forces that opposed the dictatorship initially favored warm relations with Cuba. In 1979 even present-day *contra* leader Alfonso Robelo could declare that "Cuba and Nicaragua will always be, as they have been, brother peoples" (FSLN 1979:45). While this affection did not in all likelihood extend to Eastern Europe and the U.S.S.R., it is noteworthy that in the first months of the revolution there was a broad consensus in Nicaraguan society in favor of a diversification of foreign relations that would include the socialist countries.

THE LINES ARE DRAWN: 1979-1981

Events in the period from July 1979 through early 1981 are crucial to understanding Nicaragua's subsequent relations with both the Soviet Union and its allies and the United States. Several points must be emphasized, although they will not be considered in detail here. The victorious FSLNwas, in general, sympathetic to the socialist countries, particularly to Cuba, which had been virtually the only significant sanctuary its militants had during the years of struggle against Somoza. Yet, in the period following the July 1979 overthrow of Somoza, the Sandinistas displayed considerable openness towards the United States, guaranteeing political space for the private sector and opposition parties and even seeking U.S. military aid (Matthews 1985:23-28). Even after the major escalation of the *contra* war in 1982, the Nicaraguan government expressed its willingness on numerous occasions to provide guarantees addressing the security concerns of the United States (Gilbert 1986:118-121).

The security threat faced by the new Sandinista-led government was one of the main considerations that contributed to polarizing the situation. The guerrilla force that overthrew Somoza had perhaps 5,000 full-time combatants, a motley array of equipment, no developed command structure, and virtually no aircraft. The Reagan administration and its supporters have frequently asserted that the Nicaraguan government faced no threat in 1979 and 1980 and that it therefore had no legitimate reason for developing a large army or security apparatus (*New York Times* 1986; Valenta and Valenta 1985:12). The main source of this charge is the "72-Hour Document," a report of a high-level 1979 FSLN meeting that administration supporters have frequently misquoted or cited out of context (Singer 1984; Edelman 1986:109, 122). In fact, however, the new government faced immediate difficulties from counter-revolutionaries. In July 1979, the Spanish news agency reported a fight with 1,500 former National Guardsmen near the Honduran border and noted that

> great tension is being experienced in Managua due to intense sniper fire
> by alleged former soldiers dressed in civilian clothes. The attacks, even

on the Camino Real Hotel, headquarters of the junta of the Goverment of National Reconstruction, have been staged at night (ACAN-EFE 1979a).

In August, it was reported that there were "skirmishes every night in Managua" (ACAN-EFE 1979b). Nicaragua decided to protest to the U.S. government about the activities of former National Guardsmen who announced on U.S. territory that they were organizing a counterrevolution (LATIN 1979). The *Washington Post* also reported in August that some 2,000 ex-National Guardsmen had regrouped just over the Honduran border and were carrying out sporadic raids (Krause 1979). Tomás Borge declared

> we are not seeking to set up a large army; our underdeveloped country could not afford this, to say nothing of the fact that we do not even have the power to pay for such a luxury. Still, we must consider the fact that we live in a state of constant threat. Even today Somoza is organizing his own army. We also do not know where the hostile conduct of some countries may lead (Budapest Domestic Service 1979).

Over the months these problems continued. In October 1979, twenty Sandinista miltiamen were killed in a Managua ambush (*Los Angeles Times* 1979) and there were firefights in Diriamba, Jinotepe, and Corinto (*Central America Report* 1979). In February 1980, the Honduran Army captured 270 former National Guardsmen, part of a force of around 800, that were planning an invasion of Nicaragua (AFP 1980). In June, some 200 *contras* were captured in a battle north of Managua (*Los Angeles Times* 1980). Although some Reagan administration supporters, in discussing the violent death in November 1980 of private sector leader Jorge Salazar, refer to his "*alleged* anti-Sandinista activities" (Valenta and Valenta 1985:13), others have documented his involvement in an armed group seeking to foment a coup from within the ranks of the Nicaraguan army (Christian 1986:204-213). By late 1980, the Carter administration had begun a modest "covert action" program to support the political approach in Nicaragua (Dickey 1985:78; Gilbert 1986:105). Already in late 1980, the anti-Sandinista armed group Unión Democrática Nicaragüense (UDN)Unión Democrática Nicaragüense), led by Francisco Cardenal and Edmundo and Fernando ("El Negro") Chamorro, was receiving funds from the U.S. Central Intelligence Agency (Chamorro and Morley 1985:19-20).

Borge's lament that "our underdeveloped country could not afford" an army reflected another aspect of the difficult reality facing the Sandinistas in 1979-1981. Fleeing functionaries of the Somoza regime had absconded with all but $3.5 million of Nicaragua's currency reserves and had left the new government a country in ruins. If the Sandinistas were to realize their ambitious social investment goals *and* build a modern army to defend against the very real security threat, it was necessary to spend as little as possible on arms. Nonetheless, the Sandinistas sought military aid from the United States (Matthews 1985). While they received some miniscule amounts for binoculars and compasses, it was clear by September 1979 that no significant arms aid would be forthcoming. Although Sandinista leaders had on a number of occasions expressed a preference for obtaining Western arms (and actually signed a small arms deal with France in 1981), they had little alternative to turning to the U.S.S.R. and its allies, which were willing to provide stable supplies on favorable terms (Matthews 1985). It has been suggested (Schwab and Sims 1985:454) that some of the Soviet arms Nicaragua has received have been purchased with hard currency. However, it is not likely that this is usually the case, given Nicaragua's dire economic crisis.

The situation in the intelligence area was similar. Panamanians played an important role in training the Sandinista police in 1979/1980. The Nicaraguans, however, were reluctant to accept Panamanian trainers into army intelligence because of the Panamanian National Guard's historic links to both Somoza's officer corps and the United States (Bossert 1986: 190). The FSLN had historic ties to Cuba, and Cubans rapidly came to play the key foreign advisory role in military intelligence. As Robert Matthews suggests,

> Nicaragua faced a Hobson's Choice: accept Cuban offers of military help and arouse Western antagonism, or risk taking the Panamanians into sensitive security areas. As U.S. hostility grew, and blossomed into war under Reagan, the Sandinistas must have felt that their decision to play it safe with the Cubans was a wise one (Matthews 1985:27).

Among other factors that contributed to worsening relations in 1980 were the U.S. Congress's efforts to attach what were perceived by Nicaraguans as onerous conditions to a proposed $75 million loan package promised Nicaragua (Sims 1984:60-61) and the subsequent signing of several aid protocols with the U.S.S.R. that included a party-to-party agreement for contacts between the FSLN and the CPSU. The Sandinistas' April reorganization of the Council of State to provide greater representation for FSLN-linked mass organizations provoked an outcry from the more conservative sectors of the political opposition. Reagan's election on a platform that was deeply hostile to the Sandinistas (Matthews 1985:29) and the contacts between the president-elect's staff and armed Somocista exile groups were additional motives for Nicaraguan concern (Chardy 1980).

There is also evidence that in the brief period between Reagan's election in November 1980 and the failure of the Salvadoran guerrillas' "final offensive" in early 1981, the Sandinistas shipped some arms to the guerrillas, a step that obviously aroused U.S. government anger. U.S. warnings, however, led almost immediately to a virtual elimination of the arms flow (Gilbert 1986:99-100; LeoGrande 1986:247-249), and the U.S.-sponsored militarization of Honduras that began in 1982 ensured against any significant resumption of this traffic. Nevertheless, the charge that the Sandinistas were supplying the Salvadoran insurgents continued to be a staple of Reagan administration attacks against Nicaragua and a key justification for the initiation of the *contra* war.

By 1981 the die was cast. In March, six weeks after his inauguration, Reagan issued a finding calling for stepped-up covert action in Central America (Dickey 1985:104). In April the United States cut off all economic aid and began to systematically block Nicaraguan loan requests in multilateral lending agencies (Berríos and Edelman 1985). In July, in a series of moves widely viewed as a "radicalization" of the revolution, the Nicaraguan government announced the expropriation of thirteen large firms that had been decapitalizing, promulgated a broad agrarian reform, and decreed certain limits on private sector activities (Gilbert 1986:100).

In August, literally on the same day Assistant Secretary of State Thomas Enders was in Managua with the ostensible purpose of fostering peaceful reconciliation, the FDN (Fuerza Democrática Nicaragüense) *contra* organization was founded with U.S. encouragement (Ignatius and Rogers 1985; Christian 1986:231-232). The Enders mission took place in an atmosphere of heightened tensions, and the Sandinistas, angered by the U.S. handling of the $75 million aid package and by growing evidence of CIA ties to the *contras*, were skeptical of U.S. promises of a deal. Although the Nicaraguans believed that sufficient legal guarantees existed against U.S.-sponsored attacks so as to make additional pledges unnecessary, they continued private talks for several weeks. The Nicaraguans were later reported to regret the end of these negotiations (LeoGrande 1985:430), but it was the United States that terminated the talks. When Nicaragua protested U.S. naval maneuvers off its coast in October, the Reagan administration broke off the discussions (Gilbert 1986:101). In November Secretary of State Alexander Haig refused to rule out an armed intervention against Nicaragua. Also in November the United States allocated $19 million for covert activities against the Nicaraguan government.

THE RHYTHM OF THE MILITARY BUILDUP

Any effort to examine the post-1979 Nicaraguan military buildup faces inevitable methodological difficulties (Jacobsen 1984:15; Edelman 1986). Reagan administration figures on Nicaraguan troop strength and equipment acquisitions for even the early years of the conflict have been revised upwards with each new press release (compare the arms acquisitions cited in DOD/DOS [Department of Defense/Department of State] 1985 with those cited in DOD/DOS 1986). Frequently such data are not disaggregated by important categories and instead lump together, for example, the tonnage of all arms deliveries (DOD/DOS 1985:25) or combine active-duty military and civilian militia as "forces" or both combat and non-combat airplanes under the single rubric of "fixed-wing aircraft" (DOD data cited in Coll 1985:10). In most cases, Reagan administration claims about Nicaraguan strength are substantially greater than those of sources widely respected for their objectivity in this field, such as the Stockholm International Peace Research Institute (SIPRI), *Jane's Defense Weekly* and its associated publications, and the London International Institute of Strategic Studies. It has also been reported that the CIA has presented closed congressional hearings with "much lower figures" on Nicaragua's military capability than those published by the administration (*Latin America Regional Report* 1985a; House of Representatives 1985:1133-1137).

Borge's 1979 assertion that "we are not seeking to set up a large army," reiterated on various occasions by other leading Sandinistas (Matthews 1985:25), appears to be largely borne out by an examination of Nicaraguan military acquisitions in the 1979-1981 period. During the first years of the revolution, military aid from the Soviet Union and its allies was not very substantial. U.S. intelligence figures released in 1985 showed only $5 million worth of Soviet-bloc military imports in 1979 (Krauss and Greenberger 1985). Imports during late 1979 and the first half of 1980 included Soviet ZPU light antiaircraft guns, SA-7 surface-to-air missiles, RPG-7 antitank grenades and East German trucks (Goldblat and Millán 1984:531). U.S. Defense Department (DOD) figures indicate that by the end of 1980, Nicaragua possessed a total of thirty-nine antiaircraft guns and six missile launchers (Coll 1985:10). DOD figures on Nicaragua's imports during 1980 suggest a total weight of deliveries of some 850 metric tons (DOD/DOS 1985:25), worth between $6 and $7 million (Krauss and Greenberger 1985). The same sources report 1981 arms imports of 900 metric tons (DOD/DOS 1985:25), worth an estimated $39 to $45 million (Krauss and Greenberger 1985). Most of the 1981 tonnage was almost certainly accounted for by some twenty-seven Soviet T-54 and T-55 tanks, weighing 32 metric tons each, that were acquired secondhand from Algeria (Edelman 1985:50; Coll 1985:10).

Part of the 1980/1981 buildup was simply the construction of a national armed force where none had existed, and part was almost certainly due to perceived threats from Nicaragua's neighbors and from *contras* who were already training on U.S. and Honduran territory. El Salvador, Guatemala, and Honduras all made significant purchases of fighter aircraft in 1979, shortly after the Sandinistas came to power (*Latin America Regional Report* 1985b). Honduras, with the most hostile posture of the three and the most threatening geographic position vis-à-vis Nicaragua, acquired sixteen British Scorpion tanks in 1981, not long before Nicaragua received its tanks from Algeria. The Scorpions, built in the 1970s, are considerably faster and more versatile than the T-54s and T-55s. It is only if the Nicaraguans' 1981 tank acquisitions are considered outside the context of this regional balance of power that U.S. charges of an unprovoked escalation of the Central American arms race can be sustained.

What is most interesting about the DOD data released in 1985 is that they fail to support convincingly the Reagan administration's contention that the Nicaraguan buildup *preceded* the major escalation of the *contra* war in 1982. Indeed, the jump in the weight of military imports from 900 to 6,700 metric tons in 1981/82 (DOD/DOS 1985:25) could plausibly be employed to make the opposite argument, namely that the buildup accelerated *in response to* the increased threat of attack, either from *contras* or the armies of neighboring countries such as Honduras. In either case, it is significant that the DOD data, which are not likely to give Nicaragua the benefit of a doubt, suggest a rapid expansion of Nicaragua's military capability in 1982 and only limited growth in 1981.

Belatedly cognizant of the logical problems with the arms delivery data in their 1985 White Paper, the Departments of Defense and State rely in their 1986 White Paper on estimates of troop strength over time to make the same argument (DOD/DOS 1986:19-20). The troop strength estimates, however, show major divergences from those of independent observers, such as SIPRI. According to the 1986 White Paper, in November 1981 the Nicaraguan army was the largest in Central America, with almost 40,000 troops (DOD/DOS 1986:20). SIPRI and the *Washington Post*, however, estimate that Nicaraguan troop strength at that time was 25,000—larger than the army of Honduras but several thousand less than that of El Salvador (Goldblat and Millán 1984:522; Dickey 1981). Earlier DOD figures point to a December 1981 total of 39,000 that included both active-duty forces and "mobilized militia" (Coll 1985:10). Of course it may be assumed that the Reagan administration's demonstrated tendency toward hyperbole as regards Nicaragua (Jacobsen 1984; Brumberg 1985) has influenced its troop estimates. Even allowing for a large margin of error on the part of independent experts, it appears unlikely that the Nicaraguan armed forces in late 1981 had a total strength that was significantly beyond that of the armed forces of El Salvador or Honduras.

November 1981 constitutes an important watershed, however. As the 1986 White Paper states (DOD/DOS 1986:20), Nicaragua's ambassador to the United States "claims that [then] the United States decided to assist the Nicaraguan armed resistance" (as if this were not an established fact). After 1981, the rapid growth of the U.S.-sponsored *contra* forces and the U.S. maneuvers and buildup in Honduras gave the arms race in the Central American region a different dynamic. In part, this new dynamic was determined by the necessity for security planners of whatever orientation to prepare for worst-case scenarios, even seemingly unlikely ones. In the case of Nicaragua, in addition to confronting the real and by now daily incursions of Honduras-based *contras*, this meant preparation for a conventional war with Honduras or a direct U.S. intervention, neither of which appeared particularly improbable in 1982.

The 6,700 tons of military equipment imported in 1982 were worth $80 million, according to the Reagan administration (Danby 1985:15; DOD/DOS 1985:25). This matériel included twenty more T-54 tanks, twelve BTR-60 armored personnel carriers, six 105-mm howitzers and some forty-eight ZIS-2 37-mm antiaircraft guns (English 1984a:330; Coll 1985:10). Even the Kissinger Commission report conceded that the first delivery of "sophisticated Soviet electronic gear" took place only in December 1982, more than a year after the CIA began active support for the *contras* (National Bipartisan Commission 1984:appendix, 40). By the end of 1982, Nicaragua had received an estimated total of $125 million worth of military equipment from the Soviet Union and its allies (Coll 1985:9; Krauss and Greenberger 1985), almost exactly equivalent to the $124.1 million in military aid the United States provided El Salvador in 1980-1982 (DOS 1985). Honduras, not under attack as were the Nicaraguan and Salvadoran governments, received $44.1 million of U.S. military aid in the same period (DOS 1985). The U.S. aid to Honduras and El Salvador did not, of course, include the basic start-up costs for those countries' armed forces, unlike the initial Soviet aid to Nicaragua.

In 1983/84, increased U.S. maneuvers in Honduras, CIA-directed commando attacks on Nicaragua's oil facilities and ports, and the U.S. invasion of Grenada characterized the changed context in which Nicaraguan military planners had to consider their options. *Contra* units, while unable to capture and hold territory, were increasingly shifting from border incursions to long marches of several months duration into the Atlantic and northern regions of the country. These considerations provided an impetus for further growth in the size of the Nicaraguan armed forces and in Soviet military aid. DOD figures on the size of the Sandinista military and security forces indicate a rather modest increase from 39,000 to 46,000 in 1981-1983, with a more substantial increase to 67,000 in 1984 (DOD/DOS 1986:38). CIA estimates of aid in these years are $125 million for 1983 and $250 million for 1984 (House of Representatives 1985:1134). The weight of deliveries in these years was estimated at 14,000 and 18,700 metric tons respectively (DOD/DOS 1985; Cushman 1986). Importantly, however, a classified U.S. intelligence report prepared in late 1984 concluded that "the overall buildup is primarily defense-oriented, and much of the recent effort has been devoted to improving counter insurgency capabilities" (Cited in Krauss and Greenberger 1985). The years of the most significant *contra* military successes were 1983/84, with the CIA channelling over $54 million in official aid just in the eighteen months prior to mid-1984, when Congress barred the agency from participating in the war (Inforpress Centroamericana 1986). U.S. government figures indicate that Soviet bloc arms to Nicaragua actually declined sharply in 1985 to 13,900 metric tons, worth an estimated $75 million (Cushman 1986; Center for Defense Information 1986:30). In 1986, with congressional approval of a $100 million U.S. aid package for the *contras* a virtual certainty, Soviet arms deliveries to Nicaragua rose above their 1984 level, to some 18,800 metric tons in the first ten months of the year (Cushman 1986).

A major problem for the Sandinistas has been what even the *New York Times* termed in 1985 "their small and almost antique air force" (Kinzer 1985). With the Reagan administration's repeated declarations that any Nicaraguan acquisition of jet fighters, such as Mig-21s, would be met with instant retaliation, the Sandinistas have been unable to build a modern air arm. The Nicaraguans have periodically expressed interest in the Mig-21 and even in the subsonic Czech L-21 trainer, but thus far U.S. threats have dissuaded them or their potential suppliers. Honduras and El Salvador continue to have vastly greater air capabilities than Nicaragua.

In late 1986, the Reagan administration announced that Honduras would be offered advanced jet fighters, either U.S. F-5Es or Israeli Kfirs (Gwertzman 1986). If Nicaragua were to acquire Mig-21s in response to this U.S.-Honduran move, it would invite a significant U.S. attack. Paradoxically, if Nicaragua fails to acquire Mig-21s, this will be perceived in Washington as a sign of weakness or as a lack of resolve on the part of its principal arms suppliers, the Soviet Union and Cuba.

A major qualitative change in the *contra* war occurred in the second half of 1985 with the first use in combat of Soviet-made MI-24 helicopter gunships. Nicaragua received "more than twelve" of these "flying tanks" between late 1984 and mid-1986, according to U.S. figures. Later independent reports, however, indicate that Nicaragua's total fleet of MI-24s and the similar MI-25s only reached twelve or fifteen with the delivery of six new helicopters in October 1986 (Kinzer 1986; Cushman 1986). It also now reportedly has about twelve of the less powerful MI-8 model (DOD/DOS 1986:21) and some thirty-five MI-17 troop carriers (Cushman 1986). There is little doubt that increased use of combat helicopters produced a rapid shift in the military balance in favor of the Sandinistas. Large *contra* units could no longer cross open territory without fearing attack, and many were forced back to their base camps in Honduras. By late 1985, Sandinista officials were beginning to comment that the *contras* had been dealt a "strategic defeat."

Estimating the number of foreign advisers in Nicaragua (and assessing their role) is fraught with even greater methodological problems than estimating equipment acquisitions. The Cubans have been the principal source of this assistance, with small numbers of advisers from other countries (Jacobsen 1984:17-18). In mid-1980, one U.S. intelligence source suggested that there were only "dozens" of Cuban military and security advisers in Nicaragua (U.S. Army 1980). The Reagan administration would later claim that there were 200 Cuban advisers in Nicaragua by October 1979 (Jacobsen 1984:17). As late as

1984, *Jane's Defence Weekly* put the figure at approximately 200 (English 1984b:610). In October 1984, FSLN directorate member Byardo Arce remarked that there were "less than 500" Cuban military advisers. By March 1985 President Daniel Ortega gave a precise number—786. The Reagan administration claims that there are "more than 3,000" Cuban and "more than 100" Soviet and East European military and security advisers in Nicaragua (DOD/DOS 1986:20). In some cases the Reagan administration may count as "military advisers" any Cuban civilians who have received training in Cuba's military reserves. In other cases it appears that the administration's estimates of East bloc "security advisers" include auto mechanics, doctors and dentists, and experts on bank electronic alarm systems (DOS 1986:16).

The 1986 renewal of direct U.S. military aid to the *contras* will undoubtedly lead to a major escalation of the conflict, especially if reports prove true that the CIA anticipates spending an additional $400 million above the $100 million appropriated by Congress (Morganthau et al.:1986). Such expenditures would mean that the budget for a force that initially consists of approximately 20,000 *contras* would be nearly two times Nicaragua's entire export earnings, which were projected at $232 million in 1986 (*Latin American Weekly Report* 1986). The scale of this U.S. aid is, of course, completely disproportionate to even the most outlandish claims of Sandinista support for guerrilla forces in neighboring countries.

The renewal of direct U.S. aid constitutes the crossing of a Rubicon in another respect as well. During the debate that preceded the approval of the $100 million for the *contras*, Reagan administration rhetoric reached new heights. Terming Nicaragua a major threat to U.S. security and linking aid to the *contras* to the United States' "global policy of deterrence" (Iklé 1986:2) closes the door to the continuing efforts of the Contadora group to find peaceful solutions and leaves the administration no fallback position should its policy of proxy war fail to generate results. The alternatives of a continuing war of attrition or direct U.S. intervention leave Nicaraguan military planners with only one choice: to maintain a strong defense and prepare for the worst eventualities.

THE DILEMMAS OF A REVOLUTION UNDER SIEGE

For the Soviet Union and its allies, military and economic aid to Nicaragua is a relatively low-cost strategy that promises political dividends in an increasingly nationalistic hemisphere. While support for the Sandinistas has eroded to some extent in Western Europe since the early years of the revolution, international condemnation of the U.S. role has, if anything, heightened, as the recent decisions of the World Court suggest. This has contributed to diplomatic isolation and loss of prestige for the United States and is thus consonant with overall Soviet foreign policy objectives. Finally, Soviet military aid to

Nicaragua has the very immediate effects of guaranteeing survival for an endangered revolutionary experiment and raising the cost of U.S. intervention. To the extent, however, that Nicaragua has become more economically dependent on the U.S.S.R., the price of the still-modest Soviet aid commitment to Nicaragua is likely to rise.

For Nicaragua, the U.S.-*contra* onslaught poses a number of dilemmas. The economy has been devastated by the war and the U.S. economic boycott and is also still suffering from the effects of natural disasters and the inheritance of the Somoza dictatorship. How under such conditions can a revolutionary government both defend itself and provide even minimal living standards for the population? How can the human resources be trained that might permit the country to emerge from underdevelopment when large numbers of young people must devote years of their lives to the defense effort? How can the government maintain its political support base in the face of deteriorating living conditions? How can the polarization of Nicaraguan society be addressed when a siege mentality has arisen in response to real and potential threats? There are indeed no adequate answers to these questions in the current war situation. The Reagan administration, in its insistence on viewing Third World conflicts exclusively in East-West terms, has aimed precisely at presenting Nicaragua with these painful quandaries.

REFERENCES

ACAN-EFE (Spanish News Agency)
1979a   "Pastora to Put Down Somozist Uprising in North," Panama City ACAN July 26 in *Foreign Broadcast Information Service— Latin America (FBIS-LAM)* (Washington) July 27:P8.
1979b   "Sandinistas Concerned Over Security Situation," Panama City ACAN August 1 in *FBIS-LAM* August 2:P4-5.

Acciaris, Ricardo
1984   "Nicaragua-Pays Socialistes: Vers la Cosolidation des Liens Economiques?" *Problèmes de l'Amérique Latine (Paris)* 74(4):107-126.

AFP (Agence France Presse)
1980   "Somozists Regrouping for anti-Sandinist Invasion," AFP Paris in *FBIS-LAM* February 13:P10.

Arias, Pilar
1980   *Nicaragua revolución: relatos de combatientes del Frente Sandinista.* México: Siglo XXI.

Barahona Portocarrero, Amarú
1981   "Breve estudio sobre la historia contemporánea de Nicaragua," in Pablo Gonzáles Casanova, ed., *América Latina: historia de medio siglo* (Vol. 2). México: Siglo XXI.

Berríos, Rubén and Marc Edelman
1985   "Hacia la diversificación de la dependencia. Los vínculos

económicos de Nicaragua con los países soicialistas," *Comercio Exterior* (Mexico) 35(10) (October):998-1006.

Borge Martínez, Tomás
1980   *Carlos, el amanecer ya no es una tentación.* Havana: Casa de las Américas.

Bossert, Thomas John
1986   "Panama," in Morris J. Blachman, William M. LeoGrande and Kenneth Sharpe, eds., *Confronting Revolution: Security Through Diplomacy in Central America.* New York: Pantheon.

Brumberg, Abraham
1985   "Reagan's Untruths About Managua," The *New York Times*, June 18.

Brutents, Karen
1977   *National Liberation Revolutions Today* (2 volumes). Moscow: Progress.

Budapest Domestic Service
1979   "Hungarian Radio Interview," Budapest Domestic Service, August 14, in *FBIS-LAM,* August 15:P4.

Cabezas, Omar
1982   *La montaña es algo más que una inmensa estepa verde.* Managua: Nueva Nicaragua.

Center for Defense Information
1986   "Country Studies of Soviet Influence: Nicaragua," *The Defense Monitor* (Washington) 15(5):30-31.

Central America Report
1979   "Nicaragua: Tempering the Revolution," *Central America Report* (Guatemala), October 22:330-331.

Chamorro, Edgar and Jefferson Morley
1985   "How the CIA Masterminds the Nicaraguan Insurgency. Confessions of a *'Contra',"* *The New Republic* (Washington) 193(6) (August 5):18-23.

Chardy, Alfonso
1980   "Nicaraguans Seek Access to Reagan," *The Miami Herald,* November 18.

Christian, Shirley
1986   *Nicaragua: Revolution in the Family* (2d ed.) New York: Vintage.

Chumakova, Marina L'vovna
1972   *Integratsionnye protsessy v stranakh Tsentral'noi Ameriki.* Moscow: Nauka.
1970   *Organizatsiia tsentral'noamerikanskikh gosudarstv.* Moscow: Mezhdunarodnie Otnoshenii.

Coll, Alberto R.
1985   "Soviet Arms and Central American Turmoil," *World Affairs* (Washington) 148(1) (Summer):7-17.

CPSU (Communist Party of the Soviet Union)
1976   *Privetsviia XXV s'ezdu KPSS.* Moscow: Politizdat.

Cushman, John Jr.
1986   "Nicaragua Said to Get More Gunships," The *New York Times*, October 29:A3.

Danby, Colin et al.
1985   *The Military Balance in Central America*. Washington: Council on Hemispheric Affairs.

Dickey, Christopher
1985   *With the Contras: A Reporter in the Wilds of Nicaragua*. New York: Simon and Schuster.
1981   "Sandinistas Turning to East Bloc," *The Washington Post*, November 22.

DOD/DOS (U.S. Department of Defense and Department of State)
1986   *The Challenge to Democracy in Central America*. Washington: DOD/DOS.
1985   *The Soviet-Cuban Connection in Central America and the Caribbean*. Washington: DOD/DOS.

DOS (U.S. Department of State)
1986   *Inside the Sandinista Regime: A Special Investigator's Report*. Washington: DOS.
1985   "Economic and Military Assistance to Central America 1980-1985." Washington: DOS, mimeographed.

Edelman, Marc
1986   "Soviet-Cuban Involvement in Central America: A Critique of Recent Writings," *Social Text* (New York) 5(3) (Fall):99-125.

English, Adrian
1984a   *Armed Forces of Latin America*. London: Jane's Publishing Company.
1984b   "Nicaragua Treads Path Between East and West," *Jane's Defence Weekly*, April 21:610-611.

Fagen, Richard R., Carmen Diana Deere, and José Luis Coraggio
1986   "Introduction," in *Transition and Development: Problems of Third World Socialism*. New York: Monthly Review Press.

Fonseca Amador, Carlos
1984 (1970)   "Los ataques de los falsos revolucionarios de Costa Rica nos honran," *COPAN Revista Teórica* (San José) 2-3:95-106.
1982a   *Obras. Tomo 1: Bajo la bandera del sandinismo*. Managua: Nueva Nicaragua.
1982b   *Obras. Tomo 2: Viva Sandino*. Managua: Nueva Nicaragua.
1980 (1958)   *Un nicaragüense en Moscú*. Managua: Secretaría Nacional de Propaganda y Educación Política del FSLN.
1971   "General'nomu sekretariu TsK . . . ," *Pravda* (Moscow), April 14:4.

FSLN (Frente Sandinista de Liberación Nacional)
1979   *Iremos hacia el sol de la libertad . . . Sandino*. Managua: FSLN.

Gilbert, Dennis
1986   "Nicaragua," in Morris J. Blachman, William M. LeoGrande and

Kenneth Sharpe, eds., *Confronting Revolution: Security Through Diplomacy in Central America.* New York: Pantheon.

Goldblat, Jozef and Víctor Millán
1984   "The Honduras-Nicaragua Conflict and Prospects for Arms Control," in *SIPRI Yearbook 1984.* London: Taylor & Francis.

Gwertzman, Bernard
1986   "U.S. Set to Offer Newer Jet Fighter to the Hondurans," The *New York Times*, October 31:A1, A6.

Hernández Sancho, Plutarco
1982   *El FSLN por dentro. Relatos de un combatiente.* San José: Trejos Hermanos.

House of Representatives, Appropriations Subcommittee on the DOD
1985   *Hearings Before a Subcommittee of the Committee on Appropriations (Part 2).* Washington: U.S. Government Printing Office.

Ignatius, David and David Rogers
1985   "Aiding the *Contras*: Why Covert War in Nicaragua Evolved and Why the Program Hasn't Succeeded," *The Wall Street Journal* (New York), March 5.

Inforpress Centroamericana
1986   "Nicaragua: La 'contra,' un ejercito millonario," *Inforpress Centroamericana* (Guatemala), September 4:5.

Iklé, Fred C.
1986   "The President's Central America Policy: What is the Alternative?" Washington: DOD News Release, May 29.

Jacobsen, Carl G.
1984   *Soviet Attitudes Towards, Aid to, and Contacts with Central American Revolutionaries.* Washington: Department of State.

Kinzer, Stephen
1986   "Nicaragua Assails U.S. Plan on Jets," The *New York Times*, October 31:A6.
1985   "Nicaragua's Edge in the Arms Race," The *New York Times*, October 27:E2.

Krause, Charles A.
1979   "Somoza Still Revered in Key Area of Nicaragua," The *Washington Post*, August 15.

Krauss, Clifford and Robert S. Greenberger
1985   "Despite Fears of U.S., Soviet Aid to Nicaragua Appears to Be Limited," *The Wall Street Journal*, April 3.

LATIN (Buenos Aires News Agency)
1979   "Government Protests to U.S., Adopts Trade Measures," in *FBIS-LAM* August 3:P7.

Latin America Regional Report—Mexico and Central America
1985a   "Soviet Expert Challenges White Paper," *Latin America Regional Report—Mexico and Central America* (London), March 22:5.

1985b   "Rushed Job on U.S. Nicaragua Paper: Sketchy Justification of 'Threat' Thesis," *Latin America Regional Report—Mexico and Central America*, May 3:4.

Latin American Weekly Report
1986   "Nicaragua: Soviets Hedge on Level of Support," *Latin American Weekly Report* (London), October 16:2.

LeoGrande, William M.
1986   "Cuba," in Morris J. Blachman, William M. LeoGrande, and Kenneth Sharpe, eds., *Confronting Revolution: Security Through Diplomacy in Central America*. New York: Pantheon.
1985   "The United States and Nicaragua," in Thomas W. Walker, ed., *Nicaragua: The First Five Years*. New York: Praeger.
1983   "Cuba and Nicaragua: From the Somozas to the Sandinistas," in Barry B. Levine, ed., *The New Cuban Presence in the Caribbean*. Boulder: Westview.

Leonov, Nikolai Sergeevich
1975   *Ocherki novoi i noveishei istorii stran Tsentral'noi Ameriki*. Moscow: Mysl'.
1972   *Osnovnye problemy politicheskoi istorii Tsentral'no-amerikanskikh stran (1821-1954 gg.)* (avtoreforat, Doctor of Historical Sciences dissertation). Moscow: Institute of Latin America.

Leshchiner, Roal'd Efimovich
1965   *Nikaragua*. Moscow: Mysl'.

Los Angeles Times
1980   "Rebels Seized, Nicaragua Says," *The Los Angeles Times*, June 29.
1979   "20 Sandinista Militiamen Reported Slain in Capital," *The Los Angeles Times*, October 6.

Matthews, Robert
1985   "The Limits of Friendship: Nicaragua and the West," *Report on the Americas* 19(3) (May-June):22-32.

Merin, Boris M.
1973   *Tsentral'naia Amerika. Problemy sotsial'no-politicheskogo razvitiia*. Moscow: Nauka.

Morganthau, Tom et al.
1986   "Rekindling the Magic: Reagan Wins a Congressional Victory to Aid the *Contras*," *Newsweek*, July 7:20-21.

National Bipartisan Commission on Central America
1984   *Report of the National Bipartisan Commission on Central America*. Washington: U.S. Government Printing Office.

New York Times
1986   "U.S., in U.N., Defends Aid to Anti-Sandinistas," The *New York Times*, July 3:A9.

Ortega Saavedra, Humberto
1980   *50 años de lucha sandinista*. Havana: Editorial de las Ciencias Sociales.

Pérez Bermúdez, Carlos and Onofre Guevara López
1980   *El movimiento obrero en Nicaragua* (6 volumes). Managua: Ediciones Dávila Bolaños.

"Porras, Pedro" (pseudonym)
1970   "Columna subversiva: la culata de la carabina de ambrosio," *Libertad* (San José), March 21.

Randall, Margaret
1980   *Todas estamos despiertas: testimonios de la mujer nicaragüense hoy.* Mexico: Siglo XXI.

Sánchez Sancho, Luis
1976   "Beseda s Pervym sekretarem TsK Nikaraguanskoi sotsialis-ticheskoi partii Luisom Sanchesom Sancho," *Latinskaia Amerika* (Moscow) 4 (July-August):98-112.

Schoultz, Lars
1984   "Nicaragua: The United States Confronts a Revolution," in Richard Newfarmer, ed., *From Gunboats to Diplomacy: New U.S. Policies for Latin America.* Baltimore: Johns Hopkins University Press.

Schwab, Theodore and Harold Sims
1985   "Relations with Communist States," in Thomas W. Walker, ed., *Nicaragua: The First Five Years.* New York: Praeger.

Semenov, S. I., M. F. Kudachkin, B. L. Koval', and B. T. Rudenko
1976   *Kommunisticheskie partii Latinskoi Ameriki v bor'be za edinstvo antiimperialisticheskikh sil.* Moscow: Mysl'.

Serbin, A.
1979   "Luis prodolzhaet bor'bu," *Pravda*, January 8:4.

Sims, Harold D.
1984   "Revolutionary Nicaragua: Dilemmas Confronting Sandinistas and North Americans," in Alan Adelman and Reid Reading, eds., *Confrontation in the Caribbean Basin.* Pittsburgh: University of Pittsburgh Center for Latin American Studies.

Singer, Max
1984   *Nicaragua: The Stolen Revolution.* Washington: U.S. Information Agency.

Sizonenko, Aleksandr Ivanovich
1971   *Ocherki istorii sovetsko-latinoamerikanskikh otnoshenii (1924-1970 gg.)* Moscow: Nauka.

U.S. Army
1980   "Projection of Power in Latin America by the Soviet Union and Cuba." Gainesville, Fla.: 467th Military Intelligence Detachment.

Valenta, Jiri and Virginia Valenta
1985   "Sandinistas in Power," *Problems of Communism* (Washington) 34(5) (September-October):1-28.

Vesenskii, V.
1978   "Khorkhe Martines: 'My vyshli iz boev okrepshimi,'" *Komsomol'skaia Pravda* (Moscow), October 18:3.

18

Soviet Interests in Latin America: New Opportunities and Old Constraints

W. Raymond Duncan

The October 1983 crisis in Grenada left little doubt that the Soviet and Cuban presence had been expanding in the Caribbean Basin. But the October crisis did not answer questions regarding the extent of their actual influence there, nor the direction it might take in the future, nor even what the most appropriate U.S. policy responses should be to that influence elsewhere in the region. Therefore, in the wake of the U.S. occupation of Grenada and the evidence it uncovered about the degree of Soviet and Cuban activity there, it is useful to examine the kind of situations that have encouraged the Soviets to expand their presence and/or influence in Latin America. At the same time, it equally is useful to examine the limitations or constraints on such an expanded presence or influence.

Clearly, Soviet policy in Latin America has been the product of two conflicting forces or tendencies. The first has been the obvious Soviet tendency to seize every opportunity to project its power in the region as it presented itself. Most notably, these opportunities emerged in the late 1970s when major power shifts, some violent, took place, such as the Grenadian revolution of March 1979, followed shortly by Nicaragua's *Sandinista* victory in July of the same year. The second force, equally compelling, consists of those factors that either inhibit these Soviet efforts or prevent them from capitalizing on them more fully. These include on the internal side the economic problems of both the U.S.S.R. and Cuba; and on the regional side the dynamics of Latin America's nationalism as well as its notorious political factionalism. Both forces must be appraised in order to view the Soviet penetration of the region, if such it is, in perspective.

The Soviets seek to exploit opportunities in Latin America through a variety of techniques, particularly that of using Cuban backing. To ignore the scale of these activities and their implication for U.S. security would be to

From *Journal of Inter-American Studies and World Affairs* v. 26 n. 2, May 1984, pp. 163-198. Copyright © 1984 by the University of Miami. Reprinted by permission.

disregard the very nature of contemporary power politics. This essay will examine this area of Soviet opportunism through a review of some recent key events, which began in 1979: (1) the revolutionary change in Grenada, which led to (2) Grenada's domestic coup and the U.S. intervention; (3) the revolutionary conflict in Central America, most notably in (4) Nicaragua; and (5) the Falklands/Malvinas crisis of 1982.

However, it would be erroneous to assume that opportunism alone or even an expanded Soviet presence translates automatically into increased influence. By "influence" is meant the degree to which the Soviet Union can alter the behavior of another country to benefit its own interests. Admittedly, we face enormous obstacles when we try to determine the precise degree of "influence" being wielded, insofar as we cannot "get inside" the minds of decision-makers. It is well to be reminded, though, that just because the Soviet Union may exercise some presence in a country, it does not ipso facto control that country's domestic and foreign policies.

As the United States has found in its foreign policy, the Soviets also found constraints in projecting their power into the Third World. They are bogged down in Afghanistan, are plagued by difficulties in the Middle East, are not always in harmony with their Vietnamese clients, and experience their share of pressure from southern developing countries in the North/South debate. Therefore, this essay also will undertake to examine some of the obstacles faced by the Soviet Union as they pursue an expanded relationship with the Latin American countries, such as (1) the Soviet and Cuban economic weaknesses, which work to undermine their economic aid programs; (2) Latin American nationalism; (3) the nature of Cuba's often strained relationships with Latin American and Caribbean nations; (4) the regional opposition that has developed toward Nicaragua; and (5) the restrictions that the Soviets have placed on their military commitments to both Cuba and Nicaragua.

Both of these conflicting forces that have affected Soviet policy in Latin America had their origin in the post-World War period. The Cuban revolution in particular, which created a breathtaking opportunity for Moscow to exercise new leverage in Latin America, was only one, if the most dramatic, example of the kind of pressure for change that characterized Latin America, a pressure that was finding new expression in Central America as the decade of the seventies came to a close. Not all new developments in the region necessarily were conducive to Soviet and Cuban inroads, however, even as they contributed to the undermining of the long-standing U.S. influence. A glance at this period is instructive.

DEVELOPMENT OF SOVIET INTERESTS IN LATIN AMERICA

In one sense at least Latin America fell into the Soviet lap. Prior to the Cuban revolution of January 1959, Nikita S. Khrushchev had focused his attention on the newly independent, excolonial countries of Asia and Africa.[1] However, Fidel Castro's unexpected, independent shift to Marxism-Leninism in December 1961 injected a new optimism in Soviet thinking about the future of anti-imperialist struggles through national liberation movements, extending it into the Latin American arena, where the Soviets previously had had few successes (Clissold, 1970a, 1970b; Ratliff, 1976; Levesque, 1978; González, 1974).

The Soviet-Cuban affair matured against a background of change in the rest of Latin America that created conditions favorable to an increased Soviet presence there. Foremost among these forces was the drive for economic development, which evolved out of the region's rapid urbanization, population explosion and the food shortages accompanying it, an increased skewing of income, and worsening of the ever-present unemployment. By 1973 when OPEC (Organization of Petroleum Exporting Countries) sharply increased the price of oil, all of the above problems were aggravated. The drive for economic development was accompanied by openness to political experimentation: to wit, Mexico's mixture of capitalism and socialism in the postwar period; Cuba's above-mentioned revolution; military reformism in Brazil (1964) and Peru (1968); Chile's socialist experiment (1970-1973); a leftist socialism in Guyana (1970 onward) and Jamaica (1972-1980).

The new economic growth models thus engendered opened the door for Soviet involvement, particularly in the area of trade. Soviet commerce with Latin America excluding Cuba increased from $124 million in 1970 to $4.9 billion in 1981 (Zinoviev, 1983: 6). By 1981 the U.S.S.R. was exporting approximately $178 million worth of merchandise and importing about $5.2 billion in Latin American products. Again excluding Cuba, the Soviets maintain commercial relations with at least 25 Latin American and Caribbean countries. Of these, just nine countries (Argentina, Bolivia, Brazil, Mexico, Colombia, Nicaragua, Peru, Panama, and Uruguay) account for 90% of the total Soviet-Latin American commerce. Among the nine, Argentina emerged as the Soviets' principal Latin American trading partner: In 1981 the Soviets purchased 77% of all agricultural commodities exported abroad by Argentina (principally wheat, corn, and meat), and was the single largest consumer of its red meat (Andrés López, 1983: 59).

---

[1] Castro's 26 of July Movement, first defeated in its ill-fated assault on the Moncada Army barracks in July 1953 and returned to Cuba as a guerrilla movement in December 1956, by no means enjoyed active Soviet backing, much less Soviet attempts to influence it. Nor did it receive support from the Cuban communists through the Popular Socialist Party (PSP). Initially the Soviets viewed Castro as unlikely to succeed, since they believed that sooner or later he would either be snuffed out by the United States or else accommodate to the imperialists. As late as November 1958 Khrushchev observed, in an interview, that everybody remembered the fate of Guatemala, and even though the Cubans were heroic in their struggle, it was an unequal affair (Dinerstein, 1976: 35).

The overall impact of these different forms of economic/political nationalism simultaneously witnessed a precipitous decline in the Western Hemisphere Community idea, which had assumed a mutuality of interests between North and South America. Increasingly the Latin American countries saw themselves as part of the North/South development struggle, and joined in a variety of international governmental organizations (IGOs) to exert pressure on the United States to recognize their economic demands: through the Non-aligned Movement, the United Nations Economic Commission for Latin America (ECLA), the United Nations Conference on Trade and Development (UNCTAD), and the New International Economic Order (NIEO). The Latin American countries began to define their foreign policy goals differently from the United States, as the former were more and more oriented toward North/South development priorities, while the latter continues to cling to an East/West political-ideological competition.

All of these transformations combined to present opportunities for the Soviet Union to insinuate its presence and gain influence wherever possible, hopefully at the expense of the United States. Adapting its foreign policy to the new realities, Moscow concentrated on five main types of activity: (1) to pursue any opportunity that promised to weaken the United States, short of provoking direct confrontation; (2) to establish bases for its ships, including its blue water navy as well as those engaged in intelligence-collecting, commercial fishing, and merchant marine activities as a projection of its power in the region; (3) to gain access to strategic raw materials and food; (4) to expand diplomatic, commercial, and trade relations whenever possible; and (5) to promote Marxist-Leninist models of economic and political change, hopefully communist-party-led, in as risk-free a manner as possible (i.e., with minimum financing and, again, short of provoking U.S. intervention).

Cuba has played a pivotal role in the calculation of these activities. Its geopolitical location in the "strategic rear" of the United States, to use Soviet terminology (Vasilyev, 1971: 43; Gouré and Rothenberg, 1975: 5-6), and its leftist leadership have enabled Cuba to play a key role for the U.S.S.R. as a major Latin American anti-imperialist spokesman, advocate of pro-Soviet positions, supporter of socialist models, and ally of national liberation movements. The importance of Cuba to the Soviets can be traced through their trade with one another: from a low of about $4.7 million in 1959 to about $7.4 billion in 1981, approximately 70% of Cuba's total commerce (Zinoviev, 1983:5). By 1982 Soviet aid to Cuba totalled $4.9 billion per year or an estimated $13 million per day, much of which is due to special pricing arrangements for Cuban sugar and Russian petroleum.

However, to suggest that Soviet objectives in Latin America end with the pursuit of hard currency, markets, natural resources and port facilities underestimates the full range of their policy objectives. Moscow also seeks to influence domestic internal events where possible, and to move them in directions favorable to Marxist-Leninist prescriptions for change, that is, through support of local communist parties, broad united fronts against capitalism/imperialism, scholarships for study in the U.S.S.R., trade fairs, and cultural exchange. While in the short run the Soviet Union follows a realistic-pragmatic course of projecting its presence where possible in ways that benefit its state interest, in the longer run it pursues ideological goals whenever conditions permit.

NEW OPPORTUNITIES IN THE LATE 1970S

Latin America's continuing pressures for change began to assume revolutionary proportions by the late 1970s, particularly in the Caribbean Basin countries, even escalating into armed conflict. Ever resourceful, the Soviet Union quickly perceived these developments as opportunities with the potential to advance their interests there, and moved to insert or to increase its presence either directly or through its Cuban ally.

Revolutionary Change in Grenada

Shortly after Maurice Bishop, head of the revolutionary New Jewel Movement, assumed control of the new government in Grenada in March 1979, it became apparent that its foreign policy was set on an increasingly pro-Soviet and pro-Cuban course. Soon after taking office Bishop found himself visiting Cuba to attend the Sixth Nonaligned Countries Conference as well as the Second Congress of the Communist Party of Cuba (*Granma*, 1979). In January 1980 Grenada distinguished itself by becoming the only Latin American or Caribbean country to vote with Cuba against the United Nations resolution deploring the Soviet intervention in Afghanistan (Duncan, 1982: 103). Later the same year approximately a hundred Cuban military advisors arrived in Grenada to assist in training a 2000-person army (Duncan, 1982: 103-104). It was the intention of the Bishop government to disband completely the old Grenadian army in order to build a new one based on "the people," comprised largely of unemployed youth. This new people's army was patterned after Cuba's Territorial Militia, a group organized in response to the Reagan presidency, which was perceived as a security threat by the Cubans, and the Grenadians. Bishop urged strengthening the militia as a way for Grenadians to increase their consciousness, training, and discipline to protect both their homeland and the "revolution."

Grenada looked to Cuba for assistance in other areas as well: Cubans donated fishing boats to Grenada, cooperated in agroindustries, constructed a new radio station, helped to develop a transportation network, and maintained and developed the island's electricity network (*Intercontinental Press*, 1982a). In 1981 Cuba sent 300-400 construction workers (whom they paid themselves)

to aid in the construction of a new international airport, an installation perceived by the United States as offering potential strategic significance to both
the Cubans and the Soviet Union (International Press [sic], 1982b: 2).

Not all assistance came only from Cuba, however; much came directly
from the Soviet Union, mostly in the form of aid and trade agreements, as
well as from Soviet Bloc countries. A trip by Bishop to Bulgaria, East Germany, and Libya in 1982 netted a $14 million line of credit from East Ger-
many to purchase agricultural equipment, help from Bulgaria to buy ice-mak-
ing machinery, and a $4 million interest-free loan from Libya (FBIS, 1982b).
Another trip by Bishop to the U.S.S.R. later in 1982 produced a $7.7 million
line of credit, repayable over ten years at 3% interest with provision for a grace
period in repayment, to finance construction of a satellite earth station, to
undertake feasibility studies for an east coast port, and to purchase equipment
for an improved water supply and sewage disposal system (FBIS, 1982a).
Moscow also agreed to give Grenada a gift of $1.4 million to cover purchase
of a spray plane for agricultural purposes, to provide 400 tons of flour,
clothing, and steel, and to purchase quantities of Grenadian cocoa and nutmeg
over a five-year period (FBIS, 1982a.).

Following its invasion and occupation of Grenada, the United States dis-
closed in November 1983 that it had discovered evidence that five secret military cooperation agreements had been concluded by the former Bishop government with Cuba, North Korea, and the Soviet Union. The agreements would
have provided $37 million in additional military equipment to Grenada, plus a
permanent delegation of 27 Cuban military advisors. The Soviets planned to
ship $27 million in military equipment,   North Korea $12 million in
supplies, and the Cubans would have provided training for the armed forces
(New York Times, 1983b).

In the Grenadian situation then, both the Soviet Union and Cuba utilized
the political change as an opportunity to insert their presence through trade,
aid, and advisors, and with it their influence.

Crisis in Grenada and U.S. Intervention

In September 1983 the relatively peaceful change in Grenada began to take on
more ominous overtones. By that time a power struggle, dating back to an
October 1982 Central Committee Meeting of the New Jewel Movement, had
erupted between Prime Minister Bishop and his Deputy Prime Minister
Bernard Coard (New York Times, 1983c, 1983g). Coard was known to be
more of a hardline Marxist than Bishop, apparently enjoying even closer relations with Fidel Castro and the Cubans than Bishop. It has been conjectured
that the two men differed over the degree and speed of the revolution. In late
September Bishop embarked on a trip abroad, which took him to Czechoslovakia and Cuba, and from which he did not return until October 8. On his

return the disagreement flared again, and on October 13th Bishop was placed under house arrest by fellow members of the Central Committee of the New Jewel Movement (*New York Times*, 1983g).

During Bishop's confinement Bernard Coard emerged as the new leader. This position was of short duration, since a crowd formed and released Bishop on October 19th, escorting him to Fort Rupert where he confronted the recalcitrant members of his Central Committee. The consequence of this meeting was that Bishop, three ranking members of the government, and two labor leaders subsequently were shot (*New York Times*, 1983g). General Hudson Austin was announced as the new leader and head of a new Military Council, whose first act was to impose a 24-hour "shoot on sight" curfew.

This sequence of events shocked and startled the world at large. Neighboring prime ministers (Tom Adams of Barbados, Edward Seaga of Jamaica, and Eugenia Charles of Dominica) announced their intentions not to participate in regional meetings with the new Military Council. The United States, with no embassy in Grenada, had little accurate, up-to-date information, although the brief surfacing of Bernard Coard as a leader did not presage well for future U.S.-Grenadian relations. The presence of U.S. medical students on the island and the perceived threat to their welfare in the light of the unstable and unpredictable turn of events provided the impetus for the U.S. occupation of Grenada on October 25 by 1900 U.S. Marines (*New York Times*, 1983k).

In addition to the trade and aid agreements already discussed, what was the extent of the Soviet and Cuban presence uncovered by the U.S. occupation? During the crisis, the Cuban government stated that 784 Cubans were on the island, of whom 43 were members of the armed forces: 22 army officers and the rest translators and support personnel (*New York Times*, 1983e). In addition to the 43 members of the armed forces, Havana said there were 636 construction workers, while the remainder were advisors in the fields of public health, education, fishing, transport, trade, culture, and communication. At the time of the anti-Bishop coup, the United States estimated there were 49 Soviet personnel on the island (*New York Times*, 1983g). This figure was considerably lower than that estimated by the United States during the first heated days of the occupation when the Marines captured some 600 Cubans, but continued to receive sniper fire from others.

To what extent were the Cubans or the Soviets actively involved in the coup itself? It should be noted that Cuba was not a likely participant in the coup against Bishop. The Cuban government, long a Bishop ally, denounced his overthrow in no uncertain terms:

> No doctrine, no principle or proclaimed revolutionary position and no internal division justifies atrocious actions such as the physical elimination of Bishop and the outstanding group of honest and worthy leaders who died yesterday (*New York Times*, 1983i).

At a meeting of the Cuban politburo there were even those who argued strongly that Cuba should break diplomatic relations with Grenada (*New York Times*, 1983i). These statements suggest that far from playing a direct role in Bishop's demise, the Cubans *condemned* it (*Christian Science Monitor*, 1983d). However, once the U.S. action was underway, both Havana and the new Grenadian government undertook a series of efforts to forestall it through diplomatic channels (*New York Times*, 1983g).

On the other hand, the picture involving the Soviet Union is less clear. A flurry of activity occurred between the Soviet embassy and Bishop's radical opponents in the days before the coup (*Christian Science Monitor*, 1983c). A trip to the Soviet Union by Bishop's opponent was called off three weeks before the coup, indicating that the Soviets may have known what was happening to Prime Minister Bishop (Madrid Radio Broadcast, 1983). Although the official Soviet media clearly denounced the United States over Grenada, its formal position was made at a relatively low level (*New York Times*, 1983d, 1983j). The Cubans, meanwhile, denounced his overthrow (*New York Times*, 1983j, 1983k). While Bishop was considered a "friend" of the U.S.S.R., it is known that a majority of Soviet leaders did not have great confidence in him, even though they publicly defended his policy (*Christian Science Monitor*, 1983d). If indeed the Soviets did have prior knowledge of the coup or were involved even indirectly, the case for U.S. intervention then becomes stronger from a power politics perspective.

The question remains: To what extent did the U.S. landing in Grenada help or hinder Soviet and Cuban long-range influence in Latin America? The evidence probably will not be in for quite a while.

In the short run it would appear that the Soviets and Cubans may have gained not so much from an increase in their influence as from the damage inflicted on the credibility of the United States by the immediate and widespread criticism the intervention provoked. Thus it can be argued that even though the Soviet/Cuban alliance lost an important client state, they may yet benefit from the loss of U.S. prestige in the region and even in the world.

What was the nature of this negative reaction? First, immediately following the invasion, the U.N. Security Council passed a resolution that "deeply deplored" the intervention as a "flagrant violation of international law" (*New York Times*, 1983h). The vote was 11 in favor of the resolution, with the United States itself casting the only dissenting vote. Some nations abstained (Great Britain, Togo, and Zaire), while some of our usual allies (France, Netherlands, and Pakistan) voted against the United States and for the resolution (*Washington Post*, 1983a).

Second, some of our NATO (North Atlantic Treaty Organization) allies (Great Britain, France, and West Germany) sharply challenged U.S. wisdom in taking this step, in part because they neither were notified nor consulted. Decreasing confidence from this corner may portend future problems for the U.S. with western Europe.

Third, at least fifteen members of the OAS (Organization of American States) condemned the invasion of Grenada as a violation both of international law and of the principle of nonintervention in the domestic affairs of member states. Mexico and Venezuela, leaders of the Contadora Group that had been seeking negotiated settlements to the region's turmoil, were especially critical. Rafael de la Colina, Mexico's ambassador to the United States, stated that the invasion would leave "deep and persistent wounds," while Venezuela increased its vigilance along its shore (90 miles from Grenada), and Colombia compared the occupation to the Japanese attack on Pearl Harbor (*Washington Post,* 1983a).

Fourth, while the United States claimed that its invasion of Grenada was at the request of the OECS (Organization of Eastern Caribbean States), the legitimacy of this claim was called into question. The United States had characterized the request as a "regional collective security measure," which would have justified its action by qualifying it as an exception to the U.N. nonintervention provisions. However, the OECS treaty had not been registered formally with the United Nations (*New York Times,* 1983d). Neither is the United States a party to the OECS, which deals with arrangements for "collective security against external aggression" and requires that all decisions must be "unanimous." It is also questionable whether or not the situation in Grenada can be characterized properly as one of "external aggression" in the case of the coup; nor can the decision be considered to be a unanimous one, since three of the organization's members (Grenada, St. Kitts-Nevis, and Montserrat) did not vote, and three of the members who participated in the operations (United States, Barbados, and Jamaica) are not members at all.

Ameliorating this tide of criticism and dissent are a few ripples that indicate that the opposing ranks are not as solid as first appeared. After all, seven members of the OECS did demonstrate deep concern about the overthrow of Bishop, and the overall involvement of the Soviet Union and Cuba in the region. Suriname is reported to have ordered more than 100 Cubans to leave the country in late October (*New York Times,* 1983k). Jamaica soon followed by expelling four Soviet diplomats and a Cuban journalist for allegedly spying and conspiring to kill a Foreign Ministry official (*New York Times,* 1983d).

Negative reactions from the United Nations and the Organization of American States may also merit a second look. The U.N. rebuke could be interpreted as much as a diplomatic slap on the wrist as an indication of deeply felt opposition. Many Third World countries who condemn both the Soviet occupation of Afghanistan and the Soviet-backed Vietnamese occupation of Cambodia feel that consistency demands that they also deplore the U.S. invasion of Grenada (*Christian Science Monitor,* 1983a). In Latin America a number of national leaders who publicly condemned the invasion confessed *privately* that they felt the crisis conditions obtaining in Grenada provided justification for the U.S. action, since refraining from action might have created an even more disastrous situation (*Christian Science Monitor,* 1983b). Five Latin

American countries (Chile, Uruguay, Guatemala, Honduras, and El Salvador) supported the occupation, and four Central American countries (Panama, Guatemala, El Salvador, and Honduras) who make up CONDECA (Central American Defense Council) began to investigate the legality of a joint military action against Nicaragua . . . that could set in motion a more serious loss of influence for the Soviet Union in the area.

At the very least, however, the United States has sent a very clear message that the limits of its tolerance for Soviet and Cuban involvement in the Caribbean Basin have been reached, a message that may persuade them that further provocation may lead to that direct confrontation both wish to avoid. . . . the invasion could produce more circumspect behavior on their part in the future. At a news conference on October 25, President Castro said that if Nicaragua were to face an invasion similar to that of Grenada, Cuba would be unable to offer assistance in the face of so superior a force (*New York Times*, 1983m). Similarly, Cuba itself can not depend on the Soviet Union to come to their assistance should Cuba be the one invaded.

Revolutionary Conflict in Central America

Toward the end of the 1970s, revolutionary conflict broke out in Central America, thereby providing new opportunities to the Soviets to expand influence and/or presence. The *Sandinista* victory in Nicaragua in 1979 brought to power a new radical, national, Marxist-oriented regime, characterized by close ties to Moscow's client state in the Caribbean, Cuba. The success of the Sandinistas served also to encourage a similar effort by leftist guerrillas in neighboring El Salvador, eagerly assisted by Cuba.

This Cuban assistance was underwritten to a large extent by the substantial economic and military aid it was receiving from the Soviet Union. In 1981 the Castro government received about $3.6 billion in aid from the Soviets and the Eastern European countries, which was increased to $4.9 billion in 1982, largely through the mechanism of preferential pricing of Cuban sugar and the artificially low price Cuba pays for Soviet oil (Theriot, 1982). In 1982 the Soviets provided Cuba with 62,000 tons of military equipment, the largest amount sent since the Cuban missile crisis of October 1962. Thus by 1982 Cuba had the largest, best-equipped armed forces in Latin America except for Brazil (*Strategic Survey*, 1983).

Not only does the Soviet Union funnel military aid to the revolutionary forces via Cuba, but uses more direct tactics in other areas where it seems feasible to do so. For example, Moscow uses its news media to stress the more negative aspects of the government in Guatemala: to publicize cases of large-scale killing and/or disappearances of moderate and radical political leaders, of its treatment of the Indian communities, and any other examples of its egregious behavior (Leonov, 1982). In El Salvador they have acted in a variety of ways to strengthen the local Communist Party in its alliance with the revolutionary forces opposing the military-backed government (Leiken, 1982). At the same time, the Soviets readily grant publicized interviews with members of El Salvador's guerrilla forces (*América Latina*, 1983: 24-32).

The Central American conflicts, with their overtones of sympathy for the left, have produced guarded optimism in Soviet decision-making circles vis-à-vis the potential for Third World evolution toward socialism through the mechanism of armed struggle led by guerrilla armies (Leiken, 1982). This of course was the position advocated in Cuba in the 1960s, later subordinated to a Soviet policy that emphasized peaceful, parliamentary change and broad united fronts as the most realistic means of shifting the "correlation of forces" toward socialism, stimulated by the Chilean and, one might add, the Portuguese experiences. In other areas of the world the Soviets had been willing to support direct action, backing coups, assassinations, and guerrilla movements, upgrading military assistance, and so on, but not in Latin America, where peaceful change and state-to-state relations were identified as the way to go.

The Central American successes have been the source of some policy reformulation. Unlike earlier statements, the Soviets began to refer to "armed struggle" as "most promising in the specific conditions of most of the Latin American countries" (Leonov, 1982b: 37; Smirnova, 1982). After Nicaragua, the old Cuban position and Che Guevara's emphasis on the violent road was resurrected. This in turn led to adoption of this revised Soviet line by the communist parties in Central America, from an emphasis on peaceful change and broad united fronts spear-headed by communist parties to a new emphasis on "political-military fronts" and the designation of Central America as an arena where "socialist states" are emerging (Castro, 1981: 68; Wyanovsky, 1979: 119; Leiken, 1982: 36-43). It should be noted that this was not the only policy line pursued; united fronts were still advocated in such countries as Argentina, Brazil, and Mexico, where the prospects of successful armed struggle were less positive (Mikoyan, 1980: 101).

The significant point to be made, however, is the specific linking of Cuban and Soviet support of armed struggle with a theoretical underpinning, both legitimizing, and implying a predisposition toward external support of guerrilla movements.

Nicaragua

Of the various opportunities for Soviet expansion in the region, one of the newest and most visible is that in Nicaragua. Following victory of that country's revolutionary forces in 1979, it soon became apparent that a number of the new leaders were committed Marxist-Leninists who could be expected to be receptive to strengthening that aspect of the revolution. As Nicaragua's relations with the United States began to deteriorate and its security vis-à-vis the

United States (and Honduras) eroded, Moscow with Havana sought to fill the emerging vacuum.

Toward this end Moscow signed a military agreement with Nicaragua in 1981 that, together with military aid from both Cuba and Eastern Europe, amounted to about $28 million in military equipment (U.S. Department of State, 1981). By March 1982 the U.S. Central Intelligence Agency (CIA) announced it had evidence of a Cuban aid program that included sending 2000 Cuban and 70 Soviet military advisors to Nicaragua (New York Times, 1982a). There also were estimated to be 4000 Cuban civilian advisors there.

By mid-1983 Soviet weapons deliveries to Nicaragua were estimated to total 20,000 tons, double the amounts of 1981 and 1982 (Washington Post, 1983c). The Soviets acknowledge that Managua is engaged in a military build-up, which they describe as a "legitimate" measure for self-defense against alleged American plans to destabilize the Sandinistas (U.S. Department of State, 1983a).

How justified is this view? Beginning with 1982, U.S. actions toward Nicaragua amounted to what some observers described as an "undeclared war" (New York Times, 1983o). As the United States witnessed the entrance of a Soviet/Cuban presence, it transformed its policy from one of implicit support of the legitimate Nicaraguan government to one of covert (and sometimes overt) support of that government's opponents. U.S. activities have included a $19 million covert operation of the CIA in 1982 to train ex-Somocista Nicaraguan National Guardsmen in Honduras and additional support for their anti-Sandinist operations throughout 1982 and into 1983 (New York Times, 1983m). There is also evidence to suggest U.S. support of Argentina advisors for anti-Sandinist groups who work out of Costa Rica as well as support of anti-Sandinista U.S. personnel working within Nicaragua (New York Times, 1983p). Overt U.S. activities have included a combination of aid to the anti-Sandinista military establishment in Honduras, "training exercises" and joint military maneuvers with them, as well as highly visible display of U.S. naval "presence" off both Nicaraguan coasts, Atlantic and Pacific, during late summer 1983.

In some quarters these activities are considered interventionist in violation of the Treaty of the Organization of American States (OAS) and as much a contravention of international law as the Soviet/Cuban activities in El Salvador, so much criticized by the United States.

What other "presence" has the Soviet/Cuban alliance been able to insert in Nicaragua? In 1981 Moscow opened its first diplomatic mission in Nicaragua, initiated Aeroflot service between the two countries, and donated 20,000 tons of wheat after the United States suspended its economic assistance in early 1981 by the outgoing Carter Administration. Bulgaria and East Germany donated an additional 60,000 tons of free grain that, together with the Soviet donation, more than made up for the U.S. cancellation of PL-480 grain deliveries in 1981. The U.S.S.R. also allocated $50 million in 10-year credits for the purchase of agricultural, road-building, and communications equipment, while Czechoslovakia extended $35 million, Bulgaria $20 million, and Hungary $5 million (Managua Radio Broadcast, 1981).

In 1982 Nicaragua began to draw on these credits when it purchased loaders, wagons, perforators, and other mining equipment from the U.S.S.R. (*Foreign Trade*, 1982: 2). In May 1982 Daniel Ortega went to the Soviet Union seeking more aid. While he received an elaborate welcome and some aid, Brezhnev utilized the visit to emphasize the great distance separating their two countries, and Ortega returned home somewhat disappointed with the results (International Press [*sic*], 1982a). The following year, 1983, proved somewhat more successful in that Moscow reportedly pledged another $100 million and the East Europeans $140 million (*El Nuevo Diario*, 1983). However, it must be stressed that the Soviets are distinctly unwilling to add "another Cuba" to their roster of economic dependents (Clement, 1983).

The result of all this is that it raises the question as to the extent of the Soviet/Cuban influence on the Sandinista government, both in terms of that government's willingness to follow the Soviet/Cuban political model as well as its willingness to act as their proxy vis-à-vis El Salvador. According to the thesis of the U.S. government, the Sandinistas are dogmatic Marxist-Leninists backed by the Soviet Union, and committed to promoting both totalitarian rule on the domestic front and revolution elsewhere in Central America (Ullman, 1983). Evidence cited in support of this thesis includes (1) Nicaragua's voting with the Soviet bloc on key issues at the United Nations; (2) the major role played by the Cubans in Nicaragua's armed forces, security, and intelligence networks, and the substantial Cuban presence in nonmilitary sectors of agriculture, health, education, and social services; and (3) the recently established neighborhood Committees of Sandinista Defense (CDS), apparently patterned after Cuba's Committees for the Defense of the Revolution (CDR). Additionally, Humberto Ortega, Nicaragua's Minister of Defense, has spent years in Cuba, and has stated unconditionally that Sandinism and Marxism-Leninism are the same thing (Ullman, 1983: 47). Finally, the United States argues that the guerrillas in El Salvador are allowed to use Nicaraguan territory as a sanctuary of logistical support to their forces within El Salvador, and that the Nicaraguan government supplies them with weapons (Ullman, 1983: 34-41).

Thus far, what have been the benefits of all this to the Soviets? On the practical side, the advantages appear to have been slim. Agreements have been signed that allow the Soviet Union to operate a floating workshop for ship repair off Nicaragua's Pacific coast, to allow them fishing privileges in Nicaraguan waters, and the right to conduct an extensive survey of Nicaraguan fisheries resources (Leiken, 1982: 85-87). While it is possible that the Soviets may seek additional naval bases and facilities there, it is equally possible that such an eventuality may never be realized given the strong Soviet concern to avoid provoking any direct confrontation with the United States (Osgood, 1983: 92).

On the political side the advantages are less defined but perhaps ultimately more valuable. The U.S. "interventionist" activities have provoked considerable alarm and criticism on the part of its normally friendly and sympathetic Latin American neighbors. These activities run directly counter to the efforts of some of these countries, most notably the Contadora Group (consisting of Mexico, Venezuela, Colombia, and Panama) to negotiate a peaceful settlement to the growing tensions. Both the Soviet Union and Cuba have endorsed these efforts, which leaves the United States somewhat alienated diplomatically from its usual allies.

Increased fighting inside Nicaragua in March-April 1983 led the Sandinistas to bring the matter of the U.S.-supported activities of Honduras and the ex-Somocista National Guard before the U.N. Security Council, where the U.S. position (that the Nicaraguan revolution was produced externally) largely was unaccepted. Traditional U.S. allies (Mexico, Venezuela, Colombia, Ecuador) refused to believe the U.S. charges, only to be accused of lying or purveying false information by the U.S. delegate (*New York Times*, 1983o, 1983p, 1983q). This was a new low in inter-American relations.

Thus in the longer run, the Soviet benefits prove more political than substantive, since their expanded presence has provided them with an opportunity to provoke the United States into actions ultimately counterproductive to their intended consequences: to drive a wedge between the United States and its Latin American allies, creating greater credibility for the Soviet/Cuban position rather than weakening their influence in Central America.

The Falklands/Malvinas Crisis (1982)

Although the Falklands/Malvinas dispute is certainly geographically remote from Moscow's essential Third World concerns, the Soviet Union chose to involve itself by extending political and diplomatic support to Argentina. The crisis appears to have offered a number of opportunities to Moscow: (1) It tended to distract international attention from Moscow's own intervention in Afghanistan; (2) it provided the Soviets with a useful propaganda ploy as demonstrating the U.S. lack of reliability as an ally, while (3) demonstrating their own credentials as the "natural ally" of the Third World; (4) it allowed the Soviets to point out the weakness of the inter-American system, once dominated by the United States; and (5) produced a wave of anti-U.S. sentiment in Latin America of potentially exploitable proportions (Pravda, 1983b; Moscow Television Broadcast, 1982; *Izvestia*, 1982; Moscow Radio Broadcast, 1982; Child, 1983).

The immediate practical fallout was an even further increase in already healthy Soviet-Argentine trade relations. By the end of 1982 the Soviet Union was Argentina's chief trading partner, accounting for 40% of her total exports and 70% of meat-grain exports alone. Argentina also sells tung oil to the Soviets, and has been negotiating for the establishment of binational fishing companies with processing plants on the Patagonian coast. In return, the Soviets sell railway and oil producing equipment to the Argentines, plus turbines for hydroelectric projects (*Financial Times*, 1983:4). In April 1983 Aeroflot service was inaugurated between the two countries.

Cuba also was able to utilize the crisis to both practical as well as political advantage. In the wake of the April 1982 hostilities, Castro used his leadership position with the Nonaligned Movement to call a conference in June 1982, an occasion he used to assail the British action in hopes of achieving condemnation of British "aggression," a move eventually undermined through the efforts of Jamaica. However, one consequence was Havana's successful negotiation of a $100 million trade agreement with Argentina, who also offered to send 7000 tons of wheat to help Nicaragua overcome food shortages suffered as a result of their May 1982 flooding (*New York Times*, 1982b; *New York Times*, 1982c; Havana Radio Broadcast, 1982). However, Havana was not able to parlay the same magic into much-needed trade relations with Brazil.

CONSTRAINTS ON SOVIET POWER PROJECTION

Clearly, Moscow is not the prime source of instability in Central America. To argue that the Soviets engineer the region's turmoil simply implies far more control over internal events than is the case. In fact the Soviet Union faces great limitations in projecting influence in Latin America, and its general presence in this region should not be equated with automatic control over internal decision-making. The constraints on Soviet influence merit a book in themselves, but the major outlines of obstacles to Soviet power in Latin America can be identified in broad brush-strokes.

Soviet and Cuban Economic Weakness

Neither the Soviet Union nor Cuba is capable of extending the quantities and quality of capital, technology, and trade required by the Latin American countries to meet their development needs. The Soviets and Cubans of course can extend military aid, as illustrated earlier, to regimes in need of increased defense capabilities (as in the case of Soviet increased military supplies to Cuba and Nicaragua). But extensive economic aid, trade, and developmental assistance is simply impossible for either Moscow or Havana to provide.

The Soviet Union and Eastern Europe are noted for their low level of economic aid to noncommunist developing countries. They do extend economic credits at low interest rates, but even much of this aid is not drawn due to the low quality of equipment that translates into low demand. During 1981 the Soviet Union's economic aid program fell to its lowest level in the past four years: only $450 million total in new credits extended to a few small recipients in the Third World, one of which was Nicaragua. These credits were designed primarily to promote the sale of Soviet equipment and are less concessionary than traditional development aid that provides 12-year payments at 2.5-3% interest (U.S. Department of State, 1983).

Other limits to Soviet economic assistance can be identified: They do not participate in North-South discussions; they often are absent from important international economic meetings, for example, the Cancún Summit in October 1981; and their (and East European) aid is tied to purchases from the donor (Theriot, 1982; *Latin American Weekly Report,* 1983a). Current Soviet and East European concentration on direct aid to communist countries is not likely to be reversed, although this policy may increase strains on the Soviet Union in the future. Moscow pays an artificially high price for Cuban sugar, while Cuba pays low prices for Soviet oil. The result is a loss of hard currency in terms of what the Soviets might have earned by refraining from such prejudicial trade practices.

In assessing the overall limit to Soviet influence in Latin America, a simple but major point needs to be made: The Soviets are constrained greatly in how far they are willing to go in supporting revolutionary regimes in Latin America in both economic and military terms. In light of their past economic aid record (Chile under Marxist-Leninist president Salvador Allende; Nicaragua to date), the Soviets are quite unprepared to engage in "another Cuba." They cannot afford it, and the record of economic and political "pay-offs" for them in terms of past aid recipients has been marginal at best.

As if to underscore this point, Andropov addressed the June 1983 Central Committee plenum on the issue of Soviet aid to Third World countries (*Pravda*, 1983a):

> It is one thing to proclaim socialism as one's goal and another thing to build it. Certain levels of productive forces, culture and social consciousness are needed for that. Socialist countries express solidarity with these progressive countries, render assistance to them in the sphere of politics and culture, and promote the strengthening of their defense. We contribute, to the extent of our ability, to their economic development, just as the entire social progress of those countries, can be, of course, only the result of their leadership.

As noted earlier, the Sandinistas have not been satisfied completely with the level of Soviet economic aid.

Total Soviet and Eastern European economic assistance to the Third World and Latin America is far less than the aid provided by the Western developed countries. In 1981, for example, the Soviets extended a total of approximately $450 million in new aid commitments to noncommunist developing countries, followed by $716 million in 1982 (U.S. Department of

State, 1983). In contrast, the total OECD (Organization of Economic Cooperation and Development) aid to developing countries, which includes U.S. aid, amounted to $25.6 billion in 1981 and to $28 billion in 1982 (World Development Report, 1983: 182).

The Cuban economy, meanwhile, is noted for its economic failings and for being highly dependent upon the billions received in aid from the U.S.S.R., although its record in education, health, and social welfare is impressive. Its foreign debt amounts to over $10 billion, of which about $7.3 billion is owed the U.S.S.R.; Cuba runs a persistent trade deficit, and its manufactured goods have a difficult time achieving quality control standards (*Economist*, 1982: 96). In his main address at the 1982 rally commemorating the twenty-ninth anniversary of the attack on the Moncada Army Barracks, Castro urged his audience "to do more with less" (*Granma Weekly Review*, 1982: 1). By early 1982 the Cuban government was trying to secure foreign cooperation with other countries through joint ventures in tourism, and shipping, export, and service industries—through the country's first foreign investment law.

Latin American Nationalism

Nationalism throughout Latin America, although expressed in different forms under distinct situations, limits the power of external forces to control internal events. This subject merits more attention than received in U.S. policymaking circles, where the force of nationalism frequently is underestimated in U.S. perceptions of Latin American events, while the communist factor in the East-West formulation of the problem may be overemphasized.

The diverse faces of nationalism—identity with the homeland, love of the country, consciousness of past struggles for independence, sense of a unique people with its legacy of historic events and heroes—are clear in Latin America. Nicaragua is a case in point. As Tomás Borge Martínez (Borge Martínez, 1983: 17), a founding member of the ruling Sandinista National Liberation Front in Nicaragua, writes here:

> I can affirm, with full knowledge of the facts, that neither the Cuban ambassador nor Fidel Castro, with whom we have frequently conversed, nor the Soviet leader, Yuri Andropov, with whom we have also spoken, has ever told us what we must do. To think the contrary would be to accept that we have no criteria of our own, that we are simply puppets. . . . We Sandinistas never have been, are not and never will be anybody's satellites.

Other leading Nicaraguans, who have become disillusioned with the Sandinista leadership, also write eloquently with a strong sense of nationalist identity. Arturo José Cruz, head of the Central Bank of Nicaragua from July

1979 to March 1980 and Ambassador to the United States from April to November 1981, writes that the Nicaraguan Revolution should "be the most important landmark in our nation's history" and that in the beginning it "enjoyed the almost unanimous support of the Nicaraguan people" (José Cruz, 1983: 1031). While Cruz and others are disenchanted with the direction taken by the Sandinistas, they nevertheless reflect the Nicaraguan Revolution's nationalist origins—rather than its being the product of external Soviet and Cuban influence. These deep nationalist sentiments are powerful antidotes to external control, which critics of U.S. policy believe are underestimated by Washington in its frequently counterproductive policies designed to manage the region's discontent.

Certainly Nicaragua's Revolution under Sandinista leadership rule moved in its own *sui generis* directions. Opponents of the Sandinistas are able to speak their minds, key sectors of the Hispano-Catholic Church openly oppose the regime, a kind of pluralist consensus-building operates in the government's Council of State, and about 60% of the economy remains in private hands (Ullman, 1983: 44-48). These and other features of the Nicaraguan Revolution denote something other than a Soviet-style system, but rather a quest for Nicaragua's own form of rapid change consistent with Nicaraguan realities.

Other aspects of nationalism can be identified in Latin America. Three out of the five guerrilla groups in El Salvador are known to be anti-Soviet in sentiment and leftist leaders in El Salvador insist on control over their own guerrilla operations. Cuba's own relations with the Soviet Union reflect its nationalist sentiments in a variety of ways, including (1) unhappiness with the Soviet occupation of Afghanistan, (2) displeasure with Soviet policy in Poland, and (3) disagreement over the level of Soviet economic support for the developing countries that conflicts with Cuba's leadership role in the Third World Nonaligned Movement. In Argentina in particular, key sectors of the armed forces have expressed concern about the close Soviet embrace.

Experiences elsewhere in Soviet-Third World relations bear witness to the importance of nationalism and national brands of communism. Angola, Mozambique, Ethiopia, and Vietnam have not become mere Soviet pawns in a great Soviet design, as the lack of Soviet ability to control them and their variations of national communism so vividly illustrate (*New York Times*, 1983p). Thus nationalism places substantial limits on Soviet influence in a number of issues.[2]

---

[2]   Soviet inability to control Third World client states is illustrated by various facts. Differences between the Soviets and Vietnamese have emerged over the quantity and quality of Soviet economic aid. Vietnamese economic planning, policies toward Laos and Kampuchea (Cambodia), and Vietnamese resistance to Soviet efforts at domination (Zagoria and Simon, 1982: 164). By 1979 disagreements had developed between the Soviets and Agostinho Neto, leader of Angola, owing to Neto's concern regarding excesses in Soviet and Cuban influence. In December 1978 Neto issues a public warning about the necessity to "defend the independence of the Party," and that same month fired the Cabinet minister who had signed an

Cuba's Strains with Latin American Countries

By the early 1980s many Central and South American countries increasingly were becoming concerned by the resumption of the 1960s armed struggle pattern originally pursued by Cuba, then muted at the outset of the 1970s, both rhetorically and materially, only to be resurrected after the 1979 Nicaraguan revolution. As a result, by 1982 Cuba's relations had soured with Colombia, Costa Rica, Ecuador, Jamaica (under Edward Seaga), Panama, and Peru. Panama, previously a staunch defender of Cuba, had become disturbed by Nicaragua's growing military might to the point of sending a high level delegation to Cuba to discuss the matter (Panama Radio Broadcast, 1982). Panama's concern duplicated that of other Central American countries including Costa Rica. This concern produced strains that did not help the Soviets, given the close Soviet-Cuban ties and Moscow's general attempt to improve its own diplomatic position in the region.

Cuba's diplomatic relations with its Latin American neighbors do not flow always as smoothly as might be believed. Colombia's new populist conservative president, Belisario Betancur, elected in May 1982, came to power partly on the basis of proposed renewed relationship with Cuba, previously suspended in March 1981 owing to Cuban training of insurgents for the purpose of intervening in Colombian territory. When Betancur was elected, it was thought that he would restore diplomatic relations with Cuba, important to Havana in light of its isolation. However, in March 1983 when Castro was interviewed on Colombian television (on the occasion of ex-president Alfonso López Michelsen's visit to Havana), he publicly admitted that he has trained M-19 insurgents to operate in Colombia. He also described ex-president Julio César Turbay Ayala (1978-1982) as a surrogate of the United States, sort of rubbing Colombia's nose in the ground. Thus President Betancur was forced to back away from recognition of Cuba. In another case, Cuba backed Guyana in its dispute with Venezuela over the Essequibo controversy, whereupon

agreement with Cuba providing for an additional 6000 Cuban technicians to be sent to Angola. Meanwhile, Neto moved strongly to improve relations with the United States (Zagoria, 1979: 748).

Soviet political control finds itself undermined in part by African and Middle Eastern disinterest in Moscow's brand of socialism. President Somora Machel of Mozambique, for example, counseled the newly elected, self-described Marxist leader of Zimbabwe, Prime Minister Robert Mugabe, not to set up a Soviet-style planned economy. By 1981 Machel himself determined to abandon government ownership of small enterprises and services (*Washington Post*, 1980: A17; Congressional Research Service, 1981:124). By the mid-1970s, scholars working on Soviet-Third World relations concluded that Soviet leverage on key issues of importance to the leadership of countries such as India, Indonesia, Ghana, and Egypt was "marginal at best." The editor of the study, Dr. Alvin Z. Rubinstein, concluded that this "strongly" suggested that the "gratitude of these Third World countries does not convert to any willingness to tolerate Soviet interference in domestic decisionmaking on key issues" (Rubinstein, 1975: 221, 223).

Venezuela did not join the Nonaligned Movement. Like other countries in world politics then, Cuba faces constraints and setbacks to its diplomacy that must be assessed relative not only to its standing in Latin America, but also to the impact these setbacks have on Soviet-Latin American relations.

Cuba's relations with Mexico merit particular attention, given their special relationship over the years. Since the beginning of Cuba's revolution under Fidel Castro, the Cuban government found a sympathetic sister country in Mexico with its own legacy of the 1910 Revolution. During periods of intense strain between Cuba and the United States and between Cuba and the OAS, Mexico always has continued to maintain relations with Cuba. By 1982-1983 as revolutionary upheavals pulsated in Central America, Mexico has become increasingly uneasy under the mounting regional conflict. Mexico has been especially sensitive to the refugees pouring across its border from Guatemala and into Mexico's poverty-plagued and politically sensitive southern provinces, not so far from its rich, potentially vulnerable oil fields. This escalating pressure has led Mexico City to play a more vigorous role in attempting to facilitate a political settlement in the area, potentially heightening strains with Havana over the latter's activities in Central America. The tip of the iceberg of these strains surfaced in September 1983, when two Cuban diplomats were arrested by Mexican authorities and held incommunicado for a week. It was reported that the Cuban diplomats, involved in a plot to deliver explosives to two Cuban exiles, were beaten and threatened while in custody (*New York Times*, 1983n). The Soviets and Cubans have exceptionally large embassies in Mexico City, so that the arrest of diplomats may have been intended to send a message to both countries.

In addition to the strained relationships revealed in the course of the U.S. invasion of Grenada (the OECS opposition to the Soviet/Cuban presence; Suriname's expulsion of Cuban personnel; and Jamaica's request for Cubans to depart the island), the coup in Grenada illustrated another Cuban problem. Havana was not able to control the internal power struggle of a client state, a fact that suggests no long-run guarantee of the welcome mat. The internal coup in Grenada produced a new political leadership of a type distinctly not in Cuba's interests, despite its hardline Marxist orientation. In April 1983 the surprising death of Cayetano Carpio as a result of political infighting in El Salvador eliminated yet another leader of a pro-Soviet and pro-Cuban guerrilla faction. The guerrillas in El Salvador, meanwhile, hold together tenuously against a long background of internal disputes. Internal conflict among Marxist-Leninists is not unusual, and Cuba by no means exercises control over these disputes.

Regional Concern with the Soviet Cuban Client State, Nicaragua

Available evidence suggests growing regional as well as West European opposition to Nicaragua's growing centralization of Sandinista political control during 1983, four years after their rise to power (*Christian Science Monitor*, 1983a). What has happened is that the very West European and Latin American leaders who once supported the Sandinistas have become openly antagonistic. As Daniel Oduber Quiros, former Costa Rican president and vice president of the Socialist Internationale, stated: "We are not going to keep defending a process that has become Marxist-Leninist" (*Christian Science Monitor*, 1983d). Mr. Oduber argues that this is the consensus of Socialist International leaders, including Socialist International President Willy Brandt of West Germany, Spanish Prime Minister Socialist International Vice President Felipe Gonzales, and Carlos Andrés Pérez, former president of Venezuela.

The Sandinistas also are under pressure from the region's two chief oil powers, Mexico and Venezuela. Venezuela cut off crude oil deliveries to Nicaragua in September 1982, when Nicaragua did not pay its bills, thereby leaving Mexico as the country's sole oil supplier (on 100% credit). However, as reported in the *New York Times* on August 13, the Mexican government told the Nicaraguans that future oil supplies would be contingent on Managua's commitment to pay. Indeed the Mexicans held up oil shipments in June and July 1983, releasing them only after high-level delegations arrived from Nicaragua for urgent discussions. With Mexico's own financial difficulties mounting, Nicaragua will not be able to take Mexico's oil shipments for granted. As Nicaragua comes under this kind of increased regional pressure, the cause of Moscow and Havana is not advanced.

Restricted Soviet Military Commitments to Cuba and Nicaragua

In 1983 the Soviets likely will double the amount of military aid shipped to Nicaragua during 1981 and 1982 (*Washington Post*, 1983c). These increases appear to be tied to the rising level of insurgent activity in Nicaragua directed against the Sandinistas. By no means does this indicate that the Soviets are prepared to come to the aid of Nicaragua at the risk of direct combat with the United States, as they are equally unlikely to do for Cuba under similar conditions. The Soviets have not committed themselves to the protection of Nicaragua. When the United States invaded Grenada, Soviet formal position statements were made at a relatively low level. In referring to the possibility of a subsequent U.S. invasion of Nicaragua, the Soviets merely stated their "unswerving solidarity with the Nicaraguan people," but provided far less than any solid military commitments (*New York Times*, 1983d). In the case of Soviet military responsibility to Cuba, Havana is not a member of the Warsaw Pact, and President Castro (*Granma Weekly Review*, 1982) makes quite clear that in a confrontation with the United States, Cubans

> wouldn't have the privilege of calling ourselves revolutionaries or considering ourselves free unless we were convinced that we are more than

capable of defending our nation and our Revolution from any enemy, no matter how powerful.

The Soviet presence in Latin America is by no means an omnipotent one.[3]

CONCLUSIONS

These sets of opportunities and constraints relative to potential Soviet influence in Latin America hold significant implications for an effective U.S. foreign policy. To identify Soviet foreign policy as the central source of the Caribbean Basin turmoil appears to credit the U.S.S.R. with more control over domestic events than it actually possessed. To be sure, the Soviets are intent on exploiting opportunities that advance their interests wherever possible, including expansion, influence, and control if achievable. This means support of leftist, radical-nationalist, and Marxist-Leninist groups, in countries like Nicaragua and Cuba as well as pursuit of markets and natural resources in less revolutionary settings. But the actual influence wielded by Moscow in the Latin American countries is a more complex matter, and a number of regional forces suggest that Soviet control over a wide range of domestic issues is quite limited de facto. Certainly, it can be argued that the causes of Central American instability do not arise from outside Soviet pressure.

The Soviets recognize that there are limits to their control over Third World countries, of which Latin America is a part, and that control as such may not be a feasible policy objective (Valkenier, 1979). At the same time, more Soviet writers acknowledge the lack of coordinated actions between the

---

[3]   An anonymous referee for this journal argues that the limits to influence are less persuasive than implied here. This assessment is based on the important "influence" exerted by Soviet military aid and cooperation (which may outweigh Soviet economic instruments), the case that economic aid and trade is not the best index of real or potential control, and that nationalism may not ipso facto impede Soviet influence. These observations raise important questions about influence. Previous superpower-client relations, however, suggest that provision of military aid does not necessarily lead to donor control over the recipient, as the United States discovered in Vietnam and as the Soviets have learned in Syria. Neither does the economic aid of Country A to Country B mean that Country A gains control over a wide range of issues pursued by Country B, as both the Soviet Union and the United States have learned in their relations with a number of Third World countries.

In the case of nationalism, we simply need to study more this feature of Third World relations with superpower donors such as the Soviet Union. However it must be said that Cuba's relations with the Soviet Union historically have demonstrated many examples of the nationalist force at work dating from the early 1960s, when Havana first began to extend its ties with Africa and Asia. Soviet relations with both Syria and Vietnam must contend with a variety of nationalist elements today. Undoubtedly this debate will continue. For another view of the Cuban role in the Soviet policy toward Latin America, however, see Rothenberg (1983).

U.S.S.R. and the Nonaligned Movement (with its Latin America members) than used to be the case (Valkenier, 1983; Valkenier, 1979). More recently, there have been indications that Moscow may be coming to accept the concept of a single world economic system, thus departing from its traditional perception of a world divided into socialist/communist and capitalist/imperialist systems (Valkenier, 1983). The novel feature of this apparently evolving view is that it suggests that the capitalist world does have a role to play in the future world economic order. Furthermore, the change suggests that Moscow may find that it has more in common with the Western world than it formerly believed from the 1950s through the mid-1970s. If this is so, then Soviet actions in Latin America may be viewed less as aggressive, and more as a search for economic survival in a world of shrinking resources, a world in which accommodation to some degree of interdependence is imperative.

In some respects, U.S. policy appears counterproductive. Persistent hostile actions toward Cuba, Grenada, and Nicaragua, albeit appealing as a means to counter the Soviet threat, have the effect of driving these countries more closely into the Soviet embrace than of stimulating them into more independent courses of action. Grenada, before the coup against Bishop, illustrates the point. The U.S. refusal to deal with the Bishop government in a positive way, that is, by opposing loans to Grenada by the International Monetary Fund (IMF), by keeping Grenada at arms length for over two years, and declining to see Bishop in June 1983 when he came to Washington in search of a political accommodation—suggests at least the possibility that closer U.S.-Grenadian relations might have helped to prevent the sequence of events that led to Bishop's ouster by the more pro-Soviet militants, and hence the need for the consequent U.S. occupation.

Meanwhile, the refusal to press for negotiation over a range of Central American issues and the reluctance to follow a policy of diplomacy rather than one of armed force tends to isolate the United States from its Latin American neighbors such as Mexico, Venezuela, and Colombia. In general, characterization of the region's difficulties as part of the East-West problem insinuates more control to the Soviet Union over domestic life in the region than appears actually to be the case. U.S. policy appears rooted in an overestimation of Soviet and Cuban capabilities, and an underevaluation of the constraints on Soviet and Cuban power in the region as a whole.

As the 49 Russians, 50 Cubans, assorted East Germans, North Koreans, and Libyans departed Grenada in early November 1983, the future of Soviet opportunities to expand their Latin American presence and exert some control over domestic events remained cloudy. Moscow had lost a potential key Caribbean Basin outpost and was placed on warning as to the limits of U.S. tolerance for its activities in the Caribbean Basin. They experienced unwanted confrontation with the United States, the consequence of pressing their luck beyond acceptable limits in the minds of many English-speaking Caribbean republics and more privately among several South American leaders.

Moreover, the majority of Grenadians interviewed appeared to welcome the U.S. presence, which added credibility to the U.S. action. On the mainland, both Cuban advisers and Salvadoran rebel leaders found it advisable to depart Nicaragua in large numbers following the Grenadian episode for fear of a U.S. invasion.

While the Soviets certainly lost a foothold in the Caribbean Basin, other aspects of the Grenadian crisis may have been less detrimental to Soviet opportunism than appears at first blush. The United States disseminated much incorrect information and numerous unproven assertions about the number of Soviet-backed Cuban personnel on the island, about proof that the Soviets and Cubans were preparing to "take over" Grenada, about the existence of a "terrorist training base" there. Neither did the United States provide evidence that the Soviets or Cubans had a role in the killing of Bishop and his colleagues as early implied or dispel allegations that U.S. planning for the invasion had not occurred well before the call for assistance by the OECS. As the dust settled, U.S.-West European allies continued to be doubtful both about the degree of Soviet and Cuban involvement and the specific reasons given for the U.S. occupation. Indeed this division between the U.S. and its North Atlantic Treaty Organization partners has helped to promote the traditional Soviet objective of fragmenting NATO. The U.S. occupation of Grenada then is more than an isolated regional event.

Throughout the crisis, it can be argued that the Cubans pursued a low-key diplomatic posture. They provided accurate information about the number of Cubans on the island, portrayed themselves as a country with limited stakes in Grenada (other than the safety of their citizens), and invited the foreign press in for several news conferences, at a time when the U.S. press was being prohibited from visiting Grenada (during the first days of the U.S. action). Western journalists in Havana came away with the impression that the Grenadian setback was unlikely to alter Cuba's well-known commitment to "internationalist solidarity," which will continue to benefit the Soviet Union. This assumption means that we are left with uncertainty about which long-range lessons the Soviets and Cubans will draw from their Grenadian setback and how they may seek to exploit future opportunities. Of one thing we can be certain: The Soviet quest for new footholds will be offset by the continuing limits to Moscow's influence.

REFERENCES

América Latina
1983   "La decisión del pueblo." (Julio): 24-32.

Andrés López, J.
1983   "Relaciones comerciales Argentina-URSS: balance y perspectivas." *América Latina* 8 (Agosto): 55-64.

Borge Martínez, T.
1983   "The U.S. and Nicaragua: An Aggression of Lies." *Manchester Guardian Weekly* (August 21): 7.

Castro, A.
1981   "A step toward unity." *World Marxist Rev.* 3 (March): 66-68.

Child, J.
1983   "The Falkland/Malvinas conflict and inter-American peace-keeping." *Conflict Q.* 3 (Winter): 5-20.

Christian Science Monitor
1983a   November 7: 3.
1983b   November 4: 10.
1983c   October 27: 7, 10.
1983d   October 19: 1.

Clement, P.
1983   "The Soviets in Nicaragua: cultivating a new client." Presented at the American Association for the Advancement of Slavic Studies, Kansas City (October).

Clissold, S. [ed.]
1970a   *Soviet Relations with Latin America. London:* Oxford University Press.
1970b   "Soviet relations with Latin America between the wars," pp. 1-15 in G. Oswald and A. J. Strover [eds.] *The Soviet Union and Latin America.* New York: Praeger.

Congressional Research Service
1981   *Soviet Policy and United States Response in the Third World.* Report prepared for the Committee on Foreign Affairs of the U.S. House of Representatives. Washington, DC: U.S. Government Printing Office.

Dinerstein, H.
1976   *The Making of a Missile Crisis: October 1962.* Baltimore, Md.: The Johns Hopkins Univ. Press.

Duncan, W. R.
1982   "Grenada," pp. 100-106 in R. F. Starr and R. Wesson [eds.] *1982 Yearbook on International Communist Affairs.* Stanford, Calif.: Hoover Institution Press.

Economist
1982   "Mother Russia's son." June 19: 95-96.

El Nuevo Diario
1983   Managua, Nicaragua. June 21: 1.

FBIS [Foreign Broadcast Information Service]
1982a   Latin America. July 29: SI.
1982b   Latin America. June 23: SI.
Financial Times
1983   London. February 28: 4.
Foreign Trade
1982   Soviet Union. November 11: 2.
González, E.
1974   *Cuba Under Castro: The Limits of Charisma.* Boston, Mas-
                 sachusetts: Houghton Mifflin.
Gouré, L. and M. Rothenberg
1975   *Soviet Penetration of Latin America.* Miami, Florida: Univer-
                 sity of Miami Center for Advanced International Studies.
Granma Weekly Review
1982   Cuba. August 7: 1.
1979   Cuba. September 16: 16.
Havana Radio Broadcast
1982   Cuba. June 4.
Intercontinental Press
1983   Auburn, Alabama. May 8: 2.
1982a   Auburn, Alabama. May 31: 2.
1982b   Auburn, Alabama. May 24: 3.
Izvestiya
1982   Soviet Union. May 17: 2.
José Cruz, A.
1983   "Nicaragua's imperiled revolution."   *Foreign Affairs* 61
                 (Summer): 1031-1047.
Latin America Weekly Report
1983a   London. October 14: 1.
1983b   London. March 18: 8.
Leiken, R. S.
1982   *Soviet Strategy in Latin America.* Washington Papers 93. New
                 York: Praeger.
Leonov, N. L.
1982a   "Inquietudes y esperanzas de Guatemala." *América Latina* 8
                 (Agosto): 29-39.
1982b   "Nicaragua: experiencia de una revolución victoriosa." *América
                 Latina* 3 (Marzo): 33-40.
Levesque, J.
1978   *The U.S.S.R. and the Cuban Revolution: Soviet Ideological and
                 Strategic Perspectives, 1959-1977.* New York: Praeger.
Madrid Radio Broadcast
1983   Madrid. October 16.
Managua Radio Broadcast
1981   Managua, Nicaragua. August 14.
Mikoyan, S.
1980   "Las particularidades de la revolución en Nicaragua y sus tareas

desde el punto de vista de la teoría y práctica de movimiento liberador." *América Latina* 3 (Marzo): 95-103.

Moscow Television Broadcast
1982   Moscow. May 14.
Moscow Radio Broadcast in Spanish to Latin America
1982   Soviet Union. May 18.
New York Times
1983a   November 11: A-18.
1983b   November 6: 1.
1983c   November 6: 21.
1983d   November 2: 17-18
1983e   October 31: A-10.
1983f   October 30: 20 and I-E.
1983g   October 29: 13.
1983h   October 28: A-12.
1983i   October 27: 7.
1983j   October 26: A-19.
1983k   October 16: 3.
1983l   October 10: 14.
1983m   March 28: 7.
1983n   March 23: 1.
1982a   November 15: 1.
1982b   June 7: 7.
1982c   June 4: 7.
Osgood, R.
1983   "Central America in U.S. containment policy," pp. 91-96 in A.
                F. Lowenthal and S. F. Wells [eds.] *Working Papers*, The
                Wilson Center Latin American Program. Washington, DC:
                Wilson Center.
Panama Radio Broadcast
1982   Panama City. October 7.
Pravda
1983a   Moscow. June 16: 5.
1983b   Moscow. May 14: 2.
Ratliff, W. E.
1976   *Castroism and Communism in Latin America, 1959-1976.*
                Stanford, Calif.: Hoover Institution Press.
Rothenberg, M.
1983   "Latin America in Soviet eyes." *Problems of Communism* 32
                (September-October): 1-18.
Rubinstein, A. Z. [ed.]
1975   *Soviet and Chinese Influence in the Third World.* New York:
                Praeger.
Smirnova, N.
1982   "Nicaragua: la revolución en marcha." *América Latina* 7 (Julio):
                4-12.
Strategic Survey
1983   International Institute for Strategic Studies, London.

Theriot, L. H.
1982   "Cuba Faces the Economic Realities of the 1980s." Study
                  prepared for use of Joint Economic Committee of the U.S.
                  Congress. Washington, DC: U.S. Government Printing Office.
Ullman, R. H.
1983   "At war with Nicaragua." *Foreign Affairs* 62: 1 (Fall): 39-58.
U.S. Department of State
1983   "Soviet and East European aid to the third world." (February).
1981   "Cuba's renewed support for violence in Latin America." Special
                  Report 90 (December). Washington, DC.
Valkenier, E. K.
1983   *Soviet Union and the Third World: The Economic Bind.* New
                  York: Praeger.
1979   "The U.S.S.R., the third world, and the global economy."
                  Problems of Communism (July-August): 17-33.
Vasilyev, V.
1971   "The United States' 'new approach' to Latin America." *Int.*
                  Affairs (Moscow) 6 (June) 43-49.
Washington Post
1983a   Washington, DC. October 27: A-9.
1983b   Washington, DC. October 26: A-9.
1983c   Washington, DC. July 2: 1.
1980   Washington, DC. April 14: A-7.
World Development Report
1983   New York: Oxford University Press.
Wyanovsky, R.
1979   "O stranakh sotsialisticheskoy orientatsii" (On the countries of
                  socialist orientation). *Kommunist* 11 (July): 118-122.
Zagoria, D. S. and S. W. Simon
1982   "Soviet policy in Southeast Asia," pp. 153-173 in D. S. Zagoria
                  [ed.] *Soviet Policy in East Asia.* New Haven, Conn.: Yale Univ.
                  Press.
Zagoria, D. S.
1979   "Into the breach: new Soviet alliances in the third world."
                  Foreign Affairs 57 (Spring): 733-754.
Zinoviev, N.
1983   "Dinámica de las relaciones económicas." *América Latina* 3
                  (March): 1-15.

19

Diversifying Dependence: Nicaragua's New Economic Links with Socialist Countries

Rubén Berríos and Marc Edelman

Once an area of little concern, over the past 15 years Latin America has become of great interest to the Soviet Union and the socialist countries of Eastern Europe.[1] With rising nationalism in Latin America and with detente—up to 1980—alleviating East-West tensions, the U.S.S.R. and the Eastern European countries have succeeded in expanding diplomatic relations and commercial links with most countries in the region. Key Latin American states have experienced a broader political consensus, achieved more autonomy in their foreign affairs and derived concrete economic advantages from this diversification of their foreign relations. Many countries have used their recent ties with the Soviet Union and its allies as a means of strengthening their position vis-à-vis the United States and as an alternative source of trade, credits and technical assistance. In turn, the socialist countries and particularly the Soviet Union have stepped up their commercial relations with various Latin American countries, irrespective of the nature of their governments.[2]

This study examines trade and aid in Nicaragua's post-1979 economic relations with the socialist countries. Prior to July 1979, trade between Nicaragua and the socialist countries of Eastern Europe was practically non-existent.[3] After the Sandinistas seized power in July 1979, the first socialist

From *The Journal of Communist Studies* 2:1 (March 1986), pp. 31-48. Copyright © 1986 Frank Cass & Co., Ltd. Reprinted by permission.

[1]   For our purposes, the term "socialist countries" will be used to refer to full members of the Council of Mutual Economic Assistance (CMEA or COMECON), as well as to other countries, such as Yugoslavia, Albania, China and North Korea, that consider themselves socialist.

[2]   For an interesting analysis of Soviet-Latin American relations see Cole Blasier, *The Giant's Rival: The U.S.S.R. and Latin America* (Pittsburgh: University of Pittsburgh Press, 1983). For a socialist country perspective on the role of the other members of the CMEA, see A. I. Sizonenko et al., *Los Países del CAME y América Latina* (Moscow: Editorial Progreso, 1983).

[3]   Nicaragua and the Soviet Union formally established diplomatic ties in 1944, but they

countries to open embassies in Managua were Cuba, in August, and Vietnam, in September. The Soviet Union established relations with the Sandinista government in October 1979, three months after the fall of Somoza, as did several Eastern European countries and Mongolia. Other socialist countries that extended diplomatic recognition to Nicaragua included Albania (November 1979), North Korea (December 1979), Yugoslavia (March 1980), and Poland (August 1980).

NON-ALIGNMENT AND THE DIVERSIFICATION OF RELATIONS

Although non-alignment is sometimes misunderstood as implying neutrality or equidistance in international affairs, the first meeting of the Non-Aligned Movement (NAM) in Cairo in 1961 defined the term according to a set of specific principles. Non-aligned countries, according to the NAM's own criteria, are those that do not participate in military pacts, do not grant military bases to the great powers, pursue a foreign policy based on peaceful coexistence, and support national liberation movements.[4] Ten years before the overthrow of Somoza, the Sandinistas stated that once in power non-alignment would be a guiding principle of their foreign relations. In their first major pre-revolutionary programmatic statement in 1969 the Sandinistas called for "an independent foreign policy" and stated that they would "accept economic and technical aid from any country, as long as it did not imply political commitments."[5]

Since 1979, Nicaragua has followed an independent, non-aligned foreign policy, more than doubling the number of countries with which it has diplomatic relations.[6] Diversity in political and economic relations has been central to Nicaragua's foreign policy and critical for its survival. Prior to 1979, Nicaragua had strong commercial and financial links to the United States. The Sandinistas have tried to redress this imbalance, pragmatically seeking a wider set of trading partners. Nicaraguan planners refer to the goal of diversity in

---

did not exchange representatives and the relationship was of virtually no practical significance: see interview with Yuri Volskii, Managua Radio in *Foreign Broadcast Information Service-Latin America (FBIS-LAM)*, 22 October 1979. On pre-revolutionary commercial relations between Nicaragua and the socialist countries, see Jorge I. Zumarán, "El comercio de los países latinoamericanos con los del CAME," *Comercio Exterior* (Mexico), Vol. 31, No. 12 (December 1981), p. 1428; and Ricardo Acciaris, "Nicaragua-Pays Socialistes: Vers la Consolidation des Liens Economiques?" *Problèmes d'Amérique Latine* (Paris), Vol. 74, No. 4 (1984), p. 107.

[4]   Peter Willetts, *The Non-Aligned Movement: The Origins of a Third World Alliance* (London: Frances Pinter, 1978), pp. 18-19; William LeoGrande, "The Evolution of the Non-Aligned Movement," *Problems of Communism*, Vol. 29, No. 1 (Jan-Feb 1980), p. 37.

[5]   *Programa Histórico del FSLN* (1969) (Managua: Departamento de Propaganda y Educación Política del FSLN, 1984), pp. 34-5.

[6]   Alejandro Bendaña, "The Foreign Policy of the Nicaraguan Revolution," in Thomas W. Walker (ed.), *Nicaragua in Revolution* (New York: Praeger, 1982), p. 322.

economic relations as a "four-legged" model based on ties with four groups of countries: the United States (traditionally Nicaragua's main partner); Latin America (including the members of the Central American Common Market); other developed countries in Western Europe and Japan; and the socialist and non-aligned countries. Trade relations with developing countries (for example, Mexico, Argentina, Brazil, Libya, Algeria and Iran) and with the socialist countries have been increasing in absolute and relative terms. The steady growth of these relations has coincided with a fall in the amount of U.S.-Nicaraguan commerce (see Tables 1, 2 and 3 at the end of this chapter).[7] Although the share of Nicaragua's trade with the United States in early 1985 was still almost as large as that with all the socialist countries together, the United States has lost the position of overwhelming dominance it once had in the Nicaraguan market.

Nicaragua's economic growth was among the highest in the region in the first two years after the revolution.[8] Nevertheless, the country suffers from many of the economic difficulties experienced by the rest of Central America, notably a traditional dependence on a small number of markets and suppliers. Its terms of trade—the relative price of its largely agricultural exports measured against the cost of manufactured imports—suffer from a secular decline, falling by 26.6 per cent just between 1981 and 1984.[9] The country's foreign debt, exacerbated by high interest rates, now stands at over 4,000 million dollars and in per capita terms is one of the highest in Central America.[10] In relation to exports and GNP, this debt is by far the highest in all of Latin America.[11] Because of debt rescheduling arrangements, however, interest payments which absorbed 33 per cent of export earnings in 1982 amounted to a slightly more manageable 19 per cent in 1983 and 1984.[12] A chronic current-account deficit has been running at over $500 million per annum, roughly the same amount as Nicaragua's entire export earnings.[13] Finally, meeting the country's oil import requirements of approximately $200 million per year has been a major burden.

At the same time, several particular factors exacerbate the situation. These include the destruction caused by the earthquake of 1972, the insurrection of

---

[7]   The data in Tables 1 and 2 are based on the *Boletín Estadístico*, No. 5, published by the Ministry of Foreign Commerce. Table 3 is based on Central Bank figures distributed by the Nicaraguan embassy in Washington.
[8]   Comisión Económica para América Latina (CEPAL). *Notas sobre la economía y el desarollo*, Nos. 409-10 (January 1985), p. 12.
[9]   CEPAL, *Notas*, p. 15.
[10]   *The New York Times*, 27 March 1985; José Luis Corragio and George Irvin, "Revolution and Pluralism in Nicaragua," *Millennium: Journal of International Studies*, Vol. 13, No. 2 (Summer 1984), p. 197.
[11]   CEPAL, *Políticas de ajuste y renegociación de la deuda externa en América Latina* (Santiago: Cuadernos de la CEPAL, No. 48, 1984), pp. 44-6.
[12]   CEPAL, *Notas* 1985, p. 18.
[13]   *Ibid.*, p. 17.

1978-79 (which caused material losses estimated at $481 million),[14] and the floods of May 1982 (which were responsible for $350 million in damage);[15] the theft in 1979 by fleeing leaders of the Somoza regime of all but $3.5 million of the country's hard currency reserves; the U.S. effort to block multilateral credits and first to limit and then totally embargo trade; and the channelling of 50 per cent of the state budget to defence against the *contras*.[16] The ambitious investments in social infrastructure undertaken during the early years of the revolution have in many cases been curtailed because of the high cost of the *contra* war. Finally, in an effort to use the country's limited foreign exchange most rationally, the government has instituted a multi-tiered exchange rate which has had a number of problematic side-effects, the most important of which are a disproportionate growth of the urban informal sector and a dampening of productive activity.

Given its dire economic situation—at once similar to and worse than those of its Central American neighbours—Nicaragua has sought many of the kinds of commercial relations, aid projects and technical co-operation agreements that other underdeveloped countries also pursue.[17] The international political support won by the revolution has permitted Nicaragua to establish closer economic relations with socialist and non-aligned countries as a means of meeting some of its fundamental development needs.[18]

SHIFTING COMMERCIAL RELATIONS

Following the insurrection of July 1979, the Sandinista government expressed

[14]   On the human and material cost of the insurrection see CEPAL, *Nicaragua: el impacto de la mutación política* (Santiago: Estudios e Informes de la CEPAL, No. 1, 1981), p. 36.
[15]   United Nations' figures cited by Richard Fagen, "Revolution and Crisis in Nicaragua," in Martin Diskin (ed.), *Trouble in Our Backyard: Central America and the United States in the Eighties* (New York: Pantheon, 1983), p. 141. The flood damage was equal to 70 per cent of Nicaragua's 1981 export earnings.
[16]   The 50 per cent figure is cited by Henry Ruíz, Minister of External Co-operation, in *The New York Times*, 27 October 1985. For an analysis of the economic effects of the *contra* war see E. V. K. FitzGerald, "Una evaluación del costo económico de la agresión del gobierno estadounidense contra el pueblo de Nicaragua," paper presented at the Latin American Studies Association conference, Albuquerque, New Mexico, April 1985.
[17]   Even in Central American countries that have close links to the United States, such as Costa Rica, pro-U.S. politicians sometimes raise the possibility of diversifying dependence through increased trade with CMEA nations: see, for example, Oscar Arias Sánchez, "El poder tiende a concentrarse," in Ricardo Sol (ed.), *El reto democrático en Centroamérica* (San José: Departamento Ecuménico de Investigaciones, 1983), p. 111.
[18]   For broader analyses of Nicaragua's relations with the socialist countries, which consider aspects other than trade and aid, see Rubén Berríos, "Economic Relations Between Nicaragua and the Socialist Countries," *Working Paper* No. 166 (Latin American Program, Woodrow Wilson International Center for Scholars, Washington, DC) 1985; and Marc Edelman, "Lifelines: Nicaragua and the Socialist Countries," *Report on the Americas*, Vol. 19, No. 3 (May-June 1985).

a need for reconstruction assistance and a desire to broaden Nicaragua's international economic relations. Cuba, Bulgaria and other socialist countries sent relief donations and other aid shortly after the Sandinista victory, as did the United States and numerous Latin American and Western European governments. But apart from a small trade, health and education agreement signed with East Germany on 31 October 1979, no significant commercial protocols with socialist or non-aligned countries were adopted.[19]

Ties with the socialist countries expanded in March and April 1980, in part as a response to pressure from the United States. Nicaraguan requests for U.S. military assistance were never considered, with the exception of a miniscule appropriation in 1979 for binoculars and compasses.[20] In early 1980, in a move that Nicaraguans perceived as deeply humiliating, the U.S. Congress attached a series of conditions to the Carter Administration's proposed $75 million loan package for Nicaragua. The legislation stipulated that 60 per cent of the aid would be for the private sector and that the loan could not be used in facilities that engaged Cuban personnel (such as the literacy campaign or the health system). Disbursements were to be conditional upon Nicaragua's human rights performance, the holding of elections and non-involvement in "international terrorism."[21] Nicaraguans in the private sector and government were angered both because no other country attached similar provisions to the aid it offered and because the United States had not placed such conditions on its assistance to any other country, including those where there were abysmal human rights practices and a systematic suppression of opposition that could not be compared with the situation in Nicaragua's relatively open multi-party, pluralist system.[22] On 12 March 1980, two weeks after the Senate froze all foreign aid appropriations and thus effectively postponed the $75 million loan, the Nicaraguan government announced its first high-level visit to the Soviet Union and Eastern Europe.[23]

During March-April 1980, Nicaragua signed various economic, technical and cultural bilateral agreements with the Soviet Union, Bulgaria, Czechoslovakia and the German Democratic Republic (GDR). From 1980 to 1981,

---

[19] Managua Radio Sandino in *FBIS-LAM*, 6 November 1979; Acciaris, pp. 117ff.

[20] Department of the Army, *Nicaragua: A Country Study* (Area Handbook Series) (Washington: U.S. Government Printing Office, 1982), p. 212.

[21] Harold D. Sims, "Revolutionary Nicaragua: Dilemmas Confronting Sandinistas and North Americans," in Alan Adelman and Reid Reading (eds.), *Confrontation in the Caribbean Basin* (Pittsburgh: University of Pittsburgh Center for Latin American Studies, 1984), pp. 60-61.

[22] For an analysis of the Nicaraguan political system, see Heinrich-W. Krumwiede, "Sandinist Democracy: Problems of Institutionalization," in Wolf Grabendorff et al. (eds.), Political Change in Central America (Boulder, Colorado: Westview Press, 1984). On the elections of November 1984, see Abraham Brumberg, "'Sham' and 'Farce' in Nicaragua?", *Dissent* (New York), Vol. 32, No. 2 (Spring 1985).

[23] Havana Radio in *FBIS-LAM*, 12 March 1980; *La Gaceta Oficial* (Managua), 15 March 1980; Sims, p. 61.

exports from Nicaragua to the CMEA countries more than doubled, growing from $12.1 million (2.7 per cent of total exports) to $24.8 million (7.3 per cent) (see Tables 1 and 2). Imports from the socialist countries, financed largely with concessionary credits, grew even faster, jumping from $2.0 million (0.2 per cent of all imports) in 1980 to $32.8 million (3.3 per cent) in 1981, largely as a result of $29.4 million in purchases from the GDR.[24] The amount of credits contracted with the socialist countries, however, remained relatively constant, at slightly over $100 million per year (see Table 4). This amounted to 19 per cent in 1980 and 15 per cent in 1981 of the total credits extended to Nicaragua from all sources.

The Carter Administration's $75 million loan package was finally approved by Congress in June 1980, although disbursements were held up until September, over a year after the aid proposal had first been drafted.[25] But by then the delays and conditions on the loan had already led Nicaragua to seek trade and co-operation agreements with the socialist countries. In January 1981, just after assuming office, the Reagan Administration suspended aid payments from the $75 million loan to Nicaragua because of alleged shipments of arms to guerillas in El Salvador. In February, $100 million in U.S. credits for wheat purchases were suspended. On 1 April the remaining $15 million due to Nicaragua under the $75 million loan package was cancelled.

Socialist and non-aligned countries began to increase their economic commitments to Nicaragua. In January 1981 Bulgaria agreed to provide credits worth $48.5 million for industrial machinery purchases, the installation of turnkey plants, the construction of a hydro-electric dam, and medicine. Cuba signed a $64 million co-operation agreement in April and offered to help build a large, modern sugar agro-industrial complex. The Soviet Union and Bulgaria donated wheat to replace the supplies cut off by the United States. In April, just after the cancellation of the remaining U.S. aid, Libya granted a $100 million credit that provided for scientific and cultural exchanges, reconstruction aid, technical assistance for petroleum exploration and the creation of joint agricultural enterprises.

In late 1981 and early 1982 the Reagan Administration stepped up its campaign against Nicaragua. Military pressures included the founding in August 1981, with CIA encouragement, of the main *Contra* organization, the Nicaraguan Democratic Force (FDN);[26] Secretary of State Alexander Haig's statement in November 1981 that the United States would not rule out a direct military intervention in Nicaragua; the U.S. National Security Council's authorization, also in November, of a $19 million program of covert paramilitary operations against the Sandinista government; and the destruction

---

24 Banco Central de Nicaragua, unpublished trade statistics.
25 William M. LeoGrande, "The United States and the Revolution," in Walker, p. 75.
26 *The Wall Street Journal*, 5 March 1985.

in March of two important highway bridges by FDN demolition teams, which prompted the government to declare a state of emergency.

Economic pressures in this period also grew. In November 1981 the United States used its votes in the Inter-American Development Bank to block a $40 million fisheries loan to Nicaragua. In February 1982 the World Bank suspended its aid program in the country in response to U.S. government pressure.[27] When the Reagan Administration's Caribbean Basin Initiative aid plan was announced, also in February, Nicaragua was the only Central American nation excluded from participation. In March the State Department put pressure on U.S. banks not to participate in a $130 million loan organized by a London consortium.[28] Given U.S. efforts to reduce Nicaragua's access to multilateral credits, it became increasingly clear that the country's trade pattern would be determined largely by the availability of bilateral finance and trade credits. In the face of a worsening military and security situation, obtaining military assistance also became an urgent consideration.

In April and May 1982, Nicaraguan delegations again sought additional aid and trade during visits to the socialist countries. The U.S.S.R. agreed to provide two technical assistance and financial agreements worth over $200 million, half of which was a trade credit for purchases of agricultural, mining and fishing equipment. Cuba extended a $50 million loan for sugar industry development. Bulgaria signed six trade agreements and contracts worth over $30 million that provided aid in mining, food production, port construction, hydro-electric development and the creation of joint commercial enterprises.

During 1982-84 Nicaragua's trade with CMEA countries grew in both absolute and relative terms (see Tables 1, 2 and 3). Exports to the CMEA countries rose from a total of $29.9 million in 1982 (7.4 per cent of total exports) to $55.1 million in 1983 (12.7 per cent). In 1984, however, they declined to $22.8 million (6.1 per cent). Imports expanded from $89.0 million in 1982 (11.5 per cent of total imports) to $209.0 million (26.5 per cent) in 1984. Socialist country credits, however, were only $146.0 million in 1983 (35.2 per cent of total credits) as compared with $252.9 million (46.7 per cent) in 1982 (see Table 4).

In 1982-84, part of the absolute and relative increase in Nicaragua's commerce with CMEA and radical non-aligned countries again had to do with the closing of other markets and other sources of supply and finance. In 1983, for example, the United States refused to sell Nicaragua spare parts for computers made or purchased in the United States.[29] In May 1983 the United States cut Nicaragua's sugar quota by 90 per cent, thus virtually closing the main market for the country's third most important export product. Algeria and Iran immediately announced that they would purchase the sugar that could no longer be

---

[27] *Central America Report*, 8 July 1983.
[28] *The New York Times*, 10 March 1982.
[29] *Central America Report*, 8 July 1983.

placed on the U.S. market; Mexico and the U.S.S.R. also made significant purchases at this time.[30] In the cases where cash was paid, however, the transactions were calculated at world market prices; the United States, on the other hand, pays preferential prices to Central American sugar producers.

Similarly, after Mexico began to slow its oil deliveries to Nicaragua in late 1983, the Soviet Union made its first shipment of fuel.[31] When Mexico ceased supplying oil to Nicaragua in early 1985 because of mounting unpaid bills and Nicaragua's difficulties in contracting tankers, the Soviet Union, Libya, Algeria, Iran, Ecuador and Brazil agreed to send shipments.[32] The Soviet Union, however, began at that time to supply most of Nicaragua's needs. In May 1985 reports indicated that it agreed to provide up to 90 per cent of Nicaragua's fuel needs.[33]

Although Nicaragua became a CMEA observer in September 1983 (a status that Mexico has held since 1975), no major aid commitments or commercial agreements were forthcoming. At the Havana CMEA meeting in October 1984, Nicaragua submitted a proposal to expand bilateral and multilateral cooperation, but no agreement was announced at the conclusion of the meeting. Nevertheless, although the Soviet Union and other socialist countries have until now been cautious about committing large amounts of resources to Nicaragua, it appears likely that their economic involvement will increase following the announcement in May 1985 of a U.S. trade embargo.[34]

TRADE WITH THE SOCIALIST COUNTRIES

From the Nicaraguan point of view, trade relations with the socialist countries have advantages and disadvantages when compared to those with other countries. The commercial balance has not favored Nicaragua but the conditions governing trade on the whole have been favorable. Socialist country loans to finance their exports generally involve grace periods of one to three years, payment periods of two to 12 years and interest rates of 2.5 to 7.0 per cent (see Table 6). This compares favorably with loans coming from Latin American nations, which usually do not provide for grace periods and which charge slightly higher interest. The bilateral loans contracted with Western Europe and Canada (and even the United States prior to 1981), however, have generally granted more favorable grace periods, payment periods and interest

---

[30] *Latin America Weekly Report* (London), 10 May 1985.
[31] *The New York Times*, 28 March 1984.
[32] *The New York Times*, 24 March 1985; *Latin America Commodities Report* (London), 7 December 1984 and 25 January 1985; Radio Sandino in *FBIS-LAM*, 9 March 1984.
[33] *The New York Times*, 21 May 1985. For a more detailed discussion of Nicaragua's petroleum supply problem, see Edelman, p. 47.
[34] Ironically, President Reagan announced the embargo in West Germany at the opening of an international conference on free trade. The German government had not been advised in advance of the announcement.

rates. Importantly, it is likely that rescheduling socialist country loans will be less problematic than in the case of credits from other sources.[35]

CMEA-country trade agreements frequently include an option for payments in kind rather than in scarce convertible currency. These "compensation" clauses are barter arrangements that permit Nicaragua to exchange primary products for imports from the socialist countries.[36] The commodity structure of the trade flow remains very traditional and the list of items traded is relatively short. Nicaraguan exports consist mainly of agricultural commodities, such as coffee, cotton and sesame seeds, while imports from the CMEA countries are composed of capital goods, manufactured products and fuel. Another payment modality that distinguishes the socialist countries' trade with Nicaragua, in addition to compensation agreements, is the practice of installing light manufacturing facilities that are paid for with the products they produce.[37] Thus, for example, the cost of some of the Bulgarian-built agro-industries will be amortized through the export of canned and processed Nicaraguan products.

Most compensation agreements so far have presupposed a calculation of the price of Nicaraguan goods at or near international market rates. Only rarely have CMEA countries explicitly offered Nicaragua preferential prices for its goods. An East German accord of 1984, of unknown scope, is virtually the only such agreement that has been reported.[38] Nevertheless, the long-term nature of many of Nicaragua's commercial agreements with the CMEA countries has a stabilizing effect inasmuch as demand is assured for periods of several years and prices are set at the beginning of accords and may often be maintained for the entire period, even if world prices decline.[39] On the whole, by world standards, the prices of CMEA country goods tend to be favorable.[40]

The problems affecting Nicaraguan-socialist country trade include the great geographical distance separating Central America from Eastern Europe, the historical absence of commercial relations, and the consequent lack of familiarity on both sides with the other's foreign trade institutions. Nicaraguan economic analysts indicate that difficulties have arisen in incorporating socialist country technology in an economy that has long been dependent on

---

[35]   Berríos, 1985; FitzGerald, "Estado y política económica en la nueva Nicaragua," *Estudios Sociales Centroamericanos*, No. 37 (January-April 1984), p. 266.

[36]   For a discussion of these arrangements in Latin America, see CEPAL, *Relaciones económicas de América Latina con los países miembros del Consejo de Asistencia Mutual Económica [CAME]*. (Santiago: Estudios e Informes de la CEPAL, No. 12, 1982), pp. 46ff.

[37]   Acciaris, p. 74.

[38]   *Latin American Commodities Report*, 14 September 1984.

[39]   Berríos, "Economic Relations."

[40]   Blasier, p. 64. It should be noted that because CMEA prices are usually set by central planning boards rather than by international markets, it is difficult to compare CMEA trade figures in dollars with those of market economy countries.   On the methodological ramifications of this problem, see Christopher Coker, *Soviet Union, Eastern Europe and the NIEO* (New York: Praeger-Washington Papers, 1984).

U.S. and Japanese technology and that continues to engage in significant trade
with similarly dependent neighbours in the Central American Common Market.[41] Furthermore, since trade with CMEA countries generally does not
produce hard currency earnings, it does not contribute directly to resolving
Nicaragua's pressing debt and balance of payments problems.

The centrally planned economies tend to lack flexibility in meeting small
orders, and the comparatively limited scale of their total trade with Nicaragua
has discouraged them from establishing sizeable and long-term economic ties.
At times, this has caused problems with servicing and with the supply of
spare parts for CMEA country equipment. This in turn has sometimes contributed to prejudices, particularly in the private sector, against socialist country technology. The private sector continues to account for approximately 60
per cent of Nicaragua's GNP and CMEA countries prefer to trade with public
sector entities. Thus the Nicaraguan mixed economy model itself also constitutes a limit to the growth of commerce.

DEVELOPMENT AID FLOW TO NICARAGUA

Material and financial assistance from the socialist countries has been helpful
to the devastated Nicaraguan economy. This aid has provided much-needed
strategic and civilian assistance to the embattled revolutionary government.
Military aid from the Soviet Union and Cuba, which began in 1979 and grew
substantially after 1982 as the *contra* war escalated, has been critical for
Nicaragua's survival.[42]

Technical assistance from the socialist countries has become an integral
part of their increased co-operation with Nicaragua. The U.S.S.R. has assisted
in the areas of fishing and ocean resources, geological and mineral surveys, the
construction of two hydro-electric plants, and the establishment of radio and
television services and telecommunications. There has also been a joint
Soviet-Bulgarian project to construct a deep-water port at El Bluff on the Atlantic coast, as well as Soviet aid in building an inland waterway system from
the Río Escondido to Rama and a dry dock at the Pacific port of San Juan del
Sur.[43]

Aid to Nicaragua from other CMEA countries reflects the different capabilities and specializations of the donors. Cuba, with its long experience as a
sugar producer, has assisted Nicaragua in modernizing archaic milling installations and constructing a major new mill and refinery with mechanized field
operations. Moreover, it has provided aid to the fishing, poultry and livestock
sectors. Cubans are advising Nicaraguans in areas as diverse as radio

---

[41] Ministerio de Comercio Exterior, *Nicaragua en la coyuntura económica mundial 1982*,
Vol. 1, No. 1 (1982), p. 20.
[42] For a detailed discussion see Edelman, pp. 48-52.
[43] Theodore Schwab and Harold Sims, "Relations with Communist Countries," in Thomas
Walker (ed.), *Nicaragua Five Years Later* (New York: Praeger, 1985).

broadcasting, road construction and public health. Bulgaria, with its strong agro-industries, has concentrated on setting up food processing plants and has also helped with the construction of hydro-electric stations and communications systems.[44] Bulgarian specialists have also advised the Nicaraguan Statistics and Census Institute and trained Nicaraguan port technicians. The Czechs have concentrated on providing equipment and technical advice for the textile sector and the Hungarians have done the same for the health system. The East Germans have built and equipped a technical school and provided assistance in the chemical and construction sectors and in economic planning.[45] The North Koreans have built two hospitals, and they signed an agreement in 1983 to install Nicaragua's (and Central America's) first steel mill.[46]

The socialist countries have also donated large quantities of material emergency assistance, such as food, medical supplies and hospital equipment. Cuba absorbed a Nicaraguan debt of $73.8 million which had been used to finance the construction of the ultra-modern sugar mill at Tipitapa-Malacatoya.[47] Personnel assigned to Nicaragua have included doctors, nurses, teachers, technicians and engineers. In addition, the U.S.S.R. since 1980 has provided over 1,000 scholarships for Nicaraguan students to study in the Soviet Union. Other socialist countries also, notably Cuba and Bulgaria, have offered thousands of scholarships to Nicaraguans, although the total figures, even from official sources, vary widely.[48]

Much of CMEA countries' assistance to Nicaragua has consisted of credits for the purchase of their exports. Nevertheless, the amount of such loans has not been large. In the period of July 1979 to June 1984 only 24.2 per cent of Nicaragua's credits were provided by socialist countries (see Table 5). Since 1982, however, Nicaragua has experienced increasing difficulties in obtaining credits from multilateral lending institutions. The World Bank has not offered new loans since 1982, and in September 1984 it suspended disbursement of previously allocated funds.[49] The Inter-American Development Bank, under pressure from the United States, has repeatedly denied Nicaraguan loan

[44] Since 1978, Bulgaria has co-ordinated agro-industrial aspects of CMEA co-operation with Mexico. It appears to be playing a similar role in Nicaragua: see P. Karaivanova, "La República Popular de Bulgaria y América Latina," in Sizonenko *et al.*, *Los países del CAME*, p. 58.

[45] East German economic planning assistance has been financed through credits, such as one for $26 million extended in March 1982.

[46] Managua Radio in *FBIS-LAM*, 4 August 1980; *Barricada International* (Managua), 26 September 1983.

[47] *Barricada* (Managua), 12 January 1985.

[48] Regarding the number of Nicaraguan students in Cuba, for example, FSLN Political Secretary Bayardo Arce remarked in January 1984 that there were 2,000; Junta Coordinator Daniel Ortega stated in July of the same year that there were 5,000. See *Barricada*, 7 January 1984 and 13 July 1984.

[49] *The Washington Post*, 11 October 1984.

applications, most recently in March 1985.[50] Thus the current trend is almost certainly toward some increase in the amount and relative importance of CMEA country credits. In 1984, 50 per cent of Nicaragua's bilateral funding was reported to have come from CMEA countries.[51]

CONCLUDING REMARKS

Economic relations between Nicaragua and the socialist countries have taken various forms, including trade, credits and technical assistance in the construction of a wide range of development projects. Both the socialist and the non-aligned countries have become crucial outlets for Nicaragua's exports, as well as sources of credit, technology and oil.

The experience of trade and economic relations between Nicaragua and the socialist and non-aligned countries has been favorable to Nicaragua, even though the balance of trade has been negative and in spite of some of the problems that remain to be solved. The expansion of trade and economic co-operation in most cases has generated a diversification of export markets and supply sources. It has also permitted the beleaguered Sandinista government to survive in the face of both U.S. economic pressures and the attacks of the CIA-directed *contra* forces.

There are, in principle, favorable prospects for further co-operation between Nicaragua and the socialist and non-aligned countries. In the case of the CMEA countries, trade credits have been generous. The equipment exported to Nicaragua has been acceptable, both because it is sold at lower prices and on favorable terms, and because it is less complicated. In most cases, the technology has been adequate to Nicaragua's development needs. The long-term trade agreements with centrally planned economies have a stabilizing effect by guaranteeing demand and prices for periods of several years. In the cases of the U.S.S.R. and the non-aligned petroleum-producing countries, the commitment to meet Nicaragua's oil needs has been of critical importance.

While economic relations between Nicaragua and the socialist countries have increased to a significant level, they are still limited by a number of factors. First, since Nicaragua is not a full member of the CMEA, it is difficult for the U.S.S.R. to justify major commitments.[52] Second, the Soviet

---

50   *The Financial Times* (London), 28 March 1985.
51   *Latin American Regional Reports: Mexico and Central America* (London), 3 May 1985.
52   Only Cuba, Vietnam and Mongolia, among less developed economies, are full members of the CMEA. In the Soviet taxonomy of Third World societies, the next closest group includes the "socialist-oriented states": Afghanistan, Angola, Mozambique, Ethiopia, the People's Democratic Republic of Yemen and the Congo. Other countries that maintain good relations and signed long-term friendship treaties with the U.S.S.R. are India, Iraq and Syria. Rarely referred to in the Soviet literature as "socialist-oriented," Nicaragua is considered a good friend along with Algeria, Libya and Benin, none of which have signed friendship treaties with the U.S.S.R.: see Carol Saivetz and Sylvia Woodby, *Soviet-Third World Relations* (Boulder, CO: Westview Press, 1985); Zafar Iman, "Soviet Treaties with Third

Union's ability to provide aid is limited by that country's shortage of foreign exchange and ultimately by its own declining growth rate. Third, geographical distance is a constraint on further trade. Finally, Nicaragua's proximity to the United States discourages risky commitments in a region that is peripheral to essential Soviet security concerns.

The image of the Soviet role in Nicaragua as that of an expansionist superpower bent upon the goal of "world domination" involves a "worst-case" analysis of Soviet desires and an overestimation of Soviet capacities. To the extent that aid and trade are politically motivated, the socialist countries have achieved their objective—shared by many Latin American countries—of denying the United States a monopoly of influence in the Western hemisphere. Nevertheless, the Soviet stake in the Central American region is small and Soviet analysts express concern about the dangers of reversals in revolutionary processes in the Third World.[53] U.S. policy-makers who seek to understand Central American upheavals primarily in terms of Soviet "meddling" tend to give inadequate consideration to the complex internal dynamics of societies with long histories of oppressive rule and social injustice.[54]

The United States' trade embargo, announced on 1 May 1985, declared Nicaragua to be "an unusual and extraordinary threat to the national security and foreign policy of the United States."[55] Part of the justification cited was Nicaraguan President Daniel Ortega's trip in April to the U.S.S.R., prompted in large part by the cessation of Mexican oil shipments.[56] The embargo reflects the Reagan Administration's goals of increasing Nicaraguan reliance on the socialist countries and of using that reliance to justify further intervention. The Nicaraguan's visit to the socialist countries suggests that they foresaw increased U.S. economic pressures even if the Reagan Administration's *contra* aid bill was defeated in Congress.[57]

Of all the severe economic problems that led Nicaragua to seek additional foreign assistance, the most critical was almost certainly the country's oil

World Countries," *Soviet Studies*, Vol. 35, No. 1 (1983); A. Kiva, "Socialist-Oriented Countries: Some Development Problems," *International Affairs* (Moscow), No. 10 (1984).

[53]   See Kiva, "Socialist-Oriented Countries."

[54]   Typical of this misplaced emphasis is the Kissinger Commission Report, which does not mention either Augusto César Sandino or Agustín Farabundo Martí, leaders of anti-oligarchical and nationalist movements in the 1930s in Nicaragua and El Salvador. The revolutionary movements in their respective countries today bear their names: see *The Report of the President's National Bipartisan Commission on Central America* (New York: Macmillan, 1984).

[55]   *The New York Times*, 2 May 1985.

[56]   The trip also included visits to seven other socialist countries and to Finland, Italy, Spain, Sweden and France.

[57]   Although Ortega's trip was announced shortly before the U.S. congressional vote in April, it had been planned since March. After his return Ortega stated that in planning the visit the Nicaraguans believed that the vote would not take place until May: see *The Washington Post*, 21 May 1985; Agencia Nueva Nicaragua, "Boletín Diplomático para las Embajadas de la República de Nicaragua," 21 May 1985.

shortage, exacerbated by the termination of Mexican supplies earlier in the year. Apart from securing guarantees regarding Nicaragua's oil supplies, Ortega's visit has not brought massive amounts of aid from the U.S.S.R. or the socialist countries of Eastern Europe. But it is now clear that they will provide the necessary economic (and probably military) resources to ensure the Sandinistas' continued existence. For the Soviet Union and the other socialist countries, this is a low-cost strategy that promises political dividends in an increasingly nationalistic hemisphere. It also raises the cost of U.S. intervention by limiting the effects of economic and military pressures. Trade and aid from the socialist countries are of increasing importance in guaranteeing the Nicaraguan revolution's survival. But they are only one element in a broader effort—which includes overtures to Western Europe and the Third World—to diversify dependence as a means of meeting the country's basic development needs and maintaining its non-aligned foreign policy.

TABLE 1

NICARAGUA: TRADE BALANCE BY ECONOMIC REGIONS 1980-83
(millions of US $)

		EXPORTS			
		1980	1981	1982	1983
I.	DEVELOPING				
	COUNTRIES	87.612	145.835	103.489	105.057
	1. CACM	75.429	70.813	52.120	33.476
	2. ALADI	313.000	10.816	14.530	9.120
	3. Others:	11.870	64.206	36.839	62.461
	Caribbean	7.677	9.617	8.998	4.990
	Asia	2.738	54.589	27.841	57.471
	Europe	1.455	..	..	..
II.	OECD	350.718	325.099	272.103	271.186
	1. USA	162.351	131.132	90.073	77.741
	2. EEC	129.496	98.661	95.058	110.763
	3. Other OECD	58.871	75.306	86.972	82.682
III.	CMEA	12.112	37.331	29.857	55.050
	1. Eastern Europe	12.112	24.843	28.585	36.748
	2. Other CMEA	..	12.488	1.272	18.302
IV.	Others	..	..	..	.002
TOTAL		450.442	508.265	405.449	431.295

Table 1 continued

| | IMPORTS | | | |
	1980	1981	1982	1983
I. DEVELOPING				
COUNTRIES	513.592	505.740	363.682	355.564
1. CACM	300.561	210.504	116.947	123.571
2. ALADI	179.612	260.303	211.227	189.300
3. Others	33.419	34.933	35.508	42.693
Caribbean	26.090	25.277	13.036	27.671
Asia	7.306	9.586	22.472	15.022
Europe	.023	.070	..	..
II. OECD	371.439	460.601	320.264	315.691
1. USA	243.589	262.886	147.398	156.680
2. EEC	69.638	114.472	109.144	78.449
3. Other OECD	58.212	83.243	63.722	80.562
III. CMEA	1.966	32.787	89.032	133.574
1. Eastern Europe	1.615	24.557	58.451	91.778
2. Other CMEA	.351	8.230	30.581	41.796
IV. Others	.214	.312	2.569	2.086
TOTAL	887.211	999.440	775.547	806.915

Table 1 continued

		BALANCE		
	1980	1981	1982	1983
I. DEVELOPING				
COUNTRIES	-425.980	-359.905	-260.193	-250.507
1. CACM	-225.132	-139.691	-64.827	-90.095
2. ALADI	-179.299	-249.487	-196.697	-180.180
3. Others	-21.549	29.273	1.331	19.768
Caribbean	-18.413	-15.660	-4.038	-22.681
Asia	-4.568	45.003	5.369	42.449
Europe	1.432	-0.070	..	..
II.OECD	-20.721	-135.502	-48.161	-44.505
1. USA	-81.398	-131.754	-57.325	-78.939
2. EEC	59.858	-15.811	-14.086	32.314
3. Other OECD	.659	12.063	23.250	2.120
III. CMEA	10.146	4.544	-59.175	-78.524
1. Eastern Europe	10.497	0.286	-29.866	-55.030
2. Other CMEA	-0.351	4.258	-29.309	-23.494
IV. Others	-0.214	-0.312	-2.569	-2.084
TOTAL	-436.769	-491.175	-370.098	-375.620

Source: Planning Directorate, based on the listings compiled by the Ministry of Foreign Trade and the Dirección General de Aduanas. Nicaragua Boletín Estadístico No. 5, Comercio Exterior 1982-1983, Ministerio de Comercio Exterior, 1984.

Key:

CACM	Central American Common Market
ALADI	Latin American Integration Association
CMEA:	

Eastern Europe	U.S.S.R., Poland, Czechoslovakia, GDR, Bulgaria, Rumania, Hungary
Other CMEA	Cuba, Vietnam, Ethiopia

TABLE 2

NICARAGUA: PERCENTAGE OF FOREIGN TRADE BY ECONOMIC REGIONS 1980-83

EXPORTS

			1980	1981	1982	1983
I.	DEVELOPING COUNTRIES		19.4	28.7	25.5	24.4
	1.	CACM	16.7	13.9	12.8	7.8
	2.	ALADI	0.1	2.2	3.6	2.1
	3.	Others:	2.6	12.6	9.1	14.5
		Caribbean	1.7	1.9	2.2	1.2
		Asia	0.6	10.7	6.9	13.3
		Europe	0.3`	—	—	—
II.	OECD		77.9	64.0	67.1	62.9
	1.	USA	36.0	25.8	22.2	18.1
	2.	EEC	28.8	19.4	23.5	25.7
	3.	Other OECD	13.1	18.8	21.4	19.1
III.	CMEA		2.7	7.3	7.4	12.7
	1.	Eastern Europe	2.7	4.9	7.1	8.5
	2.	Other CMEA	—	2.4	0.3	4.2
IV.	Others		—	—	—	—
TOTAL			100	100	100	100

Table 2 continued

		IMPORTS			
		1980	1981	1982	1983
I.	DEVELOPING COUNTRIES	57.9	50.6	46.9	44.1
	1. CACM	33.9	21.1	15.1	15.3
	2. ALADI	20.2	26.0	27.2	23.5
	3. Others	3.8	3.5	4.6	5.3
	Caribbean	3.0	2.5	1.7	3.4
	Asia	0.8	1.0	2.9	1.9
	Europe	—	—	—	—
II.OECD		41.9	46.1	41.3	39.1
	1. USA	27.5	26.3	19.0	19.4
	2. EEC	7.9	11.5	14.1	9.7
	3. Other OECD	6.5	8.3	8.2	10.0
III.	CMEA	0.2	3.3	11.5	16.6
	1. Eastern Europe	0.2	2.5	7.5	11.4
	2. Other CMEA	—	0.8	4.0	5.2
IV.	Others	—	—	0.3	0.2
TOTAL		100	100	100	100

Source: Same as Table 1.

TABLE 3

NICARAGUA: TRADE BY ECONOMIC REGIONS, 1984
(millions of US $ and percentage of total)

REGION	EXPORTS US$ m.	IMPORTS US$ m.	BALANCE US$ m.	EXPORTS per cent	IMPORTS per cent
USA	45.3	158.8	-113.5	12.1	20.1
CMEA*	22.8	209.0	-186.2	6.1	26.5
Central America*	32.9	88.5	-55.6	8.8	11.2
Other Latin America**	6.7	111.4	-104.7	1.8	14.1
Western Europe	138.8	169.4	-30.6	37.1	21.4
Japan	93.5	26.0	67.5	25.0	3.3
Other	34.0	26.9	7.1	9.1	3.4
TOTAL	374.0	790.0	-416.0	100.0	100.0

*   Includes Cuba
**   Does not include Cuba

Source: Banco Central de Nicaragua

TABLE 4

NICARAGUA: SOURCES OF FOREIGN FINANCE, 1979-84

SOURCE OF FINANCE	Millions of U.S. Dollars					
	1979	1980	1981	1982	1983	1984
MULTILATERAL ORGANIZATIONS	213.0	171.9	86.7	93.6	65.6	..
World	22.0	67.0	33.7	37.0	..	..
Regional	191.0	104.0	53.0	56.6	65.6	..
BILATERAL	58.7	356.8	600.9	433.1	350.0	..
BILATRAL AID BY SOURCE:						
CAPITALIST COUNTRIES	58.7	254.8	495.7	180.2	204.0	135.3
West Europe	14.6	63.3	60.2	38.7	86.7	33.5
N. America	..	..	72.6	..	..	15.7
Latin America	44.1	118.9	332.5	138.5	83.5	86.1
Africa and Asia	..	..	103.0	3.0	33.8	..
SOCIALIST COUNTRIES	..	102.0	105.2	252.9	146.0	N.D.
TOTAL	271.1	528.7	687.6	526.7	415.6	135.3

Table 4 continued

	Percentage of Annual Total				
SOURCE OF FINANCE	1979	1980	1981	1982	1983
MULTILATERAL ORGANIZATIONS	78.4	32.5	12.6	17.8	15.8
World	8.1	12.7	4.9	7.0	0.0
Regional	70.3	19.7	7.7	10.7	15.8
BILATERAL	21.6	67.5	87.4	82.2	84.2
BILATRAL AID BY SOURCE:					
CAPITALIST COUNTRIES	21.6	48.2	72.1	34.2	49.1
West Europe	5.4	12.0	8.8	7.3	20.9
N. America	0.0	0.0	10.6	0.0	0.0
Latin America	16.2	22.5	48.4	26.3	20.1
Africa and Asia	0.0	0.0	15.0	0.6	8.1
SOCIALIST COUNTRIES	0.0	19.3	15.3	48.3	35.1
TOTAL	100	100	100	100	100

Source: División de Planificación, Estudios y Control, Fondo Internacional para la Reconstrucción, Managua, 1985.

TABLE 5

NICARAGUA: LOANS AND LINES OF CREDIT CONTRACTED DURING
THE PERIOD OF JULY 1979-JUNE 1984
(in millions of US $)

	Amount	Percentage
I. MULTILATERAL ORGANIZATIONS	$632.2	25.3
CABEI (Central American Bank for Economic Integration)	125.9	
World Bank	106.1	
IDB (Interamerican Development Bank)	256.7	
Others	143.5	
II. OFFICIAL BILATERAL LOANS AND LINES OF CREDIT	1,844.7	73.7
North America	83.0	3.3
U.S.A.	72.6	
Canada	10.4	
*Western Europe**	258.3	10.3
West Germany	25.8	
Holland	57.9	
Italy	5.4	
France	64.4	
Finland	5.7	
Spain	81.9	
Austria	12.4	
Sweden	4.8	
*Latin America**	758.0	30.0
Mexico	519.0	
Venezuela	64.2	
Brazil	50.5	
Argentina	47.8	
Peru	10.0	
Colombia	4.5	
Costa Rica	37.0	
Honduras	25.0	

Table 5 continued

Socialist Countries	605.6	24.2
U.S.S.R.	262.2	
German Democratic Republic	140.0	
Yugoslavia	25.0	
Bulgaria	60.0	
Czechoslovakia	30.0	
Hungary	5.0	
Cuba	53.4	
Korea	30.0	
Africa and Asia	139.8	5.6
Libya	100.0	
Taiwan	6.0	
China	7.0	
Iran	26.8	
III. SUPPLIERS	24.6	1.0
Italy	24.6	
GRAND TOTAL	$ 2,501.5	100.0

* Specific country-by-country breakdowns not always possible.

Source: Ministerio de Cooperación Exterior, Managua, 1985.

TABLE 6

CONDITIONS GOVERNING NICARAGUA'S FOREIGN LOANS AND LINES OF CREDIT

Creditor	Range of Grace Periods (years)	Range of Payment Periods (years)	Range of Annual Interest (%)
North America			
U.S.	6-10	25-40	2-3
Canada	10	50	0
Western Europe			
W. Germany+	10	30	2.0-2.25
Holland*	4-8	23-30	2.5
Italy	2	12	4
France	7.5-10.5	10-30	3.0-10.6
Finland	7.5	25.5	0.75
Spain		1-7	8.25-10
Austria	10	30	1
Sweden		7	1.25
Latin America			
Mexico**	N.D.	1-8	6.0-6.5
Venezuela	5	20	2
Brazil		2-10	6.5-8.0
Argentina		3-10	7.5-13.5
Peru		2-5	7
Colombia***		5	LIBOR
Costa Rica***		2	LIBOR
Honduras		3	6
Socialist Countries			
U.S.S.R.	1-3	5-10	3-5
E. Germany++	0-2	2-10	4.5-6.0
Yugoslavia	1-2	5-10	5.5-7.0
Bulgaria+++	1-2	2-10	3.5-7.0
Czechoslovakia	2-3	10-12	2.5-4.0
Hungary	1.5	6	7.25

Table 6 continued

Cuba++++	3	12	6
N. Korea		3	5
Other Countries			
Libya		5	6.3
Taiwan	2.0-2.25	10	7.0-7.5
China	2-4	8-15	7-8
Iran		2	0
Multilateral Institutions			
CABEI	N.D.	N.D.	N.D.
World Bank	N.D.	N.D.	N.D.
IDB	4.5-15	11-40	1-11
FIDA	8-10	20-50	1.2-4.0
OPEC	3-5	10-15	4
Banks associated with CEMLA	N.D.	5	N.D.
Other		5	N.D.

N.D.	No Data
*	Holland financed $3 million for 8.5 years at 10.5%.
**	Mexican data refers to lines of credit only.
***	London Inter-Bank Rate (fluctuating market rate).
+	West Germany has not extended credits since 1980.
++	East Germany financed $28 million over two years; remainder over 10 years.
+++	Bulgaria financed $35 million at 2 per cent over 10 years.
++++	Terms listed for Cuba are for $49.9 million credit; $3.5 million financed at 7.5% over seven years.

Key:		
	CABEI	Central American Bank of Economic Integration
	IDB	Inter-American Development Bank
	FIDA	Fondo Internacional para el Desarrollo Agropecuario
	OPEC	Organization of Petroleum Exporting Countries
	CEMLA	Centro de Estudios Monetarios de Latinoamérica

Source: Ministry of Foreign Cooperation, Managua.

PART 4

RECONCEPTIONS

20

America's Cuban Obsession: A Case Study in Diplomacy and Psycho-History

Edward Cuddy

"No more Cubas!" For a quarter of a century, that slogan has propelled American intervention into Latin America. President Kennedy's Alliance for Progress was designed to head off more Castro-type revolutions in the region. In 1965, President Johnson crushed a revolution in the Dominican Republic, declaring that "another Cuba in the hemisphere would be unacceptable." And the Nixon plan for subverting the Chilean government in the early 1970s was motivated, in Henry Kissinger's words, by fear of Allende's "patent intention to create another Cuba."

Today the Cuban obsession continues to mesmerize our foreign policy makers. Unless we act "decisively in defense of freedom," warns President Reagan, "new Cubas will arise from the ruins of today's conflict." Consequently, he has hoisted the stars and stripes on the bloody mast of the El Salvador regime, has crushed a fledgling regime in Grenada, is making war against Nicaragua and has committed American fortunes so deeply into the quagmire of Central America that we may soon have to choose between bloody conflict in defense of repressive governments or humiliating retreat from the scene. The Kissinger Commission on Central America has urged a much greater dose of American interventionism into the region, to counter the "Soviet-Cuban thrust" there, which endangers American security.[1]

Bad enough that we must contend with limping analogies—all Latin countries rumbling with revolution are simply "new Cubas" in the making. Far worse that the original base of comparison—"Cuba"—has been transformed into a mental construct far removed from the historical reality. In the American lexicon, Cuba has come to mean a Caribbean clone of the Soviet state; the focal point for the Soviet Communist assault on the Western

[1] "Report on Central America," *New York Times*, January 12, 1984.

hemisphere; the tap root of revolution in Central America. Had it not been for Castro, declares Brian Crozier of the *National Review*, there would have been "no Cuban missile crisis in 1962, no airlift of Cuban troops to Angola and Ethiopia, no Sandinista takeover in Nicaragua, no civil war in El Salvador. . . . "[2]

Such sentiments, at best, are based on partial truths. At worst, they fuel a national compulsion which has propelled us repeatedly into the turbulence of Central America at the expense of our own interests. If we are to construct an effective Latin American policy, we must first neutralize the Cuban demon within us. The task is psychological as well as historical, requiring an understanding of the psychic factors which have ensnarled the American mind in such powerful compulsions. Moreover, to loosen the grip of the Cuban obsession is to help unravel the other compulsions which have warped our Cold War diplomacy—particularly the blind anti-Communism which has so often distorted the precise definition of American interests and the adroit use of our power in the world's trouble spots.

A good place to begin is that jagged edge where sound historical scholarship collides with the public myths of Cuban-American relationships.

Myth 1: Fidel Castro's revolution was hatched in Moscow as part of the global assault on the free world.

Few scholars would waste time refuting this myth. The pro-Russian Cuban Communist Party had abandoned its revolutionary pretensions in the 1930s when it had acquiesced in the Cuban regime. "When Castro's men captured Havana," Soviet leader, Nikita Khrushchev, later admitted, "we had to rely on newspaper and radio reports" to find out what was happening. "We had no official contacts with any of the new Cuban leaders and therefore nothing to go on but rumor."[3]

If Karl Marx had died of the measles at age 4, there would still have been a Cuban revolution bursting with anti-Americanism. Castro rode to power on a tide of revolutionary nationalism, born of deep resentment toward six decades of Yankee domination, as well as internal poverty and political oppression. "For Castro," claims Edward Gonzalez, "permanent defiance of the 'imperialist government' of the United States remains very much the essence of his revolution."[4]

[2]   Brian Crozier, "The Caribbean Scourge," *National Review*, XXXV, September 2, 1983, 1062.
[3]   Nikita Khrushchev, *Khrushchev Remembers* (New York, 1970), pp. 540-1.
[4]   Edward Gonzalez, "The United States and Castro: Breaking the Deadlock," *Foreign Affairs*, 50: July 1972, 722-37.

Myth 2: Castro's Cuba soon became the primary security threat to the United States—a puppet regime for the Soviet assault against the Western hemisphere.

Undoubtedly, Castro's firebrand anti-Americanism, his expropriation of American corporations, his growing ties with Cuban Communists inflamed the growing conflict between the two countries. But the critical question, from the beginning, was not whether the United States was endangered by the Castro revolution, but whether the Cuban regime could survive American intervention. Washington had toppled the left-leaning reformist government of Guatemala, just five years before Castro's rise to power. Cuban fears of a repeat performance were soon confirmed. The United States denied badly needed loans, pressured her European allies to refuse refining Soviet oil in Cuba, squeezed the sugar trade—the island's economic lifeline—and finally launched the reckless invasion which ended in the Bay of Pigs fiasco.

In his desperate struggle to survive "Guatemalization" by the northern giant, Castro turned to the Soviet Union. The latter eagerly responded with loans, generous trade agreements and military aid. The Bay of Pigs invasion had put the Russians on the spot: either provide effective protection against further Yankee aggression or be dismissed as a useless ally in the power struggle with the United States. Nuclear missiles, so Khrushchev reasoned, provided "the most tangible and effective deterrent" to further aggression.[5] The terrifying missile crisis of 1962 was the direct outcome of Washington's prior efforts to crush the Castro regime.

The missile crisis passed. But in the following years, there would be no let up in Washington's economic offensive against the fragile island economy. Until the mid-1970s, the United States isolated Cuba economically and diplomatically from most of Latin America, forbade American corporations and their foreign subsidiaries to trade with her, refused to service merchant ships which had called at Cuban ports, and threatened to cut off aid to nations which traded with her. Trade and credit embargoes continue to this day.

Through it all, the American public managed to convince itself that Soviet and Cuban aggression, not American belligerence, was at the root of the conflict. But many scholars and foreign observers conclude otherwise. Many marvelled at Castro's survival skills. The bearded revolutionary, according to Cubanologist, Carmelo Meza-Lago, was a "political genius" who defied overwhelming American power to turn Cuban into one of the most stable nations in the hemisphere.[6] Cuba's struggle for survival, her cardinal foreign policy

---

5 Khrushchev, p. 546.
6 Jorge I. Dominguez, "Cuban Foreign Policy," *Foreign Affairs*, 57: Fall 1978, 83-108.

objective since 1959, declared Jorge I. Dominguez, stands as one of the great success stories in modern times.[7]

Tragically, American diplomacy helped transform Cuban nationalism—a force hostile to all outside control, Russian as well as American—into a Soviet outpost in the Caribbean. Fidel Castro was like a drowning man in a pool, claimed Mexico's former President, López Mateos, who sought help from the America side. But every time he splashed over to our side, "we stepped on his fingers." Washington, he insisted, had forged the Moscow-Havana alliance.[8]

Myth 3: In pursuit of its aim of world conquest, the Soviet Union used its Cuban puppet to export revolution into Latin America in the 1960s and continues to foment revolution in Central America today.

Fierce images of a Soviet-Cuban conspiracy, pumping revolution throughout Latin America, are rooted in distorted notions which crystallized around events in the 1960s. In those years, Castro did indeed support revolutionaries on the mainland. But his policy was based on Cuban aims and executed in outright defiance of the U.S.S.R.. The Fidelista regime was struggling to survive the iron grip of commercial and diplomatic isolationism forged by the Yankee Colossus. What better way to break out of the suffocating squeeze than to subvert governments beholden to Washington.

As for the Soviets, they had little interest in Latin America, so marginal to their strategic interests, and had less confidence in revolutionary struggles there. By the mid-1960s, they had reversed their tentative endorsement of revolution to support the very governments Castro was trying to topple. Hence, rebellions which many Americans attributed to a Soviet-Cuban conspiracy, had actually embittered relations between the two Marxist states. After the death of Cuban rebel leader, Che Guevara, in 1967, Castro shifted course, patched up his ties with the U.S.S.R. and resorted to diplomacy to break the diplomatic quarantine.

Today, as then, warped notions of Soviet revolutionary conspiracies continue to control American responses to Central America. Only now, both Nicaragua and Cuba are the supposed pawns in the Russian chess game. True, the Soviets seem to have funnelled low-key support to the Salvadoran rebels. But the entire area remains outside the pale of their strategic interests, and they recognize the "primacy of the United States interests and power" as "the chief political reality in the Western Hemisphere."[9] Moreover, not even the Soviet

---

[7] *Ibid.*, 83-108.
[8] James Reston, "Mexico City," *New York Times,* December 12, 1962.
[9] Robert H. Donaldson, "The Soviet Union in the Third World," *Current History,* 81: October 1982, 313-17, 339.

Union wants "another Cuba." At a cost of over one billion dollars a year, one Cuba is plenty.

The American fixation on the Russian-Cuban-Nicaraguan connection, unburdened by nuance or complexity, blurs the more fundamental realities which should inform American diplomacy: that poverty and oppression, not global Communism, are the well springs of revolution; that it has been our allies, not our enemies, that have fomented the greatest terror and violence in El Salvador; that the internal struggles of the region are directed against oppressive regimes, not American security; that American interventionism has been a powerful spur for rebels and radicals to turn to the Soviet bloc for help.

Myth 4: Since the 1970s, the Soviets have used the Cubans to expand their strategy of conquest to the continent of Africa.

Since the late 1970s, Presidents Jimmy Carter and Ronald Reagan have vented their rage over the presence of 40,000 Cuban troops in Africa—alleged proxies of the Soviets, "constantly embroiled in every trouble spot" on the continent.[10] Once again, American spokesmen were acting more in the mold of cold-war fixations than historical analysis, distorting both the motives and behavior of their Cuban adversaries. Despite close cooperation with the U.S.S.R., Castro's African policies were fashioned in Havana, not Moscow. Soviet leader, Leonid Brezhnev, was not far off the mark when he reminded President Carter:

> You continue to complain about Cuban troops in Africa. We do not control these decisions, which are made by the Cuban leaders themselves. However, we do know that the troops are sent only in response to specific requests by the recognized governments in Angola and Ethiopia.[11]

Prompted by its own revolutionary history and ideological sympathies and seeking a more friendly international sphere in a world dominated by a hostile American power, the fidelistas have long supported African revolutions against Western imperialism. Nor have they played the mischievous role conveyed by the carping criticism of American politicians and journalists. The Cubans have built roads and staffed hospitals. When conflict between Somalia and Ethiopia erupted, Castro visited both countries, seeking a reconciliation. In Angola, the Cubans have provided military protection for its Gulf oil refineries and bolstered defenses against invading South African forces. By and large, Cuba's actions have "greatly strengthened its position with African countries,"

10 Jimmy Carter, *Keeping Faith: Memoirs of a President* (New York, 1982), p. 254.
11 *Ibid.*, p. 256.

declares Dominguez, "and thus gained the very sort of international influence
. . . that had long been a major objective of Cuban policy."[12]

"The twilight zone that lies between living memory and written history,"
writes Historian C. Vann Woodward, "is one of the favorite breeding places of
mythology."[13] Our Cuban experience fits into that twilight zone. For many
Americans, old enough to remember the traumas associated with Castro but
too young for historical perspective, "Cuba" has become a cluster of exaggerated memories of Soviet intrigue and forgotten memories of American aggression. Yet, as long as American diplomacy is under the spell of the Cuban obsession, American interventionism will be gasoline poured on a raging
fire, aggravating the violence in Central America and sabotaging our vital
interests in the process. Apart from strategic analysis, so necessary for constructive diplomacy, scholars need to explore the psychic forces which entan-
gle our foreign affairs.

A good starting point is George Serban's study, *The Tyranny of Magical
Thinking*. Adult neuroses, according to Serban, are rooted in the faulty perceptions and emotionally charged memories of childhood. A child, for example, may experience a frightening episode without understanding exactly why
the event posed a danger. Yet, the emotional charge from the trauma will
linger on, shaping future actions. "His memory retains the emotional response
associated with the feared object to which he has now been conditioned,"
blunting his ability to evaluate similar events in the future and warping his
behavioral response to them. Those emotionally charged memories, claims
Serban, can "lead to the formation of attitudes, patterns of reaction and approaches to reality that become the guiding principles for the organization of
the child's (and later the adult's) behavior."[14]

It is risky business, translating observations on individual psychology
into generalizations about society. But, with proper caution, psychology can
provide valuable insights into political processes which might otherwise escape the historian or security analyst.

Politically speaking, the critical "childhood years" for our Cuban-American relationship occurred during the five-year period between 1957-1962. With
only the haziest notions of the pressures which prodded Castro into the Soviet
orbit, American attitudes toward the bushy-bearded revolutionary congealed
during one of the most traumatic seasons of the Cold War. The ominous
launching of Sputnik in 1957 heralded the advancing nuclear capabilities of the
Soviet Union. Several crises followed in rapid succession: the Soviet downing
of America's U-2 spy plane, the Berlin wall crisis, the Congo conflict,
Russia's stunning decision to resume open-air nuclear testing, the growing

12 Dominguez, pp. 83-108.
13 C. Vann Woodward, *The Strange Career of Jim Crow* (New York, 1966), p. xii.
14 George Serban, *The Tyranny of Magical Thinking* (New York, 1982), p. 36.

revolutionary upheaval in Southeast Asia. Everywhere, it seemed—in Africa, the Middle East, Latin America, East Asia—the Soviet Empire was surging forward. And all this against the reckless rhetoric and bullying style of Soviet leader, Nikita Khrushchev. His blustering threat to "bury" America, his shoe-pounding tantrum at the United Nations, his exuberant support for "wars of national liberation," all seemed to dramatize the retreat of the free world before Soviet expansionism.

In this frenzied framework, Fidel Castro came to power and forged new ties with the Soviet Union. With the Cuban missile crisis in 1962, all the jagged emotions of the prolonged Soviet-American power struggle came to a head, transforming Cuba into an American fixation—a potent symbol of both the nuclear Damocles sword dangling over the United States and the relentless advance of Communism against the crumbling barricades of democracy. In this charged atmosphere, many Americans lost sight of Cuba's own desperate struggle to survive the onslaught of American power.

These early encounters with Castro's Cuba undoubtedly aggravated the "paranoid style" which, according to Richard Hofstadter, has permeated American politics. The paranoid individual processes information through a grid of preconceived expectations which confuses real with imaginary dangers and hinders flexible responses to changing situations. As Serban points out, paranoia is often rooted in an exaggerated sense of self-importance fostered during childhood. Deluded into thinking he is of special importance, the child develops a penchant for blaming others for his own failures—a psychological barrier for protecting his fragile self-esteem. Hence he grows up in a world filled with people out "to get him," a world of incompetent and corrupt enemies who cannot brook his alleged superiority.[15]

The American historical experience has nurtured a superiority complex which makes us vulnerable to feelings of paranoia. From the Puritan pioneers whose "zion in the wilderness" was supposed to inspire a corrupt Old World, to the Founding Fathers whose revolutionary government was deemed a model for Europe's aging monarchies, America's origins were heavily larded with notions of moral and political superiority. For three centuries, our forefathers plundered the Indian cultures, a grim record of aggression and broken promises which was turned into a story of Indian savagery, pioneer heroism and the national pursuit of freedom and Manifest Destiny. A century of isolation from Europe's power struggles reinforced ideas that we were above the greed and aggression that mired other lands in conflict. And when we finally stumbled into World War I, President Woodrow Wilson set the tone for the century: that America fights, not for base motives typical of other nations, but for the freedom of all peoples.

[15] *Ibid.*, p. 103.

No leader has bested President Reagan in catering to this exaggerated sense of self-importance. "I have always believed that this anointed land was set apart in an uncommon way," he declared, "that a divine plan placed this great continent here between the oceans to be found by people from every corner of the earth who had a special love of faith and freedom." The Soviet Union, however, is an "evil empire," the "focus of evil in the modern world," the force behind all the "hot spots in the world."[16]

The paranoic compulsion to protect a fragile self-image by lashing out at others surfaced early in our dealings with Fidel Castro. The events culminating in the missile crisis of 1962 fixed our rage on his perversity. Forgotten (probably never understood) was the fact that Castro's anti-Americanism sprung from a Cuban nationalism generated by six decades of American domination; that his collaboration with the Soviet Union was not a strategy of conquest but a desperate effort to survive American efforts to crush his fledgling regime.

This paranoic pattern continues today. Blaming Soviet-Cuban subversion for the turbulence in Central America undoubtedly answers some basic psychic needs. In El Salvador, it blurs the fact that our allies, not our enemies, have inflicted most of the terror on that blood-soaked land. In condemning the Sandinistas for betraying democracy and arming Salvadoran rebels, Reagan can ignore the prolonged American support for the Somoza dictatorship, the massive flow of American arms into the region, the governments we have manipulated or overthrown. The Administration's invasion of Grenada was carried out to a familiar drumbeat: the outrage over the murder of Maurice Bishop— even though Reagan had tried to sink his regime; the claims of an oversized runway designed for Russian jets—even though it was shorter than runways on neighboring islands; the furious fusillade over weapons cached away on the island—overlooking its defensive needs in the face of United States threats. "If we are to believe certain madmen," groaned the deposed Grenadian leader, Bernard Coard, "this tiny island, 21 by 13 miles, is a superpower . . . because the United States, the mightiest nation in the world, is trembling at us."[17]

The compulsion for control is a key concept in Serban's analysis of the obsessive, paranoic individual. Here, too, we have a rich field for exploring the affinities between the pathology of the individual and the fixations of a nation.

The well-adjusted person learns to accept losses in life. He can shift priorities and goals, tailoring them to new situations in which old patterns have been short-circuited and new opportunities are opening. Not so the obsessive-compulsive whose behavior is still molded by the tyranny of

---

[16]   Quoted in Arthur Schlesinger, Jr., "Foreign Policy and the American Character," *Foreign Affairs*, 62: Fall 1983, 1-16.
[17]   Penny Lernoux, "U.S.'s 'big stick' policy hits tiny isle of Grenada," *National Catholic Reporter*, November 4, 1983, 24.

childhood egocentrism. Such a person, Serban tells us, is rivoted by an inflexible urge to control events. Unable to adjust to the loss of control, even when he realizes his initial goals are beyond reach, he often continues the pursuit of them, becoming "progressively more frustrated."[18]

This description of the neurotic individual parallels current analysis of our Central American diplomacy. For over a century, the United States has exercised preponderant power in the Western hemisphere. Since 1850, by one count, she has intervened militarily 69 times in the Caribbean and Central America.[19] The U.S. was "so overwhelmingly influential," former Ambassador Earl Smith once admitted, that "the American Ambassador was the second most important man in Cuba; sometimes even more important than the Cuban President."[20]

Fidel Castro rode to power on the tide of a powerful nationalist impulse to break loose from foreign domination. That was the crux of the conflict: the American compulsion for control; the Cuban thrust to break loose from that control. From the outset, Washington tried to limit Castro's radical reforms. And, failing that, she tried to crush his government—first, by economic blows; then by outright invasion; finally by prolonged strategy of commercial strangulation. What Americans generally conceived as a Communist conspiracy was more fundamentally a Cuban struggle to be free of American power.

In the following years, the Cuban pattern proved contagious. For a quarter of a century, U.S. hegemony throughout Latin America has been declining. In their foreign policies, in their shifting trade patterns, in their assertive behavior at the United Nations, in the revolutions sprouting throughout the region, the Latin lands have increasingly asserted their independence from Yankee dominion.

This changing political power balance is the natural outcome of powerful indigenous forces. An old order led by pro-American elites is giving way to a new order marked by a lower level of American influence. These indigenous changes—even revolutionary movements—pose no basic threat to American security interests. And the better part of wisdom today, so many analysts claim, is a new U.S. policy which accommodates the emergent hemispheric system of declining American control.

Yet, like the paranoid people in Serban's analysis, the United States seems unable to "let go." "If we cannot manage Central America," declares Henry Kissinger, Chairman of Reagan's Commission on Central America, "it will be impossible to convince threatened nations in the Persian Gulf and in other places that we know how to manage the global equilibrium."[21]

[18] Serban, pp. 29, 30, 31, 190-191.
[19] Lemoux, p. 24.
[20] Quoted in Stephan E. Ambrose, *Rise to Globalism* (New York, 1982, 2nd rev. ed.), p. 240.
[21] Ronald Steel, "Kissinger is Skilled in Working the Dark Side of Nation's Ambitions,"

Reagan's rabid animosity toward Nicaragua, claims Richard H. Ullman, is due largely to its challenge to American dominion. The Sandinistas are "living proof that movements such as theirs can triumph over a government that . . . enjoyed substantial support from the United States."[22] In this respect, many foreign observers have likened the American to Soviet behavior: "Both seek hegemony. Neither will tolerate political diversity within its sphere of influence."[23]

The central conflict at the storm center of the Western Hemisphere, then, is not Communism verses freedom, but Latin independence versus Yankee control. As Abraham Lowenthal puts it, "The fundamental flaw of United States policy toward Latin America and the Caribbean during the past twenty years," has been the nation's failure to respond to the erosion of its "unchallenged dominance in the Western Hemisphere," its failure to "cope with hegemony in decline."[24]

Whiplashed by the urge to control the uncontrollable, the neurotic often resorts to magical thinking. He relies on ritualistic gestures rather than activity which is causally connected to desired results: the ballplayer, for example, who rubs a rabbit's foot to get a base hit, or the child who pulls the covers over his head to fend off ghosts. "From this magical approach to reality," Serban declares, "seems to stem the obsessive compulsive behavior in adulthood."[25]

"Rabbit's Foot Diplomacy" has become a marked feature in our Central American policies. Many of our actions—more ritualistic than realistic—bear no relation to desired goals or actually produce opposite results. In the name of American security, Washington persists in its hostile actions despite weighty evidence that such behavior drove Cuba into the Soviet orbit and is achieving similar results in Nicaragua and El Salvador. "The only conceivable result of American policies" in Nicaragua, Ullman warns, will be a nation "domestically more monolithic and more repressive than today and in its foreign policy more stridently anti-American, more dependent on the Soviet Union and on Cuba, and therefore more willing to do their bidding."[26] In pursuit of stability in El Salvador, the United States supports a regime which is responsible for most of the turmoil there. War is waged against Nicaragua

---

Buffalo News, July 31, 1983.

[22] Richard H. Ullman, "At War With Nicaragua," *Foreign Affairs,* 62: Fall 1983, 39-58.

[23] *Ibid.*

[24] Abraham Lowenthal, "Ronald Reagan and Latin America: Coping with Hegemony in Decline," in Kenneth A. Oye, et al., eds., *Eagle Defiant* (Boston, 1983), p. 325. See also Roland H. Ebel, "Political Instability in Central America," *Current History,* 81: February 1982, 56-59, 86.

[25] Serban, p. 30.

[26] Ullman, *loc. cit.*

on the illusory notion that it will solve problems in El Salvador. The invasion of Grenada will, presumably, preserve democracy elsewhere. Economic embargoes against Cuba will dampen revolutions on the mainland.

Across the entire region where faltering economies, huge unemployment and glaring gaps between rich and poor have fueled political conflict, Reagan has waved a magic wand: the "Caribbean Initiative." This bundle of trade and aid proposals will supposedly solve festering problems which neither President Kennedy's ill-fated Alliance for Progress nor generations of local elites could solve. And this from an Administration which tends toward laissez-faire when it comes to our own problems of poverty and unemployment.

Such is the nature of magical thinking: a foreign policy geared more to American psychic needs than to strategic interests. Living in a complex, threatening world, many people need simple explanations (however far removed from reality) which lead to concrete actions (however ineffective) to assuage the need to feel that the world is still subject to American control. Indeed, pessimistic predictions of the dangers facing the nation may be more assuring than optimistic ones, according to Robert H. Johnson. "By suggesting the need for action, they respond to culturally rooted American compulsions toward activism and believing that all problems have a solution. It is reassuring to think that by 'doing something' we can eliminate threats to our survival. . . . "[27]

Improved Central American diplomacy demands more than the careful analysis of strategic interests and appropriate policies. It demands greater psychological analysis to deal with the mental tyrannies which can injure international as well as personal relations. As a nation we must neutralize our Cuban obsession and its related compulsions, temper our fears over revolutionary change in a region where it is long overdue, adjust to the inevitable decline of American power. A measure of psychic growth is necessary to ground our policies on sound diplomatic realities.

The transition from childhood modes of magical thought to adult patterns of logical analysis can be extremely difficult. The "irrational behavior" of the neurotic, writes Serban, is deeply entangled with "emotionally laden past experiences" and "the feelings associated with these memories are likely to overpower any attempt to correct the neurotic behavior by a simple appeal to the logical rules of thinking."[28] Moreover, society itself reinforces faulty beliefs. In the absence of factual knowledge or habits of logical thought, people cling to mythical explanations, unable to tolerate the mystery of a troublesome environment. "Mankind has a pressing psychological need to explain the world; it has no such need to see it explained correctly."[29]

[27] Robert H. Johnson, "Periods of Peril," *Foreign Affairs*, 61: Spring, 1983, pp. 950-70.
[28] Serban, p. 185.
[29] Quoted from Patrick Morgan in Johnson, *loc. cit.*

An important task for historians, claims Howard Zinn, is to expose the faulty myths and rationalizations which permeate the culture, the fixed ideas which buttress the established system. In this respect, the historian functions much like the psychologist. "The therapist must attack the patient's beliefs or fears," advises Serban, enabling him to realize that his "own preconceived view of reality" and the behavior flowing from it "are responsible for his conflict with others." In the course of treatment, the patient must not simply recall events but recall the significance he had given them. Through this process of recall and reflection, pseudocausal explanations of problems give way to logical analysis of causal connections, leading to "new and more viable ways of coping with life."[30]

Serban's prescriptions are pertinent to the rigid ideology which has permeated the entire Russo-American power struggle. But the Cuban obsession is a good starting point for "Cold War therapy." It provides a sharp, manageable focus for studying the distorted notions which have hardened around our Central American diplomacy. We have persuasive testimony from Latin American allies (especially the Contadora nations of Mexico, Panama, Venezuela, and Colombia) who share our anti-Soviet concerns but challenge our anti-Communist compulsions. The rancid Vietnam experience (though a fading lesson in history) has disposed a large segment of opinion for alternative views to the compulsive anti-Communism which has catapulted us into the internal conflicts of other nations.[31]

American history, itself, provides ample correctives to the rigid dogmatism which infects our hemispheric policies. As pioneers of revolution in the New World, we should be the first to sympathize with those who have chosen the same means to end political oppression in their homelands. Our long struggle against white Anglo-Saxon conformity to achieve a pluralistic society should expand our tolerance for a continent evolving toward a wider diversity of political ideologies and social structures. And when revolutionary regimes, like the Fidelistas and the Sandinistas, fall short of their democratic promises, our own tormented history—an unseemly mixture of democratic idealism and undemocratic practice—should provide a tolerant perspective.

"Who controls the past, controls the future: who controls the present, controls the past." So George Orwell proclaimed. It was governmental control of the nation's history—the manipulation of documents so that "the past is whatever the Party chooses to make it" that buttressed the nightmarish dictatorship in Orwell's famous novel, *1984*. Against this kind of governmental power, genuine historical knowledge and reflection, broadly diffused, are the

---

[30]   Serban, pp. 192-93, 197-98.

[31]   A Gallup poll taken during the summer, 1983, indicated that 72 per cent of the American people believed that American intervention could change El Salvador into another Vietnam. Americans opposed military aid to Central America, 55 per cent to 35 per cent.

best weapons. The burden of cauterizing the compulsions which have spurred so many conflicts between the United States and her Latin neighbors is a continuing task for historians, television producers, journalists and those rare politicians graced with both the intelligence and the courage to challenge the destructive dogmas which have crystallized around our Cuban experience.

Peace activists shudder whenever Washington utters its war cry: "No more Cubas." For two decades it has been the prelude to American interventions, often to prop up old dictatorships or to install new ones. Yet, stripped of its mythology, even the critics might respond: "No More Cubas? You're Damned Right—Let there be no more Cubas!"

21

Historical Realities

E. Bradford Burns

As a historian I would like to turn back to historical perspective. We can take the long view and place events in context.

Visions of the Central American reality in 1985 are many, and they are contradictory as well. While everyone agrees that crises rock the Isthmus, disagreements on the causes and consequences abound. But as a historian I think that these crises, though the causes are many, share a common denominator. Running through them all is an anxiety about socioeconomic change. At least during the past century, any effort at change within Central America triggered international responses.

Indeed, so sensitive is the subject of change that even talk of it awakens apprehension. This is true not only within the five states of the region, but beyond Central America. Even the mere suggestion of fundamental change affects the metropolis, if only because the metropolis perceives that it does. And in the twentieth century, obviously and indisputably, that metropolis is the United States.

No serious discussion of Central America can avoid, or should avoid, the major characteristic of this region: grinding poverty for the many, and opulence for the few. No country in Central America is incapable of feeding its population, yet none does so. Central America has sufficient resources to ensure an adequate level of living for its population, yet it fails to do so. No discussion of Central America should become so abstract, should indulge so theoretically in geopolitics, that it ignores these brute economic and social realities.

We must constantly remind ourselves that the budgets of El Salvador, Honduras, and Nicaragua—their combined national budgets—are less than the budget for the University of California. The University provides for staff, faculty, and students numbering 170,000. Those three governments, on the other hand, bear responsibility for twelve million people. The economies of all five Central American nations have collapsed. None is prepared to meet the new realities of the world market. Debts strangle each and every state. In each—

except Nicaragua—hunger, unemployment, underemployment, malnutrition, and disease mount.

In 1983 a Costa Rican presidential report declared that 83% of rural Costa Ricans lived in poverty. Land distribution in a country once acclaimed as the Switzerland of Central America has become increasingly inequitable. In 1981 1% of the farmers owned 36% of the land, each holding on average *925 times* the average holding of almost half the population: 48.8% held only 1.9% of the land. In 1984 the Honduran government reported that 72% of the population suffered from malnutrition. As Rudolfo Carranza, a landless rural inhabitant with eleven children put it: "The question is hunger. Our stomachs need an answer." You might well imagine that the quality of life in rural Honduras is sobering. Half the children die before their fifth birthday. Life expectancy for those who survive is under fifty years.

The planning ministry of El Salvador reported in 1984 that 53% of children under five years of age were malnourished. Researchers at the Universidad Centroamericana José Simeón Cañas (San Salvador) said the figure was too low: reality lay closer to 80%. Salvadoran statistics indicate that between 1979 and 1983 real, minimum wages declined by 65%, while the general price index rose 97%. In 1984 both the Dirección General de Estadística and the Banco de Guatemala reported that 75% of the Guatemalan population could not satisfy their minimum needs, and 40% could not even afford a minimum diet.

These statistics suggest the brutal realities Central Americans must address. They prompted former President Rodrigo Carazo of Costa Rica to remark, "We're getting tired of repeating this, but the social unrest in many of our countries is not caused by ideologies, but by hunger."

I visited Guatemala, Honduras, El Salvador, and Nicaragua in the summer of 1985. I was very much concerned about how the Nicaraguan revolution was perceived. The major newspapers of Guatemala, Honduras, and El Salvador condemned whatever they reported taking place in Nicaragua uniformly, in unison, often and loudly. According to these papers, Nicaragua was, in addition, the source of all troubles in Central America. Nothing positive happened in Nicaragua, and nothing positive was reported.

Yet, whatever one's views of Nicaragua, the fact is the people have access to education, to health care, and to land, and they are learning to feed themselves. Surely, I thought, that fact must appeal to someone in Honduras, El Salvador, and Guatemala. So I undertook to talk to people. I speak Spanish, I can go wherever I want, and I did; and I spoke with what I call ordinary folks. In Guatemala I learned absolutely nothing: that's the silent country, the eeriest of these Central America states, for no one talks. *No one talks.* So in Guatemala I learned nothing. But in Honduras and El Salvador, thanks to conversations with women's groups, student groups, Christian-based communities, and labor unions, I asked people privately what they thought about

Nicaragua. The response was quite uniform. They knew something about Nicaragua, and it was something that was not in the press.

They knew that their counterparts in Nicaragua have access to land, food, education, and health care. They knew that. They admired it, because that is what they want. Despite the press they—the twenty, perhaps thirty, people I spoke to in Honduras and El Salvador—perceived Nicaragua as a country attempting to meet basic social needs.

HISTORICAL REMINDERS

Hunger can be abolished in Central America, but only if some basic institutions, inherited from the colonial past and strengthened in the nineteenth century, are significantly altered. The changes require a new, more imaginative leadership, willing and able to exercise the attributes of sovereign power through and for the majority. Unfortunately, the past suggests that such an imaginative leadership, speaking with a nationalist voice, is always regarded by the metropolis as a challenge. It poses a threat to the metropole-client relationship.

The United States moved to shape Central America in the late nineteenth and early twentieth centuries. Building on the Monroe Doctrine, Washington placed limits on client states, while expanding the role and control of the metropole. In 1895 Secretary of State Richard Olney affirmed the rule governing US policy when he said its "fiat is law" in the Western Hemisphere. Presidents Theodore Roosevelt, Taft, and Wilson unequivocally imposed that fiat on Central America. With few ambiguities and fewer inhibitions, Taft pursued dollar diplomacy, which he publicly defined as a policy including "active intervention to secure our merchandise and our capitalists opportunity for profitable investment." Talk like that, and the action that ensued, set precedents followed in US relations with Central America to this day.

Since 1945 client states and colonies have challenged the global metropolises. Asian and African demands led to decolonization. Latin American clients have challenged Washington and can be expected to do so more frequently. Some judge that the behavior of the metropolis makes such challenges inevitable. But even when the aim in Latin American countries is limited to changing traditional institutional structures, an overly sensitive Washington has perceived a direct challenge to its hemispheric hegemony. With the cry "the Russians are coming!", Washington flatly opposes efforts for significant internal reform, no doubt concluding—because the Soviet Union does not, in fact, establish itself in those countries—that the United States has thereby thwarted the Russians.

This automatic rejection of change carries serious dangers. In the concluding volume of *The Story of Civilization* Will and Ariel Durant write of change—in language that cannot but echo eerily in our minds. "When the group or a civilization declines," they warn, "it is through no mystic limitations of a corporate life, but through the failure of its political or intellectual leaders to meet the challenges of change." History demonstrates, alas, that every twentieth century US administration, except that of Franklin D. Roosevelt, has labelled efforts at change as Bolshevik, or communist-inspired or communist-dominated. That charge has been hurled at the Mexican revolution for decades, even though the Mexicans began their revolution about seven years before the tsar fell.

There have been five revolutions in Latin America since 1900. The United States has opposed them all. Its opposition to the distant Bolivian revolution, of course, was much subtler than its armed interventions in Mexico, Guatemala, Cuba, and now Nicaragua. US administrations have been particularly hostile to agrarian reforms that promise to give Central American people access to land and to shift the emphasis of production from export crops to foodstuffs for local consumption. Guatemala, El Salvador, and Nicaragua offer ample evidence of Washington's resistance to land reform.

The CIA overthrew the democratic and constitutional government of President Jacobo Arbens of Guatemala in 1954, castigating his land reform as communistically inspired. Colonel Carlos Castillo Armas, a counter-revolutionary put in power by the CIA, reversed the reform, returning to the former land barons that very land distributed to create a new peasant class.

At first glance, El Salvador might appear to contradict the charge that Washington opposes fundamental reform. In 1980 the US Agency for International Development wrote a far-reaching land reform program for El Salvador. But closer examination shows this case to be a bizarre study in political schizophrenia. The Salvadoran army—financed, equipped and trained by the United States—has prevented the reform from being successfully undertaken. Washington can take credit in this particular case for proposing an admirable land reform, and for preventing its implementation as well.

In Nicaragua today the *contras*, trained, financed, armed, and directed by the CIA, make rural cooperatives one of their prime targets; their goal is to destroy any evidence of agrarian reform and to suppress the reform movement by murdering agrarian reform officials. Perhaps this hostility to agrarian reform springs from the knowledge that reform would alter the political balance in Central America, reducing the power of the traditional elites and conferring some power on a new peasant class. Perhaps, too, they recognize that reform would restructure external trade flows. One would do well to reflect on the observation of former President Eduardo Frey of Chile, who said:

> The biggest threat as I see it, is that Latin America will try to stop communism by stopping reform in progress, and there is nothing bet-

ter prepared to open the door to communism than such action. We need to champion and lead reform, then we have nothing to fear.

The evidence is clear. Washington harbors deep suspicions about change and prefers traditional relations to new ones.

The Central American elites and military share the same expectations, and they have become masters at winning Washington's support. It is a case of mutual manipulation. Unable to stem the tide of change, the elites and military depend ever more heavily on the metropolis to assist them in maintaining the patterns of the past. Their tactic is simplicity itself, one that had already proven effective in many parts of the hemisphere. The elites identify any longing for change, no matter how modest, with communism. They fully appreciate the Pavlovian response of US officials to any charge that communism is afoot in Central America. Once the alert has been sounded, military and economic aid from Washington cascades over a grateful, if greedy, elite. That aid shores up shaky institutions. Washington—and many US academic specialists—refuse to believe that centuries of gross social and economic inequities might give rise to justifiable demands for change. Rather, Washington prefers to view local struggles for justice as major acts in an endless East-West drama, a never-closing stageplay that has mesmerized generations of politicians and bureaucrats. Following well-defined policies traceable through decades of Republican and Democratic administrations, the US government continues to ally itself with officers and oligarchs in a relentless struggle against change. Washington abandons the revolutionaries. It withdrew from relations with Cuba. Oblivious to any lessons from history, it repeats its tragic mistakes in Nicaragua.

POLICY

The Soviet leadership, we might imagine, is only too pleased at the unexpected opportunity handed to it by the temperamental and illogical behavior of the natural metropolis of the Western Hemisphere. Any hard-nosed analyst of international behavior must agree that weak, impoverished, small nations cannot on their own withstand the pressure of the metropolis. They must succumb to the pressure or find a protector. In Nicaragua and Cuba, US policy seems determined to create the very outcome it professes not to want: alienation of its client, which in a desperate search for a means of self-protection accepts aid from the rival metropolis. Alternatives for those Central American leaders who want to move beyond rhetoric to real reform, while retaining good relations with the hemispheric metropolis, are not encouraging. Lamenting a week of international violence in the Middle East, President Ronald Reagan remarked on 5 April 1985 that this return to violence is abhorrent. All the more so, because it is so useless. There is no military option for solving the difficult conflicts of the Middle East.

One might hope that his wisdom could be extended to Central America, where the military is, and has been, a large part of the problem.

Yet it is the military solution that Washington relentlessly pursues. Money spent on the military can only further destabilize Central America. It distorts the economies. It deflects development. It ensures further death and destruction. It radicalizes Central Americans, ever more desperate for a solution to deepening problems. There is not one single historical precedent in all the history of Central America for the windy rhetoric that a strong military will provide an umbrella for democracy. Such talk provides one more example of Orwellian newspeak. Democracy and development have no more formidable foe in Central America than the military.

In 1980 Archbishop Oscar Romero, both as a Salvadoran and as archbishop of San Salvador, pleaded with President Jimmy Carter:

> As a Salvadoran and as archbishop of San Salvador, I have the obligation of seeing to it that faith and justice reign in my country. Therefore, assuming you truly want to defend human rights, I ask that you do two things: Prohibit all military assistance to the Salvadoran government. Guarantee that your government will not intervene, directly or indirectly, by means of military, economic, diplomatic, or other pressures, to influence the direction of the destiny of the Salvadoran people.

Mr. Carter turned a deaf ear to the archbishop's plea. Mr. Reagan followed suit.

Relying upon military means for the past six years, US policy has resolved no problem in Central America. Instead, it has contributed mightily to political destabilization and economic decline. Nor have US trade and aid addressed the real problems of poverty, underdevelopment, and dependency. As in earlier episodes, trade and aid have only made matters worse. Loans have devastated the economies, creating real debt peons of the Central American people for generations to come. Investments have stripped the countries bare.

And yet, when US Secretary of the Treasury James A. Baker spoke to the World Bank/IMF meeting in October 1985, he proposed the same old programs. Baker called on the underdeveloped nations to promote growth of the export sector through private investment and lower inflation. He asked for greater austerity in countries where starvation is already widespread, where the export sector has already so disfigured the economy that only a handful benefit from it, and where public services have already been reduced to unacceptable levels. The old answers are not appropriate for hungry nations. Mindless repetition of them will not reverse the downward economic spiral for the majority.

In short, if Central America is to be saved for democracy, if economic development is to occur, and if mutually favorable relations are to be established between the United States and Central America (thereby thwarting any temptation of an extracontinental metropolis to meddle), the United States must set new priorities in Central America and adopt more realistic attitudes. Friendly relations can only be based on mutual respect, trade that benefits both parties, and an understanding and even appreciation of each other's needs and fears. Because of the great wealth and power of the United States and because the Central Americans are sensitive to the many past US interventions, occupations, and pressures, the metropolis will be called upon in this relationship to display maturity and patience to win and maintain the confidence of otherwise suspicious Central Americans. Proximity and past US conduct make Central Americans much touchier about US actions than about those of a very distant Soviet Union.

After all, the Soviets have not invaded and occupied Central America, mined its harbors, overthrown Central American governments, or even owned local property. Most Central Americans are aware that the Soviet Union built a hospital in Nicaragua, while the US-supported *contras* burned one down. Such contrasts force themselves on the Central American consciousness. In most respects, however, the Soviet Union remains an abstraction to Central Americans while the United States is an all too vivid reality.

Maturity and patience require acknowledging the region's dynamic nationalism. Many Central Americans subscribe to emotional nationalist doctrines. That nationalism has both positive and negative effects.

Nationalism calls for economic development and greater independence. Because they pursue real independence, Central Americans do not regard Soviet hegemony as any solution to their problem of US hegemony.

Negatively, nationalism attacks the United States as a major force frustrating development and compelling dependency. Consequently, nationalist rhetoric is filled with anti-Yankee slogans. US listeners often interpret the rhetoric—simplistically—as pro-Soviet. I think it voices nationalism first and anti-imperialism second.

Maturity and patience also require understanding that larger and larger numbers of Central Americans long to be masters in their own houses.

They wish to destroy institutional barriers blocking economic, social, and political achievement by the majority. The present institutions inhibit development.

Exercising maturity and patience will open our own minds to the positive potentials of revolution. Washington must overcome its paralytic fear that revolution—in and of itself—threatens US security. The fear is irrational. The

Latin American revolutions have sought to develop education and achieve healthy and autonomous societies, goals often praised but rarely achieved in the Third World. These revolutions could have been, and in the cases of Cuba and Nicaragua may still prove to be, major steps on the long road to stability, prosperity, and well-being.

If revolutions can achieve more broadly distributed social and economic justice, they can transform semifeudal societies into modern nations, working to the advantage not only of the peoples of the transformed nations but to the advantage of the people of the United States as well. Latin American nations must undergo profound changes if they are to undertake broad-based and autonomous development. Those that do so will be better neighbors, superior trading partners, and far more reliable guarantors of hemispheric security.

Ideally, with patience and maturity Washington would forge a *positive* foreign policy expressing hope, not fear—a policy of peace, social justice and development. This requires the United States to shift funds from military aid, and support instead governments and groups promoting change. The five republics vary; no one policy will suffice for all. Yet there are some general guidelines for a positive and effective foreign policy. Such a policy would address the need for agrarian pacts and political reforms, regional economic cooperation, and industrialization, and public works.

Unused or under-used land should be redistributed to create a new peasant class with access to credit, fertilizers, seeds, and technical assistance. Such a reform not only would end the unnecessary need to import food—a draining of scarce hard currency—but would create self-sufficiency. It would raise the low level of nutrition of the majority. It could also increase exports. A strong, healthy peasant class is essential for economic prosperity and political stability.

The tax burden should rest squarely upon those who derive the most benefits from society rather than, as at present, on those who already bear the heavy burdens of poverty. Indirect taxation, a major source of revenue in most of the republics, falls heaviest on the poor.

Enough has been written about prevalent human rights violations and political repression. The United States should direct its aid and friendship toward those governments that encourage political expression and make every effort to protect human rights.

The small size of the nations of Central America suggests that they could gain economic strength through complementary trade relations. Encouragement of the revitalization of the moribund Central American Common Market will expand their trading opportunities. Ready access to that expanded market should strengthen industrialization, but to be meaningful the region's industrialization must reflect local realities. It must serve local needs. First and foremost, it should be labor-intensive to provide jobs for the legions of unemployed and underemployed. Second, it must produce basic necessities for larger numbers of the population, shifting away from the present concentration on assembly plants of consumer items for the North American market.

Monies diverted from sterile militarism should flow into badly needed public works projects. Central America desperately needs hospitals, clinics, schools, vocational training centers, and low-income housing. Public works projects will supply the basic needs of the impoverished majority and at the same time create jobs.

US endorsement of the Contadora peace proposals would be a major step in restoring the tranquility Central America must have in order to carry out these needed reforms. Furthermore, it would bring to fruition a Latin American proposal for peace, strengthening a partnership of the United States with Latin America. A genuine partnership must be the foundation of any new Latin American policy of the United States.

Finally, endorsement of the peace proposals would guarantee US security in many ways. It would eliminate the threat of foreign forces—that is, non-Central American forces—being stationed on the Isthmus. In short, there are reasons to believe that a clearly enunciated, energetically applied policy, a *positive* foreign policy, encouraging peace and reform, would enjoy the support of large numbers of Central Americans, strengthen their traditional friendship with the United States, bring stability and prosperity to a restive region, and ensure hemispheric security.

The claim that the Soviet Union threatens the United States through Central America is partly a rationalization to thwart change in that region. It is partly the imposition of US priorities and fears on another region of the world. It is partly a realization of the failure of US policy among its Middle American clients. It is partly an ignorance, or a misunderstanding, of the historical, economic, and social realities of a neighboring region.

The claim unfortunately diverts our attention from the issue at hand: the need for, and desirability of, change in Central America, and a US policy that will facilitate—not frustrate—such change. From all the confusion, ambiguities, and contradictions, there emerges only one certainty: Central America will not enter the twenty-first century shackled with the institutions of the nineteenth.

22

Repentance and Reconciliation: The Road to Peace in Central America

David G. Sweet

Don Sergio Mendes Arceo, the retired Mexican bishop of Cuernavaca, likes to tell audiences in the United States that the American people suffer from a rare disease—one which, spread by us, is wreaking havoc on the entire human race. This disease is a new strain of an ancient virus, only recently identified. It strikes without regard for race, creed, gender, class or sexual preference. Its etiology is obscure, but there is evidence that it is sometimes spread intentionally by socially irresponsible persons. At times it has affected whole communities. Once contracted, the virus hardens the heart and invades the brain tissues, leaving its victims both handicapped for rational thought and prone to aggressive behavior. The scientific name of this affliction is *anticommunism*, and its consequence is interminable war. Don Sergio urges upon his listeners the need for a campaign of research and public information on the disease and, in addition, a collective self-examination leading to a change of conscience and comportment by those who suffer and cause others to suffer from it. He calls on the people of the United States to come to our senses, repent of the sins we have committed against humanity under the influence of our chronic anticommunism, seek reconciliation and thereby make peace with our neighbors before it is too late.

Peace is of course what rational human beings desire above all things—excepting, perhaps, those who profit from war, those whose vocation is war, and those who are so ignorant of war as to find excitement, recreation, or romance in it. A majority even of North Americans, accustomed as we have become to taking the preparations for war lightly, would presumably still prefer peace to war in Central America. But war is what we have wrought there; and war is what our leaders currently prefer. How, then, can we find our way to a just and enduring, genuine peace?

HANDICAPS TO PEACEMAKING

The materials gathered in this volume, examined side by side, suggest that
Bishop Mendes Arceo's observation about us is less a rhetorical device, an
earnest jibe and exhortation, than a thoughtful diagnosis and prescription.
Resolute and unreasoning anticommunism is seen here very clearly to be the
ideological basis for President Reagan's policy towards Central America. The
Santa Fé document, an early formulation of the policy, goes so far as to take
as staunch an anticommunist as President Jimmy Carter to task for having so
much as suggested to us that we might be capable of overcoming our
"inordinate fear" of communism. Most Americans, if the truth be told, have
become over the last forty years quite outspoken and pigheaded anticommu-
nists. We see communism everywhere, we are prone to identify almost any
unfamiliar way of thinking with communism, and we expect pious expressions of anticommunism and hostility toward specific "communist countries"
from our leaders. Anticommunism is taught in the schools, preached from the
pulpit, and cultivated by the mass media. Even those of us who see through
and oppose that view of the world are deeply affected by it. Anticommunism
has, after all, dominated the public discussion of world affairs in this country,
as it dominates the first seven contributions to this book, during all of our
adult lifetimes.

Nevertheless, most of us in the United States know very little about
communism to this day, and we know even less about the Soviet Union or
Vietnam or Cuba. Few of us could define the much-abused term in a satisfactory fashion, or provide an accurate description of the operations of government, the economy, or the people's way of life in any of those countries. Few
of us could explain clearly the changes in the governance of "communist"
countries that have been introduced by a Tito or a Deng Xiaoping or a Gorbachev—even though we are inclined to approve of them. This embarrassing
truth notwithstanding, ever since World War II, wherever the charge of
"communism" has been raised against a leader, a movement, or a government
anywhere in the world by our politicians and public opinion molders, we have
ceased to view those in question with the normal interest and sympathy that
human beings display towards fellow humans struggling against common ad-
versities. We have hardened our hearts, shaken an accusing finger, clenched our
fists, and prepared (or more accurately, looked around for some poor people in
this country or elsewhere to prepare) for a face-off and eventual combat. We
have done this always in the name of high principle; but in practice we have
given the world a great deal more evidence of what we are *against* over the past
four decades than of just what principles we are *for*. Worse yet, something
similar has happened to our *own awareness* of what we are about and why.

The great confusion here at home about what we are for and what we are
against is evident in our custom of using the most imprecise language we can

to talk about politics, so as not to have to think very much or very clearly about them. We talk a great deal, for example, about our support for "freedom" around the world; yet most citizens of the Third World, or nonindustrialized countries with which we have close relations, simply do not enjoy freedom as we define that term. They are oppressed by the iron heel of the very governments we have chosen to see as bastions of the "free world"— in South Korea, Taiwan, the Philippines, Indonesia, Saudi Arabia, Egypt, Turkey, South Africa, Zaire, Chile, El Salvador, and Guatemala, to name just a few. Yet our politicians, whether Democrats or Republicans, are generally as complacent about the anomaly of that situation as they are eloquent in their advocacy of an apoplectic posture towards the bogeyman of "communism" wherever he is said to have appeared in the world. This has gone on to the point at which it now seems to many of us that knee-jerk anticommunism is the normal or even the only acceptable approach to the conduct of our relations with other countries, and with revolutionary or radical reformist movements anywhere.

A consequence of this attitude toward the struggles for justice and autonomy and well-being of much of the human race is that we now live surrounded by nations who are not only envious of our wealth but deeply suspicious and resentful of our power—even where they do not feel safe to express open and explicit hostility towards our pretension to preeminence in the world. Most thinking people in the world detest what Latin Americans refer to as our government's *prepotencia*—its constant bullying and lack of good faith, and its inveterate, arrogant assumption (born of ignorance) that its own notion of anything is the correct one. We base our foreign policy on *a priori* thinking of a remarkably uninformed kind rather than on a thoughtful listening to others. We seek immediate advantage in foreign relations rather than sustainability. We bribe and threaten more than we negotiate. Proceeding in this fashion, we have failed to earn the respect and good will of our neighbors during two centuries of interaction with them; and what we have to live with today is their fear and distrust. This is truly a parlous situation; and it suggests that what the national interest most urgently requires in our times and for many years to come is a policy and process of *reconciliation* with other peoples and other governments, the only reliable avenue to an enduring peace. But we all know that unless some drastic changes are made, such a policy is not what we are going to have.

The painful truth is that rather than being chastened by this country's recent experience of declining influence and credibility in the world, rather than engaging in a much-needed process of public self-criticism and reevaluation, rather than exploring creatively all possibilities for negotiation and reconciliation with other countries, our political leaders have chosen to ignore caution and dig into increasingly defensive positions. Under their guidance, we have fallen as a nation into the habit of boasting inanely to ourselves of our greatness, flexing ever-flabbier muscles, and beating our chests in an effort to intimidate those neighbors who are still obliged by poverty and proximity to pay attention to us. In the process, we have been deceived that our government's clumsy endeavors abroad are essential to the pursuit of a chimerical "national security" which is contingent upon victory (or the appearance of victory) over the "communist" nemesis somewhere. This concern with "security" thus conceived has distracted the attention of our people from the traditional and more rational pursuit of health, well-being and happiness for ourselves and our children. That is the crabbed view of the world, and of the national interest, that requires and has foisted upon us the claim that the Soviet Union threatens the United States through Central America.

AMERICAN OPINION AND CENTRAL AMERICAN POLICY

Belligerent anticommunism is the spirit in which the United States government has conducted our relations with Central America in particular, since shortly after the triumph of the Sandinista Nicaraguan revolution in 1979. It is troubling to have to admit that the Congress, the press, and most of our people have supported this bipartisan policy without knowing much about the specific circumstances or objectives of the Central American people's struggles, or about just why it is that our country is so unfriendly towards them. Of course, not all Americans have taken that stance. There is a general suspicion in many of us, reflected regularly in the public opinion polls, that something is not quite right about what the Reagan administration has been doing in Central America and that, whatever the problem there may be, we should stay out of other people's wars and keep our boys at home. But in the absence of an opposition political party ready to advance an alternative to President Reagan's program, in the absence of a mass-circulation opposition press or television network, these public attitudes have been insufficient to change the course of public policy.

The so-called "low intensity" war that we have been waging by proxy in Central America has gone on for more than six years now, at the cost of many thousands of (mostly civilian) Central American lives and several hundreds of millions of U.S. tax dollars each year. These dollars have been paid out mostly as subsidies to the *de facto* military dictatorships in El Salvador and Guatemala, toward the creation of the vast infrastructure for a permanent U.S. military presence in Honduras, and toward the remilitarization of Costa Rica. Payments to the Nicaraguan *contras*, whether acknowledged or unacknowledged, are only a small part of the whole. So the United States is, despite the will of her people, already deeply involved in what looks like an interminable, multifront Central American war. Like the war in Vietnam, this one is likely sooner or later to require a massive commitment of U.S. air, naval, and ground forces, if a way is not found to bring it to a conclusion by negotiation. But the government of the United States has refused every opportunity for negotiation and has brought its weight to bear on its Central American client states to keep them from negotiating.[1] This policy is being pursued even in the wake of the remarkable peace initiative undertaken by the five Central American presidents meeting at Esquipulas in Guatemala in the summer of 1987. The Central American war, in the meantime, is clearly being "lost" by "our" side. It is a war about which there is, moreover, every reason to believe that it cannot (and indeed should not) be "won" by the United States.

President Reagan's warlike policy towards the aspirations of the poor majority in Central America has been vigorously opposed here at home; but even in the wake of the "Irangate" hearings, the Congress appears to be mesmerized by the President's resolute rhetoric of righteous anticommunism. Great energy and expense has gone into massively publicized inquiries into a few sleazy details of the implementation of the bipartisan anti-Sandinista policy. Yet the political risk of speaking truth to power (for example, by standing up to say in public what many members of Congress believe—that Mr. Reagan's domestic and foreign policies have been a disaster for the long-term real national interest of the United States and have been misrepresented to the public as successful), is apparently unacceptable to any professional politician. Though the elected representatives of our people have expressed marginal differences regarding the choice of an appropriate procedure for eliminating the much-reviled Sandinista government, or the amount of money to pour into the militarization of Nicaragua's neighbors, they appear in practice to be in solid agreement with President Reagan that the "Soviet communist threat" (that is, the threat of popular revolution) is increasing in Central America and that it must be stopped at all costs. To seek to "stop" this revolution, as distinct from striving to have some influence on its course, is to rely on means which, in the last analysis, can only be military.

The essays in the second and third sections of this volume make it clear that the consensus view of our political elite—that the Soviet Union threatens the United States through Central America—is based very much more on our national ideology of anticommunism than on the actual behavior of the Soviet Union, or on the nature of revolutionary struggle in that part of the world. The Soviet Union is indeed active in Central America; and the Cubans are more active still. They both provide much-needed assistance to the Nicaraguans for their national defense, and for their programs to develop their economy and their social services. They will presumably continue to do this as long as Nicaragua is threatened with war by the United States. But if these activities

---

[1]   See the article by Wayne Smith, "Lies About Nicaragua," *Foreign Policy* 67 (Summer 1987):87-103.

appear to threaten us, it is only because *we have chosen* to define the process of revolutionary social transformation in Central America as a threat to our national security.

There was an alternative view of the Central American revolution that might have been adopted by the United States. It might be adopted still. This is the view that sees in that rapidly changing situation an unparalleled *opportunity* for creative foreign policymaking—an opportunity to assist rather than resist the long-overdue transformation of tyrannical governments, profoundly unjust societies, and backward economies into vital and self-sufficient nations with which we could hope to have peaceful and mutually beneficial commercial and cultural relations over a long period of time. The United States government came with some reluctance to see Yugoslavia and China in that way, choosing respectful coexistence over belligerence, active trade over embargo. This is an attitude whose intention and consequence has been to expand rather than to narrow our sphere of influence in the world. No country was, and continues to be, a more promising candidate for such neighborly treatment than Nicaragua—where baseball is the national game, where North American customs, institutions, merchandise, and cultural products are admired, and where visiting North Americans are received with extraordinary warmth and hospitality even today.

SOME FACTS ABOUT NICARAGUA

It can readily be established by anyone willing to read for a week in the library that Nicaragua is not a communist country, and that to most informed U.S. observers it does not appear to be in the process of becoming a communist country.[2] The Sandinista government has not abolished free enterprise or private property, freedom of speech or religion; it does not hold political prisoners without trial or practice torture or capital punishment; it does not deny the public an opportunity for active participation in the political decision-making process. It has not expropriated the holdings of U.S. corporations, nor has it acted in a manner hostile to the United States. It is not in fact an enemy of this country. It has joined no alliances against us, carried out no acts of war against us, broken off no diplomatic relations, cut off no trade. Much less is it a "Soviet satellite" suffering under an autocratic pseudorevolutionary regime imposed from abroad, with key public policy decisions being made in a foreign capital. U.S. citizens enter Nicaragua freely without visas, whether as individuals or in groups; and once there they travel, take pictures, and talk to

[2]   See the general works suggested in the bibliography in the section "On Revolution and Counterrevolution in Nicaragua."

people freely, wherever they like outside the war zone and military installations.[3]

The few restrictions on the right of expression by Nicaraguan citizens are measures easily understood, however difficult to condone, as having been taken in the interest of national defense under a state of emergency in a time of war. The U.S.-subsidized opposition newspaper, *La Prensa*, was closed for a year, for example, and two seditious hierarchs of the Roman Catholic church were sent into exile. These measures were taken after those in question had given open support over an extended period to the military intervention of the United States in their country. Nicaragua does not have a drab or humorless monolithic or repressive public culture; its government does not operate in blatant disregard for public opinion by means of a system of police repression.

Nicaragua is, on the contrary, a fiercely independent country with a popular and (since 1984) freely elected government, one which is determined above all else to resist the hegemony of the United States as it would that of the Soviet Union or of any other "superpower." What is absolutely unacceptable and non-negotiable to the Sandinistas is the U.S. pretension (tantamount to the Soviet pretension in Poland) that because we are powerful it is our prerogative to place limits on the sovereignty and the self-determination of small countries in the interest of our national security. That aside, the first major objective of the Sandinista government has been to eliminate the extreme social inequality that Nicaragua has inherited from four and a half centuries of colonialism, foreign intervention, and dictatorship. Their second objective has been to accelerate the production and improve the distribution of goods and services so as to raise the abysmally low standard of living of most Nicaraguans— particularly in the areas of health, education, housing, transportation, energy, communications, and recreation. Modest progress has been made on both these fronts during the past eight years (although social inequality persists, and in many places newly acquired goods, newly built installations and newly trained personnel have been ruthlessly and purposefully wiped out by the *contras*).

The most important real accomplishment of the Sandinista revolution (apart from its sheer survival in the face of the hostility of the United States) is, however, not a material but a spiritual one. The revolution has restored to the Nicaraguan people the sense of dignity and self-esteem, and the faith in a Christian (and socialist) ideal of loving community that are evident today to any visitor. These are precious gifts indeed. The Nicaraguans had lost them in the course of a long history of humiliation and alienation, both personal and national, at the hands of the rich and powerful. But they have them today, and

---

[3] These observations and those that follow are based on wide reading and on the author's five visits to Nicaragua and some ten months residence in that country between July 1983 and September 1986.

that is why visitors envy rather than pity them, even in the midst of their terrible suffering and privation.

WHAT IS WRONG WITH U.S. POLICY?

None of the actual undertakings of the government of tiny and impoverished Nicaragua seems, upon close examination, to represent a threat to the national interest of the United States—at least as that interest would be defined after a bit of reflection by any thinking American. Yet our government has committed us to a policy of implacable hostility towards the Sandinista revolution, and towards like-minded revolutionary movements everywhere—a policy of "destabilization," of sabotage, of economic embargo, of international isolation, of "low-intensity" war. Tens of thousands of Central American people have met violent and unnatural deaths as a result of this policy; hundreds of thousands have been driven from their homes into extreme privation and permanent anguish. This is indeed a serious crime against humanity.

The policy toward revolution in Central America that we have been following under President Reagan, and under a Congress unwilling to risk effective political opposition, is of course especially exasperating and painful to behold for those Americans who have been interested enough in Nicaragua and Honduras and Guatemala and El Salvador to know something about those countries. This includes the great majority of the several thousands of professional scholars and university professors represented by the Latin American Studies Association in the United States, who have consistently opposed the policy in our public resolutions. And it includes the tens of thousands of American citizens from all walks of life who have visited or travelled or worked in Nicaragua since 1979, seen the havoc wrought by this undeclared war, read the Nicaraguan newspapers, and talked with ordinary citizens as well as with the public officials there about what the Sandinista revolution is about. We have come back home (or out of our libraries!) to find with horror that the all-too-fragmentary information that makes its way from press and government sources into the public discussion about Nicaragua is mostly "disinformation"—that is, information that is generally (and intentionally) so badly distorted as to mislead, and very often downright false. We see our people being lied to about Nicaragua and the rest of Central America every day. We see our people being called upon to support a counterrevolutionary program that we know from firsthand observation to be nothing more than a relentless campaign of terrorism against the poorest people in Nicaragua, El Salvador, and Guatemala—a program urged on by the very U.S. politicians who claim that their principal foreign policy objective is to *fight* terrorism all over the world. The Central American war is an expensive campaign of terrorism, paid for by all of us, which is directed against the majority of Central America's people.

There is another, more political, dimension to the dismay felt by the people of the United States knowledgeable about Nicaragua who are in opposition to President Reagan's war in Central America. We have read much and then gone to Central America to see for ourselves what is happening; and as U.S. citizens we have been ashamed and angered by what we have found. We have protested the administration's policies by every legal means available to us; for a great many of us this has been our principal off-hours activity or even a full-time activity during most of the 1980s. We have organized and marched and written to our representatives in Congress; we have written in the press and spoken in public, millions of words on tens of thousands of occasions; some of our number have even testified before congressional committees. We are the best-informed U.S. citizens on the particular subject in question, the only U.S. citizens who have seen the Sandinista revolution at work and are therefore in a position to provide some of the information necessary for the rational formulation of a constructive policy toward Nicaragua. Nevertheless, we have not been consulted and we have not been heard. Or if occasionally heard, we have been unable to bring about an open and informed public discussion of U.S. policy in Central America, to prevent the acceleration of the war and the wanton killing of Central Americans. Nor have we been able to persuade a single member of Congress or high-ranking government official to risk his or her career by speaking out in unequivocal opposition to this manifestly unjust war.

The reason for this resistance to information, to open discussion, and to clear thinking in high places appears to be that the U.S. political and journalistic elite, like most of the rest of the population of our country, is so deeply invested in the ideology of anticommunism that when confronted with any kind of movement for social justice and national sovereignty in a Third World country, it functions just as Don Sergio Mendes Arceo warns us that it does: it becomes incapable of rational thought and prone to aggressive behavior. One cannot imagine a more convincing image of what we are up against in this regard than the zealous Marine and self-described patriot Col. Oliver North, who, as these lines were being written, was offering unapologetic testimony to a congressional committee about his efforts to facilitate the mass murder of Nicaraguans by subverting our national institutions—and who was allowed by the legislators who purported to be investigating his misdeeds to make yet another impassioned appeal over the national TV networks for U.S. aid to the *contras*.

This situation, in the view of citizens well enough informed to be deeply opposed to the present policy of war in Central America, is a critical problem for the future of our country. It is obviously a serious handicap for the formulation and implementation of foreign policy that informed opinion and conscientious criticism not be consulted. But more broadly speaking, the present practice seems a serious threat to our democracy itself, and with it to the still-fragile hope of an emerging international system of law and order that dawned with the signing of the UN charter in San Francisco in 1948. Without accurate and generally available information, making it possible for reality to inform public participation in the political process, how can any democracy function? Without a genuine working commitment to peace, to respect for the autonomy of peoples, and to the resolution of differences through honest negotiations rather than by threats and violence, how can any community of nations function?

It is apparent from their public statements with regard to Central America that President Reagan and his principal collaborators may actually believe that in some manner of speaking the Soviet Union threatens the United States through Central America, and that this threat is manifest in the revolutionary nationalist movements that they believe the Soviet Union has launched, managed and sustained there. Our leaders may even believe that if we do not stop this "red tide" of revolution, the consequence will be revolution in the remaining "free" countries of Central America, then in Mexico, and eventually in the United States. But let us be clear that this anticommunist argument is based not upon an understanding of Central America, or of revolution, or of Soviet foreign relations. It is the fruit of our leaders' bizarrely conceived anticommunist notion of "national security" as a good deriving entirely from military power and geopolitics—rather than as a state of grace and well-being rooted in the economic productivity, the increasing social justice, and the general quality of life in the United States. Such national security thinking has been basic to United States policy towards Central America since the Eisenhower administration. Yet the policy as practiced appears to be impossible to defend with reasoned arguments in an open discussion at the bar of an informed public opinion. Astonishingly, for nearly forty years in our free country it has seldom been put to that test. The government avoids discussing the policy in forums where it cannot control the terms of debate.[4]

One strong indication that the Reagan administration's policy is indefensible is the fact that it has for the most part been carried out in secrecy through "covert" operations. Another is that public statements about it by government officials (even those of the president on national TV, and statements made in closed sessions to Congress) have frequently been lies. Another is that the policy enjoys very little support abroad, even among our more faithful Western European and Latin American allies. Another is that it has been found in violation of international law by the World Court. But the most serious shortcoming of the policy from the point of view of many thinking U.S. citizens is one that comes to many of us as something of a surprise: when the

---

[4]   It is a common complaint of the organizers of public discussions on this subject—such as the conference from which the present volume derives—that the State Department is reluctant to send a representative who will participate.

"national security" foreign policy of the United States is subjected to close scrutiny, it turns out to be startlingly un-American! The policy has, in fact, been conceived and executed in direct and intentional violation of some of the most commonly held values of our people:

1. IT IS UNLAWFUL. The policy has led us to train and equip large numbers of people in Central American countries to perform terrorist and other criminal acts against their own people—acts that are illegal in this country and illegal where they are performed. Implementation of the policy has also involved regular violations of the spirit if not always the letter of the Constitution and of U.S. statute governing the relations between the executive and the legislative branches of government, specifically removing from Congress in practice the right to declare war and control the purse strings. The policy is also in violation of many treaty obligations of the United States that have the force of domestic law—in particular, it is in violation of the UN Charter.

2. IT IS UNPEACEABLE AND WARLIKE. The basic principle on which the anticommunist foreign policy towards Central America is based is that our wealth and our military might make us strong enough to force others to do our will, whether or not we have arguments with which to persuade them. The honest negotiation of differences is therefore unnecessary. Ours is the policy of the schoolyard bully, not of the respected member of a community.

3. IT IS UNBUSINESSLIKE. The policy has led us into activities characterized by bad planning, by enormous expenditures poorly (if not altogether fraudulently) accounted for, and by incompetent execution—activities that have produced no benefit to ourselves at a great cost to our good will in the world. It has moreover committed us to throwing good money after bad for a long time still to come.

4. IT IS DISHONEST. In the public formulation and implementation of the policy the government has regularly lied to the American people, to Congress, to our allies, to the Nicaraguans and others, and (as the Irangate hearings suggest) frequently even to itself. The government alleges, for example, that its purpose has not been to overthrow the Sandinista government; that it supported negotiations and the Contadora process; and that Nicaragua has expansionist designs upon its neighbors, is supplying arms to the Salvadoran rebels, is a key link in the international drug trade, and performs genocide upon the Miskito Indians.

5. IT IS UNDIGNIFIED. The consequence of this policy has been to raise serious questions about the sincerity, the probity, the constructiveness of purpose, the knowledge and capability, the military effectiveness, and even the sanity of our national leadership in the eyes of most world opinion.

6. IT IS UN-NEIGHBORLY. Instead of offering a helping hand to needy neighbors, and acting out of respect for their dignity, their privacy, and their property, we have lied to them, threatened them, rained destruction upon them, and spoken ill of them at every opportunity.

7. IT IS UN-CHRISTIAN. Every aspect of this policy is in direct contradiction to the principles of human conduct and the ideal of a human community
in covenant with God, which evolved through the early history of the Jewish
people as recorded in the Bible, and which is expressed in the life, death, and
resurrection of Jesus Christ in whom most Americans profess to believe.

8. IT IS UNSUCCESSFUL. None of its publicly acknowledged objectives
have been achieved, or appear to be achievable.

In sum, this is a policy which, when its true nature and consequences are
revealed, must fill any well-informed, thinking, and conscientious U.S. citizen
with shame. It should also fill us with alarm.

The anticommunist policy of the Reagan administration toward Central
America and the rest of the Third World, like the policy of the Kennedy,
Johnson, and Nixon administrations toward Vietnam on which it is modelled,
has indeed been a dismal failure. It has spread untold death and suffering; it has
committed us to the maintenance of tyrannical governments inimical to every
value held dear by the people of the United States; it has sabotaged our
genuinely constructive efforts to assist some peoples in solving their pressing
problems of chronic hunger and poverty; it has ruined our reputation
(established at the cost of many American lives during World War II) as defenders of peace and freedom; it has cost us a great deal of money; it has distorted our economy and political system by tilting them towards war and away
from the well-being of the citizenry; it has given us a trillion-dollar budget and
made us the principal debtor nation in a debt-ridden world; and it has engendered among us the habit of public dishonesty and the habit of self-deception. We have in fact already paid a terrible price at home, in reduced public
services and lowered public morale, for our blind persistence in pursuing this
policy abroad for more than two decades.

The policy has, of course, succeeded in the limited way envisioned by the
more cynical of its authors. It has greatly increased the cost in suffering to
those peoples who attempt revolutionary social transformation (and are therefore defined by us as enemies); it has slowed down the process of social transformation for some of them. But it has not prevented any revolution; it has
not provided a viable alternative to revolution; it has not obviated the *need* for
revolutionary social change in most of the world's poor countries, nor has it
discouraged hungry patriots from struggling for freedom anywhere. What it has
done is make of the United States of America, a nation born of revolution, the
principal barrier and *bête noire* for all peoples everywhere who struggle for
social justice and national liberation. It is hard to see how such a policy could
ever have recommended itself to any American—if it had not been hidden in
the proclamation of our demented and disinformative, deadly and dysfunctional
national crusade against "communism." But it was presented to us in that
way, and we bought it. As a result we have we been saddled for a quarter of a
century with this wrong-minded and belligerent, un-American foreign policy,

this policy that opens and exacerbates rifts rather than cements healthy relationships with our neighbors.

ALTERNATIVE PATHS

How may we hope to restore a semblance of peace among the Central American nations and between them and us, so as to be able to devote our energies, and encourage our neighbors to devote theirs, to the search for lasting solutions to the real problems—the problems of survival and the problems of improving the quality of life—which our people and all other peoples face in common?

The situation that we face after four decades of an ineffective and un-American anticommunist foreign policy in Central America is a difficult one, but it is perhaps not as hopeless as it sometimes appears. Americans in crisis have sometimes turned for solace and enlightenment to the Bible. Were we to do so today we might turn to the passages in which the prophet Isaiah speaks to the idolatrous people of Israel "calling them to account for their transgression." The people of Israel were proud of their righteousness but complained that God seemed not to be heeding their prayers. God observed that for all of their piety they were working to serve their own interests rather than living in harmony according to God's plan. They made their employees work harder than was just, and their conduct in the world led "only to wrangling and strife, and dealing vicious blows with the fist." That was no way to live. Rather:

> Is not this what I require of you . . .
>> to loose the fetters of injustice,
>> to untie the knots of the yoke,
>> to snap every yoke
>> and set free those who have been crushed?
> Is it not sharing your food with the hungry,
>> taking the homeless poor into your house,
>> clothing the naked when you meet them
>> and never evading a duty to your kinsfolk?
> Then shall your light break forth like the dawn
>> and soon you will grow healthy like a wound newly healed;
>> your own righteousness shall be your vanguard
>> and the glory of the Lord your rearguard.
> Then, if you call, the Lord will answer;
>> if you cry to God he will say, 'Here I am.'
> If you cease to pervert justice,
>> to point the accusing finger and lay false charges,
>> if you feed the hungry from your own plenty
>> and satisfy the needs of the wretched,
>> then your light will rise like dawn out of darkness

and your dusk be like noonday;
God will be your guide continually
and will satisfy your needs in the shimmering heat;
he will give you strength of limb;
you will be like a well-watered garden,
like spring whose waters never fail.
The ancient ruins will be restored by your own kindred
and you will build once more on ancestral foundations;
you shall be called Rebuilder of broken walls,
Restorer of houses in ruins.

Isaiah LVIII:6-12

There is hope for any sinning people who can acknowledge error, be repentant, and change direction. And we the people of the United States are free even now to do just that. What we need now is a fresh new policy toward Central America—one based not on anticommunism or on anti-anything. We need a policy that is an expression of the best and not the worst values we share, one that is just in the terms familiar to most American people and that has a clear and constructive purpose, one that seeks to alleviate suffering rather than causing it—a policy of which Americans may rightly be proud. How can we arrive at such a policy? How can we change direction when we have been so long on our present disastrous course? How can we restore the breach that we have opened in our relations with our nearest neighbors, and help create a system of community with other nations in which the interests of all may be peaceably served? What would such a policy consist in?

The profound change in foreign policy that this country needs will indeed require a radical change in outlook. But it is not utopian to argue for such a change, if we keep in mind that the present policy is in fact an absolute failure from the point of view of everyone who does not actually profit from it, that a new policy is required by our long-term real national interest in viable coexistence with other nations, and that this new policy has to be based on new principles if it is going to lead to a new kind of behavior. The new and different policy that can be derived directly from the commonly held values of the American people is therefore a realistic and pragmatic one, conceived with an eye not to Armageddon, but to the peaceful and prosperous future which we all desire for ourselves and our children.

In the first place, we must abandon the pretension of hegemony—that attitude toward the world which in its sublime expressions speaks of the "special responsibilities" of power, and which at its most vulgar is Teddy Roosevelt's big stick, or the Kissinger Commission's plan for "managing" Central America, or President Reagan's fantasy that the Sandinista government might turn around to his tawdry "freedom fighters" and "say 'uncle.'" The United States is not and cannot be the arbiter of the destinies of other nations.

Hegemony is as nonviable a relationship between nations as it is between groups and individuals in any neighborhood—particularly in these rebellious times. It breeds bitterness and opposition in the weak, and shame and fear in the strong. So the first thing we need is a policy that explicitly abandons the claim to hegemony in Central America or anywhere else in the world, one that recognizes that in foreign relations we can expect to enjoy the respect and influence we have earned by our friendly behavior towards other nations, and no more.

A second needed change is a reevaluation of our view of revolution by desperately poor people in countries with tyrannical governments—that is, perhaps, most people in the world still today. Revolutions are not what we have been told they are. Here are some truths about them which, once assimilated, can help us develop a policy toward revolutions that works:

1. Revolution in some countries is *necessary*. The unjust social order that is the product of colonialism and neocolonialism in Latin America, for example, is intolerable by twentieth-century Western world standards. It is also incapable of transforming itself into a just social order by means of moderate reform programs, even when these are supported by the United States. That was a lesson of the Alliance for Progress of the 1960s. This order requires radical transformations that cannot be carried out under the leadership of presently ruling elites and that may be accomplished either by violent or by nonviolent means.

2. Revolutionary movements neither cause nor prefer violence; their goal is the radical transformation of society at the least possible cost in human suffering. But they are frequently obliged to recur to violence in the face of violent repression by an unyielding authoritarian government. The degree of violence that accompanies a process of revolutionary social transformation is in large measure a function of the past and present capacity of the government for repression. The United States could have contributed greatly to diminishing the violence that has accompanied the revolutions in Cuba, Nicaragua, and El Salvador, among many other countries, had we refrained from providing military assistance to the tyrannical governments of those countries.

3. Revolutions cannot be exported from one country to another, though citizens willing to attempt revolution in any country may be provided with weapons and training from abroad. No amount of foreign assistance can make a revolution unless conditions in the country are ripe for it—unless misery and injustice are great, the government has lost its legitimacy in the eyes of the people, ordinary citizens are sufficiently exasperated to take the enormous risks involved in supporting a revolutionary movement, and a movement appears whose program and conduct are persuasive to a large proportion of the people.

4. Revolutions are nationalist. Every revolution places the interests of the nation as understood by its leaders ahead of those of any foreigners; and it demands the recognition by other nations of its sovereignty. Such a movement

is hostile to the United States only to the extent that the United States represents a threat to that sovereignty.

5. Revolutions are socialist. They are concerned with accelerating production and distributing its benefits equitably. Each revolution will devise its own means for attempting to do this (those means devised in Nicaragua are, for example, startlingly different from those devised in the Soviet Union or China or Cuba); all countries will be interested in the lessons that can be learned from the experience of socialist revolutionary movements elsewhere. This process should nevertheless be welcomed by the United States rather than opposed, because as has been shown in China, it improves the general standard of living, diminishes the danger of war, and is conducive to the development of increased trade with the United States.

6. Revolutions are democratic in principle and purpose. That is, they abolish the control of the political process by a wealthy elite and encourage wide participation. They also reveal a countervailing defensive tendency to reconcentrate authority in a "vanguard" party or a small new group of leaders. The best guarantee that they will be more democratic than authoritarian is that they be free to find their own road in the struggle between leaders and followers, and that they not be embattled by an anticommunist United States.

7. Revolutions are constructive rather than destructive. Their purpose is to create institutions that will meet the needs of their people; and any destruction they work is reluctantly undertaken by revolutionaries as a necessary concomitant of that process.

8. Revolutions are pragmatic. They are more concerned with practical problemsolving, with defending their achievements and improving the standard of living of the people they serve, than with nursing grudges over past offenses, or with promoting hostility towards foreigners. If the United States were friendly or at least correct in our behavior toward them, we would have nothing to fear from them.

9. Revolutions are needy. They take place in poor countries lacking the personnel and infrastructure necessary for rapid economic development. Often they lose some of the few qualified people they do have by depriving them of privilege and thereby driving them into exile. This feature of revolutions is what has made of them an opportunity for the expansion of Soviet influence; but it is an opportunity for the expansion of U.S. influence as well. Revolutions provide us with an occasion for wielding influence in the way that it works best—by being genuinely helpful, as the Cubans have been in Nicaragua and Angola and as the several hundred U.S. citizens now working in Nicaragua have demonstrated that it is possible for us to be as well.

10. Revolutions are no threat to the national security of the United States. What threatens our security is our determination to prevent them at all costs (in the name of anticommunism) among peoples for whom they are the only viable alternative to ignorance, starvation, humiliation, and premature death.

Revolution, then, is conceivably and potentially a good thing rather than a bad thing from the point of view of the United States.

But in order to turn that recognition into a new foreign policy, we are going to have to turn away from sterile and self-defeating anticommunism and embrace a positive commitment, a commitment to promoting and nurturing and improving the general well-being of humankind. As the liberation theologians of Latin America tell us, we are going to have to turn away from our idolatry of death (that is, of wealth and power) to embrace the loving God that is life. Once that possibility is envisioned, once we have committed ourselves as a nation and as individuals to a practice that is based on love rather than on hatred, the Soviet threat to the United States through Central America, once perceived as the central determining factor in the formulation of foreign policy towards that part of the world, will be a hard thing even to remember.

REPENTANCE, FORGIVENESS AND RECONCILIATION

What is called for, I believe, is a 180-degree change in direction, a change from a policy that has proven to be an unmitigated disaster, for ourselves as well as for our neighbors, to a policy that actually works. But in order to have the opportunity to conduct such a policy, and to learn by doing how we as a great nation can relate to our neighbors in a manner we can be proud of, we must first find our way to *reconciliation* with these neighbors. Reconciliation is alien to the thinking of statesmen and others committed to the pursuit of power, but it is a familiar and easily understood phenomenon and goal for ordinary people. It should therefore be possible for the powerful of this country to be taught it, or called to it, by the millions of ordinary U.S. citizens who understand very well the way to achieve it. In order that reconciliation may take place between those who have fallen out, and sinned against one another in word and deed, the principal offenders must, having reflected upon their offending behavior, acknowledge it openly with signs of an honest *repentance* so that they may be forgiven by those whom they have offended. The miracle of reconciliation is that no vengeful hatred in human beings is too great to notice sincere repentance in an offending other, nor to give way to forgiveness as a natural response to it.

Reconciliation is therefore possible even between great life-destroying sinners such as the United States, the Soviet Union, and the other world powers of the twentieth century, and the bleeding peoples against whom we have sinned. It is possible between the Germans and the Jews, between the British and the Irish, the French and the Algerians, between the Israelis and the Palestinians, the Afrikaners and the South African Blacks. It is possible between the Russians and the Poles, the Czechs, the Hungarians and the Afghans; and it is possible too between the people of the United States and the

Vie.namese, the Indonesians, the Angolans, the Cubans, the Salvadorans, the Guatemalans, the Chileans, the Granadans, and the Nicaraguans.

Open and sincere self-criticism and repentance are perhaps too much to expect from President Reagan and his friends. But surely it is within our power to demand from the next president of the United States open repentance of the sins of a nation led by past administrations, a change of direction in foreign policy, and a commitment to reconciliation and peace with our neighbors. We can demand a public acknowledgement of past errors and an expression of our determination to make amends—not with cash reparations to those against whom we have transgressed, but with genuinely neighborly conduct during the decades to come. Those are the decades during which Central America's peoples will be rebuilding their societies amidst the ruins to which we have reduced them, as the Vietnamese are doing still today. They will very much need our help then, as they will that of the Soviet Union and Cuba and anybody else who is willing to lend a hand. In such circumstances, forgiveness and reconciliation are gifts that a United States with a changed heart and a changed conduct could certainly look forward to receiving from the peoples against whom we have transgressed.

A POLICY TO BE PROUD OF

What might a reasonable United States policy for relations with Central America look like? It doesn't take experts to imagine it. Any group of neighbors or friends could come up with a policy that would work just fine: no more troops, no more threats, no more shipments of weapons to anybody; an honest willingness to negotiate all differences with any country openly, and to rely on the United Nations and the World Court in the resolution of conflicts; warm support for the efforts of all countries to broaden the base of participation in their political decision-making processes; retraining and guaranteed employment for the U.S. workers who lose their jobs in war industries as we move to disarmament; generous terms for the resettlement in the United States of the generals, oligarchs, and ordinary middle-class Central American people whom we have encouraged over the last four decades to think that they can maintain a nonviable position of privilege in impoverished countries indefinitely; guaranteed prices in the U.S. market for the commodities the Central Americans produce for export, so that they can count on foreign exchange with which to finance their development projects; renegotiation of each country's debt to interest-free or low-interest loans from the United States and other governments and from the international lending agencies; modest bilateral and multilateral programs of material and technical assistance to improve economic infrastructure and social services and provide the basis for equitable and environmentally sound economic growth; support for poor countries' efforts to carry out land reforms and other redistributive programs aimed at establishing the basis for a stable social and political order; assistance programs that are all conditioned on the observance of international standards of human, political, and labor rights and respect for the ethnic autonomy of indigenous peoples; reasonable prices for the manufactured goods, food staples, and technology that the Central American countries are obliged to import from the United States; open admissions and fellowship support for Central American students who wish to pursue their studies in the United States, on the condition that they will return home after they have finished their studies, and that their home governments will guarantee them employment; encouragement of all forms of cultural and educational exchange.

The details of the new and radically different foreign policy that we must devise in the years before us are easy enough to imagine. They will follow freely upon fresh thinking in a friendly and constructive vein, unimpeded by the virus of anticommunism—thinking focused on who our neighbors are, on what they need from us, and on what we need from them. Sweden can serve as an example to us in this. If we can find in ourselves the principled boldness with which to face the consequences of our present life-destroying course of action, then we can turn sharply away from it to a view of the world that works. If that can be done during the final decade of this nightmarish twentieth century, we may live to see in our own lifetimes a United States of America that once more lives, in Isaiah's words, "like a watered garden," and whose people enjoy a reputation in the world as "rebuilders of broken walls, restorers of houses in ruins."

Bibliography

GENERAL READING ON CENTRAL AMERICA

Adelman, Alan and Reid Reading (eds.) *Confrontation in the Caribbean Basin.* (Pittsburgh: University of Pittsburgh Center for Latin American Studies, 1984).

Anderson, Thomas P. *Politics in Central America.* (New York: Praeger, 1982).

———. "The Roots of Revolution in Central America," in Wiarda (ed.), *Rift and Revolution.* (Washington: American Enterprise Institute for Public Policy Research, 1984).

Barry, Tom, Beth Wood, and Deb Preusch. *Dollars and Dictators: A Guide to Central America.* (Albuquerque: The Resource Center, 1982).

Bermudez, Lilia and Ricardo Cordova. *América Central: la estrategia militar norteamericana y el proceso de militarización.* (Mexico City: 1984).

Blachman, Morris J., William M. LeoGrande, and Kenneth Sharpe (eds.) *Confronting Revolution: Security Through Diplomacy in Central America.* (New York: Pantheon Books, 1986).

Bulmer-Thomas, V. "Central American Economic Development Over the Long Run—Central America Since 1920," *Journal of Latin American Studies* 15 (November 1983):274.

Burbach, Roger and Patricia Flynn (eds.) *The Politics of Intervention: The United States in Central America.* (New York: Monthly Review Press, 1984).

Central America in Crisis: Washington Institute Task Force Report. (Washington, DC: The Washington Institute for Values in Public Policy, 1984).

Chace, James. *Endless War: How We Got Involved in Central America—And What Can Be Done.* (New York: Random House, 1984).

Coleman, Kenneth M. and George C. Herring (eds.) *The Central American Crisis: Sources of Conflict and the Failure of U.S. Policy.* (Wilmington, Del.: Scholarly Resources, Inc., 1985).

Commission on U.S. Central American Relations. *U.S. Military Intervention in Central America.* (Washington, 1984).

Diskin, Martin (ed.) *Trouble in Our Backyard: Central America and the United States in the Eighties.* (New York: Pantheon Books, 1983).

Durham, William H. *Scarcity and Survival in Central America: Ecological Origins of the Soccer War.* (Stanford, Calif.: Stanford University Press, 1979).

Etchison, Don L. *The United States and Militarism in Central America.* (New York: Praeger, 1975).

Fagen, Richard and Olga Pellicer (eds.) *The Future of Central America: Policy Choices for the U.S. and Mexico.* (Stanford, Calif.: Stanford University Press, 1983).

Falcoff, Mark and Robert Royal (eds.) *The Continuing Crisis: U.S. Policy in Central America and the Caribbean.* (Lanham, Md.: Ethics and Public Policy Center, 1987).

Fogel, Daniel. *Revolution in Central America.* (San Francisco: Ism Press, 1985).

Grabendorff, Wolf, Heinrich-W. Krumwiede and Jorg Todt (eds.) *Political Change in Central America.* (Boulder, Colo.: Westview Press, 1984).

Leiken, Robert S. (ed.) *Central America: Anatomy of Conflict.* (New York: Pergamon Press, 1984).

————, and Barry Rubin (eds.) *The Central American Crisis Reader.* (New York: Summit Books, 1987).

Nairn, Allan. "Endgame: A Special Report on the U.S. Military Strategy in Central America," *NACLA Report on the Americas* 18 (May-June 1984):39.

Newfarmer, Richard (ed.) *From Gunboats to Diplomacy: New U.S. Policies for Latin America.* (Baltimore: Johns Hopkins University Press, 1984).

Pearce, Jenny. *Under the Eagle: U.S. Intervention in Central America and the Caribbean.* (London: Latin American Bureau, 1981).

Ropp, Steve C. and James A. Morris. *Central America: Crisis and Adaptation.* (Albuquerque: University of New Mexico Press, 1984.

Stanford Central America Action Network. *Revolution in Central America.* (Boulder, Colo.: Westview Press, 1983).

White, Richard Alan. *The Morass: United States Intervention in Central America.* (New York: Harper & Row, 1984).

Wiarda, Howard (ed.) *Rift and Revolution: The Central American Imbroglio.* (Washington: American Enterprise Institute for Public Policy Research, 1984).

Williams, Robert C. *Export Agriculture and the Crisis in Central America.* (Chapel Hill: University of North Carolina Press, 1986).

Woodward, Ralph Lee, Jr. *Central America: A Nation Divided.* (New York: Oxford University Press, 1985).

Wynia, Gary W. "Setting the Stage for Rebellion: Economics and Politics in Central America's Past," in Wiarda (ed.), *Rift and Revolution.* (Washington: American Enterprise Institute for Public Policy Research, 1984).

ON REBELLION AND REPRESSION IN EL SALVADOR AND GUATEMALA

Adams, Richard N. *Crucifixion by Power: Essays on Guatemalan Social Structure, 1944-1966*. (Austin: University of Texas Press, 1970).

Americas Watch Committee and The American Civil Liberties Union. *Report on Human Rights in El Salvador*. (New York: Random House, 1982).

Anderson, Thomas P. *La Matanza: El Salvador's Communist Revolt of 1932*. (Lincoln, Nebr.: University of Nebraska Press, 1971).

Anfuso, Joseph and David Sczepanski. *He Gives—He Takes Away: The True Story of Guatemala's Controversial Former President Efraín Rios Montt*. (Eureka, Calif.: Radiance Publications, 1983).

Armstrong, Robert and Janet Shenk. *El Salvador: The Face of Revolution*. (Boston: South End Press, 1982).

Baloyra, Enrique. *El Salvador in Transition*. (Chapel Hill: University of North Carolina Press, 1982).

Bermúdez, Fernando. *Death and Resurrection in Guatemala*. (Maryknoll, N.Y.: Orbis, 1986).

Browning, David. *El Salvador: Landscape and Society*. (Oxford: Oxford University Press, 1971).

Carrigan, Ana. *Salvador Witness: The Life and Calling of Jean Donovan*. (New York: Ballantine Books, 1984).

Clements, Charles, M.D. *Witness to War: An American Doctor in El Salvador*. (Toronto: Bantam Books, 1984).

Davis, Shelton H. "State Violence and Agrarian Crisis in Guatemala: The Roots of the Indian-Peasant Rebellion," in Diskin (ed.), *Trouble in Our Backyard: Central America and the United States in the Eighties*. (New York: Pantheon Books, 1983).

Didion, Joan. *Salvador* (London: 1983).

Dilling, Yvonne. *In Search of Refuge*. (Scottdale, Pa.: Herald Press, 1984).

Dombrowski, John et al. *Area Handbook for Guatemala*. (Washington, D.C., 1970).

Dunkerley, James. *The Long War: Dictatorship & Revolution in El Salvador*. (London: Junction Books, 1982).

Fried, Jonathan L., Marvin E. Gettleman, Deborah T. Levenson, and Nancy Peckenham (eds.) *Guatemala in Rebellion: Unfinished History*. (New York: Grove Press, 1983).

Galeano, Eduardo H. *Guatemala: Occupied Country*. (New York: Monthly Review Press, 1969).

Gettleman, Marvin E., Patrick Lacefield, Louis Menashe, David Mermelstein, and Ronald Radosh (eds.) *El Salvador: Central America in the New Cold War*. (New York: Grove Press, 1981).

Herman, Edward S. and Frank Brodhead. *Demonstration Elections: U.S.-Staged Elections in the Dominican Republic, Vietnam, and El Salvador*. (Boston: South End Press, 1984).

Immerman, Richard H. *The CIA in Guatemala: The Foreign Policy of Intervention*. (Austin: University of Texas Press, 1982).

Jonas, Susanne, Ed McCaughan, and Elizabeth Sutherland Martinez (eds.) *Guatemala Tyranny on Trial: Testimony of the Permanent People's Tribunal.* (San Francisco: Synthesis Publications, 1984).

McClintock, Michael. *The American Connection, Vol. I: State Terror and Popular Resistance in El Salvador.* (London: ZED Books, 1985).

————. *The American Connection, Vol. II: State Terror and Popular Resistance in Guatemala.* (London: ZED Books, 1985).

Melville, Thomas and Marjorie Melville. *Guatemala: The Politics of Land Ownership.* (New York: Free Press, 1978).

Montgomery, Tommie Sue. *Revolution in El Salvador: Origins and Evolution.* (Boulder, Colo.: Westview Press, 1982).

North, Liisa. *Bitter Grounds: Roots of Revolt in El Salvador.* (Toronto: Between the Lines, 1981).

Pearce, Jenny. *Promised Land: Peasant Rebellion in Chalatenango, El Salvador.* (London: Latin American Bureau, 1986).

Schlesinger, Stephen and Stephen Kinzer. *Bitter Fruit: The Untold Story of the American Coup in Guatemala.* (Garden City, New York: Doubleday, 1983).

Taylor, Philip B., Jr. "The Guatemalan Affair: A Critique of the United States Foreign Policy," *The American Political Science Review* 50 (1956):787-806.

Wheaton, Philip. *Agrarian Reform in El Salvador: A Program of Rural Pacification.* (Washington: EPICA Task Force, 1980).

White, Alastair. *El Salvador.* (New York: Praeger, 1973).

Wise, David and Thomas B. Ross. "Guatemala: CIA's Banana Revolt," chapter 11 in *The Invisible Government* (New York: Random House, 1964).

ON REVOLUTION AND COUNTERREVOLUTION IN NICARAGUA

Arce, Bayardo. *Política de la Revolución Sandinista: Una repuesta ante la política agresiva de la Administración Reagan.* (Managua: Edición del Centro de Comunicación Internacional, March 1985).

Black, George. *Triumph of the People: The Sandinista Revolution in Nicaragua.* (London: ZED Books, 1981).

Booth, John A. *The End and the Beginning: The Nicaraguan Revolution.* (Boulder, Colo.: Westview Press, 1982).

Cabezas, Omar. *Fire From the Mountain: The Making of a Sandinista.* (New York: New American Library, 1985).

Christian, Shirley. *Nicaragua: Revolution in the Family.* (New York: Random House, 1985).

Crawley, Edward. *Nicaragua in Perspective.* (New York: St. Martin's Press, 1984).

Dickey, Christopher. *With the Contras: A Reporter in the Wilds of Nicaragua.* (New York: Simon & Schuster, 1985).

Donahue, John M. *The Nicaraguan Revolution in Health.* (South Hadley, Mass.: Bergin & Garvey Publishers, 1986).

Eich, Dieter and Carlos Rincón. *The Contras: Interviews with Anti-Sandinistas.* (San Francisco: Synthesis Publications, 1985).

Everett, Melissa. *Bearing Witness Building Bridges: Interviews with North Americans Living and Working in Nicaragua.* (Philadelphia: New Society Publishers, 1986).

Grossman, Karl. *Nicaragua: America's New Vietnam?* (Sag Harbor, N.Y.: The Permanent Press, 1984).

Harris, Richard and Carlos M. Vilas (eds.) *Nicaragua: A Revolution Under Siege.* (London: ZED Books, 1985).

Hirshon, Sheryl. *And Also Teach Them to Read.* (Westport, Conn.: Lawrence Hill & Company, 1983).

Leiken, Robert. "Nicaragua's Untold Stories," *The New Republic* 191,5 (October 8, 1984):16-22.

Marcus, Bruce (ed.) *Nicaragua: The Sandinista People's Revolution: Speeches by Sandinista Leaders.* (New York: Pathfinder Press, 1985).

Nolan, David. *The Ideology of the Sandinistas and the Nicaraguan Revolution.* (Coral Gables, Fla.: University of Miami, 1984).

Randall, Margaret. *Sandino's Daughters.* (Vancouver: New Star Books, 1981).

———. *Christians in the Nicaraguan Revolution.* (Vancouver: New Star Books, 1983).

Ridenour, Ron. *Yankee Sandinistas.* (Willimantic, Conn.: Curbstone Press, 1986).

Rosset, Peter and John Vandermeer (eds.) *Nicaragua: Unfinished Revolution. The New Nicaragua Reader.* (New York: Grove Press, 1986).

Ruckwarger, Gary. *People in Power: Forging a Grassroots Democracy in Nicaragua.* (South Hadley, Mass: Bergin & Garvey, 1987).

Rudolph, James D. (ed.) *Nicaragua: A Country Study.* (Washington, D.C.: U.S. Department of the Army, U.S. Government Printing Office, 1982).

Spalding, Rose J. (ed.) *The Political Economy of Revolutionary Nicaragua.* (Boston: Allen & Unwin, 1987).

Vilas, Carlos M. *The Sandinista Revolution: National Liberation and Social Transformation in Central America.* (New York: Monthly Review Press, 1986).

Walker, Thomas W. (ed.) *Nicaragua in Revolution.* (New York: Praeger, 1982).

———. *Nicaragua: The First Five Years.* (New York: Praeger, 1985).

Wheaton, Philip and Yvonne Dilling. *Nicaragua: A People's Revolution.* (Washington: EPICA Task Force, 1980).

ON THE USSR AND CUBA IN CENTRAL AMERICA

Alexander, Robert J. *Communism in Latin America.* (New Brunswick, N.J.: 1957).

Bartley, Russell H. "The Inception of Russo-Brazilian Relations (1808-1828)," *The Hispanic American Historical Review* 56, 2 (May 1976):217-240.

————. *Imperial Russia and the Struggle for Latin American Independence, 1808-1828.* (Austin: Institute of Latin American Studies, University of Texas Press, 1978).

————. (trans. and ed.) *Soviet Historians on Latin America. Recent Scholarly Contributions.* (Madison and London: University of Wisconsin Press, for the Conference on Latin American History, 1978).

————. "Soviet-Latin American Relations: The Historical Parameters," paper delivered at the 29th annual meeting of the Pacific Coast Council on Latin American Studies, Portland, Oregon, October 13-15, 1983.

Berríos, Rubén. "Economic Relations Between Nicaragua and the Socialist Countries," *Working Paper* 166. (Washington: Latin America Program, Woodrow Wilson Center, 1985).

Blasier, Cole. *The Hovering Giant, U.S. Responses to Revolutionary Change in Latin America.* (Pittsburgh: University of Pittsburgh Press, 1976).

————. *The Giant's Rival: The USSR and Latin America* (Pittsburgh: University of Pittsburgh Press, 1983).

Bonsal, Philip W. *Cuba, Castro, and the United States.* (Pittsburgh: University of Pittsburgh Press, 1971).

Bosch, Adriana. *Nicaragua: The Internationalization of Conflict and Politics in Central America.* (The Rand Corporation, N-2119-AF, June 1984).

Brzezinski, Zbigniew. "Strategic Implications of the Central American Crisis," in Joseph Cirincione (ed.), *Central America and the Western Alliance.* (New York: Holmes & Meier, 1985).

Center for Defense Information. "Country Studies of Soviet Influence: Nicaragua," *The Defense Monitor* 15, 5(1986):30-31.

Challenge to Democracy in Central America, The. (Washington, DC: U.S. Departments of State and Defense, October 1986).

Cirincione, Joseph and Leslie Hunter. "Military Threats, Actual and Potential," in Robert Leiken (ed.), *Central America: Anatomy of a Conflict.* (New York: Pergamon, 1984).

Clement, P. "The Soviets in Nicaragua: Cultivating a New Client," presented at the American Association for the Advancement of Slavic Studies, Kansas City, October 1983.

Clissold, Stephen (ed.) *Soviet Relations with Latin America.* (London: Oxford University Press, 1970).

Coll, Alberto R. "Soviet Arms and Central American Turmoil," *World Affairs* 148, 1(Summer 1985):7-17.

Crozier, Brian. "The Caribbean Scourge," *National Review,* XXXV (September 2,

1983):1062.

Cruz, Arturo. "Implications of an Orthodox Communist Political System in Nicaragua," occasional paper, Institute of Interamerican Studies, University of Miami, 1984.

del Aguila, Juan. "Central American Vulnerability to Soviet/Cuban Penetration," *Journal of Interamerican Studies and World Affairs* 27,2 (Summer 1985):77-97.

Dominguez, Jorge I. "Cuban Foreign Policy," *Foreign Affairs* 57 (Fall 1978):83-108.

———. "Cuba's Relations with Caribbean and Central American Countries," paper prepared for the Center for International Affairs, Harvard University, August 1982.

———. (ed.) *Cuba: Internal and International Affairs.* (Beverly Hills, Calif.: Sage Publications, 1982).

———. *U.S. Interests and Policies in the Caribbean and Central America.* (Washington, DC: American Enterprise Institute, 1982).

Donaldson, Robert H. "The Soviet Union in the Third World," *Current History* 81 (October 1982):313-317, 339.

Einaudi, Luigi R., Hans Heyman, Jr., David F. Ronfeldt, and Caesar D. Sereseres. *Arms Transfers to Latin America: Toward a Policy of Mutual Respect.* (The Rand Corporation, R-1173-DOS, June 1973).

Enders, Thomas O. "Building the Peace in Central America," speech before the Commonwealth Club, San Francisco, California, August 20, 1982. *Department of State Bulletin* (October 1982):66-69.

———. "Nicaragua: Threat to Peace in Central America," speech before the House Foreign Affairs Committee, April 14, 1983. *Department of State Bulletin* (June 1983):76-79.

———. "Revolution, Reform and Reconciliation in Central America," *SAIS Review* 3,2 (Summer-Fall 1983):1-10.

———. "The Evolving Soviet Debate on Latin America," *Latin American Research Review* 16,1 (1981):107-123.

Fascell, Dante B. "Challenge in the Caribbean: The United States and Her Southern Neighbors," *NATO's Fifteen Nations* (August-September 1981):26-33.

Feinberg, Richard E. "Central America: No Easy Answers," *Foreign Affairs* (Summer 1981):1121-1146.

Gannon, Francis X. "Globalism Versus Regionalism: U.S. Policy and the OAS," *Orbis* (Spring 1982):195-221.

Gelb, Leslie. "U.S. Officials See Need for Big Effort in Salvador," *New York Times* (April 22, 1983).

Gonzalez, Edward. "The United States and Castro: Breaking the Deadlock," *Foreign Affairs* 50 (July 1972):722-37.

———. *A Strategy for Dealing with Cuba in the 1980s.* (The Rand Corporation, R-2954-DOS/AF, September 1982).

Grabendorff, Wolf. "The United States and Western Europe: Competition or Cooperation in Latin America," *International Affairs* (Fall 1982):625-637.

———. *The Central American Crisis and Western Europe: Perceptions and Reactions*. (Bonn: Research Institute of the Friedrich Ebert Foundation, 1982).

Gwertzman, B. "Kissinger on Central America: a Call for Firmness," *New York Times* (July 19, 1983).

Haig, Alexander. "An Agenda for Cooperation in the Western Hemisphere," in Sta. Lucia, December 4, 1981. *Department of State Bulletin* (January 1982):1-6.

Huntington, Samuel P. "Human Rights and American Power," *Commentary* (September 1981):37-43.

Iman, Zafar. "Soviet Treaties with Third World Countries," *Soviet Studies* 35,1 (1983).

Jackson, D. Bruce. *Castro, the Kremlin and Communism in Latin America*. (Baltimore: Johns Hopkins University Press, 1969).

Jacobsen, Carl G. *Soviet Attitudes Towards, Aid to and Contacts with Central American Revolutionaries*. (Washington: U.S. Department of State, 1984).

Katz, Mark. "The Soviet-Cuban Connection," *International Security* 8, 1 (Summer 1983):92.

Kirkpatrick, Jeane. "Dictatorships and Double Standards," *Commentary* (November 1979):24-45.

Kiva, A. "Socialist-Oriented Countries: Some Development Problems," *International Affairs* (Moscow), 10 (1984).

Krause, J. "Soviet Military Aid to the Third World," *Aussenpolitik* (English edition), 4 (1983).

Krauss, Clifford and Robert S. Greenberger. "Despite Fears of U.S., Soviet Aid to Nicaragua Appears to Be Limited," *The Wall Street Journal* (April 3, 1979).

Leiken, Robert. *Soviet Strategy in Latin America*. (New York: Washington Papers—Praeger, 1982).

———. "Overview: Can the Cycle Be Broken?" in Leiken (ed.), *Central America: Anatomy of a Conflict*. (New York: Pergamon, 1984).

Levesque, J. *The USSR and the Cuban Revolution: Soviet Ideological and Strategic Perspectives, 1959-1977*. (New York: Praeger, 1978).

Levine, Barry B. (ed.) *The New Cuban Presence in the Caribbean*. (Boulder, Colo.: Westview Press, 1983).

"Lifelines: Nicaragua and the Socialist Countries," *Report on the Americas* 19,3 (May-June 1985):33-56.

López Segrera, Francisco. *Cuba y Centroamérica*. (Mexico City: Claves Latinoamericanas, 1986).

Luers, William H. "The Soviets and Latin America: A Three Decade U.S. Policy Tangle," *The Washington Quarterly* 7,1 (Winter 1984):3-32.

McColm, R. Bruce. "Central America and the Caribbean: The Larger Scenario," *Strategic Review* (Summer 1983):28-42.

Menges, Constantine. "Central America and Its Enemies," *Commentary* (August 1981), 32-38.

Moore, John Norton. *The Secret War in Central America: Sandinista Assault on World Order*. (Frederick, Md.: University Publications of America, 1987).

Moorer, Thomas H. and George A. Fauriol. *Caribbean Basin Security.* (New York: Washington Papers—Praeger, 1984).

"National Security Council Document on Policy in Central America and Cuba," *New York Times* (April 7, 1983).

"Nicaragua: Soviets Hedge on Level of Support," *Latin America Weekly Report* (October 16, 1986):2.

Nye, Joseph S., Jr. "U.S. Power and Reagan Policy," *Orbis* 26,2 (Summer 1982):391-411.

Oswald, G. and A. J. Strover (eds). *The Soviet Union and Latin America.* (New York: Praeger, 1970).

Podhoretz, Norman. "El peligro presente," *CIDE* (Mexico) 9 (1981).

Ramet, Pedro and Fernando López-Alves. "Moscow and the Revolutionary Left in Latin America," *Orbis* 28,2 (Summer 1984):341-63.

Ratliff, William E. *Castroism and Communism in Latin America, 1959-1976: The Varieties of Marxist-Leninist Experience.* (Stanford, Calif.: Hoover Institution Press, 1976).

Reagan, Ronald. President's news conference on foreign and domestic matters, July 28, 1983.

———. "Saving Freedom in Central America." *Current Policy* 499, Bureau of Public Affairs. (Washington: U.S. Department of State, 1983).

———. "Central America: Defending our Vital Interests." *Current Policy* 482, Bureau of Public Affairs. (Washington: U.S. Department of State, 1983).

———. "Strategic Importance in El Salvador and Central America." *Current Policy* 464, Bureau of Public Affairs. (Washington: U.S. Department of State, 1983).

Report of the President's National Bipartisan Commission on Central America. (New York: Macmillan, 1984).

Rosenberg, R. "Soviet Support for Central American Guerrilla Movements as a Strategic Initiative," *SAFRA* 1984.

Rothenberg, Morris. "Latin America in Soviet Eyes," *Problems of Communism* 32 (September-October 1983):1-18.

———. "The Soviet and Central America," in Robert Leiken (ed.), *Central America: Anatomy of a Conflict* (New York: Pergamon, 1984).

Saivetz, Carol and Sylvia Woodby. *Soviet-Third World Relations.* (Boulder, Colo.: Westview Press, 1985).

Sanjuan, Pedro A. "Why We Don't Have a Latin American Policy," *The Washington Quarterly* 3,4 (Autumn 1980): 28-39.

Schwab, Theodore and Harold Sims, "Relations with Communist Countries," in Thomas Walker (ed.), *Nicaragua Five Years Later.* (New York: Praeger, 1985).

Silber, John. "Plain Talk Behind Closed Doors in Central America," *The Wall Street Journal* (February 8, 1985): 21.

Singer, Max. *Nicaragua: The Stolen Revolution.* (Washington: U.S. Information Agency, 1984).

Smith, Wayne. "Dateline Havana: Myopic Diplomacy," *Foreign Policy* (Fall

1982): 157-174.

Tambs, Lewis (ed.) *A New Inter-American Policy for the Eighties.* (Washington: Council for Inter-American Security, 1980).

Taubman, P. "Pentagon Gets Tough on Latin Policy," *New York Times* (August 5, 1983).

Theberge, James D. *The Soviet Presence in Latin America.* (New York: Crane, Russak for National Strategy Information Center, 1974).

"Transcript of the President's Address to the General Assembly," *New York Times* (October 25, 1985):9.

U.S. Central Intelligence Agency. *Communist Aid to Less Developed Countries of the Free World.* (Washington: 1977).

――――. *Communist Aid Activities in Non-Communist Less-Developed Countries, 1979 and 1954-79.* (Washington: 1980).

U.S. Department of State. *Communist Interference in El Salvador* (White Paper), February 1981. (Washington: U.S. Department of State, 1981).

――――. "Cuba's Renewed Support for Violence in Latin America," *Special Report* 90, December 1981.

――――. "President Reagan: Caribbean Basin Initiative." *Current Policy* 370 (Washington: U.S. Department of State, 1982).

――――. *Soviet and East European Aid to the Third World, 1981.* (Washington: U.S. Department of State, 1983).

――――. "'Revolution Beyond Our Borders': Sandinista Intervention in Central America." *Special Report* 132, September 1985. (Washington: U.S. Department of State, 1985).

――――. "The Soviet-Cuban Connection in Central America and the Caribbean." (Washington: U.S. Department of State, 1985).

U.S. Departments of State and Defense. "Background Paper: Central America," (May 27, 1983).

Vaky, Viron. "Reagan's Central American Policy: An Isthmus Restored," in Robert Leiken (ed.), *Central America: Anatomy of a Conflict.* (New York: Pergamon, 1984).

Valenta, Jiri. "The USSR, Cuba and the Crisis in Central America," *Orbis* 25,3 (Fall 1981):715-746.

Valenta, Jiri and Virginia Valenta. "Soviet Strategy in the Caribbean Basin," in Alan Adelman and Reid Reading, (eds.), *Confrontation in the Caribbean Basin.* (Pittsburgh: University of Pittsburgh Press, 1984).

――――. "Sandinistas in Power," *Problems of Communism* 34,5 (September-October 1985):1-3.

Valdez Paz, Juan. "Cuba y la crisis centroamericana," (Mexico City: Seminario Internacional Centroamericano, June 1984).

Valkeinier, E. K. *Soviet Union and the Third World: The Economic Bind.* (New York: Praeger, 1983).

Wiarda, Howard J. "The Origins of the Crisis in Central America," in Wiarda (ed.), *Rift and Revolution.* (Washington: American Enterprise Institute for Public Policy Research, 1984).

Will, George. "Our Central American Myopia," *Newsweek* 102 (August 1,

1983):76.

Zagoria, D. S. "Into the Breach: New Soviet Alliances in the Third World." *Foreign Affairs* 57 (Spring 1979): 733-754.

CRITIQUES OF U.S. POLICY IN CENTRAL AMERICA

Barnes, Michael D. "U.S. Policy in Central America: The Challenge of Revolutionary Change," in Andrew J. Pierre (ed.), *Third World Instability: Central America as a European-American Issue* (New York: Council on Foreign Relations, Inc. EuropeAmerica, 1985).

Bialer, Seweryn and Alfred Stepan. "Cuba, the U.S. and the Central American Mess," *New York Review of Books* (May 27, 1982):17-22.

Black, George. "Central America: Crisis in the Backyard," *New Left Review* 135 (September-October 1982):28-29.

———. "Israeli Connection: Not Just Guns for Guatemala," *Report on the Americas* 17, 3 (May-June 1983):43-45.

Bollinger, William. "Revolutionary Strategy in Latin America," *Monthly Review* 34, 9 (February 1983):27-33.

Bonner, Raymond. *Weakness and Deceit.* (New York: New York Times Books, 1984).

Brumberg, Abraham. "'Sham' and 'Farce' in Nicaragua?" *Dissent* 32,2 (Spring 1985).

———. "Reagan's Untruths About Managua," *New York Times* (June 18, 1985).

Brzezinski, Zbigniew. *Between Two Ages: America's Role in the Technotronic Era.* (New York: Viking Press, 1970).

Child, John. *Unequal Alliance: The Inter-American Military System, 1933-1978.* (Boulder, Colo.: Westview Press, 1980).

Cockburn, Alexander. "The Case of Robert Leiken," *The Nation* 241, 22 (December 28, 1985):702-703.

Ebel, Roland H. "Political Instability in Central America," *Current History* 81 (February 1982):59-69, 86.

Edelman, Marc. "Costa Rica: Modernizing the Non-Army," *Report on the Americas* 18,2 (March-April 1984):9-11.

———. "Back from the Brink: How Washington Bailed Out Costa Rica," *Report on the Americas* 19, 6 (November-December 1985):41.

"Extermination in Guatemala . . . Creating a Desolation and Calling It Peace," *The New York Review of Books* (June 2, 1983): 13-16.

Farer, T. "Reagan's Latin America." *New York Review of Books* (March 19, 1981).

Feinberg, R. E. *Central America: No Easy Answers.* (1981).

Fonseca Amador, Carlos. "Nicaragua: Zero Hour," in A. C. Sandino, C. Fonseca, *Nicaragua: La estrategia de la victoria.* (Mexico City: Editorial Nuestro Tiempo, 1980).

FSLN National Directorate. "Analysis of the Situation and Tasks of the Sandinista People's Revolution" (*72-Hour Document*), trans. by U.S. Department of State and published in Washington in 1986, available in Mark Falcoff and Robert Royal, (eds.), *The Continuing Crisis: U.S. Policy in Central America and the Caribbean*. (Lanham, Md.: Ethics and Public Policy Center, 1987).

Herring, George C. "Vietnam, El Salvador, and the Uses of History," in Coleman and Herring (eds.), *The Central American Crisis: Sources of Conflict and the Failure of U.S. Policy*. (Wilmington, Del.: Scholarly Resources, Inc., 1985).

Immerman, Richard. "Guatemala as Cold War History," *Political Science Quarterly* (Winter 1980-1981):629-653.

Kenworthy, Eldon. "Central America: Beyond the Credibility Trap," *World Policy Journal* 1, 1 (Fall 1983): 181-200.

Landau, Saul and Daniel Siegel, "Reagan's Penchant for 'Stretchers,'" *Los Angeles Times* (April 23, 1985).

LeFeber, Walter. *Inevitable Revolutions: The United States in Central America*. (New York: Norton, 1983).

LeoGrande, William W. "A Splendid Little War: Drawing the Line in El Salvador," *International Security* 6 (Summer 1981):45-47.

———. "Through the Looking Glass: The Kissinger Report on Central America," *World Policy Journal* 1,2 (Winter 1984):253.

Lewellen, Ted C. "Human Rights as Propaganda: The Political Manipulation of Central American Human Rights Data," paper presented at the International Studies Association, Washington, D.C., March 6-9, 1985.

Linowitz, Sol and Galo Plaza. *The Americas at a Crossroads: Report of the Inter-American Dialogue*. (Washington: Woodrow Wilson International Center for Scholars, 1983).

Lowenthal, Abraham F. "The United States and Latin America: Ending the Hegemonic Presumption," *Foreign Affairs* (October 1976):199-213.

———. "The Caribbean Basin Initiative: Misplaced Emphasis," *Foreign Policy* 47 (Summer 1982):114-118.

———. "Ronald Reagan and Latin America: Coping with Hegemony in Decline," in Kenneth A. Oye, et al. (eds.), *Eagle Defiant*. (Boston, 1983).

Marchetti, Peter. "The Disenchanted Liberal Stereotype," *In These Times* 9,15 (March 13-19, 1985):15.

Matthews, Robert. "The Limits of Friendship: Nicaragua and the West," *Report on the Americas* 19,3 (May-June 1985):22-32.

———. "Sowing Dragons' Teeth: The U.S. War Against Nicaragua," *Report on the Americas* 20,4 (July-August 1986):13-40.

Maynes, Charles William. "Reagan is Wrong on Central America," *Los Angeles Times* (June 12, 1983): IV-1.

Moran, Fernando. "Europe's Role in Central America: A Spanish Socialist View," in Andrew J. Pierre (ed.), *Third World Instability. Central America as a European-American Issue*. (New York: Council on Foreign Relations, Inc. EuropeAmerica, 1985).

Ortega, Daniel. *El acero de guerra o el olivo de paz*. (Managua: Editorial Nueva

Nicaragua, 1983).

Parkinson, F. *Latin America, The Cold War, and the World Powers: 1945-1973.* (Beverly Hills, Calif.: Sage Publications, 1974).

Poelchau, Warner (ed.) *White Paper Whitewash.* (New York: Deep Cover Books, 1981).

Ross, David F. "The Caribbean Basin Initiative: Threat or Promise?" in Coleman and Herring (eds.), *The Central American Crisis: Sources of Conflict and the Failures of U.S. Policy.* (Wilmington, Del.: Scholarly Resources, Inc., 1985).

Smith, Wayne. "Dateline Havana: Myopic Diplomacy," *Foreign Policy* 48 (Fall 1982):162.

————. "U.S. Central American Policy: The Worst-Alternative Syndrome," *SAIS Review* 3,2 (Summer-Fall 1983):12-13.

————. "The Grenada Complex in Central America," *Caribbean Review* 12, 4 (Fall 1983): 64.

————. "The Failure of Statecraft," in Joseph Cirincione (ed.), *Central America and the Western Alliance.* (New York: Holmes & Meier, 1985).

————. "Lies About Nicaragua," *Foreign Policy* 67 (Summer 1987): 87-103.

The Southern Connection: Recommendations for a New Approach to Inter-American Relations. Ad Hoc Working Group on Latin America, Transnational Institute. (Washington: Institute for Policy Studies, February 1977).

Ullman, Richard H. "Plain Talk on Central America," *New York Times* (July 10, 1983): E21.

————. "At War With Nicaragua," *Foreign Affairs* 62 (Fall 1983):39-58.

Walker, Thomas W. "Nicaraguan-U.S. Friction: The First Four Years, 1979-1983," in Coleman and Herring (eds.), *The Central American Crisis.* (Wilmington, Del.: Scholarly Resources, 1985).

Index

About the Book

Assertions that Nicaragua's policies and political dispositions threaten U.S. security, critiques of that claim, and assessments of Soviet and Cuban activities and capabilities in Central America are represented in this unusual collection. Not intended to be a dispassionate volume, the book presents lively and informed argument—a diversity of views and evidence—so that the reader may judge the charges and countercharges and form an independent opinion. An extensive bibliography is included.